TILLIE OLSEN

TILLIE OLSEN

One Woman, Many Riddles

Panthea Reid

RUTGERS UNIVERSITY PRESS

NEW BRUNSWICK, NEW JERSEY, AND LONDON

Library of Congress Cataloging-in-Publication Data

Reid, Panthea.
Tillie Olsen : one woman, many riddles / Panthea Reid.
     p.   cm.
  Includes bibliographical references and index.
  ISBN 978-0-8135-4637-7 (alk. paper)
  1. Olsen, Tillie. 2. Women authors, American—20th century—Biography. I. Title.
  PS3565.L82Z86 2010
  813.' 54—dc22

                           2009006026
A British Cataloging-in-Publication record for this book is available from the British
Library.

Frontispiece/photograph © by Jill Krementz; all rights reserved. [30 May 1977]

Permission to publish excerpts from her unpublished letters and papers granted by
© Tillie Olsen.

Permission to publish selected Tillie Olsen's letters from The Tillie Olsen Papers
(M0667) courtesy of Department of Special Collections and University Archives, Stanford University Libraries.

Visit our Web site: http://rutgerspress.rutgers.edu

Manufactured in the United States of America

For John
Always

CONTENTS

ACKNOWLEDGMENTS

In the more than a decade I have spent writing about the long and complicated life of Tillie Olsen, I have accumulated many debts. The first is to my husband, John Irwin Fischer, who has been inconvenienced by but marvelously supportive of this project. As always, he is my very best, most meticulous reader and advisor. I also appreciate the help of my son Reid Broughton, the attorney who drew up my contract with Tillie Olsen, and my daughter, Hannah Fischer, of the Congressional Research Service, who uncovered some really obscure bits of information for me.

I am deeply indebted to the National Endowment for the Humanities for my 1999–2000 Fellowship for University Teachers, awarded to write this biography and edit a collection of Tillie Olsen's letters. And I thank the College of Arts and Sciences and the English Department at Louisiana State University, which cooperated with the Endowment to free me of academic duties for an entire year to work on these projects.

I owe much to Tillie Olsen herself. Since 1997, she willingly endured my visits, letters, and phone calls and responded eagerly to my queries. Somewhat less eagerly she gave me permission to quote excerpts from and use information gleaned from her unpublished papers. Julie Olsen Edwards officially granted me access to all materials in the Tillie Olsen Archives. Julie Olsen Edwards, Kathie Olsen Hoye, and Laurie Olsen Margolis have sent me photos, shared memories, clarified details, and answered my almost endless queries. Tillie's eldest daughter Karla Lutz chose not to be involved in this book. I respect her choice but regret not having her assistance. I am grateful for help from her daughter Jessica Lutz, from Julie's husband and daughter Rob and Rebekah Edwards, and especially from Laurie's husband Mike Margolis, who showed extraordinary patience with Tillie and with me.

Among Tillie's siblings, Gene Lerner assisted me in the task of uncovering the European family background of the Lerners and Goldbergs. After interviewing his sisters in 2000, he shared their recollections with me; in 2001, he wrote "From Czarist Russia to Omaha, Nebraska, and Beyond: The Story of the Lerner Family Over More Than One Hundred Years," now at Stanford. I spoke once with Jann Lerner Brodinsky, and she wrote me what may have been her last letter. Harry Lerner died before I began this work, but his children Howard and Susan have been most helpful. I exchanged many letters with Lillian Lerner Davis and interviewed her early in 2002 and have visited and corresponded with her daughters Caroline Eckhardt and Rivka Davis. Vicki Lerner Richards Bergman answered many questions and sent me copies of the letters, inscriptions on books, and articles on Tillie Olsen that Tillie sent her. Her son Cory Richards has also shared his recollections with me. Gretchen Spieler, great-niece of Abraham Jevons Goldfarb, has been most helpful in tracing family records and finding photographs.

My very special thanks go to William McPheron, William Saroyan Curator for British and American Literature at Stanford University Libraries. He and I cooperated on getting friends and family to donate their letters from Tillie to Stanford, letters on which I rely here and will use to edit the *Selected Letters of Tillie Olsen*. Over the years, McPheron answered my countless questions with care and grace and facilitated my access to the Tillie Olsen Papers and the Lerner Family Papers at Stanford.

Writers, artists, and friends who have been especially generous with their time include Sandy Boucher and Mary Anne Ferguson, who carefully annotated Tillie's letters to them; Ann Hershey, who shared her experiences while she was filming *Tillie Olsen: A Heart in Motion*; Edith Konecky, who consulted old letters and diaries to help me date Tillie's activities; Alice Walker, who entertained me and shared vivid recollections; Diane Wood Middlebrook, who gave me Tillie's mark-up of her chapter on Anne Sexton and Tillie Olsen; Ruth Vance who drove me around San Francisco to view the many places where Tillie settled in her peripatetic life there; Ann Goette, who read several chapters with wit and insight; Leonda and Arnold Finke, who entertained me and my family with a sculpture tour. Three extraordinary women have been wonderfully supportive professionally and personally: Rosalie Siegel, my agent; Lisa Jerry, my copyeditor; and Leslie Mitchner, editor-in-chief at Rutgers University Press. My thanks to Rosalie, Lisa, and Leslie, as well as the press's efficient and responsive staff.

In choosing illustrations, I have preferred to use previously unseen (or rarely seen) photographs and also ones that tell a story. Here my friend Al Aronson has offered invaluable help. He carefully took illustrations I provided that came from old glossy photos, e-mail attachments, museum and library records, and even a 1934 newspaper clipping and assembled them into a visual narrative of clear and telling pictures.

I thank Roberto Trujillo, head of Special Collections at Stanford, Annette Keogh, who has taken William McPheron's position on his retirement, Mattie Taormina, head of Public Service, and the wonderfully helpful librarians Polly Armstrong, Glynn Edwards, and Joe Geller. My list of other librarians and staff members who have been most helpful must begin with Bill Lynch of the Magazine and Newspaper Center at the San Francisco Public Library, who uncovered countless newspaper articles and photos for me, and Jane Knowles, archivist of Radcliffe's Schlesinger Library, for tracking down photos, clippings, and previously lost sources.

I will not try to distinguish between archivists who answered a few queries and those who answered many, but my thanks go to the following: Kathy Kienholz of the American Academy of Arts and Letters; Peter A. Nelson at Amherst College; Jane Parkinson at Banff; Genevieve Troka of the California State Archives; Barbara Miller at California State University, Fullerton; Jean Ashton of Columbia University; John E. Haynes of the Library of Congress; Leonard Greenspoon and Fran Minear of Creighton University; Cristina Favretto at Duke University; Michael Lampen at Grace Cathedral; Sandra Taylor of the Lilly Library, Indiana University; Mary Fellman and Dotty Rosenblum at the Jewish Community Center, Omaha; Susan E. King at Jewishgen.org; Glenna Dunning of the Los Angeles Public Library; Elizabeth Michael, Joe Bills, and Brendan Tapley at the MacDowell Colony; Robert Machesney at Macmillan, United Kingdom; Mike Milewski at the University of Massachusetts, Amherst; Tracey Baker of the Minnesota Historical Society; Thomas M. Verich and Jennifer Ford at the University of Mississippi; Tom Bickley of the National Endowment for the Arts; Jane Aikin of the National Endowment for the Humanities; Oliver Pollak of the Nebraska Jewish Historical Society; Julie Cobb of the Newberry Library; Stephen Crooks, Philip Milito, and Isaac Gewirtz at the New York Public Library; Geoffrey D. Smith at Ohio State University; Bonnie Marcus of Poets and Writers; Jane Knowles, Renny Harrigan, Jennifer Lyons, Sophia Heller, and Jeanne Winner at Radcliffe; Alycia Vivona of the Franklin D. Roosevelt Presidential Library; Tom Carey at the San Francisco Public Library; Lynn Bonfield, Jeff Rosen, and Susan Sherwood at San Francisco State University; Wendy Bousfield at Syracuse University Library; Daniel Traister at the University of Pennsylvania; AnnaLee Pauls of the Princeton University Library; Cathy Henderson and Tara Wenger at the University of Texas, Austin; Amy Coenen of Women's Liberation Studies Archives for Action; Steve Siegel, the Poetry Center of the 92nd Street YM-YWHA; John Lennox and Sean Smith at York University.

Several people on this list of additional people I thank asked me to hurry up and finish so they could read this book before they died. I regret that I did not finish in time for some of them.

William Abrahams, Kathie Amatniek (also Sarachild), Ted Atkinson, Bobbi Ausubel, Joanne Trautman Banks, Frances Blumkin Batt, Eve Beglarian, Frank Bergon, Liana Borghi, Sandy Boucher, Linda Bowers, Blanche Boyd, Faye Bradus, Aaron Braude, Adele and Sam Braude, Edward T. Breathitt, Esther Brown, Lloyd L. Brown, Rosellen Brown, Dorothy Bryant, Susan Cahill, Gladys Cajka, Carl Cannon, Virginia Cannon, Stacy Carlson, Tom Cline, Robert Coles, Sara Coulter, Tara Craig, Kiana Davenport, Anthony Dawahare, Pele de Lappe, Robert DeMaria, Deborah DeMoulpied, Arlyn Diamond, Roberta Braude Diamond, Annie Dillard, Bob Eisenberg, Candace Falk, Allen Fink, Leonda Finke, Kathleen Finneran, Karen Goldfarb Fisken, Ruth Stein Fox, Marge Frantz, ChaeRan Freeze, Joanne Frye, Marvin Gettleman, Trudy Glucksberg, Mildred Goldberger, Lennie Goodings, Vivian Gornick, Susan Greenberg, Doris Grumbach, Clarinda Harriss, Judy Hogan, Carol Holmes, Florence Howe, Mary Gray Hughes, Camille Hykes, Minette Louis Katz, Helen Kelley (Sister William), Maxine Kong Kingston, Annette Kolodny, Douglas Konecky, Milton Konecky, Richard Kostalanetz, Carole Goldfarb Kotz, Maxine Kumin, Jane Kyle, Elinor Langer, Paul Lauter, Merloyd Lawrence, Jane Lazarre, Ursula Le Guin, John L'Heureux, Gordon Lish, Michael Lyon, Rachel Lyon, Dotty McCaughey, Eileen McClay, Jill McConkey, Peggy McIntosh, Paul Mandelbaum, Jane Marcus, Hanna Margan, Elaine Markson, Michelle Matz, Maude Meeham, Lea Mendelovitz, Howard Meyer, Noland Miller, Michael Millgate, Valerie Miner, Maria Teresa Moevs, Mary Jane Moffat, Mark Morris, Faye Moskowitz, Jim Murray, Sarah Murray, Tema (Thelma) Nason, Yvonne Noble, Joyce Carol Oates, Elaine Orr, Cynthia Ozick, Nancy Packer, Grace Paley, Hanna Papenek, Ruth Perry, Lorna Peterson, Jayne Anne Phillips, William Piehl, Marge Piercy, Jo-Ann Pilardi, Judith Plaskow, Sara Poli, Linda Pratt, William Pratt, Jonah Raskin, Maia Reim, Malcolm Richardson, Norma Rosen, Deborah Rosenfelt, Sidney Rosoff, Alexander Saxton, Jenni Schlossman, Budd Schulberg, Dick Scowcroft, Nancy Schimmel, Cynthia Blumkin Schneider, Raymond Screws, Elaine Showalter, Alix Kates Shulman, Barbara Sirota, Alan Soldofsky (Sr. and Jr.), Susan Stamberg, Peter Stansky, Catharine Stimpson, Barbara Swan, Anne Taylor, Ray Thibodeau, Karen Ticot, Harold Tovish, Robert Treuhaft, Genevieve Troka, Scott Turow, Darlene Unrue, Les Valentine, Linda Wagner-Martin, T. Mike Walker, Jack Wesley, Fred Whitehead, Bill Wiegand, Jan Wilkotz, Joan Williams, Laird Wilcox, J. J. Wilson, Debra Winger, Jeanne Winner, Joyce Winslow, Nellie Wong, Charlene Woodcock, Doug Wixon, Rachel Wyatt, Betty Jane Wylie, and Mitsuye Yamada.

NOTE ON THE TEXT

Tillie Olsen's handwriting was tiny and peculiar. With much practice and many magnifying glasses, I think I've learned to read it, but I apologize in advance for any mis-transcriptions. To ensure the coherence of quotations from her letters and journals, I have taken a few liberties: normalizing spelling and punctuation, except when the original oddities convey meaning: saying "enuf" for "enough," capitalizing for emphasis, or eliminating all capital letters for de-emphasis. When I tried to replicate her habit of using spaces instead of punctuation, the result was so confusing that I substituted normal punctuation. While I have silently corrected most quirks of Tillie's prose, I have preserved the oddities of writings by her parents and Rae Schochet to illustrate their often poetic efforts to learn English. Also, I have preserved Abe Goldfarb's phonetic spelling of Yiddish English. I have mostly left these letters as they were written, sometimes inserting the intended word in brackets and on rare occasions have added "[sic]" to clarify that the error was in the original. The early and late years in Tillie Olsen's life tend to blur together, and so I do not divide them chronologically. Between 1926 and 1989, however, each chapter spans a specific number of years; I separate the end of one year and the beginning of another with a line-break, mentioning the new year soon after the break.

The letters and papers of Tillie Olsen form a vast archive in the Department of Special Collections at Stanford University that holds her diaries, writings, scrapbooks, and much more, including many letters to her, alphabetized by author's name. The Tillie Olsen Papers are abbreviated here as TOP, with a box number indicating their placement. I read some of Olsen's papers before they were deposited at Stanford, which are cited as "Tillie Olsen, private papers." They too are now at Stanford but have not yet, I understand, been classified. Tillie's brother Gene Lerner deposited various historical documents (including letters, records, and his own writings) about the family at Stanford. They are identified as "Lerner Papers." Letters to the author are abbreviated as "to PR."

All correspondence to and from Bennett Cerf and Donald Klopfer of Random House Publishers (including letters from Tillie Lerner,

William Saroyan, and Sanora Babb) are from the Random House Collection, in the Rare Book and Manuscript Library of Columbia University. The Berg Collection of the New York Public Library holds early drafts (or "makings") of *Yonnondio*, the 1928 school reprimand signed by Sara Vore Taylor, and Tillie's letters to Nolan Miller. Blanche Knopf's memos and letters about Tillie Olsen and Olsen's letters to Knopf are in the Knopf files at the Harry Ransom Humanities Research Center, University of Texas at Austin. The Humanities Research Center also holds Anne Sexton's papers, including Tillie's letters to Sexton, Sexton's copies of Tillie's "copy-outs" (transcriptions of and notes on important passages), and a transcription of Tillie's 1963 talk at Radcliffe. Tillie's letters to Malcolm Cowley are in the Malcolm Cowley Papers (Box 49, Folder 3018), Newberry Library, Chicago. The Seymour Lawrence Collection at the University of Mississippi holds Tillie's letters to Lawrence and his to and about her, including correspondence with her agents. Tillie's letters to Jerre Mangione are in the Department of Rare Books and Special Collections of the University of Rochester Library. Tillie Olsen's letters to Richard Elman are in the Special Collections Research Center, Syracuse University Library. Olsen's many Guggenheim applications are property of the Guggenheim Foundation; permission to quote from these materials is granted by the Guggenheim Foundation and G. Thomas Tanselle, vice president. I thank Robert Coles for permission to use some of my article on Tillie Olsen from *DoubleTake Magazine* (Spring 2000) and Leonard Greenspoon for permission to use some of my article from *Studies in Jewish Civilization* 18.

Permission to quote from the Tillie Olsen Papers and the Lerner Papers is courtesy of Department of Special Collections and University Archives, Stanford University Libraries. Permission to quote from the Anne Sexton and Alfred A. Knopf papers is thanks to the Harry Ransom Humanities Research Center, the University of Texas at Austin. Permission to quote from the Seymour Lawrence Collection is thanks to Archives and Special Collections, J. D. Williams Library, University of Mississippi, and to Sidney Rosoff. Permission to quote from the letters of Bennett Cerf, Donald Klopfer, William Saroyan, and Sanora Babb is thanks to Random House Records, Rare Book and Manuscript Library, Columbia University. Permission to quote from early drafts of what would become *Yonnondio*, from Tillie Lerner's 1929 high school reprimand, and from Tillie Olsen's letters to Nolan Miller are courtesy of the Henry W. and Albert A. Berg Collection of English and American Literature, The New York Public Library, Astor, Lenox and Tilden Foundation. I have also used the Jerre Mangione Papers, Department of Rare Books and Special Collections, the University of Rochester Library, and the Richard Elman Collection, Special Collections Research Center, Syracuse University. I thank all those institutions for granting permission to quote from their holdings. Diarmuid Russell's words are reprinted with the permission of Russell and Volkening Literary Agency. Rob Cowley has kindly granted me permission to quote from Malcolm Cowley's letters to Tillie Olsen.

ABBREVIATIONS

AFL	American Federation of Labor
CIO	Congress of Industrial Organizations
CP	Communist Party
CS	Criminal Syndicalism
CP-USA	Communist Party of the United States of America
CWA	Civil Works Administration
ERA	Equal Rights Amendment
FBI	Federal Bureau of Investigation
FDR	Franklin Delano Roosevelt
HUAC	House Un-American Activities Committee
ILWU	International Longshoremen and Warehousemen Union
IPP	Independent Progressive Party
LA	Los Angeles
MIT	Massachusetts Institute of Technology
MLA	Modern Language Association
NEA and NEH	National Endowments for the Arts and for the Humanities
NOW	National Organization for Women
NPR	National Public Radio
NRA	National Recovery Administration
PR	Panthea Reid
PW and DPW	*People's World* (also *Daily People's World*)
PWA	Public Works Administration
SERA	State Emergency Relief Administration
SFSU	San Francisco State University
SUNY	State University of New York
TMAR	*Tell Me a Riddle*
TO	Tillie Olsen
TOP	Tillie Olsen Papers at Stanford
UCSC	University of California at Santa Cruz
USSR	Union of Soviet Socialist Republics
WPA	Works Progress Administration
YCL	Young Communist League

TILLIE OLSEN

PROLOGUE

The enigma of Tillie Lerner Olsen is intertwined with the enigmas of the twentieth century. Neither can be labeled cavalierly. Neither can be explained succinctly. In answering here, as best I can, the riddle of Tillie Olsen, I hope I have also helped to untangle some puzzling knots of the last century's triumphs and failures.

She was named Tybele, became Tillie, and claimed that her real name was Matilda. She had three different last names: Lerner, Goldfarb, and Olsen, though she admitted to only two of them. She adopted aliases: Theresa Landale, Theta Larimore, and Amy. As a teenager, she had countless nicknames: including Piggy (for appetite), Curly (for frizzled curls), Encyke (for knowledge), Windy (for talkativeness), Faun (for impishness), and Bacchante (for hedonism).

At eighteen, Tillie wondered to her diary: "With dozens of selves, quarreling and tearing at each other—which then is the natural self?" She concluded, "None." She was a "hell-cat" in the 1920s, an earnest revolutionary during the entire 1930s, the "most sought-after writer" in America in the mid-1930s, a war-relief patriot during World War II, a crusader for equal pay for equal work in the mid-1940s, a stay-at-home mom with a baby-boomer during the rest of the 1940s, a victim of FBI surveillance in the 1950s, a storyteller who foregrounded the struggles of mothers and ordinary men and women in the late 1950s, a figure in the Civil Rights, feminist, and antiwar protests of the 1960s and 1970s, a feminist icon in the 1980s and 1990s, and in her twilight years a beloved emblem of one woman's power to change the world.

Tillie Olsen and her family, separately or together, participated in or were affected by the major events and movements of the last century: rebellions against the czar, immigration from Eastern Europe, anti-Semitism and xenophobia during World War I, the rise of socialism and communism, the Depression, 1930s strikes, the New Deal, the first American Writers' Congress, Hollywood's leftist phase, World War II, the founding of the United Nations, the Nuremberg Trials, labor-movement rivalries, House Un-American Activities Committee hearings, the Cold War, "back-to-the-kitchen" pressures on women, the decline of the labor movement, the rise of feminism, integration, affirmative action, and the founding of academic programs in women's and minority studies. Not only did these events, pressures, and value-shifts mark the life of Tillie Olsen, she shaped the best of them through her activism, her journalism and nonfiction, and her extraordinary fiction. As a telescope reveals patterns in remote galaxies, her story makes remote events more accessible. In turn, the prism of history illumines the mysteries of her being.

Though Tillie Lerner once called herself, "Your American Tragedy," she lead a long life filled with success. The American Academy of Arts and Letters cited her in 1975 for creating a "poetic" prose that "nearly constitutes a new form for fiction." Her books *Tell Me a Riddle*, *Yonnondio*, and *Silences* sold about 100,000 copies apiece, and her stories, especially "I Stand Here Ironing," are reprinted each year. She did not publish the novels or collections of stories and essays she promised, but nearly everything she did publish became, as Robert Coles has written, "almost immediately a classic." On National Public Radio in 2006, Scott Turow explained that in Olsen's fiction "paragraph after paragraph achieves the shocking brevity and power of the best poems."

Over the years, she gathered disciples who called her "Saint Tillie," our "national treasure," and "Tillie Apple Seed" for planting the seeds of women's studies. The founder of the Feminist Press called her the "Mother of Us All." In the 1990s, when she returned to her hometown, a reporter proclaimed that a "legend" had walked Omaha's streets.

On 4 February 2001, I introduced that legend at Louisiana State University by quoting from an FBI report on her supposedly subversive work establishing publicly funded day-care centers, authoring an unemployment bill for disabled veterans, urging women to vote, and holding meetings in her house to which most people came on foot. Such accusations had hurt Tillie and Jack Olsen in the 1950s but greatly amused the audience in 2001. After I concluded, eighty-nine-year-old Tillie Lerner Olsen stood on the stage alone. When she announced that she would read "I Stand Here Ironing," a ripple of applause passed through the standing-room-only crowd. She stood near the podium, without leaning on it. A spotlight on her silver hair shed radiance around her chiseled face. Wearing no glasses, she held a book in her hand but hardly looked at it. She recited the whole story with passionate intensity. Her deep humanity made the FBI's quibbles seem not only dated but also absurd.

For more than three years, at that time, I had been investigating the many faces of Tillie Olsen. I knew by then that she was a subversive rebel, a compassionate crusader, and a superb performer. I was discovering that those were but three in a galaxy of selves ranging from the heroic, the inspiring, the generous, the self-effacing, the self-denying to the self-aggrandizing, the petty, the vain, the manipulating, the extorting, and the fabricating Tillie. She modestly asked that I call her by her first name but immodestly insisted that I cite her fiction's profundity.

Now, eight years and countless inquiries after her magnificent performance at LSU, I think I have come as close as a biographer can to answering the riddles of one extremely complicated woman's life and times.

CHAPTER 1

ESCAPES

1880s–1916

"Race, human; Religion, none."
—Tillie Olsen, "Tell Me a Riddle," 1960

On 14 January 1912 in Omaha, Nebraska, a baby named "Tybile," Yiddish for little dove, was born to Ida Goldberg and Sam Lerner. The name echoed the universal symbol of the peace that Ida and Sam expected America to provide. The two of them seemed indistinguishable from other Russian Jewish immigrants in North Omaha: Yiddish-speaking at home, hard-working yet poor, sacrificing for their children. These parents, though, were unique, themselves the stuff of legends.

Baby Tybile grew up as Tillie Lerner, coveting stories about her parents' impoverished origins and their defiance of the czar's Cossacks in the failed 1905 Russian Revolution. As Tillie Olsen she spun stories true to her parents' essential characters as iconoclasts, idealists, and reformers in a movement that eventually toppled an ancient and corrupt regime. In 1924, when she applied to attend night school to better her English, Tillie's mother wrote:

> I see again the old destroyed houses of the people from the old country. I hear the wind blow through them with the disgusting cry why [.] The poor creatures ignore him, dont protest against him, that soulless wind dont no [know], that they are helpless, have no material to repair the houses and no clothes to cover up their bodies, and so the sharp wind['s] echo-cry falls on the window, and the windows cry with silver-ball tears seeing all the poor shivering creatures dressed in rags with frozen fingers and feverish hungry eyes.

That compassion for "poor shivering creatures" and her hopes for a world of only one race—the human—profoundly affected each of her six children.[1]

Public records, histories, and family recollections fill in details that Tillie Lerner Olsen did not know. Her father, Samuel Lerner, was born in December 1884, her mother, Hashka Goldberg, in January 1885.[2] The Goldberg family lived in the hamlet of Osipovichi in Bobruisk within the Minsk Province. Though this area was 50 percent Jewish, Jews had no rights, no voice beyond the shtetls. Farmlands and major cities were closed to them.[3] In such shtetls, houses were jammed together, as were people and animals. A single dwelling might include a workshop and house an extended family. With streets rarely cobbled, carts and animals kept the lanes and alleys constantly churned. Hashka's father, Zalman Goldberg worked in the logging business and was called "Rebbe," as perhaps a rabbi, or simply an old man who enjoyed respect and authority.[4] His wife, Raisa Gisha Shapiro Goldberg, enjoyed neither. No one remembered anything specific about her, except that she bore Zalman five daughters and three sons.[5] She taught her daughters to share housekeeping and mothering duties for the family, to work a Singer sewing machine of the type imported from America in the 1870s, and to master their religion's intricate domestic rituals.[6]

Hashka Goldberg accepted all of her mother's lessons except the last. She resented that girls were confined, undereducated, and expected to preserve Jewish traditions, while boys escaped the home to study Torah. Hashka Goldberg detested the men's prayer "thank God I'm not a woman." When people were starving and their protests brutally suppressed, the prayer "*Dianu*"—it would be enough—infuriated her. She confided to her second son that she had been eighteen when she "threw god out of the house."[7] She also took herself out of the house.

The Lerner family lived in Minsk Province, too, but closer to the city of Minsk. Mendel Lerner and Yetta Bok Lerner had five daughters and one son, Samuel. Mendel made a modest living at diverse enterprises—a flour mill, a café, and a school. An apprentice worked the treadmill and ground the grain in a pattern dating from the Middle Ages.[8] Officially the bar-café's operator, Mendel left its running to his wife Yetta, who had to be cagey to avoid arrest because Jews were forbidden to sell liquor. Gene Lerner heard that Mendel forced two daughters, Chaika and Rose, to help their mother in the café, even when patrons regularly pinched their bottoms and squeezed their breasts. These daughters detested the patrons and resented the father who failed to protect them. At the *kheyder*, or small Jewish home school for boys, Mendel himself taught all the subjects.[9] He did not teach his daughters because women needed only minimal learning to preserve Jewish traditions in the family. The lone son Samuel was the tallest Lerner, smart, handsome, and, even as a boy, a clever punster. At his father's school, he enjoyed preferential treatment, even as he chafed under his father's religiosity.

Tillie Lerner Olsen recalled none of that information, but she did tell a story about discrimination and oppression. She said Sam could not swim but only dog-paddle, with "just a head moving through the water" because, as a boy taking a dip in the river, he had had to pile his clothes on his head to keep Gentile boys from stealing them. She combined that tale with one of paternal oppression. Her grandfather discovered Samuel swimming naked, but Mendel waited until before Sabbath observances, when, as she said, "the men all went to the baths. In front of everybody, he beat my dad unconscious." Then Samuel's father rubbed salt in the wounds, carried him home, and locked him in the chicken coop. Tillie said, "My illiterate grandmother knew her man, and she gave him some schnapps" to put him to sleep. She said her grandfather was "very tired" because he was "a poor porter," like one in the Yiddish tales of I. L. Peretz, who worked for long hours, his back "creaking under his heavy burden." In Tillie's story, her grandmother "got the key and she went and washed off all the salt and comforted my dad. And then she put the key back," while Samuel's father slept off the "schnapps."[10] Her story offers some puzzles: If Mendel Lerner were a desperately poor porter, he would not have had "schnapps" to drink; nor would the chicken coop have had a lock and key. Nor would the worn-out old man have been able to beat his son unconscious and carry him home.[11] However illogical this tale, poverty, discrimination, paternal cruelty, and maternal kindness remain its key elements.

Gene Lerner found that Samuel, after attending his father's *kheyder*, was one of few Jews authorized to attend Russian school in Minsk, where he encountered western, secular ideas and distinguished himself in languages and mathematics. As a Jew, though, he was barred from college. While Jews were denied education and were terrorized by pogroms, letters from emigrant Jews extolled freedom and opportunities abroad, especially in America. Four members of Samuel's maternal family the Boks (his grandmother, two uncles, and one aunt) set out for new beginnings in America together. Mendel Lerner feared that Samuel might follow and abandon his parents, Russia, and Torah. For Jews like Mendel, as Karl Marx said, religion was the only consolation in a cruel world.[12] Samuel was not consoled.

Jewish groups in New York and Chicago networked with organizations in the hinterlands to resettle immigrants westward.[13] After risking their lives to leave Russia for New York, the four Boks (renamed LaBook) risked their security in 1904 to travel a thousand miles west of Manhattan to an alien midwestern city named after an American Indian tribe, the Omaha. That same year, Samuel risked his life to join a largely Jewish reformist defense league, the Bund. Tillie's older sister Jann (after rejecting the name "Fannie") interviewed Sam in his old age and recorded: "1904—Dad joins Jewish self-defense."[14] Young men like Samuel joined the Bund to help overthrow the czar and establish democracy in Russia. Young women like Hashka also joined because, at least in theory, the Bund was committed to sexual equality in a postrevolutionary world.[15]

In 1939, in California, Tillie met a cultured former Russian revolutionary, Genya Gorelick, who had shown solidarity with ignorant laborers by working "in a match factory. She slept a couple of hours a day in primitive factory barracks" to prove that women could live independently of oppressive men. Genya's son, Al Richmond, wrote that his mother had felt a "romanticized asceticism: the pure revolutionary was above marriage, sex, or any solely personal gratification." Like Genya, Hashka Goldberg meant to forsake sex and marriage for the cause of justice. She began to travel on foot, at considerable risk, beyond the shtetls of the Minsk district. She read Yiddish and taught herself to read Russian novels. The more she witnessed oppression of women, the more dedicated she was to improving their lot, whether or not they were Jewish.[16]

Given the prevailing assumption that women were apolitical and ignorant, young women could sometimes be more effective in the Bund than men. Women often carried secret manifestos, hidden beneath shawls and voluminous skirts. They stood guard during meetings, sounding the alarm in time for radicals to hide subversive papers before Cossack troops arrived. Women helped organize workers in match factories, cigarette plants, lumber mills, and sewing shops to demand better working conditions. Men and women, probably including Hashka and Samuel, joined to write, act, and sing in pageants appealing to workers' longing for better lives. Probably Samuel and possibly Hashka helped write, print, and distribute underground newspapers.[17] The Bund encouraged young men and women to spend Sabbath afternoons in the woods learning to use clubs, daggers, and old revolvers, or so wrote Genya's son. In such forest gatherings, young revolutionaries broke Sabbath restrictions, defied parental, religious, and state oppression, wielded romantic weapons, vanquished brutal Cossacks in pantomime, and planned a better world. Being with like-minded members of the opposite sex in a wild and unchaperoned setting carried its own excitement. Hashka and Samuel joined such activities, but Jann recorded only that Samuel "met Mother in Minsk."

In the campaign for decent treatment for women, Hashka traveled with a young Greek Orthodox woman named Olga. One day, when Olga was speaking in Minsk, word got to officials. Before the rally could be moved or dispersed, a troop of Cossacks on horseback charged the crowd. With women screaming and scattering before the horses, Hashka witnessed in horror as the Cossacks' horses trampled Olga to death. Hashka kept a photograph of herself, clinging to Olga, who stares confidently into the camera. Later, the picture hung prominently in the Lerner's home. Gene knew the brutal tale of Olga's death, but Tillie preferred to think that the photograph showed her mother with Genya.[18]

On 22 January 1905, Czar Nicholas ordered a brutal crack-down on St. Petersburg workers who marched on the Czar's Winter Palace carrying a petition for better working conditions and voting rights. Troops armed with swords and rifles met the petitioners and killed about 130. This "Bloody Sunday" confirmed world opinion that only revolution might improve Russia. Genya Gorelick rallied crowds with her eloquence and inspired them by her dedication. The Cossacks viciously suppressed rebellion and jailed both Genya and Samuel Lerner, who narrated this story to Jann, who in turn summarized: "Jewish self defense no match for Russian military." She wrote "Dad, 20 yrs old caught, involved in 1905." Jailed, Samuel was "kept in a separate cell for 6 mo. while waiting for trial." Hashka was "in Kiev during his arrest," though she could be arrested as a Jew for being in that city. The revolution of 1905 had failed. The beautiful and erudite Genya remained incarcerated for six years. In another jail, the handsome and clever Samuel faced a worse fate: he was to be sent to Siberia to waste the rest of his life in forced labor.

Samuel told Jann that he "escaped in 1905 during war with Japan, dressed as a college student with a false mustache." Tillie told a more dramatic tale: Before he was to be marched away, an entourage of women came on visitors' day with the apparent purpose of bidding Samuel farewell. Among the group were Hashka Goldberg and Samuel's sister Rose. In the melee of well-wishers and grieving relatives, Rose and Hashka extracted a dress, shawl, babushka, and other female apparel from about their persons. When they left the prison, there was an extra woman with them. Tillie's version of the tale ends, "and that was my dad." Though the Bund had mapped out a path for him, Samuel sneaked home to bid his mother farewell. Knowing she would never again see her only son, she became hysterical. His father struck him for refusing to kiss the Mezuzah. Samuel left home weeping for his mother and cursing his father.[19]

According to Jann's notes, an enlightened government official hid Samuel in his home for two weeks. The Bund was fragmenting between inclusive Menshevik and rigid Bolshevik factions. Samuel had no use for the Bolsheviks, led by Vladimir Lenin. In Polotsk near Poland he worked to organize workers against further pogroms. Meanwhile, his sisters escaped both the bar-café and Russia. Chaika Lerner married Hyman Swartz and Rose Lerner was engaged to Lazer Wolk, so the four left together for America.[20]

Given public foment for improved living conditions and basic rights, on 17 October 1905, a desperate Czar Nicholas II announced modest reforms. Rumors spread that he had granted equal rights to Jews. Reforms backfired, as seven hundred pogroms and anti-Jewish demonstrations, in the fall of 1905, followed. The police and army did not protect the innocent, lest they be accused of defending Jews against Russians. Czar Nicholas refused to pardon any revolutionary. If caught, Samuel Lerner was headed for execution, but he said a courageous government official tipped him off that his rearrest was to serve as a lesson for other prisoners contemplating escape. Despite the danger, Samuel sought Hashka and prevailed upon her to abandon her intention to forsake sex and marriage in the cause of justice. Whether they made love, they did make commitments.

After that extremely hazardous rendezvous, with the Bund urging him, as he told Jann, "to leave country—[he] left for London. Stole across border by help of secret agents. Party paid expenses & his father helped." In Tillie's account, as a "poor porter," his father had no money to help but cursed Samuel instead. In her siblings' account, the Bund instructed Sam to walk across the border from Poland into Germany. Non-Bolshevik Bund members hid him near Berlin for three weeks; then he traveled by train to Bremen, and from there sailed to England. He strolled the streets of London, picking up the language, and observing differences between the elegance of Mayfair and the deprivations of east end slums. He learned about socialist reforms in governance. Jann wrote that Sam's mother died soon after he left; her "unfortunate death [was] due to scare" for him and a resulting epileptic fit. Tillie, liking to believe that Sam's mother died in the 1920s, said that Sam covered his mother's picture with black cloth. Jann's note confirms, however, that Sam knew his mother died shortly after he left Russia.[21]

However these stories varied, no one doubted Samuel's love for his mother; and no one doubted that his skills at languages and wily impersonations helped him escape Russia and acclimate to England. Himself an actor, Gene said Sam learned English well enough to take part in a repertory theater company named after Jack London, whose novel *People of the Abyss* exposed the horrors of London's slum life. Sam played bit parts for room, board, and an introduction to socialism. He was inspired by William Morris, who aimed to restore dignity to the working man by teaching traditional crafts. Armed with knowledge of British English and English socialism, Samuel left London in summer 1906 and boarded the vessel, *St. Paul*, in Southampton. He arrived in New York on 9 September 1906 and was met by his sister Rose, now married to Lazer (renamed Louis) Wolk. Meanwhile, Hashka Goldberg's older sister Chodeh, with her husband Morris Braude and their two young children, had left Russia for Baltimore.

Changes in family names among immigrants were more the rule than the exception. When Samuel's sister Chaika Lerner Swartz immigrated to the states, customs officials anointed her with the Anglicized name of "Ida," and when Hashka's sister Chodeh Goldberg Braude immigrated to the states, customs officials dubbed her "Ida," too. Before long, Sam was able to send Hashka a ticket. She arrived in the port of New York in June or July 1907, on the *Rindam*, sailing from Rotterdam. Before she could join Sam, customs officials christened her too with a new American name—Ida.[22]

Ida had no English; Sam had no connections in New York. As immigrants, they took menial jobs. Ida worked as a seamstress in an oppressive New York sweatshop, and Sam took probably even more demeaning jobs. They were desperately poor, frustrated, and lonely, but America was not a place for protest, especially when they could leave the slums for opportunities in the west. A year after she arrived, Ida and Sam decided to follow his family. Though the plains of Nebraska bore no relation to the forests of Minsk, this underpopulated state seemed to offer Russian emigrés a wealth of opportunities.

By the time Ida and Sam reached Nebraska, forty-one years of statehood had doubled its population. With wooden Indians standing outside western outfitters, Omaha was the "Gate City" to the American west.[23] It presided over the center of a vast web of rail lines stretching the length and breadth of the nation. From the West, the rails shipped cattle and pigs to Omaha slaughterhouses; from the East and South, the rails brought workers to man the meat-processing industry. In *Yonnondio* Olsen wrote that the "fog of stink smothers down over it all." The stench spoke "for the packing houses, heart of all that moves in these streets."[24] Avoiding those smelly South Omaha streets, Ida and Sam joined the city's rapidly growing Jewish population, in North Omaha.[25]

On 18 December 1908, in Omaha, Samuel Lerner filed his Declaration of Intention to become a citizen of the United States of America. He and Ida presented themselves both officially and unofficially as a married couple. Ida, however, considered the marriage bond an affront to the dignity of women. Not until 1942 did she wear a wedding ring; however, Ida did not ever marry Sam Lerner.

Congregating around North Twenty-fourth Street, Omaha's Jewish families created an environment reminiscent, except for its prosperity, of old world vocations. Jews ran tailor shops, shoe shops, groceries, Kosher delicatessens, clothing stores, and other family businesses. As of 1909, there was even a Jewish peddler's union. Different synagogues, reflecting their congregations' Lithuanian, Hungarian, German, and Russian backgrounds, occupied former Christian churches, as those congregations moved west to more affluent suburbs. The City Directory of 1909 listed Ida Lerner as a tailor for Sam's uncle Reuben LaBook at 2623 Caldwell, a North Omaha residential and business address. Sam first appeared in the 1910 Omaha City Directory, with a modern job as elevator operator in a grand building downtown. A cousin of Ida's had married Israel Beber in Minsk; now they too arrived in Omaha.[26] Then, much to Ida's irritation, her sister Chodeh Goldberg Braude and her family left Baltimore and moved to Omaha. As rigid and orthodox as their father had been, Chodeh took advantage of her age and relative affluence to lecture against Ida's egalitarian values. Had she known that Ida and Sam were unmarried, Chodeh would have denounced them both.

A cheap trolley ride from North Twenty-fourth Street brought residents to Omaha's prosperous "miracle mile" of wide tree-lined avenues, handsome municipal buildings and parks, and a magnificent high school, atop a downtown promontory.[27] Some ten blocks west of the Jewish nucleus, handsome houses with turrets, gables, and mansard roofs advertised their owners' eminence. Because Ida and Sam distrusted such testimonies of wealth, they were gratified to find that the Workmen's Circle, an American Bund, was so active in Omaha it split into several branches.

Ida and Sam's first daughter was born in Omaha on 23 February 1910. Admiring the beauty of nature's creatures, Ida chose the Yiddish name "Fegele," meaning "little bird," for her first baby. Doctor Jefferson presided at the birth of the healthy baby; he became a friend of the family, but in 1910 he knew them so slightly he thought they were "white-German." Ida and Sam soon adapted an English name for Fegele—"Fannie." Unable to find meaningful work, Sam became a peddler and probably joined the peddler's union.

Almost two years after the birth of Fannie, on a frigid 14 January 1912, another daughter was born to Ida and Sam. Before long, the eyes of Tybile, little dove, had lightened to a sky blue, and her head was covered with thick curls. If Sam had hoped for a son, his disappointment was quickly mollified by this second child. With her name Anglicized to Tillie, she distinguished herself by babbling as a baby, talking early, walking early, always demanding, and usually getting attention.

Ida and Sam did not register the births of their two daughters. Perhaps they remembered the ways of the old country, where birth registrations cost fees and subjected families to poll taxes, the draft, and other interferences.[28] Perhaps they were afraid of disclosing their unmarried state. Perhaps they were intimidated by anti-immigrant resentment. Or perhaps they did not understand the requirement to register births.

Sam soon traded in his push-cart for a clerking job with a pawnbroker on North Twentieth Street.[29] To Ida, pawn shops represented the worst of capitalism; they had nothing to do with the dignity of work and dealt only with trading worldly goods for cash, transactions that benefited only the broker. The city's exploitative factories, crowded ghettos, and pawn shops seemed almost as corrupt as New York sweat shops. Ida and Sam wondered if the open land further west was pure and untrammeled. He was a restless young man, but one with a life-mate, if not a wife, and two daughters. If he could not clear the middle border of rattlesnakes, or herd cattle on the open prairie, or pan for gold in California, then he thought he could farm the midwestern plains. He wanted "to experience the open spaces, to own land, and to farm" precisely because, Tillie speculated, Jews had been forbidden to do so in Russia.[30] Two events in March 1913 made farming seem actually practical.

On 20 March 1913, branch 173 of Omaha's Workmen's Circle reacted to a nationwide 25-percent hike in the price of meat by planning a Kosher meat cooperative. Those plans to benefit both producers and consumers would put Ida and Sam's socialist ideals to practical use. Three days later, however, a tornado, hitting Omaha late in the afternoon, cleared a swath about a quarter of a mile wide and seven miles long. Arriving without warning, this black, twirling, funnel-shaped cloud bore no resemblance to any European storm Ida or Sam had ever experienced. This "Easter Sunday Tornado" tore buildings from the best residential areas to the west of town into the poorer northeast, where Ida, Sam, and their little girls lived. Their neighborhood was severely damaged, while the Jewish area further north of them was devastated. More than 350 people were injured and 185 were killed. Survivors were hungry, exposed, and terrified. Municipal agencies, churches, synagogues, and the Workmen's Circle struggled to alleviate the misery. At the Jewish Relief Station at 1604 North Twenty-fourth Street, volunteers who spoke both Yiddish and English helped immigrants, like Ida and Sam, find private and public assistance.[31] In this crisis, socialist schemes for a meat cooperative and more shared commerce were forgotten.

The *Omaha Bee* soon filled its front pages with news about emergency efforts, and its back pages featured advertisements for loans to pay for repairs and ads like the following from 31 March 1913: "Farm Hands. Laborers furnished free of charge to employer. Evans' Employment Office, 1617 Dodge." Sam responded and was hired as a farm hand. In her family history, Jann Lerner recorded: "Farm right after tornado." While Sam would be a laborer "furnished" to a land-owner, Ida could plant a garden, raise chickens, and feed the family with home-grown vegetables and fresh eggs. Their girls could play in fresh air. And Ida could enjoy her third pregnancy far away from the stench that occasionally floated north from the Omaha slaughterhouses. So Sam contended.

In Omaha and the nearby countryside, time was now reckoned as "before the tornado" or after it. For Ida, time must have been similarly divided. Before the tornado, she had achieved some comfort in Omaha. She lived in a poor neighborhood, but so did the extended family. All spoke Yiddish together, and, even if Ida and Sam eschewed religious observances, familiar customs reassured them, as did the Workmen's Circle.

After the tornado, Saunders County, Nebraska, offered no such reassurances. The town of Mead, about thirty miles west of Omaha, might have been on a different continent. At Mead's Union Pacific depot, the anxious couple (Ida not yet showing her third pregnancy) and their two daughters were met by Charles Burmeister.[32] He and his wife owned 320 acres of farm land in Marble Precinct, about half way between the towns of Mead and Memphis, stretching west and east without stream, or hill, or even tree.[33]

If Omaha was in part cosmopolitan, dynamic, Jewish, and hilly, Marble Precinct was rural, slow, Christian, and flat. Roads were not laid out, as even cow paths are, following such natural phenomenon as valleys or rivers; instead, they followed an abstract grid of right angled intersections, unnatural impositions onto an uneventful landscape. From Mead, Burmeister drove south, then east, then south, and then east again past a schoolhouse to get to the small tenant house on the east end of his farm. The emptiness of the landscape, with its artificial crisscrossing of roads, was almost as much a shock as the tornado had been. Sam quickly settled his family on Burmeister's property and went to work. Though monotonously flat, these plains, enriched by wind-deposited silt, were amazingly fertile.[34] Here the American dream of investing hard work toward owning land seemed a possibility. In *Yonnondio*, Tillie Olsen captures the lure of farming:

> Days falling freely into large rhythms of weather. Feet sinking into plowed
> earth, the plow making a bright furrow. Corn coming swiftly up. Tender
> green stalks with thin outer shoots, like grass. . . . Drama of things growing.
> You're browning, children, the world is an oven, and you're browning

in it. How good the weariness—in the tiredness, the body may dream. How good the table, with the steam arising from the boiled potatoes and vegetables and the full-bellied pitcher of milk.

That picture of joy and plenty would, however, elude Ida and the children. After his escape from prison, Sam had become a happy-go-lucky guy. If he took a horse-drawn buggy into Mead once in a while for supplies, then he would be sure to chat with the postmaster and general store owner, ingratiating himself into a community of men, who marveled over Mead's new-fangled improvements. Even after the assassination in Sarajevo of Archduke Franz Ferdinand and Austria's declaration of war on Serbia on 28 July 1914—events plunging Europe into war—Mead residents were more conscious of the electric lights, water tower, fire hydrants, and a one-cylinder electric generator their town now sported.[35] Burmeister's tenants, however, had no such modern improvements. As Tillie Olsen wrote in *Yonnondio*: "'I tell you, you cant make a go of it. Tenant farmin is the only thing worse than farmin your own.'"

Since late in the past century, local newspapers had carried populist editorials applauding socialist Eugene Debs and lamenting tenant farmers' situations.[36] Socialist values affected farmers who worked together as harvesting crews, traveling from farm to farm, helping everyone bring in the crops, with the aid of a threshing machine owned by a single farmer. Tillie remembered such "cooperative harvesting. My dad was well known and liked. He was good company, very jovial."[37] Jann explained, "My father was fluent in English and always spoke to the men on the porch, never inside. Only once do I remember visitors that Mom knew."

Except for those one-time visitors, Ida had no social life at all. She spoke to no one other than her little girls and Sam. With Sam working in the fields as long as daylight lasted and visiting with men folk afterward, the former crusader for women's rights found herself oppressed and lonely. Of course, country women gathered for quilting bees and canning sessions; they cooked for community picnics and sang in the choirs; but all such activities centered in the usually Lutheran churches. Ida had no interest in, time for, or access to them. She was a Jew who spoke only Yiddish.

Prairie grasses and wildflowers (lilies, buttercups, poppies, capers, golden rod, and clovers) could be lovely. In several beautiful passages in *Yonnondio*, Tillie Olsen recalled Ida's delight as the mother shows her children blossoms from catalpa trees: "look inside, there's black and gold and blue markings, beautiful. And the tiny glass thread standing up as if they was flowers themselves. Yes . . . they do feel velvet inside." Such moments are rare in *Yonnondio*, as they were in Ida's time on the farm. If Sam borrowed a horse and buggy, it was not for a pleasant drive in the country but to buy Burmeister's supplies. While Sam worked in the fields, Ida had water to pump, wood to chop, fires to stoke, bread to bake, eggs to gather, chickens to feed, behead, pluck, and bake, meals to fix, a privy to clean, floors to scrub, and clothes to wash in water warmed on a wood stove and hung out to dry. The kitchen seemed always clouded with steam and festooned with wet clothes flapping from lines above the wood stove. Tillie remembered Ida always washing, cleaning, cooking, and nursing a baby.[38]

Both Lerner girls were exceptionally bright, but little Tillie was outgoing, as Fannie was not. While Fannie's feelings were repressed, Tillie's were irrepressible. Even as a toddler, Fannie felt eclipsed in her parents' affections by the cute little Tillie, with her curly hair, big blue eyes, and amusing ways. But soon both girls felt displaced in their parents' affections by the birth of a little brother, Harry Victor Lerner.[39] He was the first Lerner child with the middle-class honor of a birth announcement. On 4 December 1913, the *Wahoo Wasp* noted: "Born to Samuel Lerner and wife, a boy on Fri., Nov. 28."[40]

Relieved to have given Sam a much-wanted son, Ida still experienced the new baby as another burden. She had no energy for and no outlet to the causes that had animated her since just after the turn of the century. Fannie soon learned to keep the baby distracted while her mother did chores. In her old age, Jann recalled her mother rather dramatically as "emotionally disturbed." Ida was "overwhelmed in foreign surroundings, not knowing the language, afraid of her neighbors, on a farm where she was even frightened by the animals, one child after another, all alone, no one to hear her lamentations and anger, I the only one." There was another cause for fear: tornadoes in flat prairies of Saunders County were even more a threat than in Omaha.

Less than two when baby Harry was born, Tillie did not react as Fannie did. She stomped her feet and said "No!" She sobbed when she did not get her way. She sought her father's attentions when her mother was nursing the baby, and her mother's when her father was working. Then, barely more than a year after Harry's birth, Lillian Lerner, named after Ida's favorite flower, was born on 14 December 1914. The Saunders County records list the Lerner residence as Mead; Samuel as a farmer, Ida as a housewife; their ages are, respectively, thirty and twenty-nine.[41] With four babies born in less than five years, Ida was, Jann recalled, always "holding a baby in her arms, with a toddler beside." Tillie remembered "three kids sleeping all in the same little room," while Ida kept baby Lillie with her to nurse. At some point little Tillie began to speak with a stutter—perhaps her way of competing with little babies who gurgled and cried but did not talk. Her major means of competing, though, was to charm.

In winter, the climate was cold enough for a Mead ice plant to thrive by hoarding ice for the summers when the temperature often exceeded 100.° The summer of 1915 was different. While German and British troops were decimating each other and the countryside with a novel new weapon—mustard gas—nature took vengeance upon the Nebraska plains with relentless rain and chilling cold.[42] Clothes would not dry although the wind blew relentlessly. Tillie remembered, "we had a cellar, with double doors almost flat with the ground, they sloped up at an angle. It was called the cyclone cellar." More than once, the whole Lerner family had to dash under the house and huddle in the dark cyclone cellar among potatoes in barrels, sauerkraut and pickles in stone jars, pots of butter and jars of milk, waiting with whatever creatures dwelt there until a tornado passed by. After false alarms, "one terrible" tornado became Tillie's first precise memory.[43]

Ida had had to suppress her yearnings for the secular and feminist utopia that she envisioned, thanks to the Bund and the Socialist Party. What with childbearing, house work, farm work, exhaustion, and loneliness, she was desperately unhappy. Still, little Tillie could amuse her mother with clever questions, odd mixes of Yiddish and English words, and a flair for picking up tunes and making up ditties. Tillie became, Jann resentfully remembered, "everything" to their mother.

As Tillie became more loquacious, Fannie became more silent:

My thoughts were always unspoken. I lived among the chickens, the cows, the horses, the trees, the flowers, the birds, the corn fields, the sky, the winds, the frightening thunder. My mysterious father, whom I rarely saw, I hoped to find in the corn field, but I did see him when I came to the barn to get the fresh, warm milk. On the farm my father gave me a wonderful dog named Shep. The first auto I ever saw on our road ran over the dog. I can never forget that. I still feel the pain.

She remembered that in the tenant house there were no pencils and papers "so one day I was sent to the country-school." It was 1916.

In Europe that summer, the desperate British launched a massive, disastrous attack on German defenses in the Somme. The French had been hopelessly weakened, and the Allies war effort bogged down (literally) in trenches. Europe began to fear that this war would never end—that Western Europe would hemorrhage itself to death. Pressure was mounting on President Wilson and Congress for America to rescue the Allies and help win the war. As pacifists, Ida and Sam were alarmed by growing militarism and tensions between the German Burmeisters and some of their neighbors.

In Saunders County, school began in midsummer so that pupils could be let out at harvest time or in bad weather; in July 1916, Fannie began attending school #38.[44] Records named her as "Fannie Lehrner" and her father as "Sam Lehrner"; the misspellings suggest the teacher's disinterest. The forty-three children enrolled in the little schoolhouse ranged in age from four-and-a-half to nineteen, with mostly German and Swedish surnames.[45] Three children younger than Fannie enrolled, but each attended with a significantly older sibling. Four-year-old Tillie did not attend. Fannie walked to school by herself, hoping that sometimes a family would stop its wagon and offer her a ride, but they rarely did. She was "unhappy, as was the teacher for having a Jewish child." While the war roused anti-German feelings in much of the United States, at School #38, suspicion turned against the lone Jewish "foreigner."

Later, Tillie reconstructed those times: "Well, you see we were pacifists. And my older sister was already in first grade. There was no kindergarten out in the country. We had stones thrown at us, because we wouldn't buy war bonds. I remember that very clearly."[46] That supposedly clear recollection actually grafts later history back onto 1916. War bonds were not yet on sale; her sister did not mention stones; nor was Tillie harassed. Only Fannie walked the half mile to attend school alone; thus, she was vulnerable, while Tillie, who stayed home with their mother and the babies, was not. Her retelling, then, inserts Tillie herself into history and recasts her as another victim.

Sam Lerner had many reasons to be disenchanted with farming on the Nebraska plains. The clearing, plowing, planting of land, the harvesting and hauling of crops, and the feeding, milking, and sometimes slaughtering of animals (all for someone else's profit) hardly met his romantic ideas of living close to the land. That work neither brought him closer to farm ownership nor did any Progressives seem able to change the tenant system in which he was mired. His eldest daughter refused to go back to the country school. And his life-partner was utterly disenchanted with him.

Although Jann's phrase "emotionally disturbed" seems too strong for Ida's situation, there is no doubt that she was depressed. Living conditions in the tenant house were almost as bad as those in the shtetls. The virtues of a democratic system were invisible because unnaturalized immigrants could not vote; tenant farming bore no relation to the pastoral ideals;

and her crusading lover seemed transformed into another patriarchal oppressor who used her for sex and child-rearing. Furthermore, her first daughter had met with the same racism from which Ida had fled halfway around the globe.

Tillie would say that her parents disdained "the orthodoxies and traditions of the past; they believed that if you loved each other, you lived together."[47] Their utopian dream—based on love, trust, and equality—was, however, disintegrating. Sam did love and admire Ida, but his happy-go-luckiness led him to laugh with the farmer-hands, not to cry with Ida. He might have faulted himself for enticing Ida to America with utopian dreams, only to oppress her with domestic cares. Sam did not realize how much he needed Ida intellectually and ethically. He did know he needed her sexually. In summer 1916, she became pregnant once again.

Somehow, out of her loneliness and misery and fatigue, the fierce Ida who had defied her father and thrown god out of the house reemerged. She must have denounced their life and blamed Sam. He had to concede that tenant farming had not been pastoral, healthy, or inspiring and that Ida had borne an unfair burden of toil. After the harvest was in, sometime late in fall 1916, the Lerners packed their belongings and left.

At the Union Pacific station in Mead, with whistles shrieking, the family trudged through clouds of steam to board a train headed east. Tillie could remember all six of them piled into four narrow seats to save fares, though Ida was so swollen she could barely make room for little Lillie on her lap. Carrying all their earthly goods in boxes and cardboard suitcases, the Lerners, humiliated, returned to Omaha. After a three-and-a-half-year experiment in country living, they had to seek the care of relatives.

Little Fannie had internalized her schoolmates' xenophobic message. Though she had escaped the farm and the country school's anti-Semitic bullies, she remained a frightened child. Little Tillie, not yet five years old, was unabashed. Fancying that a wind child was "caged in me," she longed to uncage that child and soar.

CHAPTER 2

REALITY RAISED

1917–1924

I remember us all at that age (but not just when I raised reality and inked my self eyebrows—and hair long enough to cover 'the shame' of such ears—).
                                        —Tillie Olsen to her younger brother, 1985

At the beginning of 1917, the Lerners were lodged in a tenement house on North Twentieth Street, cramped quarters that frustrated the wind child in Tillie, which "struggled, choked and twisted to leap out and run with the wind whenever it heard the wind's voice."[1] With four little children, the eldest under seven and another on the way, Ida was harried and worn. Though the air was not so clean nor the produce so fresh, Omaha offered excellent schools, good teachers, free kindergartens, and free evening classes for adults. It also offered water, sewer, and electrical services, a fast trolley line, and Jewish cultural events.

In January 1917, Ida walked her first daughter the few blocks to Kellom School to begin the first grade. Three days later Ida also enrolled her second daughter, not quite five years old. The girls walked to school, and Tillie loved scampering along mornings and afternoons with neighborhood children, who chattered in odd combinations of Yiddish, Russian, and English. She skipped ahead of her sister, who was glad to be freed of the country kids who had made her so miserable and also of boisterous little Tillie.[2]

The girls had been in school just longer than a month when, on 21 February, Ida gave birth to her fifth child. Turning seven two days later, Fannie felt protective of baby Morris. Five-year-old Tillie had no interest in another baby. The wind child in her sped through lessons and asked funny questions and jollied the other children along, to the amusement of her father, who encouraged her antics, and her kindergarten teacher, Miss Metz. Ida felt protective of Tillie, partly because they almost shared a birthday,

21

but mostly because the five-year-old was the liveliest and seemed the most promising of her children.[3]

When the United States officially entered World War I in April, young men from all walks of life flocked to enlist. Patriotic parades sent them off as heroes. Liberty Bonds went on sale. School children saved pennies to buy War Savings Stamps at 25¢ each to help defeat the Huns, but Fannie and Tillie were forbidden to waste time collecting war stamps and told to concentrate on lessons. While Fannie finished the first grade, Tillie finished all of kindergarten and half of the first grade in the spring term of 1917. The wind child was propelling this special little girl toward something momentous.

By the time baby Morris was starting to crawl and the school year had begun in fall 1917, the Lerners had moved to a substantial house at 2512 Caldwell Street. Though only a few blocks further from Kellom School than their former lodgings, the new house meant the girls had walk to school by crossing North Twenty-fourth, a bustling street bordered with shops, filled with peddlers' carts and pedestrians, and traversed by a trolley line, with a few honking automobiles zigzagging in and out of traffic.

Other than the hazardous walk to Kellom School, Caldwell Street offered a promising environment for the Lerners. Samuel's aunt Chaika LaBook Sokolow lived a block away. Across an alley and around the corner from the Lerners on Twenty-fifth, lived the Steins, who ran a small grocery down on North Twenty-fourth. An African-American Baptist church sat beyond the Stein's house, on the corner of North Twenty-fifth and Hamilton. Up Caldwell, sat a "mysterious, silent nunnery, Catholic and closed." Tillie's younger brother recalled it as "imprisoned by a high concrete wall and stifled in a disturbing silence." The exuberance of the African-American church and the silence of the nunnery made puzzling studies in Christianity for the Lerner brood. The rituals of Judaism seemed almost as mysterious.

As news of American casualties abroad reached home, patriotic fervor intensified. Tillie remembered a parade when an effigy of the German kaiser was prodded into a fire, burning the kaiser, it seemed, alive.[4] Rampant jingoism made pacifism seem un-American, immigrants suspicious. A rash of "homestead massacres" threatened poor immigrants with death or deportation. As justice was under threat in the United States, in Russia justice seemed finally accomplished when the 1917 Bolshevik revolution ended czarist rule. The assassination of Czar Nicholas II and his family, however, fomented fear that Bolsheviks or communists, so named for advocating community control of work and property, had wider aspirations. In America, the Communist Party (CP) was small and splintered, but President Wilson's Attorney General A. Mitchell Palmer scapegoated it as an enemy of freedom. In 1918, Palmer even had socialist Eugene Victor Debs arrested for violating the Espionage Act, though he had only given an antiwar speech. Debs defended himself in court with a classic, eloquent, but futile argument; he began a ten-year jail sentence in April 1919.

Even in an anti-immigrant, antipacifist environment, the Lerners were resourceful. Sam painted or repaired houses to barter for food staples and for cloth, which Ida sewed into clothes. Ida cooked, Lillian remembered, "nutritious meals on very little money. In those days soup bones were free to regular customers, beef liver cost almost nothing." From the butcher's offerings and a kitchen garden, Ida made simple meat dishes, healthy soups, and leafy green salads without dressing, which made Sam protest, "What am I? a cow?" Fannie helped Ida clean and chop vegetables, and, when Ida could catch her, Tillie played marbles and jacks and teased her younger siblings with words she knew and they did not.[5]

Morris promised to be Ida's last child, for she now practiced birth control.[6] Her liberalism, in birth control, religion, and politics fueled an explosion with her sister. The Braudes were Zionists, conservative, and "anti-Negro." The Lerners were liberal, socialist, and antiracist. The Braudes moved further west to a "two-story house on a hill" that seemed a veritable "castle."[7] Ida stopped speaking to Chodeh Goldberg Braude.

When World War I ended on 11 November 1918, the Allies congratulated themselves on having made the world safe for democracy. In the brief euphoria before reparations that sowed seeds of another war, an era of humanity and tolerance seemed to be dawning. In Omaha, voters turned out the corrupt long-time mayor and elected a reform ticket. The rails brought African-Americans from places like Birmingham, Alabama, and Nashville, Tennessee, to Omaha. As they earned enough money to bring their families, too, many blacks moved from South Omaha to the predominantly Jewish and eastern-European North Omaha. Soon the Lerner children all had black friends, some with grandparents who had survived slavery. In her later years Tillie often commented, "I'm so old that I've talked with ex-slaves."[8]

By January 1919, when Harry Lerner registered for kindergarten at Kellom, Sam had a new profession, a "confectioner." With his business registered at 2512 Caldwell, he kept the sugars, syrups, dyes, bags of nuts, and other supplies in the basement or in a little barn behind the house and used the kitchen for cooking candy. The children all helped shell almonds and peanuts in their kitchen, and once "there was a huge vat of chocolate put in the middle of our living room." Sam stirred while the children sprinkled almonds into the vat.[9]

By the end of the spring term, seven-year-old Tillie was promoted to the second half of the third grade. She felt cleverer than Fannie and cousin Aaron Braude, who often stopped at the Lerners' on his way home from Long School, supposedly to use the indoor toilet but really to enjoy a healthy snack from his Aunt Ida and candy from his Uncle Sam. He did not stay, lest his mother punish him for associating with supposedly Bolshevik cousins.[10] Always "chanting meaningless jingles to myself," Tillie composed a little poem called "Moon":

> The moon was a round red lollypop
> stuck in the sky for the clouds to lick,
> the cloud children liked it and ate it all up,
> 'til there's nothing left but this stick.

The poem displayed a delight in words, a lively imagination, and a comic view of loss.

Ida and Sam thought the prohibition amendment absurd, but Ida was exhilarated by the other 1919 amendment, giving women the vote.[11] She and Sam could not vote, however, because they were not citizens. Postwar harmony and tolerance soon disintegrated as Attorney General Palmer blamed workers' strikes in the "Red Summer" of 1919 and mysterious bombings in eight cities, including Washington, D.C., on communists. He argued that Russians had brought down the czar and could do the same to the president. He began deporting immigrants, like Emma Goldman, for speaking out against war and intolerance. Rumors that blacks were all strike-breakers heightened racial and labor tensions. Then the *Omaha Bee* announced "Black Beast First Sticks-up Couple" in the "most daring attack on a white woman ever perpetrated in Omaha."[12] That inflammatory headline brought the arrest of a former packing-house laborer whose severe rheumatism had incapacitated him for work and also, common sense suggests, for sexual assaults. On 28 September 1919, the city was convulsed in racist hysteria. A huge mob set fire to the courthouse, tried to hang the reform mayor, did hang the accused man, and dragged his remains downtown to the intersection of Seventeenth and Dodge streets. About 11 P.M., it set what was left of the corpse on fire. Federal troops belatedly arrived to keep order. [13] In his Yiddish newspaper, the *Omaha Jewish Bulletin*, Isaac Konecky castigated citizens for brutality to blacks and intolerance of Jews.[14]

Sam realized he needed more than English fluency to prove himself a good American. He took three responsible steps. First, he bought a house.

For $2,000, Sam became owner of 2512 Caldwell Street in December 1919.[15] Since 1917, Ida had made the house theirs, tending flowers and vegetables in her backyard garden, growing grass in the front yard around a lovely maple tree, and sewing curtains for the windows. Still, her name was not on the deed, which assigned the property to Sam and his "heirs and assigns forever."[16]

Sam's second move was joining, on 5 January 1920, branch 173 of the Workmen's Circle, aligned with trade unions, socialism, the Bund, and the *Jewish Daily Forward,* the largest Jewish paper in the world. The Circles appealed to the Lerners' commitment to justice, their need for security, with low-cost insurance policies, and, to Sam's sense of self-worth, which peddling and farming had undermined.[17] Before long he became treasurer of branch 173 of the Workmen's Circle and then secretary of the state Socialist Party.[18]

Sam's third self-protective act was to become a citizen. In November 1920, the United States of America issued a Certificate of Naturalization for the Lerner family, which listed Ida as Sam's wife and named their five children. This certificate was not processed in time for Sam or Ida to vote in the 1920 election, so they missing voting for Eugene Debs, who ran from an Atlanta prison cell and received 919,000 votes—his record in his five tries. His feisty campaign overshadowed those of Democrat James M. Cox and Republican Warren G. Harding, but the barely qualified Harding was elected president.

While Sam was busy establishing his American credentials, Ida spent much of her time caring for her fourth child, who was hit by a speeding car when Sam took the children to visit their Braude cousins in affluent western Omaha. Lillian's slow recovery set her apart from what Morris would call "the swirling eddy" of Lerner passions "to salvage the world" or "achieve grandeur." She also stayed outside rivalries that pitted Harry against Morris and Fannie against Tillie and aligned Fannie and Harry with Sam, Tillie and Morris with Ida.[19]

Another property deed, dated 29 March 1921, suggests some alteration in Sam's relationship with Ida. For "One Dollar and other good consideration" Sam completely signed over the house to "Ida Lerner, my wife."[20] He told Morris that she would have a baby, and Morris recalled turning cartwheels in the back yard, singing "new life is coming here!" The five Lerner children were winter babies, born between late November and mid-February. On 26 August 1921, another girl, the Lerners' only blond and only summer child, was born. They named her Yetta, after Sam's lost mother. Morris called her a girl of "sunshine beauty."[21] All her life Tillie delighted in calling her "my baby sister." Whether she planned this pregnancy, Ida, like everyone else, was delighted with this baby girl.

The ground floor of the Lerner house included a living room, dining room, and kitchen, stretching from front to back on one side. On the other side were a large bedroom for the senior Lerners and now baby Yetta, a bathroom, and a small bedroom for Morris. Upstairs Fannie had her own room, and Tillie shared an open bedroom with Lillian. These rooms had windows overlooking the front porch's roof. From the open bedroom, a few steps led up to a raised platform looking back over an alley. Harry claimed that space as his own, and Ida soon curtained it off to separate him from his sisters.

By the 1921–1922 school year, Lillian was almost ready to begin school, but Ida feared for the little girl to cross streets, so she registered her at Long Elementary School, on their side of North Twenty-fourth Street, and prevailed upon the school board to have her older children transferred there too. In September 1921, Fannie, Tillie, and Harry began at Long, though six-year-old Lillian still stayed out. The three older children's registrations list Sam's profession as, respectively, a merchant, a confectioner, and a clerk. City Directories list him as president of the Silver Star Candy Company. No longer were vats of candy bubbling on the kitchen stove on Caldwell Street. Sam relocated his candy company to 1604 North Twenty-fourth, the same one-story building that had housed the Jewish Relief Station after the 1913 tornado. Sam expressed a socialist belief in the dignity of craftsmanship in creations like sugar flowers and candy vases, one of which Tillie remembered breaking.[22]

Whenever she talked about Long School, Tillie always mentioned framed pictures of nineteenth-century American writers, "those white bearded men who happened to be abolitionists." Most of them, like Oliver Wendell Holmes and William Cullen Bryant, had three names, which amazed her, she said, because she did not know anyone with three names; she apparently forgot her brother Harry Victor Lerner. Ralph Waldo Emerson lacked a beard but had the requisite three names and reformist politics. His poem "Redemption," Tillie said, should gratify African-Americans who yearn for reparation "because the poem's last line is 'Pay them!'" Also attending Socialist Sunday School, Tillie said her education brought her "closer to our own country's revolutionary past, an anti-slavery past"; it offered "a real sense of the times when our country tried to live up to democratic ideals."[23]

Those ideals of racial and political tolerance were jeopardized on 31 May 1921, in Tulsa, Oklahoma; after yet another charge that a black man had assaulted a white woman, the Ku Klux Klan went on a rampage through

Tulsa's black neighborhoods.[24] Then, in Omaha, a strike in meat-packing plants turned violent and racially vindictive.[25] Sam was too good a friend to his diverse neighbors to feel threatened. He even counted the cash register's take in front of the store's lighted window. Fannie often walked there after baby-sitting to urge him home. One night she witnessed a man grab her father. Though a pacifist, Sam successfully held off the robber until the man hit him on the head with a brick. Fannie screamed until "the police came. Then an ambulance came, he was treated, then taken home. Mother was in shock, kept crying desperately."[26] Neither Ida nor Sam blamed the man but instead the poverty and injustice that brought him to rob. Once, when a strange black man opened the Lerners' unlocked front door, Ida simply said, "Sir, you have the wrong house" and the man left.[27] Pacifism, though, was rarely so useful a weapon.

Like Chodeh Braude, many people tried both to deny the existence of injustice and to escape its persistent results by moving away from economically disadvantaged neighborhoods. Like Palmer, many blamed immigrants, blacks, and communists for social unrest and called for deportations and arrests. Socialists, like the Lerners, chose to work for better living conditions for all. The Lerners sheltered their black neighbors during the 1919 riot. In 1921, branch 173 of the Workmen's Circle sent $49.10 to support the packing-house strikers. Debs was released from prison on Christmas 1921, by President Harding, who was in no danger of being called soft on Reds. Pushing for radical changes in the capitalist system, the CP courted Debs. He, however, condemned Bolshevism and remained a socialist. The CP then labeled Debs and Workmens' Circle members "social fascists" for being middle class.[28] To Ida and Sam communists were as guilty as Attorney General Palmer of bending truth to fit ideology.

Thanks to gifts and volunteer work from craftsmen like Sam Lerner, the Workmen's Circles finished the Labor Lyceum, on North Twenty-second, in August 1922. Wives formed a Ladies Labor Lyceum Club, but Ida was too outspoken for the ladies and remained a member of the mostly male Workmen's Circle. The Lyceum's auditorium, which seated 250, hosted local performances, informative free lectures on secular topics, and traveling Yiddish theater.[29] The Lerner children practiced singing and invented silly plays at home in their "Cosy Club." Ida taught them harmony, and they often sang Yiddish songs at the Lyceum. In *Yonnondio* Tillie wrote about singing when "the separate voices chorded into one great full one," an ecstatic experience of bonding and transcending. Rather than bonding with her brothers and sisters, though, Tillie teased and taunted them and left them with her chores.

The Labor Lyceum also sponsored various leftist groups, like the Young People's Socialist League, led by Eugene Konecky. Born in 1898, he was the son of Isaac, editor of the *Omaha Jewish Bulletin*. In *Bulletin* installments, the Koneckys attacked racism and classism in the Jewish community, but their attack on a "Jew Klux Klan" went so far, the Jewish establishment shut down the *Bulletin* in April 1921. Eugene took a job as publicity manager for the Woodmen of the World's new Omaha radio station WOW. He had married in 1919, had a son in 1922, and had a book of poems accepted, including one, "Infidelity," which hinted at the handsome young man's outside activities. Assistant editor for the Woodmen's *Sovereign Visitor* magazine, he was hailed as Omaha's most promising literary talent. He was certainly its most accomplished self-promoter and adman.[30]

Sleeping downstairs, Morris would hear his parents arguing in Yiddish in the front bedroom. He would yell, "Be quiet! Act like grown-ups," and they would tell him, "You go to sleep." Though he knew little Yiddish, Morris recognized Tillie's name in their arguments. Yetta remembered, "Tillie's faults were overlooked. Ma would argue with Dad about it, saying he was too tolerant." Lillian recalled, "My mother tried to persuade him to take some action regarding Tillie, to no avail." Lillian thought that Ida "couldn't control Tillie," who thus got "out of doing work," which usually fell to Fannie instead.[31] Fannie once refused "to do some ironing that Mama asked me to do. And when she asked me to wash the kitchen floor, I got angry and told her to get Tillie to do it. Mama and I had an argument but I didn't give in. So Dad went ahead and washed the floor." Fannie "had responsibility I accepted. Tillie had none—and none was requested. . . . Tillie was Mama's prize."[32] Before long, Yetta took the little downstairs bedroom, and Morris moved up to share the curtained off room with Harry.

While Fannie did chores, Tillie walked from Long School downtown to the public library, through heavy revolving doors, where "crowning the mid-part of the stairs . . . you couldn't help but see this huge painting of Willa Cather." In cool paneled rooms, she read her way through Julius-Haldeman paperbacks and *McGuffey Readers*, which since 1836 had taught generations of American young people not only to read and write but to value virtues like honesty, kindness, sharing, and thrift.[33] Such old-fashioned virtues seemed inadequate in the face of 1920s injustice and the growing economic gap between ordinary citizens and the very rich.

Even if they resented preferential treatment given Tillie, the younger Lerners were glad for her attention, though she spoiled word games by continuing to read the dictionary after looking up a word. When she showed them constellations in the night sky, she seemed to be showing "off what she called her culture and her vocabulary." Her lengthy explanations silenced them. The boys especially resented that she got away with pranks for which they were punished. Once Lillian was horrified to witness a whipping Sam gave the usually well-behaved Harry. Ida "never whipped, never shouted," but she offered few hugs or kisses beyond babyhood. Morris described the Lerners as "a Jewish Radical Puritan family."[34]

Ida still stayed up late at night reading the Yiddish papers and waiting for Sam. She did so much housework herself, it seemed to Lillian, so her children could take advantage of their educations. She looked over their school work not to criticize but, it seemed to Morris, to better her English and to learn poems, like Longfellow's "Hiawatha," with its rhyme and rhythm and romantic vision of native Americans. Loving opera, Ida delighted in recordings of Caruso, Galli-curci, and Schumann-Heink that she played on the record player Sam purchased for her. Her talented children improvised on a piano which sat on the front porch in warm weather, covered with canvas against rain. When Yetta was only three, she invented her own melodies, rather as little JimJim in *Yonnondio* sings when he can make only "a shadow of the real words, but the melody came true and clear." Tillie was a friend to the younger Lerners when she sang on the porch with Lillian, danced with Morris and Yetta, and played games like "ring around the rosie" in front of the neighbors.

As Ida became increasingly active and confident, her arguments with Sam were no longer private. She often stood at meetings in the Labor Lyceum to condemn some policy; then Sam would arise to defend it. Or he would suggest an expedient solution to a problem, and she would rise and disagree with him. These public arguments made enemies for Ida and mortified her children, all except Tillie, who relished the drama. Gene Lerner recalled that Ida respected her children's "independence to develop ourselves in whatever direction we chose. With the exception . . . that she approved Tillie's determination, 'I'm going to be somebody.' Mother, at that time, was still young and to have a child who was going to be famous, she welcomed it, anybody would. But we were never ordered to do things. She had such very strong principles, but she never tried to force her principles on us—Harry's religious feelings for example." Harry was becoming a believer, and the atheist Ida did not interfere. Like the purple irises she planted in front of the porch, that reappeared each year, she let her children flower as they would. Sometimes, though, her most prized flower seemed more like a virulent weed.

Sam's politicking, as financial secretary of the Nebraska State Socialist Party, enabled him to bring Eugene Debs to Omaha at the beginning of the

1924 presidential election. Almost sixty-eight, Debs's term in prison had weakened his health but not his eloquence. On 10 October 1923, he told a mixed audience of 1,500 at Omaha's city auditorium that "only the poor remain long in the prisons of our land." Furthermore, he said, all war is "waged for commercial reasons." In chanted phrases, he named influential groups, starting with Wall Street financiers, who "didn't go to the war" but sent the young and the poor.[35] Sam managed to have his oldest daughters mount the stage after the talk and present Debs with roses. The talk was a triumphant example of the eloquence, passionate oratory, and socialist values that would be Tillie's for the rest of her life.

Meanwhile, Tillie had outgrown poetry such as "Moon." When she was eleven or twelve she wrote a poem called "Pet of the Fairies" which ends: "And their song is the song only I may hear—I am the one mortal they do not fear." In her eighties, Tillie would type the following commentary: "All my poems of that summer (1923? 1924?) were like this—quiet lyrics, very simple and unaffected. I think that if I had been left alone, and had not read certain 'poetry' I would have very soon found a real means of self expression and become a good poet." She blamed the "grand, tragic style of poetry—Tennyson's 'I'm to be queen of the May.'" She also blamed Eugene Konecky for encouraging her not "to express myself at all."[36] Even as an old woman, Tillie remained utterly blind to the egoism of seeing herself as the fairies' "pet," the only mortal the fairies need not fear.

The Council of Jewish Women offered classes in English and citizenship, and Kellom school offered free night classes for immigrants, both of which Ida attended in 1924.[37] Her workbook's lined pages include conventional exercises in spelling and penmanship. She copied important facts for immigrants to know and a number of truisms: for example, "Honesty is the best policy," and "The true American believes that liberty does not mean to do what you like," a concept Ida did not apply to Tillie. However tentative was her command of the niceties of English, Ida's introspection and questioning of injustice were precise. On 6 December 1924, she wondered why she could not "make clear to my-self the reason what makes it so hard for me to write a composition when there are so many things around us to arouses questions." Among her exercises in sentence-making were: "I love to study English. . . . I wich [wish] to leave Omaha; I left Russia." Disappointed in Sam and apparently in Tillie too, she did leave home, writing a practice letter, on 9 December 1924, to "My Dear Mother" from "2419 Franklin St. Omaha Neb."

The next day she was back at the Caldwell Street address, explaining to "Dear Teacher" her difficulties in studying and her recollections of the old country: "I am glad to study with ardor but the children wont let me, they go to bed late so it makes me tired, and I cant do my lessons. It is after ten o'clock my head dont work it likes to have rest. But I am in a sad mood I am sitting in the warm house and feel painfull that winter claps in to my heart." She described (quoted here in chapter 1) the "poor shivering creatures" in the old country.[38] At the end of her notebook, Ida included an original composition:

> It is told of the olden days, the people of that time were building a tower, when they were on the point of success for some reason they stopped to understand each other and on account of misunderstanding, their hopes and very lives were buried under the tower they had built. So as a human being who carries responsibility for action I think as a duty to the community we shall try to understand each other. This English class helps us to understand each other, not to feel helpless between our neighbors, serves to get more respect from the people around us. We are human beings trying to understand, we learn about the world, people and our surroundings.

On a draft, Ida added: "to ask questions [so] that superstition must vanish" and "to not forget what was [history] so to know where we must go together." Those admonishments against superstition and forgetfulness were secular ways of combating injustice. Privately she still maintained that "God and the human heart are a contradiction."[39]

Sometime near the mid-1920s, Sam became a house painter. He might have left the candy business because he was more devoted to Workmen's Circle and Socialist Party business than to his own or because being beaten had dashed his entrepreneurial instincts, or because what Aaron Braude called his "kind-hearted" candy gifts cut too far into his profits, or perhaps because, as Lillian thought, Sam preferred unconfined, "outdoor physical work." At any rate, he redirected his considerable artistry and sense of color from creations like a greenish-white sugar lily to house painting and decorating.[40]

Meanwhile, however much she stammered, Tillie's verbal powers were gaining her a reputation. She sometimes attended the African-American church around the corner and sang gospels songs with verve. She was a whiz at punning and the word games she practiced on the younger Lerners. She was called down the street to write letters for Sam's aunt, Chaika LaBook Sokolow, who remained largely illiterate in English. After school, she read anything she wanted in the public library, including Lafcadio Hearn, who had disregarded caste taboos to visit with Japanese fishermen and laborers and write their folk tales.[41] Reading Hearn, Tillie realized how rarely books depicted the deprivation and injustice that undermine society.

In May 1924, she heard about an event that threatened society in another way. Riots could be explained as reactions to injustice and ignorance, but there was no logical explanation for what privileged young men Nathan Leopold and Richard Loeb did to Loeb's fourteen-year-old cousin. When headlines announced that they confessed to murdering the boy for a thrill, as an experiment inspired by Nietzsche, the country shuddered over what seemed a new species of evil. In September, attorney Clarence Darrow saved the duo from the gallows, securing sentences for them of life plus ninety-nine years in prison.

All school children memorized poems, but Tillie's memorizing skills were so extraordinary that she was chosen to recite for the graduation ceremony at Long Elementary School in December 1924. She said that Aunt Chodeh Braude respected her recitation skills and sat on the front row at the ceremony. Tillie's siblings and surviving Braudes all doubt that story, for her presence would have been a direct insult to Ida, who still did not speak to her sister.[42] Whoever attended, Tillie did recite the assigned poem, Longfellow's "The Day is Done" with its sense that poetry should soothe until the "cares, that infest the day/ Shall fold their tents, like the Arabs/ And as silently steal away." Then she startled officials by reciting an unassigned poem, Spartacus's speech to the slaves.[43] Clearly, she sensed a disparity between literature as solace and as provocation. Equally clearly, she had learned to use a public platform and a captive audience to promote her own values. The wind child had morphed into the rebel, who disobeyed instructions, the crusader, who protested slavery, and the performer, who exploited her stage presence. She was not quite thirteen.

Sometime in this period, a professional photographer took a portrait of the four eldest Lerner children sitting on a bench in a formal pose, each staring at the cameraman.[44] Fannie wore a cotton print dress and dark stockings, while the younger three wore fancier white outfits and white stockings, symbols of Ida and Sam's American success. Clearly, the children were told to be still, to fold their hands in their laps, and to look at the camera. Three of the children managed to keep their hands folded, but not Tillie. Always the good girl, Fannie seems oblivious to the monkey business Tillie is making. Not so Harry, who was watching Lillian's lap, where Tillie's hand has slipped through the crook of her elbow to tickle the little girl's hand. Though she seems tempted to giggle, Lillian resists her big sister's mischief-making. The photo shows Tillie undermining conventional good behavior and pretending to have done nothing of the kind.

Even more curious evidence in this photograph is Tillie's later make-over of her own image. In the Jazz Age, she redrew herself. Over her naturally curly hair, she inked in a flapper image of straight bobbed hair, short bangs, and heavy dark eyebrows and eyelashes. Some sixty years later, when her younger brother sent her a copy of this photograph, she replied: "I remember us all at that age (but not just when I raised reality and inked my self eyebrows—and hair long enough to cover 'the shame' of such ears—)."[45] Tillie had raised reality and reinvented herself. She would continue doing so.

CHAPTER 3

MAGNETIC PERSONALITY

1925–1929

"And I would that this Squeaky typewriter could squeak some squeaks for me."
—Tillie Lerner, "Squeaks," in the Central High *Register*

The Tillie Lerner who dumbfounded officials by rebelliously reciting Spartacus's speech was intimidated at first when, just thirteen, she entered Omaha's Central High in January 1925. This giant edifice was built around the old high school, which was then demolished, leaving a central courtyard, where students gathered between classes, unobserved by townspeople on the streets below.[1] Although Tillie said that only she and a black minister's son transferred to Central from Long, about 5 percent of its graduates regularly did so; certainly all the Lerner children attended Central. Fannie was enrolled in commercial courses, and Tillie in a college preparatory curriculum.[2] The sisters might have taken the trolley from North Twenty-fourth to North Twentieth, above which Central loomed.[3] Instead, the girls walked the ten or so blocks, but not together.

Gathering in the courtyard at Central, co-eds talked hip flapper jargon, sang jazzy tunes, and practiced the Charleston. When one girl pointed out that Tillie was wearing her hand-me-down dress, Tillie was humiliated. In her diary, she reflected that a sense of inferiority was "growing deeper—not at all good for young 'uns like me." Rather than succumb, like Fannie, Tillie vowed to pursue the secret of popularity and also "keep some of me back as the amused spectator."[4] While she amused herself testing schemes for becoming popular, she amused a larger audience in a comedy called *Spooks*, produced at the Labor Lyceum in 1925. Eugene Konecky was the playwright.[5]

As radical as his father, Konecky blamed injustice on "the monster of organized capitalism." He founded a men's reading group to study: the

New Masses, a weekly featuring political articles, poems and stories, cartoons, and letters; the *Modern Quarterly,* a more academic journal of literary criticism and socioeconomic analysis (both first published in 1923); and the *Daily Worker,* a newspaper begun early in 1925 in New York City. He encouraged the reading group to see "rich Jews in Omaha" as reactionaries against whom only a communist revolution could create justice.

Wealth of course was not monolithic, as Ida recognized. It dehumanized her sister Chodeh, whose children one after another ran away from the loveless but grand Braude home.[6] Another immigrant Jewish woman named Rose Blumkin had begun peddling and then, with her husband, opened a second-hand clothing store on North Twenty-fourth, where they made capitalism work by advertising, selling in volume, cutting prices, and, as Rose said, telling the truth. Ida detested her sister but respected Rose Blumkin, who helped send Tillie to camp and hired her to coach Frances Blumkin, six years her junior, in singing and acting. Tillie would "write plays, would direct them; she was the prop man. She was the musical director." Though Frances "always got to be princess," Tillie always got to be impresario.[7] She was not intimidated in either the theatre or the library, where she memorized reams of poetry, and read the dictionary, Greek and Roman myths, and endless novels and biographies, especially of women.

As she blossomed into a young womanhood, Tillie looked as unusual as she acted, with her impish face, framed by thick curls. Her eyes, as her younger brother wrote, "never seemed to stick to one color. They were gray, they were green, and at times they were close to the sky blue color of Mama's eyes."[8] One day Ida began a mother-daughter talk about "the female anatomy while dissecting a chicken." Ida compared Tillie's body to the hen's because "there were a lot of little eggs in this particular chicken." Having explained sexual basics, Ida quizzed her about whether "slavery was a good thing—not for the slaves, of course." Ida wanted Tillie to understand that the horror of slavery did free slave-owners for leisure, a necessary element of culture. Tillie began to weigh the benefits and liabilities of capitalism, as illustrated in a *Comrade* cartoon depicting Andrew Carnegie as a devil who earned fortunes oppressing steel mill workers and as an angel who gave $41,000,000 to fund libraries.[9] Trying to solve this conundrum, Tillie compared Ida's sense that wealth can create culture and Eugene Konecky's sense that wealth always corrupts.

At a 1925 Workmen's Circle picnic, Tillie was enjoying the rare experience of lying with her head in her mother's lap, while women gossiped about out-of-town Yiddish performers, who were billed as man and wife but rumored to be unmarried. Some said the couple should not perform and one woman even said they should be run out of Omaha. Then Ida lifted herself up, upsetting Tillie: "My mother, she was furious; one of the things she said I'll never forget: 'Anna Karinina under the wheels for such as you.'" Ida's reaction, as much as the couple's unmarried state, caused a "great scandal," especially when Ida was rumored to be only Sam's common-law wife.[10]

Early in 1926, Tillie wrote a series of poems for her baby sister, titled "At Fourteen Years" after herself.[11] She read poetry to Yetta and "took [her] to the movies and would buy cartons with sweet pickles or stop in a hamburger joint to buy hamburgers with onions," food Ida did not cook. She took Yetta and her best friend Ruth Stein to parks, where she read while the little girls played catch. She took Yetta, Ruth, and Morris to the end of the street-car line, where they slid on dead leaves down mud paths toward the Missouri River. Fannie was too busy working, Harry too studious, and Lillian too fragile for such goings-on. Tillie played charades and word games with Lillian and named constellations in the night sky for her.[12] Ida clipped out articles in Yiddish on music, literature, and politics from the *Jewish Daily Forward*. Tillie took her as a model for culture and Sam as a model for revelry. He bought a Model T Ford and showed it off around town, often with Yetta and Ruth Stein in the back seat. In warm weather, they snapped off the plastic window panes and wiggled their bare feet out the windows, as Sam chuckled with them at the reactions of people on the streets.[13]

Before long, there were three exceptional Lerner siblings at Central. Harry, a seriously religious student who missed school only to attend Hanukah, Passover, and other religious observances at the Steins, often took Yetta with him. When the principal at Central asked Ida to justify one child's keeping the Jewish holidays when the others did not, she explained that her children were free to develop their own beliefs. Ida tried always to instill an open mind. For example, her tastes in music embraced opera, classic composers like Hayden and Bach, Yiddish and Russian folk songs, and spirituals like "Go Down, Moses" and "Swing Low Sweet Chariot," which she learned from Tillie's forays to the African-American church around the corner.[14] She invited Tillie to stage with her a Lerner-only performance at the Lyceum. Ida taught the children Yiddish songs like "Tsoom Hemmerel," and Tillie directed Morris in dancing a "mean kazatscha to the music of 'The Peddler Song.'"[15] The Lerner family review culminated in a chorus in which Ida's soft soprano led the children to harmonize in the upper registers, while Tillie's full voice swooped down into an alto counterpoint. Wild applause thrilled Tillie, the accomplished singer-director, Morris, the star singer-dancer, and Ida, the visionary who believed in music's holiness.

Registering for the new academic year, Fannie listed Sam's occupation as a painter; Tillie raised reality by calling him an interior decorator. She also raised reality by nicknaming Konecky "Shelley," after revolutionary poet Percy Shelley. Konecky now sponsored a reading group for girls. Overtly, he wished to educate them about the exploitation of the poor by the rich; covertly, he wanted power over young virgins.

After making a C and then a B, Tillie began making As in English. She signed onto the staff of the school paper, the *Register*, where she snuck jokes onto the ends of columns. They were so clever she was soon allowed to create her own humor column. She called it "Squeaks" and wrote under a byline, "Tillie the Toiler."[16] The column took a silly perspective on wealth and poverty: "We're calling money 'John' these days—we're not familiar enough with it to call it 'Jack'"; or "scientists claim paper money has germs; we shouldn't worry—we're safe."

By January 1927, the twenty-nine-year-old Konecky had begun an ever-closer tutelage of fifteen-year-old Tillie, who began writing him as "Dearest Gene." She read the lives and works of famous revolutionaries in thick volumes like the *Liberator*, *The Comrade*, and *Cry for Justice*; the latter was edited by Upton Sinclair, introduced by Jack London, and organized by topics such as "Toil," "Revolt," and "Martyrdom."[17] She read Konecky's writings, including a Freudian argument about sex and the ego, which provoked Tillie's long poem, called "With Adolescent Eyes," dated March 1927.

The "Squeaks" column soon gained sophistication: "Every time I get the ends to meet, somebody moves the middle." She wrote a take-off on Tennyson's "And I would that my tongue could utter/ The thoughts that arise in me"; Tillie's version was: "And I would that this Squeaky typewriter could squeak some squeaks for me;/ O well for the happy reporters who frolic about at their play,/ But I? I must sit and wildly rave some wilder squeaks this day." As her squeaks got wilder, Tillie was "transformed into popularity."[18] She delighted classmates with satires on learning: "this Shakespeare. Always ravin' about mercy, and then keepin' on writing plays for poor high school students to suffer through. But he must've been a good football player, anyhow, judging from his long run plays." Students loved her assaults on their enemy: "the teacher should apologize if she calls on you when you are unprepared."[19] Despite her hand-me-down clothes, her loud stammering voice, and her radical sympathies, Tillie had become a character. She accepted her popularity as license to do or say anything, almost.

She was keeping diaries in an odd assortment of composition booklets, memo pads, and spiral notebooks, large and small, rarely dated consecutively. They include poems, bits of stories, drafts of letters, and reflections offering an unusual glimpse into the life of a female adolescent genius in 1920s America. She described these diaries as the expression of a "terrible force" that prompted her "to write reams & reams. (Perhaps that's what people mean by an inspiration.)" She assessed her inspiration comically:

> I have written 19 poems (there I go misusing the word poetry again) in the past three days—average 4 minutes a poem; I have also written four columns of Squeaks, three bitter tirades against colds, tea-lemonade, & musterole; one short short murder story; thirteen book reviews on books I never read; three imaginary conversations with (respectively) Satan, Rabelais, & the author of Elsie Dinsmore: I have written a dime novel entitled Dore Deirl Dickette, the poor little sewing ripping girl (not saying whether it was wild oats she sowed, neither,) I have not written any letters (which I should've) nor have I worked on my play, nor have I written in my diary. But, as one says to the hostess, 'I've enjoyed myself immensely' (adding to oneself: considering the wretched circumstances.)

Admitting driving Fannie "almost mad," she signed herself "Your Seemingly Optimistic, Really Pessimistic, Truthfully un-Earnest, and Boldly loving friend, Tillie."[20]

The ability to be truthfully un-earnest and honestly self-satirical emboldened Tillie the Toiler to joke: "Why teachers go crazy: 'Homer is the guy Babe Ruth knocked out'"; or "'I didn't do any outside reading because it was too cold.'" She showed a command of logic and also of lawlessness in her "Jocular Geometry," testing her theorem: "A Bootlegger is a necessity. Proof: a. Necessity knows no law; b. A bootlegger knows no law; c. Therefore, a bootlegger is a necessity." Her "Mottoes & Sayings" included: "Plutarch: I regret that I have not more lives to give to my country. Jonah: You can't keep a good man down. Helen: So this is Paris. Sir Walter Raleigh to Queen Elizabeth: Step on it, kid."[21] The "Squeakeress" was seduced by her own personality.

> if anybody could be classified as "precocious" she was it. She read more books than there were in any library. In fact, if she kept on stealing books from the public library and the Central High Library, she'd soon have more books hidden in the cellar of the house than remained on the shelves of the libraries. She read philosophers like Schopenhauer and Nietzsche. She turned *Thus Spake Zarathrustra* into "Thus Spake Tillie Lerner." She read Katherine Mansfield and Emily Dickinson, and she relished the poetry of Sappho. She was very superior to the rest of us. And if you didn't realize it,

she'd not be afraid to straighten you out. Mama was proud of her. She was Mama's favorite until Mama began to realize that Tillie was a real problem. Tillie was a liar.[22]

She certainly lied about her age: after listing it correctly in the ninth grade as 14 January 1912, she then made herself five months younger in the next three grades by listing her birth-date as 14 June 1912. Altering reality was intoxicating, as was "being unpredictable. One day she would wear a very long dress, the next day a very short one. Nothing seemed to stop her. Whatever she thought was right [for her], she did." One friend remembered that in a little shop owned by a suspicious old man, Tillie once lifted her skirt and peed on the floor. She had become a "hell-cat." Lillian recalled that Tillie "mostly went her own way. Sometimes she had meals at home but her social life was usually away from the house." Forgetting about capitalist corruption, she now hung out with a crowd from affluent, gentile neighborhoods.[23] She pulled younger friends into her orbit. Marian Duve, Anel Creel, and Ruth Fox were all in the class a year behind Tillie's. Marian lived in a part of town called "Dundee" among imitation Gothic and Tudor houses. Her father was an executive in the meat-processing business. Anel Creel's father had important political connections and was advertising manager of the Eppley Hotels.[24] Ruth Fox's father owned an automobile dealership. Other affluent friends were Agnes Jensen, two years younger than Tillie, and Jeanette Gray, three years younger. Short curly-haired Tillie thrilled to take down Agnes's long blond or Jeanette's long black tresses in tentatively erotic times. In her poem "To Agnes," she wrote of "the faces of women in the moment of orgasm." Looking back on such poems Tillie later recalled boating with Agnes: "your long body stretched stem to stern . . . and your coiled braids down, undone, the 5 feet of golden hair unbound trailing in the blue Carter Lake water as I rowed round and round." She realized "my body loved you too" and wondered if she had felt similar lesbian impulses for Marian: "whom I loved so—passionately and innocently."[25] Tillie seemed a Pied Piper leading the girls into a free-thinking, rebellious world, while they were secured by wealth from any repercussions of misbehavior.

The sibling most like Tillie, Morris was likewise capable of mischief. He told a story about sneaking into the ball park as a youngster, once being spotted, and "jumping into the governor's box with the police after me." He told Governor Bryan (brother of William Jennings Bryan), "I love baseball, but I don't have any money. So I sneaked in and the police are trying to throw me out." The amused governor invited him to watch the game in his box and to visit the capitol of Nebraska. A few days later, Morris rode the bus to Lincoln alone, and the governor "personally showed me around the capitol."[26]

The odd thing about that story is that it aroused Tillie's competitive instincts. She recalled: "I was 15 and ran away from home; spring; all in an April evening" to "see the capitol." Though Tillie often stayed out very late, when she did not come home at all, Ida panicked and had Sam call the police. In Lincoln, the next day, a social worker saw her hanging around the capitol. Her vague answers to queries were suspicious, and her short curls and elfin face matched Sam's description. He drove to Lincoln in his Model T and fetched her home. The law-abiding Harry said, "you made Ma cry—why did they want you back?" The adventurous Morris said, "what did you let him bring you home for?"[27]

Tillie vowed to practice "one simile every night," and she was thrilled by a "*compliment!* Gene [Konecky] said tonight—'you're the only girl I've ever been out with that had intelligence *and* sex appeal.'" Tillie objectively questioned that assessment: "methinks me back—on our conversation—we had discussed movie actors and actresses, cars, movies, and sundaes—nope, nothing about the Einstein theory, or Keyserling's latest book, although afterwards we discussed Will Rogers and Mark Twain—that is Gene talked and I listened."[28] Not much given to self-assessment, Tillie was mostly thrilled over Konecky's compliments to her intellect and sexiness. She made a sassy use of his theories at the Orpheum Theatre, singing "Side by Side" with a young man and pantomiming "swinging along the road . . . striding side by side." When he sang "Oh we ain't got barrels of money," the irrepressible Tillie made comic asides like "No, only 17 cents but we'll go on, 'a singin along.'"

In 1927, the Jewish Community Center wanted to stage a play based on the Book of Esther, which would have to include the story of Hamon who convinced the king, Queen Esther's husband, to murder all Jews in his kingdom. The problem was that "the Jewish Community Center couldn't find anybody to play Hamon. Until—who agrees to play Hamon?—Tillie!" Her role playing "the most hated person in the Jewish religion" confirmed suspicions that the Lerners were not "true Jews." Ida had already condemned the Center for its materialism and self-righteousness.[29] By playing Hamon there, her special daughter seemed to have been corrupted by materialism and exhibitionism.[30]

Tillie copied aphorisms as models for "Tillie the Toiler": Oscar Wilde: "One should always be in love—that is why one should never marry"; Bourget: "Flirting is the virtuous woman's way of being sinful. The sinful woman's way of being virtuous"; Chloe: "It is time we should part my dear Sue,/ For *your* character's totally lost/ And *mine's* not sufficient for two";

Ben Franklin: "'Women are books,' says Hodge. 'Then would mine were an almanack, to change her every year.'" The theme here is sex, not marriage, impropriety, not convention. She saw herself as a nihilist, not reading "a single book except Nietzsche & Schopenhauer for *17 days*—."[31] Thanks to Nietzsche, via Konecky, she could disregard values like propriety, ownership, and truthfulness.

She planned a serious play "*Transitions.* 3 acts" to illustrate that the only non-neurotic people "are the proletarian. The only positive thing—movement." She listed topics lifted from communist literature: "Individualists—to hell with them . . . the liberal—contemptibly weak. Sex-mad. Fascist. Degenerated." Her problem, predictably, was making drama out of such ideas. After writing the words "Act I," she gave up. She was better at vivid imagery—frost on a window pane, "crinkled like the skin of boiled milk" or black twigs outside "thickened with white fur" of snow—than theory.

A diary entry comparing attractions between magnets and lovers suggests that Tillie was feeling under sexual, as well as political and literary, pressure from Konecky. She tried romance: "a thin silver serpent rushes through her flesh, when his bare hands touch her. They lie down. . . . The sun flowed in waves over her & throbbed against her naked body." Hiding such writing from her sisters, she had "terrible fits of depression."

Several factors contributed to "tense times" at home, including Ida's frustration with Sam, Tillie's wildness, and, according to her brother "the things she did to Fannie."[32] When they anglicized their eldest daughter's name, neither Ida nor Sam knew that fannie was slang for female buttocks, but to Fannie that name was just another unfair insult; so she renamed herself "Jann." From her after-school secretarial work, Jann bought herself nice office clothes, which Tillie, without petty bourgeois prejudices, felt free to borrow. Ida fretted and scolded, but Sam mostly chuckled at Tillie's pranks.

Ida and Sam, who referred to each other in public as "Mrs. Lerner" and "Mr. Lerner," continued to argue. She objected to his using decorating skills to paint the houses of the Blumkins and others, not theirs; he responded that he needed to earn a living. She objected that, in the evenings, he changed his paint-stained clothes for a suit and tie and left for Workmen's Circle and socialist meetings; he thought she preferred reading the papers and their children's school books. She feared that he compromised with communist-leaning members of the Workmen's Circle; he wanted to keep the Circle together. She was furious when he made peace with her enemy, a man named Forman. She objected, Yetta recalled, to "women at meetings flirting with Dad"; he insisted that he was and always would be faithful to her.[33] She argued that he must discipline Tillie, but he was no more able than Ida to control Tillie.

Once Ida packed a bag and left to stay with her cousin Rachel Beber and then with Sam's sister Chaika Lerner Swartz. After a brief period away, as Tillie noted in her diary: "Mama came back, a little more embittered, a little more broken, but still the same mama." Tillie recorded that Ida had said of the Swartz marriage: "what a 'go' they made of it," giving Tillie one of her "quick, stabbing flashes of understanding, which I so often get in family people . . . Oh to write them, to write them!"[34] She grasped that stories about actual people make better drama than conflicts between abstractions like the proletariat and the liberal. That recognition formed an epiphany: she would be a novelist.

In May 1927, sixteen-year-old Aaron Braude began "bumming" to Los Angeles. Tillie described him as "wandering here & there, a restless shadow, all his quick charming wit & fine clear head, ground out on the hard wheel of the world." Connecting wealth with inhumanity, she told her diary, "Oh I *hate* Auntie Braude. Damn her & her fat complacent smug cruelty, & her slow quenching of all the good in her children."[35]

That summer, bored with a typing course at Omaha Tech, Tillie yearned "to know another mind, luminous, fiery crystal, to see it turn, flashing and shining." Returning from his paper boy job, Morris sometimes saw her arriving home late at night in a fancy car driven by a liveried chauffeur, proof that privilege could trump antibourgeois theories. Her antic ways attracted Ruth Fox's brother, E. D., who owned a small two-seater plane and took her flying.[36] Thrilled by their godlike power, Tillie wrote a poem, "Air-Plane Ride," in which she sees flight as too exciting to be scary.[37] She intended not to be seduced by the romance of flight. Since "goods become soiled, even in the touching, the inspecting," she resolved "I will not show, unless you wish to buy." Still, another poem dated from summer 1927 begins: "Come here. I give to you my breasts, my arms." Flight (with wealth) had become an aphrodisiac. In her diary, Tillie said she took "my first lover," apparently E. D. Fox, who probably did not have a mind like a fiery crystal.

With such a wealthy beau, Tillie needed to dress more fashionably. Ruth Stein remembered that Tillie freely "borrowed" Jann's clothes, "whatever she needed. Then Jann would have a fit." Under the influence of Marx, Nietzsche, and Konecky, Tillie felt liberated from bourgeois morality. Lillian recalled that "Tillie would not work, but she would swipe anything she wanted from Jann." At last to "mollify Jann" and stop Tillie's thievery, their father put a lock on the door of Jann's bedroom.[38]

The case of Nicola Sacco and Bartolomeo Vanzetti captured the news that summer. Anarchists, these poor Italian immigrants had been framed as murderers and sentenced to death in 1921. After years of postponement, major American writers rallied to their defense, but Sacco and Vanzetti, still maintaining their innocence, were executed by the state of Massachusetts on 22 August 1927. Eloquent editorials, impassioned stories, powerful plays, and poignant poems (one of which Tillie claimed to have written) could not save Sacco and Vanzetti, while Clarence Darrow, well-paid by the Leopold and Loeb families, had saved two confessed cold-blooded murderers from the death chamber. Konecky used the two cases emphasize that under capitalism wealth beats ideals. Tillie had no wealth, but the example of Leopold and Loeb, buttressed by readings in Nietzsche, did suggest that some individuals might be above the law.

After young Fox left Omaha to return to college, ending his summer fling, Tillie wrote a melancholy poem, dated "Autumn 1927," comparing her heart to autumn's dead leaves. Her "Prayer in Desperate Need" asked the wind to blow away clues "that hold remembrance of our love." She dated it November 1927. She sent a copy to Marian Duve, in "desperate need" of her support. She wanted to "arise from my death (?), lemonade-tea, handkerchief strewn bed & toddle with thee to Gene's. He wants to see some of my late poetry, & my 19 risque poems along with a dozen other of my autumn poems will be presented to him—& he'll decide little Tillie has no more promise as a poet, but Marian will be by to comfort." Konecky marked her poems "broad, profound," and Tillie began calling him Genius. He however offered similar compliments to Jeanette Gray, who soon published poems in the *Omaha World-Herald*.[39]

In 1927 Omaha saw the opening of a picture palace called the Riviera, decorated with a Moorish motif and a ceiling with "twinkling stars." There, Frances Blumkin, coached by Tillie Lerner, won first prize in a gala talent show.[40] Tillie needed fine dresses for performances at the Community Center, the Orpheum, and the Riviera. (One diary entry mentions her own "very dirty" clothes and her need for "hosiery, Silks, woolens, Curtains, blankets, undies.") Underwear was important since Konecky apparently became her sexual as well as political tutor in December 1927. When she had called him Shelley, perhaps she had in mind Percy Shelley's abandoning his wife to elope with feminist Mary Godwin, about six weeks before her seventeenth birthday. Despite Konecky's marriage, Tillie was ready to elope with him about six weeks before her sixteenth birthday. Jann's things were no longer available for "borrowing," thanks to her locked door, but one afternoon, while Jann was at work, Tillie concocted a story that convinced Harry to climb out the window from the open bedroom, edge along the roof over the front porch, and open Jann's window. He walked through her room and left her door unlocked. Tillie entered and came out with Jann's new dress and silk stockings.

Finding her best dress missing that evening, Jann went out on the landing, according to Lillian, and screamed at Ida, who was mystified. Having once seen Sam whip Harry, Lillian did not want to witness more punishment so she did not tell. Tillie had again proved herself beyond petty bourgeois morality. She offered narcissistic advice: "Don't suffer all your life; don't be unpopular. But that's what's so different about me. I have a magnetic personality. Got it for fifteen days free trial." Jann had had enough of Tillie's magnetic personality and Ida's indulgence. She rented a small room away from home and continued working and going to school. Tillie got Jann's room, which she decorated with a gold Buddha squatting amid a forest of candles.

By the time she turned sixteen in 1928, a brazen Tillie the Toiler offered a cynical "sure-fire recipe to become popular": Students should "sneak in the lunch room line. . . . Don't carry around books, borrow them from somebody else, when needed. Never take down assignments, the other fellow will be only too glad to show his to you." She would "not shut up for a bit, but we might consider it for two bits."

Soon, however, Tillie had problems against which her personal magnetism was no help. On 11 March, she wrote about discussing Anna Karenina's illicit affair with Ida. A month later, Tillie went on what was intended to be a harmonious good-bye picnic with Jeanette Gray and Konecky. Tillie took off her shoes and stockings and "took down Jeanette's hair," as in more innocent days. After their picnic lunch, they "climbed a windswept hill" together. But Jeanette left Tillie, and "then he went to *her*." Hoping that he would elope with her, Tillie was so upset she ran about in her bare feet digging up dirt and flinging it into the wind in a madcap attempt to recapture his attention. Back in town, she begged Marian Duve to visit her, but Marian's parents had ordered her to steer clear of Tillie Lerner.

Tillie withdrew from school on 11 April 1928 officially because of illness.[41] Someone arranged for her to leave Omaha for a farm near Sioux City. In her diary, she gave no hint of how she got there but mentioned "the family that I am staying with" and tried to cheer herself over "meeting with handsome farmer who served in war: nearly overpowered with the good wishes and pie of a family." Like Mother Nature, she felt like soiled goods. She was pregnant. A note from Marian, saying that an "elusive fairy something" in Tillie made her a terrific children's playmate but would ill-suit her for motherhood, suggests that Tillie confessed her secret to Marian.[42]

By summer, Tillie felt hysterical regret over desiring and/or causing the death of a girl-baby. She wrote a revealing autobiographical poem.

Influenced by T. S. Eliot's "The Waste Land," she saw the farm's fecundity as cruel. She described the natural world in images of female sexuality: pregnant earth, ecstasies of buds, full-bellied clouds, swollen breasts of hills. Tillie first titled that poem "Any Woman, After Miscarriage." Then she crossed out "Miscarriage," substituted "Abortion," and added "for me." Another poem "The Mother Who Died too" is initialed "E. M. T." for "Edith Matilda Thomas." It begins, "She was so little—little in her grave." More poems mention graves, death, and corpses. Later she noted, "after this I wrote no more till the fall of 1928."[43]

All her life, good girl Jann resented that bad girl Tillie got away with everything, even an unwanted high school pregnancy. Jann

> never had a date when in Omaha as a result of Tillie's escapes, looseness, which somehow got into the papers. I didn't want to be tarred with her brush. Tillie lied, lied, lied. She took my only decent dress and wasn't punished. She stole my silk stockings which I bought from my earnings. She never worked. When the book theft at Central High was discovered, she said I was the thief and got Mother and [the Dean of Girls] to believe her. She stole books from the Public Library too. The police came to the house, found them in the basement but she wasn't punished."[44]

Morris thought that the police decided "not to prosecute Tillie—partially I think because of Mother's terrible reaction."[45] Tillie's hell-cat ways were unraveling Ida's dreams.

Late in summer 1928, Tillie wrote Marian: "I arrived from Sioux City a few hours ago—I am tired, the wind washed on the car windows, and Mr. Forman sang old forgotten tunes, all the way down; and as the day groped away thru the rain, I kept thinking of you. Marian, why didn't you come? I *needed* you. I love you still, but you will never again be necessary to me—no human will." Tillie crossed through her next lines, but she left the end of the paragraph: "I must be free-free!" She caught herself "weeping. It is hard to lie"; then she crossed out "to lie" and substituted "to shut out everything."[46] In her despair, only writing might restore well-being: "nothing must keep me from my work—nothing," but she was "still crying." She sent Ruth Fox "some very tragical nonsense last night" with the excuse that she became "more crazy than usual" at night. She was so distraught that a woman named Meryl Friedel reached out to her. A pioneer radio announcer and manager of the Midwest Radio Advertising Service, she invited Tillie watch her broadcasts and share her troubles. Tillie did go to the radio station, but she still shut out the truth; she knew that Meryl Friedel was Konecky's colleague.

With nothing left to lose, Tillie transformed poetry readings with the younger girls into transgressive sessions, the group itself into a latently lesbian Sappho Club. The girls dared to smoke, though Marian admitted to Tillie, "Gosh, I sure get hungry when I smoke." While the parents thought the girls were learning poetry, Tillie spoke about sexual passion. Marian admitted, "I don't believe I've ever really been kissed in the sense you might mean." For Marian, comforting but titillating "pal kisses are the best."

Having returned from his run-away trip to California, Aaron Braude was surprised when Tillie invited him to "indeed an unusual event" in the basement of a large house with six or seven "of Tillie's peers. We gathered in a semi-circle & by lamplight I was treated to poetry readings. Some of the poems had social & political undertones. This setting and its ambiance gave me an eerie feeling. It resembled a scene of a Bohemian gathering, some place in Greenwich Village, of like-minded people that I have often read about. I felt enveloped in an aura of mystery. I was totally lost & definitely out of place." Tillie wanted to shock him, if not with girls kissing each other, then with radical politics and poetry that "certainly wasn't Edgar Guest or Henry Longfellow." Duly shocked, he was surprised that an older man, clearly Konecky, was "in charge of this gathering."[47]

On 15 August 1928, the Socialist Party of Nebraska held its convention in Omaha, endorsing the national platform with Norman Thomas of New York for president and the Nebraska platform with Samuel Lerner for lieutenant governor. Campaign literature made the progressive argument that the "trend toward the centralization of wealth and power" need not be "destructive and oppressive"; instead, it could "be the means of vast social betterment."[48] This argument for reform, not revolution, infuriated Communists, who wanted to overthrow the whole capitalist system.

Tillie returned to Central High in fall 1928 in a chastened mood. Jann had graduated, but there were still three Lerners there. Lillian explained, "Tillie was still at Central when I was a freshman," but neither she nor Harry had "any contact with her there." Marian was forbidden to see her so Tillie wrote her about her roller-coaster emotions. She confessed "it's *very* trying being so exalted one day and so desperate the next." She had had "them 'low-ho-down bloo-hoos.' But I feel almost normal now, like Tillie, the Squeakeress. It is just three short weeks ago that I was terrible Tillie?" Having survived what she called an "emotional *hell*," she resumed her Squeakeress voice: "We have still to hear about the absent-minded professor who forgot to flunk anyone."

When the Communist campaign manager in Omaha publicly accused socialists like Sam of being "supporters and defenders of the capitalist system" Tillie found herself alienated from her father, who spent much time that fall defending Socialists against accusations that they were, with Democrats and Republicans, tools of capitalism. Harry and Morris passed out campaign materials around town and even outside stockyard fences, where neither had ever been before, beneath a huge sign declaring ARMOUR. Norman Thomas himself hired a convertible to parade through Omaha streets with Sam Lerner and, in the back seat, seven-year-olds Yetta Lerner and Ruth Stein, waving to the crowds. The *Daily Worker*'s post-election headline read: "Hoover, Choice of Wall Street, Elected President, Big Communist Vote, Socialist Party Loses Heavily." The loss ended Sam's career in electoral politics.

That fall, Tillie put a photo of Virginia Woolf on her desk, imitated Woolf's stream-of-consciousness writing, copied passages from Katherine Mansfield's journal into her own, and parodied Gertrude Stein. A new journalism instructor, Anne Lane Savidge praised the "Squeaks" column, but Tillie satirized even her in an allegory called "The Three Tigers." Though being derelict or insubordinate in her literature course earned her a C in English, she made As in her other classes.

Almost twelve, Morris sold newspapers in a shabby downtown district. On one bitter night, a woman named Pearl invited him up to her hotel room for hot chocolate when he got too cold, so long as he first knocked on her door. When he told about Pearl's kindness, Tillie urged him to ask her home and Ida agreed. After she came for supper, Tillie informed him that Pearl was "a whore," a word he did not know. Then she "told me, and I broke down in a rage because I could not put together the idea of the generosity of this woman with something that was considered so bad." Later he reflected that Tillie had manipulated "this confrontation . . . to see what kind of reaction she would get." She was experimenting with real people, as a playwright or novelist would with characters.

In a dated and typed November diary entry, Tillie addressed a scissors grinder outside her window calling "'Scissors tew me-end, scissors tew me-end.'" She scribbled, "Oh scissors man, I wish you were a-crying 'Hearts to mend, hearts to mend.'" She wanted an iron heart that could "never be hurt." Tillie the Toiler countered her depression by affronts on middle-class morality: she advised her fellow students to "do your Christmas Shoplifting early" and offered them "fast words/ That aren't one bit nice." Her own "fast words" formed a carapace over her heart, broken over losing lovers and baby.

Words could be not only a carapace but a lifebuoy so Tillie vowed "nothing must keep me from my work—nothing." She began 1929 reading a *Daily Worker* claim that "Communism is Hope of Women Workers." It printed pictures of women revolutionaries, including Rosa Luxemburg, and called for "An Anthology of Revolutionary Poetry." Tillie responded with a poem arguing that artistic beauty was useless without a social message. In a barrel outside a used bookstore, she discovered three old issues of the *Atlantic Monthly*. Attracted to a long, unsigned story called "Life in the Iron Mills," in the April 1861 issue, Tillie bought the set for 10¢. The "Iron Mills" story exposes the underside of industrialism, the exploitation of workers. A middle-class female narrator invites the reader into a grimy slum to hear the story of a "furnace-tender." This untutored natural sculptor made art out of "korl," waste from the steel-refining process, but was doomed to an early death. Still depressed, Tillie started a story about a girl nicknamed "Fuzzy," whose dire poverty dooms her, like the sculptor in the old tale.[49]

Tillie's academic subjects were highly rigorous that spring.[50] Her English teacher was the formidable Sara Vore Taylor, who taught, as Tillie would say, a "condensed equivalent of a very good college course in English literature." Taylor authored her own style book, considered "the Bible for our study of proper use of the English language." Tillie absorbed its principles of proper English usage but did not always follow them, as she made superlatives like "most favoritist" and "bestest." Nor did she follow the rules for "proper" classroom behavior. Tillie the Toiler brazenly claimed to have "all ready got my poetic license for 1929," a license to challenge authority and "always be littlin'; Always be littlin." After she belittled her choral music teacher in "Squeaks" and sassed her during glee club practice, Tillie was ordered to leave class. Walking out, she turned to scream, "I'd hate to be your husband!"[51] The chorus tittered, but Tillie the Toiler noted, "Laugh and the class laughs with you, but you stay after school alone."

Tillie's story began oddly with Fuzzy's death. A middle-class girl named Ruth had befriended the poor girl and nicknamed her "Fuzzy," thanks to her "inflated halo" of wild hair. After Ruth left town, friendless Fuzzy was vulnerable to a book-loving young man who "completed his seduction" with a car ride; she ended the resulting pregnancy with an abortion.[52] Fuzzy had wanted to write about the lives of "girls in the factory" but caught pneumonia haunting cemeteries and died. Autobiographical importations (fuzzy hair, seduction by a fancy vehicle, and an abortion) show Tillie unable to invent on paper and unable to conquer loss.[53] Like her Fuzzy, she roamed cemeteries with her girlfriends, and rumors spread that she encouraged them to laugh and dance on graves. Other rumors accused her of being sexually promiscuous, "really hot stuff," and of her urging her girl friends to experiment sexually.[54] That advice produced unintended consequences when Jeanette bragged that at fourteen she had lost her virginity to the almost thirty-year-old Konecky. Heart-broken, Tillie recorded his aphorisms: "Prejudices are confidences in our opinions. One is a virgin only when there is a possibility of one's not being. She knows a lot, but she hasn't lived it.—The Genius." Tillie wanted to prove that she could live "it," of life, without inhibitions, but her reckless behavior created more rumors and more tensions at home.

In her diary, Tillie noted that Sam was "in damn surly fit," perhaps because both his second daughter and his partner were sources of middle-class outrage. Ida wore no wedding ring, and a rumor about the Lerners' nonmarriage circulated. (Once when Morris would not let Ruth Stein practice on the Lerners' piano, she retorted that his mother wasn't his father's "real wife.") Mr. Forman once met Ida on the corner of Caldwell and Twenty-fifth and spit onto the pavement. Walking around her as if she might contaminate him, he called Ida a prostitute, her children "bastards."If this were the Mr. Forman who brought Tillie back from Sioux City in 1928, knowledge of her disgrace confirmed his opinion of Lerner "bastards."

Having nothing else to lose, Tillie became more confrontational in school. She wrote poetry condemning "book-feasters, culture-lovers" who ignore the hungry and desperate.[55] Miss Taylor thought that "U.S. literature did not exist" and Carl Sandburg was a disgraceful excuse for a poet. To "confirm her worst suspicions," Tillie invented a parody, supposedly a "new poem" by Sandburg. In "Any Man," she expressed her own (and Sandburg's) egalitarianism but offended Miss Taylor's elitism with lines like "Don't think I ain't got no song." Tillie expected that "Any Man" was so bad Miss Taylor would recognize it for a parody, but Taylor "didn't know the difference."[56] She was ecstatic, as were other seniors who gossiped that Tillie Lerner had fooled its most venerable English teacher.

Tillie sassed, belittled, ridiculed, and fooled her teachers with "a sense of humor she could turn to anything. They *couldn't* get her. That's what made them so mad. They thought she was psychopathic!" as Anel Creel heard later and then wrote Tillie. Anel also confided that teachers "used to take me aside and inquire about my 'queer choice of friends,' but then I answered back . . . I knew you and they didn't, so shut up. I said it more subtly, however."[57] Tillie faced a belligerent cadre of teachers and parents who conspired to keep nice girls from making the "queer choice" of Tillie Lerner for friend.

In a Shakespeare class, Tillie told her diary: "I up & give 'To be or not to be'—again I fool my teecher; she thinks the glazed, oh-what's-the-use look in my eye & the hopeless expression on my face is due to my 'wonderful' acting ability—she told me my pathos when I said 'the pangs of despised

love' was unusual in one so young—the class snickered—and Tillie
giggled." The class suspected and her giggles confirmed that seventeen-
year-old Tillie knew more about the pangs of love than Miss Taylor.[58]

At the end of April, the senior English class was studying *Hamlet*, and
Taylor "had given us this very passionate and really beautiful lecture ... along
the line of how carefully [crafted he] was, how there were no contradictions
in Shakespeare." In response to that formalist sense of artistic perfection,
Tillie asked: "how come" Hamlet can refer to death as a "bourne from which
no traveler returns," when he has "just in the scene before been talking to
his dead father?" Questioning the bard's logic and consistency was heresy
to Taylor. Morris recalled that "Taylor was so angry over T's contradiction
that she threw the Shakespeare book at her, ordered her to leave and to go
to [the dean of girls'] office and to never come back." [59] Tillie's recollection
was vague: "that was a semester when I was not being."[60] Her "not being"
meant refusing to be a "nice" girl. After kicking Tillie out of her class, Sara
Vore Taylor filled in the following notice: "To Parents: The work of Tillie
Lerner has not been of passing grade in English IX during the past month."
She left blank the line designed for an explanation. The report was mailed
to "Mr. Samuel Lerner" and dated 30 April 1929. Tillie did not report to the
principal's office. Apparently expelled, she walked out of Central High.[61] In
Central High's 1929 annual, her picture was separated from the graduating
seniors, without explanation, except for the line "*Tillie—the unfathomable.*"
Morris remembered "our parents were mortified by the expulsion." It led to
her "separation from family, physical and emotional."[62]

Ida and Sam insisted that she make up for lost credits by attending
summer school and for past indulgences by taking on her share of household chores. Tillie wrote Anel Creel, then in New York with her politically
prominent family: "I has been ... taking care of our whole fambly." She
claimed that her life was uneventful, except "ever once in awhile 'Make
Whoopee.'" Still Tillie was feeling "awfully rebellious." Friends spurned her.
She told her diary she was "constantly ill. But *I must write.* ... it is all I
have." By mid-August 1929 Tillie felt like her "own cemetery & undertaker
& corpse & ghost."[63]

More than seventy years after Miss Taylor threw *Hamlet* at her, Tillie
mixed up that story in a hodgepodge of references to Konecky and
Jeanette.[64] She often slept over at 2023 Burt Street, a grubby little bungalow
Konecky rented and registered as the "City Talmud Torah of Omaha."[65]
That religious registration was a cover for Konecky's leftist meetings and
amorous assignations. He now "shacked up" with Jeanette Gray, making
Burt Street a churning caldron of emotions for Tillie.[66] Trusting Konecky as

Jeanette's tutor and knowing nothing about Burt Street, Mrs. Gray forbade Jeanette to see Tillie.[67]

Writing Marian, Tillie tried to reclaim a happy-go-lucky persona: "To wit (where *did* that funny expression originate? 'to wit'—sounds like a toast to me)." Seemingly uninhibited, she listed her nicknames and pretended that "Matilda" was her real name:

"Item 1-Tillie (but of course, nobody ever *could* call me Matilda for more than 17 minutes). Item 2-Windy (cause I chattered so much, I guess.) But all the kids what used to call me that are lost, strayed, or stolen. There's nobody left except Gene Konecky, now that charges me with that. Item 3— Moosquin . . . It means "faun"—Berny Szold has the same fancy—always calls me wood-sprite, faun, Bacchante, etc.). . . . Item 4-Mims (My camp name—God only knows why). That's all that really matters, tho' I've had temporary unimportant ones like Encyke (short for Encyclopedia), Curly, Piggy (!) (how I hate to confess it)."

Admitting to being called "wood-sprite, faun, Bacchante" by the artist Bernard Szold,[68] Tillie did not admit being the thief, miscreant, sexual adventurer, or the Pied Piper whose influence mothers and teachers feared. She called herself: "Your American Tragedy."

Hiding out on Burt Street, Tillie revised her Fuzzy story, modeling it more on "Life in the Iron Mills," with surrealistic descriptions of poverty and delirium.[69] Like Tillie, Fuzzy has "hair enormous around your head, a great spread of it, like the painting of Phoebus by someone or other." Like Tillie, Ruth longs to "express myself. Once, only once." Like Tillie, Fuzzy has "quarreling parents," but they are more desperately poor, ignorant, and neglectful than Sam and Ida ever were.[70] Like Tillie, Ruth narrates Fuzzy's story to "transfix you forever into the stone of words." Ruth insists "not you I weep for," but that remark begs the question: if not for Fuzzy, then for whom? Perhaps for Tillie.

Anne Lane Savidge, Tillie's former journalism teacher, reached out to lonely Tillie and apparently ended up sleeping with her. In September 1929, Tillie recalled "that night when I lay beside her, with her heart under my hand beating like a tortured, caged bird." Wild hair, odd ears, changeable eyes, and unpredictable clothes made Tillie a head-turner. She wrote Marian: "I was very meekly standing in the dime store waiting for Jeanette, when a little man with hands like a girl's suddenly pounced upon my hair & picked it up above my ears—I stood very still. Suddenly he shouted: 'where's the pointed ears? My God, the perfect Pan face, &

she has no pointed ears.'" Hired to paint a portrait of Jeanette, the artist
Bernard Szold joined Konecky's group and courted the head-turning Tillie
with book talk and a gift of gold earrings from Spain.[71] As Tillie vowed
to "never to work again—to starve or whore first," she abandoned any
pretext of respectability and moved in with Szold. Marian cautioned: "This
man Szold . . . pretending to bring out your genius that was so delightfully
human before, is killing it, actually killing it, and satisfying his own appetite
meanwhile. Like a weasel."[72]

Perhaps Marian's remark, probably her own ignominious situation, and
certainly the desire to write brought Tillie to wonder "What's it all about?
Life, I mean." After a visit to her Braude cousins, she mentioned how
each, even "Babbitt Sammy," seemed isolated. Wanting to know what they
were thinking, she longed for a "quick,stabbing" flash of understanding,
like the one that she experienced when Ida told about the Swartz's
marriage, that would enable her "to write them" into a family novel.[73]
Suddenly being Szold's mistress seemed a self-betrayal. He was "a poseur,
a fool, empty, empty. And I—oh hopeless. I am really caught too—physically." She freed herself by moving home, where she appropriated one of
Harry's school assignments to lament no longer feeling "the sharp sting
of words." Her only consolation was: "Schopenhauer says all persons of
genius" are alienated.[74]

During the 1920s, under the Harding, Coolidge, and Hoover admin-
istrations, the poor had suffered while the rich had grown ever richer, at
least until the stock market crashed. The downward spiral of Wall Street
investments, which began in early September 1929, set up economic repercussions affecting not only the wealthy but every worker in the country;
economic injustice became an urgent issue.[75] A 6 November 1929 *Daily
Worker* article, "Women Share Soviet Power," convinced Tillie of the Soviet
system's benefits, especially to women. Communism offered her a resurrection from her "own cemetery" of isolation and despair. She advised
herself to "consider the interests of the Party as the supreme good and
judge moral values as petty bourgeois prejudices."

Sitting alone, late in 1929, Tillie reflected on: "two years, two years since
my mad leaving of home—one year since my first lover—& now—I am
tame, domesticated." Her math was inventive: the "mad" leaving home for
Lincoln was in the spring of 1927, her first lover was that summer, and her
second lover was late in 1927 or early 1928.[76] Whatever the accounting, the
diary entry shows resignation. Near year's end, she sat by an open window
in freezing cold, feeling "so ugly tonight." Even her diaries, spread out on
a table, looked "like tombstones" in a cemetery.[77] Even as she wondered
how she could squeeze life "into creeping black words," Tillie began

squeezing her handwriting down to a size seemingly too small for much life or legibility. She wondered: "Oh why must a man think that just because you've given your body, all you want in return is a few tinsel words, a bit of flattery—why starve you only with that? Why withhold what he shares in ordinary friendship to another man?. . . I don't think that because a man desires me, or I yield to the desire, that that is a reason for spoiling the friendship." After Fox, Konecky, Szold, and perhaps others, Tillie wanted friendship and free love.

Saying she burned a juvenile novel, she made one composition book into a rare consecutive diary—from late 1929 through part of 1930.[78] On a snowy Saturday night Tillie noted that she "Went to Genius's. Meryl there too; and Jeanette." She began sublimating her passion: "the feeling I have for Gene is like that Mary Magdalene must have had for Jesus." Though he cheated on his wife with Tillie and on Tillie with Jeanette, Tillie's sympathies were still with Konecky who, she thought, suffered in "so thick a mist of pain." With a demanding job now as editor-in-chief of *The Sovereign Visitor*,[79] a wife Eva, two sons, and a very young mistress, Konecky tried to divert Tillie's Mary Magdalen-like devotion by critiquing her poems, recommending radical readings, and conversing about "Shakespeare & dreams & Communism & happiness."

Tillie spent the weekend of 7 December 1929 in Sioux City with Freda Rosmovksy, whose parents, socialist friends of the Lerners, may have helped connect Tillie with the farm family back in 1928. Noting the high bluffs composed of fine loessal soil on the way to Sioux City, Tillie remembered "the hills, standing shoulder to shoulder" and her lost child: "The snow that covers you will also be my shroud." Her mood improved, though, after returning late at night and feeling "so good to be in my shabby room again—candle light, glints and shadows, books and papers sprawled careless everywhere." Kissing her golden Buddha, she worried if her mind would "ever play & ripple & flash, like Meryl's like Gene's." She got some sort of a job and then, in an odd gesture for an atheist Jew, she went to mass on Christmas night 1929, sensitive to a Marxist irony: "all thru the beautiful frail music, clink; clink of money being collected."

Near year's end, a woman named Rachel Goldfarb Schochet came to visit her sister Lizzie Goldfarb Resnick in Omaha. Their Russian-Rumanian parents, Bernard and Clara Goldfarb, fleeing oppression for the dream of justice and prosperity in the USA, arrived in Minnesota in 1903, with Rachel, Lizzie, and seven-year-old Abraham. The next year, at sixteen, Rachel married a thirty-six-year-old man named Phil Schochet of Faribault. Soon the other Goldfarbs moved to Omaha, where they were naturalized in 1911. Two more Goldfarb children, Nahman and Betty, were born in Omaha, where Lizzie married Joseph Resnick. The Goldfarbs lived in North Omaha, only a few blocks from the Lerners' future home, but by 1919 the Goldfarbs had migrated to a farm near Stockton, California, leaving Lizzie in Omaha and Rachel, called Rae, in Faribault, where she made a home for her brother Abe before he volunteered in World War I.[80] He trained in Florida and El Paso, but the war ended before he saw action. He spent time in Mexico, attended college, and by 1929 lived on College Avenue in Berkeley, California. He had a reputation as a radical writer and associate of V. F. Calverton, coeditor of the *Modern Quarterly*.[81] He regularly sent poems and book synopses to Rae, who claimed that she need not read the books, after her cultured brother's explanations of them.

When Rae and her daughter Ethel Schochet arrived in Omaha that December, Lizzie Resnick invited Eugene Konecky to meet them. He arrived with Jeanette, who seemed to Rae "like a scared rabbit . . . scared to say anything for fear I would write to Eva." After Jeanette asked about Rae's older husband, Rae chuckled to Abe in untutored but wise English that Jeanette would be in "the same boat" if she married Konecky, who had indoctrinated her to mouth "comunisticly inclined" slogans.

Abe Goldfarb had reason join his older sisters and niece, who both adored him, in Omaha. Rae amused him with her outspoken opinions and wacky spelling. Now her picture of a like-minded, fellow radical with a well-indoctrinated young mistress made Omaha seem less stodgy than he recalled. He arrived in Omaha by train, met his family and called on the Creels, with whom he had Mexican connections.[82] He attended Konecky's "Jewish Men's discussion group," and then Konecky invited Abe, who was thirty-three, and Ethel Schochet, who was seventeen, to attend a meeting of the Sappho Club. Rae thought Abe needed "plenty attention" and should marry a "charming housewife." Tillie hardly fit that bill, but she was brilliant, funny, impishly beautiful, had literary talent in need of shaping, and was not hung-up over schoolgirl notions of propriety and virginity.

For Tillie, December had been a "sleepwalking month" on an unidentified job among the bourgeoisie who made "respectability and vulgarity an apology for lack of brains." She felt "a horror of people closing over me" and wondered "where *are* they? My people with the infinite sympathies & delicious absurdities & swift daring minds—warm & sensational & alive—where are they?" Abe Goldfarb, with his twinkling eyes, full sardonic mouth, brilliant mind, and leftist commitments promised to be one of her people, one who might save her. She wrote ambiguously, "Mine never came on December 31st midnight."

CHAPTER 4

REVOLUTIONARY
AND MOTHER

1930–1933

You have a powerful logical mind which will serve you in good stead as an international revolutionary—a greater Rosa Luxemburg, for you are really creative.

—Abraham Jevons Goldfarb to Tillie Lerner Goldfarb, fall 1932

Though Goldfarb did not appear on New Year's Eve, he did so soon afterward and established a "deep flow of understanding" with Tillie. By 4 January 1930, she felt "all new—high tide. Hope. Ghosts laid," the ghosts of her entanglements with Konecky. Like another Shelley, Goldfarb opened a path to revolutionary action. On a train with him to Lincoln, she showed off her talent for political writing by aping a child's voice naming things she wanted, illustrating how capitalist advertising manipulates human desire. Tillie joined the Young Communist League (YCL) and, on 11 January, wrote, "Goodbye, my girlhood. Tears I do not weep for all I have never had." When she returned and told her parents she was a Communist, Sam remarked "at least she's not joining the capitalist class." Though Ida had said, "I'd rather see you dead than a dirty Communist," she conceded that at least Tillie was "not joining the floggers against the flogged."[1]

On 14 January 1930, when the *Daily Worker* prophesied that the worsening economic crisis was bringing forth a new order, the Lerner house, under snow, seemed expectant, "like a woman with child, near her hour." The Lerners never made much of birthdays, but for her eighteenth Tillie made herself a dinner party. She "cleaned & ironed & brot in coal" and set the table with a white cloth and candles. Marian Duve was invited but only dropped in "for an instant," looking "sleek and successful" while her chauffeur waited outside. Ida suspected the dinner to be a Communist event and refused to sit at the table, though Sam and Morris did. Tillie recorded the arrivals: "Gene; then J & A & D." Her guests were certainly Eugene Konecky and Jeanette Gray, who looked, Sam whispered to Morris, like a black-haired witch. "D" was a visiting cousin. The guest called "A" was Abe Goldfarb. The evening was "all so gay and unreal" it met Tillie's expectations and filled the void in her heart.[2] The next morning, she left home with Abe.

In a tiny leather book she wished herself "Happy Birthday. I wish you . . . not alone happiness, but deep genuine [? an illegible word]." She reflected on "the intimacy of two people who are essential to each other" and theorized that true surrender required "a belief in one's own essential freedom." After a "sunrise gorgeous as an Arabian shawl," the west appeared a "country that only great souls could live in."[3] She was exhilarated by her surrender to this handsome, mysterious, great soul. He knew Russian, Spanish, and Marx, and spoke flawless English in a hypnotic voice. He had been born in Budapest, perhaps had joined the Mexican Revolution, and was perhaps a writer.[4] In California's lush Central Valley, Tillie wrote in her little black diary only "Tuesday. Stockton." There Bernard and Clara Goldfarb raised artichokes on their modest farm.

Outraged, Ida and Sam quickly figured out that their daughter had run away with Goldfarb. They contacted Lizzie Resnick who telegraphed her parents, who got Tillie on a train home. Abe must have been furious that she would forsake him, like a schoolgirl, because her parents ordered her home. Her "unbearable happiness" had lasted only about ten days. "Wretched," she tried to read the *Modern Quarterly*, which Abe had assigned her, thinking: "Christ! How ignorant, how stupid I am! Paragraphs I had to read over and over, names that were as unknown to me as Uranus is to man; words as unintelligible to me as Arabian. . . . The surprising knowledge of so many people—and I so stupid, so ignorant . . . But I belong! I swear it! I swear it! . . . . Slowly, every day, the veil lifts from my eyes." Tillie felt still bonded to Goldfarb: "Life is so terrible—& *we* must make it beautiful. We, who are perhaps alone in this universe." Abe had said, "in art there are only revolutionists or plagiarists"; she decided like him to be a revolutionary.[5]

Her parents insisted instead that she be a schoolgirl. Enrolling at Central High on Monday, 27 January, she listed her place of birth as "Nebraska," the date as 14 January 1913, taking a year off her age.[6] On her first school day, brazen Tillie made trouble by quarreling with her teacher. She felt she had nothing to lose because Abe did not write; Konecky kept his distance; Marian was a "Judas, Judas," and high school seemed irrelevant when the

Daily Worker detailed the "Tasks of the Young Communist League" to foment revolution. Tillie withdrew from Central High for the third and last time on 31 January. She and Abe had been alone together; now she was just alone.

She sought Konecky's guidance by resurrecting the ghosts of their relationship. He now was less a Shelley than a Christ, whose voice moved "thru dark Gethesemanes . . . crying against injustice and pain and mutilation & the world." She yearned to: "take you in my arms tonight/ And give your tired heart rest/ And let you sleep, your tired lips on my breast." He tried to deflect her adoration by appointing her "the official reader & rejecter of manuscripts for the *Sovereign Visitor.*" He suggested books by Jean Toomer, Erskine Caldwell, e. e. cummings, and Robert Cantwell, and also a book about the sexual origins of art, texts Miss Taylor would hardly have recommended. Meryl Friedel warned Tillie against further involvement with Konecky.[7] To her, though, he "might have been Christ crucified on the cross, as he talked to me."

Tillie was reading about the superman or overman in "the lonely Nietzsche," while "downstairs Mama & Daddy jabber in empty planes of sound—about me." Belatedly, they tasked her with chores, like washing "endless greasy dishes." Near despair over Tillie's misbehavior, Ida fled again, making Tillie consider "my family history." She sought to define her "*true* opinions" on literature, true art, the relation between the sexes—issues proving she was now appreciating the *Modern Quarterly.*[8]

In early March Tillie was still waiting to hear from Abe and also from New York, where she applied for a job. Taking a temporary job at Parnassus, Fine Books, Tillie could scorn "rare books, catering to exquisitely fingered people, with faces like ancient drawings" but be amused by sexual innuendo. When a customer examined a "purple covered" volume of Symons's poetry, Tillie asked if he was passionate about covers. "'Over covers?' Satyr like, he grins—'Oh no, under 'em.'" That night she sat naked in her window, with rain in her hair. She prowled around Central High, knowing that students who had adored the "Squeakeress" would have nothing to do with her now. After Ida returned and explained herself, Tillie's "respect for Mom grows." Ida's mind was "as tough & pliant & keen as one of her kitchen knives—until she is a mother again," scolding Tillie. She still hoped that Abe "will come, but no letter."[9]

On 18 March, the socialist mayor of Milwaukee spoke in Omaha against prohibition. Then with Omaha's mayor he went to tea with the prominent socialist Samuel Lerner. When the mayors arrived at 2512 Caldwell Street, a crowd of blacks and whites gathered to admire their limousine.[10] Tillie was unimpressed by this show of capitalist excess and socialist solidarity. The letter from New York arrived but said "out of question," thus burying her prospects. She heard nothing from Abe. She had no older women counselors because Anne Savidge blamed her for turning Marian Duve into "*a hysterical neurotic*" and Meryl Friedel had taken a radio job in Chicago. Home was "absolute hell—seven highly strung individuals that should never have been more than casual acquaintances forced into daily contact—and so each inevitably maimed."[11] Anel Creel was publishing. Jeanette rubbed Tillie "like sand paper." Konecky advised, "Dont compromise—*keep* yourself," but she felt so battered she could not find a self. In March and early April poems, she covered her bruised emotional selves with images of armor.[12]

No longer trying to deflect Tillie's adoration, Konecky soon lit "the old flame" of her passion. By 15 April, she felt "like a candle in the wind, Gene. . . . Heavy where his hands lay on my breasts . . . Smothering where his lips lay on mine." She was "deliciously, deliriously MAD. And I love him." They spent two weeks in a sexual "white heat," until he tried to extinguish the flame of passion.[13] Feeling emotionally bludgeoned, Tillie turned to the YCL for consolation. It sent her to preach in Ottumwa and Des Moines. For texts she used Marx and Konecky, especially his "America: The Land of Delusion," which denounced the injustice of having "65% of the total population, own only 5% of the wealth."[14] She gained confidence as she rallied, like the Pied Piper, unemployed but ignorant drifters. She rationalized: "if the profundities of Jesus could be mouthed by empty fellows, so can the profundities of Marx." After a month, she returned to Omaha, ill and exhausted.

Konecky counseled her "*keep* yourself" and "be natural!" She wondered if such bromides applied, "If naturally one is a primitive, uncivilized animal, loving, and hating and lusting too deeply."[15] She was "dozens of selves, quarreling and tearing at each other—which then is the natural self?" The adoring self, reading Konecky's *Secrets of a Book Reviewer*, thought her "words would be desecration."[16]

Tillie tried job hunting, without success because no employer believed her "glib lie" about experience. She admitted it was "a bad life I have been leading since I swore that day never to work again—to starve or whore first, so damn sick today." Konecky came to her rescue with a new scheme. She said, "Goodbye, dear room, this [will] be the last time I write in you"; on 16 June she and Jeanette boarded the train to Chicago. Meryl Friedel took the young women into her eighteenth-floor apartment, where Tillie marveled at "skyscrapers for neighbors, the lake for a footstool, and wind as our constant visitor." Chicago should be a city "in which to laugh and live and love and forget—and find myself, and lose myself."[17] She lost herself, however, in another "mad turmoil" of sexual intrigue. Konecky arrived and confessed that he still desired Tillie. Jeanette was less like sandpaper, more like a knife. A man named Ben seduced Tillie, thanks to "Ben's foolish delusion that Meryl is sexless."[18] Then she felt she "must have" another man "as an antidote for Ben." She posed for an artist and seems even to have slept with another man because he could "do so much for Gene." Friday, 27 June, was "one of the most terrible days of my life." Tillie had vowed to starve or whore; she had done the latter. Fifteen days after arriving in Chicago, she wrote "July the first. I love Gene."

Meanwhile, Jann Lerner accepted a secretarial job with the Navy in Washington, D.C., where she stayed with her aunt Rose Lerner Wolk. She had to change trains in Chicago so "Mama asked me to find out what Tillie was doing. I found her posing for nude pictures!"[19] Tillie felt so liberated she not only posed in the nude but counseled her older sister to read a "*very* elementary text" called *Sexual Life*. Jann told their parents, who sent Harry to Chicago to bring Tillie home. She penciled in a notebook, "My God, how dared they send Harry here?" She thought she should save him, but he was as unavailable to Communist salvation as she was to his attempts to bring her home. Tillie's poem "Chicago Mist-Night" shows both her depression and the influence of Sandburg and Eliot: "dead cities curl in the fog, dead people crying in the wind, and the scrapers turn white." She did not blame CP men for taking advantage of her because she too used Nietzsche to justify amorality. She did blame Meryl Friedel's affluence: "18 stories up, two maids, well-fed, well-clothed—*what am I doing here?*"

Friedel was so outraged by Konecky's dalliances she informed Eva Konecky, who hired a detective to tap the Burt Street hangout's phone. Scandal succeeded where Harry had failed. Tillie rushed home to face "questions, questions, recriminations" and to wonder, "how can I look him in the face?" Faulting herself for Konecky's misdeeds, as a reader of Nietzsche, she saw him as an overman, beyond criticism. Alhough he had taken advantage of and betrayed her, she still loved him.

In the second half of July, Tillie left her diary blank, while she traveled for the YCL, often jumping on boxcars, with poor vagrants, to avoid train fares. Rumors circulated that she was living like a hobo, staying in empty rooms with cardboard boxes for furniture.[20] In one such room, she commandeered a new Omaha phone book to use as a scrapbook. Typical of the absolutist messages she pasted in it were a flier of "Directives on the Recruiting Drive by CP-USA," a cartoon labeled "Bodies by Ford," showing a conveyor belt flattening the bodies of job-seekers, and a clipping saying "Lenin Points the Way!"[21] She collected stories about Communist good deeds.[22] She got a job "setting up boxes" at an ice cream company, perhaps in Des Moines, but objected to working conditions and got "laid off today—my fault. I shouldn't have kicked."[23]

When public outrage over Konecky's behavior reached Rae Schochet, she wrote Abe: "I supouse you remember that youngster you introduced Ethel to when in Omaha that dark eyed poetes. . . . My God does Gene have to rob the cradle in order to satisfy his desires." While agreeing to a large alimony settlement and losing custody of their sons (ages eight and three), Gene continued to "satisfy his desires" with the fifteen-year-old Jeanette.[24] To Rae, the "genius Eugene and his theory of free love" were crazy.

Both Kansas Cities, on either side of the Missouri River, were rife for rebellion, and so the CP invested considerable human and limited financial resources there, the center of Party District 10, which included Kansas, Missouri, Nebraska, Iowa, Oklahoma, and Texas. By mid-October, Tillie was assigned to an Armour meat-packing plant in Kansas City.[25] For once, she admitted class prejudice: "I cant bear—what? . . . the women I work with? The horror of their own lives? the Smell?" Such bourgeois revulsion made her accuse herself: "You see—reality frightens you." Still, like a convert to a fanatical religion, she told herself that her "only life is in the movement. I must help."[26]

Even while traveling for the YCL, Tillie took a moment to send her Fuzzy story to artist Phil Sharpe. He replied with ungentle insight, seeing it as "a top-heavy superfluously embellished record of an adolescent's bewildered feelings." He asked her to "reassure me that you wrote the epic when you were fourteen years old."[27] Dejected, Tillie "crept to the cemetery, sat on my favorite tombstone, (Amanda Parker—The work she did will follow after her) (poor woman)."[28] Tillie now blamed words: "how can you torment me so?" As if she had had the abortion to write, she asked, "Have I not bled, have I not killed for you?" Her handwriting got even smaller, less legible. She was "too goddam ill to do anything" so her writing remained "in my head." She vowed, "I *must* go away. Here my heart will not let me alone. . . . I feel too much. Perhaps Abe."

Seriously ill, Tillie "had a delightful fantastic picture of me summoning my body before the Society for Prevention of Cruelty to Animals, & having it arrested. . . . How revolting that I egotistical, proud, independent should have to be its abject slave." From the "sloping top" of a tombstone, Tillie seemed well enough, dreaming "of the great works I would do—and of how I would help lift the burden from the masses, and of how full my life had been of experience, if not in happiness, & I dreamt of Abe—& I loved Gene, & J . . . & then I skipped home to the rhythm of the St. Louis Blues . . . laughing." After she wrote "perhaps Abe" and dreamed of him, he reappeared. Tillie celebrated herself: "One of the terrible things about me is that I can feel more in five minutes than the average person does in a lifetime." With Abe, on Christmas Eve, she "rambled downtown" in Kansas City's West Bottoms. They "walked across the Leavenworth bridge" and "watched the green & red lights like fallen stars, & the shining silver of the rails, & the smoke lowing from factory chimneys, from trains."[29]

Abe had finally broken Konecky's spell. Tillie wondered what a relationship with him would "mean to me." She inked over several lines in her diary but left a reference to "the news" and new plans. By 26 December, she was in "ecstasy. I cannot write or think," though she knew "I will come to him so tired, so shattered in health."[30]

On 3 January 1931, "Jeanette's birthday," Konecky drove Jeanette, Tillie, and another man to Fremont, Nebraska. He "brought us rattles, baby bottles, etc." Tillie "thought of Jevons" (Abe's middle name, which she began using privately). These baby items were for "us," so possibly both young women were pregnant. Though she had vowed to whore rather than work, Tillie took a job in metal working, stamping rivets "on the punch press" but soon quit thanks to a "foolish fear of my hand or fingers getting cut," again faulting herself for being bourgeois.[31] She asked her diary if the "chameleon that tried to fit everybody else's conception . . . [was] really me?" She vowed to redeem herself: "1st health. 2nd no more festering–1 year has been enough, the New Masses has shown me the way, 3rd to go to trade-school if Calif doesn't pan out."

California, however, did "pan out," as at last did Abraham Jevons Goldfarb. They eloped and on Valentines Day, the justice of the peace of Reno, Nevada, issued a plain marriage certificate: "Abe J. Goldfarb of Stockton California and Matilda Lerner of Omaha Nebraska were joined in lawful wedlock on 14 Feb 31." However else they celebrated, Tillie bet a dollar in Reno's slot machines and lost it. The newlyweds then traveled to Stockton, where they moved into the run-down farm house with Abe's recently widowed mother. With a background in auto mechanics and Marxist theory, Abe knew little about farming; nevertheless, this period was restorative.

Abe's notes on Victorian literary figures, typed on paper from the Berkeley campus's Stephens Student Union offer clues about his Marxist approach to literature. He attacked Tennyson "for blind obedience to capitalistic regime." He praised Dickens's "masterpieces" for exposing the "abuses of his time."[32] Such opinions informed his penciled-in changes to Tillie's Fuzzy story, which she retyped and tried to publish.[33] She described her "simple rural existence" to Marian, who replied that it sounded "gorgeous." In her poem "She lies on the March Grass in the Arms of Her Beloved," dated March 1931, Tillie celebrated her contentment with "Your lips quiet on my lips—How still my heart." She only feared that peace with her beloved might spoil her for "life's haggard pain."[34] She wrote home that she was babysitting for a sweet family and was in love with Abe Goldfarb. Sam Lerner quickly instructed her, "inform us at once you desition," her decision to marry Abe. In a postscript, Sam instructed, "Let Abe write to us. Mother has mailed you some package give something of it to Abe and to Mrs Sweet." Tillie wrote a lyric celebration of March "our beloved month." Then her tone changed. She wrote dark stories that worried Abe and Anel Creel, to whom she sent them: "The Realist" includes a description of "necrophilia." In another, the "click of the typewriter is the rattle of skeleton's bones." In her diary, she said that a "thin ghost of a wind" was "simply bursting with the secret." But she felt "such depression—life is too strong for you; it takes life to love life." Possibly, Tillie's secret was pregnancy, but she felt too ill to bear a child and too remorseful to have another abortion.[35]

The situation in Kansas City had gotten so bad that unemployed men selling the *Daily Worker* were arrested, sent to the "municipal farm," and horribly mistreated for being Reds. Such flagrant abuse offered the CP-USA an opportunity to set up a Communist training school.[36] On 11 March, the *Kansas City Star* ran an article questioning the CP "School?" It said that Paul Cline, "Communistic organizer for Kansas City," was on the faculty, as was his wife "the violet-eyed Clara Spear." Students, mostly American-born, included "two Negro students." In the 10¢ March *Party Organizer*, Paul Cline wrote that in Kansas City he was developing leaders "from below!"[37]

In early May, Sam sent an account of "daily worries" at home.[38] Tillie replied that she and Abe were getting married. Never having married, Sam was in an awkward position: "we dont believe in ceremonies as [did] our grandfathers." Still, he and Ida would like for Tillie and Abe to marry in Omaha. They "did not have much pleasure yet" but instead "a lot of grief, suffering and worries," mostly from Tillie. Then she gave him more grief with the news that she was already married. Sam sent a long mixed-message letter, greeting "Our dear children Abe & Tillie! Dear Son Abe!" However, "against you we are complaining, your actions in this case [form] more wrong against your Mother and Father and the rest of the family. . . . Have tried to impress on your mind to think and then act, not act and then think but sorry have failed." He blamed himself for not disciplining his wild daughter. His was now the "voice of a broken heart."

In July, Anel Creel invited Tillie and Abe to join her at a California Humanist Group retreat. Tillie was too ill to attend, perhaps because she was near to or recovering from childbirth.[39] She claimed not to be jealous over an article, forwarded from home, headed "Publishes in 'Poetry' at 16." Showing a dramatic photo of Jeanette, the article said Harriet Monroe, editor of *Poetry: A Magazine of Verse*, had sent a personal letter "to Eugene Konecky, who has been tutoring Miss Gray." Tillie chuckled over the euphemism "tutoring" but consoled herself that *Poetry* published purist writing, passé in troubled 1931. Before long, Tillie and Abe were back in Omaha, where they tried sharing a home with Konecky and Jeanette on South Thirty-third Street. Visiting the Resnicks, Ethel Schochet came by and was invited in, apparently by Konecky. Shocked, she wrote Abe that she saw nothing of "the old Abe Goldfarb (I secretly worshipped)." She had once been "insanely jealous" of her mother's devotion: "She would pore over the dictionary for hours trying to learn how to express herself intelligently in her letters to you." Now "the once immaculate Abe" lived with two women who preferred "mad pictures of sensuous bodies" to cleanliness. Abe was "a genius. I honestly admit all four of you are," but genius did not excuse dirt. Lacking the courage to send her screed; Ethel hid it in her hatbox.[40]

Writing Anel Creel, Tillie raised reality by making that same house sound "deliciously Bohemian." Otherwise, Tillie seemed so gloomy; Anel was glad she was merely ill, not dying. Tillie habit of using initials and unidentified names exasperated Anel: "Who may be Gene and J.? Absolutely all I know of thy friends and relatives are Marian [Duve], Harry [Lerner], and your husband. Any other names are Greek, and initials are—hieroglyphics." Tillie's habit of "meticulously" scratching out whole lines made letters incomprehensible, while her "tiny, tired little" letters made them illegible.[41] (For seven more decades, Tillie's correspondents would make the same complaints.)

By September, Tillie had recovered enough to become, like Jeanette, one of the "new promising comrades" Paul Cline was recruiting in Kansas City. Abe became a traveler for the CP in District Ten. Konecky kept his Omaha WOW job to pay alimony. Scotsman George Stalker became party leader in Omaha, and a section organizer named Stanislaus was sent from Omaha to Kansas, where he quickly seduced Jeanette. She saw her seduction oddly as betraying "the movement viciously." She discussed her affair "very calmly with Gene and Jevons," and the men excused her because Stanislaus had "the party halo about him"; their reaction implied that loyalty to the

CP superseded loyalty to her lover.[42] Then Konecky proved his loyalty by marrying Jeanette on 2 October 1931 in Hiawatha, Kansas. An Omaha paper printed her picture, dressed as Hiawatha, and noted that Konecky's "bride will be 17 years old January 3."

With exploitation, poverty, and even starvation rampant, the CP-USA had a chance to change the system. Tillie would remember that in the 1930s people "could electrify the consciousness of the nation" against unemployment and such injustices as the "Scottsboro Boys," nine African Americans convicted on trumped-up charges of raping two young white women in Alabama. The party planned a Hunger March, with caravans of suffering citizens gathering in Washington, D.C., in early December to protest starvation in America to Congress.[43] Amid horrors and injustices, the Communist movement gave Tillie "hope: beleaguered, starved, battered, *based* hope." Like a *Daily Worker* author, she could say "The Revolution Made a Person Out of Me."[44] It also promised to make a writer out of her.

In Kansas City, Missouri, under the name Teresa Landale, Tillie wrote a dramatic account of a young man's speech: "We can not eat battleships, we can not eat promises, we demand work at good wages, unemployed relief, unemployment insurance." Then "Fern Pierce, 16, and Ellen Allen, 18," began to speak but were arrested. In Tillie's account, the "crowd immediately surged about the [CP] leaders as a bodyguard," leaving the "baffled cops" standing "helplessly by while the crowd cheered time after time for the Hunger Marchers, Freedom of Tom Mooney, and the Communist Party."[45] That powerful account shows Tillie following the party imperative to write dramatic and publishable journalism. For the Unemployed Councils, she wrote songs and skits, following an "agitprop" formula, combining agitation and propaganda about a Kansas City sweatshop or "plague spot."[46] She was sent to a plague spot, a tie factory in Argentine, Kansas, a late nineteenth-century mining settlement, near the Santa Fe Railroad tracks and a silver smelter ("Argentine" being Latin for silver). She joined Argentine's Communist Council, led by David Dawson. Tillie soon was enough of an insider to criticize CP "Wrongs" such as "Orders from above in Hunger March," "Loose Organization," and "factionalism." In early November, Theodore Dreiser headed a group of prominent American writers, including John Dos Passos and Malcolm Cowley, to investigate working conditions in the coal mines of Harland, Kentucky. In Kansas City, needle workers at Liberty Garment Company went on strike. On 7 November, the *Daily Worker* reported that in Kansas City, "Police Raid Red Offices to Stop Council's Work." Arrested and soon released were Paul Cline, David Dawson, and thirteen others, probably including Tillie Lerner.[47]

While writers and laborers described "mass starvation" in the Kentucky minefields to an appalled New York audience, the *Kansas City Star* printed a cartoon showing the Dreiser investigation sinking into quicksand. The *Star* ignored what the *Daily Worker* described as the "second full-time training school held in District 10," from 1–31 December, to be led by Paul Cline and Harry Winston. A brilliant and cultured immigrant, Cline struggled to prove his proletarian credentials. Cline's wife Clara Spear, a poor factory girl, claimed he taught her: "big words, introduced me to American literature. I carried my dictionary like a religious person would carry the Bible." Winston was a blind African American who believed in education "based upon the teachings of Marxism-Leninism . . . [and] the spirit of proletarian internationalism."[48] The school offered courses "in the History of the American Working Class, Public Speaking, Negro Work, Agrarian Work," and the importance of reading "the *Daily Worker* and Party litera-ture." One student circulated among others to guide "the discussion, to clear up controversial points, to maintain discipline among the students while they were studying." Tillie Lerner was that leader. She wrote Abe that her major fault was being "too capable." Still, the students "nearly all like me a helluvalot—one or two are distrustful because I have not been in jail & passed out leaflets on cold nights. . . . Most students are homeless types and the tragic thing is I have no time to develop [indoctrinate and mold] them." Though irrepressible Tillie was reprimanded for "superior flippancy," revolutionary Tillie did not question a communist catechism, which asked, "Have not Party interests ended by deadening all my discrimi-nation between moral values?" The correct answer was "yes."[49] Certainly, the CP big-wigs who had taken advantage of her in Chicago had displayed deadened moral values, but Tillie was too indoctrinated to object.

That December, while Clara Spear Cline was touring the Soviet Union and Abe traveling, Tillie and Paul Cline seduced each other. She later wondered if handsome Paul recalled the passionate Tillie: "her ears & nose & slush-eaten feet were frozen, & her round breasts frozen hard (unless you slipped your hand into her jacket & loved them." She recalled "if you were kind, you put her chapped hands into your leather jacket pockets, & rubbed life into them." If he "were cruel, the snow crunched under her feet, & got into her shoes, & that good old flame of luv that roared in her veins or that dark fire of despair they write about didn't keep those feet warm." She desired Cline in a "primitive sense—sweeping everything away, all sense, all heart, all mind, obliterating them. . . . I 'loved' him: a dumb thing cried 'Paul Paul' always." However many lovers she had had, she let loose her animal sexuality with only three: "Gene & J [Jevons] & Paul. Yes."[50]

Before the CP school ended, students took jobs and tried to convert fellow workers to Communism. Tillie was distributing "leaflets to meatpackers at Swift's in a near blizzard, for the Young Communist League" when she was arrested on a charge of "making loud and unusual noises." Argentine's 1891 City Hall, a cupola-crowned stone edifice, housed police and fire departments and a basement jail, from which chain gangs trudged daily to break up rock in a quarry.[51] The dank basement held female "criminals"—both leftist agitators and prostitutes, whose pimps, in cooperation with the police, bailed them out on Saturday nights. Political prisoners like Tillie were left in cold, rat-infested cells without charges, lawyers, or trial dates.[52]

Tillie's hours at sewing machines and on assembly lines, followed by after-hours organizing, leaf-letting, skit-writing, and love-making (mostly it seems in the snow) had sapped her strength. The various illnesses and weaknesses, threatening for years, caught up with her. She recorded the "cold freezing about me quietly, making the fever so insufferable." Left to molder in jail, her bitterness was as vehement as her passion: "you sonovabitch. O Do you remember sweet T, Paul, sweet Tillie with her hair so brown, who laughed with delight at each smile that you gave, & trembled in fear of your frown?" After Tillie's fellow prisoners spread news that she was coughing up blood, authorities released her to Fern Pierce and Red Allen, who took her to their rooming house and permitted her only to read the *Daily Worker.* Tillie was so indoctrinated she hailed, "O Communism—how you came to those of whom I will write—more incredible & beautiful than mama," another instance of the abstract trumping the personal.[53]

The beginning of 1932 and Tillie's twentieth birthday passed unnoticed. Racked by fever, she was sometimes delirious. On 21 January, she lay near the rooming house's front window, fixated on the drooping pods of a catalpa tree. Like a purist poet, she speculated that the reality of the cigar-like pods "all depends on one's vision. When I was a child I saw them as the lovely fringes of a dancers dress." Now they seemed "dying fingers and worms." In late January, she penned a poem "Bitter of heart, hunched by the window."[54] Bitterness could be illuminating: "my own foulness revealed," but it did not reveal the foulness in an ideology that dispensed with conventional morality. Ravaged by fever and guilt, Tillie seemed near death, so Fern and Red contacted Abe, who rushed to her. Though the passion she felt for Paul Cline had surpassed what she had felt for her husband, he appeared in the guise of rescuer, saving Tillie. She vowed: "Whatever I feel Jevons must be made happy. Do I love him? I do not know. Only time can answer the question, but every day asks, 'is gratefulness, a realization of splendid character, love'?" After "a hasty exit," Abe and John Dawson took Tillie north, to Omaha.

Unannounced, she and Abe arrived at 2512 Caldwell Street when only Ida and Morris (almost fifteen) were home. The year before, Sam had welcomed Abe as his son, but Ida had not. Morris noticed that, under his overcoat, Abe "dressed very well. . . . silk shirts and ties. I could have cast him in a film as a gangster." He shook Abe's hand, but Ida would not speak to him. Abe took the marriage license from his coat pocket and, in a "deep rich voice," explained to Ida that it proved he and Tillie were married. Thinking Reno hardly a place for marriages, Ida assumed the license was a fake and tore it up. She asked Morris to leave the room." Tillie and Abe soon left, cast out into the snow.[55]

Humiliated, they fled to the Burt Street address, now listed as the residence of George Stalker, organizer. While Goldfarb, Dawson, and Stalker involved themselves with CP recruitment, Tillie stayed indoors. Coughing less, she hand-printed fliers. One read "Against Evictions! Against layoffs, wagecuts! Against Boss 'Justice,' Against lynchings, Jim-crow!! For Unemployment Insurance!!!!" It summoned a crowd of nearly one hundred on 4 February 1932 to Jefferson Square in downtown Omaha.[56] The *Omaha Bee-News* reported that "John Dawson of Kansas City, an organizer for the Trade Union Unity League, A [G] Stalker, and J Feldman [perhaps A. J. Goldfarb] were among the speakers in Jefferson square and at City Hall." Accompanying the article were photos of the crowd at City Hall and of a woman, identified as "Theta Larimore, 2023 Burt Street." Despite her cough, Tillie roused the crowd: "'What becomes of the women who lose their jobs?' She shouted. 'Save their respectability,'" an odd association of unemployment with whoring. The photo shows her with a puffy, far from faunlike, face.[57]

She hand-printed a flier, "Young Workers Come to the Red Valentine Dance": Workers Center 2023 Burt, Sat Feb 13th Russia's Valentine to Young workers." Spaced inside a hand-drawn heart were impossible promises of a six-hour work day, "Equal Pay for Equal Work," no unemployment, a month's paid vacation for "all under 24!," and "Free Education!" Valentine's Day itself was the Goldfarbs' first wedding anniversary, so Jeanette and Gene Konecky hosted a party, inviting Tillie's cousin Roberta Braude but no Lerners. At sixteen, the youngest person there, Roberta felt timid in such a "wild" and "giddy environment." She was too young to recognize illegal alcohol but did note loud music, wild dancing, and lots of flirting. She met a woman from Chicago (Meryl Friedel) and found Abe so handsome he looked like a movie star. He seemed romantic until they met in a back room, and he planted a kiss on her mouth.[58]

While hidden on Burt Street, Tillie "worked steadily on shorthand, the scrapbook." After the death of Harry Simms, a young protester in the Harlan, Kentucky, miners' strike, she "wrote a wretched poem on Harry Simms which could be used as mass recitation." She tried writing about Joe York, a YCL district organizer, "murdered in class war." She hand-printed a flier to the "Negroes of Omaha" urging them to protest the "legal lynching of Jess Hollins," a black man sentenced to death in Oklahoma. The CP-USA recruited African Americans and made some, like Henry Winston, leaders.[59]

With the CP, however, good work for the poor and underprivileged and personal relations too were means toward an end—revolution. Fern Pierce, for example, advised "Comrade Tillie" to "ignore your surround-ings—I mean your mother, Storms [Jeanette]. Cain [Konecky] and even Jevons" who were personally unimportant given the need to "read *Daily Worker* everyday" and prepare for revolution. A doctor, however, saw the personal toll Tillie was paying and ordered her to care for herself instead of the YCL. Then Abe proposed that they journey to Fairbault, Minnesota, where Rae and Phil Schochet lived alone in a big empty house. Whatever Tillie thought about revolution, she relented, hiding memories of Paul Cline "who kissed my hair under a wintry sky."[60]

Tillie read Jonathan Swift to learn political satire, practiced shorthand to "equip myself to be of value," and tried to reverse her "inefficiency, procras-tination, idle planning, lack of perseverance." With "Jevons to help," she vowed to "only care about my sick body," but even health was in service of ideology: "to be a good Bolshevik I need health first." She destroyed papers to "bury the past here, leave it here to rot, not drag the evil corpse after." She rejoiced: "I do not feel ill—only happy. I am leaving—leaving this place of horrors." Thinking "how indebted I am to Jevons for taking me away to Faribault," she also wrote "in love again."[61]

Tillie and Abe Goldfarb rode the train from Omaha to Faribault, arriving when "Workers Urged to Vote Communist in March 15 Election in St. Paul." A quiet town of nearly 13,000, in southern Minnesota's lake region, Fari-bault was known as the "Athens of the West." The Schochets' house sat alone on a large corner lot in a tree-lined section near the center of town. Their son Nahman (named after Rae's younger brother Nahman Goldfarb) lived in northern Minnesota. Their older daughter Sarah (Sally) lived in New York City with their younger daughter Ethel, born, like Tillie, in 1912.

Phil Schochet owned the Faribault Iron & Metal Company, which he described on a letterhead as "wholesale dealers in scrap iron, rags, rubbers, metals and bones" with "Hides, Pelts & Wool, Tallow and Raw Furs a Specialty." More simply, Phil ran a scrap iron and rag and bone junkyard, one of the few business not decimated by the worsening depression. Meanwhile, Rae earned her own cash from the Theopold-Reid Company, wholesale grocers and importers by selling dried and fresh fruits and sometimes other mail-order foods (including ducks) to her neighbors.[62] With her own income and her children grown, Rae had begun hitch-hiking alone in the late 1920s. She did what she pleased and said what she thought. She listened to news, opera, and entertainers like Jack Benny on the radio, which she called "this godsend instrument." She adored Abe and kept his brilliant letters, thinking that, if he became famous, they would make "a complete book with a good ending."[63] She wrote that her "heart swells with pride when you tell me that I still am your Mother father sister and above all your friend." At forty-four, Rae saw herself as a "lady of soothing hearts." She brought Clara Goldfarb from Stockton to Minneapolis to live near relatives. Then Rae settled down with her sixty-four-year-old husband Phil to make a home for Abe and his ailing wife, who arrived when the winter was just ending: "We had the middle bedroom, and there was even snow when we first came, and the branches of the tree outside the window were skinny and naked. You had such a quiet, deep house." Abe soon became a traveling salesman and cleaner of rugs and involved himself in Minnesota CP activities.[64]

At the Schochets' home, Tillie coughed up "less and less" blood, "and I write." Glimpses of the Swartz and Braude families had provoked her desire "of to write them." Now she invented a family named Holbrook and began a novel about them. She envisioned child protagonists: "O Mazie & Will & Ben. At last I write out all that has festered in me so long."[65] For Abe she linked creative, political, and sexual excitement. She said she was "mentally much stimulated" by reading Marx and "suddenly became extremely aroused sexually, thinking of you." She needed "sexual release very much. Mentally I am too much alive, [having] gigantic ideas, & arguments on every subject." Privately, however, she admitted being plagued by "the past—Paul & Gene—the cruelty," presumably theirs to her. Still, she felt a "curious, infuriating, humiliating, longing for Paul. Just a physical thing I cannot conquer." Despite her letter to Abe about longing for him, she told her diary that longing for Paul was "Why I can't take J[Jevons]."[66] Burying these pages in Ethel's hatbox, she unearthed Ethel's screed from the summer before. Tillie was appalled to read Ethel's denunciation of the filth and debauchery in which Abe had seemed to be existing with Tillie, Jeanette, and Eugene Konecky.

With music playing on Rae's radio and outside "the feel of spring" in the air, Tillie forgot her regrets and shame to find life at last "wonderful." While Abe, the Schochets, and doctors worried about her health,

Bolsheviks, like Red Allen, worried about her political contribution. Red even wrote Tillie to "stop coughing up that blood, that red blood; the workers' flag is deepest red & yours has better places to be shed than in that sour smelly handkerchief." While Red cared about "the work, the revolution," Harry Winston bucked the bureaucracy to get Tillie a party transfer to Minneapolis.[67]

Once she recorded wanting "Abe passionately in a 'bitey' way. There was no mind; none, none." She assured him that her "monthlies are over" and urged him to "come down Sunday—manage it somehow." Abe arrived in Faribault, while Rae took their mother to Omaha to see Lizzie Resnick, who had had a baby boy, whom Abe called "Leetle Bernie." As loyal brother and husband, Abe delivered boxes of apricots, prunes, and mixed fruit to Rae's customers, collecting almost $25, despite "hard times."[68] And he painted to Rae a picture of domesticated bliss: "Tillie is ironing the clothes: the duck came out fair—not done enough and quite small—but we did justice to it—Phil felt that you were gypped on the weight of the ducks. Everything hotsie-totsie.... Atmosphere here splendid for Tillie—She will soon feel well enough to start on her novel."

In Omaha, wanting to heal the "idiotic" family break that Tillie and Abe had fostered, Rae took Lizzie to the Lerners: "found the Father gone to a meeting but Mother was hom also the children. They all seem to know me said I looked like my picture. The little girl Yetta is real sweet and Morris was quite talkative and we got real chumy. The older girl [Lillian] was busy typing but she smiled sweetly and the older boy [Harry] was nice too." Ida and Lizzie did "most of the talking," convincing Ida that Tillie was, after all, married to a nice Jewish man from a good family. Rae was pleased that Tillie and Abe were "getting quite chummy with my husband. You know he is not such a bad sort after you know him in fact he is a good heartet soul." The good-hearted Phil sent Ethel "a good word for Abe's wife." Having no better notion of Tillie's writerly ambitions than of her rampant sexuality, he noted: "Since Mother is gone, we eat together. She keeps house."

When Rae and Lizzie next visited on Caldwell Street, they found the Lerners "all kind of exitet" because Jann had sent Lillian money to visit Washington, D.C., after graduation. When Sam drove the women back to Lizzie's, Ida went along, news that inspired Tillie to send a conciliatory letter home, which Yetta found so illegible "even if I did not burn it—posterity could never decipher a word." On 4 May 1932, Tillie wrote one line in her diary: "I am pregnant." Soon she confessed: "I need—Jevons. Yes, Jevons. ... He at least looked down in mercy & compassion, even gave me a hand to rise. ... So it [is] fair for me to have his child—I am not my own."[69]

Reading "gigantic" novels by Dos Passos, Dreiser, and Cather made Tillie feel "dwindled."[70] She took "a few poems of the first eighteen years of my life" and sent them to Harriet Monroe of *Poetry: A Magazine of Verse*, adding the non sequitur, "I am pregnant." She said she had revered the "false" dawn that *Poetry* had epitomized in purist writing, but she would no longer ignore the subhuman working conditions of the poor. Moore did not reply to this young revolutionary's bizarre submission and scolding.[71]

The Schochet home gave Tillie joy, as "such a lived in place. All of Rae's little stories about people, about herself carry some deeper significance," as Tillie wanted to connect her own scenes to larger meanings: "Mazie & her brother in dank March woods. Clouds like bellies—remembrance of he blood & agony of creation." In a letter to "Abe Darling," that she for once dated (31 May 1932), Tillie described walking with Rae on an "aphrodisiac night, restless & splendid." Pregnancy brought contentment, though also nausea and inertia, but "at least I am creating a child."

In an April 1932 radio speech, Franklin Delano Roosevelt promised that, if elected, he would intervene to ease the burden on the poor "Forgotten Man." Still, many leftists distrusted FDR's private wealth and big business connections, believing that he would protect the wealth of the few against the needs of the many. That summer, William Z. Foster, Communist presidential candidate, spoke in Minneapolis, and Tillie took Rae to hear him. Fearing a police raid, Rae wore Abe's American Legion pin as protection. Foster's campaign signaled the high watermark of sympathy for the CP-USA. His denunciation of acquisitive capitalism highlighted the irresponsibility in President Herbert Hoover's *laissez faire* economics. Calling out the army, under General Douglas MacArthur, to drive World War I veterans seeking promised bonus pay out of D.C. proved Hoover's callousness. Malcolm Cowley later wrote that sending the army against the heroes of 1918 should have provoked "a revolution in itself."[72] Though Roosevelt became the Democratic candidate, more than fifty prominent writers, critics, and academics endorsed Foster for president.[73]

Forgoing her hell-cat and promiscuous ways, Tillie assured Abe that the "hectic feverishness of K. C." was over and she longed to "give you your child." She begged "forgive me that past." In his silk shirts and handsome suits, Abe seems to have functioned as CP theorist, not as a recruiter of impoverished, unemployed, poor white and black laborers. When he did speak at one unemployment protest, he did not move the crowd.[74] Tillie counseled him that "polished methods" can drive "'want-to-think' youngsters away. They want to feel equal & talk." Abe, however, equated spontaneity with lack of preparation, an "inherent" weakness of Tillie's.

In Duluth, where a clerk allowed him to use the YMCA's typewriter, Abe sent his "Beloved" a long, loving letter (the only extant one of his to her). He saw a future with "you well and happy, a glowing mother, a noted novelist, a keen communist theoretician (of course, you will have lots of studying to do), and a splendid revolutionary—living a rich, vibrant life. Your poetic gift will blossom forth into immortal song and your imaginative intellect will create noble novels. But you have a powerful logical mind which will serve you in good stead as an international revolutionary—a greater Rosa Luxemburg, for you are really creative." Other than noting a "rather stiff" dentist's $50 charge, the entire letter expressed adoration for his "beloved wife" from "Your devoted husband, Abe." By late summer, he and Tillie were contentedly together in Minneapolis.[75]

At the Lerner home in Omaha, contentment was no longer possible. Though Yetta had begun the summer with no complaints except that Tille's handwriting was too tiny, the circus too expensive, by her eleventh birthday on 26 August, she had a life-threatening ailment. A terrible skin disease on her left leg began dramatically when her parents were out of town at a socialist meeting. Yetta became delirious, and Ruth Stein was too terrified to help. When Ida returned, she quickly got a doctor to the house, but he advised cruel treatments, like drilling holes in Yetta's foot or amputating it.[76] Ida "absolutely refused." She put Yetta in the front bedroom, and she and Morris alternated "staying up all night to put hot pads on the leg every couple of hours" for months.[77]

On Broadway that October, a musical review called *Americana* became the first popular entertainment to "treat the wreckage of the Depression seriously." Its touching song, "Brother, Can You Spare a Dime," soon became the "worldwide anthem of the Great Depression."[78] With Hoover campaigning for reelection further to the right and Roosevelt to the left, writers and intellectuals began turning from Foster to FDR.[79] On 1 November 1932, he soundly defeated Hoover, Foster, and Norman Thomas. A "New Deal" seemed possible. The CP-USA had lost its chance to change the system. Josef Stalin further weakened the CP with an "accelerated" purging of "conciliationist elements."[80] Fern Pierce wrote that "Cline has been removed—because of weakness of his work in the election campaign." A reformed Tillie sent Abe "a whole chorus of halleluias concerning Cline. And a cupple [sic] more echoes for your paragraph on it."[81]

Late that fall, Ida wrote Tillie a letter of reconciliation, saying how happy she was to know that she had friends ("reel good frinds"). Ida said that hard times made her language "even wors." Thinking "maybe your a mama already," she wanted Tillie's child to know that her being quiet ("my beng kvaet") was not because of a cold heart. Touched by Ida's laboriously written English, Tillie brought her own approaching motherhood into her novel. When young Mazie is forced to take a job in a steamy candy factory, older women nurture her, sometimes singing or telling stories of Italy, and a kind pregnant woman lets Mazie put a hand on her belly to feel the mystery of a baby kicking.[82]

Awaiting the birth of her child, one November day Tillie wrote a startling list of "things I love about me. The baby-fulfillment. Writing and my books. My mind . . . has priapism—it has so much exciting it to an erection. Today it aches, too many orgasms of thought, that's why I lay in bed all day. Priapism is no joy." Omitting the "orgasms of thought," Tillie rewrote her experiences for Ethel: "When we walk in the fog, Abe and I, late in the night after he comes home, it is as if only we two existed, till shredding the night a train comes whirring with its knives of light and sound." She reflected: "To Jevons I am a soft breast. To your mother, a secure desk to pigeonhole her doubts and secrets in, to the movement an efficient and ingenious machine, to others, a mind, to my baby sister, a hand in the dark." Full of self-love, Tillie could also be so insecure and frightened that "Jevons quit work and came and stayed with me" one day.[83]

Abe wrote his brother Nahman that he was earning a "few shekels here and there on odd jobs." Rae "did a wonderful thing—she peddled her fruit and purchased a lovely crib," which could be passed on to a second baby. Other relatives were so "shamed by such generosity" they promised more gifts "so our expenditure for the heir has been almost nil." A friend named Tom Courtney, whom Abe called "Saint Thomas," gave them $50 to take care of the "necessary birth expenditures." Abe was "extraordinarily happy," and Tillie "looks lovely. We expect the baby any time—but he seems damned slow in coming out. I guess he knows already what a lousy woild he's going to be in—can hardly blame him." Renewed health should "liberate [Tillie's] tremendous energies intellectually. . . . She will finish her novel as soon as she is well." That letter shows Abe a proud, though paternalistic brother, husband, and father-to-be. But when Lizzie Resnick sent baby things, used by little Bernie, Abe haughtily refused to be a "victim of charity." The Resnicks were "stupid swine," possibly kindhearted, but "empty and moronic."

Counseling Abe to change his "arrogant disposition," Rae went to Omaha to patch up relations with the Resnicks and report to the Lerners on Tillie's pregnancy. Sam was in the doldrums because, with house painting a luxury, his income was almost nonexistent. Rae called Tillie "your highness" and suggested she "develop the art of" writing her family.[84] She assured Abe that women survive childbirth better than their husbands.

Rae was home when Tillie went into labor, and Rae, as she later recalled, "stayed near your bed and I thought you were so brave." Karla Barucha Goldfarb was born on at 12:40 A.M. on 20 December 1932. Her birth certificate lists her as a full-term legitimate baby, born to Abe J. Goldfarb (not employed) and Matilda Lerner (homemaker). For once, Tillie listed her age correctly—as twenty, but Abe said he was twenty-seven, when he actually was thiry-six.[85] The baby's first name derived from Karl Marx and Karl Leibnecht, who, Abe told Nahman, had been "slaughtered by the German reactionaries in 1923"; her second name, Barucha, was Hebrew for "praise."

Tillie responded to the newborns in the hospital ward "wailing in their blatantly physical hungers" with such an excess of mother's milk she used a breast pump to "extract milk for the other babies." Abe got a job in northern Minnesota so Rae and Phil took Tillie and baby Karla back early in 1933. Sometimes Tillie felt she should paste stickers that read "Fragile, Handle with Care" on her breasts and head and back. She needed Abe to "hold me, help me." Visiting her daughters in New York City, Rae was impressed with a speech by Tillie's "Cousin Sam Beber," now a judge.[86] Having recently married Sue Clark, Nahman Goldfarb checked out the Stockton farmhouse, at Rae's request. He told her that it was livable; he told Abe that it could hold both their families.

With Yetta Lerner spending 1932–1933 out of school, mostly in bed with a tent over her foot, Tillie did better at writing her family; she even sent a birthday cake to Morris. His reply, addressed to "Dear T., Abe, and Karla, with Love to Rae," told about life on Caldwell Street during the worsening depression. Sam was "almost broke, no work for a time." Harry, who had graduated in 1930, had enlisted in the Civilian Conservation Corps and now worked at the Socialist Party Office. Lillian was taking piano lessons, for "free, for we can't afford no spending of money" so he was especially grateful for the dollar bill Jann sent for his birthday. Ida had received a letter from Russia "so horrible that she cried for two days. Two of her nieces are dying, and two have died. They are all starving. Mama asked me to ask you if you could send even a dollar here to help them pay for a doctor." He begged Tillie to send the birth announcement she had "promised Mama."[87]

Tillie wrote Abe that their precocious baby "pumped up my buzzim [bosom] with pride." Phil had "bumped down" from the attic a relic from the past—the Schochet baby carriage. Karla purred and "cooed whole symphonies." Tillie tried and rejected modern tactics like letting her baby cry until a scheduled feeding time. She set a happy scene, with a spring robin "chirruping and singing ... Downstairs Karla coos and the radio pours overpoweringly sweet music into my veins." Karla's father was ecstatic over "angelic, magnetic, dynamic Karla whose physical precocity amazes us every moment." With "rare beauty," she was at seven months a "little erotic sensualist." Her mother was a grown-up sensualist, who laughed at a book that defined "debachery and licentiousness" as having intercourse more than once a month. (Justice Woolsey's lifting the obscenity ban on James Joyce's *Ulysses* helped Americans ridicule sexual prudery.) Reading Dreiser's sexually explicit *Dawn*, she wrote Abe that Dreiser "writes, god-damn it, exactly like you, only somewhat simpler."[88] Though she chaffed under his criticism, Tillie accepted Abe's temper as "an integral part of your character." Meanwhile, Karla drank from a glass with "never a drop spilled, & grins between each sip."

The depression had put a quarter of Americans out of work. Reposses-sions and evictions sent homeless people into makeshift shacks. Teachers and preachers were paid in local produce. Middle-class citizens waited in breadlines for food to feed their children. Despite their poor showing in elections, party members like Abe and Tillie rationalized that unemploy-ment, including his losses of "carpet-beautifying" and "advertising man" jobs, meant that "the revolutionary era is beginning—we are at the end of an epoch," as he wrote Nahman. In Germany on 6 March, Hitler assumed absolute power, and by April the Nazis boycotted Jewish merchants and expelled Jews from symphonies and art groups. In the *New Masses*, "noted American writers" protested "Nazi atrocities" and warned "against fascist danger in U.S.A." In a *New Masses* cartoon, a $ on his tie, Roosevelt embraces female versions of Hitler and Mussolini. But the *New Masses* and the CP had FDR wrong. In his inaugural address of 4 March and later radio talks, he inspired such hope that citizens began redepositing their savings in failed banks.[89] Still, Tillie thought Phil Schochet's "faith in Roosevelt" naïve. She planned for her choppy scenes from Mazie's childhood to become chapters leading up to a strike, precipitating a massive revolution, unlike the incremental changes FDR could inspire.

For the Fourth of July, Joe and Lizzie Resnick melded the families into harmony by bringing Ida to Faribault. She sang lullabies to her granddaughter, told about Yetta's recovery, and worried about Karla's protruding navel, blamed on an enlarged appendix or a hernia, but Tillie assured her mother that there was no emergency. Rae entertained the family by reading aloud a yellowed letter from Bernard Goldfarb about troubles in old Russia. She made "Funny face," as Tillie now called the baby, "vociferous—answering to everyone—with resultant shrieks of flattered delight." Ethel and Tillie danced under the trees in the dark to music on the radio. Unable to sleep, Tillie later wrote such lovely details to Abe. When she went outside and burned the last of her sparklers, however, she confessed in her diary a "sudden memory of Paul."

Abe was away during the weeks on a new job, and the devoted mother kept a baby book, informing Abe when Karla began eating vegetables and could "crawl all over—watching the ants." When she heard the unsurprising news that Jeanette was divorcing Konecky,[90] Tillie feared her own "punishment for a wasted life." She felt a middle-class longing for "tranquillity, quiet, children, friends, time to write" but also a radical commitment to "the bloody years ahead." Party readings instructed her that "more is lived in one day of revolution than ten years of peace," but her personal joy in baby, husband, and the Schochets' home made such abstractions less compelling.

When Nahman Goldfarb proposed that Tillie and Abe join him and his bride in California, Abe replied: "T. is thrilled by the idea of isolation in Stockton—she is finishing her data on her baby book, and is impatient to finish her novel—and the beginning of it is splendid. She also plans on writing articles for shekels and of course her poetry." Abe himself might begin a "longdreamed of novel" as well as "multitudinous diatribes on ze system." Soon, Tillie and Abe did set out for California, stopping in Omaha on the way. Rae mailed Abe a "5 spot to get the necessitys for Barucha and T," and he sent updates on Karla that made Rae "lonesome for that sweet sugar plum I could kiss her, but I gues she has others who love the darling as much." She told him that a master of ceremony at a Greenwich Village gathering of artists, musicians, and poets, "wrote something on your style. Ethel made a copy."[91]

Two and a half years since Ida had torn up their marriage license, she welcomed Abe, Tillie, and especially their baby. Despite straightened circumstances, she and Sam fed the Goldfarbs, and Karla charmed the Lerner and Resnick extended families.[92] There seems to have been only one inharmonious moment. Morris later recalled that while he was "sitting on the toilet, Abe Goldfarb came in and told me I should seek out older women, and I could learn about sex from them." Abe's "hallucinating" talk about sexual initiation with older women so revolted the sixteen-year-old he could hardly leave the bathroom.[93]

Regretting Karla's departure, Rae reflected that "the Goldfarb clan did inherit a restlessness from dear old Dad," who had rebelled "against the

Romanian and Russians he cursed them for the injustice and mishandling the Jews, and also by traveling from place to place." Passing through the backsides of cities, these restless Goldfarbs saw through train windows homeless people clustering in shanty-towns full of so-called Hoover shacks. Crossing the drought-ravaged plains, they sped past encampments of farmers fleeing the Oklahoma dust bowl for a better life in California. Tillie was glad to return to the old Stockton farmhouse and resume a "simple rural existence" like the one she had lived with Abe in the early days of their marriage. She was pleased to share the house with Nahman and Sue, both in their twenties, both smart college graduates. Sue, a pretty woman with blond hair and an eager smile, was pleased to have married into this family of Jewish intellectuals and thrilled that little Karla quickly warmed to her.

Roosevelt had just launched the Civil Works Administration (CWA) to restore people's dignity with work relief and the economy with circulating funds. Abe applied at the Stockton office and immediately was hired to help administer the program. He hired Tillie as his part-time secretary and put Nahman on the payroll too. Sue loved staying with precocious Karla and encouraging her ventures in walking and talking.

Tillie now had the supportive circumstances to write: love and encouragement from a stable family; a safe job that kept her only minimally busy; and freedom to read and work on her novel. After living a "bad life," after promiscuity, prison, and pleurisy, she had managed a secular redemption. She had thought she must be a Bolshevik in her personal life. Now she saw that she might achieve a broader redemption through her proletarian fiction. She was buoyed by Abe's faith that she would be "an international revolutionary—a greater Rosa Luxemburg." She was sustained by his belief that Tillie Lerner Goldfarb was "really creative."

CHAPTER 5

EARLY GENIUS

1934

The work of Tillie Lerner is going to be the inevitable extension of the work of such writers as Dos Passos and all the other movement writers.
—William Saroyan to Bennett Cerf, 11 September 1934

By the beginning of 1934, federal agencies were getting people back to work (the Civil Works Administration alone employed four million workers), but the depression was too broad for a quick fix. However impoverished, half of all American families owned radios, and most gathered by them on Sunday evenings to hear President Roosevelt's reassuring "Fireside Chats." Almost everyone could sing along with Bing Crosby's "Brother, Can You Spare a Dime." Many took the song "Remember My Forgotten Man" as a sermon.[1]

With large-circulation magazines like *Vanity Fair* and the *Saturday Evening Post* still publishing fiction mostly about an untroubled middle-class, a host of new small magazines promised stories and poems about forgotten men and women. Proletarian novels presented horrid bosses, horrendous injustices, and heroes striking and demanding a workers' paradise. Appealing to the ideologically committed, they were easily forgotten. Tillie's proletarian characters Jim and Anna Holbrook have a smattering of education (what daughter Mazie calls "edjiccation"), toil doggedly, and want a better life. Tillie scoured the Stockton Public Library for articles about the misery of the American worker and the benefits for the Soviet worker. She even proposed emigrating to Russia, a notion that made Rae scold Abe for marrying someone "even more" radical than he. Rae argued that, when Roosevelt supplied Abe with bread, butter, and dollars, Tillie should not try to undermine his government. Tillie herself feared that domestic contentment kept her from overturning the system.

In the *New Masses*, she read a letter telling women who "buy embroidered children's dresses labeled 'hand made' they are getting dresses made in San Antonio, Texas, by women and girls with trembling fingers and broken backs." The author ended: "I want you women up North to know. I tell you this can't last forever. I swear it won't."[2] Though she had written skits and poems about other miscarriages of justice, only this picture of victimized women provoked a powerful poem. Borrowing cadences, phrasing, and actual names, she rewrote the letter as "I Want You Women Up North to Know." In her rendition, the embroidered dresses are "dyed in blood, are stitched in wasting flesh." The "bourgeois poet" might see a seamstress's stitching as an "exquisite dance," and the purist poet might depict her cough as "accompaniment for the esthetic dance of her fingers." But this radical poet saw her as a victim of capitalist exploitation. Calling for a Soviet-style "heaven on earth," Tillie sent the poem to *The Partisan*, the magazine of the West Coast John Reed club.[3]

Then on Valentine's Day, their third anniversary, Abe's CWA boss wrote "AJG" to "kindly advise your men" that they were out of work until Congress appropriated more funds.[4] Only earning twenty-five cents an hour as a "lackey steno," Tillie blamed her lost job on corrupting wealth "in the heart of Franklin Dealout Richvelth and his C. W. A." Meanwhile, San Francisco longshoremen kicked union bigwigs out of their convention and chose an ordinary Australian dock worker named Harry Bridges as leader. Tillie and Abe attended a rally led by a strong handsome longshoreman who looked about Tillie's age. His name was Jack Olsen.[5]

When Tillie read that the fascist Austrian government of Dollfuss slaughtered socialist rebels and closed schools "to keep children off the hazardous streets," she no longer felt hampered by domesticity but fired up to write. In rapid order she turned out two anti-Dofuss poems and sent one, called "There Is a Lesson," to the *Daily Worker*.[6] A new magazine, the *Partisan Review*, called for fresh proletarian voices;[7] so Tillie retyped her first chapter, signed it "T. Lerner," and popped it in the mail to editor, Philip Rahv, who immediately accepted half of it, which he titled "The Iron Throat." He asked T. Lerner for a self-description. Tillie replied to "Dear Comrade Rahv" with two proletarian self-versions:

Age, 21 (born 1912) Home state Nebraska. Y.C.L.'er on leave of absence to produce future citizeness for Soviet America—Karla Barucha. Or if you want to be more garrulous: Father state secretary Socialist party for years. Education, old revolutionary pamphlets laying around house (including the Liberators) and Y.C.L. jailbird—'violating handbill ordnance'

Occupations; Tie presser, hack writer (honey and its uses in the home, etc), model, housemaid, ice cream packer, book clerk.[8]

Tillie was honest about being born in 1912, not about all the other details.

Rahv's reply shows party intellectuals' eagerness to connect their theory with working-class experiences: her actual "activity in the Y. C. L. and work in factories" proved that "proletarian literature isn't growing in a vacuum." In March, the *Partisan* printed "I Want You Women Up North to Know" and the *Daily Worker* printed "There is a Lesson," which the *Partisan* reprinted in April. "The Iron Throat" appeared in the April/May *Partisan Review*. With four publications in just over a month, Tillie Lerner had made a sudden and sensational entrance onto the leftist literary stage.

"The Iron Throat" begins with the scream of whistles calling workers into a Wyoming coal mine. Dialogue shows the degrading effects of poverty, exhaustion, and hopelessness on Anna and Jim Holbrook. Tillie used what she had learned at Central High about Virginia Woolf's stream of consciousness to delve into six-year-old Mazie's mind:

> "I am a knowen things. I can diaper a baby. I can tell two ghost stories. I know words and words. Tipple. Edjiccation. Bug dust. Superintendent. My poppa can lick any man in this here town. Sometimes the whistle blows and everyone starts a runnen. Things come a blowen my hair and it's soft, like the baby laughing." A phrase trembled into her mind, "Bowels of earth." She shuddered. It was mysterious and terrible to her. "Bowels of earth. It means the mine. Bowels is the stummy. Earth is a stummy and mebbe she ets the men that come down. Men and daddy goin in like the day, and comin out black. Earth black, and pops face and hands black, and he spits from his mouth black. Night comes and it is black."

Though she included some preachy addresses about capitalist exploitation, her descriptions were poetic, her interior monologues brilliant. Her most autobiographical elements, other than Anna's "kike blood," are Mazie's precociousness and Anna's bitterness. At her request, Rahv sent a copy to the Lerners in Omaha. Morris took "The Iron Throat" to Judge Sam Beber,[9] who praised her "brilliant and original style" and "*powerful sentences*," comments that vindicated Ida's long-suffering belief in Tillie's genius.

Without CWA jobs, Abe and Tillie briefly went south to organize farm workers in the Imperial Valley, leaving Karla with Sue, and Tillie began writing about the "100,000 homeless who trek up and down the valleys

of California" during picking season.[10] On 9 May, longshoremen coordinated strikes and closed two thousand miles of west coast shoreline.
They protested working conditions, like trudging between hiring halls in
predawn hours to beg to work twenty-four or more hours, nonstop.[11] Tillie
was rapturous: "there was a night in Stockton when I walked down the
road for the paper when the sun lay dispersed, over the yellow stubble,
and the wind in the dry weeds—and I lifted out the paper and over the
page a headline streamed—STRIKE CALLED, STRIKE CALLED—and the
fierce exultation beat up in me." That fiery exultation melted Tillie's secular
redemption as mother and novelist. She vowed to join the San Francisco
strikers, "health be damned."[12] She asked first Rae and then her youngest
sister to come to San Francisco to care for Karla. Yetta had recovered from
her infection to become a lively preteen who sang and danced to tunes like
"Ah, But Is It Love?" and "Inka Dinka Do."[13] Though she made all As, Yetta
cared for popularity and larks, which California might offer. An uncle was
going west on 7 June, so Ida agreed to let her youngest daughter go along.
Yetta wrote Tillie, "Goody!!"

Tillie and Abe got party transfers and took an upstairs apartment in a
pretty little house with a Queen Anne window at 73 Diamond Street and
soon got Nahman and Sue, who was pregnant, to join them in San Francisco.[14] Sue kept Karla when Tillie took the trolley to party headquarters,
in a converted store at 27 Grove, a block from the Civic Center, where the
party published the weekly *Western Worker*.[15] Frenetic activities on Grove
Street and on the docks created for Tillie "unbearable tension, when in
an hour, years of events were packed, when people grew up overnight and
blurred class lines reared sharp."[16] She promised to write about the strike
for the *Partisan Review*'s 1 August deadline.[17] Abe got a job with the State
Emergency Relief Administration (SERA), which prompted Rae to joke
"now he is the Capitalist and I might ask him for a loan." When radical
youth organizations declared Memorial Day 1934, National Youth Day, the
YCL put Tillie in charge of some 250 kids, whom she led to a rally, where
the police attacked them. When the *San Francisco Examiner* blamed unions
and youngsters for police violence, Tillie, who was unharmed, had a ration-
ale for yoking the children's and longshoremen's causes together in a great
crusade against injustice.

One night when searchlights spanned the sky, she did try a purist
description "Blue—the pure blue of a star, long fingers of light—I run to
the kitchen window; suddenly they begin moving, suddenly the sky is mad.
Falling, shifting, straightening, the tall slim stems weave over each other."
She pledged: "Yes, I shall be a writer. Descriptions every night. To write

alone again, to live alone. To take my walks and see the city in day, in night. To closet this in me and feel it move."[18] The focus of these literary ambitions was less protest than the desire to be alone to write.

About two weeks after Youth Day, Tillie's baby sister arrived in Oakland on the Union Pacific railroad and took the ferry across the bay, marveling at the stars' reflection in the water. Yetta's excitement quickly dimmed, though, because Abe, not Tillie, met her at the dock. She enjoyed trolley rides by tall skinny houses on the San Francisco hills, but was frightened to find she was sharing the Diamond Street apartment with Karla and Abe because Tillie had moved out. She "never saw" Tillie. The mysterious Abe "kept going in and out," making her "uncomfortable," especially after he made a pass at her.[19] She knew no curses to replace "Goody!"

Tillie's fellow crusaders included strike organizers Dave Lyon and Jack Olsen, each a year older than she. Lyon was a University of California graduate student in journalism, who had covered the Youth Day crackdown for the *Western Worker*.[20] Olsen was the Communist Party candidate for the Fourteenth Senatorial District. He had been a U.S. citizen since his birth in 1911 and a California resident since 1929. In his statement of fitness for office, he said he had been "arrested many times for fighting for relief for unemployed youth and against war preparations. If elected I will carry these issues into the [state] senate." The YCL paid his twenty-dollar filing fee. The party instructed him to memorize and then destroy messages.[21]

A mass meeting on 19 June jammed the Civic Auditorium with strikers, who rejected a strike-ending compromise. As tensions threatened to explode, Tillie called for women to petition the chief of police "to permit peaceful picketing on the waterfront." Instead, the mayor called out the entire police force and hired extra men for a showdown on 5 July. Like Russian cossacks, police on horseback charged into the lines of placard-carrying men blocking the ports. In a union newsletter, Tillie wrote that the strikers "put up a great battle, *without arms*, against police bullets and tear gas bombs." In the melee, two strikers and one bystander were shot to death, a hundred people were hospitalized, and countless others were injured on the day that would always be known in San Francisco as "Bloody Thursday."

On the next Sunday, some forty thousand men and women marched behind a truck carrying coffins up Market Street. Tillie wrote about: "a longshoreman—a World War Veteran—and a dead man. ON STRIKE SINCE THE NINTH DAY OF MAY, 1934," who was "A MARTYR TO THE CAUSE OF LABOR."[22] FDR and his "Brain Trust" advisors, fearing violence would jeopardize the country's recovery, sent an assistant secretary of labor to mediate the strike. Uninterested in mediation, a transplanted Australian Communist named Ella Winter saw the strike as harbinger of the "coming Workers' Revolution in America."[23]

At the 1919 peace negotiations, as an assistant to American lawyer Felix Frankfurter, Winter had met the older muck-raking journalist Lincoln Steffens, whose *The Shame of the Cities* had branded public bribery, later called "pay to play," as treason. Steffens had visited the Soviet Union and exclaimed, "I have seen the future and it works." He and Winter married, had a son in 1924, and in 1927 bought a house in Carmel, California. Dubbed the "Getaway," it had become a haven for reformist writers and artists. Through his 1931 autobiography, Steffens led many young people to communism.[24] After the carnage of "Bloody Thursday," he and Winter kept tabs on efforts to "Break the Shipowners' Dictatorship" with a general strike called on 16 July. Tillie wrote a flier telling strikers not to mediate or arbitrate but to "SPREAD THE STRIKE" that crippled the city.

The *Partisan Review*'s third issue proclaimed that Granville Hicks's *The Great Tradition* had launched a "revaluation of America literary history" to depict economic truths. Hicks's dictum provoked the *New Republic* to assign Robert Cantwell (author of the ironically titled *Land of Plenty*) to see if the new magazines were avoiding or showing depression realities. Tillie soon got a surprise invitation from famous writer, editor, and former expatriate Malcolm Cowley, who asked her to submit a story to the *New Republic*. She was too caught up in spreading the general strike to respond.

San Francisco shopkeepers posted signs saying "Closed till the Boys Win," and the unions controlled the delivery of essentials such as milk and bread; otherwise, they locked down the city.[25] Union leaders struggled to coordinate the strike, prevent violence, and preserve appearances. (Photographer Dorothea Lange's pictures show strikers wearing brimmed hats, suit jackets, and often ties.[26]) Tillie worked at party headquarters and in a makeshift haven on Ellis Street, sleeping on floors, eating irregularly, and typing into the night to produce the anonymous *Waterfront Worker*, countless bulletins with appeals like: "Graduates what now? Jobs? Relief? Peace? Join YCL, 37 Grove St., SF," and skits, like one with ship owners singing: "They'll say what ever I say, Betray when I say betray."[27] So much frantic activity almost completely repressed her writerly ambitions, her maternal feelings, and even her rampant sexuality, though she did harbor a yen for Jack Olsen.

National publicity about the strike alarmed Rae, who thought Tillie and Abe should quit working "under cover," care for Karla's "apendics," and remember "the most deserving of all Tom. Do you correspond with him the poor sucker."[28] Tillie was not about to quit. She was exhilarated to be working with Olsen in a swirl of reform projects. Though his campaign literature said he was "forced to leave school," he had graduated from Alden High School in New York State in 1928, moved to Los Angeles with his family, the Olshanskys, and had Anglicized his name to "Olsen." Like Abe, he was a Communist of Eastern European Jewish descent and a handsome guy. But while Abe was a theorist, Jack was a laborer; while Abe could be explosive and arrogant, Jack was easy-going and sympathetic; while Abe thought of Tillie as the next Rosa Luxemburg, Jack saw her as herself, a political firebrand who was talented, beautiful, and passionate. She was also, of course, a married woman.

Under prodding from Rahv, Tillie wrote that she was in Stockton when "streaming headlines, *Longshoremen out, Riot Expected; Longshore Strike Declared,* made an exultant rhythm in my blood. And I stood there in the yellow stubble remembering Jerry telling me quietly, ominously" about strike plans. This "Jerry" was an amalgam of Abe (living with her in Stockton) and of Jack (loading "cargo five times the weight" others could carry and refusing to be hired "in a slave market begging for a bidder"). She titled this account "No Strike is Ever Lost" but abandoned it for the more urgent job of producing bulletins about workers' demands and cutting stencils of songs like "Industrial Union's Call" and "Chiselers' Sorrow." She learned "What to do if your mimeograph is Broken Up During a Strike."[29]

In Europe, Hitler was on the march, Austria was convulsed in civil war, and Mussolini was mobilizing troops. In America, the west coast was paralyzed. As beholden to big money as the oligarchies Steffens had exposed, city officials condoned attacks on strikers and Communists because, as the 17 July *Chronicle* reported, "Reds Plotting Revolt." After vigilantes beat "Communists' furniture into matchsticks," newspaper baron William Randolph Hearst's *Chronicle* gloated "REDS TURN BLACK AND BLUE." Tillie responded with a jingle "You may wonder where is Hearst/ you may wonder if he's burst,/ with the hatred of the reds,/ you may wonder is he dead."[30]

Closed docks created such a downward business cycle that the general strike soon succeeded. By 19 July, maritime unions were recognized, "fink" hiring halls were eliminated, and 20,000 men were back at work.[31] The Communist Party reopened its Grove Street headquarters. It claimed credit for procuring decent working conditions for longshoremen, launched voter registration campaigns for candidates like Olsen, and construed the strike's success as the beginning of the end of capitalist exploitation.[32] The landlady of the Ellis Street apartment fretted over the ongoing clack of typewriter keys and the rolling thump of mimeo machines. She called the

anti-Communist police squad, which stormed the place on 22 July. Tillie
gave a familiar alias, "Teresa Landale," and listed the Grove Street address of
the CP as her home. Sixty years later, she wrote: "no warrants, up the stairs,
the thunder of their feet. Five of us jailed, I the only one of my sex."[33] On
23 July, the *San Francisco Examiner* reduced the conflict to "Americanism
Versus Communism."[34] It saw "Divorcee Shoots and Blinds Fiancé in Love
Quarrel" as less offensive than Judge Lazarus's releasing "58 Held as Reds."
It praised Judge Steiger for taking prisoners with "asserted Communist
connections" off relief rolls. The paper named unreleased arrestees David
Lyon, Harold Johnson, Jack Olsen, and "Theresa Landale," who "said she
attended U. C. one year."[35] All demanded jury trials. Tillie was jailed with
the socialite who attempted murder in a "love quarrel." Male comrades were
thrown in a pen a floor below.[36] They sang up the pipes the "Internationale"
and songs like "You ain't done nothing/ If you ain't been called a Red."[37] At
Olsen's suggestion, they also sang "Let me Call You Sweetheart."

Lincoln Steffens wrote Secretary of Labor Frances Perkins (the first
woman cabinet member): "there is hysteria here, but the terror is white, not
red." He blamed "the incredibly dumb captains of industry" for abusing
workers and Hearst for fomenting hysteria and encouraging fascism at
home.[38] With prisoners "held as vagrants under $1,000 bail each," the Inter-
national Labor Defense sent attorney George Anderson to defend them. In
Oakland, California District Attorney Earl Warren presided at a meeting
decreeing that publications critical of capitalism or favorable to communism (like Ella Winter's 1933 *Red Virtue*) should be taken off library and
school shelves. Although police were exonerated in the "Bloody Thursday"
killings, Steffens and Winter were put under surveillance and even accused
of trying to "make pinks out of children" and of not disciplining their ten-
year-old son.[39]

Under the title "To Face Jury," the *San Francisco Call Bulletin*, on 25
July, ran a photograph of "Theresa Landale." The photographer caught
Tillie raising her hand to her mouth. Her remarkable eyes stare back at
the photographer in defiance.[40] With her hair cropped very short, she
looked handsome but frightened. The same day that the *Bulletin* printed
her picture, the *New Republic* ran Robert Cantwell's article on "Little
Magazines." Among some 200 stories in 50 magazines, he said "there
is one fragment (by Tilly [sic] Lerner) so fresh and imaginative that
even a cautious critic can call it a work of early genius." He praised her
"metaphors distilled out of common speech [which] are startling in their
brilliance." Though he misspelled it, Cantwell equated the name Tillie
Lerner with genius. (No wonder Cowley had asked her to send a story to

the *New Republic.*) Cantwell, then sequestered with Winter and Steffens, had no idea that this "early genius" was incarcerated in a San Francisco jail cell.

Cantwell's endorsement caught the attention of publishers who suspected that Hemingway's tales of foreign adventurers and Fitzgerald's of the decadent rich were out of touch, while Faulkner's novels appeared bizarre, southern, and apolitical.[41] In his *U.S.A.* trilogy, John Dos Passos addressed depression realities, but experiments with narrative form were costing both Faulkner and Dos Passos a wide readership. Lerner might be the one writer who could make the ravages of the depression accessible and affecting to a wide audience. With no Tillie Lerner in the Stockton phone book, publishers hounded Rahv, who shared the Diamond Street address with several publishers, including Donald Friede and Jerre Mangione. They telegraphed her, and Mangione also wrote: "I suppose you realize by this time that half the publishing world is on your trail. I blush to confess that I've been one of the bloodhounds."[42] He got no reply.

Tillie was stuck in jail with a cell mate singing "Keep Young and Beautiful If You Want To be Loved" and advising her to buy face creams to preserve her youthful complexion. More compelling were serenades from Olsen, Lyon, and other male prisoners. The right-wing press urged Roosevelt to deport "Reds," but Secretary Perkins maintained that deportation was not a means to get rid of "alien agitators." In Sacramento "28 Red Suspects" were charged with "Criminal Syndicalism" under a 1919 bill suppressing labor unions. San Francisco and Sacramento jails could well have been tools of a fascist state.[43]

When Attorney Anderson visited the San Francisco jail, he made the sensational discovery that Theresa Landale was Tillie Lerner. She gave him a letter to Cantwell, who spread the sensational news to Steffens, Winter, and Cowley that his "early genius" was the jailed "Landale." Then Cantwell retold the tale for the *New York World-Telegram*. Steffens and Winter paid Tillie's $1000 bail and set her up on Dolores Street, with instructions to write about her arrest. Tillie could stroll along a palm-lined boulevard down to Dolores Park for sunshine and supplies, but she was otherwise confined to her hide-away. Winter and Steffens shared this address only with Cowley and Bennett Cerf, of Random House.[44]

Back in 1925, Cerf and Donald Klopfer, at ages twenty-seven and twenty-three, had purchased the Modern Library from Horace Liveright. After making a huge success of its inexpensive editions of classics, the two young men launched Random House to publish fine books by contemporary writers, including James Joyce, Gertrude Stein, Robinson Jeffers, Eugene

O'Neill, and Marcel Proust. Cerf and Klopfer had just signed William Saroyan, a young San Franciscan with a sunny attitude toward America's troubles. They were eager to add important authors of all political persuasions to their list.

Cerf wrote Tillie, and she replied on 6 August that publishers' many overtures tempted her to cut her novel "into parts." It was not set in a mining town but "wanders over South-Dakota farmland, western Nebr. beet fields, Sioux City packing house strike, a state detention home for children, and then settles down in the working section of a large mid-west city." Her present tense implied that the novel was complete, though she admitted its second half had problems. Still, "if some miracle happened, and I can get three hours a day for writing, I could re-work it in two or three months easy." Her Dolores Street address was "hot," so he should next write to General Delivery. Cerf was elated: A woman's perspective on so much of depression America was just what America and Random House needed.[45]

The Tillie Lerner story became an even bigger sensation when the *New York World-Telegram* printed Cantwell's story. He said the "fire-eating" Judge Steiger had condemned her as a mental case (thanks, probably, to her stutter). The judge demanded to know if Tillie had rejected her American education for communism; Cantwell quoted her retort: "'No,' she said, 'but I've become pretty well converted since my residence upstairs'—meaning the jail." He said the police beat "up the four boys there and took them and the two girls—Tillie Lerner (Teresa Landale) and Marian Chandler—to jail." He urged readers to write lawyer Anderson "that she is not a vagrant but a writer of high talent."[46] From New York, the *Daily Worker* featured stories of Tillie Lerner's arrest and of African-American Langston Hughes's being "driven" out of Carmel. Thanks to Steffens, it managed a phone interview with Tillie, who said she had "written since the age of 10, she says, 'when I grinded out an Eddie Guestian ode for Eugene Debs who dandled me on his knee.'" She hoped to publish her novel "in a very cheap edition" so that poor people could "get a crack at it."[47] With competition intensifying, Friede telegraphed that he and his partner were Tillie's "BEST PUBLISHERS."[48]

Her first obligation was to tell the horrific story of her arrest so she explained: "It was Lincoln Steffens who commanded me to write this story. 'People don't know,' he informed me, 'how they arrest you, what they say, what happens in court. Tell them. Write it just as you told me about it.'" In isolation, she finished quickly and then described other prospective articles for the *New Republic*, which asked to see "the fragment 'No Strike is Ever

Lost' and the one about the hysteria of the tie-factory girls." Cantwell wired Cowley her arrest story.[49]

Tillie expanded "No Strike is Ever Lost" as if she were again chaffing under Steffens's command: "Do not ask me to write of the strike and the terror." Nevertheless, she told of the Youth Day and of events "crescendoing" to the Bloody Thursday "massacre" and the General Strike. Not on the "battlefield," she had had to piece together "words of comrades, of strikers, from the pictures filling the newspapers." Now on an unspecified battlefield, her words were "feverish and blurred." She simplified her title as "The Strike."

With both the arrest and the strike pieces finished, Tillie left the secret Dolores apartment around 10 August, bought a doll for Karla, and walked to Diamond Street. She recalled when "I came back" after her summer's absence, Karla "woke from her dream, & seeing me standing there, began to weep, horrible, racking tears, & would not be caressed, even by the doll. Clutching me as if she were drowning." Tillie experienced paroxysms of love and guilt. She tried to placate Yetta by dubbing her with the unethnic name "Vicki" and taking her to Carmel to meet Winter and Steffens, Robert Cantwell, William Saroyan, and Langston Hughes, who was not "driven" out of Carmel after all.[50] When Tillie posted "The Strike" to the *Partisan Review*, on Monday, 13 August, she found at General Delivery a special-delivery letter from Bennett Cerf.

Cerf sent her a dozen Modern Library books free and offered to gamble a "$200.00 advance immediately against a 15% royalty on your novel." On 14 August, the *San Francisco News* called Tillie Lerner, alias Teresa Landale, "the most sought-after writer in the United States." It ran a sketch of a jailed demure young woman, supposedly Tillie.[51] She, Abe, Karla, and Yetta then moved to a studio apartment at the back of a tall Victorian house on Broderick Street, an address Winter and Steffens kept secret from everyone but Cerf. When the *New Republic* sent a check for Tillie's arrest story, Steffens wrote "Darling": "Dont cash it yet—keep it for your trial and wave it under the nose of the DA."[52]

Regardless of the Bill of Rights, the *Examiner* and the *Chronicle* justified mass arrests, book burnings, and vigilante attacks with the claim that strikes were "preparation for the armed insurrection." Abe and Tillie, along with comrades like Rahv, Hicks, Lyon, and Olsen, preferred words to guns. After belatedly discovering that Tillie Lerner was one of the "vagrants" arrested in late July, William Saroyan called on lawyer Anderson. The son of long-suffering Armenian immigrants, only four years older than Tillie, Saroyan was a more assertive high school dropout. He pontificated that writers ought "to forget rules . . . , to spurn adjectives . . . , to learn typing for speed, and, above all, to live life to its emotional peaks."[53] He assured Cerf that Tillie would survive "the fascism unharmed."

Her trial began on 20 August with Anderson using a barrage of supportive publications, letters, and telegrams to establish that Tillie Lerner was "a writer, not a vagrant." The *New Masses* sponsored a New York rally for the "new genius T. Lerner," at which Ethel Schochet showed off Tillie's photo and conferred with Philip Rahv about a publisher for her.[54] For once thinking like a capitalist, he said Tillie should sign with the firm that offered her the most money.

After a day at her trial, Saroyan took the streetcar home with Tillie, and they exchanged writing samples. Saroyan's claim, in "Seventy Thousand Assyrians," that there is only one race—babies, before they are taught language and difference—reminded Tillie of Ida's insistence that there was only one race—the human. Still, she flirtatiously insulted him, wondering if he were a fake. Surprisingly, Saroyan said, "I probably was." (He had just earned $100 from *Vanity Fair* for a glib story based on a cousin starving in Brooklyn. Saroyan told Cerf he sent the cousin $15.) Despite Tillie's proposal that her novel be printed in "a cheap edition, fifty cents or so, so that it will reach the masses," Saroyan advised Cerf that she would be a good investment because "she hates rather beautifully."

In the *New Republic* Cantwell now described "Literary Life in California" as so repressive that Tillie Lerner (spelled correctly) spent time "dodging the police" rather than writing. The *Examiner* and *Chronicle* reported that, on 22 August, the jury hung in the case of "Mrs. Theresa Landale." Still, she, like gangster Al Capone, could face jail. Then Judge Beber in Omaha appealed to a jurist in San Francisco, arguing that sentencing her would subvert justice, that literary genius required encouragement, and that the accused was his cousin. The retrial was cancelled and Tillie released, though Dave Lyon and other Reds remained jailed.[55] She would say she was released as "a good mother with a good character record." Rae knew better—Tillie should thank Judge Beber "for his help ha ha ha."

When she returned to the Broderick Street apartment, Tillie found another special delivery from Bennett Cerf, who was publishing a one-volume edition of Lenin's writings. With Lenin and Lerner on its list, "Random House should certainly win the attention of every radical in the country." Meanwhile, a fellow SERA worker introduced Abe to Louis Freedman, west coast representative of Macmillan Publishers, whom Abe brought to Broderick Street. Random House's gift of twelve books and its offer of $200 appealed to Tillie, but Freedman said Cerf and Klopfer were "just publishers of fine books and modern library—never had any real sales." It would be "ruinous" to sign with Random House.

With Karla cuddling, Abe making love to her, and the country's best publishers begging to sign her, Tillie's mood was euphoric, until Sue Goldfarb gave birth to a stillborn baby after four days of agonizing labor. Tillie was saddened and guilty too, especially after Sue wrote her as "dear generous, thoughtful, thoughtless Tilda."[56] To compensate, she vowed to write "something of Sue, lying there in the hospital," and "something of those other mothers." She recalled her painful reunion with Karla and losing "that *other* one." She lamented "my baby, my little baby, dont die, why did you die."[57]

Saroyan wrote Cerf about Tillie: "the mob is supreme to her. To me one mob is as bad as another, and I hate them Communist, Rotarian, Presbyterian, Armenian, American, any cockeyed kind." Still Saroyan promised to "run right down to her place and have another talk," which he did on 27 August. He was there when Abe appeared with Louis Freedman, who offered Tillie an advance of $500 "to pay for her daughter Karla's [hernia] operation, and to enable Tillie to get across the bay to Berkeley and have a house with a garden." After Freedman and Abe left, Tillie confided in Saroyan that "she'd rather go with Random House." He helped Yetta ready her bags for her return to Omaha and wrote Cerf that the whole Lerner family "is brilliant; six children, and all remarkable. Yetta was thirteen a couple of days ago but has more sense than three college graduates."

Jail time had weakened Tillie's stamina; then Karla's hysterical greeting and Sue's loss had upset her emotional balance; and now the tug of war between rival publishers further aggravated her weakened lungs. She ended up in St. Luke's Hospital with a rattling cough and high fever. Meanwhile, Jack Olsen received more than eight thousand votes in the primary, hardly a challenge to the winner's 171,000 votes or proof of capitalism's downfall.[58] On 29 August, the *New Republic* printed Tillie's "Thousand-Dollar Vagrant." She presented the judge as a benighted dullard, the policemen as racist beasts, who beat a "red bastard," saying "we know you're all Jews or greasers or niggers." One promised to "take the whole bunch of you, pour oil over you, and burn you up like they do the niggers down south." She included a perhaps teasing (certainly thoughtless) bit of dialogue with one "bull." He asked, "'You married?' I don't answer. 'You're Jack Olson's [sic] girl aren't you? Aren't you?' I don't answer." Sue thought Abe was irritated by the "awful strain of Party work." Actually, he was jealous over that reference to Olsen and Tillie's camaraderie with Saroyan. Cerf wanted to "PERSUADE YOU TO COME

WITH RANDOM HOUSE WHERE I CAN HANDLE YOUR BOOKS PERSONALLY
WONT YOU WIRE ME COLLECT BENNETT CERF."

When Morris Lerner wrote for the *Weekly Omaha Jewish Press* an article
on Cantwell's praise for "The Iron Throat," he listed honors won by all
six Lerner children, reminded readers of Tillie's comic "Squeaks" column,
claimed that her story appeared in the *"Parisian Review"* and was "living
in San Francisco with her husband and their 8-months-old daughter."
(Citing Karla's age as eight rather than eighteen months was a typo;
renaming the *Partisan Review* as the *"Parisian Review"* was intentionally
self-protective.[59])

Morris also wrote a long articulate letter to Tillie; she regretted that her
jail sentence would reflect badly on him, Yetta, and Karla and vindicate
teachers who still considered Tillie "a liar, a cheat, a thief, a radical." A
published novel should acquit Tillie and prove that she was "working for
humanity & at the same time for a beautiful child & a brilliant husband."
A Jewish English teacher planned to read Mazie's soliloquy to her class
as a superior "example of analytical thoughts running through a child's
mind," but Sam Beber thought that, if she planned to make "Mazie a radical
organizer in her later years & have her attempt to save the world," it would
be a "most mediocre & worn-out plot . . . which would be read only by
your Communist friends."[60] Tillie could not think of another ending when
she was ill and half a dozen publishers hankered to see a whole novel,
immediately.

On probably 28 August, Cerf upped the ante: "WILL GIVE YOU FIVE
HUNDRED DOLLARS ADVANCE IMMEDIATELY AGAINST STRAIGHT FIFTEEN
PERCENT ROYALTY ON YOUR NOVEL AND WILL SEND YOU MORE LATER IF
YOU NEED IT PLEASE WIRE ME AT ONCE COLLECT AND IF SATISFACTORY WE
WILL MAIL CONTRACT BENNETT CERF." However tempting Cerf's offer was,
pressing hospital bills compelled Tillie to sign with Macmillan.[61] Saroyan
regretted that Random House had lost "my pal Tillie: really the swellest gal
imaginable." She and Abe used Macmillan's advance to move to Berkeley,
where they rented a basement apartment in a handsomely shingled house
on Spruce Street.

The austere cover of the next *Partisan Review* carried the words "TILLIE
LERNER, 'THE STRIKE'" in large black letters in a broad red stripe on
the cover.[62] Rahv sent a copy to "S. Lerner" in Omaha. Rather than having
her novel sold for fifty cents a copy, she now told Cerf that she wanted
wealthy people to buy it at $2.50; poor people to read it in libraries. She
said her arrest had provoked Abe's firing.[63] Though she had signed with
Macmillan and taken its money, she told Cerf: "if you really think you're the

best publisher for me, I'll take your word, and hope I'm not a sap." She put the letter in her purse and took it with her the next day, 11 September, when she saw Dr. Ralph Reynolds. After hearing that her lungs were healing, she walked to Saroyan's place.

They lunched, visited art galleries, sampled book stores, and walked in the park, where they could see piers erected for an amazing suspension bridge to be called "Golden Gate." When Saroyan took her to dinner, all the while singing the praises of Random House, she showed him her unmailed letter.[64] Thrilled that his "pal Tillie" might not be lost, he insisted she mail the letter to Cerf immediately. As soon as she took the ferry to Berkeley, Saroyan fired off an airmail letter informing Cerf that the battle was not over. Tillie's book would sell even to "people who don't give a God damn about the Communist movement." He believed that "technique with her as yet is instinctive, subconscious; she simply writes, slam bang, and no fooling around: which is swell." (He did not know that Tillie had written rapidly only when confined by pregnancy in 1932 and cloistered by Winter and Steffens in early August 1934.) Though she was "not easy to figure out," Saroyan guessed that Cerf could "convince her Random House *is* her publisher." He took up the gauntlet and wired Tillie that he could send the "necessary funds for you to repay Macmillan" its $250 with "no strings attached."

Tillie wired Random House: "ACCEPT OFFER WILL EXTRICATE MYSELF IMMEDIATELY UPON RECEIPT OF MONEY LETTER FOLLOWS GLAD TO MEET KLOPFER." (Donald Klopfer was on his way west.) Cerf recorded in his diary: "20 Sep Tillie Lerner wires acceptance of our terms" and sent another $250. She canceled her contract with Macmillan, splurged on a radio and a jar of her former cell-mate's expensive face cream, waited for Klopfer, and worried that she might be pregnant. "The Strike" brought Tillie more fame; the *Partisan Review* quickly sold out; other magazines begged for stories and articles.[65] Tillie had none, so she sent the *New Masses* one of her YCL pamphlets, thinking message should trump art, but the *New Masses* rejected it. Then a letter from Freedman, sent to "Mrs. A. J. Goldfarb" on Broderick Street and forwarded to Spruce Street in Berkeley, announced that Macmillan could not and would not release her.

As soon as Donald Klopfer arrived in San Francisco, he and Saroyan rushed across the bay. Tall, handsome, and only ten years older than Tillie, Klopfer treated the Goldfarbs to dinner, reassuring Abe and delighting Karla, whom he referred to as "Carla," missing the Marxist connection. When he produced a contract, Tillie used his expensive fountain pen to sign her name in legible letters. She left the date blank. With some fatherly words, Cerf wired Tillie another $250. Returning Macmillan's advance, she was $250 to the good. She felt like a successful capitalist—until Macmillan insisted she was still its property.

Tillie seemed like a tiny boat caught in the wakes of two ocean liners. Her affairs were "so bawled up" Saroyan considered recruiting "some new genius" like Dave Lyon.[66] Then Freedman, as Tillie wrote Cerf, "sleuthed me down" in Berkeley and scolded her like a child for making a "ghastly mistake."[67] At Macmillan's urging, Granville Hicks sent her a letter saying that, though Macmillan was a "rather stodgy house," it still published his *Great Tradition* and would publish his biography of John Reed. Wanting nothing to do with stodginess, Tillie proposed to demand $1000 of Macmillan, which would force it to release her. Appalled, Cerf warned her that demanding more money than she had agreed to would make her seem "an insincere little bitch." He suggested she plead poor health to Macmillan, as she did on 15 October, which was also the publication date of Saroyan's *The Daring Young Man on the Flying Trapeze and Other Stories*. After mailing Macmillan her excuse, Tillie spent the rest of the day celebrating with Saroyan. They chased about San Francisco and huddled, she wrote Cerf, in "an alley eating persimmons and having a fight because he tried to tell me poverty had virtues and shouldn't be abolished." He said that Tillie remained "very much" active in the Party but would be freed "for about six months after she reports some trials in Sacramento, or something: she hates to feel like a writer and is afraid her pals in the Party won't like it if she stays away from them." He had thought she was "not easy to figure out," but he had succeeded. She had internalized the notion that, being individualistic, writing was elitist and isolationist. Then Cerf advanced on the "Lerner battlefront" by inviting Tillie to pose for a Random House jacket cover. Though flattered, she defiantly wore her YCL uniform for the photo, while meekly assuring Cerf "the arm band and hammer and sickle won't show." She promised to get the first half of her novel typed for Random House. Then she telegrammed: "THEY REFUSE TO RELEASE ME WIRE NIGHT LETTER WITH SUGGESTIONS." She felt like the "first case of rigor mortis in a still alive and suffering being."

She joked about her "almost collapsed body," but then she did collapse after apparently another abortion.[68] From her bed, she dictated to Abe a long letter telling Cerf that she had been assigned to cover criminal syndicalism trials "for the Party press," but the job would delay her only "a few weeks" and give her "momentum to tackle that impossible second half." She assured him Saroyan's *Young Man* was selling "like hot-cakes." Like a film treatment Billy Wilder sold as he fled Hitler and like Hollywood's *Stand Up and Cheer*, Saroyan's fiction distracted Americans from the doldrums.[69] Tillie's novel would compel them to understand causes and solutions to depression doldrums.

Tillie dictated a letter to Granville Hicks, with a copy to Cerf, saying she had had a 104° fever and needed "dough for the hospital, etc." She also suggested that when she signed with Macmillan she had "no idea it was binding." Her "frankly revolutionary" novel needed a smaller, less capitalistic publisher. Still bed-ridden, Tillie studied news about the upcoming criminal syndicalism (CS) trials of eighteen men and women. Defendant Martin Wilson, a lawyer for the International Labor Defense, out on bail, was making speeches connecting the "Vag" arrests of Tillie and others to the CS "Frame-Up" trials.[70] She was appalled to read in the *Western Worker* that CS convictions would effectively outlaw strikes and finish the labor movement.[71]

As a teenager Tillie had been inspired by Upton Sinclair's exposé of the meat-packing industry in *The Jungle*. Now his campaign for governor of California, under the slogan "EPIC"—"End Poverty In California"— proposed to give jobs to the unemployed, a formula challenging CP candidates. In the *Young Worker*, Jack Olsen wrote an article illogically branding Sinclair as a "cog in the same machine of the ship-owners, land corporations and industrial associations." Both Tillie and Olsen saw Sinclair's sin as converting from the Socialist to the Democratic, rather than the Communist, Party.[72]

Tillie's promise to spend only "a few weeks" on the criminal syndicalism trials ignored her actual assignment: to send the International Labor Defense "all clippings" about the trials, to write articles for the *Western Worker* and the *Young Worker*, to send carbon copies of "every story you write . . . plus an article for" the December *Labor Defender*, and to make a pamphlet on the trials.[73] She began pasting clippings into a San Francisco phone book and sent the second half of her first chapter to the *Anvil: The Proletarian Fiction Magazine*, which announced it would publish "'Skeleton Children,' a novelette by Tillie Lerner."[74] Already a famous novelist (without a novel), Tillie had been floating on publishers' praise; now she was sinking under commitments to them.[75]

In a second letter to Hicks, with a copy to Cerf, Tillie opined that Random House authors Proust, O'Neill, Jeffers, and Stein were "guys that stink with decay," while Saroyan was egotistical and ignorant of communism. (She advised Hicks to tutor him.[76]) Still, she preferred Random House to Macmillan. She reiterated a familiar distinction between art, being unsure "about the art of my book," and message, being "sure [it] is propaganda." She also made a startling admission: "I'm ashamed to say I haven't been working on the book—as a matter of fact haven't touched it since I wrote it a couple years ago." She had started to work on it in Stockton just before she and Abe had "moved to Frisco which meant I could be active in the movement again—and I forgot about the book." Though she had forgotten to be a novelist in the flush of being a revolutionary, publishers had convinced her to resurrect it during her three-month leave of absence from YCL work.

While she panned Gertrude Stein for stinking with purist decay, Cerf was entertaining Stein and her partner Alice B. Toklas before their tour of the States.[77] Still Cerf took time to tackle the "Tillie Lerner business" with a visit to *New Masses* offices on East Twenty-Seventh Street and a lunch with Hicks, who felt "rather full of The Strange Case of Tillie Lerner." Reluctantly, he promised Cerf that, though Tillie's contract was "legal as all hell," if she broke it, he would keep Macmillan from suing her.[78]

On 3–5 November, in the rambling terraced Getaway overlooking the Pacific, Ella Winter and Lincoln Steffens entertained various notables and Tillie, Abe, Karla, and Sue Goldfarb. With Winter and Steffens providing a phone, Tillie took the dramatic step of placing a call across the continent. On 5 November, Bennett Cerf announced that Tillie Lerner was forsaking Macmillan to become a Random House author. In *Controversy*, Winter gossiped about movie stars and Tillie Lerner who had "wanted to walk on the beach, and to know whether great men always look great."[79] Steffens was, Winter wrote Tillie, "very fond of you and believes in you, and your gifts." Winter warned: "so don't squander."

Before the election, Hollywood moguls had launched a campaign to smear Upton Sinclair as a Communist and coerced employees to contribute to his Republican opponent, who won handily. Communist candidates made hardly a showing.[80] Democrats increased their strength in the U.S. House and Senate. On 6 November, while votes were being counted, Abe drove Tillie to Sacramento, where they arrived "just in time" to hear African-American Angelo Herndon, who had been jailed in Georgia in 1933 under an outdated law against slave insurrections. Out on bail and en route to visit Tom Mooney in jail, Herndon was telling people about his outrageous arrest and other miscarriages of justice. After the speech, Tillie and Abe discovered, she wrote Klopfer, that the "battered portable I've always used to click out my stuff on was heisted out of the car last nite along with the little radio I splurged on first thing I got your advance—and was so damn tickled about."

In Sacramento, a sympathetic family offered Abe, Karla, and Tillie a room. She wrote Klopfer that Abe would transcribe eight chapters when she finished covering the trials. A year ago she and Abe and Karla had "bummed into Stockton" with "$6.75 in the world plus a typewriter, and nobody had ever heard of me." She was giddy because 1934 had been "a lot better—dazzling in fact, except we don't have the typewriter. By next year this time I'll have a book out, and it looks like all sorts of other things."

With Hicks on Random House's side, Macmillan at last capitulated. On 9 November, Tillie wired Cerf: "OBTAINED MY RELEASE HORRAY." He wired back "BEST NEWS WE HAVE HAD AROUND HERE IN WEEKS." The contract between Modern Library Inc. and Random House and Tillie Lerner of Spruce Street Berkeley gave her a five-hundred-dollar advance and 15 percent of earnings, a sensational offer for a first novel and a promising moment for a democratic American literature. Klopfer announced "a great marriage between Tillie Lerner and Random House," which encouraged Rae Schochet to claim kin and demand a free copy of "that book Ulises" [James Joyce's *Ulysses*].

Back in August, Tillie had assured Cerf that if she had "three hours a day" she could finish in three months. Almost three months had passed, but Cerf and Klopfer had received nothing of the novel, and their telegrams were returned. Finally, she remembered to write that she was "with Jevons in Sacramento. Will send 8 chapters." She covered a grand jury hearing for the *Western Worker*, making an odd equation of stuttering and lying: "Fake Witnesses Stutter Their Parts Despite Many Careful Rehearsals."

While the Hearst papers continued to fulminate about a Red menace, leftist papers presciently described fascism's threat, protesting Nationalist China's forcing peasant rebels on a "Long March" to an outlying region. In Austria, Dollfuss was "Slain by Nazis," and the *Young Worker* warned "World War Looms." When Berlin was chosen site of the 1936 Olympic games, the *Young Worker* recognized that Hitler intended to make "Games a Fascist Tool" for the master race. The *Western* saw criminal syndicalism trials as harbingers of American fascism. The *Young Worker* predicted a German alliance with Japan "FOR WAR." The *Western* saw that messianic leaders, like Huey P. Long and Father Coughlin, cultivated followings in hopes of becoming American Hitlers.[81] Nobel Prize–winning novelist Sinclair Lewis ironically called his satire on Long and Coughlin *It Can't Happen Here*.

Klopfer warned Tillie not to get "into a mess with the authorities," but one night she skipped out on Abe and Karla with Mike (probably Mike Quin) to paint "Smash the Criminal Syndicalism Frameup" all over town. When the police approached, Tillie and Mike scaled a fence and hid in a Catholic school's tubelike fire escape. After the cops left, Tillie began coughing. She confessed to Klopfer: "when it comes to painting slogans or plastering up stickers a madness overcomes me." She went to Dr. Reynolds, who told her "absolutely *not* to go back to Sacramento." Cerf and Klopfer were relieved; she could get back to her novel.

Word spread that Tillie had had an "attack" so Ella Winter invited her to Carmel to make party contacts.[82] On Saturday, 17 November, Tillie (with Winter, Steffens, and Abe too) "went up to the city to meet Doletsky the head of Tass," the Russian news and propaganda bureau, who invited Tillie to Moscow.[83] She promised Cerf to spend "eight hours a day on" her novel; although the second part would be "tough to tackle," she planned to finish by the end of February.

Relieved by illness from covering the trial, Tillie took Karla to Stockton, while Abe stayed on in Sacramento, perhaps taking over her journalism assignment. Resurrecting the frayed pages written in 1932, she had to admit to Cerf they now seemed "sorta childish." She told Cerf it was "just as well" she had one more assignment and was "not working on the novel." She belatedly realized that sending Cerf a copy of her letter saying major Random House authors "stink with decay" had been tactless. Cerf claimed he was "not the least bit peeved" by that remark, but he was irritated because she was "harder to keep up with than a Mexican jumping bean."[84] He quipped: "Donald says you are very good-looking. Is he on the level?" Her novel should be "item No. 1 on the Fall 1935 Random House List." Tillie need not worry over "financial matters for the next two months."

From Sacramento, Abe assured Tillie "remember, I am always your friend." She tried to write an article for the *Labor Defender* but "tore it up in disgust." She wrote the *Defender* a letter supposedly from Abe saying that his wife Tillie Lerner was too sick to write. Forging his signature, she admitted to him that she was a "liar." She was being "good to" Karla and "making her things to eat." She insisted, "I will be alright," words which suggest how distraught she really was. She needed to feel "no have tos. Just the novel."

Though Tillie told herself to "do the poverty & beet field chapters first," she needed to "outline article."[85] She had gotten a letter from the county jail, which she used for a *Young Worker* article. Don Bigham wrote that his mother worked in a cotton mill and died of pneumonia. Tillie reworked the facts: "his mother, with the lint of the South Carolina cotton mill strangling in her lungs, coughed to death one night, leaving him an orphan." He said he "worked in a bakery after school hours from the age of nine." Tillie said he learned a "lesson in child labor when he was nine and earned his board and keep by greasing pie pans until the early hours of morning."[86] Printed as "Why They're Trying Don," her specific details and dramatic style created more empathy than any courtroom journalism could have managed.

Abe was husband, mentor, and always friend, but Tillie blamed her writing troubles on domesticity. Around 10 December, she left him for San Francisco, taking a room on Rhode Island Street. At 37 Grove, she was greeted as a jail bird who had established the brutality and bigotry of San Francisco police, the journalist who had exposed the injustice in the criminal syndicalism laws, the fiery speaker who could convert crowds, the novelist who would tell the proletariat's story, and the most beautiful of Communist crusaders.

With Klopfer "itching to see those first eight chapters of the novel," Tillie outlined: "The childhood. Hunted. Poverty, the drinking, swaggering father, but proud; Anna, hard, bitter, strong; the children, and their own bitter suffering. Migratory—the freight car boxed in from Portland to Minneapolis. The Hole Up." Her sense of Anna's bitterness was lifted from a surprise letter from Ida, who felt "so unlucky" to be unable to "control" written English, as Tillie could in "The Strike." Ida insisted that Sam was "my tragade [tragedy]." He was so busy politicking for the Workmen's Circle, Ida felt alone, and "I dont here mats [hear much] of Fame" (apparently Tillie's fame). Though she had "somesadisfaksun" [some satisfaction], Ida felt "boren to be dad a lif" [born to be dead in life]. Tillie saw this bitterness as "the burden of being poor and a mother."[87]

Sue Goldfarb had recovered enough strength to be "ready for Karla" so Tillie left her daughter with Sue and listened for her characters to resurrect themselves: "after the streetcars are quiet, the solitary footsteps, the voices that walked into my room and waited there for me to finish and start them." She had to cope with unconnected pages, sloppy notes, and "gaps. Why didn't I type it carefully, make carbons [and] put it away."[88] Looking over her typescript, she noticed that Abe had crossed out a talky query, "could you not make a cameo of this and pin it onto your aesthetic hearts?" Abe's editing encouraged her to delete such comments and convey her message indirectly, in conversations, descriptions, and dramatized events.[89] Tillie sent Klopfer two of the promised eight chapters; she said she had lost the rest.

On probably 17 December, after midnight, Tillie retyped jottings in her notebook as a frenzied meditation on writing: "Fever over the body, an unearthly glow, a burning. Faribault in late winter, in early spring. Such pain. Rae's voice 'lie still dont you know you came here to get well.' But the words swollen big in me like a child. My people lashing about blindly. And suddenly I am writing. Blurred days, voices or warning; tears that drowned somewhere in the throat, and Joe York's face, flaming and dissolving in a mist, urging me on like a flag." Acknowledging the troubles of "my people" as catalysts for her writing, she vowed to "harness" herself into creativity. The next day she wrote Cerf a cooler letter saying that her Rhode Island Street address was good for three months, unless the party went "underground," a clear admission that she was not devoting herself exclusively to writing. She said she was more mousy than good-looking but kept others "in a sort of daze so they never really get a good look." Photographer Willard Van Dyke got a good look and produced exuberant pictures of Tillie in a cotton dress, bought at J. C. Penney's at a "79¢ sale."

Alone, Tillie wrote Abe "only forgive me." Images of his love and kindness flooded over her, as she recalled "the Xmas walk" in Kansas City just before they eloped. Suddenly, she felt guilty and longed to see him.[90] For Christmas, she sent Klopfer a bubble pipe from Karla and Cerf a "real literary classic" by Angelo Herndon, whose message was "You Cannot Kill the Working Class." She took Karla back to the Stockton farmhouse, where she found birthday presents for Karla from Rae and the Lerners.

Since Cantwell's article had thrust Tillie into the limelight, she had been arrested, jailed, and released, hospitalized with lung trouble, had collapsed after an abortion or miscarriage, campaigned for Communist candidates, covered the CS trials, and gotten sick again. She had spent weekends in Carmel, met the Soviet head of Tass, written time-consuming, feverish letters, involved herself in party agitations, and seesawed back and forth in her relations with publishers and Abe. Cerf and Klopfer were used to dealing with literary geniuses, but Tillie was zanier than most. She was undisciplined, high strung, full of excuses, and passionate. She might be an untutored genius who disdained apostrophes, but she wrote authentically from the working classes. Her prose achieved a beauty and power unmatched by proletarian writers like Jack Conroy and Josephine Herbst. She might put others in "a sort of daze," but Cerf and Klopfer knew the ropes. Her novels should indeed become the "inevitable extension" of socially relevant work by Upton Sinclair, Theodore Dreiser, and John Dos Passos. She might even rival Dos Passos's and Faulkner's experiments with narrative form and thus conquer the divide between art and ideology. The year 1934 had been a turning point for the country and an *annus mirablis* for Tillie Lerner. She promised to send Cerf and Klopfer the first half of her novel early in the new year.

CHAPTER 6

GREAT FEMININE HOPE

1935–1936

Now look here, don't you worry about my "underground" work that ordinary people can do, etc. or my giving up writing—I know what I'm doing and what's more I'll wind up a real proletarian writer which is more than 80% of these writing under that name are.

—Tillie Lerner to Rae Schochet, early 1936

By 1935, folk songs, plays, movies, and "Popular Front" culture had heightened the country's social awareness.[1] Led by FDR, many Americans now blamed greedy rich tycoons for the Great Depression. In New York City on 6 January, an audience of 1400 people at the opening of Clifford Odets's *Waiting for Lefty* shouted "STRIKE, STRIKE, STRIKE!!!" Performed around the country, the play, like San Francisco's general strike, encouraged the working classes to demand better working conditions. Like Clifford Odets, Robert Cantwell, and other proletarian writers, Tillie planned a strike to provoke a crackdown, which would ruin the Holbrooks and inspire Mazie to become a reformer. Tillie's Random House publishers imagined that Mazie would help create a better world. Editors at the *Daily Worker* expected her to foment revolution. Capitalist editors admonished Tillie not to sacrifice art for ideology; Communist comrades warned against sacrificing ideology for art.

Overwhelmed by contradictory demands and fed up with trying to be a grown-up writer and a dutiful wife and mother, Tillie fled back to San Francisco.[2] On New Year's Eve she had, she told Cerf, a "swell time" at a YCL affair. She danced "for the first time in years, looked about 16 years old, & afterward tramped around all night," flirting with Harold Johnson, Peter Quince, and perhaps Jack Olsen.[3] Buffeted about by cold winds, she and the young men sang raucously and saw the sunrise glinting on the piers and cables of the future Golden Gate Bridge. Her all-nighter

produced her "old admirer flu, very persistent, & a new suitor, pleurisy."
She sent Random House two chapters: "No use keeping them around to
wait for the other 4 to be copied," making six, not eight chapters. Senior
editor Saxe Commins found emotional content of her two chapters "true
and believable," not her technique. Seeing Tillie as an untutored genius,
he advised Cerf and Klopfer not to "cramp her style" by criticizing her.
Cerf telegraphed "VERY EXCITED ABOUT FIRST TWO CHAPTERS KEEP IT
UP LOVE BENNETT."

Cerf's telegram inspired Tillie to tackle her "damn" third chapter, but
she belatedly admitted that a "long time" had passed "since I was supposed
to have worked on it." She would add more chapters "*if* I survive a speech I
gotta make & flu which still has me in its clutches." Though "supposed to"
suggests "pretended to" and speech-giving meant she was still politicking,
she assured Cerf that nothing would stop her writing now. She thought
she could finish by "late March. Early April anyhow" and naïvely expected
her novel to be on book shelves by summer. Having run through her
$500 advance, she rushed the sloppily retyped third chapter to Random
House and asked for more "spondulicks." On 16 January, Cerf praised the
"glowing and alive" new chapter but worried about sustaining Mazie's
perspective. Tillie could "write like a streak!" like Faulkner, who told a
fawning admirer, "'well, ma'am, I just do the best I can,'"[4] Tillie followed
suit. Thanks to Cerf, she spent her twenty-third birthday reading Faulkner
for the first time.

Offhandedly, she told him, "my husband and I have separated." She left
her sickbed to raise her fists, yell about worker's rights, and sing songs like
"Banks of Marble" about weary farmers, miners, and seamen who will "own
the banks of marble/ No more guards at every door/ And we'll share the
vaults of silver/ That we all have sweated for."[5] When she "fainted and got
awfully delirious" at a rally, a friend took her to Stockton and "telegraphed
for Jevons to come down from Sacramento and take care of Karla and me."
Tillie enjoyed an aura of martyrdom, like Rosa Luxemburg or Joe York.[6]
She wrote Cerf she needed to enter a sanatorium in Phoenix. Her failure to
mention the half novel she had promised early in the new year made Cerf
wonder if illness was at least in part an excuse.

Tillie signed the *New Masses*' call for an American Writers' Congress
to meet in New York City in late April.[7] She telegraphed Cerf on 22
January: "BROKE PLEASE SEND MONEY AIR MAIL SPECIAL DELIVERY
LETTER FOLLOWS. TILLIE LERNER." He sent her another $100.[8] She wrote
him that her novel should have two parts, "B.C. (before Communism) and
After." She thought the "B.C." part worked "because it was all lived over

and known." She admitted that the second part was "just surface stuff," not that it was unwritten. She painted a pitiful picture of herself begging, not "can you spare a dime?" but "'Have you got a nickel for carfare?' With Funnyface along its particularly effective. I only approach fat ladies. Also have got two bucks YCL money." Appalled, Cerf sent Tillie "another check for $200," telling her to make it last, to learn "how to type a manuscript," and to "*go ahead and write your book*."⁹ In early February, Tillie replied in a tiny scribble with only a few phrases readable: "my fault," "my writing crystallized," and "I'm not going to leave it as it was three years ago either." Flummoxed by her handwriting and the admission that she had not worked on the book in three years, Klopfer praised her at least for having her plan "crystallized."

By 21 February, Tillie was in Venice, California, a beachfront suburb of Los Angeles frequented by old-world Jewish retirees. She left Karla and Abe behind. His selflessness, she told Klopfer, reminded her: "I owe him absolutely everything one can owe to another human being—he really has 'made me what I am today'—but it's like adolescence, when you have to break with your parents, this was my second growing up." She begged Klopfer for "another $400" to "go right away for debts, the typewriter, and Karla's hospital bill."¹⁰ Long before corporate publishing, he and Cerf could make their own decisions. Fearful that Tillie's mostly unreadable scribble signaled depression, they sent her $400. Cerf decreed that "the only lady author on the Random House list must be kept happy at all costs!" Tillie replied, "evidently Gertrude Stein aint no lady."

With both publishers and comrades claiming her, the tide of fame and fortune that had carried Tillie for half a year began to feel like an undertow. After Abe sent a letter that "clouded tears into my eyes, dear, strong, like the one who had written it," when Japanese magnolias were "in blossom," Tillie took a train from Venice to San Francisco, rode the streetcar, and then walked to "a sudden open flung door—and Sue, dear Sue, like a light, like a fire." Reunited with Sue, Nahman, and Karla, Tillie spent a few days trying to work on her fourth chapter. Then she took Karla over the bay to Stockton and Abe.¹¹ This reunion produced an effusive letter to Rae about wanting another baby. Rae was skeptical: "I still remember Barucha's [Karla's] reception, which was not so bad, but it certainly was uncertain, of course then [back then?] you had Tom."¹² Tillie was still sick, so Abe took her back to sunny Venice, where she settled with Karla among "a lot of oil wells & ocean (the latter 2 blocks away)" in a "nice little dump." She sent her parents the first letter in years. On his return, Abe stopped at the Getaway, provoking Winter to write Tillie, "what happened to you this time?" Winter reminded her that "Bennett Cerf has a lot of money and now that they think you are such a good publishers' bet for them it's certainly up to them to keep you till the novel is done."[13]

When John Strachey, a British Communist, stayed at the Getaway after lecturing to two thousand people in San Francisco, Winter arranged for him to meet Tillie in Los Angeles after his debate with philosopher Will Durant, now an anti-Soviet lecturer.[14] Tillie heard the debate, dined with Strachey, and gave him parts of her novel, wrapped in paper and string.[15] She revived a comic voice, hardly used since "Tillie the Toiler," for Karla, who reported to Klopfer: "my ol mamma . . . has got me tied to the close-line sos I cant wander un discover the worl. otherwise its swell here. i yam gettin chocolate brown, an take footbaths in the oshun [ocean]." Like any two-year old, Karla was demanding. Like any young mother, Tillie was frazzled. Like few mothers, she attached her daughter to a clothesline. Like few, she was always overcommitted and often ill. Strachey's verdict on her manuscript was that she was a writer, but "whether you are a *good* writer or not" was debatable. He counseled her to finish, publish, and then "write something better."[16] Disconsolate, Tillie fled into a storm, mixing her tears with rain and creating a self-inflicted relapse.

Her excuse for signing with Macmillan in August 1934 had been that she needed "dough for the hospital," but she had not paid her bill. Dr. Reynolds had vouched for her, and now the hospital was dunning him $22.25 for "hospitalization, x-ray plate of her chest, blood count, Wasserman test [for syphilis] and urinalysis during her stay at St. Luke's Hospital in San Francisco." After Reynolds appealed to Cerf and Winter, the capitalist Cerf offered to advance Tillie money so she could keep her promise to the doctor. The Communist Winter asked friends to contribute to Tillie's bill.[17] Feeling justified in "cheating the hospital out of their chance to cheat me," Tillie rationalized that the hospital did not deserve payment because its ambulances were used to get scab laborers past the picket line in the waterfront strike. Reynolds said such rationalizations were just how Tillie Lerner "looks at things." She had looked at policemen as "dumb bulls" so she was "shocked" when smart, honest Sacramento policemen found and returned her stolen typewriter and radio.

Tillie's inspired ending for chapter 4 has Anna screaming in childbirth and Mazie trying to divert "her mind to a time of dancing when laughter rose like froth." If creativity kept flowing, Tillie need not "labor over and rewrite" and could finish by July. She said she was "definitely out of the movement for six months anyhow" and assured Klopfer that "the comrades . . . don't even [know] I'm around."[18] She told Cerf, however, that

YCL headquarters always knew her location. She sent Random House a list of disasters to befall the Holbrooks, before, during, and after "The Strike."[19] She conscientiously planned chapter 5, in which the Holbrooks retreat from a farm to an Omaha-like city. Jim Holbrook loses packing-house jobs, Anna and the children get sick, and Mazie fails at school. Tillie wrote a scene with Jim sitting "confident on the employment bench" until impoverished old men make him feel "the fear of growing old, of being useless." For his epiphany, Tillie used a letter from her father, who was surprised by Tillie's "sudden kind act" of writing and showing that she felt "very deeple [deeply] the tragedy of the 'forgotten man.'" She drew a house plan, labeling corners so the sun could rise and set consistently. She charted the children's ages and planned a scene when Will and Mazie laugh at Charlie Chaplin as Little Tramp, then go home to find that Anna has killed herself. She dated this work "Venice, Calif. March, 1935."[20]

Privately, Klopfer and Cerf lamented that her parade of disasters showed little trace of the "Iron Throat's" brilliance and confirmed Commins's doubts about her plotting skills. Klopfer joked to her that her four chapters were "so good that they depressed me for a couple of days." Cerf suggested she give Mazie "a few good breaks here and there."[21] To Klopfer, she listed expenses for a new typewriter, her 1934 hospital stay, and an operation for Karla's tummy.[22] Whatever Tillie told her publishers, she went to Hollywood Communist meetings and met, among others, Harry Carlisle and Sanora Babb, left-leaning writers of fiction and film.[23] One day, they appeared at her "dump" and did "some fancy talking" to convince her that she should accompany them to the first American Writers' Congress. Tillie told Klopfer the trip would take three weeks and be "gratis." She would "leave Funnyface with Jevons" and write on the road.

Perhaps Tillie really thought the trip to New York would only delay her novel by three weeks, but her editors recalled that her November journalism was also to have postponed her novel only "a few weeks." Perhaps Tillie really believed that she would spend evenings writing her novel, but her editors remembered she was to have written daily and to have sent eight chapters in late 1934 or early 1935. Perhaps Tillie really thought sentences would "just rip out of her," but Cerf and Klopfer knew good writing is rarely so effortless. Perhaps Tillie believed that Random House would "keep" her indefinitely, but Cerf and Klopfer were her publishers, not her bankers. They began to suspect that Tillie had squandered their money and trust. Had she lied all along about having a complete novel? Or did she equate mapping out a novel in her head with writing it? Cerf had warned her she would seem "an insincere little bitch" in playing Macmillan for more money; he now worried that the "little bitch" was playing him.

Tillie attended an "inspiring" talk about Ukraine, with its "bumper crop; and on all the collectives such prosperity and happiness."[24] Actually, Ukraine had been plagued by famine, mass starvation, and even state-sanctioned murder, but Tillie preferred the fabrication to the realities exposed by Will Durant. Probably at that lecture, Paul Cline, her Kansas City lover, now director of the Communist Party in Los Angeles, reentered her life. At the end of the scene with Jim and the old men, Tillie scribbled "Paul, Paul."[25]

Klopfer thought Tillie was "crazy" to come to the Congress, but he sent another $200. He joked that the rest of her novel would be "depressing enough to send me into a decline for a few years, but still it should be an important book" if she did not try to get "the whole Communist" argument into it, as Josef Stalin was trying to do with the influential American movie industry.[26] Sanora Babb and Harry Carlisle had written themselves out of poverty and now intended to expose the abuses of wealth in movie scripts, as Stalin expected.[27] Tillie badly needed direction in her muddled life, which traveling with them would offer, at least literally.

Unable to convince her not to come, Cerf invited her to meet Gertrude Stein. In an oblique reference to Stein's lesbianism, Bennett cautioned, "Keep your pants on when you speak to Gertrude. Remember that politics is not her long suit." Carlisle and Babb had instructions to head to New York by way of Gallup, New Mexico, a mining town, where a labor organizer had been arrested for inciting a strike. During the trial, a huge crowd of impoverished miners and their families gathered to hear the outcome. In the melee that followed a guilty verdict, shots broke out; two miners and the sheriff fell dead to the ground. The whole crowd of hapless miners was charged with murder.

While Abe set off with Karla for Omaha and Faribault, Tillie set off with the scriptwriters for Gallup on 9 April. Squeezed into Harry's roadster convertible, she was thrilled to pass the grand forests near Flagstaff, though she thought she might freeze in her flimsy cotton jacket.[28] They found Gallup a virtual war zone, where Labor Defense investigators had been kidnapped, beaten, and left to die.[29] In a letter to Abe, Tillie detailed brutalities toward women and children, Slavs and Mexicans—all at the hands of police and "gun thugs" hired by mine owners. She bought a "little indian doll for dear funnyface," called Abe an "angel," promised "letters every day," and said she would return in "just a few weeks" since the "car makes good time, 40 miles an hour average." She begged, "Please kiss Karla for me—everytime I see kids playing—I feel so damn homesick." She sent a nostalgic poem, "There was a dream, they called it Stockton." She urged Abe "above all write me."[30] She was playing the roles that most touched him: the activist writer and the needy, once again loving wife.

At two-and-a-half, after traveling halfway across the country with her nearly-forty-year-old father, Karla was glad finally to be cuddled in Grandmother Ida's soft lap. But she was confused after her father left for Faribault and her mother appeared with two strangers, spent a night, and vanished, again swooping in and out of Karla's life. She enjoyed a grandmother who sang lullabies, like "Byushkibyu," a grandfather who told silly jokes and riddles, and aunts who read picture books to her.[31]

In Chicago, the Hollywood threesome stayed in "fifty-cent hotels, visited factories to talk to the workers, and looked up [author] Nelson Algren." The terror in Gallup had hardened Tillie's convictions. She chided Babb for being too liberal, too individualistic, and too ignorant of Marx.[32] Babb was offended by such lectures and by her "sleeping around with fellow leftists—by Sanora Babb's standards Tillie seemed quite 'loose' sexually."[33] Tillie enjoyed Carlisle's easy-going ways, working-class origins, and sexy charm. Along the way, party members took them into their homes. In New York, playwright and producer Albert Bein and his wife Mary turned over a bedroom to Tillie and Harry. Still humiliated by Strachey's lukewarm response to her novel, Tillie asked Bein about writing plays. He later sent love to "Harry and yourself," the script of his *Let Freedom Ring*, and a warning not to give up her novel to try to break into the theater.[34]

On the evening of 26 April 1935, in Mecca Temple, a domed and elaborately tiled Shriners' convention hall just south of Carnegie Hall, the Congress opened with a plea for the 216 participants to join an International Union of Revolutionary Writers.[35] Tillie was invited to speak at an upcoming session. Delegates debated whether they wrote for workers or for everyone, whether unschooled writers were more authentic than sophisticated ones, whether proletarian writers could borrow techniques from bourgeois writers, and whether message always trumps art.[36] Jack Conroy was so far on the side of message he claimed "a strike bulletin or an impassioned leaflet" could be literature. In her speech, Tillie declaimed that "what we get out of our material" means more than craft. She demanded "death to culture by capitalists." She rushed from speech to caucus to party in a flurry of political agitation, self-importance, and sexual excitement.

Just after the Congress began, Bennett Cerf entertained "Tillie Lerner, Jack Conroy & a mob of Communists" at a nightclub called the "Black Pit" before taking some to dinner at a fancy restaurant. When homeless people were begging for food, Tillie was appalled by restaurant charges on food and cocktails.[37] Though his comment about a "mob" of Communists was in his private diary, Tillie intuited his disdain. When Babb praised his charm and generosity, Tillie attacked his culture and wealth. Babb denounced Tillie as a Communist patsy, and Tillie denounced her as a capitalist tool.

With writer Meridel Le Sueur, Tillie was named an advisor to Jack Conroy's *Anvil*. She attended an editorial meeting, near Madison Square Park, before Bennett Cerf's dinner party.[38] In his diary, he described the party as a hotel "dinner for 15 & party for 50 for Gertie Stein, over at 4 A.M." Among the invited dinner guests were composer George Gershwin, stars of stage and film Miriam Hopkins and Sylvia Sidney, novelist Edna Ferber, photographer Carl Van Vechten, and young celebrity authors William Saroyan and Tillie Lerner. But Tillie debated the *Anvil*'s future so long she missed the dinner. Arriving just as Gertrude Stein and Alice B. Toklas were leaving, she hid her embarrassment by ducking into the ladies' room. There one other face met hers in the gilt-framed mirror. Previously twenty feet high on the silver screen, this image was now just Tillie's size. The gorgeous face with big sad eyes belonged to Sylvia Sidney, star of *City Streets* and *Jeannie Gerhardt*. Tillie was speechless.[39] Later she was flabbergasted to see Sylvia Sidney affectionately embrace Bennett Cerf.

Though the party lasted until the wee hours of the morning, Tillie met Cerf at Random House the next morning, asking him for more books and more money. Cerf began writing a "$50 buck check." Then he looked up from behind his handsome desk to ask, do you know "how much you've drawn?" Hoping to introduce her to eastern culture, he offered her a three-day, expense-paid experience of New York. She declined, saying that spending money on New York's cultural sites seemed "such a waste" when she claimed she needed "money for the trip and to send home for Jevons and Karla."

Then Cerf lunched at the posh "21" Club, and Tillie joined writers and workers in the annual May Day Parade. She was no longer the tragically languishing girl too sick to write. She was a dazzlingly vivacious marcher. Legends circulated that she had been raised in poverty, had left high school to support her impoverished family by working in factories, had been jailed for exposing capitalist oppression, and had sewn her Young Communist League uniform with her own needle. She wore, Conroy remembered, "a red scarf in the Soviet Youth manner" that rippled as she marched along Broadway; all the while she exuberantly swung her body and chanted, to the beat of heels smacking the pavement, "we write for the working class."[40] The *New Masses's* coverage of the Congress included a double-page spread of cartoons, sketches of anonymous onlookers and named writers, including Jack Conroy, Malcolm Cowley, and Granville Hicks. The cartoonist drew only two women, Josephine Herbst and Tillie Lerner. His Tillie in profile, with short, wild hair brushed back, emphasized a large nose and large bosom. Hers was the only cartoon with a body, which looked nothing like her; it must have been drawn from word-of-mouth.[41]

Sanora Babb recalled that the trio "were all poor, broke, though I had $70, and paid the bills." Their trip which began "happily, did not end so."[42] After Tillie's lectures on her Marxist failures, Sanora hitchhiked back to California. Tillie and Harry rode back together. He appropriated her experiences in lectures on "Terror in the West! San Francisco, Sacramento—Gallup."[43] They returned to Los Angeles forty days after leaving, which she told Cerf were "the most maturing five weeks in my life." She wired: "ARRIVED HOME IMPECUNIOUS SEND SPONDULICKS AIR MAIL SPECIAL DELIVERY LETTER FOLLOWS AFFECTIONATELY TILLIE LERNER." She said nothing about finishing her novel in July or indeed anytime.

Bennett Cerf had been caring, polite, generous, and patient. Now he was mad. On 22 May 1935, he outlined facts: His $500 advance was generous, especially for a first novel "not yet even written." If priced at $2, her book would "have to sell over 3000 copies to earn back to you the advance already paid." In eight months, she had sent in only "a draft of the first few chapters," all in need of revisions. By writing a "really fine proletarian novel," she could do more for communism than by trying to foment revolution. He would send another $50 to make an even $1000 but no more until she submitted a draft of the whole novel. He could not respect her "amazing conviction that Communism is the answer to all the world's ills," when it kept her from "the path that an important novelist should follow." He ended his letter: "That's that." Before his letter arrived, Tillie wired for "THIRTY DOLLARS IMMEDIATELY RENT ETC."

Next she wrote Cerf a nearly-eighteen-hundred-word reply to his "That's that." She said she had "fallen for" his line about supporting her and now was worried about "how to keep alive." In addition to such "hokum," she painted a pitiful picture of being reduced to picking vegetables in 100° weather in Stockton.[44] His offense was not realizing that the communist movement was "a life and death necessity—and the only realistic thing."[45] Earl Browder too had told her "the book was the best thing I could do for the movement now and hurry up and get it out";[46] but now a "crippling feeling I can't write" was inhibiting her. She promised she would not to "go to a unit meeting till the book is done." He could check by writing "Jack Olsen, D.O. [District Organizer], Y.C.L, 37 Grove St., Frisco."

Among Tillie's surviving letters and notes that can be dated 1935, this is her only mention of Olsen, whose family lived in Venice.[47] Now she wrote Cerf that "a too turbulent state" kept her from writing. Presumably, Abe had discovered that Carlisle had been part of her "maturing" experience and that she had a yen for Olsen. She dreamed that Karla was sleeping restfully in her coffin, and she scribbled about Abe: "I begged him to shoot me for sleeping around."[48] Instead, he walked out on her. For the second and final time in 1935, she said her marriage was over.[49]

On 27 May, Cerf telegrammed: "WIRING YOU FIFTY DOLLARS THIS MORNING . . . DO YOU REALIZE THAT YOU HAVE ALREADY DRAWN EQUIVA-LENT TO TWENTY DOLLARS A WEEK FOR ONE SOLID YEAR THINK IT OVER BENNETT." Tillie pleaded "Karla's tummy," though she had earlier claimed a hospital bill for fixing it. Then she asked Sanora Babb for a handout. Unbeknownst to Tillie, Babb wrote Cerf about Tillie's sad predicament: the "rent due and the landlady threatening eviction, her husband still hunting a job everyday, with a baby to be taken care of—all this, and it isn't easy to write anything." Furious, Cerf explained to Babb that he had advanced Tillie $1000 since September and had not seen "a word" of her novel in two months. He wondered what Tillie did with money and time, other than "rushing around in helter skelter fashion yelling for the cause." He asked Babb to "go over to Tillie with Harry Carlisle and tell her to finish her book and to keep her mouth shut until she has it finished. I have no intention of seeing her starve while she is doing that work."

Tillie felt further pressure to write. The *New Masses* invited her to review Agnes Smedley's *Daughter of Earth*. The *Anvil* expected her "to deliver" stories from Harry Carlisle and herself. Peter Quince advised that her marital breakup was "unimportant alongside the good you may do the *Anvil*." Ella Winter gave her Saroyan's book to review. Despite her claims, Tillie did none of the above, nor did she work on her novel.[50]

Leftists thought Roosevelt's choice of wealthy Joseph P. Kennedy to head the new Securities and Exchange Commission presaged an end to reform. They thought, like the dog in the RCA picture, FDR was following "His Master's Voice," the voice of big business.[51] New limits on corporate power and guarantees of $12 a week for workers on federal programs proved otherwise; the U.S. Chamber of Commerce therefore accused FDR of trying to "Sovietize America." FDR's opposition to racial discrimination was buttressed when the Supreme Court reversed the sentences of the nine

"Scottsboro Boys" because black people had been excluded from the jury that sentenced them to the electric chair.

When Cerf's account of Random House's $1000 in payment to Tillie reached Sanora Babb, she saw Tillie's pitiful tale as an extortionist ploy. She wrote Cerf that Tillie "places [party] activity before writing" or truth. He next offered Tillie $10 a week for twenty weeks so she could "go ahead and do the first-rate novel that we have been expecting." Taking the $10 allowance as an insult, she replied, "Sure, let's call it quits."[52]

Tillie had no taste for bourgeois extravagances, other than expensive face cream. She had bought a radio, a typewriter, and a couple of 79¢ dresses. Moving her few boxes and other possessions cost little. She rented a cheap "dump" by an oil field. If she had expensive dinners, she did not pay for them. Trains and buses were inexpensive. Babb had paid for the trip east; Carlisle's car was free. Cerf's $50 had covered their return. When relief workers had only recently gotten raises from $40 to $48 a month, Tillie had burned through $120 a month, none of it, apparently, on a hospital bill for Karla. She had told Klopfer that she and Abe "split" their funds, so maybe she gave him half of Random House's cash advances. More probably, she filled Party coffers, sharing the wealth of capitalist publishers Cerf and Klopfer with the YCL.[53] In the first half of 1935, she had lived like a yo-yo; she loved and then left Abe; moved back and forth between San Francisco, Stockton, and Los Angeles; kept and abandoned Karla; involved herself in party demonstrations and with another man; swore she did nothing but write; finished four chapters; worked on a fifth; and took more than $1000 from Random House before calling her contract "quits."

Powerful Hollywood connections, perhaps Ella Winter, perhaps Paul Cline, now a tennis friend of Charlie Chaplin, got her assigned to the Hollywood branch of the CP-USA, which operative Stanley Lawrence set up to recruit scriptwriters. He paired her with Budd Schulberg, who had attended Dartmouth, traveled to the USSR for a writers' congress, and stuttered. Alienated from the extravagant life that film moguls like his father, B. P. Schulberg, lived and offended by the industry's destruction of Upton Sinclair's gubernatorial campaign, Budd Schulberg had returned to shake up Hollywood.[54]

By summer 1935, joining the Hollywood Communist Party was thought to signify conscience and intellect, often hypocritically.[55] Still, a blend of Marxism and New Dealism inspired more socially aware movies.[56] Literature too turned from the exotic to the ordinary. William Faulkner, John Steinbeck, Josephine Herbst, Zora Neale Hurston, Jack Conroy, Erskine Caldwell, Robert Cantwell, Meridel Le Sueur, and Langston Hughes, among many others, wrote about plain people in small towns. Sandburg's 1936 collection *The People, Yes* epitomized a fresh social consciousness. The party construed this trend as a tribute to Marxism. Progressives and liberals saw it as a return to essential American principles of "liberty and justice for all."

As head of Paramount, B. P. Schulberg was reflecting this trend in *Crime and Punishment* and hedging his political bets by starring the liberal Melvyn Douglas in a light comedy *And So They Were Married*. When Budd Schulberg invited Tillie to a party at his father's mansion, she brought Karla. A two-year-old was so unusual at a Hollywood party, the senior Schulberg made a fuss over her. (Tillie later made a little parable: instead of talking film, flirtation, and finance, B. P. Schulberg, "who had had affairs with Joan Crawford and half a dozen other stars, had a pillow fight with Karla."[57]) If cute Karla could charm the big film magnate, beautiful Tillie could convert Hollywood personalities to communism. Her job was to look gorgeous in a 79¢ dress and deplore the fabulous salaries film moguls and top stars earned, while behind-the-scenes laborers earned pitiable wages for long and unpredictable work hours, and hard-working writers earned pittances, often for cleaning up others' scripts.[58]

Budd Schulberg introduced Tillie to Hollywood writers with leftist leanings, among them Dorothy Parker, Tess Slesinger, Frank Davis, and Marian Ainslee. Known for witty poems and stories and clever repartée in the *New Yorker*, Parker was a prolific scriptwriter and an adamant opponent of fascism and Nazism. Though Tess Slesinger's *The Unpossessed* satirized Communist devotees, her scripts reflected concern for the underdog.[59] After divorcing Bette Davis, MGM producer Frank Davis became a leftist sympathizer married Slesinger. Marian Ainslee had been a "captionist," who wrote lines for silent film star Greta Garbo; now she wrote for the "talkies."[60] An anonymous note instructing Tillie to invite Marian Ainslee to a meeting with "Comrade Lawrence and Mildred Ashe," wife of Harold Ashe, party organizer, shows that Tillie's job was introducing acquaintances to Party operatives who would make the hard "sell."[61]

Though Tillie's sad tale of lacking money for rent would no longer work on Babb, Klopfer, or Cerf, it did work on Marian Ainslee, who invited her into her grand home overlooking the Pacific in Playa Del Ray. Her housekeeper now watched Karla. The only child among creative and adoring adults, the long-neglected, headstrong girl was gleeful, as was her frazzled mother, who cashed Cerf's $10 checks but did not write him. She told Ainslee she had finished her novel. At summer's end Ainslee responded to the hard sell by following a path advertised in the *New Masses* for tours "giving a rounded picture of Soviet Life."[62] She left her ocean-view house, with Tillie and Karla in residence, in Frank Davis's care. Stopping in Manhattan, she called at Random House. Relieved that the classy script-writer was caring for his recalcitrant nonauthor, Cerf confided in Ainslee that he was engaged to Sylvia Sidney. He wrote Tillie, delighted that "you and the baby are now settled in a pleasant home and that you are able to work without so many of the worries that were besetting you. . . . [and that] you are almost finished with the manuscript of the novel." If so, Random House could have it in print by spring 1936. In early September Marian Ainslee wrote Frank Davis from Russia, hoping he enjoyed the house and was becoming "Karla's devoted cavalier, though you may want to throttle her occasionally." She had intended "to get a coat for our child Karla in New York, but didn't have the time. So you [Frank] can have a nice holiday in a children's shop—but no eagles or stars and bars on the sleeve." Not mentioning Tillie, Ainslee seems to have assumed, with Davis and the housekeeper, responsibility for Karla.[63]

On 8 September, Huey P. Long was assassinated in the Louisiana state capitol, a skyscraper he had built largely as a monument to himself. FDR and Congress were working to undermine the appeal of leaders like Long by further improving Americans' quality of life. The 1935 Emergency Relief Appropriation provided more funds to get people back to work. The Works Progress Administration created jobs, building schools and hospitals, damming rivers and developing parks. Federal One provided work for professional artists, including writers, and made culture available around the nation. Government camps promoted decent treatment and new jobs for migrant workers. The Social Security Act saved America's aged citizens from poverty in a pact between workers and retirees. FDR knew that the more satisfied and hopeful Americans became, the more irrelevant were militant fascist or communist leaders.[64]

As soon as Cerf's engagement became public, Saroyan wrote that he could hardly wait to say "superciliously, Why, God damn it, you rats, my publisher is the lover and husband of the most beautiful girl in America." On 1 October, Cerf recorded in his diary "SYLVIA IS MRS. CERF!!!!!!" Three days later he only wrote "Happy!" Ainslee had eased his mind about Tillie, whom he courted with lunch on 5 October at the Los Angeles Biltmore. Though she had called her novel and her contract with him "quits," she now told Cerf that she was writing and trying "not to describe [Anna's] state," to make scenes seem "more in a dream," to limit the amount of "detail needed," and to finish. Delighted to hear that Tillie was actually going to finish her novel, Cerf saw that she was invited to numerous parties celebrating his marriage. One night's dinner included Dorothy Parker, Tess

Slesinger, Lucille Ball, William Saroyan, a "guy named Schulberg," and Tillie Lerner. Cerf pointed out that a Broadway play called *Dead End*, set in East Side slums, was stirring audiences with its exposé of the destructive effects of slum housing. Tillie's novel would be even more stirring and powerful, should she finish.[65] On the back of a flier about a benefit for the *Young Worker*, she scribbled new ideas for scenes set in the "dump, the school playground." She attended a posh Hollywood cocktail party, perhaps instead of the benefit, with Cerf and Sidney near the end of October.[66] When Cerf climbed "into the airplane at the Glendale Airport" he left Tillie and his bride together "at the railing" and waved good-bye.

In the 28 October issue of *Pacific Weekly*, Ella Winter said Cerf had come to Carmel, "on leave from his honeymoon with Sylvia Sidney," who was "making 'Trail of the Lonesome Pine' in Southern California, the first outdoor picture in color." Cerf had visited Tillie Lerner "who is doing her first novel for him."[67] Because Tillie had not reviewed Saroyan's *The Daring Young Man* for *Pacific Weekly*, Ella Winter gave her Henry Roth's *Call it Sleep* instead. When Tillie wrote she was unable to review Roth, an exasperated Winter published her entire statement anyway:

> No use, I'd like to do this review, but I'd probably be a flop—can't manage to make it. Anyhow, you know what I feel about Roth's book—the writing may be swell and the psychology of the child hero, but the picture of working class children is slander. The old stuff—the one tender lily flowering out of the dung heap—the old biologic sport, sensitive, intelligent, imaginative, not like the vulgar, nasty, stupid, other little boys and girls. The bourgeois world will love this book—it comes up to their ideas of what workers' kids are like. Maybe New York kids are different, but the ones I know possessed imagination and originality and courage and "honor." Henry Roth doesn't give you any idea these other kids had potentialities. I think the conversation at the end overheard in the streets is bad, too.[68]

Despite empty words like "swell" and "bad," Tillie wisely insisted that talent is not class-determined. Here she articulated one of the best aspects of communism. In assaulting class distinctions, it created hope for the disadvantaged. By preaching the dignity of all work, it instilled pride. When communism preached the equality of all work, whether picking peas or writing a novel, however, it troubled skeptics, like Hollywood director Elia Kazan and scriptwriters Clifford Odets, Budd Schulberg, and now Sanora Babb.

When Marian Ainslee returned from the USSR, she brought a black dress for Tillie, "Cossack style with red silk lining, which showed as I walked." With Tillie dramatically swishing the dress to swing open and show her legs, Greta Garbo called her "the beautiful Cossack." Perhaps Ring Lardner, Jr., had Tillie in mind when proclaiming that "The Most Beautiful Girls in Hollywood Belong to the Communist Party."[69]

Beautiful and talented Hollywood comrades were supposed to be excused from foot-soldier activities like selling newspapers, marching in protest parades, donating "Red Sundays" to the cause, organizing strikes, and laboring with the working classes.[70] A letter to Tillie from a comrade (apparently Dorothy Ray Healey) told about laboring on the "night shift in asparagus, we start at six in the evening and usually finish 6:30 in the morning." When the canneries were slack, the women "had to pick 30 pounds of peas to fill a hamper and were paid twenty cents a hamper." Poor women, often migrant workers, suffered terribly from such grueling work. Middle-class comrades joined them to show solidarity and urge them to strike and join the party. Laborers, however, sensed that such solidarity was more theoretical than actual and often wanted dabblers in communist theory expelled from unions. In San Pedro, Jack Olsen sided with the workers and proposed that they should lead the YCL and start "a real Pacific Coast youth paper."[71]

When Tillie became "sick in bed for first time in a long time," she had a revelation: high-powered friends, posh parties, and elegant surroundings were evil. With this epiphany came "the knowledge of death . . . on that big bed at Marian's that looked on the sea." In a tiny notebook, labeled "Nov 1935—Tillie Lerner," she wrote of time as "water into which one must drown." She seemed to regret "the days since I have not written," but still she did not write. She felt threatened for the "first" time by death, but perhaps that was only another excuse. [72]

After her "last day in bed," 21 November, Tillie fled Marian's house as if it were a den of iniquity. She forswore bourgeois pleasures. She abandoned her writing career. Reversing the "direction my life was going," she was born-again, into the party.[73] She sent Karla to Omaha, with a box of Communist books, a gift of questionable value to the Lerners. She said good-bye to "all that has been. . . . Karla there in the train. Goodbye, goodbye. No more of the old vows—only a few to keep."[74] Her redemption as writer, wife, and mother long behind her, Tillie typed a letter telling Rae that she or her family could raise Karla if they followed communist precepts.

Tillie began speechifying, working on assembly lines, and organizing in a canning factory.[75] (She spoke of standing hour after hour, sealing caps on jars of hot canned vegetables.) She heeded Jack Olsen's plea for a paper written from the working classes. Together they put out a mimeographed newsletter called the "Spirit of '76." Headlines suggest her concerns: "Peace," "Abolish Jim-Crow CCC camps," and "Help the Young Friends of Ethiopia against the murderous onslaught of fascist-robber Mussolini."[76]

Tillie regretted only that if she did not write about women who cook and sew and clean or hold low-paying jobs as maids or factory workers, while caring for children, they would "die with me." She addressed them, "listen to me, I loved you as few of the living have." She hoped these forgotten women would somehow know "this is she—Tillie Lerner."[77]

Tillie left Los Angeles on New Year's Eve, and Winter's early 1936 "They Tell Me" column began:

> Tillie Lerner came through Carmel on a flying trip complete with hitch-hiker and news of her novel finished and sent to Random House. To the hitch-hiker she entrusted her (borrowed) car for the night, while she sat up bewailing the fact that the novel was no good, that she should never have written it, that she wasn't a writer, and wondering whether any other writer had ever felt like her. She got her car and hitch-hiker back in the morning and Bennett Cerf reports that he does not share her feelings about her novel. It will appear early in the spring. She will send [actually had sent] her three-year-old daughter to her folks in Omaha and move to San Francisco shortly.[78]

The hitchhiker was Jack Olsen. Tillie had seemed a high-flyer, too flamboyant for him, until he first kissed her as 1936 began.[79]

Having heard nothing from Tillie since she and Sylvia Sidney waved good-bye at the airport, Bennett Cerf was outraged by Winter's column. Either "Ella Winter was dreaming," or Tillie lied. He told Tillie she could be a great writer, if she ever got her personal life in order. She replied: "I have decided not to publish this book. It's too lousy. I guess there isn't anything more to say. I will keep in touch with you—Tillie." After a year and a half of promises, now $1200 in advances, countless assurances that she was almost finished, and many excuses, Tillie had reneged. In mid-January, Cerf suggested that she let her editors decide whether or not her book was lousy.

She did not reply. She moved to 1292 Fell Street in San Francisco, home of Celia (Seevya) and Harry Dinkin. Like Ida and Sam Lerner, the Dinkins had left Russia after the 1905 revolution. Now their rambling old house was part family home, part boarding house, and part recruitment center.

They offered shelter to their daughters, boarders, free loaders, and seamen. Other establishments, like a "Welcome Hotel," used drawings of sketchily clad women to lure sailors.[80] Harry, "Mom" Dinkin, and the YCL lured them with a homelike atmosphere and a heady mixture of flirtation and communism.[81]

In Omaha, three-year-old Karla now slept in the Lerners' downstairs bedroom. Jann had long since left home. Morris had put aside acting dreams to write "threatening letters to customers in arrears on their monthly payments" for a Chicago automotive parts company.[82] Harry, Lillian, and Vicki lived upstairs. In the Civilian Conservation Corps, having graduated from Omaha University, Harry attended Creighton University's law school at night; Lillian, a stenographer, was engaged to Joseph Davis, a New Yorker studying medicine at Creighton.[83] Vicki attended Central High. A photo shows a largely unchanged living room, with picture of the frowning Mendel Lerner and the smiling Raisa Gisha Goldberg on the wall, faded velvet curtains, and Ida's worn horsehair-upholstered arm chair. She tried to discipline and Sam to entertain Karla, but neither could control the willful little girl, who one day walked down Caldwell Street and around the corner onto Twenty-fifth.[84] Lillian happened to be home to catch her, but tension over Karla's waywardness and her future rattled the senior Lerners, who felt ill-equipped to raise the headstrong and needy child.

Toward the end of January, Tillie sent Cerf an account of the "strange life" she was living as a working-class woman. She loved this humbling life, which she defined as "making an honest living for a change (milliners' apprentice)," implying that novel-writing was dishonest. She said she was "working on a book I really love doing, being with my kind of people." She apparently referred to a social history, not a novel, and Marxist workers, not high-flyers, like Cerf and Sylvia Sidney, who were already divorcing. Cerf replied that Random House was merging with Smith and Haas, acquiring William Faulkner and forming "one of the finest rosters of modern writers," including the most "important writers on the radical wing in all the world." She would be in "good company," if she ever finished her novel for Random House.[85] She sent nothing.

Tillie had typed the letter about Karla to Rae in December but had not mailed it until January. When it arrived, Rae rushed south to see Karla and began a sixteen-page letter from Omaha's Hotel Paxton on 24 January 1936: "You so and so, even after you finally typed a desent letter you couldn't make the envelope at the same time and send it out." Tillie's request that Karla be raised in poverty "so that she will recognize want and suffering when she grows up," made Rae call Tillie "you little idiot" and a fanatic "about this [Party] organizing." Ida and Sam were so worried about the "danger you put yourself in" that Rae urged Tillie to "type a letter to your folks." She felt "sorry when I see a little page of yours filled with fly specks no one can read it not even Yetta. Why in hell don't you write larger, mine is bad spelling and all that but at least one can get something out of it." She scolded, "you have choosen your road by breaking up with Abe."

Rae passed on Omaha gossip: Konecky was assistant stage manager under Billy Rose for the Rodgers and Hart musical *Jumbo at the Hippodrome.* Jeanette had remarried and was on leave of absence from the YCL to write, while Tillie who had:

> proven that you can help the cause more with your pen, went back to underground work, that so many ordinary people can do, you who are not strong enough, who can't take care to even eat at the proper time or the proper food, you who shouldn't exite yourself on account of your headaches, you who were ordered time, and time to lead a calm life. Oh go to the devil, you'l never do the right thing, that is why you had no business to marry leagally or bring an ofspring and don't you dare to have another . . . well Karla is just a sweet baby and very good at that but when she says *no* she means it and she is so attached to your Dad she follows him every where but I wouldnt worry about her, she's alright.

Tillie should "stop raving about proletarian and Capitalist" and let Rae's childless son and daughter-in-law adopt Karla, for "as long as you sent her away from you, you shut up." Rae expected an airmail reply, but Tillie asked for time "to make up my mind. . . . the only thing I agree is she belongs in your family, because she certainly is every inch a Goldfarb." To Rae's inventively spelled and oddly punctuated letter, Tillie countered: "Now look here, dont you worry about my 'underground' work that ordinary people can do, etc. or my giving up writing—I know what I'm doing and what's more I'll wind up a real proletarian writer which is more than 80% of these writing under that name are."

She was following Marx, as was her new best friend Miriam Dinkin, Harry and Seeya's daughter, a machine operator and, according to her grandson, a true "lefty (a hard-boiled Bolshevik, actually)." While she and Tillie discussed Lenin's views on the "woman question," other comrades were more interested in sexual than in Marxist freedoms. The Dinkins gathered young people who "felt a great deal of camaraderie—and certainly shared beds." [86] Tillie confirmed that assessment by labeling a notebook "1936 Dinkins in S. F. sleeping around."[87] From ports far and near, sailors recalled Tillie's "plenty sex appeal."[88] Courting her and Mariam and Lillian Dinkin were Finnish Arne Matilla and Harold "Mink" Johnson.[89] Dave Saunders, who wrote a seafaring column called "Rip Tides" and one called "Diary of a Class Conscious Seaman" for the *Western Worker,* asked Tillie, whom he called "Wench" and "Vixen," to keep the night of 6 May, when he would dock, free for him.[90] Another sailor sent Tillie an idea for an "agit-prop" play and proposed to meet her but "don bring jack"; he sent "love and other things, dont tell jack."[91]

Despite the sailors' testimonies of love and desire, exotic gifts, and tales of Mexico, Honolulu, and Singapore, Tillie could not forget Jack Olsen's New Year's kiss. With credentials as a Communist organizer, would-be politician, ordinary dock-worker, occasional vegetarian, and fellow jailbird, he was ideologically compatible. Only a year older, he was sexually compatible. While her parents disapproved, Rae Schochet scolded, and Bennett Cerf denounced, Jack did not judge Tillie.[92]

Valentine's Day 1936 was the fifth anniversary of Tillie's marriage to Abe Goldfarb, but she was thinking of neither Abe nor their daughter. She was anticipating making love with Jack Olsen. They hitched rides and then trudged into the snowy mountains near Fresno, where they rented a little cabin and built a fire against the blustery snow outside. With their bodies warmed chiefly by lovemaking, Jack aroused in Tillie, she would say, the lust she had felt for Abe. Jack too gave her "sexual release." Exhausted and content in their isolated cabin, Tillie pledged faithfulness to him on this Valentine's Day, "that hitch-hiking (our honeymoon) trip."[93] Jack adored her but not as Abe had. (Ethel Schochet said Abe had treated Tillie "as some goddess instead of a mortal."[94]) Jack's love was more down-to-earth. Also, his work was more above-board, as a photo and newspaper article on his job dispatching workers in a reformed ILWU hiring hall proved.[95] Tillie reveled in their shared political activities. [96] She relished the order, security, and sexual pleasure he brought her. She skipped the assignation with Dave Saunders.

When the *Western Worker* reported "People's Front Wins Votes of Spain: Communists Seat 14 in Parliament," Tillie and Jack felt that the choices they had made, for not only each other but also the world, were vindicated. They saw the Popular Front's modest victory as proof that ordinary people would choose communism if they could. In America, people were opting for decency and fairness. In Hollywood James Cagney, Dorothy Parker, and Donald Ogden Stewart held a benefit for new trials of the "Scottsboro Boys." The *Western Worker* mounted a campaign to repeal the Criminal Syndicalism Act. In New York, a committee promoted the very books that

German Nazis had burned. Granville Hicks made John Reed a martyr for communism.[97] With four Olympic gold medals, African-American track star Jesse Owens foiled Hitler's plan to exhibit the "master" race's superiority. The Screen Writers Guild agitated for the rights of ordinary Hollywood workers, as well as for those of writers.

Since Rae's January visit to Omaha, Ida Lerner had been considering the younger Schochets' adoption proposal. They might be good parents, but they lived in northern Minnesota. Though Tillie thought Karla was "every inch a Goldfarb," Ida wanted her to remain a Lerner. She decided that Morris must return Karla to Tillie. He was not happy with the assignment, but he could not disobey Ida. When his one-week vacation began in late June, he rode the train from Chicago to Omaha. Ida advised him: "if you are forced to choose between tenderness and love, choose tenderness." Family photos show Ida beaming tenderly with Morris and Karla. (They also show that Karla's hernia had yet to be treated.)[98] On a train called "The Zephyr," able only to afford a single seat, Morris struggled to keep Karla entertained all the way to California. In Oakland, Tillie greeted her with kisses and hugs, and Morris took the returning Zephyr to Chicago, not knowing where Tillie lived or with whom. She was then openly living with Jack Olsen. Even the sailors who lost her to him admitted that he was the man for her.[99] None of the sailors knew that she was married to someone else.

Jack showed a healthy blend of kindness and sternness to the three-year-old,[100] and Karla soon called him "Daddy." Once again settled, Tillie considered restarting her novel, though she had not worked on it for more than a year. She outlined ten chapters, planned to end with a sequence called "The Poem," and vowed this would be "the last novel I write in this manner—piecemeal." She would send chapters to Random House, even if they were only sketched in "the lousiest manner."[101]

That July, however, Spanish generals staged a coup against the Republican Parliament in the name of nationalism. Tillie and her comrades were exhilarated, as they had been in 1934 when police brutality created sympathy for victims. This good-versus-evil example pitted the legitimately elected leftist government against military fascists. In the United States, about 2,800 volunteers rallied for Republican Spain, and Tillie again abandoned her novel. Seeing fascism "not only [in] Spain, but China, and Germany, and Italy and Brazil," she rededicated herself "to build a united front."[102]

Rae had converted the rooms, where Tillie and Abe slept in 1932 and 1933, into an apartment whose rent enabled Rae to travel to Mexico and California. Abe was now courting a beautiful woman of Tillie's age named

Frances Schmulowitz, from Oakland. He traveled between San Francisco and Los Angeles in a nefarious life, organizing for the film union, the Music Corporation of America during what the *Western Worker* called, on 7 September, a "Great Awakening of Labor in Los Angeles." Charlie Chaplin's film *Modern Times* hilariously exposed how factory assembly lines dehumanize laborers but unintentionally encouraged AFL craft unions (of musicians, upholsterers, and painters) to disparage blue-collar unions (of factory, shop, and garment workers). This class split in the labor movement soon became a vicious, even bloody, rivalry.

In late August, the Communist Party in American ordered Tillie to return to Los Angeles, to support Republican Spain, and to work for party candidates. She obediently moved, writing for party papers and making speeches for Earl Browder for president, Harold Ashe for Congress, and Louis Rosser for the California Assembly."[103] While teaching at a workers' school, she told students to buy "Lenin Speaks to the Youth" for three cents, and Browder's *What is Communism?* She promoted pamphlets with titles like "Happy Days for American Youth" and novels about economic injustice, none of which were written by women. Though party officials reprimanded her "obsession with personal affairs," she listed the "gauge of what's a good party member" as full-time devotion.[104]

In the 1936 presidential election, the Republicans fell back on underhanded advertising techniques. Browder tried to convince the public that "Communism is Twentieth-Century Americanism." Roosevelt cast Republicans as "economic royalists," the "haves" who had wrecked American prosperity for their private profit. Against them, Democrats created an alliance of "have-nots" and progressives, a new generation of Americans who held "a rendezvous with destiny." People who had not bothered to vote in 1932 came out in droves for Roosevelt and the New Deal. He won by a landslide.[105]

John Steinbeck and Carey McWilliams were writing about the plight of migrant farm workers, making Tillie's 1934 potential "Imperial Valley" article obsolete.[106] She was off the board of *Pacific Weekly*. She had published nothing since her one-paragraph response to Henry Roth, except anonymous journalism in party papers. She attended a Western Writers' Congress in San Francisco, but the press did not mention her.[107] A Random House advertisement in *Pacific Weekly*, however, listed a forthcoming book by Tillie Lerner. Seeing it while at the Congress, she fired off a telegram to Cerf, worried that Abe had finished her novel for her. Cerf would hardly publish without contacting her, so whether or not her novel would "be published, depends, of course, upon you." He continued: "I credit you with sufficient power of imagination to make it unnecessary for me to tell you Donald's and my opinion of your conduct in this whole affair."

Tillie wrote Cerf from in Los Angeles on 24 November. She explained her conduct: "in the new life I was leading the Tillie Lerner who had publishers was very remote, and it was easier not to write." She might have meant that it was "easier not to" inform her publishers or that it was "easier not to write" her novel. She referred to the epiphany that had shown her the way to become an "honest" worker. She had become "active on the waterfront, and secretary of the Waterfront Branch of the Y.C.L." She said that since August she had worked in Los Angeles and San Pedro, campaigning four days a week. The other three days she said she did "nothing but write, write like I've never done before." She did not say what she was writing. Nor did she mention Karla. She did say she intended to be "a true working class, a true revolutionary writer." The "direction my life was going" in Hollywood had prevented becoming one, but "I have found my way." Working with ordinary laborers would make "a writer of me." She hoped Cerf and Klopfer would someday be proud of her books, "and so [be] somewhat repaid for all the grief I have been for you." That note of contrition extended to her personal life. She gave four-year-old Karla her first birthday party, for which Ida and Sam sent a toy piano, Rae an accordion, along with orders to deal with Karla's tonsils. Before leaving California, Rae met Abe in Stockton and admitted being "kind of nasty" to him, for Karla's sake. She asked Tillie "to think over Jevons request for a divorce seriously." Tillie should do so in "justice to all concerned," especially Karla, Abe, and Frances, who was pregnant.

Tillie's expectation that working in fields or factories and organizing workers would make "a writer of me" assumed that authentic experience with the working classes was preliminary to writing and that message trumps artistry. Cerf did not comment on such assumptions but appreciated the "note of optimism in your letter which was singularly lacking from letters that we got just before you dropped out of sight entirely."

Though Random House had won the battle with Macmillan to publish her novel, over two years and $1200 later, it had lost the battle with the Communist Party for Tillie's soul. To her, communism remained a "life and death necessity—and the only realistic thing." Sixty-five years later, Budd Schulberg could recall Tillie Lerner in the mid-1930s only as "the great feminine hope of Communist letters."[108]

CHAPTER 7

DEAD AND RESUSCITATED EGO

1937–1939

Why can't I "pour it out—tell the truth? And I know all this I deserve—for the falseness that was in me."

—Tillie Lerner, journal [late 1937]

For New Year's 1937, from a Los Angeles address on Whiteside Avenue,[1] Tillie sent Cerf and Klopfer a postcard picturing a man passed out on a bench. A woman in a frilly dress is asking "Are you a Dead One?" Tillie scribbled, "I guess the dead one is me," at least to Random House. Her sense of extinction echoed the country's fears. New Deal reforms had reached a dead end, the country was slipping back into recession, the world into fascism. Supposedly demilitarized after World War I, Germany's mighty army occupied the Rhineland. Italian bombers attacked Catalonia, Spain. Tillie and Jack briefly escaped such worries at a rowdy New Year's Eve party in the smoky *Western Worker* office on Washington Avenue. They danced and boozed it up, celebrating the *Worker*'s fifth and their first (unofficial) anniversary. Recalling their kiss outside the Steffens's Getaway, Tillie said she regretted not making love the previous New Year's Eve.

More than a year after its command performance at the White House, *Dead End* opened to the public in Washington, D.C., Morris Lerner, who had renamed himself Gene, played "Milty," a juvenile delinquent displaying "the horrors of improper environment," as he explained in a letter to Eleanor Roosevelt. She reciprocated by encouraging FDR to tackle the problem of urban slums.[2] He was hampered however by aged Republican Supreme Court justices, who repeatedly ruled New Deal programs unconstitutional. FDR now proposed adding liberal younger justices to the Court.

Congress rejected the plan and accused FDR of "court-packing" and dema-
goguery.[3] An anti-Roosevelt backlash benefited conservative Republicans
and southern Democrats and seemed to open a door for Communist influence. Like the Pied Piper, Tillie recruited new members, founded new YCL
branches, organized YCL dances, sold *Western Worker* subscriptions, and
helped Jack at the San Pedro port.[4] She typed up bulletins and calls to action
and ran them off on a mimeograph machine at 3019 Winter Street, clearly
a party address, as Ethel sensed after Tillie said she could always be reached
there.[5] Her frequent speeches praised plebeian "Trade Unions" who joined
the Congress of Industrial Organizations (CIO) after the more elitist and
reputedly corrupt American Federation of Labor (AFL) ousted them. Her
outlines include uplifting but vague phrases like: "United in the rearguard,
like the vanguard, We Shall Win."[6] Her notes outline "false neutrality,"
"Catalonia—1,600,000 refugees," and fascism's threat to "our children." Her
lines are often powerfully cadenced: "Black shirts and German passports;
Italian bombs and German bullets." She challenged audiences not to "stay
home, as if nothing is happening in Spain." But Tillie herself sometimes
struggled "to be absorbed to believe in what I am doing."[7]

Reports from the Soviet Union detailed dire stories of oppression and
brutality, worse, some said, than any atrocities the czar had committed.
Such reports tested party loyalty, especially when Stalin exiled Leon Trotsky,
who had led, with Lenin, the 1917 October Revolution. Mainstream papers
in the States saw Trotsky's exile as proof of Stalin's villainy; leftist papers
linked Trotsky with Hitler, Judas, and even John Wilkes Booth.[8] Abe Goldfarb labeled Stalin's critics as "counter-revolutionary Trotskyites." He wrote
Rae, now on her way west, a grandiose letter calling his sister "Diana of the
Chase—nimblefooted skirted gentleman of the road—oh fair wanderer
on this frenetic mundane sphere." More practically, he thought Rae was a
trustworthy friend, unlike "certain unpleasant individuals who have taken
advantage of my patience and kindness." He meant Tillie. He hoped to offer
Rae a "haven of security whenever you come to L.A." She had no more need
for Abe's haven than for his inflated rhetoric. She rented a room in San
Francisco and got a part-time job.[9] When Jack traveled to San Francisco's
CP headquarters, he at last met Rae and assured her of his love for Karla as
well as Tillie.

Bennett Cerf reacted to Tillie's zany card by remarking that she could
write something really big once she got "such trivial things as sex out of
your system." Cerf's remark made her further reconsider—not sex—but
"what I am doing," especially writing anonymous, throw-away bulletins
instead of "something really big." Giving art and ambition one more chance,

she petitioned party bureaucracy for time off and was granted a few months to resuscitate her proletarian novel, with a 1 June deadline. Tillie, however, worried that writing fiction was bourgeois, a worry she let leech into her resolve.[10]

Tillie's ambition to write was further interrupted when she discovered once again the hazards of unprotected sex. She told Karla she had a baby in her stomach. She could hardly take care of her four-year-old, much less a new baby, though female comrades sent baby gifts and promised help. She faced the "knowledge of failure, of my pregnancy. Strength, strength. I have the hardness in me to break what is necessary to be broken." Just then Tillie received a report from Random House's bookkeeper: her debt for the "advance to date" was $1201.98.[11] When Jack was sent to New York on party business, she summoned the "hardness" to break her pregnancy, at least her third abortion. Later she recalled the lost child as the "dead rich baby," with its unused baby gifts.[12]

Tillie's spirits lifted a bit when she got a reprieve from Cerf, who had his bookkeeper send a notice: "author agrees to deliver ms when ready." Calling Cerf "comrade psychoanalyst," Tillie said Jack had shrugged off his "impudent" remarks about her sex life by asking, "what do you expect from a guy like that?" Cerf retorted, "How the hell" did the "Jack" she mentioned "know what kind of a guy I am?" To Jack and their comrades he was a wealthy capitalist and hence an effete man.

Without editorial guidance from Abe and babysitting from Sue, Ida, and Rae, Tillie found writing was harder than ever. Her excuses for not writing had included poor health, her hyperemotional state, and party work. For the first time, Tillie's excuse to Cerf was domestic: "a job a child and a house to keep alongside," but she was not even feeding Karla well. She claimed that septic poisoning kept her from writing for two and a half weeks and that the novel was "DONE except the going over." She said, "I hafta have a book for you by June 1st at the latest or I'll be disgraced forever as far as the movement and myself and everything that means anything to me is concerned." Cerf concluded that the movement meant more to her than her contract with and debt to Random House.

Along with about eight thousand others in Los Angeles, Tillie was thrilled to hear André Malraux speak about the Spanish people's heroic defense of democracy and freedom. Now a Random House author, Malraux's opposition to Franco made Tillie feel indeed a "dead one" and regret no longer being Random House's most "promising young novelist." Calling herself "Tillie the Moocher," she asked for more free books.[13] Cerf sent her ones by Malraux and Angelo Herndon, now also a Random House author, thanks to Tillie's recommendation. Rather than stimulate her writing, however, these gifts made her admit that others were saying what she "should have." Her own novel had captured the Holbrooks' heart-wrenching struggles, rendered little Mazie's mind-boggling insights, and offered breath-taking descriptions, but those achievements seemed dated when Josephine Herbst had "gone beyond me" to address the threat of international fascism. In late April, Nazi planes bombed the Basque town of Guernica and machine-gunned fleeing citizens. But in May, Congress passed the Neutrality Act, preventing the United States from sending military aid, even to Spanish Loyalists. Tillie could not bear to "read the accounts of Spain anymore. 70 school children bombed in Spain." With murderers winning in Spain, her stamina sapped by her latest abortion, Jack often away on party business, Karla a resentful child, and her novel endless, in several senses, Tillie could not settle back to writing. News that Abe and Frances Schmulowitz had a daughter, born on 15 April 1937, and that he named the baby Olive Schreiner Goldfarb, after one of Tillie's literary heroes, did not lift her from a slough of despondency.[14]

Realizing that Rae was in San Francisco only temporarily, Tillie rushed a special delivery letter begging Rae to take Karla back to the Midwest. Rae was furious that Tillie never wrote, then suddenly wasted "stamps on specials," and treated her like "a jumping bean." She said Ida Lerner was planning to head for California herself "because you don't write and when you do you still don't say anything." Then Tillie fired off a special to her parents, saying that Karla was in Rae's care, that Jack was her new husband, and that Ida was not needed. Ida accepted Tillie's "monkey business," as Rae called such ruses, and Rae agreed to take Karla away if Tillie would first have her tonsils out. Rae instructed "make sure you see the docter immediately."

When Rae came down to Los Angeles in May, Tillie turned Karla over, with hardly a word. Such rudeness to Rae paled, though, in comparison to Tillie's neglect of the almost emaciated Karla. Rae took Karla to say good-bye to Abe and cursed him for not seeing to her welfare. Then Rae took her undernourished niece to see Sue and Nahman Goldfarb in San Francisco. Since 1933, Sue had been a surrogate mother for Karla; since 1934, Karla was a surrogate for her lost child so Sue spent every day for a week taking Karla to the zoo, to merry-go-rounds, and to parks, feeding her treats all the while. When Rae and Karla arrived in Omaha on 7 June, the Lerners were shocked that Karla weighed little more than she had the year before. Rae wrote Tillie that Karla was delighted to see her grandparents, her Uncle Harry, her Aunt Vicki, and her Aunt Lillian, whose husband, medical student Joseph Davis, seemed to Rae "a very nice sort."[15] When Karla asked why they left her mother, Rae offered the hollow answer that Tillie had to be alone to write.

Despite saying that it was "DONE," Tillie produced no novel on the first of June. That month, at the second American Writers' Congress, theologian Reinhold Niebuhr accused Communists of fanaticism in their "mighty excommunication" of Trotsky. Ernest Hemingway was more appealing to the leftist writers as he declared himself "actively in the fight against fascism."[16] Tillie was not invited to this Congress; her reputation had vanished. She wrote Cerf that she would finish "sometime, sometime." She hoped sending Karla back to Omaha would "give me a little more, not only time but energy." She also made a startling confession: "will it please you to know that when I think of the time that I dribbled away that year I had nothing to do but write I go slightly crazy?" That year was 1935 after her flashy appearance at the Writers' Congress in New York when she was living on Random House's money and Marian Ainslee's support. Though she had had "nothing to do but write," Tillie instead had dribbled her time away proselytizing for the Hollywood Communist Party. Cerf replied that he and Klopfer were not "surprised to hear that your book wasn't finished yet. You have disappointed us so often that we have come to take it as a matter of course." Perhaps her book would "be so good that it will wipe away a great many unpleasant memories."

Tillie had confessed honestly to Cerf, but her ability to go beyond confession to introspection was limited. Rather than the "movement work" that had kept her from writing, she now blamed "that ruinous first taste of fame." She so twisted logic that the opposite of fame was selflessness. In another epiphany like her late 1935 one, she decided to "kill my ego. Then I can build one."[17] She sold subscriptions for the *Western Worker*, organized men and women in shipping and the automotive industries, and wrote the mimeographed *Mariner* for the San Pedro Branch of the YCL.[18] On 24 June, the *Western Worker* printed a letter from Paul Cline, "L. A. Communist County Organizer," praising these activities, without naming Tillie. She seemed indeed a dead one, having practically killed her identity, as well as her ego, as the party required.

Among the important accomplishments of the Works Progress Administration were programs making art, music, theatre, and writing accessible all over America. The Federal Writers' Project boosted the writing careers of Jack Conroy, John Cheever, Saul Bellow, Ralph Ellison, Richard Wright, and Eudora Welty (as a photographer), among many others. Tillie does not seem to have been among them, though she would say that she collected stories of Hispanic immigrants in Los Angeles for the historical records project.[19] With America's economic recovery in jeopardy, however, by August 1937, FDR cut WPA funds in half and virtually shut down the CWA. The Federal Reserve tightened credit. Unemployment rose. The stock market almost collapsed. The CP-USA offered no viable solution to the looming crisis. The common worker was again a forgotten man or woman.

After a week in Omaha, Rae took Karla to Faribault, where she "didn't seem to mind" being away from her mother. Tillie was too frazzled to send, as promised, a box of Karla's belongings and, Rae suspected, even to "keep up the house." In July, Harry Lerner penned a letter for Ida asking Rae about Karla's weight. Rae said the little girl was better, thanks to cod liver oil in her juice and milk and egg yolks in homemade ice cream. Rae wrote to Tillie a stream-of-consciousness letter about bathing Karla "about 6 times a day the little black monkie she is cute but oh how she can talk and if my voice gets stern she whimpers and says you are not getting angry, then of course I have to laugh and say oh no." About Tillie's inability to write, Rae wondered: "Who did it this time?"

After Ethel returned to Faribault in the last stages of pregnancy, she assumed Rae's role of scolding Tillie for her "out of sight out of mind" approach to Karla. Ethel instructed "BE A MOTHER FOR GODS SAKE." Karla was talking about a baby brother, so Ethel wondered, "did you or didn't you tell her there was a baby in your stomach?" When Ethel's baby Benita was born on 9 August, Rae was shocked that Karla already knew "all the details" about babies and sex. When she took her niece to see Edgar Bergen, in a Minnesota appearance, Karla astounded her aunt by understanding that the unruly Charlie McCarthy was really a dummy whose voice was Bergen's. Karla gravitated to the "Pied Piper" story about the messianic leader who "got the rats out then took the children in the mountain you should hear her tell it when she looks at the pictures." Though she understood something of sex, ventriloquism, and mesmerizing power, little Karla still refused to eat. A visiting nurse found Ethel's baby healthy but Karla, at four-and-a-half, fifteen pounds underweight. Ethel exclaimed that her family would have done "better by Karla than" Tillie and that Karla could sue her mother "for breach of promise." Tillie responded with a card to Karla, saying that the San Pedro sailors "all ask me—where is KARLA—is she being good—is she happy—is she acting like a big girl and your MAMMA says yes and hugshugsloveskisses."[20]

Desperate for attention, Karla used her pitiful looks to finagle toys, trips to shows and movies, and ice cream treats. Her ability to wheedle costly favors made Ethel charge that "Karla sure doesn't show any PROLETARIAN upbringing." She was "a little conniving queen," who lies and "looks you straight in the eyes while doing it." Karla certainly lied about eating, as Rae later discovered when she cleaned her silver tea set and found the sugar bowl, creamer, and cups each "half full with food which Karla put in when I went out from the dining room and she used to tell me she ate it all up the rascal it was moldy and there was [everything] from buttered bread to egg yolk cheese potatoes and what not." In another run-on phrase, Rae told Tillie about getting a literary "key" to James Joyce's *Ulysses* because "Good God what a book I thought I'd never finish much less understand." The "key" made sense of Joyce's stream-of-consciousness novel, even as it vindicated Rae's peculiar writing style.

Worried about Karla's health, Ida came to Faribault to take, with Rae, the little girl to a doctor. He advised that Karla's tonsils should be removed, as Tillie had failed to do, and that they should keep the truss over her navel so her hernia would not rupture. After getting more scolding, Tillie promised that she and Jack would take better care of Karla. Ethel set out terms: "If things pan out the way you want them to about Jack and jobs, Karla is yours. If not, not. But ferhevvenssake [for heaven's sake] don't keep changing her from east to west to this and that home [and] relative and so on." Rae sent Tillie a similar ultimatum: either become a good mother or lose Karla. Awaiting Tillie's commitment, Ida took Karla to Omaha.

During these hassles over Karla's future, Tillie continued giving emotionally charged speeches about German and Italian attacks on villages like Catalonia and Guernica. She sang songs like "Abraham Lincoln Walks Again." She connected American "traditions of liberty" with "the Party of Lenin [which] is leading the way!"[21] She could so fire up a crowd that many sailor friends, including Georgie Kaye and Jack Eggan, volunteered for the Abraham Lincoln Brigade. She led them to believe, as Eggan wrote, that the Brigade would restore the duly-elected Republic of Spain. At home, the criminal syndicalist detainees achieved a long-delayed release.[22] In Los Angeles though, that victory for union organizers was undermined by escalating class rivalry between AFL and CIO unions. The president of the Theatrical Stage Employees, an AFL affiliate, reportedly appointed Chicago hoodlums to intimidate studio workers to join, while CIO unions fought to keep them.

A week or two after Ida returned to Omaha with Karla, the Lerners sent her back to Tillie in Los Angeles. On 13 October, they telegraphed "Mrs Jack Olsen," at the Winter Street address, all that they had: "KARLA LEFT ON CHALLENGER WEDNESDAY TEN FORTY AM SHE WAS HAPPY AND LIKED

STEWARDESS WHO WAS EXPECTING HER PLEASE WRITE IMMEDIATELY
ABOUT HER ARRIVAL LOVE. LERNERS." After four and a half months away,
Karla must have been happy to be met by "hugshugsloveskisses" but
terrified when her mother collapsed in pain. Soon Tillie was admitted to
the Los Angeles General Hospital for an appendectomy.[23] Comrade Lou
Rosser wrote, "how does it feel to be minus that great contraption which
god gave you your appendix." He was planning a cocktail party at the state
convention for "free loaders" or "youth leaders" like Tillie. He suggested
that she "hurry up and get well Jack is worrying his head off. It shows he
loves you—so do I when my wife is not looking."[24]

Rae wrote Tillie that Abe's Los Angeles friends Jerry and Sylvia reported
that he was "not sorry for the years spent" with Tillie, though she had "taken
advantage" of his devotion.[25] In mid-November, Tillie began a 1,200-word
reply, mentioning a short story that had given her "enough strength to break
with Abe."[26] She listed paralyzing health troubles, including a "zipper" or
incision that drained and would not heal.[27] Karla tried extortion on her
incapacitated mother by saying Rae had taken her "to the movies three
times a day, supplied her with an endless stream of ice cream and kept her
happy with every toy the kids ever heard of." Though they could not afford
such treats, Tillie assured Rae that she and Jack were being responsible
parents, establishing discipline, and even converting Karla into "a voracious
eater." They were "leaving for Frisco this Sat. morning." Testifying "Rae, one
of the richest things in my life has been knowing you," Tillie begged "don't
curse me any more." At the end of this letter, she noted that she was not
leaving with Jack but "staying on another week" in Los Angeles, while he
took care of "getting settled" in San Francisco. She ended disconnectedly,
"I have a fever."

In San Francisco, Jack found joblessness at its highest point "since the
termination of the 1934 strike," according to the *Western Worker*, which
soon printed Dorothea Lange's photo of a migrant worker with her baby
(later known as "Depression Madonna") with the headline: "SPECTRE OF
RENEWED DEPRESSION HAUNTS AMERICA."[28] With unions unable
to staunch the reopened wound of unemployment, tensions deepened
between the AFL and the CIO. In Hollywood, the battle for control of
workers escalated. Abe Goldfarb had had Hollywood in mind when he
wrote Rae about hoping "to earn enough" to provide a haven for her, as she
had for him over the years. He may have fought the AFL, which had its own
paper, the *Los Angeles Citizen*, to combat the CIO's *Western Worker*, which
called AFL unions dues-collecting rackets that used the tactics of Al Capone
and Hitler.[29]

At the very time Tillie justified to Rae her decision "to break with Abe," he was found dead. On 17 November 1937, just after six in the morning, two police officers noticed a light in a culvert under a bridge just north of San Fernando, California. They found Abe Goldfarb "crushed under an overturned light sedan." One paper said, "Goldfarb was en route to Hollywood after visiting his wife and baby in San Francisco." He carried letters, a key, and a billfold with his social security card and $37.50 in cash. He listed himself as a salesman and as "sec. music corp."[30] The Los Angeles County Coroner reported that he had a "crushing injury of thorax" and a "probable basal fracture of skull. Auto ran off a bridge—accidental." In a one-car crash, a "basal fracture" at the back of the skull seems at odds with a crushed chest. The coroner was too busy or corrupt to make a more careful investigation, but the injuries may suggest foul play.[31] Perhaps Abe was a victim of the AFL/CIO rivalry for Hollywood union members. Or perhaps he had simply driven off the road in the middle of the night, catapulting himself and his car into the culvert below. Rumors circulated that he had committed suicide, had been eliminated in some union or CP squabble, and even had been set up by Tillie. She was in Los Angeles without Jack and remained there into December.[32] She had believed that the good of the party justified any misdeed, when capitalists like Leopold and Loeb could get away with murder. Her diaries now expressed crippling guilt. She wondered why she could not "pour it out—tell the truth. And I know all this I deserve—for the falseness that was in me." Then she inked out lines that might have explained that falseness. She did leave legible a question: "why A. hit so hard?" And she promised someday to answer that question.[33]

She also typed up a bizarre page labeled "This that has happened in your lifetime Karla." She imagined painting on a room-size canvas "so the eye could see it all at once." Rather than paint, she wrote a surrealistic word-picture of elegant figures in tuxedos and evening dresses eating, drinking, and dancing on a platform, with one "couple making love on a couch" and a girl leaning over "despairing, every line of her fingertips of the one fallen hand in the blood." The platform is "sustained by a fountain spray of blood."[34] Clearly, this picture was an allegory for Tillie's, not Karla's, life. It is consistent with revulsion at her pampered Hollywood existence and her "ruinous first taste of fame." Still, the "spray of blood" remains a mystery, unless it refers to Abe's death.

About six years later, Tillie told her family only "he died."[35] She later insisted that she had been a single mother, sometimes saying that Karla was the child of a passing fling with a drifter. Before she deposited her papers at Stanford, she tried to scratch out Goldfarb's name wherever it appeared. She did not keep the letter from "AF of L Sam." In a 1937 notebook, she asked, "How much does the comrade's personal life have to do with his movement work. . . . Death—puts people in their proper places." She even wrote that "torture is just, because a poor man's life is one long torture. And all who teach poor men to bear it—all the Christian priests & everyone else ought to be punished. They don't know."[36] Such rationalizations help clarify Communist disregard for the personal but do not solve the riddle of why Tillie tried to erase Abe Goldfarb from her life.

Seeing Lillian Hellman's film adaptation of *Dead End*, Tillie felt less like the good working girl, played by Sylvia Sidney, than the unscrupulous gangster, played by Humphrey Bogart, who is denounced by his mother in words that Hellman could have stolen from Rae Schochet. In poor health, desperate for stability, paralyzed by guilt, Tillie fled Los Angeles with Karla that December for San Francisco and Jack. In lodgings near Telegraph Hill and then the rough western addition, the threesome clung together. Tillie was often in tears, virtually incapacitated by awareness of the "falseness that was in me."

The *Western Worker*'s success enabled its transformation into a paper called the *Daily People's World*. Determined to overcome tears and guilt, to revitalize herself, and reclaim her writing identity, Tillie asked Al Richmond, managing editor, for a job. He offered a theater-reviewing post, giving her a free ticket to San Francisco Opera Guild's rendition of Gilbert and Sullivan's *Pirates of Penzance*. She could both mingle with San Francisco's elite theatergoers and judge them in the review she wrote near year's end.

In San Francisco, the *Daily People's World* debuted on 1 January 1938. More artful and inclusive than the *Western Worker*, the *DPW* covered the arts, sports, and local, national, and international politics. It featured poems, stories, historical essays, comic strips like "Little Lefty," and columns like "Seeing Red" (by Tillie's friend Mike Quin), "Women's Slant," and "Behind the Screen," an insider's view of Hollywood. Its first issue included Tillie's review.[37] She noted that the targets of Gilbert's wit, "pompous and corrupt officials . . . exist today as they did fifty years ago." She regretted that Sullivan "was heaped with honors," while Gilbert was "despised" by queen and establishment. Still, Gilbert's satire had "reached the ears of the masses" and ripped open the "veil of holiness and wisdom" from the ruling class. Tillie's class-conscious exposé echoed Marxist Abe's literary analysis and her early distinction between Longfellow and Spartacus. At long last, it recaptured something of the pizzazz of her youthful "Squeaks" column.

When party operatives on Winter Street in Los Angeles forwarded a letter from Random House, Tillie trembled lest Cerf might want his money back. Instead of recriminations, though, he assured her, "you need fear no terrible reproaches from me because we have long since despaired of ever getting a novel from you." Tillie replied that, if he came to San Francisco, she could always be found through *People's World*.[38]

Now twenty-six, Tillie found reviewing self-affirming. On 3 and 11 February, she accused actress Pauline Frederick of "melodraming" and praised Clare Boothe's *The Women* for blasting "Feminine Leisure Class" and proving that only "working girls" are honest. She labeled *The Wave*, a film about Mexican fishermen, with subtitles by Dos Passos, "one of the greatest motion pictures of all times, of all countries" because it showed the "thrilling power" organizing brings to oppressed people. When Richmond assigned her an article on Benjamin Franklin, though, she filled a bag with notes but could not meld them together, until she tried projection. Appearing on 17 February 1938, her much-revised article depicts Franklin as a man who rejected Britain's "glory and prestige" to choose rebellion. Her Franklin was not a wealthy entrepreneur and investor; he could well have been a Communist.

Back in Hollywood, Cerf's diary was a "Who's Who" of film and literary stars, including Dorothy Parker, John Steinbeck, Robinson Jeffers, Budd Schulberg, and Charlie Chaplin. Later in San Francisco, he met Tillie Lerner at the Palace Hotel on 22 February. Cerf was so genial she went along when he was driven over the Bay Bridge to visit Eugene O'Neill. Over a free lunch, she argued that Tom Mooney could write an even more sensational book than Angelo Herndon, who had visited Mooney in 1934.

On returning home, Tillie dashed off an article titled "Noted Publisher Here: To Visit Tom Mooney," in which she gave Cerf a makeover. Her Cerf claimed that Mooney, now appealing his 1916 conviction, was his personal hero. Her Cerf admired books published cheaply for the Russian masses. Her Cerf found Harry Bridges, the "most exciting and colorful person in the West," an opinion, she remarked, that "kind of puts Hollywood and his two western authors, Nobel Prize winner Eugene O'Neill and Carmel poet Robinson Jeffers, in their place." She had made her father a spokesman for meat packers and Ben Franklin for egalitarianism; now her ventriloquism made Bennett Cerf the voice of communism. He and Klopfer, signing radical writers like Lerner, Malraux, and Herndon, had hoped to democratize and invigorate their publishing list. But by 1938, it seems unlikely that Cerf would be saying, as Tillie claimed, "the Left is where the great literature of tomorrow is coming from."[39] He did arrange, on 25 February, to be driven over the "new Golden Gate Bridge to San Quentin where [he] had a one hour talk with Tom Mooney," who was uninterested in writing his story for Random House.[40]

Remaking others in her own image was, for Tillie, an enabling psychic strategy, but remaking Josef Stalin was a more daunting task. He used intimidation, vindictive arrests, and brutal sentences against traitors, defined as anyone who criticized him. Despite evidence that the Moscow Trials were atrocities and Stalin a despot, Tillie tried to reconstruct him as chiefly a foe of counterrevolutionaries.[41] Rumors that Stalin and Hitler might collude undermined such rationalizations, so Tillie cheered when the *Daily Worker* blasted the "filthy falsehood that the Soviet Union was considering an agreement with the bestial Nazi regime."[42] Hitler proved his bestiality by invading Austria. Former president Herbert Hoover proved his by visiting Hitler in March, an act showing Tillie that capitalism was indeed in cahoots with fascism.[43]

By writing reviews and living a more ordered life, Tillie was recovering from the guilt that had incapacitated her in late 1937, but world events still threatened her emotional stability. She could not recapture the mood of a "rainy spring here in S. F. in that pre-Spain world." The fascists bombed Barcelona on 24 March, and the "magic" of spring was "emptied" by news of another "vast exodus of women and children" from bombed-out Spanish villages. After another stock market dive, Roosevelt began reviving the WPA, the PWA, and other federal agencies, increasing employment and putting dollars back into circulation. He instructed Congress "BOOST PEOPLE'S INCOME."[44] By June, he signed fair labor legislation that outlawed child labor and established a minimum wage of 25¢ an hour (Tillie's CWA wage in 1933–1934), to rise to 40¢ in two years. FDR had preempted what was left of the Communist Party's altruistic agenda.

The Left wing turned its attention to Republican Spain's battle against fascism. Clifford Odets and Sylvia Sidney donated ambulances. The League of American Writers auctioned manuscripts, including one of Hemingway's, also to buy ambulances, but the *New York Times* refused to publish a writers' petition opposing the U.S. embargo on Republican Spain.[45] The House of Representatives created a Committee on Un-American Activities to uncover fascism in the United States, but Chairman Martin Dies of Texas, under pressure from the Hearst papers, reinterpreted his mission as ferreting out Communists. In California, HUAC, as it came to be known, became a fascist force, as it listed, for example, all *Peoples' World* writers, including Tillie Lerner, as subversives. It scoffed at censure from the League of American Writers.

After making the capitalist Cerf a Communist, Tillie made Clifford Odets seem a capitalist, perhaps because he had left the Communist Party. She dismissed his *Golden Boy* for lacking a "feeling of bitter economic necessity." She wrote no more reviews for *People's World*. She would say that she worked thirty hours a week "for Western, a temp agency, to manage hours for Karla. Desperate about writing time." She took odd jobs: "hotel maid and linen checker, a waitress, solderer of battery wires, and jar capper." She attempted to order her life: "3 nights YCL, 2 nights soc. [socializing] and Jack. Leaves 2 nights for me." The most they could afford for rent was: "$20 unfurnished, 24 furnished."[46] Sometimes they camped out in someone's spare room, entwined together on an army cot. With little privacy or time together, as Tillie gained strength, she and Jack resumed a passionate sex life. They intended to avoid pregnancy, but she sometimes forgot to use her pessary and that spring became pregnant again.[47]She felt guilty over losing other babies and neglecting Karla, but she believed herself too ill to bear a child so she scheduled another abortion. Then, at the end of May, Tillie's chest x-ray reported that she was free of TB.[48] The next week, *People's World* reprinted Käthe Kollwitz's lithograph "The Mothers," with commentary about her understanding the "sufferings of motherhood and childhood under capitalism." Tillie proceeded to the abortionist's office, but with Kollwitz's "The Mothers" searing her eyes and memories of Ida, Rae, and Karla searing her heart, she ran out of the office, still pregnant. She consoled herself that Jack could care for them and that motherhood could be redemptive.[49]

In Munich, British Prime Minister Neville Chamberlain ceded Czechoslovakia to Hitler.[50] *Daily People's World* on 1 October saw "a permanent alliance of Great Britain with Nazi Germany." On 10 October, the paper warned "HITLER THREATENS FRANCE." Japan had invaded China and remained in occupancy. Britain seemed "ready to Cede Europe to Nazi Grip." Americans were becoming so frightened that radio audiences panicked on 30 October 1938, as Orson Welles's Mercury Theatre aired its adaptation of H. G. Wells's *War of the Worlds*, about an invasion from Mars.[51]

Four and a half years after Tillie had ridiculed "Franklin Dealout Richvelth," the *DPW* put faith in him, insisting that FDR "Won't Yield on New Deal." Communist candidates did not dare attack him but lost elections anyway.[52] Democrats made a "Clean Sweep" in California, electing liberal Culbert Olson governor. Nationally, conservatives made gains by arguing that reform had gone far enough and that inflation was now the threat to recovery. Congress cut the New Deal social programs FDR had refortified. Just when *DPW* announced that Pearl Buck was "1st U. S. Woman to

Capture Nobel Prize," it described "Nazi Fury," destroying synagogues and Jewish shops. With broken glass reflecting rampant fires, 9–10 November became known as "kristallnacht," crystal night. Pogroms against Jews spread. Hitler threatened France. Loyalist lines along the Ebro River were faltering, but the United States did not lift its embargo on Spain, much less oppose Germany. HUAC considered artists like Orson Welles and Communists like Tillie and Jack more a threat than Hitler.

Tillie tried to turn her fervent speeches about Spain into articles. In letters to the Olsens, Georgie Kaye had proclaimed that the Spanish Republicans were about to "wipe fascism off the face of Spain." Jack Eggan had killed "ignorant peasants misled by the phony capitalists." Now he wished he could kill the fascist dictators, "men who cause war and who get fat from it and not their puppets."[53] Despite her private informants, public articles, and pages of notes and outlines, Tillie could not convert her speeches into publishable articles. Also, the heaviness of late pregnancy sapped her energies, even while the baby within promised a new beginning.

During the holidays, Tillie and Jack sent Karla to his parents in Venice. For the first time in a year, Tillie wrote Ethel, inviting her to San Francisco. Ethel replied that she would bring little Benita, join the Writers' Project, and leave Tillie home with "Karla, Bonny and Whatsisname," not the arrangement Tillie had in mind. Ethel admitted she would "never be the genius, the something T. Lerner was acclaimed," but she refused to be Tillie's maid.[54] Tillie was upset by Ethel's past-tense reference to her genius. News that her brother Gene Lerner won third prize in a nationwide drama-writing contest, played one of the "Dead End Kids," and had gotten Eleanor Roosevelt to address a forum at George Washington University, where he was on scholarship, did not improve Tillie's self-esteem.[55] Then she heard that Jack Eggan was killed near the banks of the Ebro.

Tillie had seen Eggan, an orphan who had become a boxer and a poet, as proof of human potential, but fascist forces had turned potential into dust. Tillie wrote of "the sterile wind" which "layed him down." She made a more defiant note: "We fight again. Hunted. You drive our seed deeper."[56] She meant that the seeds of reform and rebirth would grow to fight again. She planned to name the baby "Jack" after his father and Jack Eggan. But after a difficult labor, a daughter was born to Jack and Tillie on 27 December 1938. They named her Julie. A sailor friend teased them about having "only a girl," who would still show "revolutionary tendencies."[57] Dubbed "Gazoonie" by her parents, a word that soon produced gurgling happiness, baby Julie showed no rebellious tendencies. After assaults to her lungs, digestive track, and reproductive system, childbirth had jeopardized Tillie's health again.

Still, she felt a blissful flood of contentment with this baby. Soon she began, as with Karla six years before, trying to be scientific about motherhood. She recorded when Julie "tried to suck thumb. Partially supports head."

At year's end, the *Daily People's World* celebrated a "Leftward Trend" in the "Best Books Written in '38": Hemingway's *The Fifth Column*, André Malraux's *Man's Fate*, and Richard Wright's *Uncle Tom's Cabin.* In bed with her baby, Tillie felt little connection with the masculine experiences of those "best" writers. She imagined a book about immigrant women, like Ida and Rae, as a universal democratic mother: "in the most elementary sense no USA would be here without her, she gave life to the life of the continent." Her story could "break our heart."[58] Her own heart near breaking over such unnamed women, Tillie vowed to be a better mother to Karla and to baby Julie.

By early 1939, the CP-USA was in disarray. It had led the way in opposing racism and fascism and defending Republican Spain. It had helped to improve workers' lives and to convince most citizens that the government bore responsibility for the well-being of its people. It had, however, become a bureaucracy.[59] It refused to credit Democrats, socialists, liberals, religious people, charitable institutions, or ordinary caring citizens for improving the lot of Americans. Two 1939 *DPW* headlines suggest its tactics: "Hitler Lies and So Does Dies" and "Hitler Hoover Trotsky Join Hands."[60] Equating Martin Dies with Hitler and Hoover with Trotsky and Hitler was illogical, but logic was already absent from attempts to deny Stalin's brutal purges and collective farms' failures. Tillie was so overwhelmed by postpartum depression that, as she later told Rae Schochet, she was "too sick to know what was going on."

Early in the year, Rae came to see Nahman and Sue Goldfarb and check on Karla. When Rae heard that her youngest sister was seriously ill, however, she left abruptly; once again Karla to felt abandoned. A new house to live in, rather than rooms to camp in, made her a bit more secure. At 61 Alpine Terrace, up a heart-stopping incline and steps, Jack installed Tillie, Karla, and the baby; friends helped move their modest accumulations, including boxes and bags of Tillie's books and papers. Money was so scarce that they often held parties to solicit contributions toward the rent. As Tillie recovered from childbirth, friends from L.A., including Lou Rosser, joined them for a "tribute to Union Labor," as *People's World* put it, on Treasure Island, in San Francisco Bay.

As she emerged from the fog of depression and ill health to learn "what was going on," Tillie was horrified by a *DPW* headline: "World's Best Singer Jim-Crowed." Daughters of the American Revolution had refused to let

"Marian Anderson, Negro contralto" sing in Constitution Hall. Resigning her membership, Eleanor Roosevelt arranged for Anderson to sing at the Lincoln Memorial. Advertised "For All the People," the Easter concert attracted an integrated audience of 75,000.[61] In Harlem, Billie Holiday soon recorded "Strange Fruit," an eloquent protest against lynching in the American South. Tillie had challenged audiences not to "stay home, as if nothing is happening in Spain." But she was staying home while others fought racism in America.

A line from a song for Jack's twenty-eighth birthday, on 16 March 1939, applauds "our Franklin sneering loudly at Der Fuehrer and his boys." Other spirited verses sung at the surprise party mention "your gorgeous Lerner, Till" and the "sixty thousand million steps which lead to Olsens on the hill." People were poor but hopeful: "without benefit of money—let no bounds know our joys."[62] Such good cheer was soon demolished by the news that Republican Spain had fallen. Thanks to America's nonintervention, the lives of many idealists had been lost, in vain. When a dispirited Georgie Kaye returned, Tillie and Jack made room for him on Alpine Terrace; he repaid such generosity by helping around the house, often changing Julie's diapers while singing "I am too young to die."[63]

Jack's birthday also saw *Daily People's World* publish Dorothy Parker's "You're Doing Fine Baby, But You're Not doing Enough." Tillie took those words seriously when, despite Kaye's help, she spent her time "performing senseless & revolting work in order to continue to exist."[64] Needing help, she asked her youngest sister if she wanted to attend college in California, but Vicki wanted "down-to-earth information" about colleges, which Tillie failed to supply. Her parents scolded her for not sending news. Jack had no steady employment. They might lose their house. Ethel and Vicki had each refused to be her housekeeper. When Karla finally had her tonsils out, her tongue got infected. Tillie had bleeding ulcers or colitis, and a sulphur drug made her sicker. Finally, Jack's teenage second cousin named Pauline moved in to help. The chaotic household then included three adults, a teenager, a six-year-old, and a baby. Jack landed a temporary job back on the waterfront.[65] Still, the times were so "nightmarish" that by summer Jack "up and shipped us (Julie included) down to his folks," the Olshanskys.[66]

Sun, sleep, and food, along with the Olshanskys' nonjudgmental love, helped revive Tillie. She wrote Jack that she "started scribbling; I yam better guttily speaking; and oh its so heavenly not to be trembling with exhaustion by the time supper starts." She was sleeping late "without even taking out 10 minutes to miss your arms & legs around me. I eat enough to make

Georgie's appetite look 'delicate.' So does Karla. So does Gazoonie." Jack's
mother Bluma was so ill she ran from people on the beach who asked about
her health, but she so adored her first grandchild "you'd a thought" Julie
was "a second Lenin." Tillie gushed: "(I love your mom & dad) (also their
eldest son)."

As she recovered strength, Tillie wanted people to know that "*we* were
the ones who fought Hitler . . . at every step fought against and warned . . .
that there is a way to stop Hitler, our way, and it will be the only way." She
was right that communism had opposed Hitler from the beginning, but
she was too partial to notice how the party had corrupted its cooperative
values. It had, for example, condemned Budd Schulberg's *Liberty Magazine* story "What Makes Sammy Run" as individualistic, not "proletarian."
Furious over its dictatorial tactics, Schulberg resigned before the party
expelled him.[67]

The new Democratic governor of California pardoned Tom Mooney,
appointed activist film star Melvyn Douglas to the Welfare Board, and
made Carey McWilliams head of Immigration and Housing. At the close
of Steinbeck's novel *Grapes of Wrath*, Tom Joad goes into hiding, promising
to be "ever'where" fighting poverty, starvation, and injustice. This 1939
American epic about history and redemption reinforced Tillie's awareness
that other writers had "gone beyond me." Frank Capra's *Mr. Smith Goes
to Washington*, with Jimmy Stewart playing the earnest hero, affirmed the
three quintessential American documents: the Declaration of Independence,
the Constitution, and the Bill of Rights. The best of New Deal legislation
together formed a fourth essential American document, a declaration of
responsibility for public welfare. But the Dies committee's investigations of
Communists and even New Deal proponents undermined these documents
with fascist tactics. Jack's father started keeping all his "necessary" lists in
one envelope that could be "destroyed in half a second." Tillie advised Jack
to "follow your pop's example."

From the Olshanskys, Tillie courted Rae's goodwill with news that Karla
was "all animation & movement & plumping out." There were "several
1905'ers (real ones)" living near the beach, including two former "central
committee members of the Bund till 1921." One was Genya Gorelick, Al
Richmond's mother. Walking with Tillie, Genya told about being imprisoned by the czar in 1905 and by the Bolsheviks after 1917. Later, Tillie talked
about Genya's suffering under the czar, not under the Bolsheviks.

Jack worked only sporadically on the waterfront so Tillie sent advice
about getting food stamps and a relief number, avoiding the landlord,
renting out Karla's room and a couch for twenty dollars, and confiscating

Georgie's paycheck to "throw it at the landlord." She rationalized borrowing from Jack's father: "we'll pay it back someday." For their sex life, not their pocketbook, she begged "Jackie darling, darling Jackie—say to hell with everything, & come down for 2 or 3 days—and sleep with me in the big bed of your father & mother in the sun." She was "terribly drawn to you, same attraction as to Abe but this [is] a won-out passion." Her desire did lure him to Venice. They posed on the beach, Tillie in a sexy two-piece bathing suit, arm-in-arm with Jack and his brother Leon. She looked happy, well-kept, and energized. Suddenly, the "old miracle" revived: "I started writing last night." She tried painterly images: "the lemon and gold pier lights very clear in the twilight, the long slow line of the breakers from Ocean Park to Venice, and the ocean, swollen and rustling and glinting with green and crimson light." She thought of writing an "ulcer story" about Genya with "the Venice pier" as background. If she had "managed that hour a day" writing her novel, she might now be able to write about women like Ida, Rae, and Genya, but she had not.

By summer's end, Tillie returned with the girls to the house on Alpine Terrace.[68] A letter from Rae awaited her with news that Rae's sister, just three years older than Tillie, was dead. Tillie replied sympathetically and assured Rae that she and the girls were well, although their house was "too much for me right now. Any energies I have left I want (have) to give to writing." She had begun a book after Julie's birth, "before I got sick with the sulfanilimade" and was "working on it again. Just three hours a day." Jack was "working at odd jobs since you left. Out of the warehouse and the culinary halls. He's getting as muscled as a circus strong man." Now he taught at the California Labor School and finally got a full-time job in Merchants Ice and Cold Storage warehouses.

Back in 1937, Tillie had been reassured by the *Daily Worker*'s attack on the "filthy falsehood" that Stalin might by aligned with "the bestial Nazi regime." On 23 August 1939, however, that falsehood turned into truth, as the Soviets signed a nonaggression pact with the Nazis. Hitler ceded the Baltic States to the USSR, and Hitler and Stalin split Poland, then Germany invaded Poland. World War II began. Hitler's villainy was beyond question. Of Stalin's, Tillie still took no notice. Earl Browder rationalized that the Stalin-Hitler pact contributed to peace. When the League of American Writers refused to protest the Stalin/Hitler alliance, many writers, including Granville Hicks and Malcolm Cowley, resigned from the League. Many comrades resigned from the party. Neither Tillie Lerner nor Jack Olsen, however, resigned.[69] Still obedient to the party, she followed its orders to return to Los Angeles during October and November. There, as Matilda

Lerner, she checked out books from the public library, using the party's Winter Street address.[70]

Tillie had sent spirited letters from Venice in the past summer mostly to Jack, without writing her parents at all. Angry and worried, Ida apparently boarded a train, sitting up all the way to California. She had not seen Karla since she and Sam put the tiny girl on a train to Los Angeles in October 1937, so she was relieved to find her granddaughter no longer emaciated and Jack earning a reliable income. Perplexed to find Tillie and the baby gone, Ida apparently did not complain about a pain in her stomach.

For at least five years, Tillie had used Karla's "tummy" as an excuse for her own dereliction. Now Grandmother Ida insisted that Karla must have her long-postponed appendectomy and hernia operation. Perhaps this was when Ida wrote a grim poem in Yiddish, lamenting "I cry, 'Come, Help Me,'/ But no reply to my cry."[71] Apparently, Jack did hear her cry and rushed Ida to Mount Zion Hospital, where she was operated on for gall stones, on probably 27 November. He got word to Tillie, and she sent a special delivery letter to Sam, who responded on 29 November 1939 to the "unexpected tragedy." He and Ida had recently moved from the old Caldwell Street house to a larger house at 3419 Lafayette Avenue, a shaded street in a hilly, more affluent part of Omaha.[72] He had "mortgaged everything I could" and now had "no work." Still, "Mother should get the best treatment obtainable." He sent fifty dollars and asked Tillie to postpone other bills "till Ill be able to pick up a little work. Mother must not know any financial burden." His concern was that Ida "shall not worry."[73]

Jack, who had recently become an official in the ILWU, wanted Tillie home. She faced another ultimatum: either remain in L.A. as a Communist operative or disobey party orders and return to her family. This time she followed her heart. Ida went back to Omaha, Julie turned one, and Karla turned seven, an event she celebrated wearing a Mexican dress from Rae. Tillie began following the "Women's Slant" column in *People's World*, tallying expenses, listing "cheap meat cuts," and noting penny-pinching recipes mixing meats with cornmeal, cracked wheat, potatoes, or polenta. She joined a "Women's Committee to Lower the High Cost of Living" and vowed to "scrub kitchen floor." Her notebooks became a mish-mash of political and maternal issues. She mixed up "notes on history of Socialism in U.S." with a "pattern for how to make panties."[74]

Thanking "the old vigorous Rae" for Karla's birthday dress, Tillie tried to allay worries: Karla had started the first half of the third grade and was making perfect grades in every subject except spelling. Tillie made a little socialist parable about Karla: though a boy friend in the third grade gave her presents, she fell for a first grader who gave her nothing. Karla added a note to her "Dear Auntte Rae": "I wish I could see you and bonnie." Signing "love Karla" and making Xs for kisses, she sounded lonely.

Believing that the party took precedence over personal loyalties, Tillie had neglected one child and aborted others, been unfaithful to her husband, hidden her marriage, invented another to the man she loved but left according to party dictates. She had skipped out on debts to doctors, hospitals, and landlords. She had taken Random House's money but sacrificed her literary promise for party organizing. Near the end of 1937, she had not been able to "pour it out—tell the truth." Since 1938, however, Tillie had tried to balance party loyalties and family responsibilities, but in November 1939 her absence at the party's behest imperiled both her daughter's and her mother's health. In late 1939, an abashed Tillie realized that she must be more responsive and responsible to loved ones and to her own gifts. The question remained, however, whether she had frittered away not only her time but also her talents.

CHAPTER 8

WAR–RELIEF HEROINE

1940–1945

After all it is my livelihood, my contribution to society, and my reputation.
—Tillie Olsen to Jack Olsen, April 1944

To Tillie, former president Herbert Hoover's 1938 Berlin meeting with Hitler had proved that capitalism was in cahoots with fascism. Hitler's 1939 awards to Henry Ford and Charles A. Lindbergh confirmed her theory.[1] Stalin's 1939 nonaggression pact with Hitler, however, shook her either-or assumptions by putting communism in cahoots with fascism. As 1940 began, Germany occupied Austria, Czechoslovakia, and most of Poland, Italy occupied Ethiopia and Albania, and Spain was a military dictatorship; only Britain and France were left to fight the Nazis. The United States seemed disinterested, Tillie despondent.

With the outside world at risk, she settled with Jack, Karla, and Julie in the first floor of 50 Divisadero Street, a pleasant ginger-bread-trimmed frame house. Committed to being a better mother, she read nursery rhymes and invented ditties, took her daughters to Buena Vista Park, helped Karla with spelling words, and introduced her to *Little Women*. After Jack left early for the docks and Karla for McKinley Elementary School in a freshly ironed dress, Tillie was left with toddler Julie and chores like hand-washing clothes, squeezing them in a "mangler," hanging them out, ironing them, cooking meals, and cleaning house. The "house & Karla & Julie" made life a "duty, the kids. Money bungling." Even sex, "the flesh as Jack sees it," seemed a duty. She felt incapable "of furnishing my emotions into words" and accused herself: "you relapse to motherhood & scratches on paper." One scratched story idea was about a preacher who was a "unit organizer" and kept party notes in the Bible, mixing up Marx and Jesus. One was about "women who kicked their husbands out of bed & into the picket

142

line." She imagined another about Spanish-speaking migrant workers who tell bilingual priests about abuses from their bosses, only to have the priests protect the bosses. A neighbor remembered Tillie "wouldn't show anybody anything she wrote," perhaps because she invented dramatic situations but not resolutions.[2]

Between Tillie's twenty-eighth and Jack's twenty-ninth birthdays, they made a February excursion into the Sierra Mountains that soothed her domestic frustrations. They encountered such lovely snow they felt like "hibernating up there," as she wrote Rae Schochet on the first day of spring in an unusually affectionate letter. She reassured Rae about Karla, who looked "after Gazoonie," beat Jack at Chinese checkers, and could "wheeze out recognizable tunes on the harmonica." She was still "original at spelling," a flaw Tillie jokingly blamed on Rae. Tillie said she was "working on a book now about your generation of foreign born women," but her plans were "loose and feverish."[3] She recalled Faribault "that spring I was pregnant with Karla and wrote the first part of the Holbrook book, and was so sick. We had the middle bedroom, and there was even snow when we first came, and the branches of the trees outside the window were skinny and naked—You had such a quiet, deep house." To that nostalgic note, Tillie added, at the top of page four, two questions: "Have you heard anything at all from Abe? Did I tell you I'd broken the news to Karla about her having had a daddy before Jack?"[4]

Astonished to receive a long, legible letter from Tillie, Rae replied with news of her newly bourgeois life, taking a Delphian self-improvement course, presiding over the local League of Women Voters, listening to opera on the radio, and driving a new Dodge. But "as for Abe. Not a word in all these years since that May [1937] when I last saw him in Los Angeles. Should you get any news where he is I would like his address. It seems strange that I should be writing to you and not be able to locate him. Life does funny trics to human beings some very strange and puzling." It was indeed strange and puzzling that, two years and four months after Abe's death, Rae had not heard of it; strange that Tillie had not mentioned him; and even stranger that Tillie asked if Rae had heard from him.[5]

Finally closing the tumultuous Abe chapter of her life, Tillie vowed to "pull myself together." She volunteered for the ILWU's Women's Auxiliary and for the PTA at Karla's school. Her work table was a muddle of books, toys, newspapers, memo pads, scribbles of favorite quotations, and abortive story ideas. Library books told the life stories of great men and of a few significant women. They offered, however, no models for a book about unknown immigrant mothers, like Ida and Rae.

Charlie Chaplin's *The Great Dictator* delighted her, not only because people said she looked like the heroine, played by Paulette Goddard, or because Chaplin's slap-stick suited her zany sense of humor, but because the film ends with a plea for all races and creeds to overturn a system that "makes men torture" and has "poisoned men's souls." Most Americans, however, lost the impact of Chaplin's warning as they chortled over his hilarious, cinematically effective, satire on Hitler (as the Dictator of Tomania) and Mussolini (as Emperor of Bacteria).[6] Chaplin's antics encouraged Americans to think of the real dictators as buffoons, though France had now fallen to the Axis powers and Prime Minister Winston Churchill claimed to have little but "blood, toil, tears, and sweat" and the Royal Air Force to defend Britain against a German blitzkrieg.[7]

Vicki Lerner wrote Tillie that Ida had learned to "'live' in her own right." She and Sam were founders of a new Labor Lyceum; Harry, now a lawyer, had spoken about pacifism at its dedication, but he had drawn number thirty in the draft lottery, and Ida was terrified that he would be drafted.[8] Gene's Washington University graduation address was read into the Congressional Record, and Senator John Thomas of Idaho had put Gene on his staff.[9] Vicki had a boyfriend, Sonny Richards. If her list of family accomplishments served as a rebuke to Tillie, so did her suggestion that the "folks would like a grandson."

That September, Hitler sent as many as two hundred bombers over London most nights, demolishing power stations and rail lines. After intoning his CBS broadcasts from a rooftop with "This is London," Edward R. Murrow described in appalling detail the Nazi "blitz" of that great city. Tillie and Jack and their friends hovered around suitcase-sized radios fearing that fascism was vanquishing civilization. With former Agricultural Secretary Henry Wallace as running mate, FDR won an unprecedented third term against Republican Wendell Willkie. Relieved, Tillie now felt bypassed by "modern war & modern politics." She vowed to resurrect herself as "a living, acting part of the world."[10]

Her colitis, however, landed her in Mt. Zion Hospital late in 1940. In a last letter to Rae, she said she had just needed to escape chores and sleep "12 hrs. a day."[11] She read Hemingway's *For Whom the Bell Tolls*, about brave Spanish peasants and the Americans who fought for them.[12] She heard Edward R. Murrow describe valiant firefighters' battle to save St. Paul's Cathedral. Confidence, like Chaplin's in *The Great Dictator*, that dictators will die, but liberty will never perish, now sounded empty.

Tillie's time in Mt. Zion strengthened her stamina and her will. After her twenty-ninth birthday in early 1941, she cleared her desk and found off-and-on child care for Julie. She began a new activist phase from home, typing skits and a school newsletter for McKinley's Parent Teachers Association. She supervised rehearsals, organized meetings, and applied for a job but worried, "what kind of a mother are you?"[13]

Though the United States had supplied Churchill with WWI navy destroyers and FDR spoke of America as the "great arsenal of democracy" against fascism, the United States still did not intervene. In his January address to Congress, FDR spoke of defending American freedoms of speech and religion and from want and fear. A month later, Woody Guthrie recorded "This Land is Your Land," subtitled "God Blessed America." John Ford's film of *The Grapes of Wrath*, with Henry Fonda as Tom Joad, suggested that good Americans could survive the worse of plagues, despite the villainy of such capitalists as publishing magnate Hearst, exposed in Orson Welles's *Citizen Kane*. But publishing giant Henry Luce, in a *Life* magazine manifesto, defined America's destiny as a global empire which would make the twentieth "The American Century," a disturbing vision of hegemony.

Budd Schulberg had heard that Hollywood comrade Stanley Lawrence was assassinated in Spain, not by Franco's forces, but by the party.[14] Schulberg concluded that Communists were as evil as the capitalists he depicted in *What Makes Sammy Run*, who think that "going through life with a conscience is like driving your car with the brakes on." Tillie's recognized herself in *What Makes Sammy Run*, not as a conscienceless Communist, but as the "gal all the critics were nominating a couple of years back to write the great American novel."[15] Now her great novel was lost, but she had declared "first duty = better world." Abandoning any thought of making her "scratches on paper" into real stories, she began protesting the high cost of living, the health risks attendant on milk and meat shortages, the burdens left to working mothers, and forces depleting children's self-esteem. Elected president of McKinley's PTA, she asked herself: "is that what you really want to be a club woman? Are you building politically?"[16] Actually, she was. Chameleonlike, she had switched selves again, now becoming dynamo defender, not of the CP, but of women.

On 10 May, the German blitz hit such major landmarks of civilization as the British Museum and the Houses of Parliament. "March of Time" newsreels showed appalling devastation. Nevertheless, at the June American Writers Congress, Richard Wright, Ralph Ellison, and Cary McWilliams, among others, argued that the United States should cure racism at home before fighting it abroad. Then on 22 June 1941, Hitler broke his pact with Stalin. As Hitler began a march east toward Moscow and south to the

Black Sea, exterminating Jews and Bolshevists along the way, the League of American Writers suddenly abandoned neutrality, as did the American left.[17] Fearing the recently passed Smith Act, which outlawed subversive organizations, both the CP and the CIO established their patriotism by calling for the United States to join the Allies.

From a CP plenum in San Francisco, Jack wrote Tillie that members cheered to hear that Britain would aid the Soviet Union against Germany and that China would aid the USSR should Japan attack. A "Louise" suggested that the CP cooperate with the PTA to advance social agendas, a move that would validate Tillie's work and put her back into the political arena.[18] At a CIO Congress in Los Angeles, Tillie put on extra face cream, pulled her curls up with combs, donned a shoulder-padded suit, and became a presence.[19] Now that Germany and Russia were enemies and Britain and Russia were allies, Tillie was invigorated. She parlayed PTA work into the presidency of the California CIO Ladies' Auxiliary, membership on a new CIO War Relief Committee, and chairmanship of a board on price-rationing in case of war.

While Tillie remained at the CIO Congress, comrades Don Healey and Dorothy Ray invited Jack over for dinner and games of gin rummy.[20] Then Jack dined out twice with, improbably enough, Harry Lerner. Back in 1930, Ida and Sam had sent Harry to check on Tillie in Chicago. In July 1941, they encouraged him to check on Tillie in San Francisco and to bring Karla for a stay in the big house on Lafayette Avenue. Jack borrowed five dollars to share "a good French meal" at North Beach with Harry and advised him about San Francisco gifts for Ida, Sam, and Vicki. They avoided talking politics.[21] When the Lerners telegraphed that Harry's draft case was "suddenly coming up," Jack quickly drove him to the "Frisco side" of the Bay Bridge. From there, Harry hitchhiked to Omaha, without seeing Tillie or bringing Karla to her grandparents.

On his return, he wrote Tillie about the Lerners' "spacious well-kept yard, with flowers and grass greener than any in California. The house so spotless, with floors waxed, new covers on the front-room set, and the refrigerator well stocked, and Jewish bread." These compliments to Ida's housekeeping were a slight to Tillie's, as was the invitation: "all this is what Karla can have, to her enduring good and remembrance." He congratulated Tillie on having Jack for a husband. Vicki (whom he still called "Yetta") was marrying Sonny Richards in a religious ceremony "performed at home." Tillie was too busy in her new CIO roles to attend, so Sam wired forty dollars for Karla to come alone.

Often derelict about paying bills, Tillie and Jack and the girls moved at least twice in 1941 and ended back on Alpine Terrace.[22] Having distinguished himself for fairness and toughness on the docks, Jack became ILWU business agent and education director. He sat on the ILWU draft board. He began teaching an "official union class on Historical Problems with the CIO," trying to remake the CIO's historical anti-war, anti-imperialist position into a pro-"people's war" stance.

Jimmy Durante's absurd comedy *You're in the Army Now* encouraged American neutrality until, at dawn on 7 December 1941, the Japanese bombed Pearl Harbor, virtually eliminating the American fleet. Roosevelt declared that that day would "live in infamy" and that "righteous might" would retaliate. The United States declared war on Japan. Though his troops were bogged down in mud and snow short of Moscow, Hitler declared war on the United States, which declared war on Germany and Axis Powers. Americans became almost universally prowar. Men in Jack's union began volunteering.

Back in Omaha, the draft board rejected Harry Lerner's plea to escape military service, but as a pacifist lawyer he enrolled in administrative quartermaster training and soon was stationed with the Army Air Force in India. Joseph Davis volunteered for the Army Medical Corps. Like Ida, Gene believed nothing justified war's brutality. He left his senate post to work in New York for the Women's League for Peace and Justice.[23] With her family, Tillie fervently hoped that twenty-six different but "united nations" might outlaw war and guarantee global peace, justice, and religious freedom.

After Pearl Harbor, the big three automotive industries turned to producing tanks; factories ran day and night making ships, planes, and rubber tires. While tin cans were recycled, bobbi pins, zippers, and rubber bands, along with refrigerators and cars, were unavailable. Women went on assembly lines in arms factories and "manned" jobs like driving streetcars. Families planted private "victory gardens" so big farms could feed the troops. Red meat was mostly reserved to keep up soldiers' strength so people ate cottage cheese or processed meat products like Treet and Spam, mindful of ditties like "save your scraps to beat the Japs." They put orange dye in cheap white oleo to make it look like butter. The government rationed gas and issued each person a book of stamps for an allotment of meat, eggs, sugar, milk, and coffee. After years of feeling too ill and frazzled to write or work effectively, Tillie was now too busy mixing PTA, CIO, and domestic responsibilities to note her thirtieth birthday on 14 January 1942.[24]

In February, when Sam and Ida went to New York City for a Workman's Circle convention, Gene bought Ida a green coat with a fur collar to replace her customary black garb. Afterwards, she giddily confided she was thinking of marrying Sam. Gene said that, after nearly thirty years and six children, marriage would be "the funniest comic act in history." Still, he thought Ida might wear a wedding ring so he and Lil collaborated to buy a ring that Vicki and Sam chose.[25]

In March, radio KYA, the ILWU's station, interviewed Tillie and a butchers' union officer. Without stuttering, she urged listeners to support FDR's cost of living controls and not pay more than the controlled price of, for example, 49¢ a pound for boneless round steak. She explained that violating controls would create a black market and inflate prices; ordinary people would be unable to afford meat; their families would be malnourished; sickness would cause absenteeism at work and school.[26] She spent most of 1942 making speeches on topics like "emergency milk relief" and arguing that rationing should benefit soldiers but not rob civilians of health.[27] Though liberal Culbert Olson had lost the governorship to anticommunist Earl Warren,[28] Tillie remained defiant. Like Vice President Henry Wallace, she hoped cooperation would make the twentieth, not the American Century of Empire, but the "Century of the Common Man."[29]

When Tillie wrote her parents that she had had a health relapse, Sam invited her to recuperate in their "lovely," too-large house. He warned her not to send the girls alone because caring for three-year-old Julie would be "tough on mother." Tillie could pay her hospital bill with the forty dollars he had sent Karla. She took the train to Omaha and, despite Sam's warning, left both daughters and promised that Karla would take care of Julie. Then she sped back home. In the first issue of the *ILWU Dispatcher*, on 18 December 1942, a gossip column called "Hot Cargo" noted: "JACK OLSEN finally got off to a well-earned vacation. It's a honeymoon too because he and TILLIE are such busy little bees that they've never gotten 'round to it before."[30] Tillie was not sick after all.

The *Dispatcher* sent women mixed messages. Almost every issue included a photo of a sexy woman in a bathing suit, and the "Women's Work" page printed menus, sewing patterns, and articles like "Pretty Legs? Use union hose." It also affirmed "Sex Equality Vital to Production." It endorsed free after-school child care so "Mama" could be "Free to Build Air Planes." It applauded strong actresses and called female defense workers the "women behind the man behind the gun." It printed pictures of "Rosie the Riveter" holding a rivet gun, showing her biceps, and keeping a powder puff handy.

As 1943 began, *Time* magazine named Joseph Stalin "Man of the Year" for 1942 for his "tough guy" refusal to succumb to Hitler. Many Americans who thought of Stalin as Satan were upset by *Time*'s choice and even more offended to be fighting with, not against, Stalin. Ida begged Gene to get Eleanor Roosevelt to warn FDR against Stalin.[31]

When Labor groups planned a "march inland" to recruit members along the way, vivacious Tillie led the marchers, and a comrade remarked to Jack that she was "built like a brick shithouse." The marchers spent a night in a big warehouse in Lathrop. Titillated by bodies breathing nearby, by the risk of discovery, and the thrill of exhibitionism, Tillie sought out Jack's body. They made love, without light and without protection.[32]

After a month in Omaha, Karla and Julie took a train back to San Francisco, and Ida went to D.C. to help Jann with her family. Left alone, Sam lamented to Tillie: "You, after many years of desertion came home with lovely two grandchildren [and] did not even give me a chance to catch [?] news of life and extraordinary developments in our material and spiritual world." Sam had his suspicions about Tillie's "spell of sicknesses" and speculated there "must be some error in Heaven. I'll look into it if I'll be ever in there." To Karla and Julie he wrote: "you have given me happiness while you were here."

Hollywood was creating a new genre of female-reporter movies, played by stars like Claudette Colbert, Rosalind Russell, and Katharine Hepburn.[33] Tillie followed their example and in early February joined the staff of the *Labor Herald: Official California C.I.O. Newspaper.* Instructing readers to "Watch Close," she explained how price ceilings were misused to exploit the consumer. Her article on "Price Gouge Rackets" shows an articulate Tillie effectively yoking women's issues to the war effort. She took charge of the CIO Council for Child Care. She wrote public letters supporting emergency milk supplies and a leftist woman candidate. While running a canteen at a USO center, she publicized "labor's role in the war" to servicemen otherwise inclined to be "predominately anti-labor." She had become a powerful publicist for her causes and herself.[34]

At a June 1943 convention, the massive ILWU made a crucial pledge not to strike during wartime. The "Hot Cargo" column offered a personal angle: "Jack Olsen (S. F.) was right in the groove, jitterbugging 'n everything. . . . But mama Tillie made a martyr of herself by staying away from the Chinese Banquet to teach a consumer class." Tillie also skipped the Chinese food to avoid nausea. She was pregnant. She and Jack called their expected son "little Lathrop."

Aided by ordinary citizen's sacrifices, the military used brilliant intelligence, inspired battle plans, massive troop deployment, and rapid arms manufacturing. After Mussolini was arrested in a bloodless revolution, Roosevelt, in his "Fireside Chat," on 28 July 1943, proclaimed that the "angered forces of common humanity" had turned back barbarity and corruption. He assured listeners of the "first crack in the Axis" defenses. Soon Italy withdrew from the war, at least on paper.[35] It seemed that the pestilence's spread might be stopped, dictators might die, and liberty might not perish after all.

That summer, Tillie sank under a wave of "physical exhaustion." She was too "feverish" for anything except "practicals": recipes for cooking, child-rearing, CIO and PTA organizing, and fall campaigning.[36] On 7 August 1943, the Office of War Information invited her to join a "Housewives Panel" to report "what women are saying" about rationing problems, price control, commodity shortages, and other civilian supply issues. Unbeknownst to the FBI, she apparently became a special War Office informant.[37]

That fall Karla entered a handsome public school overlooking the bay; the school was named for Kate Kennedy, who had used her positions in the public school system to war against ignorance. Kennedy's example reminded Tillie that "women's work" could make a difference. In the *Dispatcher,* "Sister Tillie Olsen contributes her own prized special recipe for a Victory Special for the months ahead":

> VICTORY SPECIAL: Recipe for more meat in the pot, more milk in the ice box, more bread on the table. To make a good Congress Victory Special, the housewife first must shake well Congressmen who are putting arsenic in the home front porridge. Then add a pinch of letters, telegrams and a dash of delegations. Place in a high pressure cooker and steam thoroughly. If the first try doesn't take, don't get discouraged. Add more letters, wires, delegations and a dash of pepper. Most essential of all, apply even greater pressure. Prepared singly the recipe is difficult to master. It brings best results with community participation. If all attempts fail, remember that new Congressmen will be on the market again in '44.

A decade before, Tillie would have condemned such a "recipe" as an effete liberal attempt to work within the system. Not only had the CP and the CIO become prowar, so had Tillie, as long as women's issues were at the heart of the war effort.

Tillie's ten-month baby did not arrive until 17 November 1943. "Little Lathrop" turned out to be, as the nurses told her, "just" a girl.[38] On 28 November in Sam's reply to a birth notice he suggested that the "Mother of Three" was setting a record for a "female tribe." He addressed the baby as "nameless" and advised that, while children give parents pain, sleepless nights, and many worries, they give grandparents "only pleasure and great joy" and "birthday worries" about presents. He counseled Tillie "we hope by now you are about fully recovered to assume your duties first of all as mother and also spare a few minutes to write us a letter we should be able to read." The healthy baby was not "nameless" for long—she was Katherine Jo Olsen: "Katherine" for Käthe Kollwitz, Katherine Mansfield, and Kate

Kennedy. She was "Jo," at Karla's request, for the outspoken hero of Louisa May Alcott's *Little Women*.[39] Sloughing off the weight of her strong predecessors, the baby was soon just "Kathie." Vicki sent congratulations, saying no more about their parents' wish for a grandson. After marrying, Vicki and Sonny Richards visited her siblings in the east and then settled with the senior Lerners at 3419 Lafayette Avenue.[40] She was thrilled that Broadway producers were reading Gene's plays.

As 1944 began, Karla won a prize for an essay answering how children can support "Our Armed Forces?" They could sell war bonds and play "games with our wounded" at hospitals and, most important, "kids can help their mothers."[41] On 7 January, a *Herald* headline confirmed accusations about Hearst's fascism by saying he made a "Deal With Hitler." By 21 January, a resilient Tillie was the on the "1944 Manpower Committee of the California CIO Council."[42] FBI informants considered her "extremely active in the affairs of the Communist Political Association in recruiting new members and sponsoring campaigns for Communist candidates for public office."

That February, the *Labor Herald* announced that Jack Olsen would teach a course on "You and Your Union" at the California Labor School.[43] With students volunteering to battle tyranny (and brave soldiers regularly depicted on the silver screen), however, Jack began to feel cowardly for not volunteering.[44] He also felt left out of Tillie's busy life. She seemed hardly to need him so he visited the U.S. Army office, renounced his deferment (as an older family man), and enlisted. Furious Tillie felt abandoned, but sensible Tillie admitted he was wise not to consult her. Because only wives got military benefits, she proposed marriage. The small ceremony was on 29 February 1944 in the Chapel of Grace, Grace Cathedral, on San Francisco's Nob Hill. A left-leaning Episcopal canon officiated. On the wedding license of Tillie Lerner and Jack Olsen, she acknowledged Abe Goldfarb as her former husband, herself as his widow.[45]

The *Dispatcher* and *Labor Herald* had long called her "Mrs. Tillie Olsen" and "Sister Tillie Olsen" and for years her father had sent letters to "Mr.& Mrs. J. Olsen" so she did not publicize the wedding. She did tell her parents about Jack's enlistment and asked to borrow $1000 for a house and a piano. For some years, Sam had been buying, fixing, and selling old houses for profit, but the work "played to much on my nerves." Now he worked "for 40.00 a week 10 hours a day and 6 days a week. It is hard work and I do not like the job. Am used to be a free man." He could only help her buy the piano.

On 11 March, the ILWU honored business agent Jack Olsen for joining the ranks of some three thousand Local 6 members already inducted into

the Armed Forces. The *Dispatcher* printed a photo in which Jack clasps
Tillie tightly around her waist. While he looks rather besottedly at her alone,
Tillie's eyes cut away from him to give the cameraman a penetrating stare.
At thirty-two, she was hardly faunlike; she was gorgeous. On 16 March 1944,
Jack's thirty-third birthday, "the house was swarming with people all who
came to say good luck and come back Jack." He and Tillie and the three
girls made a hasty move from Alpine to an apartment over a shop at 903
Castro Street in a multi-ethnic neighborhood. Jack expediently resigned
from the Communist Party. Before he went into training he and Tillie spent
a last night in a cabin near San Jose.[46]

By the beginning of April, Jack had joined Company D, 81st infantry
for training at Camp Roberts, south of Salinas. His enlistment somehow
validated Tillie to her parents. On 4 April, Sam wrote her, "my worries
are over and you are forgiven." He hoped: "now since you'll be in a [CIO]
office, may we expect letters oftener and typed if possible, easier to read."
He wrote Jack that his generation was "still dreaming" of the reforms he
and Ida had fought for in 1905. With Joseph Davis a major in the medical
corps stationed in England, Sam and Ida would soon have two sons-in-law
on the European front and a son in India, all doing their part to vanquish
the curse of fascism.

Jack's presence had been a stabilizing and enabling influence. Now his
absence was empowering. Tillie began working as Northern California
director of the National CIO War Relief Committee. On 7 April, the *Labor
Herald* printed a dashing photograph of her, with her long wavy hair piled
above her face, her eyes cut to the side, and her lips closed in a provoca-
tive smile.[47] It printed a photo of Tillie offering a bearded man a choice
of razors to make him a properly clean-shaven sailor. Questioning price
ceilings and championing well-regulated rationing, Tillie made nutrition
a front-page political issue. Complaining about taking "work home with
me—deadlines to meet," she wrote Jack she ought to begin her speech "on
labor participation" like "Jimmy Durante—I will now deliver a few appropriated remarks."[48] She enclosed "family" clippings, mostly about her.

Jack's absence greatly eased Tillie's financial burden. Not only was she
paid for her CIO work and *Labor Herald* work, but her marriage certificate
entitled her to funds from the Office of Dependency Benefits. Her first
allotment arrived barely a week after Jack left, and she enjoyed an "orgy
of paying people back." She actually "put aside this week's salary" to hire
her first housekeeper, though she would have to borrow money to pay the
utility bill because the lights had been turned off when she forgot it.[49] Tillie
moved freely in more prestigious circles. She lunched with a "big shot of
the State War Chest." She dashed off outlines for improvised speeches. She

sent Jack quick little "tidbits," amusing family narratives, lively accounts of her hectic activities, and erotic love letters.

Needing to travel for the CIO Red Cross blood drive, Tillie took driving lessons, put down $100, and agreed to pay $44.89 a month for a used car she dubbed "the heap." She opened a checking account to keep herself "on my strait jacket budget." She became a "financial juggler," firing one housekeeper and hiring another. Coming home to little Kathie was a delight: "darling little mugwumple is brrrrrrring out little singy noises—such a cozy sound, like a teakettle." She had her own stationery headed: "National C.I.O War Relief Committee, Mrs. Tillie Olsen, Northern California Area Director, 150 Golden Gate Avenue."[50] Also an air raid warden, she owned her own gas mask.

In 1937, Tillie's vow to kill her ego had caused negligence, guilt, and despair. By 1944, she had rehabilitated herself by reclaiming her ego. In one letter she told Jack, "I want you terribly." But she also said she needed to talk about her work before next making love: "after all it is my livelihood, my contribution to society, and my reputation." She remained enough of a party insider to hear a speech titled "Teheran cancels Munich." "Teheran" referred to the November 1943 meeting in Teheran, Iran, when the "Big Three"—Roosevelt, Churchill, and Stalin—planned a two-front final assault against Germany.[51] The speaker told party leaders that "Teheran" really meant that the Allies would make territorial concessions to Stalin.

Tillie churned out love letters and official reports and left her home full of "dirt, noise, disorder."[52] She had to clean it before she hired another helper because the five-room upstairs apartment would not hold a live-in housekeeper. Shuffling "999000 other clamoring *musts*," Tillie postponed a rendezvous with Jack but wrote that their "dearest little Katushikins" was "the best and patientish baby Jackie—all polkadotted with chickenpox, but so good and smily and grateful if you toss a come-to-think-of-it-you-exist look at her." She would not get a driver's license until 5 May, but drove anyway, "stalled her twice—once sputtering up the Castro Hill—most embarrassing."

After reading this tally of professional obligations, domestic worries, childhood sickness, and illegal driving, Jack finagled a furlough. He hitchhiked to San Francisco, hopped on trolleys, and surprised his wife and daughters. The bigger girls were so elated they hardly let him be alone with Tillie. She was thrilled by love-making but aggravated that, after he left, she had to stay up until dawn speed-typing an overdue report.[53] She feared Jack "must think I am a most disarranged, disorganized, disorderly female which honest I really am not." She made a "stern resolution" not to procrastinate writing other reports.

Jack's cousin Pauline had married in 1940 and lost her young husband just after their baby was born. Now she turned to Tillie for a yeasty mix of casual hospitality, lively music, political arguments, and madcap jokes. One evening Tillie's cousin Lou, one of the Omaha Braude sons who had run away from home, also appeared, and Tillie shared with them inside information that "Teheran" meant establishing classless worker states in Eastern Europe. She managed a brief rendezvous with Jack on 13 May, south of Camp Roberts, at the Paso Robles Inn, the "half-way point on Highway 101 between San Francisco & Los Angeles." After "three speeding hours" in bed, he hitchhiked back to camp. Tillie drove up to Salinas on CIO business. Next she started for New York City on the San Francisco Overland Limited for a CIO convention. Jack regretted she was going three thousand miles away.[54] Still he wrote Karla, his "biggest girl," to thank her for staying "without your mama and daddy" and taking care of "Katushie" while "Mama and Julie are away." Tillie did not, however, take Julie with her, though she pretended she did.[55]

On the train, Tillie assured Jack that there were only "20 days to go" before they were together again. She described Wyoming and Agnes Smedley, who "grew with such pain, and never flowered." Speeding over the plains, she recalled running away from home alone in 1927 and with Abe in 1930.[56] From Chicago, she took a train to D.C., to join the Office of War Information's "Housewives Panel." She visited the old Senate Chamber and the Lincoln Memorial and then took a night train to New York, arriving at seven on the Saturday morning, 27 May. She called Gene to ask if he were a famous playwright; then she fell asleep in her tiny room in the Hotel Wellington, south of Central Park. She woke to collect a check from CIO headquarters, post a note to Jack, and prepare for dinner.

As an upcoming playwright, Gene arranged for a glamorous dinner atop a building across from Central Park. With Albert Bein and a young actress, they sat in "a windowed corner." As the Park became a dark mystery and the city a sparkling temptation, Tillie felt "the town submissive at our feet." Afterward, she met CIO delegates who demanded "Teheran talk (from me)." She wrote Jack that she had once tried to "crack this town" but was "rooted solid now" in, presumably, San Francisco with him, but her CIO celebrity mothered "bad ambitions" to "be somebody in this pile of rock."

At the conference, Tillie made a rousing argument about communism's crucial place in America's "Big Push" toward victory. Then she and other activists traveled to the Hudson Shore Labor School, near West Park, New York. Teasing Jack about the "attractive" guys there, Tillie assured him that she was "corseted in indifference—tonight had quite a time (tho I enjoyed it) holding off some wolves." The retreat officially ended with a "campfire picnic beside the Hudson" and antics that lasted until dawn. Tillie got back to the City in time to send Jack a postcard of the Washington Bridge with a promise that their sexual reunion on Saturday, 10 June, would dynamite the bridge cables keeping them apart. She sent Jack a contract apparently making her a spokeswoman for the CIO.

Learning to fire a bazooka was almost as traumatic for Jack as reading "that contract you sent, forced myself to. That's all I can say about it." Apparently trying to redirect her ambition, he went on to say how "damn proud" he was of her writing, by which he did not mean newspaper or speech writing. Tillie's whirlwind of prominent appearances and crusades, however, had supplanted her desire to write a novel, a book on the universal mother, or even short stories. She left New York on Sunday, spent a night in Chicago,[57] met "rank and file" workers at the local ILWU office, and Monday evening "boarded my train early—hoping to sleep" before reaching Omaha, after hectic days in D.C., New York, West Park, and Chicago.

At 5:30 on Tuesday morning, 6 June, however, the porter "trumpeted it thru the car" waking everybody: "'that Day is here—we're giving it to 'em now—we's started across.'" The Allies were crossing the English Channel to retake Europe from Hitler. The porter's D-Day call roused Tillie to rush to the club car for more news. Approaching Omaha, she heard that Allied forces had diverted the Germans with fake raids. Eighteen thousand British and American parachutists had landed in Normandy, clearing the way for amphibious tanks that brought 155,000 Allied troops ashore in one day.

When Tillie got to 3419 Lafayette Avenue, probably by taxi, she found Ida alone; Sam, Vicki, and Sonny Richards were all working. At first, drama queen Tillie treated five letters from Jack as lost treasure and "like a miser I counted and recounted my gold." Ida was not impressed: after all Jack was still in training camp, and Tillie could see him when she got home. Admonishing Tillie, Ida said, "she won't go to a wedding unless she can be the bride or to a funeral unless she can be the corpse." Tillie wondered if the phrasing were original with Ida, who replied, "gay avek, original, shmoriginal, alts hat been gasagt—something about how many thousands of years mankind has had to say things."[58] Tillie disliked Omaha's newly "opulent look," meaning her parents' house with its wide porch, fish scale shingles, gabled roof, and large rooms, at odds with her preferred image of Lerner poverty. When Sam got home, they heard that Germans had pinned down Americans only on Normandy's "Omaha Beach."

Tillie was in San Francisco by Friday when a friend, driving up Castro Street in a truck rented for a "REGISTER TO VOTE campaign," serenaded Tillie "over a loud speaker."[59] By Saturday, Allied forces secured the Normandy beachhead, including Omaha Beach, and were retaking France;

other troops made a triumphant entry into Rome; Stalin's forces met German troops on the Leningrad front; and Tillie spoke exuberantly to the Columbia Steel Workers local. She "didnt stutter—I made em laugh—they clapped like hell when I was thru—some *stood up when I left*." Tillie joked to Jack: "maybe I'll grow up to be a capable person someday after all." Her speech was on 10 June, the day she had pledged to have explosive sex with Jack. He was hurt that Tillie had met the steel workers instead of him, according to her contract. He had reason to resent her being a "capable person," talking about "placesyourwifehasbeen," and flirting with "wolves" or "swell guys." After he got this letter on Monday, 12 June, he showed up on Castro Street.[60] Tillie described his appearance as a "miracle." She raised reality in comic accounts getting the story "better all the time." Smashing the heap's fender embellished her tale of pratfalls, though not, she claimed, of pleasure.

People's World, the *Labor Herald*, and the *Dispatcher* accompanied news of Allied triumphs with accounts of Tillie Olsen's. She started a summer CIO camp where children would discuss "democratic objectives of the postwar world," "the four freedoms," and the "races of mankind." She placated Jack with news that Karla was going to the CIO camp, Julie to daycare, and "Katush" was smart. "Maybe its just mamma paid attention to her for two whole days but by this noon she'd learned three parlor tricks: clucking back to your clucking sounds; hissing back to your hissing; and waving bye-bye." Jack was hardly placated by her conclusion: "Maybe she's a Lerner after all." Sundays at the Castro Street apartment mixed Count Basie's, Duke Ellington's, and Glenn Miller's music, children's make-believe, cheap food, and dirty dishes; debates among war-widows and a few men focused on "what to do with the German people," "secretary-boss relationships," the meaning of freedom, and amnesty. She wrote Jack that a 25 June was a "typical Sunday discussion—except you weren't here."

Meanwhile, on 22 June 1944, FDR signed the GI Bill of Rights, designed to make medical care, mortgage assistance, and educational support available to former soldiers. Not only payback for soldiers' service, the GI Bill was social engineering—designed to prevent a postwar relapse into poverty and unemployment. At a Fourth of July party, Karla read aloud the Declaration of Independence that Tillie had sent from D.C. For Jack the Fourth of July was "an exotic special day" because he received "five V mails from New York, Washington, the train to Omaha." Still the little free forms did not allow for much news, and Jack complained: "I don't like V mail. Don't like the lack of space. Don't send me V mails Tillie—they don't get here any faster than regular mail."

He was due for a ten-day furlough before going overseas, and Ida wrote one of her rare letters: "Dear T if jack is moving through Omaha take the car and the children and meet him in Omaha. Love Mother. Write to Morris [Gene]." Tillie had a staff, traveled widely in northern California, and worked "13 hours/day." One of 495 delegates to the 1944 CIO convention in Los Angeles, she wrote Jack "two days at the convention are a *must* for me."[61] After the convention, she met him for another "second" honeymoon, this one in a beach cabin at Santa Monica. On 6 September, they were in San Francisco for his reunion with the girls and the ILWU.

Jack's speech to the ILWU, covered by the *Dispatcher*, was on labor and the war effort. The "Hot Cargo" column observed: "By the looks of Jack OLSEN, the Army's done him good—like a couple of love birds, he and Tillie flitted off for another 'honeymoon' 'fore Jack left for Alabama."[62] The column listed body parts for the "Body Beautiful"—naming members with the most notable head, neck, heart, hands, and so on. The list ended: TILLIE OLSEN—'The Shoulders,'" a polite way of saying "breasts." While they drove down to Camp Roberts after the ILWU meeting, Jack begged her to follow him to Alabama.[63] She was traveling so much for the California CIO's "Xmas blood donor campaign" that she needed a higher gas allotment.[64] He left, alone, for Camp Rucker on 15 September.

Like a heroine in a boss-woman movie,[65] Tillie was confident enough to publicly confront ILWU leader Harry Bridges. "Sister Olsen" argued that the CIO should first assist returning soldiers domestically, for example, in getting maternity and infant care, before it promoted union membership. That fall the CP ran no one for president against FDR. As the "Hot Cargo" column explained, the ILWU "usta wear strike bands and carry picket cards—now we wear ROOSEVELT buttons and carry [Democratic] literature."[66] With Harry Truman, Roosevelt won a fourth term. The *Dispatcher* gloated: "Stunning Rebuke to Red-Baiters."

Tillie's family life was squeezed in between politics, public service, letter-writing, and visitors. She and the girls entertained Jack's brother Leon Olson and his bride Reeva Pearlstein before he shipped out to the Pacific.[67] Sometimes Whitey Gleason, a merchant marine, showed up, usually drunk. Tillie would add a plate for supper and stay up late describing her stressful life to Whitey, who would spend the night on her sofa while sobering up, take the girls out for expensive treats before his money ran out, and vanish.

In November, her prominence in the Red Cross and the CIO enabled Tillie to take her first commercial flight for a conference in New York City.[68] Knowing Jack's company would stop in New York on its way abroad, she told the "Hot Cargo" columnist that she was meeting him and told him to write her in care of Lillian Davis, the Bronx. She implored him not to insist that she "stay young and beautiful." After all she was "almost 32—a 26 inch waist, that's true, but no baby face—but I'll stay *yours* Jackie."[69] When Tillie arrived in the blustery cold city, she heard a "magnificent speech" but observed "poisonous gossip & climbing & clawing," incompatible with the CIO's "inspired & inspiring front." She was so conspicuous and "young and beautiful" she had her "picture taken half a dozen times." She was so caught up in the politics and the excitement of being photographed in her new hat and smart business suit that she did not call her sister.[70]

Meanwhile, Jack and his company did indeed arrive in New York, and he did call Lillian, who insisted he come to meet Ida and Sam, who were planning to retire to a farm that Lillian and Joe Davis were buying near Poughkeepsie, New York. Sam had not met Jack, and Ida had seen him briefly in 1939. Both were grateful that he had provided a stable home for Tillie and the girls. Both were touched that he was risking his life to combat fascism. No one knew where Tillie was. On 10 or 11 November, Jack took the subway into Manhattan and trudged along Broadway in hopes of running into his wife who had just vowed "I'll stay *yours* Jackie." Then he shipped out for Europe. Tillie's out-of-sight-out-of-mind failure to call her sister had sent her husband off to war feeling abandoned. Family praise for Jack seemed to indict Tillie for forgetting him.[71]

Tillie's return was delayed when a snow storm grounded the plane in Cheyenne, Wyoming. Still she was home before Kathie's first birthday, on 17 November. A letter from Jack, mailed from New York on Saturday, 11 November, awaited her. Tillie admitted, "I was in New York Saturday." She felt she would "go crazy I think—imagining all the *ifs* how I could have sought you out somehow." But she had not. Her guilt was heightened by a "Hot Cargo" column "TILLIE OLSEN just aint gonna let the Army take JACK away from her—now she's in New York visiting him." Then a letter from her father made her feel worse. Sam had "said goodbye to Jack, my son whom I have seen for the 1st time of my life for only a few seconds, even did not have a chance to talk with him. Will I see him again in reality? I said goodbye and kissed him. I still see him, but only in imagination." He implored, "let us keep us together." Contrite Tillie wrote Jack that Karla and Julie had cried because "you and I had missed each other." At Thanksgiving, Jack's new sister-in-law Reeva wrote that she was keeping "your old lady company by banging away a few words" on Tillie's typewriter. Tillie was scribbling with a pen "in her own inimitable illegible way her daily communique to a guy who is sorely missed at Ye Olde Bedlam." By then, he was seasick in the middle of the Atlantic.

By December, he was in England. He and his buddies expected to hear a

Glenn Miller concert before they shipped out for France and were horrified to hear that Miller's plane had vanished over the English Channel.[72] Tillie sent a "New York love song," a fantasy about making love with him after a chance meeting. She said a snapshot of him in his uniform spoke "such a physical language. I cant look at it without flaring up—you know how your shirt is open to the collarband I find myself pulling it all the way down opening it to your smooth chest, your [shirt] open to feel that smooth body."[73] Tillie's New York fantasy brought Jack to "escape to the privacy of his bunk" to reread her letters and apparently masturbate. But she also stuffed one letter with clippings about prominent men in the CIO. She told about a British officer who tried to seduce her. For him, "the proudest thing in my life is that you love me and hang on to me and won't have any other guy but me." Still, her references to men made him "so damned jealous of you." When he heard nothing, he was even more uneasy.

When Jack practice-fired live mortars in England, Tillie ended her CIO blood-drive with a record number of pints for the GIs. She drove Reeva, Pauline, and the "kidlets" to Venice and "we 6 females sang much of the way—even Katush."[74] Singing joyfully and driving erratically, Tillie barely escaped several near accidents to "the heap" and its "precious cargo." Her patriotic work had not quite defanged the FBI, which asserted that she was still active in the Communist Party, the ILWU, and the PTA. Her husband, "Jacob Olshansky, a Communist, is in the army."[75]

Tillie's description of her New Year's Eve dress, with a black top that "fits like a glove" above a "white frothy skirted business," worried him, though she promised to wear it when he returned "just to seduce you with."

The crack in Axis powers that FDR had announced in the summer of 1943 had throughout 1944 become an ever-widening chasm. With victory now a near certainty, on New Year's 1945, after nine months of training, Jack finally arrived on the front, apparently in the Ardennes.[76] Secrecy was crucial. Though Sam begged Tillie "to keep us in better mood" with news of Jack and to "Please! Please!" write, Tillie knew little to say. Jack could tell Tillie about "the Russians 91 miles from Berlin. . . . As usual a lot of the men are too optimistic—'20 miles a day, 100 miles to go, Berlin next week.'" Now that the Soviets were proving their value to the West, Jack even grabbed news bulletins before Tillie's letters. He yearned "to read and re-read the words, 'the final push to victory.'" By 31 January, Jack could tell a little about the Allied squeeze on Germany and Japan:

> Russians 45 miles from Berlin. MacArthur near Manila. . . . we've been
> sitting here with our ears glued to the phone waiting for news flashes,
> cussing every time something goes wrong with our wire. And reliving with

gusto the full important world-shaking things we'll do at home—among them soaking in a hot tub for an hour, eating at a table with a white cloth on it; wearing riotous colors as far removed from OD [olive drab?] as possible *and* crawling into a clean bed with sheets, cuddling up to your old lady. Peace—it will be wonderful. . . . Remind me to name our triplets Ike, Mac and Joe.[77] If I get home soon I'll be in debt to them for the rest of my life. Me and a few hundred million others.

Jack had not yet heard that Soviet troops had entered Auschwitz-Birkenau and found more than seven thousand barely-alive survivors among piles of skeletons. The death of a single German, murdered for trying to kill Hitler, distressed him as much as the death of Eggan.[78] Jack confessed to Tillie "falling in love with you was the swellest thing that ever happened to me." When she did not write, he felt almost as "miserably physically homesick" as the "bad time" in New York when he "knew you were there and I couldn't get to see you."

With the Allies closing on Hitler from the west and the Soviets from the east, Jack was "trying to keep pace with the delirious whirlwind news. Like the Tennessee kid who sleeps next to me says, 'seems like pretty soon those Krauts won't have no room left to run it!'" He was "planning to breathe a little prayer for [Generals] Montgomery and Patton and then dream of the day you'll lift the phone and hear me tell you to meet me at the Ferry building and drive me home."

Tillie's housekeepers kept quitting for higher-paying wartime factory jobs, but she managed a rousing thirty-fourth birthday celebration for Jack with "just your wife and your daughters—we had steak like you like it and raw onions (even Julie ate a smidgin of one in honor of you) and chocolate fudge cake with 34 candles and each one sang happy birthday and then all together (even Katushie la-la-ed along) and then the kids wrote letters while I put Katush to bed, and then they put on a show in your honor." After pulling his heart strings with that story, Tillie pushed his panic button with another: she had gone out afterward with men "for a drink to you—we all had several—with toasts."

In San Francisco in early April, labor and business officials gathered to hear a speech and impromptu concert by activist Paul Robeson, whose powerful baritone voice so soothed differences between the CIO, AFL, and the Chamber of Commerce that they pledged, the *Dispatcher* said, "postwar industrial peace" and a "new era of jobs." When Robeson followed an African-American lullaby with a Russian one, Tillie felt near tears as she remembered Ida singing that very song.[79]

Though Jack assumed he would remain a "buck private" forever, thanks to his Communist record, he was promoted to private first class, earning forty dollars, "approximately 15 smackers a month more in my pay envelope. Most of which I ought to be able to send home." He would not say what he had done to win an infantry combat medal.[80] He admitted to feeling damaged by "the horrible destructive job of killing and keeping from being killed. The fact that the job is almost done doesn't make it any more pleasant."

On 12 April, radios broadcast the news of Franklin Delano Roosevelt's death. That evening, when ILWU Local 6 officers arrived in the Civic Auditorium, they found the janitor, dead of a heart attack, on the floor; his radio still played Samuel Barber's *Adagio for Strings* along with the terrible news.[81] The ILWU meeting became a memorial for the leader now described by the *Dispatcher* as labor's "best friend." Hunkered down in bunkers all over former German territories, American soldiers wept freely. FDR's death distressed Jack "more than the news of any military reverse ever did." Roosevelt was "the symbol and voice of true unity" in the world. Whether President Truman could live up to FDR's legacy remained to be seen.

Needing to escape "the noise, and terror and filth of the front," by 15 April Jack got a leave to Paris, where he bought Tillie a book on Picasso, an artist who had for them been rehabilitated from purism by his antifascist *Guernica*. Walking along the Seine among clinging couples, Jack found Paris "without my girl" painful. She asked if he remembered when sex had warmed their bodies against the snow. Not only did he recall it, he relived "it, as well as most of our lives together, over and over and over again." He was not consoled by her too late regret, "Wish I'd gone to Alabama." She told about trying to stop "money bungling" and having "whoosed over to Richmond [California] today an invited guest at the new-formed Council of Social Agencies [CSA]." In her stylish suit and jaunty hat, Tillie was treated "as if I was Eleanor, Duchess o Windsor, Ingrid and Dean Gildersleeve all in one."[82] Clearly, her ego was very much alive now.

News of German efforts to exterminate Jews and other "undesirables" proved that fascism was worse than even Tillie had believed. When the British entered the Belsen concentration camp, they counted 35,000 corpses. Among the survivors, as Tillie quoted to Jack from local papers, "one or two feeble wasted arms came slowly up and gave a 'v' sign." She realized that first-hand encounters with horrors would henceforth be "the setting" behind their lives.[83] Now, she felt "gladder for what you are doing" than if he had lived out the war in security. After seeing human extermination, Jack spoke only of digging trenches. He craved diversions in innocent "descriptions of your day and stories about the kids."

When representatives of fifty nations met in San Francisco that April, Harry Truman appointed Eleanor Roosevelt as U.S. delegate and called on them all to be "architects of the better world." Tillie took her daughters to the Opera House to see strange new flags in wild colors and designs posted among familiar red, white, and blue geometrical patterns flapping together in the wind. Julie cried with Tillie because the United Nations was "going to stop the world from ever having a war again."[84]

Before the month's end, Mussolini was shot by Italian partisans. His body, along with his mistress's, was hung upside down in Milan. Written in his fortified bunker, Hitler's own account of events still blamed the entire European disaster on the Jews. He committed suicide on 30 April. Victory over the Third Reich was tainted in the West, however, by the news that Stalin had taken the concessions of the Teheran agreement as license to renege on democratic commitments. Churchill objected, but Truman and Generals Eisenhower and Marshall acquiesced to Soviet control of countries reclaimed from Hitler, including Czechoslovakia, Poland, and Hungary.[85]

On 6 May, the *Chronicle* ran a story "Witness to Horror," showing gruesome photographs of piles of bones and bodies found in Buchenwald. Even Edward R. Morrow had "no words" for horrors that proved humankind so brutal. Hoping May would be Jack's last month "in hell," Tillie distracted him as requested with an account of the children's performance for Reeva on Leon's birthday. Her "weakness for talk" with anyone who showed up in what Reeva called "Ye Olde Bedlam" continued. She and other war-widows often speculated about the "unreal" prospect of renewed married life. Managing family and job, playing a star role in war relief and peace efforts, functioning independently, and being an often-photographed personality, Tillie could hardly imagine dwindling into a mere wife. She would have to cease "slapping cream on my face (the rare times I remember) and going to bed whenever I feel like (instead of waiting up till you come and then being hauled to bed whether I want to read or not) etc. etc." She claimed, "I still say I can hardly wait." This letter was "as untidy and disorganized and cluttered as the rest of my life."

Victory in Europe Day was 8 May, after, Tillie counted, "five years, nine months, eight days."[86] Jack wrote that the "artillery went dead on V-E day over here." He was awarded the Bronze Star for unspecified "valiant feats of arms against the enemy." At a V-E Day observance in Karla's school, her sixth grade teacher read aloud one of Jack's letters.[87] By 23 May, he was in Germany, on "an occupation job." He mentioned the "magnitude of the destruction" but understated its impact as "extremely sobering."

Tillie was such a bigwig she was invited to submit credentials for *Who's Who in Labor*. Out of gratitude to FDR and Eleanor, she identified her political party as Democrat. She dated her marriage correctly as 29 February but incorrectly as 1936 rather than 1944.[88] On 8 June, the *Labor Herald* reported that Tillie Olsen was bound for New York for a National CIO War Relief Staff Conference. Despite a warning from Lillian not to burden Ida, Tillie deposited all three girls in Omaha with Ida, Sam, Vicki, Sonny, and their new baby.[89] Then she rushed on to New York. With a CIO raise, she felt "awfully prosperous" but promised Jack not to "go out & blow it wildly."[90]

Tillie may have represented CIO Post-War Planning at the UN organizational meeting. She sent the girls to the Olshanskys and was gratified to hear Eleanor Roosevelt propose a Bill of Universal Human Rights, based, it seemed, on the very ideals Ida had championed all her life. Tillie recalled being "there on that big evening [26 June] when they opened the United Nations."[91] Then she hurried to Los Angeles for a CIO board meeting, where she aired ideas about unemployed disabled veterans.[92] Joining the girls at the Olshanskys, she shared letters from Jack and urged him to write more about himself, "can't have enuf."

Toddler Kathie was unsettled by her mother's absences, by tiresome train rides to different sets of grandparents, then by having her mother rush off as soon as they got home. Not yet two, Kathie already proved a clever schemer by "stripping me of my coat hat shoes earrings every thing representing going out—the second I come home." Jack felt a less comic, manly resistance to Tillie's activism. He did not "want you to get a Purple Heart for over working yourself. I'm selfish enuf to want the best of you for myself. That's the only reward I'm demanding for time spent in the army." He had worn out her pictures by imagining making love with her. By August, he could send home "another thirty dollars toward realizing our post war dream," a home of their own. He hoped Tillie had written more letters than he had received. He was trying to be less jealous, more proud of "the active part you're playing."

At the Potsdam Conference outside Berlin, beginning on 17 July, the Big Three leaders discussed dividing up Germany and finishing the war with Japan. To Churchill and Stalin, Truman confided that the United States had developed a new bomb of horrific proportions. With Japan resisting surrender, Truman believed that the new bomb could save more lives than it lost. On the morning of 6 August, an American B-29 bomber, the "Enola Gay," dropped an atomic bomb on the city of Hiroshima, crushing its buildings and eradicating most of its people. A second bomb on the city

of Nagasaki killed more than forty thousand civilians in a few minutes.[93]
A special edition of *Stars and Stripes* proclaimed in "six-inch letters 'Japan quits.'" After V-J Day, Jack would not be transferred to the Pacific: "Only four months ago I was fearful I wouldn't live to see the next morning. Sweating out night after night the last ditch artillery the Germans spat at us."[94] He signed his letter, "Goodnight my girl—with adoration and hunger—Jack." An unreligious Jew, he was so homesick and war-weary, he dreamed about, "Christmas together, maybe."

A few days later, Tillie was walking down to Market Street, joyous that war was vanquished and peace would prevail. She was singing to Kathie "an old country lullaby, created by a woman who never knew that she was a composer, many many centuries perhaps ago." When she stopped at a newspaper kiosk to read bold-faced war news, Tillie saw a "little item in the paper about that peculiar light that had never been seen on earth before. All everything thousands of years of civilization had built up, and everything had been destroyed. And there were no lights except the irradiated light of bodies burning."[95] Tillie later isolated that moment as an epiphany, a sudden recognition that she must write once more against "destruction and on the side of life. Utterances on what I call the Side of life."[96]

The CIO had contributed to the Allied war effort by its no-strike pledge, by raising a quarter of a million dollars for War Relief, by contributing 25,000 pints of blood, and by sending more than five thousand Local 6 men and women to the service. Now the CIO expected "pay-back": V-E Day and V-J Days should be followed by "V-U," Victory over Unemployment Day. The CIO planned a massive Labor Day parade, on 3 September 1945. Everyone was to wear a union button; women were "required to wear a dark skirt and white blouse." Instead, Tillie wore a conspicuously tight white skirt and blouse and a red cap. During solemn announcements, she felt someone grab her cap and spun around to find Leon, just back from the Far East.[97] Tillie proved herself as much of a show-off as her outfit suggested, if a comic letter to "Tillie Olsen—you scum" can be believed:[98]

> I was telling good ole Lindsay that Tillie woman is slightly off her nuts
> as I just cant figger out what got into her going around like a hot bitch
> in short whitetights skirts and white tight swetters which although they
> don't have built-ins a la Lana Turna do serve the purpose and make all the
> guys in the labor day parade feel uncomfortable ifyagetwhatImean and
> then that damn redhat which no one can quite figger out except that my
> personal thought is that she just didn't come [comb] her hair and that's

why she gave me those goddam blackblueand purple marks on my arm and pinched Leeons buttocks for pulling sed red hat off. Period.

According to "Hot Cargo," these shenanigans distracted from a public tribute to Jack.

On 12 September, in Singapore, Japan unconditionally surrendered. News leaked that America had interned 110,000 Japanese people in California camps, a report confirming Ida's belief that war brutalizes all participants. In Europe, Allied forces tried to meliorate brutality by rehabilitating and resettling concentration camp survivors. Harry, now a retired lieutenant colonel, was put in charge of one thousand such "displaced persons" at a camp near Stuttgard.[99] From a new address, a block further out Lafayette Avenue, Sam begged Tillie to send news of Jack "for the cause of your mother."[100] She knew only that he was in France, guarding German prisoners and shepherding them to trial.

Tillie ironed her girls' dresses and packed their lunches in the mornings and continued traveling in "the heap" for the CIO War Relief. (She went, for example, to Crockett, Rodeo, and Martinez, northeast of San Francisco, all on one day.) In a well-publicized speech, she proclaimed that "labor is uniting the many nationalities and veterans and workers in a program of full employment."[101] When her job took her to Los Angeles at September's end for another "smoky mangled State War Relief Committee meeting," she dropped the girls off with Jack's parents. She wrote him that Bluma hated her aged body, her "betraying crippling carcass," so Tillie said she felt "hellish dumping the kids there, she's not strong enuf." Still, she habitually depended on others' generosity, even when she knew better. This time Tillie rationalized that Karla would be "a godsend" of a helper to Jack's mother, as Karla at almost thirteen was to Tillie herself.

Tillie described herself to Jack as "your not-deserving-you Tillie," while he was her "very loved and needed Jack." Then "Hot Cargo" reported on 5 October that "Somebody read that JACK OLSEN's outfit is expected back in a month, so here's hopin.'" Tillie said she feared that Jack would "shudder at the sight of me now." Still, her letters were mostly "get-you-home" letters and "dog-tired I love you notes." She worried: "Jackie if it will be longer how can I go on? Help me. When you were in combat that used to help—all our hardships [were] small in comparison—but I'm all drained now." She knew that news of her professional successes, other men's interest in her, and family troubles, like Kathie's asthma attacks, disturbed Jack, but her "hop-around-mind" kept sprinkling such disconcerting information into love letters.

Even her story about a women's weekend in a forest cabin south of Santa Clara was not quite reassuring. She took Pauline and Kathie, who was "afraid that her mother will leave her—the familiar pattern in strange places (L.A., Omaha)." One woman was mad because her lover was leaving her for the wife he had not seen in years; another was ruefully happy, having lost her husband and found a new lover; another was ecstatic over a "just returned husband." Tillie said she and Pauline had listened "like hungry doves" to these "women in love" with such longing she dared not look at Jack's photos, "I am too vulnerable," an only half-reassuring remark. Kathie had become a "hilarious" mimic, and the girls invented pantomimes in one "dress-up fever" after another.

She told more consoling stories about riding with Leon Olson, Reeva, and the girls to see his parents for the first time since he was demobilized. For Tillie, the drive down was "a long memory-drenched physically beautiful ride" recalling their several "honeymoons." When they arrived at 4:30 A.M. Avrum Olshansky was waiting for them and Bluma awakened to begin "pillowing Leon's head on her lap & crooning. Dad hungrily watching Leon—not taking his eyes off him for a minute." Tillie closed her narrative: "Bub I wish I had you tonight—Your red-eyed, exhausted, so-loving girl."

As she looked down from her Castro Street window, Tillie saw the mixed race neighborhood bustling again. Returning soldiers and their families were buying property and reopening shops. The war had revitalized American industry, and the GI Bill enabled millions of returning soldiers to participate in a healthy economy. As demobilized veterans tried to readjust to domestic life, Tillie's War Relief work became even more demanding. She turned her publicity skills from nutrition and peace to labor and veterans.[102] She sent Jack good news about a CIO victory over the AFL, but she warned him that the ILWU was losing its concern for individual workers.

One evening, after a long work day, Tillie cooked "a Jack Olsen supper" for a returning soldier. They had "steak & baked potatoes & salad & peas & apple pie & cheese & Burgundy." The older girls were offended by Kathie's being "very very affectionate" to the wrong returning soldier. Karla had dance classes and friendships in the Castro neighborhood. She adored Jack, but his absence did not distress her as it did Julie, who was almost seven. She painfully printed out letter after letter to Jack, who usually replied jointly to both big girls. When he sent a letter to her alone, Julie so treasured it she took it to bed every night until she wore it out.[103]

Tillie sat up late most nights typing speech outlines, reports, and letters. One night she sang along with a Count Basie tune on the radio, drank warm milk, checked Kathie's breathing, and stared down at the city and over at Twin Peaks. She begged Jack to confide in her his experiences escorting former S.S. officers to trial and to "please please cry on my shoulder." His daily letters made her guilty for "gypping" him when she failed to write. Leon had decided to become a printer's apprentice and advised her about GI Bill financing; Tillie speculated "in 4 years—oh-boy—he can start lending us money again."

Jack was supposed to board ship on 1 December, so Tillie proclaimed 1 November "The first day of the last month without you." Then, on 4 November, papers announced that the 66th Division was one of those "not scheduled to come home in 1945."[104] When Tillie read the "cruel news," she scribbled: "I want you so *now*," but she warned Jack that she was not glamorous in her Mother-Hubbard nightgown and his bed slippers. She hoped, "it just *cant* be more than 7 weeks for you." Papers ran articles on the "Lucky Guys" who were returning from war and launched campaigns to "Bring Our Troops Back!"[105] Tillie "got me two bargain hats." She asked, "Darling what kind of robes do you like on females? Silky jobs, quilted jobs, sexy jobs, pinks, blues, prints or what? What colors do you like on, for me?"

December holiday crowds signed petitions to President Truman and Congress to bring all troops home. To the irritation of HUAC, the California Labor School gave tuition, housing, and subsidies under the GI Bill of Rights. Tillie hoped that *The Story of G.I. Joe*, though not so good a movie as *All Quiet on the Western Front*, would imprint on people's hearts the terrible price of war.[106] The *Dispatcher* argued that the atom bomb's formula should be entrusted to the United Nations so the destruction of Hiroshima and Nagasaki would never be repeated.

Then the "Hot Cargo" column reported: "Get the Welcome Mat out—JACK OLSEN is on his way home—called TILLIE from Virginia and she hasn't been able to talk sense since" (no doubt a snide reference to her stammer). Jack was in California by Friday, 28 December, when Tillie got a "darling note" from him, saying he was slightly drunk. She sent him a "special dollar" for ten more beers. Still, Jack might as well be in France, except that she would soon hear his voice on the phone saying "drive me home."

By the end of 1945, Tillie felt no more inclination to kill her ego. Her vitality, smarts, dedication, and what Jack called her turbulence had made her a celebrity in War Relief efforts. She had transformed herself into a joyous mother and a passionate partner, roles that he loved. She was also now a prolific journalist and an effective political force, roles about which he was decidedly ambivalent. She was thrilled that Jack would soon add balance to her life. Still, she had no intention of giving up "my livelihood, my contribution to society, and my reputation," even for him.

CHAPTER 9

EX-GI'S IDEAL WIFE

1946–1950

What kind of threat was I? Was Jack? What the hell could we do?"
—Tillie Olsen to Panthea Reid, 28 October 1997

Traveling about like a tumbleweed, Tillie had almost lost touch with the Dinkin family, but she wrote a poem when she heard of Harry Dinkin's death, which she read at the funeral on New Year's Day 1946 in Petaluma. She drove home to find her girls ecstatic because they'd heard from Jack; he had a weekend off. Tillie piled her sexy new nighties in a suitcase, drove the older girls to the Olshanskys, and left Kathie with a housekeeper. On Friday, 3 January, she picked up Jack. Hardly able to keep their hands off each other, they rushed to a nearby coastal resort at Morro Bay, where they spent three days sharing walks by the Pacific, hopes for world peace, and their long-suppressed sexual life. Tillie returned Jack to camp and then drove down the coast, finding her in-laws and two girls peeved with her for keeping Jack to herself.

After their happy weekend with all its "physical beauty," Tillie wrote Jack to say that she harbored longings that still "struggle in me to be said." The "trip down, L.A. again" had reminded her of "old old unsatisfied hungers" and ambitions. Jack soon got his final release, and Tillie drove to fetch him home. Julie remembered, "Karla and I made big letters spelling WELCOME HOME DADDY and glued them up the stairwell of the house at 903 Castro where we lived. I remember Kathie being so confused about who this Daddy person was."[1] By 11 January, "Hot Cargo" reported that "it's all Mellowness at the OLSON [sic] household since JACK is home again—hope he'll be in circulation soon."

Friends Ruth Sutherland, who had written the zany letter about Tillie's Labor Day antics, and Mary Lindsay took a vicarious interest in Tillie's and Jack's sex life. Lindsay loaned them her apartment in Sausalito with many innuendos about their disinterest in getting out of bed. She wished them "Happy oneymoon, chillen." Sutherland wrote, "rumour also has it the Olson [sic] Rendezvous of Joy and Rhythm is running smoothly and without loud shrieks."[2]

The country too was back together and running smoothly. Salaries had doubled. The forty-eight-hour week was standard. The "Big Three" were making cars again. Other industries were soon manufacturing rubber tires, building materials, refrigerators, electric stoves, and fur coats. Butchers again sold sirloin steaks and whole hams. Unemployment was almost nonexistent. Wartime scarcities had enforced frugality and saving; even Tillie Olsen bought war bonds. America was ready for a spending spree and a party.

The Olsens' apartment hosted what seemed a continuous party. Friends and neighbors dropped in to welcome Jack home with food, drinks, and boisterous songs. Led by the Olsen girls, children improvised one performance after another. In all this hubbub and joy, Tillie tried to recall the things that "struggle in me to be said." She had been a CIO director, a war relief celebrity, a reporter for the *Labor Herald*, and a teacher at the California Labor School. In the heady postwar atmosphere, she expected to continue such activities, enhance her reputation, and increase her fame.

Women had, as the *Daily People's World* proclaimed "Met the Test of War with Brilliant Achievement." Tillie was chosen to teach a class on welfare benefits at the California Labor School. The *DPW* reported that "certain bourgeois women's leaders" proposed that childcare centers "not be made permanent."[3] Tillie figured that only women without children or jobs or with hired help would think child care unnecessary. "Back-to-the-kitchen" pressures now were threatening wartime feminist accomplishments. Her father asked if she were "still on your job. Or home to housekeeping?" He and Ida sounded free of housekeeping pressures, after visiting Jann in D.C. and Lillian in upstate New York and staying in the Hotel Times Square. Sam told Tillie that a British nurse named Clare Schmoclair, decorated for service during the London blitz, was working with Harry in the displaced persons camp.

When former *Herald* writers returned from the front, they expected to get their old jobs back. Like Rosie the Riveter and other women war-workers, Tillie lost her job, possibly her first experience of gender discrimination. In her YCL work, her sex, as well as her brains, had earned her special treatment. Random House was extraordinarily generous and patient partly because she was a woman writer. She was assigned to recruit in Hollywood in part because she was so vivacious and sexy. She left Hollywood to take up lowly jobs, but she did so at her own choosing. Her femininity helped make her a prominent CIO War Relief hero. Now femininity cost her her job. Tillie did not, however, intend to be among the unemployed who simply went home to housekeeping.

She had applauded concessions made to Stalin at Teheran. Eastern European countries, however, taken from Germany, were becoming Soviet satellites, as was Korea, taken from Japan. That March at Westminster College, in Fulton, Missouri, Winston Churchill gave an alarming speech about dangerous Soviet influence upon Iran, Turkey, and "all the capitals of the ancient states of Central and Eastern Europe." He proclaimed: "an iron curtain has descended across the continent."[4] His implication was that a totalitarian USSR sought next to take over the western world. Stalin was said to have spied inside the United States, even during the war. Many Americans believed that communism now threatened American peace and security. Tillie and Jack saw fascism as America's real enemy. They were impressed that, now married, Harry and Clare Lerner were escorting displaced persons to the Nuremberg trials to testify against the Nazis.[5] They were personally shaken by reports of previously unimaginable atrocities but gratified that obeying orders was no longer an excuse for crimes against humanity. At home, HUAC was acting like Germany's Secret Service in Hitler's early days. Eleanor Roosevelt protested its "Gestapo tactics." Screenwriter Dalton Trumbo accused HUAC of "witch hunting." The Daily People's World called it the "Un-American Committee."[6] Cancerous paranoia deemed even Marxist idealists like Tillie and Jack as "spies" or "traitors."

Not only had Tillie lost her Herald post, she soon lost her teaching post at the California Labor School because, under the GI Bill, it needed credentialed teachers or "top-notch" experts.[7] Jack felt secure in his old job as "local director of publicity and education," as the Dispatcher announced on 22 March. Editing the ILWU Bulletin, he worked with American Printing and Lithographics on layouts. He insisted that the 18,000-member Local 6 provide equal employment opportunities for African Americans and open leadership roles to women and minorities. He taught underprivileged workers to read by studying newspapers. He successfully campaigned for Kaiser Permanente to provide health care for union members. Busy doing such good work, Jack did not notice that Teamsters, the AFL, and the FBI were infiltrating the ILWU and the CIO.

After serving in Europe, Al Richmond returned, something of a war hero, to again edit the Daily People's World. He increased circulation with commentary from such notables as Woody Guthrie, Meridel Le Sueur, and Ring Lardner, Jr. Tillie was eager to convert her anger over being fired into journalism on women's issues. On 18 April, Richmond added to his list of celebrity columnists with a "series of weekly columns by an old friend of many of our readers—Tillie Olsen."[8] Her first "TILLIE OLSEN SAYS," subtitled "No Time for Household Hints," argued that the central issue facing postwar America was making women's traditional positions as homemakers "consistent with the fullest contribution of women as human beings."

After the ILWU's annual ball at the end of April, the *Dispatcher*'s "Hot Cargo" columnist wrote: "JACK OLSEN escaped the soup and fish by having to run 'round taking pictures, and naturally TILLIE escaped the flowing gown by having to run around after JACK," an allusion to Tillie's revealingly low-cut gown. Her second "weekly" column on feminist issues appeared two weeks after her first. Writing about the "Struggle to maintain women's wartime gains," she overstated women's "real gains" as true job parity, but then said that that progress was being reversed.

Tillie followed that argument a week later with a column on "Wartime Gains of Women in Industry." She wondered what had happened to "those women who yesterday drove the busses and the cabs and the streetcars; who ran the lift jitneys and were the repairmen and the machinists and the shipbuilders; who've been closed down on, or laid off, or canned, or replaced?" She answered that they were waiting in unemployment lines for twenty dollars a week, checks that would run out after six months. She announced provocatively: "There's a new job for jobless women." Their "real housecleaning job" was to sweep away discriminatory laws and practices. She invited responses.[9]

While Tillie was frantically gathering data, working to meet deadlines, trying to lose neither the renewed romance of her marriage nor the glamour of her public persona, Richmond printed a query from a mother torn between being politically active and caring for her baby. Tillie advised the woman to "relax and have fun with your baby." She saw a "political value to 'surrendering' to motherhood" because being "WITH" other mothers enabled a woman to influence them. On 3 June, *DPW* printed: "AN ANSWER TO TILLIE OLSEN." This working mother felt Tillie did "not answer the problems of working class women. The bourgeois clichés which she uses have no place in *The People's World*." She said that "Mrs. Olsen" used a capitalist trick, covering her politics with pabulum about "loving your baby." Women needed to understand their subjugation, not to be told "about staying home and loving it."

Being called bourgeois felt like being stabbed, but Tillie acted unwounded in her next column, headed "TILLIE OLSEN SAYS: Back to the slave shops?" Women had receded back to "laundry, food processing, textile, and needle trades slave shops where the pay is 65 to 80 cents an hour and the work can't be matched anywhere for speed up and physical exhaustion." She blamed such "piecework" jobs for women on the AFL and on California's "Warren-administered Department of Industrial Welfare."

Meanwhile, Jack's brothers Max and Leon were getting job retraining under the GI Bill. Leon became a printer's apprentice, Max an accountant. Soon he invested in a small trucking company called Global Van. Thinking of vast accumulations of war goods and supplies around the world which needed shipping home, Max patented a new concept—container shipping. Jack had no desire follow his younger brothers and launch out into new fields. The traumas of killing and almost being killed, of discovering death camp atrocities, and of guarding unrepentant Nazi prisoners had taken a toll. He was grateful to be safely home with his wife and daughters and back at his ILWU post.

In her first "TILLIE OLSEN SAYS" column, Tillie had written about making domestic duties consistent with "the fullest contribution of women as human beings." She had gone on to make a landmark argument for equal pay for equal work. She had undermined her position, though, by first overstating workplace gains and then by telling mothers to stay home. Throughout June, controversy about her raged in *DPW*'s pages. She never returned to the challenge of women's full humanity. "TILLIE OLSEN SAYS" did not reappear.[10] Her "hop-around-mind" had undercut her polemics as it occasionally had her love letters. Perhaps she wrote too rapidly to think through the implications of her assertions. Or perhaps speech-making had spoiled her for argument-writing.

That June, a *Dispatcher* cartoon showed Truman much too tiny to fill FDR's shoes. In the Chinese civil war, Truman's government endorsed the authoritarian Chiang Kai-shek government, while the USSR aided Mao Tse-tung's Red Army. President Truman fired former Vice President and current Secretary of Commerce Henry Wallace for his leftist sympathies.[11] Truman also authorized bomb-building laboratories, which imported former Nazis scientists to develop ever-more-deadly bombs.[12] The United States and the USSR were carving the globe into rival spheres of influence. Republicans accused the California Labor School, where Jack was listed as ILWU contact person, of being a tool of the USSR. California's twelfth district sent Republican Richard M. Nixon to Congress.[13]

Tillie had written that women's "real housecleaning job" was to clean up discrimination against women. But feeling pressure from Jack to give up speech-making and traveling about, she gave in. She had seen a "political value to 'surrendering' to motherhood," but her Christmas list suggests little political concern, as it inculcated housewifely values: for Kathie—toy dishes, $1.39, toy stove, $1.79; for Julie—toy washing machine $1.89, tinker toys $2, books 25¢ and up, toy refrigerator $1.59, toy sink $1.49, books $2, doll 75¢. At fourteen, Karla got a finger paint set $2, a pencil set $2, pants and socks $2.[14] Tillie had become an ex-GI's ideally compliant wife and mother. She was launched on her only intentional pregnancy.

In January 1947, Tillie turned thirty-five. She was no longer a fiction writer. She was no longer a public presence. She was no longer a journalist. She no longer had a maid. She was literally a housekeeper. In April she and Jack bought, under the GI Bill, their own home at 70 Laidley Street, on the edge of the Mission District. This funky house built into the rim of a hill had a garage on the bottom level, with an odd room over it, two flights of stairs to the front door, another flight to the main floor, with its living room and kitchen, and another up to the bedrooms. The neighborhood was Hispanic, with Mexican, Samoan, and Hawaiian residents, along with a few Russian, Anglo, and black families. Though the Hawaiians and Samoans bickered constantly, the lively mix of cultures fascinated the Olsen girls. They enjoyed a superb view of San Francisco and were high enough to escape most fogs. Julie felt she at last had a "real childhood home."

In March, while HUAC collected names of more than a million suspected Communists, President Truman signed a bill calling for a loyalty check on all government employees. In June, he did object to a "slave-labor bill," but Congress overrode his veto and passed the antilabor and anti-Communist Taft-Hartley Act, a betrayal, the *Dispatcher* said, of labor veterans who had fought fascism abroad, only to be victimized by it at home.[15]

Tillie read in *DPW* that Woody Guthrie and his wife were also about to have a baby, a little musician who would play the people's music. Her own baby should be born after the Guthries' in late July or early August.[16] HUAC now turned against Hollywood for creating people's heroes, like Little Orphan Annie and Ma and Tom Joad. It objected to James Cagney's plans to film Dalton Trumbo's antiwar *Johnny Got His Gun*.[17] HUAC deemed portraying ordinary folk as heroic and war as brutal as un-American.

Expecting another ten-month pregnancy, Tillie was surprised when her labor began on time. Back in 1945, on the battlefield, Jack had imagined naming their triplets "Ike, Mac and Joe." After her hardest labor, on the fourth of July, Tillie brought forth a girl. She joked that the on-time baby was her "premie" who should be called "Glorious Fourth Olsen," or "Glory" for short. Neither she nor Jack, though, was feeling patriotic about American glory in 1947. Karla and Julie wanted to name the baby from

Little Women so Tillie settled on the name of its most appealing young man, Laurie.[18] Union men teased Jack about having "nothing but girls," but her daughters congratulated themselves for being now four "little women."[19] The entire American postwar culture endorsed Tillie's decision to be a stay-at-home mother. The bigger girls were thrilled—Julie even thought of Laurie as "my baby." Secure as a union officer, Jack could support the family.[20] A patronizing zeitgeist decreed that GI's wives owed devotion and gratitude to their husbands, and Tillie followed the decree: "To Jack—with love ... to be with you every minute of the day—every hour—as my heart is, your wife."[21]

Nursing, bathing, and changing a baby, while cleaning and cooking for a family of six, drained her energies, however, as did innumerable visitors. Whitey Gleason took the Olsen house as his personal port in a storm; Leroy King, a black youth, "one of Jack's kids," stayed longer and learned to read under Jack's guidance.[22] A typical list of chores was "soak diapers; wash a day's supply; straighten house and upstairs; cabbage soup in morning; soak beans; and 2 hours in linen closet." Tillie tried to study "election Material—issues, background," but she could campaign only sporadically against Taft-Hartley or for the only woman running for San Francisco Board of Supervisors.[23]

She was appalled to see the ideals of peace and brotherhood in the Declaration of Universal Human Rights being "done in" by paranoia.[24] As Stalin cracked down against dissidents and democracy in Eastern Europe, Truman launched a "Cold War" against the USSR. The State Department fired anyone even accused of being a security risk.[25] Under Taft-Hartley, union members who did not sign loyalty oaths lost their jobs. To Henry Wallace the "Century of the Common Man" had become the "Century of Fear."

After Representative Richard Nixon claimed that Communists were taking over America through Hollywood, the government censored more and more movies, including Charlie Chaplin's satire on modern corruption, *Monsieur Verdoux*.[26] In late October, a contingent of Hollywood personalities chartered a plane to D.C. to protest HUAC's "un-American investigation." Some actors, including Humphrey Bogart, Lauren Bacall, and Gregory Peck, protested; others, including Ronald Reagan, wanted communism outlawed in Hollywood. In an absurd distortion of the legal system, HUAC prohibited ten writers and directors from testifying, then cited them for contempt, and finally sentenced them to the penitentiary.[27] Tillie clipped out photographs of the "Hollywood Ten" and of protestors urging "Save the Bill of Rights." She kept articles about this inquisition, including Samuel Ornitz's assertion that "entombing" such creative people was a desecration of human rights.[28] When they listened to HUAC hearings over the Mutual Broadcasting Company, Tillie and Jack trembled, lest they hear their own names.

The Olsens' mood lightened some when Ida and Sam traveled west to see the new baby. Sam proved his usefulness by telling riddles and jokes to the older girls and repainting much of the Laidley Street house. Ida proved hers by washing, cooking, caring for the baby, and telling Tillie and the older girls of her dreams for them. The girls had green jumpers with embroidered flowers, which they wore for pictures taken by Al Addy, then, thanks to Jack, a photographer for the ILWU paper. In a revealingly low-cut dress, Tillie snuggles happily against Jack.[29]

Tillie's mood darkened, however, when she looked beyond her family. By the end of 1947, Republicans and southern Democrats had colluded to undermine New Deal economic reforms. The Nuremberg trials had revealed experimentation on and extermination of human beings. Lynchings in the American South, mass killings in Africa, inquisitions in America, and a race for a superdestructive hydrogen bomb were almost as horrific. World peace seemed a false dream in a nightmarish world.

Wartime movies had featured strong women as reporters and professionals, even as bosses. Movies in 1948, like *June Bride*, suggested that women were happiest marrying and staying at home with children.[30] Turning thirty-six on 14 January 1948, Tillie felt victimized by an antifeminist zeitgeist. Now fifteen, Karla was so busy with school, dancing, girlfriends, and boyfriends she was no longer a reliable mother's helper. At nine and four, Julie and Kathie loved to play with six-month-old Laurie, but they were hardly reliable help. Plagued with serious asthma attacks, Kathie sometimes needed more care than the baby.[31] Tillie did all the cooking and cleaning. The girls wore heavy cotton dresses with petticoats, which took hours to dry and iron. Tillie hand-washed wool clothes because dry cleaning was too expensive. However ravishing the view from Laidley Street, getting groceries and other purchases up the steep hill and steps was an ordeal. However aware Jack was of the rights of minorities and women, he did not share many household chores. However much scriptwriters for radio's *Father Knows Best?* meant for the show's title to be a question, audiences took the program as a prescription for women's subservience to their wiser spouses. Tillie yearned for the days when she was a bigwig, had a housekeeper, and lived as she pleased. In 1945, she had promised she couldn't "have enuf" of Jack when he came home, but the excitement of their reunion was being replaced by the drudgery of being his wife.

Tillie's typewriter sat on a table in the living room by the stairs going up to the bedrooms. The girls used the table too, so it was always piled with books, papers, and homework assignments. Pictures of Virginia Woolf, clipped from book jacket covers and taped to the wall, presided over that table and another desk in her bedroom. Depressed over her endless chores and the country's paranoid suspicions, she tried to find consolation in rereading favorite authors like Emily Dickinson, the Brontës, Willa Cather, and Katherine Mansfield. She also read less well-known women: Olive Schreiner, Sarah Orne Jewett, Mary E. Wilkins Freeman, Dorothy Canfield Fisher, Elizabeth Madox Roberts, Genevieve Taggard, and Agnes Smedley. On "copy-outs," she jotted down favorite passages. She thought of talented Jews, like Einstein and Freud, who had escaped the concentration camps and wept for the millions who had not. She felt ambivalent about the founding of Israel, but she was certain that far too many talents were lost to the world through extermination, discrimination, poverty, and toil. With GIs returning, Tillie had lost her jobs and hence her prominence because she was a woman. Though she had used a bevy of excuses for not writing, had called it quits on her novel, and had not tried creative writing in years, Tillie now blamed her failure to write on domesticity and discrimination. She wondered "how many women writers' lives" had been reduced to "that same mass, wad of notes beguns scrawls unfinisheds" that were in her notebook of story ideas. She called it a "death notebook" because she could not resurrect those story ideas.

Unable to write, Tillie began following the rest of her own *DPW* advice. She made friends with Hispanics and African-American women and counseled them about child care, education, benefits, and job opportunities.[32] When she attended a Conference on Child Welfare, however, she heard an infuriating argument that American women made poor mothers because "the United States mother is all too likely to find preparing a formula, washing diapers and getting meals a poor substitute for her previous participation in the business or professional world."[33]

When progressives and labor formed a third party, the ILWU voted to support the Independent Progressive Party and its presidential nominee Henry Wallace. Tillie advised neighboring women and Kate Kennedy PTA members to join the IPP, though the Mindt-Nixon Bill violated the Bill of Rights by threatening Wallace supporters and IPP members with jail. In October 1948 telephone polls predicted that Republicans Thomas Dewey and Earl Warren would easily win the presidency and vice presidency. Instead, Harry Truman and Alben Barkley won the November election, and Democrats gained a majority in both houses of Congress. Wallace carried no state, while the racist "Dixiecrat" Strom Thurmond carried four. J. Edgar Hoover, director of the Federal Bureau of Investigation, suggested to Truman that he defend himself against charges of being soft on communism by using the 1940 Smith Act "to outlaw the Communist Party and, by extension, any publication presumed to be published under the party's aegis."[34]

Tillie, eager to see carols as expressions of "the people's culture," took the girls to a Christmas carol program at the California Labor School.[35] She and Karla planned a family Christmas performance; baby Laurie was baby Jesus, and the older girls portrayed a mix of secular and religious figures. Neither religion nor family, however, seemed capable of lifting Tillie's spirits. Her imagination now seemed the "graveyard of the unwritten."[36] She stared out "the window my face transparent with the city thru it" and wondered if she was any more substantial than her reflection.

After being such a war-relief dynamo, such an outspoken women's rights journalist, such an enthusiastic G.I. wife, and such a devoted, but exhausted mother, Tillie determined that her substantial self was actually her writing self. Her powerful 1930s novel was lost and out of date. It occurred to Tillie that she might write again not about a universal mother, nor about horny widows, Marxist preachers, militant wives, or abusive priests, but about her own personal experience. She set about practicing "accurate chronicling; how it was it was said; the look on the face and the set of the body." She told herself to have "no illusion" but "batter it out." She wrote an anguished beginning about a neighborhood Hispanic boy who got a "life sentence" in kindergarten when a teacher labeled him "incorrigible." She wanted to comfort Karla, an "insecure, groping, tremendously self-focused adolescent daughter," whose dark straight hair marked her difference from the blond curly-haired Olsen girls. However, "all the necessities of daily living, the clamor of what is alive and dear and has claims on me," kept Tillie from time with Karla. Her subsequent guilt, she realized, was a motherly emotion that not even her favorite women authors had written about.[37]

In January 1949 the FBI recorded data on Tillie, her parents, and siblings. It asserted that Tillie's father, "SAMUEL LERNER, [was] alleged to have been banished to Siberia from Czarist Russia for operating a secret radical press."[38] The FBI turned even school children into informants who reported that sixteen-year-old Karla "continuously makes pro-Communist statements." On 28 February 1949, J. Edgar Hoover wrote to the chief San Francisco Special Agent about "OLSHANSKY, TILLIE, NATIVE BORN, COMMUNIST. Aliases: Mrs. Jacob Olshansky, Tilly Olsen, Tillie Olson, Tillie Lerner Olsen, Mrs. John P. Olsen, nee: Tillie Lerner."[39] Among the accusations in her updated file was that she had publicized "gains women were making in industry."

After her thirty-seventh birthday, Tillie tried to turn practice descriptions into salable stories. In one tale, two little girls stay in the bathroom so long two big girls accuse them of being "bad." Neither little girl understands what was "bad," but one (based on Kathie) confesses to her sympathetic mother. In another story, based on Pauline's loss of her husband, Tillie revived a line from twenty years before: "don't die, why did you die?" Then she added a salacious twist—burning with desire, a widow considers advertising: "wanted, by 32 year old widow, horny man, does not even have to be good in bed, will teach." The widow plans to seduce her boss, but he fires her, and the story ends anticlimactically. Another story depicted a mother's exhaustion from tending to a retarded son. Under the name "Emily Hulot Olsen," Tillie submitted one or more story to the high-paying *Ladies' Home Journal*, whose motto was "Never Underestimate the Power of a Woman." Because these stories ran completely counter to the postwar image of women's power as homebodies, the editors apparently did not even reply.[40]

Tillie made herself an authority on free cultural opportunities for her girls, including museums, galleries, libraries, outdoor concerts, and movies. (They saw Disney's 1940 *Fantasia* at the California Labor School.) The older daughters also attended the Peters Wright School of Music and Dance, where tuition was based on income. Still Tillie asked Sam and Ida to help pay for lessons. Her impecunious state contrasted with three siblings' successes. Having helped rehabilitate and relocate thousands of displaced persons, Harry and Clare were treated as saints or deliverers.[41] Gene had made, Sam exclaimed, "$800.00!" writing a radio series "This is Europe," which was broadcast every Saturday evening. As a Merchant Marine, Gene now was bringing food to wartorn Italy. Lillian's husband Joseph Davis had established a medical practice near Poughkeepsie, New York, and the Davises lived on Apple Blossom Farm, in Duchess County. Pleased that Tillie's girls were "so exceptional talented in various fields," Sam regretted that he could not help. That April, he and Ida moved into a cottage behind the Davises' Dutch colonial, with a view of rolling hills, ponds, and rare trees cultivated there. Ida started a flower garden and imagined living out her days on the farm.[42] They had hardly gotten settled, however, before Sam decided they were too dependent on Lillian's family and too isolated. He campaigned to move to a Workmen's Circle home for the elderly, but Ida wanted to stay in Duchess County. After almost five months of squabbling over leaving or staying in upstate New York, Sam sent Tillie a postcard: "we bought a house at 1227 Randolph Street N.W." Near Jann and also Sam's sisters Rose and Chaika, the D.C. rowhouse was a compromise between Ida's isolated farm and Sam's communal haven.[43]

Inundated by suspicion, states began forming their own HUAC committees. In 1949, the California Committee on Un-American Activities labeled "the (Independent) Progressive Party as the above-ground organization of the Communist party." The Teamsters Union infiltrated the ILWU. According to Tillie, the ILWU had held free elections from "rank and file union" members. Thanks especially to Jack, it was remarkably free of racism and sexism.[44] The Teamsters, though, represented top-down thuggery that thrived on keeping its members ignorant and claimed to be anti-Communist.[45]

Probably in fall 1949, Tillie argued in a speech for the PTA that fascist countries "try to teach children simple blind obedience," but democracies should teach them "to think for themselves, to search for facts, to weigh conflicting viewpoints, to face problems, to make sound solutions, and to act on them." She urged parents and teachers to provide a "strong sense of the brotherhood of man," regardless of race, color, or creed. She did not mention gender equality, perhaps because "women" were assumed to be part of "mankind" or perhaps women's rights were too controversial in 1949. She ended on a surprisingly Christian note: "Tell them, yes, truth was crucified once, and put in the tomb; but on the third day it arose and lived; survived those that scourged and mocked it." The Inquisition was meant to curb the Renaissance, "to prevent the spread of these terrible ideas of science and democracy; but it failed." Then she spoke of a new inquisition in which un-Americans suppressed freedom in the name of patriotism.

At the beginning of 1950, Sam sent a letter that made Tillie feel superior to Jann, who was in such financial straits that she might have to open a boarding house. Her brothers, however, were enjoying enormous success. Harry was moving to Bethesda, Maryland, as an attorney for the Veterans Administration. Sam exclaimed that "Eugene!" was "now in Paris France." In the competitive Lerner family dynamic, Tillie quickly sent a newspaper article and photograph of her as an especially attractive, prosperous-looking matron. The article about "Mrs. Jack Olsen, PTA President, Kate Kennedy School" described achievements remarkable in 1950: PTA membership doubled under her leadership; 80 percent of mothers participated in school affairs; a free neighborhood playground opened; class size was reduced to twenty-five students; a kids' galosh exchange was set up before the rainy season. In addition, Tillie organized an evening session so working parents could meet the superintendent of schools.[46] The PTA selected her, with three others, to attend a six-week workshop at San Francisco State University, ostensibly on human relations. The real focus was freedom of thought, especially when Senator Joseph McCarthy was defaming anyone who thought differently from him. (He thought the entire Democratic Party was infiltrated by Communists and brandished a list of 205 supposedly "card-carrying Communists" working in the State Department.[47])

Sam and Ida were impressed by the photo of Tillie, but Sam worried how she was making "ends meet when Jack is not working." HUAC and McCarthy had spread the rumor that Commie dockworkers might smuggle in guns to launch an insurrection. Knuckling under to the FBI, the Smith Act, the Taft-Hartley Act, and the Teamsters, the ILWU had thrown Jack Olsen, former union officer, former decorated soldier, and former Commie, to the wolves.[48] Tillie later protested: "what kind of threat was I? was Jack? What the hell could we do?"[49] Nevertheless, an anti-Communist zeitgeist condemned them. Chilean poet Pablo Neruda warned of a "hangman" working like the Gestapo in the former haven of democracy. Tillie and Jack felt the noose tightening around their necks.[50]

Gene Lerner's pacifism, war exemption, and homosexuality also made him vulnerable to HUAC so he returned to the states only briefly to see the family in the East. The liberation of Rome in 1944 had begun an Italian-American romance of both real and vicarious Roman holidays. With America so hostile and Italy so friendly to Hollywood and the dollar, Gene capitalized on his show-biz and Italian experiences to launch an Italian-American film agency with Hank Kaufman. On 10 April 1950, Lerner and Kaufman invited the Davis and Lerner families to celebrate their departure on the SS Liberté. Ida feared that she would never see Gene again, but, after seeing "what a palace you were sailing on," she returned to D.C. somewhat reassured.[51] She and Sam promised Karla that her Uncle Gene would help her pursue her surprising new ambition: called "funny-face" as a child, she now wanted to be a clown.[52]

Tillie identified not with Gene's "fantasy life" but with Agnes Smedley's ruined one. After Mao Tse-tung's Communists took Peking in 1949, General MacArthur accused her of being a Soviet spy. Hounded by accusations, she died in May 1950, just before North Korea invaded South Korea. Tillie clipped out Smedley's obituary and copied her on male fascism: "I would rather be a prostitute than a married woman. I could then protect, feed, and respect myself, and maintain some right over my own body."[53]

One evening in June, Tillie was ironing clothes for her daughters, looking out the kitchen window at a purple sunset, singing a Woody Guthrie ballad to herself, when the phone rang. Upon answering, she heard her friend

Jean Wortheimer talking about a radio commentator named Tarantino, who had named Tillie Olsen as a "dangerous communist operating in the Kate Kennedy District." As the phone kept ringing, Tillie began a letter to the superintendent about being dubbed "dangerous" (she used red ink for that word). She wrote that "after ransacking my recent past the best I could come up with were the following activities," which included a lunch for teachers, a library project, a newsletter, neighborhood playgrounds, PTA growth, and an inoculation program. Of course, the 1941 Communist state plenum had named the PTA as "one outfit we got to work in." For Tillie, at least by 1950, such work did not mean fomenting revolution. She still considered improving the lives of children and their families as a humane and basically Communist enterprise.[54]

She did not expect one "reaction to Tarantino": the PTA silently took her name off its citywide executive board. It did send her, without fanfare, to the Human Relations Workshop that summer. Though the San Francisco State University was south of the city, with ordinary architecture and raw landscaping, Tillie was "thrilled to be on a college campus." With three-year-old Laurie in tow, on the bus Tillie pointed out the busy people walking dogs, the beautiful clouds, and the hills dotted with scrub oaks. She could bring Laurie because SFSU had a campus child-care center. Laurie's pleasure in new little friends and a caring staff reminded Tillie how outside help makes child-raising easier and more fun. The workshop offered a "different relationship to people than I had ever had before in my life."[55] Shocked in one session to hear colleagues talk about "lower class" people, Tillie asked, "Why not say 'working class'?" She recovered "a sense of how much I had to contribute."[56]

With Julius and Ethel Rosenberg on trial that summer for sharing atomic secrets with the Soviets, public employees were forced take loyalty oaths verifying, not only that they supported the Constitution, but also that they were not and had never been members of the Communist Party. Civil servants were fired for not signing.[57] Richard Nixon resigned his congressional seat to fill an unexpired Senate term.[58] His name appeared more and more in California papers. The names JACK OLSEN and TILLIE OLSEN disappeared.

The ILWU could not expel Jack, but it could send him back to the waterfront. Every morning, he had to appear in a hiring hall and wait for a warehouse job. Knowing that Jack would insist on enforcing contracts, his former employer at Merchants Ice and Cold Storage refused to hire him. Labeled a commie, Jack kept getting laid off from the jobs he briefly held.[59] Tillie's "ever modest Jack" had always fought for others better than for himself. The war experience, which he still would not discuss, had drained his resiliency. Against a national intolerant, anti-Communist crusade, he could not make a living. Knowing that "the kids were calling 'food, daddy, food,'" Jack felt like a failure. And so did Tillie. In October 1950, for Jack's father's seventieth birthday, she gave a talk asserting that ordinary "people will win against the ruling class."[60] Her optimism rang hollow, given the growing capitalist success of Jack's brother Max, the capitalist and artistic success of Tillie's brother Gene, and the socialist failures of Tillie and Jack. She picked up odd jobs and tried to fend off "economic wolves" demanding payment on the mortgage, loans, and bills. She paid a personal toll, lamenting "how much it uses up of me the morning running from place to place to cash checks to put in the bank to cover the checks I cashed to cover the checks I cashed."[61] Money juggling brought more fines, fees, and ever higher interest rates, sliding the Olsens into an economic downspout.

Then Paul Cline reentered Tillie's life. Still handsome and witty, he had left his wife to marry a woman named Helen Oprian, who sold advertising for the *DPW*. Cline prospered selling Johns Mansfield asbestos siding to cover (and save) the weathered frame exteriors of San Francisco's Victorian houses. His charm and success, not to mention his house with a turret on Lower Terrace, down from the tops of Twin Peaks, seem to have resurrected Tillie's feelings: "from the other place I could see the tower under which you lived—here I have not that torture." Such sentiments violated the image of the GI's ideal wife. She felt a "traitor" to Jack.[62]

America's postwar shopping spree had inflated prices and left citizens awash in personal debt. Currents of fear had eroded postwar euphoria. Debates about putting the A-bomb genie back in the bottle when Truman asked Congress for a billion dollars to develop a hydrogen bomb. Wide-circulation magazines like *Colliers* and *U.S. News and World Report* advised readers to prepare for an atom bomb attack by building basement bomb shelters and hoarding supplies; schools conducted air raid drills and gave children metal name tags so their dead bodies could be identified after the bomb.[63] In his Nobel Prize address, William Faulkner regretted that "There is only the question: When will I be blown up?" When she looked out her window onto Laidley Street, Tillie saw people newly suspicious of each other and frightened for their futures. Her ability to write what she wanted seemed broken under the dual zeitgeist of antifeminism and anticommunism. She had jotted down "whatever is worthy of recording—for half an hour a day—[only] to be destroyed afterwards," but she feared that her jotting "says nothing and re-says nothing [despite the] shaping of twenty years." With an empty bank account, only pick-up jobs, and a family of six to feed on meager woman's wages, however, she could not make much of her "beguns" and "unfinished," though her old talents and ambitions had begun "flexing and groping again."[64]

A virtual tsunami of fear and suspicion had washed away American freedoms and almost submerged Tillie and Jack Olsen. The happy prospects they enjoyed after he returned from war and the postwar ambitions she had struggled to voice now seemed like treasure lost on the floor of the sea. Tillie recalled "1950, that's when it all ended."[65] Her ambiguous "it" referred to dreams for an America of freedom and tolerance and joy. It also seems to have referred to her vision of writing stories about the lives women actually live.

CHAPTER 10

VICTIM AND REMAKER

1951–1955

I keep on dividing myself and flow apart, I who want to run in one river and become great.

—Tillie Olsen, 1953–1954 notebook

Tillie faced the New Year in a state of dread. Gleeful reports of U.S. successful testing of a massively destructive hydrogen bomb appalled her, as did flag-waving over "police action" in North Korea, which bombed villages, refineries, ports, and infrastructure. After an FBI agent confessed, in the *Saturday Evening Post*, that he had worked undercover in the "dirty" Communist Party, Hollywood validated its anticommunism with *I Was a Communist for the FBI*. Mickey Spillane wrote pulp fiction about a tough guy ridding America of "red sons-of-bitches who should have died long ago." Malcolm Cowley called such writing paranoid and sadistic, but Spillane was a repeat best-seller, not a good sign for Tillie's "beguns" to become successful fiction.

Jack saw no chance of "becoming a full time officer again, or, at any rate, having the kind of influence I had had." He had edited the ILWU bulletin and enjoyed "playing around with lead and ink" so he approached the owner of American Printing and Lithographics. Grateful for the $32,000-a-year in union business Jack used to bring him, the owner agreed early in 1951 to take him on as a registered apprentice. Jack soon "got 2 checks—one as apprentice, another from the government," under the 1944 GI Bill. The total was "approximately what I used to make as a warehouseman," not as a union officer. The former "mover and shaker" in a powerful union now had to do homework at night and was, like any apprentice, called "boy."

At thirty-nine, Tillie was so overwhelmed by chores that a fish bowl full of dead guppies was yet another instance of "defeat by the minutia of everyday living." On Saturdays, she still managed to walk with her girls downhill to the Mission Library. After loading up on books, they rewarded themselves with trolley rides home. Their book-reading, however, struggled against popular culture. Cookbooks showed smiling housewives emerging from kitchens in high heels and pretty dresses with platters of food for a seated husband and children. If her girls went to Saturday afternoon matinees, they saw movies, like *Ma and Pa Kettle* and *Cheaper by the Dozen*, whose huge families implicitly condemned both birth control and professions for women.

When Paul Cline and Helen Oprian had married, they sent Helen's daughter Virginia to her father in Detroit to escape anti-Communist reprisals.[1] Now she joined her mother and Paul in the turreted house down Twin Peaks. In January 1951, Virginia enrolled in Mission High School, where Julie Olsen befriended her. When the Cline family visited the Olsens, Virginia observed that Tillie was "not much of a cook." Perhaps having Cline in her house frazzled her. Certainly, Tillie wondered how a former Communist leader like him escaped the witch hunt that was ruining the Olsens.

In their mixed-race neighborhood, the Hawaiian girls taught seven-year-old Kathie hula dancing and the African Americans taught her jive-talk. After school, her pals played records and danced at the Olsens, with little Laurie stomping and clapping in time. When the Olsen girls wanted to do homework or read books, however, their ethnic friends usually vanished. Tillie lamented codes that make one set of children study and others skip school. President of the PTA, she campaigned against bomb drills and organized a genteel "Kate Kennedy Celebration."[2]

When Genya Gorelick died, Tillie wrote a poem regretting "a time when one says 'my people' and cannot mean the whole human race." On 16 March, when U.S. forces recaptured the ruined Seoul, the fate of untold Koreans reminded her of generations of Russian Jews, forebearers whose remains were "shoveled underground" and forgotten. She ended her poem to Genya with a note: "it isn't a poem you want to write; it's a speech."[3] She was, however, now too controversial a public figure to be invited to give speeches. For Al Richmond, sadness, disillusionment, and anger came in a succession of blows. Just after his mother's death, the FBI raided the *Daily People's World* offices, arrested Richmond, and confiscated records, including Tillie's columns on women's rights. Richmond was sentenced to a year in jail for "conspiracy to teach and advocate the violent overthrow of the U.S. government."[4]

HUAC was enticing anti-Communist witnesses by promising leniency. On 20 May 1951, Clifford Odets named names of former Communist associations and escaped jail. Playwright Lillian Hellman wrote that she could not "and will not cut my conscience to fit this year's fashions." Before HUAC on 21 May, she did not name names and somehow escaped jail. On 23 May 1951 Budd Schulberg was called. He felt justified in naming a dozen or so Communists because the CP had tried "mind control" on its members, including him. He would claim that he only repeated names already exposed, but Schulberg was the only person to name "Tillie Lerner."[5] Still, the FBI did not connect this "Tillie Lerner" with the "Tillie Olshansky" or "Tillie Olsen" it had been snooping on since 1944. When it made the connection, she would be at risk.

Jack's brother Max expanded Global Van on a huge plot of empty land outside of Anaheim. His absorption in money-making created Olshansky family tensions, especially when Jack's belief in an equitable distribution of wealth had cost him his job. Karla missed most Olshansky get-togethers, partly because she was an "Olsen" in name only and partly because she was an independent teenager. In June 1951, thanks to savings and her Lerner grandparents, she went to camp in Denver to take clowning classes.[6]

Battered by anticommunism and antifeminism, Tillie found even her vocabulary broken. She began keeping a list of her "significant slips": she said that someone spoke with "odor," when she meant to say "ardor"; she tried to quote someone but said to "vote" him; she offered the advice to "remember what you are and what you resent" when she meant "represent"; and she proclaimed, "I've got to live now," when she had intended only to say that she had "to leave now."[7] She did not examine the disillusionment and fear behind such slips.

Tillie Olsen, like Brer Rabbit, "lay low," still sensing a noose around her neck. When Al Addy's wife cut her hair, she easily got Tillie chatting about her activities, but then the woman would ask, "'Did the party tell you to do that?' And I always would be incredulous." It turned out that the FBI was paying Al Addy to join the Teamsters and help undermine the ILWU. After Al Addy testified to HUAC, Tillie realized her hairdresser had reported to the FBI and "to the PTA on my supposedly subversive activities."[8] The anti-Communist zeitgeist remained virulent in 1951.

Tillie was terrified early in 1952 to answer a knock on the door and sign for an official-looking document. But the dreaded subpoena was addressed to Jack, whom Al Addy and Lou Rosser had named as a Communist. Rosser also named Lincoln Steffens, Ella Winter, who had married Daniel Ogden Stewart in 1939 and fled to England in 1951, and Langston Hughes. Tillie wondered if Rosser had ratted on her husband to pay her back for ignoring his flirtatious 1937 letter. She also wondered if the FBI had paid for the cocktail party he gave back then. When Jack came before the California committee, he made a statement of noncooperation, as eloquent as Lillian Hellman's.[9]

Desperate to make ends meet, Tillie finally got a full-time, apolitical job, writing copy for the California American Automobile Association (AAA), on Van Ness Avenue. She scanned the papers hoping that the names "Tillie Lerner" or "Tillie Olsen" did not surface again in the American inquisition. She resented that the trickle of public outrage was channeled mostly toward the prosecution of ten famous Hollywood talents. She tried to hide her fears from her daughters, who, after school, would "play ball or paper dolls or do our homework or read our library books, but, really, we were just waiting for her." After "whirlwind" dinner preparations and somewhat calmer dinners, Tillie packed lunches and ironed dresses, "helping us to assemble school projects or Halloween costumes or whatever the crisis of the week might be."[10] Her daughters loved her wacky ways and thought her the "funnest" mother they knew, having no inkling that Tillie's wackiness served as a lid over a deep well of despair. In snatched moments alone, Tillie copied out favorite lines of poetry and recorded her depressed moods and fears.

In summer 1952, Karla "flew the nest," as Tillie would say.[11] She had expanded her clowning and dancing to take courses, including creative writing, at San Francisco State University. Worried about her nineteen-year-old daughter, Tillie thought a story could be written about her. In a notebook she jotted down: "House full—Laurie almost kindergarten—Worked part time later full time—Tried to learn my craft." She soon discovered, however, that the craft of story-writing was more complicated than she had known. Recalling their goodness to Karla, she sent her parents an invitation to visit, apparently her first letter in a year and a half. Surprised, Sam regretted "the way my old age have treated me" making him too tired to travel. He was now financial secretary of the Franklin D. Roosevelt Branch of the Workmen's Circle, and Ida a leader in the D.C. Progressive Women's Club. The outspokenness that had been a liability among Omaha women was an asset in D.C., and Ida often gave talks in Yiddish about Russian history, Yiddish and Russian writers, and her ideals of justice.

As a veteran who had joked about naming a son for "Ike," Jack was pleased that General Dwight D. Eisenhower was running for president, until Richard Nixon became his running mate. Tillie and Jack admired Democratic nominee Adlai Stevenson, whom Nixon smeared as an "egghead." They cheered to read that Charlie Chaplin, before fleeing to Europe, said Americans had been brainwashed into apathy when neighbors were "attacked, libeled, and ruined" and children were "taught to admire and emulate stool pigeons, to betray and to hate." Intellectuals predicted that an

Eisenhower victory might enable a McCarthy dictatorship.[12] Others wore "I Like Ike" buttons and equated Stevenson's subtlety with communism. Eisenhower and Nixon won by a landslide. Then Eisenhower set about extricating American troops from a Korean quagmire.

Late in 1952, the FBI finally connected the accused "Tillie Lerner" with "Tillie Olshansky." Though it misdated her birth as 1911, the FBI discovered that her first husband was "Abraham J. Goldfarb." It found the actual date for Jack's and Tillie's marriage on 29 February 1944. It identified Karla as "subject's child by her first marriage." The FBI said Tillie had been "active in the Young Communist League," had had "very late" Communist activities at CIO conventions and the California Labor School, but had "never held a high position in the Party." Reconciling its picture of a Commie traitor with her "numerous positions in welfare work on state and local levels" was problematic. The FBI requested J. Edgar Hoover's permission to interview her.

In January 1953 Hoover granted authority "to interview Olshansky." The FBI inquired at the San Francisco AAA office, which soon guaranteed that Tillie Olsen's employment "would be terminated in the very near future." AAA fired her in March, supposedly "due to a reduction in force." Though Stalin's death weakened the Soviet threat, the FBI still hounded American Communists. Like Jack, Tillie was thrown to the wolves. Unlike Jack, she carried the weight of the household on her shoulders. She had to take Kathie to Kaiser Hospital's Permanente Clinic "4 or 5 times a week for allergy testing" and treatment.[13] Laurie was an easy little girl, as musical as her sisters, but Tillie had to take her along to meetings and juggle child care for her when she got a job.

Scatterbrained Tillie often forgot to put out the garbage for its monthly pick-up. So on 16 April when Kathie heard a knock and looked down and saw two figures in the gathering dark, she called out "Garbage, Ma, garbage, garbage!" Tillie rushed down three flights of stairs with garbage bags in both hands and flung open the door. Two men in dark suits, tight collars, and dark ties greeted her. She dropped her garbage in the bin and invited in the men, who were clearly not garbage collectors but FBI agents. One agent "was very much surprised at the subject's friendliness." However cordial, Tillie was defiant. She predicted that in two years the government would not be "investigating such cases as hers." She said no more and terminated the interview.[14] After slamming the door, she collapsed on the stairs; her courage had drained away. Two months later, when the Rosenbergs were executed, she wondered if she were next. In Korea, millions of peasants were dead, the countryside desecrated, only to have the July 1953 armistice reestablish the prewar North-South Korean boundary. Anti-Communist

Earl Warren, who had presided over the wartime internment of Japanese-Americans in California, became chief justice of the Supreme Court, in time to preside over the desegregation case, *Brown v. Board of Education*, which would be reargued in December. She might be asked, "Are you or have you ever been a member of the Communist Party?" Tillie would have to answer, "yes." She feared internment.[15]

In Italy, the Kaufman Lerner Film Agency was capitalizing on the romance of "Hollywood on the Tiber."[16] The agency represented Audrey Hepburn, who won the Best Actress Academy Award in *Roman Holiday*, secretly written by blacklisted Dalton Trumbo. Gene hobnobbed with stars like Hepburn and Ava Gardner and personalities like Harry Truman's daughter Margaret. His parents and other sisters loved to hear him name-drop on transatlantic calls. Tillie did not. She thought Gene had disobeyed Ida's advice "never lose touch with the simple people."[17] Once when Gene rang D.C., Sam was away looking over a Workmen's Circle Home in Media, Pennsylvania. Ida spoke more openly than usual and then sent Gene one of her rare hand-written letters; she was thrilled that he could make his voice "fly 3500 miles." She no longer cared "to go places to se[e] people," but she did care about history and humanity. She asked if Gene thought the Romans and Greeks had attained a better world. To her, each individual seemed like a tree in a dense forest that a lantern can illuminate with only tiny circles of light.[18]

Back in D.C., Sam lamented to Tillie: "we have no future, we are living in the past." He recalled their "youthfull life, which was so rich with idealism, romanticism and purpose. The struggle for existence after our marriage the raising of our family under such a poor living condition in the spirit of our Ideas. Happy to say our sacrifice was worth while our children are normal." Sixteen grandchildren were "something to be happy about," but "day and night the memories of the past" obsessed them, "mother especially." Sending fifty dollars, he hoped that "your situation will change to better and more happy days." His letter reminded Tillie that art and idealism survive even when people do not. She did not want to be merely "shoveled underground" like unidentified holocaust survivors. She wanted to begin again "writing—something of us to exist after death."

She confided in a journal: "15 years of our lives tangled & interwoven & each amputated root hurts." Probably she was then pulling up her roots in the Communist Party and reviewing the past from Abe's death through Karla's present emergence as a resentful but accomplished teenager. She knew that story ideas like the one about the horny widow were trivial, but profound new insights, like one about a Hispanic boy who gets a life sentence in kindergarten, were too socially complex to compress into a short story. Besides, Tillie admitted to herself, her ideas offered "themes & no stories."[19] A story about Karla, however, should be compassable. Of course, it would be domestic, when most American fiction was adventurous and macho. Whether domestic fiction could be "great" was another matter. Tillie vowed to make it so.

Battered by informers, paralyzed by fear, harassed by housewifely duties, Tillie turned forty-two early in 1954. She was so good-looking she could pick up extra money modeling for advertisers. With Jack still an apprentice, though, Tillie was forced to take other jobs to pay the bills. Her fragmentary private notes reveal her deepening frustration with money, home, and children. Sometimes she felt stories festering inside. Sometimes she tried to write in her sleep. Sometimes the girls seemed like drowning creatures grabbing onto and wrecking her barely refloated lifeboat:

> In Kafka's work: like a squirrel in its cage ... at night ironing and jotting down after children in bed ... deep night hours for as long as I could stay awake never a spot of my own ...
>
> Pushed by the most elementary force—money—further more impossibly away from writing ... Compulsion so fierce at night
>
> brutal impulse to shove Julie away from typewriter
>
> voices of kids calling—to be able to chop chop chop like hands from the lifeboat to leave me free ... My conflict—to reconcile work with life ... Time it festered and congested postponed deferred and once started up again the insane desire, like an aroused woman. ... conscious of the creative abilities within me, more than I can encompass ... 1953–54: I keep on dividing myself and flow apart, I who want to run in one river and become great. ... [20]

Determined to reclaim greatness, Tillie called on Arthur Foff, Karla's creative writing teacher at San Francisco State. She told about being a *cause célèbre* in 1934 and showed him beginnings of a story about Emily, a stand-in for Karla, who feels "corroding resentment" over her upbringing. He was so impressed he let Tillie sit in on his class.

In 1954, 75 percent of Americans still believed that Communists should be stripped of citizenship and almost half believed that Communists should be jailed as un-American. In March 1954, Edward R. Murrow finally exposed Joseph McCarthy's witch-hunting tactics on the CBS television program *See It Now*. Neighbors called Tillie and Jack down the street to view the broadcast, which included film clips of McCarthy browbeating witnesses for not being *true* Americans. Volunteering to babysit free for neighbors who owned televisions, Julie brought back news of *Father Knows Best*, which appeared on TV in 1954 (without a question mark), and of America's most popular TV program, *I Love Lucy*, sponsored by Philip Morris. Tillie was distressed to learn of the insulting picture of women such shows promulgated and of the insulting image of corrupt dockworkers in *On the Waterfront*, a film by Elia Kazan and Budd Schulberg, both of whom had squealed on Hollywood Commies.[21]

Sam's pride in Gene, who had escaped the witch-hunt, irritated Tillie who had been run to ground by it. When Gene flew to Hollywood and then San Francisco where he stayed at the Mark Hopkins Hotel on Nob Hill, Tillie was away and so missed ten-year-old Kathie's response to her "magical" uncle. Kathie found Gene, with a scarf dramatically draped around his neck, the first "fabulously well-dressed" man she had ever seen.[22] Sam was proud of Gene's "happy life" and business "adventure," which Tillie knew was both a business and sexual partnership with Hank Kaufman. She hardly noticed when Sam said Ida was "complaining. But nothing serious. I think just age. Hard to get adjusted to it."

That April, Tillie fell down a whole flight of steep stairs at 70 Laidley, calling out as she bounced down, "Don't worry girls, I'm alright." Her daughters took her call as an amusing instance of resilience. Tillie herself converted the fall, emergency room visit, and fifteen stitches into an opportunity. Her doctor signed papers giving her six weeks of disability pay, which she called her "Dr Raimundi fellowship."[23] At last Tillie had an opportunity to develop the Karla story beyond a teenager's "corroding resentment" into a tale of resilience. Such a tale would be self-exonerating, too, if Tillie could tell it without admitting that Karla had been mailed like a package between Los Angeles, Omaha, and Faribault so that Tillie could work for the party, that she had become undernourished while with Tillie, not someone else, and that Tillie would have given Karla up to the Schochets if they had promised her Marxist upbringing. Tillie revised herself into a mother suffering from more socially acceptable guilt: as a poor, working, and single mother who left her daughter with a neglectful babysitter, let her be sent to an inhumane convalescent home, and displaced her daughter with younger children. Visited by a school counselor, the mother ruminates on her responsibility as she stands ironing.

Assuming that the chief justice was a racist, Tillie was astonished on 17 May 1954 to hear Earl Warren reading on the radio the Court's unanimous decision that the "doctrine of 'separate but equal' has no place in the public schools." Citing the Fourteenth Amendment, the Court said that segregation by race in public schools denies Negro children equal protection under the Constitution of the United States of America. With

McCarthy exposed and segregation outlawed, the zeitgeist seemed to be changing.

Calling her Karla story "Help Her Believe," Tillie kept rewriting to connect the mother's meditation on her daughter with the age "of depression, of war, of fear." The mother/narrator admits balancing Emily and her blond half-sister "so badly, those earlier years," yet Emily has emerged as a vital new self, even able to clown.[24] Emily excuses not studying because "in a couple of years when we'll all be atom-dead," and test scores will not matter. Projecting her own guilt onto the anonymous mother allowed Tillie to both cope with and displace it, to use and avoid autobiography. Her powerful final sentence is a secular prayer against victimhood: "Only help her to know . . . that she is more than this dress on the ironing board, helpless before the iron." Tillie herself was a helpless victim of McCarthyism; at issue was whether she could also be resilient.

Writing "Help Her Believe" prompted Tillie to send pictures of herself and Karla to her parents, and Sam responded, "Can you people still spare the time and come for a visit if we will help you out in 200 to 300.00. Take a pencil and figure out." Tillie accepted in a special delivery letter, and Sam quickly sent money to bring the Olsens east that August. He competently sent train schedules and phone numbers and explained how to stop in Poughkeepsie to see Lillian, to navigate New York City, to board a train at Penn Station to D.C., and to wait at Union Station, where he and Ida could meet them.

The five Olsens took the ferry to Oakland, where they caught a train to Omaha. They stayed there a night or so, meeting Vicki's husband Sonny Richards and children Sandy, Cory, and Scott. They marveled at the Art Deco Union Pacific train station, which Tillie said Sam had helped paint. Then they boarded a train to Chicago, thence to New York City, and thence to D.C. They did not stop to see Lillian and her family because, Kathie thought, her Aunt Lillian had distanced herself from the leftist Olsens. Actually, Tillie had distanced herself by ignoring Lillian's pleas to write their parents and not to tax Ida. Also, Tillie did not want to relive her 1944 failure to call Lillian, a failure which had sent Jack off to war feeling abandoned.[25]

When the Olsens arrived in D.C., they did not trouble Ida and Sam but hailed a taxi. Kathie, not yet eleven, had never seen really old buildings or ridden in a taxi. The thrill soon faded, however, as the driver drove through a slum. When Jack asked what he thought about the Supreme Court's *Brown v. Board of Education* decision, he began a diatribe against "niggers." He threatened to "start Civil War II" rather than let his kids go to school with "animals." Jack shushed his appalled daughters. When they arrived at the Lerners' house, Jack explained why he had silenced his daughters: "You can't change people's minds if you don't know what they think." While the Olsens visited monuments and museums and saw the slave cottages behind Lee's Arlington mansion, they discussed the Declaration of Independence, the Bill of Rights, the Constitution, and the best and worst of the American experience.

They enjoyed returning in the evenings, hot and tired from sightseeing, to the Lerners' new house at 5024 2nd Street, N.W., a three-bedroom, three-bath rowhouse, not far from Rock Creek Cemetery, with porches, a recreation room, and two showers.[26] The girls were delighted by the big house and the fruits and vegetables in Ida's garden. The family went to Bethesda, as Ida and Sam did on Sundays, for dinner, and the Olsen girls met cousins they didn't know they had.[27] There Tillie suddenly envisioned a novel about her family: a couple, like Ida and Sam, would be survivors of the 1905 Russian Revolution; like Ida and Sam that summer, they would be sixty-nine and would have lived together forty-seven years; like Ida and Sam, they would argue about moving to an old folks' home; like Ida and Sam, they would have six remarkable children in very different financial circumstances.[28]

On the way back, the Olsens' layover in Chicago was just long enough for an excursion to the Field Museum, where a guard disapproved of taking young girls to a controversial exhibit on the development of the human fetus, but it enabled Kathie to comprehend the bodily changes she and her friends were experiencing. The Olsens' absorption in the exhibit made them almost miss the train to Omaha. Afterward, Kathie penned a letter to her grandparents from the "San Francisco Overland": "Aunt Vicki and Uncle Sonny took us on a picnic at Carter Lake and did we have fun. We saw where mommy was born and where she went to school." She retained a "glowing" memory of the trip's eye-opening insight into history, politics, biology, and family. It served as a major civics lesson.[29]

Kathie then entered James Lick Junior High. One of her best friends, African American Josephine Benion, went elsewhere. When Josie was about to be confirmed in the African Methodist Episcopal church, Tillie tried to reunite the girls by taking Kathie to the ceremony. They were the only white people in the congregation. Kathie had never heard of, much less seen, people in the "throes of religious ecstasy." As the choir sang Gospel music and the preacher intoned rhythmically, Kathie saw people around her crying, yelling, even writhing on the floor of the small, closed-in church. Feeling suffocated, she hyperventilated and seemed to faint until Tillie got her out into the air blowing up from the Bay. Kathie reveled in the attention because it was a "big deal" to be alone in the car with Tillie, but she felt alienated from Josie.[30] Though the Court had ruled against segregation, Kathie and Josie had self-segregated.

Julie was a junior at Mission High, where she inspired an after-school group that prepared skits and musical presentations. Among the group were Rob Edwards and T. Mike Walker, who worked after school in a restaurant his usually drunken father ran. One Sunday, Mike went to a movie with Julie, and Tillie and Jack included him in their family dinner. That was a "shock" for Mike: "I think it was the first real 'family' I ever saw in action. They were talking, laughing, joking, teasing, telling their stories of the day, being listened to with respect, being responded to with love. They discussed literature, music, film, and politics. They wanted to know what I thought, what I believed, what authors I was reading." Given his dysfunctional family, Mike was in love with the Olsens, who sent him home with "books to read and a heart full of hope."

Sam wrote that Ida had gotten sick the day after the Olsens left, but they had been "happy having you here even for such a short time." Though they had met in 1944, this visit offered Sam his "1st opportunity to get acquainted with Jack. I admire him, a nice boy." Gene picked up on news of Ida's sickness with a "personal prayer" for her health.[31]

For Arthur Foff's writing class, Tillie made notes for more stories, including one about "Whitey. Marriage." After the Clines' visit, she admitted, "I wrote nothing of Paul & the emotions in all of us—the silence that entwined us." On one of Foff's hand-outs, she added notes on "point of view" and "transition," artistic issues she needed to master. In class, she talked so much that the legally enrolled undergraduates protested that she was monopolizing their class. Then Foff began holding private sessions with Tillie and heard how family obligations interfered with her writing. For instance, that October Avrum Olshansky died. Leon came over to Laidley to sit with Jack on the stairs, and both of them wept. But the burden of caring for the widowed Bluma fell on Tillie.[32]

Tillie did put time with her mother-in-law to good use. When Bluma slept, Tillie let story ideas "flood" over. She sent Jack a few pages, and he responded with praise for the "beautiful, beautiful words you asked me to type up for you."[33] Tillie now felt confident that shaping beautiful words into stories would rescue her from the fear and depression that had sapped her strengths. Still in Venice, she worked on a story about Whitey Gleason and another about Kathie and Josie. Sam wrote her on 16 November 1954 to console "our Jack" and share news that "the Dr said it is nothing to be alarmed about Mother's lump. And me and Mother are feeling fair. Do not worry about us we have no chronical diseases." Tillie, apparently, did not reply.[34]

After she returned from Venice, Tillie had to rush Kathie to the clinic for a serious ear and throat infection and then had to watch over her. She bombarded Foff with woeful tales about family troubles and writing problems. He suggested that she organize her life and apply for a fellowship, which would pay her to do nothing but write. Tillie doubted that such a magical opportunity existed, but she became a believer when the mail included an application form from Stanford's Creative Writing program.[35] When she realized that Stanford required a recommendation, though, she feared no one would recommend a Commie and that the FBI would keep her out. Foff did recommend her; Tillie accompanied her application with a copy of "Help Her Believe."

Toward the end of November, Sam wrote to congratulate Karla on being on a dance tour and to remind her how much he and Ida had loved her since she was a little girl. Sam also wrote Julie who was "a president of a class, a poet, a writer, organizer, and entertainer all in one isn't that wonderfull." With her older daughters thriving, Tillie exulted in "writing down fast—letting flood the stories I have—I am having a happy time . . . half the time I am crying with a fulfilled joy." She acknowledged that formerly she had taken misfortune as a stimulus to writing: "maybe I am going to have to abandon the kind of pain with which I wrote before." She was "beginning to heal." Her mood improved even more with the news that the U.S. Senate censured McCarthy.[36]

While her creative juices flooded into the sailor and segregation stories, Tillie had little energy for her complicated "grandfather-grandmother" story. Nevertheless, she paid attention to news of Sam and Ida's trip to Omaha in January 1955. Though Ida's "tension and fatigue" showed, Vicki wrote Tillie that Ida was "in 7th heaven being back in Omaha," while Sam fretted about missing important Workmen's Circle meetings in D.C., worries that "irked Mom." Vicki did not know what was wrong with Ida's health.

In 1955, television's *Ozzie and Harriet, Leave It to Beaver*, and *Father Knows Best* still showed Anglo-Saxon families without discord, anger, or sex and mothers barely able to function outside the home. Philip Morris produced Marlboro Man advertisements. McDonald's franchises opened nationwide and made identical hamburgers all across the country. HUAC subpoenaed Arthur Miller because his play *The Crucible* exposed the mass hysteria behind the Salem witch trials of 1692 and, by implication, HUAC's 1950s trials.[37] Alcoa Corporation withdrew regular sponsorship from Murrow's controversial *See It Now*. Cracks were, however, showing in American conformist porcelain. A group of self-described "Beat" poets in New York and California shocked the public with drug-induced, unconventional, and irreverent poems. Actor James Dean and singer Elvis Presley became hugely popular precisely because they were rebels.[38]

At Stanford, a male graduate student almost discarded Tillie's "Help Her Believe," apparently assuming it was as conventional as *Ozzie and Harriet*. Then a young faculty member recognized just how unconventional was the story of a woman who does not know what is best. He personally delivered Tillie's application to Wallace Stegner. On 1 April 1955, Tillie answered the phone and heard a strange voice saying that his name was Stegner, he was head of Stanford's creative writing program, and Tillie Olsen was one of three Jones Fellows in creative writing.[39] She first thought it was an April Fool's joke. When she realized it was not, Tillie seized her chance to become at last a great writer.

Sam wrote in late April "Mother is about the same complaining once in a while but nothing serious"; she just had indigestion, pains in her lower abdomen, and spells of weakness. Despite Sam's assurances, his references to Ida's "lump" and complaints seemed ominous. Tillie made a Mother's Day call, but Sam and Ida were spending the month with Lillian, Joe, and their daughters. After they returned, Sam wrote Tillie about "pears, a few cherries grapes and mulberries, some strawberries in our garden we have tomatoes, beets, beans, peas, corn radishes and cucumbers. Roses and other flowers." Ida had proved herself indeed, in Gene's words, "Nature's friend."

Ida's complaints continued until she had a colonoscopy, removing benign polyps. In a letter to her regular doctor, dated 22 July 1955, the specialist said that Ida was not "having enough trouble to justify any [further] surgical interference." He suggested "avoiding highly seasoned foods, roughage and fats or greasy foods. Try to impress on her the importance of chewing her food well." She should rest "with her feet elevated."[40]

When Whitey Gleason dropped in on the Olsens, Julie, who had been his "special kid," was now "frightened (very) by his drunkenness." She had great empathy for her friend T. Mike Walker, who was homeless, but not for Whitey, who created his own homelessness.[41] Tillie was holding down a job and stealing moments to work on her story about Whitey's interaction with her family. She used autobiography: a "house on a hill" with "innumerable" steps; a tired mother (named Helen); a kind but stern father (named Lennie); economic troubles; three daughters, the youngest (Allie, based on Laurie), the middle one (Carol, based on Kathie), and the eldest (Jeannie, based on Julie), offended by the embarrassingly drunk sailor.[42]

Tillie chose the title "Hey Sailor, What Ship?" She revised to try and mute autobiography.

She sent her parents some photographs from an Olsen family camping trip, and Sam replied in August that Ida was improving but her medical expenses were "hard on me." He complained about his own health and the need to plan "for our short future," by moving to a Workmen's Circle home. He was pleased that Karla was embarking on a dancing and modeling career. He and Ida were proud of Joseph Davis's clinic and of Gene's "spacious 5 room office in Rome, elegantly furnished" and his "contracts for Brazzi for $400,000."[43] At the end of August, Sam sent a postcard assuring Tillie that "Mother is improving but very slow." Karla visited her grandparents on her way to New York, but Ida was furious to learn that Tillie had sent Karla to stay with Sam Braude, the cousin Tillie had called "Babbitt Sammy" back in 1929.[44]

That August, tired of sleeping in car trunks and on friends' porches, T. Mike Walker asked if he could stay with the Olsens, in the odd empty room squeezed between the garage and their lower floor. He got a job with U.S. Postal Service, thanks to Jack's help, paid minimal rent, and became a member of the Olsen's extended family for nearly a year. He and Julie played piano and guitar, picking out songs almost every night from Woody Guthrie, Pete Seeger, Odetta, and the Weavers. Why did Tillie, who had recently written that she felt like chopping off the hands of children clinging to her lifeboat, willingly add another child of sorts to her household? Her magnetic personality of course thrived on having people drawn to her. Also, obligations could be revised as excuses.

Tillie reportedly was surprised to learn that she would need to attend classes at Stanford. Once details were ironed out, though, she began making twice-weekly bus rides from San Francisco to Palo Alto and Stanford University's gorgeous Italian Renaissance campus.[45] Her fall seminar was taught by Richard Scowcroft, four years her junior, a Harvard Ph.D., and author of social novels, most recently *A View of the Bay*. Among graduate students at such a prestigious university, Tillie feared that she would be scorned for being forty plus and diploma-less. The class of ten or so students, as Bill Wiegand remembered, had no such problem. They understood that Tillie had had experiences as "a journalist before the war, in politics, and domestically." In casual wash-and-wear slacks, she also "looked great."

Scowcroft taught by reading students' stories out loud, suggesting only with a nod, or the lack of one, his opinion, and then asking for students' reactions. Wiegand remembered that on probably the second class meeting, a "dark and lowering day," Scowcroft read "Hey Sailor," beginning as Whitey "gropes for his glass" and "digs into his pockets to see how much he has left." His hands tremble and he wonders, "Where'd it all go?" The one true harbor for the fictional Whitey has been Lennie and Helen's home, but Jeannie dismisses him as "just a Howard Street wino now." The story's political implications avoid Soviet expansionism, as Whitey "never got ashore in Korea" but instead to sites of western exploitation. Whether the students caught the allusions, as Scowcroft read on and the storm raged outside, they were touched by Whitey's response to Carol's plea to "tell Crown 'n Deep." Tillie has him stand, swaying, and recite much of the Jose Rizal's 1896 "Valedictory": "*O crown and deep of my sorrows/ I am leaving all with thee.*" (Novelist and hero of Philippine independence, Rizal had promised that his voice would live even after the Spanish executed him.) Though Whitey represents stifled dreams, Rizal's words affirm that dreams need not die. The story ends as the fog lifts so Whitey can see "the tiny house he has left, its eyes unshaded. . . . Then he goes down." He literally goes down the hill and metaphorically into oblivion, leaving Lennie and Helen without him but with dreams of a better world. Only as Scowcroft finished reading the last words asking "*Hey Sailor, what ship? Hey Marinero, what ship?*" did the story's intensity, like the storm outside, abate.[46]

A teaching assistant in creative writing named Hannah Green heard that an older student named Tillie Olsen had written a transfixing story. Perhaps expecting a mentor, Hannah sought out Tillie. Formerly an undergraduate at Wellesley, where she had studied with Vladimir Nabokov, Hannah quickly discovered that her literary connections far outstripped anything that Tillie could imagine. Soon Hannah, though fifteen years younger, became Tillie's confidante and mentor.

When she wasn't traveling to Palo Alto, a reinvigorated Tillie made housekeeping entertaining by singing to loud music on the record player. She encouraged neighborhood kids to visit and took notes on black English: "why don't you hep you own brother—you so highamighty" or "whose gonna do it if I dont—without a man." Her notebooks mix Gospel music and "jive talk, jelly belly, geezy, peezy" with references to grieving figures in Käthe Kollwitz's drawings, quotations from Civil Rights leaders, and assertions she planned for Alva, the African-American mother: "Why I doin it for? . . two people treats we like peoples we peoples too."[47] Tillie set her story in an African-American church, where Helen and twelve-year-old Carol are the "only white people" attending the baptism of Parialee (Parry) Phillips. Her prose reaches a pitch of rhythmic intensity, as "the music leaps and prowls" and voices hit Carol's ears in "great humming waves." When Carol faints, Alva says, "'You not used to hearing what people keeps inside, Carol.'" Then Alva recalls being abandoned and led out of darkness by a little child (presumably Jesus). Later Helen tells Lennie about Carol's fainting in the black church and Jeannie's caustic remark on "sorting," or voluntary segregation. Carol and Parry become further alienated by puberty and high expectations for Carol, low ones for Parry. As the story ends, Helen reflects: "*It is a long baptism into the seas of humankind, my daughter. Better immersion than to live untouched.*" Helen herself longs for the nonjudgmental strength the African-American fellowship provides. Tillie titled the story "Baptism."

After Gene called D.C. to inquire about her health, Ida wrote on 27 September, thrilled to "hear your voys [voice] it made me so happy to feel you ner [near] me." Thinking that Sam had soured on the world, she remarked, "I am glad the children don't no [know] him as I do." She sent love to Gene and Hank, along with a blessing: "Somewhere in us is the neshoma [Yiddish for "soul"]. Your voys [voice] will follow me always[.] tink [thank] you son."[48] Three days after writing, despite the specialist's advice that she should keep her feet up but required no further "surgical interference," Ida and Sam boarded a train for Poughkeepsie, where Joseph Davis had arranged for her to check into Vassar Hospital. Tests there disclosed incurable gall bladder cancer and called for immediate surgery. Lillian tracked down Gene in Monte Carlo where he was negotiating a new contract with Rossano Brazzi. Through the static-filled international connection, he heard isolated words: "Mamma ... operation ... cancer ... incurable ... months." He broke down, cursing the Nature that Ida had cherished.[49] All the Lerners, except Tillie and Gene, traveled to Poughkeepsie for the operation in the first week of October.

While Tillie waited for news about her mother, her fellow writing students were abuzz over news that Allen Ginsberg read his epic poem "Howl" in San Francisco to wildly enthusiastic members of the Beat Generation. Shattering all definitions of literary propriety, Ginsberg seemed a new Walt Whitman. Tillie identified with the beginning of "Howl": "I saw the best minds of my generation/ destroyed by madness/ starving, mystical, naked. . . ." She, however, felt victimized by class and gender, while the Beats had victimized themselves mostly with drugs. Soon they became to literature what Elvis was to music.[50] Tillie feared her revisionary domestic fiction might already be upstaged.

The hospital released Ida on 18 October, and Lillian brought her mother home to Pleasant Valley. When the front door swung inward, Rivka Davis recalled feeling a wave of pleasure seeing her tiny grandmother in the doorway below. Soon grandmother Ida was installed in an upstairs bedroom, and grandfather Sam began joking and teasing without frightening little Rivka, then four years old.

Then a remarkable event transpired, as Lillian wrote Gene: "Ma says that for the last couple days, a tune has been running through her head which sends her back through the years to a time when she was perhaps not even two. And she wants me to send on to you her thoughts regarding that event of so long ago. She feels you could write up the event in a much better way—as she cannot express herself well in English. Could it be the basis for an article or story?" Ida was revisiting childhood rituals, hearing ancient tunes, and sometimes singing them in Yiddish. Fascinated, Lillian took notes in shorthand and wrote Gene that she might have missed "a few little things" but her notes were essentially accurate. Despite her lifelong atheism, Ida now felt that Jewish culture should not be "lost to the new generations." "Momentous occasions" like wedding celebrations that lasted days should be remembered. "Mom feels we should have some knowledge of and contact with our past. And she hopes someone in the musical field will revive the dances and music from those days when she was in the old country. Ma is anxious to know what you think about all this." Though Harry and Vicki had found comfort in Judaism, Lillian regretted being kept "so ignorant in these matters." (She might have but did not blame Ida.) She sent Gene and Tillie carbon copies of this transcription:[51]

The sparks were laid on the road of tens of years ago—the greater part of a century. Somewhere on a country road there was a gathering of many people—to bring together two people. And everyone, it so appeared, was very conscious of his part in this important event. A few chords have since followed me all these years—all my life; the joyfulness from those chords which breathed with spiritual sparks from the hearts of the people there. Excitement was awakened in me when I saw "Glory Brigade," as it seems to me the dance in that was taken from the wedding festivities I remember from so long ago. The "little flutes" played music so human and so buoyant, that these last couple of days it is as if I was there again at that wedding, and again only a year or two old, watching two groups of people moving, pushing, making motions in some kind of dance, with the bride and groom in the middle, surrounded; and the music was exhilarating and it electrified the air.[52] I have always had a longing for that music and that dance—which I think was reproduced in "Glory Brigade."

I know a few people who know about these old weddings: my sister-in-law in Palestine knows the old tradition; also Haike [Chaka Lerner Swartz, Sam's older sister], she used to go and dance, Mrs. Stein [too].

Ida asked, "When it is something that has been in me for 70 years, why is it not something worth while from a 'spiritual' standpoint?" At eighteen, Ida had "kicked god out of the house." At forty, she had said, "God and the human heart are a contradiction." At seventy, she used the Yiddish word for "spiritual."[53]

Tillie immediately wrote her mother:

> Have Lil and you (we hope we hope) managed some more time together for what is such a happy partnership—your talking and she transcribing it so beautifully. Your notes on the old country wedding with its dances and music have been read and re-read, not just by Jack and me and the kids, but by some of our friends. We were very moved by them There are two things I don't quite understand: what is Glory Brigade, where did you see it (stage, TV, movie?) and in what sense do you use the word "sparks" (the sparks were laid on the road of tens of years ago). Mom, will you please talk with Karla about the dancing and music? She often does her own choreography, and may figure out how to track down the music, if it is on records. Gene, too, may know people in the musical-dance world who may be of help. Certainly in the music, the dances, if lovingly done, there would be communicated some of the special quality of exhilaration you write.

Little Rivka sat by her grandmother's bedside for hours, singing songs, stroking her hair or arm, chatting about pretty flowers. Gene flew from Rome to help Lillian and comfort their mother. Lillian could not "talk freely over the phone" lest Ida hear what the family was trying to hide; but Ida knew she was dying and asked to see each of her children.[54] Gene planned to take her first to Bethesda, where she could see Jann and Harry and Clare, then to Omaha, where she could see Vicki and Tillie. Tillie agreed to meet there, but, according to Gene, wanted to bring Kathie and Laurie, too. Vicki insisted that Tillie come alone. Haunted by the picture of "My mother—her death bed—singing herself lullabies," Tillie wrote Lillian a rare conciliatory note, thanking her for that image.

In November 1955, the FBI recorded that Tillie Olsen was "reportedly giving less support to CP." Scowcroft found her completely apolitical by then, but he had no idea whether she was being politically expedient, thanks to McCarthyism, or artistically savvy, thanks to reading works that were undated by political concerns of one time or place. When Scowcroft asked students to evaluate each other's submissions, Tillie always found ways of "endorsing and encouraging" others' writings. She submitted no new work, so Scowcroft called her into his office to inquire why, after the success of "Hey Sailor," she had not turned in any other work. Stammering a little, Tillie told him that she was working on a long story but could not write because her mother was dying. He and she walked among palm trees and bougainvillea, and he consoled her by saying, "of course you can't write under such stress." They sat on a pebbled stone bench by a fountain, and she sobbed, "but I must write." So he said, "OK, do so." But then she wailed, "but I can't." Sometimes he played both roles, saying "you can't; you must; you can't; you must." His best advice was to write about what upset her so—her mother's approaching death. Forty-five years later, he recalled "much of my relationship with Tillie was conducted through a veil of tears." Wallace Stegner repeatedly observed, "Tillie is in a tizzy." She seemed always near hysteria, unable to write.[55]

Gene and Lil and Ida had their picture taken in the melting snow in front of the Davis's house. Then Gene and Ida flew from Poughkeepsie down to New York City, where they rested in a hotel for three days. Ida, he recalled, "was getting weaker" and "could go no further" than Bethesda.[56] A nurse of natural intelligence and empathy, Clare Lerner helped Ida settle into a guest bedroom and cared for her mother-in-law. When Gene called California with the news that Ida could not travel to Omaha, Tillie said she could not afford to fly to Washington. Exasperated, Gene sent her five hundred dollars.

When Gene and Sam started going through Ida's papers, they found Ida's old English class notebook from 1924–1925, which Sam gave to Gene. Ida mumbled to Gene: "One day I want you to go to Russia and bring back some of its earth. It does not belong to Stalin." She regretted being so hard on Jann and depriving her children of Jewish traditions. She even "in her dying days, wrote that Til should be writing a book about me!!!!!" Gene said he "had myself a near-hysterical laugh" at the idea of Tillie honoring him. Feeling himself "Ida's closest friend," Gene said a tearful good-bye to the woman he most admired on earth. Before he left, Ida whispered, "You will be my ambassador to the family." Then she wrote a last shaky scribble stressing the "need of caring for Karla."[57]

Progressive Women's Club members waited patiently in Harry and Clare's living room until Clare thought Ida could handle a last visit from each. (One woman was amazed that the dying Ida comforted her.) Harry and Clare translated from Yiddish a note Ida dictated. The women's kindness reminded her "of the spirit of the Workmen's Circle in its early days" and showed "how deep the seeds were planted by our early founders and leaders. It could be that unknown to us, this is the secret that holds us together."

Tillie scheduled a last-minute emergency trip late on Christmas Day; she changed planes in Chicago and then arrived in Detroit at one in the morning on 26 December. After a night in a luxurious airport hotel, she was to leave Detroit that afternoon, fly into New York and then Washington, but she begged for better arrangements because her mother was dying. Her sad tale got her the last seat in a first-class cabin on a nonstop flight to D.C. She wrote her family about her "gorgeous bath & shower before luxury breakfast in hotel" in Detroit and compared magazines available in first class with those in economy class. She sounded not at all proletarian. She arrived in Bethesda the night of 26 December.[58]

She found Clare in charge, Harry almost hibernating, and Sam as help-less as the children. The Lerners had just celebrated Sam's birthday, so their daughter Susan, almost eight, retained a specific memory that her grand-mother was semiconscious and hardly able to speak.[59] Trying to control her sobs, Tillie spent a few days by Ida's bedside with notebook at hand. The image of Ida's death bed vision not only haunted her but had become, to paraphrase Faulkner, the only image in life or literature that would move her very much.[60] She wanted desperately to recreate the "happy partner-ship" Lillian had managed with Ida in October. But Ida was apparently beyond revisiting old world recollections of songs and customs for and with Tillie.

Lillian responded to Tillie's note of thanks saying: "over the past years Mom felt closer to Gene and to you, as she felt you two had a better under-standing of her poetic and sentimental nature." Both wrote about Ida's death, and Tillie became obsessed by the image of "My mother—her death bed—singing herself lullabies." Oddly enough the notebook containing that phrase includes another: "Why A. hit so hard—that was what I was to write of & I have not kept it," apparently a vow to write about Goldfarb's death.[61] If she were thinking of Abe in 1955 when she said goodbye to her mother, the link between the two deaths must have been guilt, for she had rarely seen or written Ida and had abandoned Abe for other men and the Communist Party's requests. Now with Lillian's narrative of Ida's extraordi-nary vision, Tillie had a chance to redeem herself by writing of Ida's death and perhaps later of Abe's.

CHAPTER 11

GREAT VALUE
AS A WRITER

1956–1961

There is no Tillie Olsen. [Your stories are] the only identity you'll ever have.
— Nolan Miller to Tillie Olsen, 19 November 1957

After a tearful leave-taking, Tillie remained haunted by images of Ida's shrunken frame propped up on pillows, her blue eyes still steely but her voice almost silenced. Harry wrote that Ida had revived only enough to ask "very pointedly" if Tillie had written. Otherwise, "mother has visibly weakened since you left, and seems resigning herself." Vicki visited, as did Lillian, who wrote Tillie that Ida was "too tired to talk to me, only once she said my name."

Tillie returned to Stanford to greet Malcolm Cowley, now teaching her writing seminar. He had published her "Thousand Dollar Vagrant" in the *New Republic* in 1934 and had been a prominent figure in leftist intellectual circles. Now a senior editor at Viking Publishers, he had started its "portable" series, including the *Portable Faulkner* and the *Portable Hemingway*. Editing a novel by Jack Kerouac, Cowley was on the lookout for other unconventional writers. "Help Her to Believe" appeared in *Stanford Short Stories*, with a note on its composition and in *Pacific Spectator*.[1] Scowcroft sent it to his agent, Diarmuid Russell, who asked to see more of her writing. Tillie did not respond.

On 29 January 1956, Ida Goldberg departed her passionate and frustrated life.[2] She had insisted on having no ceremony, Jewish or otherwise. Of her six children, only Harry attended her burial. Tillie wrote her siblings that when she had last seen their mother, Ida had asked for her jewelry box and indicated that Jann should have her wedding ring, Clare should have carved ivory pieces Harry had sent from India, and Tillie could have whatever she wanted. This story presented ample grounds for embellishment: the sacrificial Tillie, who took only "single earrings for the kids to play with"; the fabricating Tillie, who told Ida she "would have lots of occasions to wear jewelry"; and the deserving Tillie who could have any of Ida's jewelry.[3]

Riding the bus to Palo Alto, Tillie was surrounded by cacophony of voices, young and old, black and white, Asian and Hispanic, rich and poor. Eavesdropping, she noted that such a lively mix of people would be criminal in the American South. In Montgomery, Alabama, Rosa Parks was in jail just for sitting at the front of a bus. Now a bus boycott, led by young Reverend Martin Luther King, Jr., challenged Montgomery's white middle class to choose between prejudice and profit. The early 1950s façade of conformity, propriety, privilege, and prejudice had cracked. Teenagers listened, not to elders who called Elvis Presley obscene, but to Elvis singing songs like "You Ain't Nothing but a Hound Dog" on their own transistor radios.[4] Tillie loved Elvis for his sexy rhythms and crossover songs that promised an interracial harmony now lost to Kathie and Josie.

In her grandparent story, Tillie made David and Eva near stand-ins for Sam and Ida, their children stand-ins for her brothers and sisters: Jann became the frustrated Clara; Harry and Clare became Paul and Nancy, who live near the old couple and entertain them on Sundays; Gene became Sammy, who is a smart-aleck; Lillian and Joseph Davis became the affluent Hannah and Phil; and Vicki became Vivi, who lives in Ohio and has four children. In her last stories, Tillie had based Helen and Lennie on herself and Jack. In this story, Helen vanishes, and Lennie becomes the son of Eva and David. Tillie added a son, Davy, who died in World War II. In her narration of the old couple's visits to their children, she injected such animus that Cowley told her to show "warmth to someone."[5]

Though Tillie did not criticize others in class, over coffee she counseled young Dick Elman to show more "social perspective" in his writing.[6] Sometimes Hannah Green drove Tillie home, up route 82, hearing about her struggle to come to terms with her mother's death and to write her grandparent story. Though feeling poorly, thanks to "absence of Mother," Sam set out on the journey originally planned for Ida. He went to Jann's, to Lillian's, and with Harry and Clare to Vicki's. He remained in Omaha after Harry and Clare left, reclaiming his prominence in the Workmen's Circle and amusing Vicki's children.

At the Olsens' home T. Mike Walker made his breakfast after the family left and noticed each morning that the kitchen waste basket was stuffed with sheets of paper, typed and then scribbled over. To Mike's eye, the same pages showed up "in the trash day after day" until he realized that Tillie's deletions, restructurings, and retypings were a painstaking way of improving each sentence. Meanwhile, Julie had applied to and was accepted at private Mills College in Oakland, where she would be a "token poor kid."[7]

As her Stanford time was ending Tillie finally sent Russell her three unpublished stories. He dismissed "Hey Sailor" as another drunken sailor story. An Irishman knowing little of American race relations, he disliked the segregation story "Baptism." He would "try" to place her grandparent story. Rebuffed, Tillie feared she would never become great, never redeem herself through writing. Again through a veil of tears, she turned to Scowcroft, who suggested she write Nolan Miller, a writer, teacher, and editor of the *Antioch Review* and a new book of college writings. Tillie stalled and then wrote Miller, as if under command: "Mr Scowcroft (Stanford) said to send this." She enclosed "Hey Sailor, What Ship?"

Miller received hundreds of stories each year, most of them about undergraduates' tribulations. A bachelor, who lived with his mother and deaf brother, he was touched by Tillie's tale of loneliness and troubles. Accepting it immediately, he asked if she knew about agents, publishers, grants, techniques to turn stories into novels, and the conventions of punctuation.[8] Tillie joyously called him a straw like "the one the drowning clutched." She had no time to write, nor could she "*inflate*" her story into a novel. She began pouring out her troubles to the far-away, literary, lonely Miller. She said she should not use "overwrought words like: implacable, ravening," but she did.

When Sam Lerner left Omaha for San Francisco, T. Mike Walker moved out.[9] In the evenings, Julie played the guitar and coaxed Sam to sing along. On weekends, Tillie and her girls took Sam on walks about the city. On Labor Day weekend, the Olsens took him camping at Big Sur. Unnerved by a query from Miller about her unconventional writing style, Tillie left the the beach to type up, on her portable typewriter, a defense of her odd syntax and lack of quotation marks. Miller quietly corrected punctuation to "Hey Sailor" but followed her by omitting quotation marks.

After Julie left for Mills and Sam for D.C., Tillie bragged to her siblings that their father had come to her seeming "at least 100, feeling already a dead man and waiting only for the physical finish." He had gained two pounds and was "fifty years younger when he left." He had talked lovingly of Ida as a young woman, and Tillie had jotted down his recollections to add to her grandparent story. She began riding early morning buses downtown to take dictation for the California Society of Internal Medicine.

Raisa Gisha Greenglaz Goldberg, maternal grandmother, c. 1900. Courtesy of Gene Lerner.

Mendel Lerner, paternal grandfather, c. 1904. Courtesy of Gene Lerner.

Ida (then Chaika)
Goldberg with Olga,
c. 1904. Courtesy
of Gene Lerner.

Jann (then Fannie),
Tillie, Lillian, and
Harry Lerner,
c. 1922. Courtesy
of Gene Lerner.

Rae Goldfarb Schochet, Tillie and Abe Goldfarb with baby Karla, 1933. Courtesy of Gretchen Spieler.

Sample page from "Us," intended to be a proletarian novel about the Depression, 1933. Courtesy of the Henry W. and Albert A. Berg Collection of English and American Literature, The New York Public Library, Astor, Lenox and Tilden Foundations.

Tillie Lerner in a cotton dress bought at J. C. Penney's "79¢ sale." Random House publicity photo, November 1934. Courtesy of Random House Records, Rare Book and Manuscript Library, Columbia University.

To Face Jury

Theresa Landale, 21, former University of California student, arrested in a communist raid according to police, whose demand for a jury trial was granted.

Tillie Lerner, alias Teresa Landale, "To Face Jury," San Francisco Call Bulletin (25 July 1934). Courtesy of the Magazine and Newspaper Center, San Francisco Public Library.

*Ida Goldberg [Lerner],
with Gene Lerner
and Karla Goldfarb,
June 1936. Courtesy
of Gene Lerner.*

*Tillie and Jack in Venice,
California, 1939. Courtesy
of Julie Olsen Edwards.*

Tillie Olsen, 1944.
Courtesy of
Julie Olsen Edwards.

Tillie with Jack
in uniform, 1944.
Courtesy of
Julie Olsen Edwards.

Ida and Sam Lerner, in backyard of, possibly, their new home in Washington, D.C., late 1940s. Courtesy of Gene Lerner.

Olsen family with Ida and Sam Lerner, December 1947. Courtesy of Julie Olsen Edwards.

Tillie and Jack, with Laurie, Kathie, Karla, and (kneeling in front) Julie, c. 1949, on the porch at the Laidley Street house. Courtesy of Julie Olsen Edwards.

Ida Lerner with Lillian Lerner Davis and Gene Lerner, early December 1955. Courtesy of Gene Lerner.

Tillie Olsen, c. 1961.
Courtesy of Julie
Olsen Edwards.

Lithograph of Tillie Olsen
by Barbara Swan, c. 1963.
Courtesy of Alan Fink.

Sample page from "My Mother's Dying Vision," 1977. Courtesy of Department of Special Collections and University Archives, Stanford University Libraries.

Tillie and Jack at the Karl Marx Memorial, Highgate Cemetery, London, 1979. Courtesy of Julie Olsen Edwards.

Tillie Olsen, photograph by Leonda Finke, January 1981. Courtesy of Leonda Finke.

Lerner siblings Vicki, Jann, Tillie, Harry, and Gene in Bethesda for the wedding of Howard Lerner and Elizabeth Goll, 1989, photograph by Lillian Lerner Davis. Courtesy of Gene Lerner.

Tillie Olsen at home in Berkeley, California, 2000. Photograph by Panthea Reid.

Tillie Olsen, 2006, photograph by Jesse Olsen Margolis. Courtesy of Jesse Olsen Margolis.

Tillie still felt a victim of her demanding family; Jack was "restless if we see no-one."[10] She wrote Cowley that "sustained writing is not possible for me with a family *and* work." She even proposed piteously that Stanford had been a mistake because "all the agony of getting back into writing and the wrench having to leave it" had turned her life into melodrama. She sent Miller "Baptism," and he forwarded it to poet Karl Shapiro, new editor of *Prairie Schooner,* a literary magazine from the University of Nebraska.

In November, Tillie went to Los Angeles to help Jack's sister Eva, who danced the night away before having her leg amputated. Tillie instructed Jack to open mail from *Prairie Schooner* and not tell the girls if "Baptism" were rejected. Instead, Jack soon told the whole family that it was accepted. Miller thought she must be a real writer "who can't stop writing just like breathing persons can't stop breathing." Such a theory might be true for a bachelor like Nolan Miller or a childless traveler like Katherine Anne Porter, not a working mother like Tillie.[11] The rough version of the grandparent story that she sent to Miller played on Jack's name by calling Ida's old-world shtetl "Olsana." Miller thought her narrative "most depressing and 'unrevealing.'" It was "far too long" and plagued by a "failure of form." She told "too many stories" about "too many of the children." It needed "*one* pattern." Perhaps she had "too *much* talent" and needed "to *use* your talent, not let it use *you*."[12] Maintaining that her story was not depressing, Tillie insisted that Eva would give David "back the sense of his life, and for her—transfiguration."

She was distressed when Nikita Khrushchev, new Soviet premier, denounced Stalin as a brutal despot, then she was appalled that October, when Khrushchev smashed a Hungarian uprising as brutally as he said Stalin had acted. CP-USA comrades like Tillie had excused purges, denied atrocities, and justified expansionism. Now they confronted undeniable evidence that the Soviet Communist oligarchy was every bit as ruthless as most Americans claimed. Another anti-Red backlash helped reelect Eisenhower and Nixon over Stevenson and Estes Kefauver. While Jack struggled in the last months of apprenticeship, Tillie worked as a stenographer for the medical society, plugged into an earpiece which shattered her nerves, ruined her hearing, and paralyzed her talents. Only now could they afford a car (a Nash Rambler) and a washing machine. When Kathie had an asthma relapse, exhausted Tillie sat up nights with her. She felt utterly alienated from writers "who can't stop writing."

After months of typing her bosses' imprecise, jargon-filled prose, Tillie begged Sam for two thousand dollars and a chance to write. His reply tells much about her plea:

Hard working woman. 9 hours a day and then some. Husband. Children, a sick lovely child in Hospital. Company. Boss. 2000.00 [sic] or more looking for time to write Story. dishes, washing machine, Insurance card, writing a letter to dad. Steps to Clinic. My! My! Where are you getting So much energy. How long can you keep it up & you are a Human being and a woman at that. . . . isn't there a way to divorce your boss. Stay home and take it a little easier it will pay in a long run. Am worrying about you, can I help in some way.

By the end of 1956, he seems to have fulfilled her request.

By January 1957 Ida's gravestone was set. After a year of mourning, adjustment, and reflection, it was time for a memorial service. Sam's problem was simple: "as you know Mothers wish was, no rabbi, no ceremony, no speeches, but how can you perform a unveiling without it? Just come to the cemetery pull off the canvass and leave it is strange. What is your Suggestion?" Tillie had none. Ida's memorial was blessed not by a rabbi but by a member of the Progressive Women's Club, who spoke of Ida's courage, her devotion to the labor movement, and "her dedication to a more just and better world. . . . I can almost see her now as she once stood in the Lyceum reading before us from the writings of Peretz. With what feeling and understanding she communicated the author's meaning and purpose."[13] After Harry sent her this eulogy, Tillie decided to take her old couple to Venice, where she placed Jeannie, too. Thus, Tillie revised autobiography by keeping herself out of this tale and substituting Julie (as Jeannie). Her initiative flagged though when Malcolm Cowley regretted that Miller had gotten her stories published in college magazines that paid only about $12.50 apiece "when they are worth thousands."[14] With the Supreme Court declaring segregation unconstitutional in schools and on buses, "Baptism" might indeed have earned "thousands" in a magazine like *Harper's* or the *Atlantic*.

In February 1957, Jack finished his six-year apprenticeship as a "boy." But the typographical union voted "86 for, to 32 against" Jack's admission. After a newsletter editorial called the vote a "Sorry Spectacle, Indeed!" embarrassed officials did grant Jack journeyman status, though the high negative vote indicated residual anticommunism.[15] When FBI agents again knocked at Laidley Street, Tillie slammed the door on them.

However much Tillie said she craved isolation, she still drew people to her like a magnet; for instance, a young Englishmen named Michael Millgate discovered Tillie that June after Cowley suggested he contact the Olsens for a firsthand account of the American labor movement. He found the Laidley Street house in pandemonium. With the stereo playing, people chattering and arguing, and Tillie blurting out an unexplained paean to Harry Bridges, Millgate gathered her importance but had no idea what she was talking about.[16]

In exuberant moods, Tillie made light of household chores. She wrote silly "lunch-box" poems to accompany her family's sandwiches. To polish the hardwood floors, she would "put on socks and skate back and forth to the rhythm of music," to the delight of her girls. The record player was always, "booming out everything from Ike and Tina to Mahler."[17] A less exuberant Tillie took trolley and bus rides to work, spent long hours typing medical reports, shopping on her way home, and carrying groceries up the hill and then up three flights of stairs to the often crowded Laidley Street rooms. The girls hungered for their mother's attention, Jack for her love, and she for time alone.

The Putnam edition of Miller's *New Campus Writing No. 2* appeared early that summer, with one contribution from Stanford: Tillie Olsen's "Hey Sailor."[18] When Miller said she had only published one story,[19] she retorted, "I had several items published in 1934," but she still self-censored her life by not naming the "items." She suppressed her radical past because the FBI was still muscling businesses to get rid of Communist employees. That summer it called on the internal medicine society, which soon fired Tillie.[20]

When "Baptism" appeared in *Prairie Schooner* (her third story in just over a year), Tillie expected her life to be transformed, but nothing happened, except that Kathie was mad at her for "ripping off" her life story without asking. Tillie felt besieged. Her daughter turned on her. Miller undersold her stories. The public ignored them. The medical society fired her. She would never earn a living as an author.[21] Stress exacerbated her ulcerative colitis, landing her in Mt. Zion Hospital. From there, she wrote Miller a barely coherent letter claiming that it was "good to burn at last with fever instead of with unused power." She threatened to take a permanent job and stop deluding herself about becoming a full-time writer. She wrote Miller, calling "Baptism" "this grave, courtesy of Nolan Miller. They die published but they die not written." She wrote of three books "imprisoned" in her imagination, apparently: her abandoned thirties novel for Random House, one about her neighborhood, and perhaps the story about "why A. hit so hard."

She stayed in Mt. Zion long enough to reclaim some equilibrium, but she refused to look for a job. If they were careful with household expenses, then Jack's paycheck could support the family, and Tillie could be free to write. Instead, she hatched a scheme to sell their house, buy a trailer their Nash Rambler could pull, and travel the country with the younger girls. The Laidley Street house was the first they had owned, the home where they had brought baby Laurie in 1947 to auspicious postwar prospects for all humanity. Selling it would be wrenching, but Tillie was adamant that they should sell it and go on the road. Her pleading convinced Kathie and Laurie that traveling would be a lark, Jack that he could work wherever they were. He agreed, with trepidation, to abandon his hard-won printing job, forget financial worries, and sell their house. Why did Tillie push this zany scheme? Her old Marxism may have convinced her not to get too invested in property. She liked to bend people to her will, to prove herself a sort of overwoman. Home-schooling should make amends for stealing Kathie's story and regain her status as the "funnest" of mothers, but she must have known that she could not write on the road.

While they waited for the sale to take place, the Olsens sorted and stored books, records, treasured furniture and mementos, and many, many boxes of Tillie's papers. She arranged for Kathie and Laurie to do fall school work by correspondence. Ten years of mortgage payments had added little collateral to their GI Bill down payment, but they bought an affordable trailer, with a little dining room table, which folded away to become a bed for the girls. There was a bed for Tillie and Jack. The Olsens drove first to Lake Shasta, near Redding, California. Jack posted his union card and easily got a job as a linotype operator at the *Redding Record Searchlight.* The three females mostly stayed by a lake, where they swam and hauled water for cooking. After a while, the family moseyed up the coast on Highway 5 and ended up in a trailer park near Seattle. Again, Jack posted his card and got work. Kathie recalled that they stayed there about a month. To the FBI, Tillie's "whereabouts were unknown," until in Seattle she cashed a check from the Society of Internal Medicine, which informed the FBI. The girls enjoyed swimming, reading, and Tillie's constant company, but the prospect of traveling the USA quickly lost its appeal. The Olsens drove back and parked in a hillside trailer park in Colma, south of San Francisco. Kathie hated being so far from her friends, detested the long bus ride to Mission High, and was "scared to death" by ninth-grade classes in the big new school. She was so miserable and angry that in October the Olsens moved back to the Mission district to rent what Tillie called "an immobile home."

Settling in, she admitted: "O Tillie this is so childish when you should be writing—can we put electric stove on counter—o shit shit shit—trapped— your own goddamn fault." Even as she made that rare admission of fault, she also saw herself as slave or victim: "remember Tillie how much of the past has been not writing . . . the freed slave . . . must heal where the shackles were."[22] She did not fault herself for the camping excursion, which surely was more self-defeating than settling into a rented house was. When Seevya Dinkin died that October, Tillie was touched by Dinkin's eulogy in which her grandson said that death "can be beneficial."[23]

When the USSR sent the first satellite into space, Tillie secretly gloated, but the FBI became more vigilant.[24] She sought books like someone marooned on the desert starving for sustenance.[25] In the *Letters of Emily Dickinson,* she discovered that Dickinson had read the anonymous story Tillie had treasured since she was seventeen. Thrilled that she and Dickinson had read the very same story in the very same magazine, Tillie was even more elated to read the footnote: "Rebecca Harding Davis's *Life in the Iron Mills* appeared in the April 1861 issue of the *Atlantic Monthly.*"

Miller countered her remark about "Baptism" being buried thanks to him, with flattery. He claimed that Tillie was a "better maker" than Katherine Anne Porter, who used "always the same voice." In each of Tillie's stories, he found "a different voice." He even said: "there *is* no Tillie Olsen." Having no idea how many times Tillie had changed colors, he supposed her stories were "the only identity you'll ever have." Pleased that, being jobless, she could write, he cautioned not to equate time with happiness: "what results, though, that's happiness."

When "Help Her to Believe" was named among 1957's *Best American Short Stories,* with a new title, "I Stand Here Ironing," Tillie was, as in 1934, besieged with requests from publishers.[26] Viking had just published *On the Road,* the Beat novel Kerouac claimed to have first written in three weeks. Cowley assumed that Tillie would be Viking's next sensation, but he was disconcerted by her report: the fall had been a "happy time, 11, 12, 13 hours a day and night" reading. She said she "grew a novel and bred conviction about my great value as a writer (little substantiation in what was written)." Like Bennett Cerf earlier, Cowley believed in Tillie's talents and spent considerable energy encouraging them, but, like Cerf, he needed to see writing, not excuses. He wondered why she had spent the fall reading, not writing, and what she meant by growing a novel. She sent her grandparent story to *Discovery,* which rejected it for offering "unrelieved human suffering."[27] Tillie told Cowley she had done "nothing those happy months to protect towards a future," a confession echoing the one made to Cerf about the time "I dribbled away that year I had nothing to do but write." She lamented burning "with unused power" but avoided using it when she had the chance. Financial troubles also undermined her. Capital from selling the Laidley Street house was vanishing. Though Julie was on scholarship at Mills, the younger Olsen girls needed support, while Karla was largely independent and married to Arthur Lutz. Julie remembered the Olsens were often "broke, [lived] close to the edge, truly working class, sometimes poor."[28] By December, Tillie was forced to take another job.

On 14 January 1958 Miller, not knowing it was her forty-sixth birthday, gingerly reminded Tillie that "Eyes are on you. Now." Still obsessed by the image of Ida on "her death bed—singing herself lullabies," Tillie imported Lillian's translation of Ida's remarkable vision into her narrative. Remembering Miller's advice that she needed "*one* pattern," she cut massive sections from what she now called her "Riddle" story.[29] She insisted to Miller that it had been a "novel, novel length. Not that it was 'cut' or 'selected,' it was distilled." Now it had "form, carefully worked out and selected form."

After Scowcroft called to insist that she must write, Tillie wrote him about neighborhood disasters, including insanity, deaths, inheritance troubles, and a marriage that ended in loathing. Envisioning a novel about such misfortunes, she said she needed to go away to somewhere "cheapest, furthest yet most accessible."[30] She next sent the "Riddle" story to Cowley, whose reply mostly thrilled her: she had "that gift of extracting almost chemically pure emotion, so concentrated as to be almost unbearable, out of a complications situation." Her last few pages were "terrific." He told her to use family stories as background, "unless you're going to write a whole novel about these people." Saying she was "essentially a novelist rather than a story writer," Cowley offered her a Viking advance, which would barely "support even a bachelor writer, let alone a married one with four children." Tillie recalled Agnes Smedley's words about preferring to be a prostitute rather than a married woman. She said she had written several thousand pages but reduced whole scenes to a paragraph, or a sentence, or nothing at all. Thus she was "a short story writer, I leave things out." She did not want to remake her novella into a novel by "padding, fattening, putting back what was cut away."

Tillie claimed that she had been "very close to a novel" before she went back to work in December, but "figuring out the handling had yet to be done." Did she really believe that being close to a novel but not "handling" it was equivalent to writing it? Or was she simply playing for sympathy as a great writer who had been victimized by the "anesthesia of 15 hour days in which the job and family use me up." She pronounced that writing was now "gone except for longing sometimes on a bus." Cowley was horrified: "You haven't told me why you had to go back to work, fifteen hours a day." Such hours were illegal. Her family should appreciate that she must write as she was "born to do." He would sign her with Viking when she was "ready to work definitely on a book."

After the *Three Faces of Eve*, for which Joanne Woodward won the Best Actress award, popularized the notion of multiple personalities, Miller suspected that he rightly guessed "there *is* no Tillie Olsen." Tillie now sounded unhinged: "I have a new pair of pointed orange shoes. I spray on Spanish Geranium (Lanvin). It is late night the second after it was early morning, and I sleep instantly and well." Her driver's license had expired, and "writing is as if it never were." Worried that she might self-destruct, Miller and Cowley nominated her for a Ford Fellowship for "writers over thirty." Cowley told her to expand "the Riddle story right away." She might win a Ford Foundation award; she might win a Saxton grant; [31] she might get a residential grant from Yaddo in the East or Huntington Hartford in the West—either providing "free board & lodging." But she must write. She filled in the Ford application and sent her father what he called a "devoted note of a few words" about her literary success.

By May, Tillie announced to Cowley that her grandparent story, now "Tell Me a Riddle," would be ready to submit to publishers in August. By the New Year, she could have ready a collection of stories unified, not by Helen's family, as in "Hey Sailor" and "Baptism," but by geography, the street they lived on.[32] She could quit work in October, if he sent her $200 a month to write "some of the books that are in me," which would make literature "the deeper." Cowley told her to gather her published and unpublished work for an "option contract" with Viking, offering $500 in advance and "an additional $500 *on acceptance*" of a *finished* book.[33]

Blanche Knopf of Alfred A. Knopf had heard that Stanford had been "nursing" a promising woman writer, so she queried Wallace Stegner, who sent a cold assessment, based on Tillie's partially invented self-history and his observations of her "tizzied" state:

> she is past forty; married very young and abandoned by her longshoreman husband; married again to a man who was for a long time an important official in Harry Bridges' ILWU, but who belatedly got stricken with how he was wasting his life, and apprenticed himself to a printer for six years. Tillie has four or five children, one or two of them grown, and when she was here as a fellow she had a lot of emotional and domestic troubles that handcuffed her as far as writing went. She was writing stories then, or trying to. What she wrote was superb, but she didn't write much. I am quite sure she has no commitment to any publisher; I am fairly sure she doesn't have a book.

Knopf thought Tillie sounded "difficult but perhaps we can pull a book out of her." Tillie sent Knopf her stories, with a note about "trying to assemble myself for the several months writing time I will have after the middle of October." Then Jack came down with Meniere's Syndrome, a disease of the inner ear that left him literally imbalanced.[34] After having "survived all this year for this writing time," Tillie saw Jack's illness as "cruel proof" of her defenselessness "if I continue woman, mother, responsible human being in our economic circumstance." She quoted Emily Dickinson on the "drowning not so pitiful as the attempt to rise." She contemplated drowning or leaving, but did neither.

Instead, she asked Gene Lerner for five hundred dllars, so she could secure "real writing time—away by myself." More delays "after five years of such postponements" would destroy her. Here she obscured the fact that her Stanford fellowship had been in the last five years and that she had spent the summer of 1957 traveling and the fall of that year reading and postponing writing. She sent the Guggenheim Foundation a "rough-draft" application three days late, asking for "economic freedom" to "begin a long gestated novel of San Francisco."[35] Then she sent a more precise plan to the Ford Foundation. Her novel, set in San Francisco, would focus on

> two family clusters, and through them, the varied lives that touch theirs: the work they do; the children—the schools (in which it is pre-decided before the kindergarteners' first day that only a few will be "academically fit" and all is conducted accordingly); the neighborhood—rooted and transient, working people mostly, conglomerate: Latins, Anglos, first generation and foreign born, newly moved in Negro and less recently migrated CIO's (Cal Improved Okies). . . . Although the weight of the material is enormous, it will be told through compression and selection of what illuminates.[36]

Recommenders raved about her talent and deplored her finances. None pointed out that, though the novel had "gestated" for twenty years, she said she intended "to begin" it.

Late that fall, Tillie sent a revised typescript of "Tell Me a Riddle" to Gene with an ingratiating letter thanking him for handling Ida's bequest of one hundred dollars for Karla, who had had "the rare quality of Mom's love and concern [in] the naked, impressionable year when she was three." (Here Tillie reduced the many times she sent Karla back to Ida and Rae to the one time Gene had been involved.[37]) She insisted that her story was not just "the story of mother's death"; its characters are "not those we know. Yet mother *is* in it—something of the incorruptibility and beliefs that were hers." She still needed five hundred dollars.

Tillie telegraphed Gene on 8 January 1959: "PLEASE CABLE IF LOAN REQUESTED IN LETTER POSSIBLE LOVE TILLIE." He sent the five hundred dollars.[38] By this time she had won a residential fellowship in the country mansion of Huntington Hartford, more than four hundred miles south of San Francisco in Pacific Palisades,[39] offering a dramatic ocean view, the company of serious artists, and free room and board. Moving in around 20 January 1959, rather than write the novel she had promised, she revised "Tell Me a Riddle" again, though she had promised to finish it the previous August.

She worked to convey "the physical manifestations" of Eva's illness within the "fibre" of Holocaust death trains, the irradiation of Hiroshima, and 1950s atom bomb evacuation drills for school children. David considers "*slaveships deathtrains*" and the American inquisition. He wonders how, amid horrors, they had "believed so beautifully," or "so . . . falsely?" Tillie projected her own frustration onto Eva, who wants "*at last to live within, and not move to the rhythm of others.*"[40] Tillie deepened "Tell Me a Riddle" through allusions to literature and scripture, especially Deuteronomy 27:8 in which stones and laws "shall not perish." In her novella, "stone will perish, but the word remain."[41]

As she was painstakingly subtracting family allusions and adding universal ones, Tillie got an astonishing call from the Ford Foundation. She had received one of five prestigious fellowships, which would support her for two full years so that she could be "free to concentrate solely upon creative work." The other winners were James Baldwin, Bernard Malamud, Flannery O'Connor, and Katherine Ann Porter.[42] She hardly noticed when Guggenheim Foundation rejected her. She sent her father a special delivery letter telling him that she and four famous writers had won Ford awards. Sam wept, drank a glass of wine, and called the family, as she intended. He wrote Tillie what she most yearned to hear: that Ida "would be the happiest of all, but I will bring her the news when I will be there." Tillie's award at last justified Ida's early faith and the later support of people who believed that Tillie Olsen could indeed make literature "the deeper." Cowley, though, reminded her that her first duty was "putting words on paper."

While Tillie was at Huntington Hartford, Jack was so lonely and resentful that he called every night.[43] He had recovered from his ear troubles enough to take Kathie and Laurie to visit their mother one time. Fifteen-year-old Kathie typed a revealing note on the machine Huntington Hartford supplied Tillie: "I WISH THAT WE ALL COULD LIVE HERE. . . . Mama is happy. We are happy. My mother looks really good." Seeing that "daddy is kissing mommy," Kathie knew that Jack had missed Tillie much more than she him.

At last Tillie brought love into her narrative. David recalls taking Eva "in his arms, dear, personal, fleshed, in all the heavy passion he had loved to rouse from her." Eva recognizes again "her springtime love (who stands beside her now)." Dying, "her hand reached across the bed to hold his." Tillie closed with "their hands, his and hers, clasped, feeding each other." Their love and forgiveness is echoed in Jeannie's affection and in Eva's "Russian love song of fifty years ago." Eva sings of old beliefs, just as Ida Goldberg, after a lifetime of atheism, spoke of Jewish spirituality and the soul. Like the ancient songs and customs in Ida's reveries, Tillie Olsen's final narrative affirms a "*joyous certainty, that sense of mattering.*" About five years since she began and nine months after she had promised to finish, Tillie sent "Tell Me a Riddle" to agent Russell.

She also made a brilliant expansion of "Baptism" to include the poignant scene when Parry brings Carol, sick in bed, homework assignments written for her "cause I mightn't get it right all right." In a stream-of-consciousness passage, Parry reflects on a teacher's assumption that her mother was Helen's maid. The "sorting" that Jeannie talks about has humiliated Parry, though she does not say so. In "Baptism," Helen reflects on the "*special history of the Negro people.*" Revised as "O Yes," Helen thinks of the "*religion of all oppressed peoples.*" Tillie finished on 15 May 1959 and wrote Cowley, "*I am into the novel*—helplessly, happily—I am going home tomorrow." She wrote Miller: "*I am into the novel!*" Her departure date then was 20 May.

The Ford money, which began in August 1959, offered Tillie at last the magical conditions she needed for writing. First, however, to make up for her four months away, she splurged on a two-week family camping trip up the Smith River in northern California, where the Olsens found an abandoned sweat-house and upended graves with bones and skulls spilling out.[44] Back in San Francisco, she and Jack used their leftover Laidley Street capital and the Ford payments to build a new house. He finally had a reliable job working "nightside on the *Chronicle*," an arrangement that gave Tillie quiet time during the days. Pleased that Russell had placed "Tell Me a Riddle" in a noncollege collection called *New World Writing*, Cowley wanted her to sign with Viking for a collection of her four current stories with three new ones and the novel that she was writing.[45] She told Miller that she had struggled out of "that place where courage fails." She envisioned courage, though, as going away to "do my own work, no letters, no relationship." Instead, the hassles of building and moving seem to have absorbed her all that fall. Jack was her most loyal ally, but she began plotting separation: "motherhood wifehood over for me."[46]

As the fifties drew to a close, the cloud of conformity and repression lifted. Ginsberg's *Howl and Other Poems* was declared not obscene. Jack Kerouac published "The Philosophy of the Beat Generation," and the word "beatnik" became current. The Hollywood blacklist of CP members was revoked. African-American Sidney Poitier was nominated Best Actor. Dalton Trumbo converted Howard Fast's *Spartacus* into film and at last was listed in the credits. *The Diary of Anne Frank* exposed Holocaust horrors and was nominated for 1959's Best Picture award. James Agee and Walker Evans's sharecropper study, *Let Us Now Praise Famous Men*, was being reissued to become a bible of moral and artistic nonconformity.[47] The Food and Drug Administration approved birth control pills. Instead of hounding a 1930s activist like Tillie, J. Edgar Hoover set the FBI on Civil Rights leaders, including Martin Luther King, Jr.

Using United Nations "Fountain of Peace" cards, Tillie invited friends to drop by on Sunday, 3 January 1960, at the new house on Swiss Avenue.[48] Julie played the guitar, people sang, men sawed down trees for a new subdivision on a nearby hillside, and Jack left for a job at the *Chronicle*. Tillie spent the afternoon ushering guests into her first personal writing room and advising them to apply for grants.[49] She had a year and a half of Ford support left. Though pleased to have her own study, Tillie was near despair over the enormous novel she had promised to write on her Ford money.

When *New World Writing* appeared, it included not only "Tell Me a Riddle" but also a first short story "Dancing the Jig" by poet Anne Sexton. Though she had never heard of Tillie Olsen, "Tell Me a Riddle" awed her. On 5 April, she apologized for her feeble story when Tillie's novella "shines out like a miracle."[50] Startled to hear from the younger, glamorous eastern poet, Tillie responded cautiously: "that you *wrote me*—I cherish. I know some of your work and honor it." Now Anne Sexton's name could be added to the list of supporters expecting something great from Tillie Olsen.

Tillie paid no attention when Gene brought their father to Los Angeles for a Valentine's Day broadcast with Rossano Brazzi and other Italian stars on television's "Dinah Shore Show." Tillie's illnesses and expensive dental work deepened the Olsens' money troubles.[51] They also heightened her writing troubles. By late June, with thirteen months of Ford money left, Tillie had overcome bronchitis but not writer's despair. She resented the fame accruing to drug-addicted, womanizing, self-indulgent Beat writers. Kerouac's notion of "spontaneous prose" offended hers of polished prose. To Hannah, she worried "about womanhood—my situation," but conventional womanly sentiments bubbled up when Karla and Arthur Lutz made her a grandmother.[52] Moreover, Tillie wondered if "what I am trying to do is beyond my present powers."

That fall, Tillie heard the presidential debate between the Republican Richard M. Nixon and the Democrat John F. Kennedy. Because Nixon had vaulted to political power by overriding the Bill of Rights with a "Red-scare," she was terrified that he would win. Kennedy, handsome son of Joseph Kennedy, was a war hero, a writer, and an idealist. Overcoming her distrust of the wealthy to vote for Kennedy, she was relieved by his victory.

When Cowley invited Tillie to a party in Palo Alto, she was a celebrity: "Tell Me a Riddle" had won the O. Henry prize as the year's best story, but Tillie's new fame provoked the FBI to reopen her file because "as a writer she is in a position to influence masses of people." *Esquire* magazine invited her to a writers' symposium where she met J. W. Lippincott, head of J. B. Lippincott, who might print a series of short story collections. If Lippincott published her four stories by themselves, then Tillie could not only forget her deal with Viking to publish a larger collection but also be free to work on her novel. Cowley told her about an intriguing front-page article in the Sunday *New York Times*; inaugurated by Radcliffe College's President Mary Ingraham Bunting, a "test program" "aimed at opening opportunities for gifted" or "intellectually displaced women."[53]

Tillie bought Anne Sexton's *To Bedlam and Part Way Back*, and on 6 or 7 November, late at night, wrote a card to Sexton. Tillie called Sexton "dear related to me" because Tillie also felt her mental equilibrium at risk. One "November noon," Anne replied: "Your letters look like poems. . . . —Your writing is so tiny and perfect that it looks as if a fairy with a pink pen and rubies in her hair had sat down to write to me." Anne begged, "tell me your life."[54]

Thirteen-year-old Laurie had suddenly gotten tall, thin, and, as Tillie wrote Hannah, "for the first time in her life unhappy; too close to me (still my love)." A passionate activist, Kathie joined the Quakers and picketed against capital punishment and for racial equality.[55] Now at SFSU, Julie worked to pay for her expenses, was engaged to Rob Edwards, her high school boyfriend, and as an excellent student and devoted daughter gave mimeographed samples of prose and poetry distributed in English classes to Tillie. She miscalculated, however, with a family Christmas play set in a "cave shelter, after the atom bomb has exploded." Knowing that the bomb really could destroy humanity, Tillie was shaken by her daughters' "unaccustomedly dank" play and depressed over the fate of humanity and of her writing.

On 26 January 1961, after midnight, alone in her room, Tillie replied to Anne's "November noon" letter.[56] In three single-spaced typed pages, Tillie wove a tapestry of hardships: "A 'low status' neighborhood; many Latin American, Negro, Samoan, first generation Irish & Italian, families. . . . Up at six, breakfast in shifts, lunchpacking—then if no one ill, or it isn't a holiday, or any of the other ORs, the day for work until four, sometimes longer or an evening—depending on housework load, shopping errands, people, current family or friend crisis." She was trying to write about how society deprives the poor of "a sense of worth, of potentiality, of community."

To Hannah Green, Tillie had feared that her all-encompassing novel might be "beyond my present abilities (and circumstances)." She hoped, however, that outside help would change those circumstances. Meanwhile, President Kennedy tried to address censorship and sexism by appointing Edward R. Murrow director of the U.S. Information Agency and Eleanor Roosevelt chair of a President's Commission on the Status of Women. Sam fretted that his children had problems "even Kennedy" could not solve.

Tillie's problems resulted from promising Huntington Hartford, the Ford Foundation, Cowley, Viking, and her many supporters a novel addressing society's injustices. Under pressure, she had said she was "into" the novel. Now torn between a ravening desire to write and a paralyzing fear that she could not, Tillie despaired. She wrote "to Nolan, your little note graved it. Life is a constant distortion that does not even allow for reflection as to what it distorts from." She told Hannah: "I have nothing to write in a letter." Preyed upon by some unnamed force, feeling her talents rotting and her prospects still-born, Tillie stopped writing altogether. She was admitted to Kaiser Hospital in early or mid-February.

By 23 February, Cowley had heard that she had "had to be hospitalized." In early March, Dick Elman wrote Tillie that he was handling literary programs at Pacifica Radio, KPFA, in Berkeley, and might interview her. When Jack turned fifty in mid-March, Julie wrote a poem and read it aloud in Tillie's hospital room. As she began to recollect herself, Tillie asked Jack to bring her a yellowed copy of a 1941 *New Republic*, which included Glenway Wescott's essay on F. Scott Fitzgerald; Wescott argued that Fitzgerald's failure to "conserve or budget" his strengths had caused his 1936 "Crack-Up." Though she had no interest in Fitzgerald's tales of privilege, Tillie now identified with him, apparently as a survivor of a crack-up. Further recollecting herself, though still hospitalized, Tillie scribbled a note to Elman, and on 27 March he asked, "why are you hospitalized?"

Tillie was in hospital for at least a month (between Cowley's hearing that she had to be hospitalized, Jack's birthday, and her note to Elman) or almost two months (between early February and late March). Released by the end of March,[57] she trembled to recall "what I could-have-been." She felt like a victim: "I know now the earth is flat. And though there is no god, [there is] a giant thumb that preys on earth [and] every day selects and flings over the blind edge me or my brother. . . ." She started a "new notebook—my new small notebook—with my new small shattered brain."[58]

Daughters Julie and Kathie are sure that Tillie had an attack of colitis so severe they "almost lost her." But her hospital stay was surely longer than even terrible colitis would require. Her reference to "my new small shattered brain" possibly suggests shock treatment, a frequent prescription for creative people, especially women, in the grips of depression.[59] Her daughters find that suggestion offensive. They, however, did not see the despondent letters she wrote to others or the severely depressed, sometimes delusional, diary entries she wrote to herself.

In April, out of hospital and mending, Tillie needed to pull herself together. She did so using a familiar remedy, rereading a vast assortment of "old loved books." She listed some fifteen of them to Miller.[60] She empathized with Virginia Woolf's bouts with manic depression and was gratified that the elite Woolf had written an introduction to an anthology of "working women's lives."[61] She wrote Miller: "I did not answer because of incapacity," or "fever inthemorningANDfeverinthenight." She described herself as "o.v.s.k.w." which she translated nonsensically as "Too occupied ironing shopping motheringcleaningformorethan occasional v. superior k. woman."[62]

The little spiral notebook, kept by "my new small shattered brain," shows Tillie in chaos. She lamented "the creative process—not a faucet—2 years now." She complained about fellowship "breadlines" that spoiled writers with transient security. She did make a realistic query: "why do I let work be last?" Then she shifted blame to her reasons: "2. Jack—1. Family life." Another muddled note reads: "not economize, sexual, or literary means to *save* w. c. [working class] life." Though she acknowledged Jack's "support & companionship," she longed for "a different life." She closed these pages with an upside down statement on "the importance of the underline."[63] She was barely coherent.

By 20 May, Tillie wrote two coherent letters. To Cowley and Viking Press, she wrote, "I bitterly regret that I am not able to meet my commitment to deliver a finished work of fiction by June, 1961." To Anne Sexton, she promised to exercise self-control and "demonstrate brevity." Her Ford money was running out so she would have to "leave writing (for a job, to earn money)." She had reneged on Viking, but Lippincott would republish her four stories in one volume in late summer. The novel she said she had been "well into" two years before was unfinished, possibly not even begun.[64] Tillie registered as a "temp." She wrote Scowcroft about working in an assortment of jobs for "Electrical Supply & week before Obrien

Spotorno & Mitchell (really Zolezzi and Abrams) & this week Cancer or Abbey Rents: Sickroom & Party Equipment!" She reflected on her failure to write the broad social novel she had promised:

> I wanted to go back again—the 20 intimate years—changes I have seen—the Okies of the depression—what has happened to the Negroes that came up from the south during the war and after—to the longshoremen as they went from the ragged edge to respectability and abundance . . . the impact of television, the effect on cowbilly and the other untainted [music?], and how so far only rock and roll remains. I had wanted to talk about my work, I who have been a job wanderer, almost 100 offices . . . I was there the morning that five year old Johnny Ramirez was sentenced to San Quentin let Riesman talk of anomie, I know what produces it; I was there, I still am, transfixed; I am engorged with all this material, it is not yet ordered or assimilated, I wrote what might be simpler to handle, the approach to what must follow.[65]

Tell Me a Riddle had been simpler to handle because she made a powerful distillation from known family events. The vast compass of the book she intended to write seemed beyond her powers of conceptualizing, ordering, and integrating. Her helplessness provoked Hannah Green, though busy with her own work, to check proofs of Lippincott's *Tell Me a Riddle*.[66] Hannah's help reminded Tillie of the usefulness of weakness.

Meanwhile, the Radcliffe Institute for Independent Study announced that it had appointed twenty-two women from the Boston area as fellows for 1962–1963; their academic fields ranged from archaeology to physiology to theology to the arts. One winner had, as the Radcliffe press release put it, "no formal college training." She was Anne Sexton. If Sexton could become a Radcliffe fellow without college, Tillie imagined she might also, if she lived in Boston. Because she did not, she considered the admittedly "crazy" idea of borrowing money so she could live there alone and write.

Tillie slowly regained her vitality. After Julie Olsen and Rob Edwards ordered standard wedding invitations beginning "Mr. and Mrs. John Olsen invite," Tillie spunkily dashed off a fresh invitation, which Jack typeset: "Our Julie is marrying Rob Edwards on Saturday, August 19th. Please come rejoice with us. . . . Jack and Tillie Olsen." The couple sent formal invitations to one group, informal ones to those in harmony with their "hippie wedding," outdoors in Napa Valley. They wrote their own vows and dressed casually, promising fresh, unconventional, equal relations between men and women.[67]

At summer's end, *Tell Me a Riddle* appeared, and Tillie sent free copies to friends and supporters.[68] But her little book seemed a mockery when she was condemned to a secretarial job now in an attorney's office. She identified with the fate of Freedom Riders, who were jailed and beaten for registering black voters in the American South. She clipped out an article about California youths who beat to death a twenty-seven-year-old teacher the boys thought "queer."[69] Tillie felt bludgeoned herself as she transcribed legalese, while Jack set type at the *Daily Pacific Builder.*

In September, when Anne Sexton entered the first class of Radcliffe Fellows, Tillie asked about the Institute. She made a Guggenheim application, describing her project in four words: "Finish my book ('novel')." She expanded her plan with promises about the novel that she had privately feared was beyond her: "I intend to give myself completely to the finishing of this book, on which (except for the present interruption) I have been working since the fall of 1959, and for which I have been storing up material (a conscious storing) most of my life. It is a 'social' novel." She hoped "to move the reader to that comprehension which alters" and "to make it literature." Under the official category for marital status, Tillie wrote "separated."[70]

Tillie hardly noticed when Sam Lerner moved to the Workmen's Circle home in Media, Pennsylvania.[71] She may not even have written her youngest sister when, in November, Sonny Richards died, though Harry wrote her that Vicki's son "whose Bar Mitzvah was only last month, now said the Kaddish for his father." Harry was offended because Tillie omitted such Jewish rituals from her novella. Her siblings were furious that she had made Eva and David poorer, bitterer, and less loving than Ida and Sam. They resented the way she had defaced her brothers and sisters of their accomplishments and fame.[72]

Tillie was burdened, she wrote Hannah, by "the 9 hour chunk of job and our crowded disorganized household (seven) and all the daily mustgetdones." Arthur, Karla, and baby Ericka had moved in while they looked for a San Francisco apartment. Tillie said that only on bus rides and during sleepless nights could she think of words "unwritten on the book." She wrote her father that she had had to sell her typewriter. From the old folks' home, he quickly sent her two hundred dollars. When she sent New Year wishes to the Scowcrofts, Tillie said she might go to Boston. She did not mention Jack.

Then she heard that *Prize Stories, 1961: The O'Henry Awards* was reprinting "Tell Me a Riddle" as the year's best story. The *Los Angeles Times* raved about her collection.[73] The *San Francisco Examiner* printed a photo of Tillie reading to baby Ericka and insisted: "Mrs. Olsen talks, as she writes, with compassion for people trapped by the economic, social and cultural problems of our time." It quoted Tillie on women: "the American standard of living forces a family to have two checks," and "it's no accident that until two or three decades ago the only well known women writers were old maids." Tillie sent a copy to Dick Elman with revealing emendations. She crossed out the "dis" in "distinguished" and added "ex" to make "extinguished." Correcting a reference to her "book of four short stories," she reversed herself to call it "3 short stories 1 novel." She was outraged over the paper's report that "money from the Ford Foundation that enabled her to stay home and hire household help while she wrote is gone." Tillie scribbled in "What help?" The article also quoted her admitting, "It's criminal that I don't write easily and quickly."[74] When the 29 December 1961 issue of *Time* listed the "Year's Best" nonfiction, fiction, and poetry, it named nine works of fiction, including books by Graham Greene, Walker Percy, J. D. Salinger, John O'Hara, and Tillie Olsen. *Time* called the four stories in *Tell Me a Riddle* "delicate as fugues." Despite a distorted account of the generations in "Tell Me a Riddle," *Time* put Tillie Olsen firmly in the literary limelight. Still, she blamed the system, including marriage, for killing her novel.

Back in 1953–1954, she had regretted "dividing" herself into so many different streams when she wanted "to run in one river and become great." Now she recalled her many lost selves. The Communist zealot was as long-gone as the white blouses and red ties of YCL uniforms. The shipyard agitator and neglectful mother were as lost as the 79¢ flowered Penney's dress. The zany cut-up was as discarded as the short skirt and risqué top of the 1945 Labor Day Parade. The sexual tease was as obsolete as the "HOT CARGO" gossip columns. The devoted wife was as forgotten as the nightgowns bought for a postdemobilization honeymoon. The charity activist was as passé as the rakish hats she had worn for press photos. The defiant accuser of the FBI was as buried as the garbage she threw out when the agents called. The student who could only talk to Scowcroft through a "veil of tears" had evaporated with the tears. Tillie wanted to discard the harassed wife and mother role and get to Boston, alone. Her riddle considered which self would reappear. Could she discard the roles of procrastinator, excuse-maker, and victim and prove her "great value as a writer"? Could she write the great novel that would alter the social consciousness of America and the world?

CHAPTER 12

EGO STRENGTH

1962–1969

I cannot even say: novel.
It takes from all literary forms, but is its own.
—Tillie Olsen, "On my 'Work in Progress,'" 28 July 1965

As 1962 began, Tillie was torn between triumph and despair. She had written one of the best books of 1961, but now she was writing only patients' case histories as she trod the corridors of San Francisco General Hospital. Radcliffe forms, sent by Anne Sexton, included the promising news that fellowships would be awarded to non-Bostonians. Tillie called upon her "Old Reliable, Fall Back Upon" recommenders and a new one, Annie Wilder, a psychiatrist. In her application, Tillie promised to finish a "social novel" and lamented having only *Tell Me a Riddle* "to really plead for me." Actually, she had Anne Sexton pleading to judges that Tillie Olsen's tough life and profound writing excused the vagueness of her application.[1]

About the time Tillie turned fifty on 14 January, Dick Elman arranged for John Leonard to interview her on KPFA in Berkeley. Her powerful performance of "I Stand Here Ironing" and "Hey Sailor, What Ship?" testified to her recovery.[2] She broached the idea of going to Boston alone and vowed to Hannah Green, "I *will* live east this fall." But she then added "perhaps Jack Laurie also." Among her recommenders, Annie Wilder wrote of her "remarkable ego strength and ego integrity," but Scowcroft admitted that she had done "rather little" with her Stanford and Ford grants.

Her KPFA recording brought an unexpected award of five hundred dollars from the National Institute for Arts and Letters, enabling Tillie to quit her hospital job.[3] She told Scowcroft about her desire to live alone in Boston: she would say "I love you (that part no lie) [and will] come back, I'll never leave you again—and try like hell to believe my lies." Jack, however, did not believe her. She spent the five weeks her surprise payment had purchased in tearful wrangling. Finally, some combination of love, loyalty, and need prevailed. Tillie agreed that Jack would come east with her if she won a fellowship. They would sell their new Swiss Avenue house, pay off debts, and live on Jack's probable salary of one hundred dollars a week and her probable Radcliffe income. Having made no progress on her novel, Tillie took another job.

Then she heard, unofficially from Anne and officially from Constance E. Smith, director of the Radcliffe Institute, that she had won a fellowship. Kathie was resentful, Julie needful because she and Rob had what Tillie called a "little comanche—Julie's new morsel of life."[4] But Tillie wanted to be free of motherly and grandmotherly duties. Enrolling Laurie in Putney School in Vermont, she insisted it was not a "class" school. A press release said that Tillie Olsen would work "full-time" in Cambridge on her novel.

After the house sold, she and Jack quit their jobs and with Laurie piled into their old car for the drive east, pulling an overstuffed U-Haul trailer, thanks to five hundred dollars for relocation costs from Cowley and the Viking Press. They slept under a tent in trailer camps, visited in Omaha with Vicki and her children, and stopped in Media, Pennsylvania, to see Sam Lerner. Tillie made a dramatic entrance at the residence, embraced her aged father, and sang folk songs with Laurie, who played the fiddle to entertain the old folks. On 23 July 1962, Sam regretted that their "so called concert robbed our valuable time to be together," an insightful observation that Tillie had substituted showmanship for intimacy. Sam now sounded as much a depressive as Ida had been, an inheritance Gene Lerner acknowledged to Jann, who was moving to Boston too: "depression seems to be a characteristic of many of the Lerners. I share it."[5]

The three Olsens moved into an apartment within walking distance of the Institute. Jack became a printer at the *Cambridge Chronicle*. Tillie took Laurie to hear impromptu concerts near Harvard Square, watch rowers sculling on the Charles River, and copy inscriptions from tombstones in the St. Auburn Cemetery, which reminded her that lost "Jews in the Russian wastes" had no tombstones. Jann had entered Boston University, thanks to Gene's help, so after Tillie and Jack drove Laurie to Putney, they invited Jann over. She told them about taking serious academic courses and even gym.[6] Jann showed the Olsens slides from her recent visit to Rome, which, she wrote Gene, "gave me a little edge of confidence & ease with Til—to feel that she desired to experience something *I had* & she not!"

After a young black man named James Meredith was denied admission to the University of Mississippi, Tillie expanded her file of clippings about racism in America.[7] While Elman replayed her reading "O Yes" as a comment on integration, Attorney General Robert F. Kennedy intervened in Mississippi to see Meredith admitted and protected by U.S. marshals. White citizens and students rioted, however; twenty-eight marshals were shot, and two people were killed. While Meredith, a black man, convicted on a trumped-up charge of false voter registration,[8] explosively entered the University of Mississippi, Tillie Olsen, a Jew, once arrested on a trumped-up vagrancy charge, quietly entered Radcliffe, the Woman's College of Harvard University.

Returning Institute Fellows included painter Barbara Swan and poets Maxine Kumin and Anne Sexton, who called themselves the creative "equivalents" of fellows from academic fields like theology, mathematics, and archeology. Among the seventeen new fellows were Tillie Olsen and sculptor Marianna Pineda. The Institute was lodged in a yellow frame house, on the edge of campus. Its attic was divided into tiny offices for fellows who worked at desks. At a formal tea, on 21 September, while Director Connie Smith welcomed new fellows, they eyed each other.[9] Most fellows had graduated *magna cum laude* from prestigious colleges; many had Ph.D.s; Kumin, Swan, and Pineda had done postgraduate work; almost everyone had a famous husband.[10] Tillie could barely stammer her credentials as wife of a printer, mother of four, holder of many jobs, and writer of four stories. Still, Sexton rushed to welcome Olsen and Pineda into the band of creative "equivalents."

Tillie took possession of a stuffy upstairs office by pasting up her sacred pictures, including one of Anne Sexton. Overjoyed to see herself in Tillie's hall of fame, Anne proposed they walk and talk about poetry. These two beautiful women made a striking couple—Anne barefoot, dangling her sandals over her shoulder, Tillie in sensible shoes, pants, and a blue tee-shirt. Tillie was such a strong "source, teacher," Anne felt re-empowered as a writer, while her adoration helped confirm Tillie's ego strength.[11]

Beginning on 14 October, Tillie and Jack hovered near radios, fearing that, after American spy planes discovered missile installations in Cuba, President Kennedy would retaliate with a nuclear bomb, but instead his statesmanship averted disaster.[12] In a "creative notebook" Tillie scribbled ideas for stories or her novel about Jeannie. Noting her "first grey pubic hair," she also named people who began writing late in life.[13] She soon learned that Marianna Pineda was the daughter of a Boston banker, while her husband, fellow-sculptor Harold (Red) Tovish, was of Russian-Jewish immigrant stock. Marianna told Tillie about Red's giving her "Tell Me a Riddle" for bedtime reading. When she neared the end, she had begun reading aloud. The image of the old couple lying side by side, joined by clasped hand and an I.V. drip, by love and death, had convulsed the two into sobs. In each others' arms, they affirmed that Tillie Olsen was truly a great writer.[14]

Tillie appreciated how the Pineda/Tovish marriage strengthened each partner, while Anne's marriage to Kayo Sexton, who thought poetry a waste of time, undermined her ego. Posing for Barbara Swan boosted Anne's confidence, but listening to Maxine Kumin explain Freud made Anne feel un-intellectual because, like Tillie, she was self-educated by ardent but random reading. Anne used her beauty and bravado to cover her insecurities, as Tillie did. The other artists reached out to her, taking her on museum and lunch excursions and to dinner parties in their affluent suburban Boston homes. Jack went to work at four in the afternoon and returned after midnight, missing such goings-on.

As the fall progressed, scholars and creative artists split apart. The scholars found Tillie shy, unsure "how she got there." When theologian Ursula Niebuhr voiced her suspicion of absolutism, Tillie kept quiet about her communism, but with a simpatico friend, she conjured up a visit to the USSR where she claimed she had marveled at economic successes.[15] At Putney's Parents' Day that fall, Tillie and Jack seemed the only working-class parents. The featured speaker, economist John Kenneth Galbraith, talked about human competitiveness and selfishness, as exemplified in *Lord of the Flies*. Suddenly, Tillie stood in the middle of the auditorium to stutter to Galbraith, "You are wrong sir!" As her voice calmed, she asked if he had never seen children comfort each other, proving that compassion is "one of the deepest human impulses . . . Hatred and violence are learned behaviors in a society that devalues people." Laurie thought her mother would "go on forever" but was relieved when women gathered afterward to thank Tillie.[16]

Jack was quiet as Tillie talked, unsure of his place at Putney or Cambridge. He had no interest in talking mathematical physics, music theory, or theology with (mostly) high-powered husbands at Institute parties. Even Tillie's friends were unsure whether Jack lived with or just visited her. When Bluma Olshansky died on 18 November 1962, Tillie stayed home to console Jack. Otherwise, she tried to minimize distractions by sending out laundry, buying prepared food or restaurant dinners, and keeping some distance from Jack, to his irritation. She started to leave her office door open and invite other women in to chat. She was distressed by news that a sociologist was studying fellows to find if their achievements "reflected the influence of strong fathers." Tillie cited *A Room of One's Own* and the suffragists Elizabeth Cady Stanton and Susan B. Anthony and accused Radcliffe of endorsing man-centered "suppositions which we are fighting all the time!"[17]

In 1962, "in Harvard's Widener Library, in the Cambridge and Boston public libraries: in old volumes, not taken out for years," Tillie browsed at will. She found that there was no biography of Rebecca Harding Davis, who had balanced motherhood with an enormously productive writing career.[18] Tillie knew that major women writers had no children. Researching nearly forgotten women writers, she was unsurprised to find that most were also childless.[19] Now, at fifty, Tillie was essentially childless, economically supported, and free to write, as she had been at Huntington Hartford. But in her "creative notebook" she jotted down little more than fragments.

When Laurie came to Boston for the holidays, the Olsens invited Jann over. She assumed Tillie and Jack were secular Jews, like their parents, so she was shocked to find that they had a huge Christmas tree with "various decorations figures and packages!! Those wrapped by Laurie were especially interesting for she drew or super-imposed lace or other objects on them all." Jann also reported to Gene that, even at Radcliffe, Tillie said she "gets no work done." Still, she had "no time to visit" Sam, whom Jann insisted they call for his seventy-eighth birthday. Tillie had forgotten to defrost the turkey, so they did not eat "until almost 11:00 at nite—but it was good." Though oddly Christian, the evening promised improved relations between the sisters.

Viking's decision not to publish her collection of what Cowley called "so few but marvelous stories" was confirmed after Lippincott lost money on *Tell Me a Riddle*.[20] On New Year's, Tillie promised Cowley that she would finish her novel by the end of 1963. She imagined Jeannie saying that horror and pity have taken "the place of justice & reason, which have become powerless." She imagined Lennie "choking and choked [over] the lies or injustices." She considered "God's with his nightmare—Jew concentration camp. Negro Lynching or the African horrors. All nuclear war." She had woven such disasters into the fabric of "Tell Me a Riddle," but weaving them into new fiction would be redundant. Fearing she could no longer join personal stories to universal issues, Tillie, like Anne Sexton, identified with Ray Charles's recording "Born to Lose," especially the line "Every dream has only brought me pain." Despondent over the "pain of not writing," near a crack-up, Tillie spent "a day fighting destroying myself."[21]

Radcliffe fellows were saddened to hear that young American poet Sylvia Plath had died in England on 12 February of pneumonia. Then they were horrified to learn that Plath had asphyxiated herself by putting her head in an unlit, turned-on gas oven. Sexton and Plath had together audited Robert Lowell's poetry class at Boston University. They shared literary ambitions and a "lust" for death, which Tillie sporadically felt too. She and Sexton were furious that Plath's husband, poet Ted Hughes, seemed to have covered her suicide to protect his image, a heartless example of male chauvinism that gave Tillie a new impetus to write.

Years spent imagining that time, money, and peace would enable her to write her great social novel had given Tillie a magical view of writing. Four months at Huntington Hartford, two years of Ford subsidies, and a half-year at Radcliffe had not produced a novel. So, on 15 February, Tillie applied for a one-year renewal. She again admitted that she might have "attempted what is beyond my powers," but she blamed years of writing others' "business-ese and legalese." She said she wanted "to read greedily and unrestrained," attend lectures and cultural events, and "to write certain pieces on Woman, Thomas Wentworth Higginson, the importance of failure, the two Emilys (Dickinson and Brontë), education, race."[22] The focus of this application lay entirely in nonfiction, in research and writing about women and social issues. The Institute renewed her fellowship for another year with a stipend of $7,000.

The Radcliffe fellows' seminars were held in a large room, made from the house's original living and dining rooms. Fellows sat about on sofas and chairs eating lunches, listening to the presentations, and asking questions. Tired of being nagged for a title, angry over Plath's recent death, and depressed by her inability to produce a novel, Tillie blurted out that she would talk on the "Death of the Creative Process." On 15 March she brought her copy-outs to the session. Shuffling through them, she lamented creativity "atrophied, thwarted, murdered, yet undeniable." She wished there were a "kind of paralysis psychiatry" for writers like herself. She cited Fitzgerald's The Crack Up. She told about Rebecca Harding Davis whose brilliant "work sleeps in the forgotten." She proclaimed "almost no mothers have created literature, so far." She ended autobiographically, saying that the Ford Grant "came almost too late." Her new novel had "stammered into a first coherence" but at a "cost to the quality of our family life." She painted herself as a dedicated writer: "the book became my center, engraved upon it, 'evil is whatever distracts.'"[23] Her talk was repetitive, self-indulgent (lasting at least two hours), and self-excusing. Other fellows were irritated that she went on so long and left no time for questions, but Sexton recalled "if anyone had stopped her, I would have chopped their head off." Craving enlightenment, she borrowed Tillie's copy-outs and reflections and, with a secretary, spent the summer transcribing them.[24] This talk opened a new way to "write": Tillie could read from cards and bits of paper, ad lib between quotations, have the whole recorded and transcribed, and then edit it herself. Her talk created such a stir, the *Boston Globe* asked to interview her. Insisting that husbands were not "becoming sissified" by wives' career gains, she expressed an early 1960s impulse to be feminist without seeming antimale or antimarriage. In *The Feminist Mystique*, Betty Friedan was more strident about women's sacrificing talents and aspirations for husbands and "occupation: housewife." Both tapped into a groundswell of female resentment.

The new feminism impacted the Marianna Pineda, who began a series of *Oracle* statues studying "women's new awareness of what their roles have been and what they might be."[25] Undergraduates wanted to talk about feminism so Tillie helped organize an informal seminar on women's futures, led also by Sister William, a Ph.D. student in English, who wore the full habit of a Catholic nun, and Hanna Papanek, a sociologist working with David Riesman at Harvard.[26] Most Radcliffe students who attended felt themselves too talented or privileged to have career problems, so the seminar did not last long, but still it absorbed time, as did writing recommendations.[27] Tillie's *Globe* interview provoked Seymour Lawrence, who was about to start a private Boston publishing firm, to invite her to lunch. She declined, saying her father was ill. When Cowley inquired about progress on her novel, she admitted that she was "in trouble" with it.

Then Kathie turned up in Cambridge, staking her claim in a mother who now seemed "owned by the world."[28] She enrolled in a month-long drama class in Cambridge and amused her parents and her Aunt Jann, whom she often visited, with comic acts and lyrics like (in Tillie's rendition) "walk right in plotz right down baby let your nose run on." Cowley hoped Tillie's Radcliffe year had been "propitious for work." It had not.

At the end of the spring term, Tillie and Jack retrieved Laurie from Putney and moved to the working-class neighborhood of Arlington, Massachusetts. Then Jack and Laurie drove, without Tillie, back to San Francisco, where they shared a room in Julie and Rob's apartment, sleeping and baby-sitting in shifts. When Annie Wilder came to visit in Arlington, Tillie introduced her to Anne Sexton, who impulsively announced, "I'm in love with you already!"[29] A jealous Tillie squandered much of her summer in emotional entanglements with the two Annes. She was worried enough about her addled brain to try to learn Annie's "system" to "prolong the attention span" and overcome mental fragmentation. She read at Radcliffe's expense, charging paperbacks of classics and handsome sets of editions from Grolier's Book Shop to the Institute.[30]

At the end of that summer, on the steps of the Lincoln Memorial, before 250,000 people, Joan Baez sang "We Shall Overcome," soon the anthem of the Civil Rights Movement. Then Martin Luther King, Jr., gave probably the greatest American speech since Lincoln's Gettysburg Address. Invoking the Declaration of Independence, the Constitution, and the Emancipation Proclamation, King envisioned a dream of racial harmony to come. In Arlington, Tillie listened exultantly.

After Jack and Laurie came back east, Tillie combined driving Laurie to Putney with a pilgrimage to New Hampshire and the home of elderly scholar Theodora Ward, whose family had known Emily Dickinson's.[31] Jack got a job printing on the night shift at the *Boston Traveler*. Still hoping she had not lost her mind, Tillie asked the Institute to subsidize her for an Evelyn Wood course on "how to write better and faster."

The murder of four black girls in a Birmingham, Alabama, church bombing dashed hopes for King's dream. This horror further distracted Tillie, who clipped out hoards of articles on racism, including one about MIT and Harvard students who challenged administrators to hire blacks in positions other than as janitors and cooks. When President John F. Kennedy was assassinated on 22 November 1963, Tillie felt the country's dream had turned into a nightmare. She was not mollified when now-President Lyndon Baynes Johnson appointed Chief Justice Earl Warren to preside over the official investigation of the murder. Death and life again intersected when Karla's second daughter, Jessica Lutz, was born on 2 December 1963.

About the time Tillie turned fifty-two in January 1964, the British firm of Faber and Faber republished *Tell Me a Riddle*, despite its poor sales with Lippincott. Tillie had promised Cowley to finish her novel by the end of 1963. Instead, she now wrote him that it might be "dead." She titled her spring 1964 seminar presentation self-reflexively "Two Years" offered only a hodge-podge of quotations and excuses.[32] On a spring visit to Hannah Green in New York, Tillie found Diarmuid Russell irritated with her for stringing Cowley along. He passed her to his junior colleague Harriet Wasserman, who insisted that Tillie must get something new into print. Tillie proposed the "Death of the Creative Process."

Jack was eager to go home in June, but Tillie said she needed more time alone to finish the long-promised novel, though she had just told Cowley it was "dead." When Connie Smith secured $2500 from a private foundation to support Tillie for the summer, she praised Tillie's "concern for people and their ideas." Barbara Swan gave Tillie her lithograph of Emily Dickinson and drew one of a kind, maternal Tillie. Not all Radcliffe fellows thought Tillie Olsen so kind, however. Some thought her tiny handwriting emblematized holding back; they called it "micrographia" and snickered when she said she wrote small because she was too poor to afford paper. Some accused her of "holier than thou" self-righteousness. Some thought she used past deprivations to secure current privileges. And some, except Marianna Pineda, tried to call in various loans.[33]

Tillie sent parts of her 1963 talk to Wasserman, who submitted it to *Harper's Magazine* in May. Connie Smith found Tillie a place to housesit for the summer. Jack resigned his job and began separating his things out of the load they had hauled across the country two years before. After Jack and Laurie, with the framed Emily Dickinson, headed west, Tillie wrote Scowcroft she had procured "the first time in my life alone."[34] She sent Cowley some pussy willow blossoms with news that she was staying in Cambridge "for the summer, not to interrupt the book," which she said was now "moving again." She was under both publishing and sexual pressure. A letter she sent Jack in June had so aroused him he could not sleep. With "50, 60 nights to go," he was overcome with desire: "it's all sex."[35] Tillie avoided telling him she wanted to stay more than sixty days.

National mourning after the murder of President Kennedy had given President Johnson a chance to heal the wounds of racism and poverty. He pushed through Congress major progressive legislation for a "Great Society": a Civil Rights Act, a "War on Poverty," and Medicare and Medicaid. He campaigned for reelection as a man of peace. Boycotts, sit-ins, voter-registration drives, and Freedom Rides challenged Americans to defend the equal rights of all citizens. Bob Dylan's prediction that the "times they are a-changin'" might be a harbinger for a new era of peace and justice. The murder of three Freedom Riders in Philadelphia, Mississippi, however, suggested that entrenched racism was unchangeable, King's dream an illusion.

In August, *Harper's* accepted Tillie's essay but requested massive revisions, condensations, transitions, and clarifications of "cloudy" phrases. It had accepted an article in need of so much revision because of her reputation, the timeliness of her topic, and her gender.[36] After Tillie saw Laurie back to Putney, she flew home at September's end, avoiding Cowley and leaving Radcliffe a Grolier's book bill exceeding $172.

After settling in with Jack at another place on hilly Alpine Terrace, Tillie described her return to both Hannah and Nolan Miller as "ill-timed." She had botched a last visit with the Tovishes. The airlines had broken her typewriter. Her summer grant gave her no book allowance. The Institute sent her an "S.O.S." about missing library books. She went to a memorial for Jack's mother in Los Angeles. She sent but withdrew a vague request to the Guggenheim to do "creative writing." Barry Goldwater, Republican nominee for president, had reputedly proposed to "erase" Vietnam; Lyndon

Johnson promised to end the war so Tillie was relieved at his election. She was present at the birth of Julie and Rob's baby boy.[37] Marianna Pineda sent a check to pay Tillie's book bill, "no worry about paying back," so the year ended on an improved note.

Still, Tillie could not pull ideas for her novel together. As she turned fifty-three early in 1965, she imagined that, if only she were alone, she could finish. Hannah Green suggested the MacDowell Colony, America's oldest artists' community so Tillie applied there. Meanwhile, voters who had believed in Johnson's peace promises were horrified when he sent combat troops to Vietnam. While antiwar "teach-ins" grew around the country, Tillie Olsen won peace and quiet at MacDowell for April and May.

She packed a typewriter and suitcase, with a large assortment of books and papers, flew into Boston, and somehow got all her stuff on a bus to Peterborough, New Hampshire. She fell in love with the quaint New England village and the MacDowell center. Founded early in the twentieth century on 450 acres of woodlands and meadows, MacDowell featured a columned Colony Hall for administrative offices, kitchen, and dining hall, where artists came for impromptu entertainments, phone calls, and family-style breakfasts and dinners, with basket lunches delivered to their isolated cabin studios. Separate residences for men and women included bedrooms and extra baths. Mostly built in the 1920s, some cabins were still without plumbing; all were without telephones. In the modest New Hampshire cabin Tillie had her long-desired uninterrupted space and time.

She felt, however, like an unopened bottle of champagne, "stoppered." She could not "open a notebook, look in a folder without [confronting] the undones, the embryos." The worry, "am I really done for?" threatened to engulf her. At Laurie's graduation, Tillie told her troubles to fellow-writer Carolyn Kiser, mother of one of Laurie's classmates. Begging for a MacDowell extension, Tillie followed a private protocol: she needed tranquility and support, promised to write a novel, won support, did not write, blamed "circumstances," and sunk into despair. She wrote, "I may never survive."[38] The Tovishes feared that, like Sexton, who was revising poems titled *Live or Die*, Tillie was suicidal. Red advised her to distance herself from Sexton and Wilder.[39] He saw Tillie as handicapped by a "masterpiece syndrome," a debilitating fear that she could never match the brilliance of *Tell Me a Riddle*. He cautioned that such fear might, like quicksand, pull her "under as an artist."

As she seemed about to sink, Seymour Lawrence, Inc., sent a lifeline. From a one-room office at 90 Beacon Street, Boston, he and his wife Merloyd Lawrence were publishing major writers, with Delacorte and

Dell Publishers handling production and distribution. Their first author was Katherine Anne Porter. On 16 June, an old black Rolls Royce lumbered up in front of Colony Hall, and a heavy-set, gruff-looking man asked for Tillie. He endeared himself by saying that Katherine Anne Porter had recommended her and by stuttering. He regretted that *Tell Me a Riddle* had gotten little publicity. If she signed with him, he promised to handle her books effectively and profitably.

When she left MacDowell's after about six weeks of extended time, Tillie was still "stoppered," though Lawrence had already begun selling her to Dell publishers as if her novel were complete. He said that Viking had advanced $2000 for it but that she was unhappy "with her editorial relationship there." He did not suggest why she might be unhappy with Cowley, who had waited six years for her to produce a novel. Lawrence proposed a $3500 advance on signing and another $3500 on delivery of her "full-scale novel, panoramic in scope and with a broad range of people and dramatic incident." Famous writers could be counted on for blurbs "to launch the novel."[40] He bought her loyalty by declaring "Tell Me a Riddle" "one of the most beautiful stories of our time" and by paying Laurie's tuition to Reed College. When Dell asked about her novel, Tillie replied that describing it would betray "what, for me, is necessary working reticence." (Her reticence might have been modesty, secretiveness, or a cover-up.)

Meanwhile, rioting in Harlem and the Watts District of Los Angeles expressed black anger over economic inequity, police brutality, and rampant injustice, but the riots provoked a white backlash. Johnson escalated bombing in Vietnam. Disaffected, "hippies" chose an alternate, often drug-induced reality. Some moved into communes, where they shared chores and often partners. The Communist in Tillie approved such experiments in communal living; the mother in her feared Kathie or Laurie might join one.

Tillie finally let Cowley know that she had signed with Lawrence Inc., saying it was "unfettered" while Viking was "primarily a business concern," an echo of the comparison she made in 1934 between Random House and Macmillan.[41] Furious, Viking's president replied that Viking had generously "offered her a contract simply because we felt that she was a fine writer." It had released her to publish her four short stories elsewhere because that seemed in "*her* interest at the time." She had won grants thanks to Malcolm Cowley's support. Viking had "advanced money to her beyond the total stipulated on delivery of her completed manuscript (this without seeing one shred of script)." It had "waited three years, without complaint, beyond the delivery date specified in the contract." A contract was "clearly from Mrs. Olsen's point of view a totally meaningless scrap of paper," an observation that Bennett Cerf had made almost thirty years before. Cowley fumed but kept quiet.

Sam Lawrence knew that Tillie was highly emotional and terribly unreliable, but he and Merloyd were so essential to Laurie's education that he felt sure she would produce for him. Jack was away days, working in a factory of two hundred printers, setting type for all the telephone books in the western United States. Kathie had gone back to Boston to stay in the Tovishes's basement apartment.[42] Tillie assured Lawrence that "as soon as we deliver Laurie to Reed," she would "be alone" and hence able to write.

In October *Harper's Magazine* began a two-part supplement on "The Writer's Life," with articles by five famous writers "and others." Tillie joked that she had a new name, "Ann Dothers."[43] She was disturbed by an article appearing with hers, titled, "The Foundations: A Welfare State for Writers?" The author saw a trend away from grants to "socially conscious" writers and toward grants to the "cerebral and 'alienated'" writers of the 1960s. On 13 October, Tillie wrote the Guggenheim Foundation that she would apply late since the *Harper's* article "threw me off," one more example of her ability to blame circumstances. Five days later, she sent the Guggenheim her statement of intention: "the creation of enduring literature. Possible only with economic wherewithal." She explained: "The book begun during the Ford award time (I cannot say 'novel' for it takes from all literary forms, but is its own) is what I work on now. . . . I am bound to it."

The Olsens moved to a "cheaper place" on O'Farrell Street, in mid-November. The posthumous release of Sam Cooke's song "Change is Gonna Come" voiced hope to end violence and intolerance. Tillie hoped for change in a "good work year."

In the first week of 1966, Tillie wrote doggerel to Nolan Miller: "66 my harvest year/ nothing better interfere." She wrote the Guggenheim, "I can no longer face daily problems AND write." She asked for her fellowship to begin in September, but the Guggenheim soon notified her that she had no fellowship. She was set further off balance by news that sister Vicki had flown to London, where Gene introduced her to famous people, including Robert Graves, author of *I, Claudius*, and actress Ava Gardner. Then at the Kaufman-Lerner villa, Casa Bianca, outside Rome, Vicki met actress Anna Magnani. In the cheap apartment on O'Farrell, Tillie felt outclassed, but she was vindicated by a grant from the National Council for the Arts. She used the money to rent an impressive place in Carmel Valley for herself alone. It was a "mirror of an old place with sun and sunset view," the Steffens' Getaway. Though Ronald Reagan's election as governor of California might mean surveillance, as in 1934, in 1966 Carmel offered

Tillie isolation and freedom. Lawrence promised that Richard Kostelanetz, who had not included her in Dell's *Six Great Stories of the Sixties*, would include her in a new edition.

Rather than tackle the novel she said she was "bound to," Tillie worked on a novella called *Requa*. Recalling the abandoned graves in the American Indian community on the Smith River that she and Jack discovered back in 1959, she has the orphaned Stevie's uncle take him to a place called Requa in March 1932, just when Abe had taken Tillie to Rae Schochet's "quiet, deep house." In one letter Tillie told Lawrence that she had finished both "Requa" and two more stories; in another she said that she would finish "Requa" by the end of 1966. She admitted to herself, "I have lived in the time of the LIE most of my 54 years." She instructed herself "alright broken self, piece together enough" to depict "real children's colonies" shaped by race and class.[44]

She was half-elated, half-terrified when late in the summer of 1966, Kathie was arrested in a protest against car dealers and restaurants that refused to hire black employees in show rooms and serving areas. Among arrestees singing "We shall Overcome" was Susan Lyon, who introduced herself as the daughter-in-law of Tillie's 1934 fellow arrestee Dave Lyon. Kathie was amused to tell Tillie that her former comrade had just published *Off Madison Avenue* and had reengineered Philip Morris's sales with the hard-box, rugged "Marlboro Man" image. He reputedly described Lenin as the consummate ad-man and said that if he could not influence people for the good he would settle for the bad.[45] He had turned, Tillie concluded, into the worst of capitalists.

She wrote her father that "Kathie the jail bird was sentenced to 60 days." Sam Lerner was "proud of our third generation of jailbirds. Hurray for Kathie!" At eighty-one, he was serving as "Chairman, Secretary and Treasurer" of the Workmen's Circle home, doing translations from Yiddish, and publishing the home's journal. At the end of August he wrote Kathie: "your place is in the free world an honorary seat not in jail. Still am proud of you. Your father and Mother, Your Grand Fathers and Grand Mothers were revolutionaries. they fought for Freedom, Free speech, and thoughts for a World of Broderhood and peace. . . . Your activities for a better world should be honored not punished." Ida and Sam's six children all carried on their parents' idealism. Now at Goddard College, Jann was writing about reshaping curricula to encourage better human relations.[46] Tillie had written *Tell Me a Riddle* and sought more equitable living and working conditions for women and minorities. After years relocating war's displaced persons, Harry had dedicated himself to keeping Yiddish language and literature alive. Pacifist Gene's glamorous business was devoted to healing relations between cultures. Lillian hosted World War II refugees, brought sick strangers into her house, and nursed them back to health. Vicki remained in the Workman's Circle and retained her prolabor political ethos. All the Lerners kept their faith in knowledge, education, and music.[47]

About this time, Jack and Tillie bought a third-floor apartment at #6 1435 Laguna Street in St. Francis Square, a cooperative union-sponsored development. They now had a large living-dining room, a tiny kitchen, a nice-sized bedroom and bath, two small bedrooms, the narrow one to be Tillie's study, and a second small bath. A living room balcony overlooked a public garden and playground; two bedrooms looked out on Laguna Street and down to the Chinese Consulate. The development was "dedicated to the ideal that all races, religions, and beliefs can live together in harmony." San Francisco's still-anti-Communist police force dubbed St. Francis Square "Red Square."

After Tillie wrote Carolyn Kiser, now at the National Endowment for the Arts, that she had viral pneumonia, Kiser "eased, as promised," according to Tillie, her application, another example of sickness's usefulness. Sending Lawrence "three marked up TMARs" and tapes of her radio recordings, Tillie expected a secretary somehow to collate the scribbled-in corrections with the tapes for an enlarged *Tell Me a Riddle*, but she had "no Requa yet" and "perhaps not at all."

Diarmuid Russell, pondering the riddle of Tillie Olsen, wrote Lawrence that "Tillie's an odd woman—she wrote me sometime ago that in my writings to Lippincott I should keep your name out of it and whatever they answered I should report to her and not to you. Dashed if I know the reason for all this since it all started with your desire to re-issue the stories." Perhaps Tillie thought that Lippincott would charge less if she had no publisher or perhaps she contemplated leaving Lawrence. Undeterred, when Lippincott handed over the copyright of *Tell Me a Riddle* for $525, Lawrence planned to "publish the enlarged edition of *Tell Me a Riddle*, with the three new pieces" in 1967. Tillie gave up her place in Carmel for Christmas with family. She sent out a pile of New Year's cards, but Dick Elman said her handwriting was "like jottings from a Dead Sea Scroll." He could only decipher something about troubles that kept her from writing.

On 13 January 1967, the day before she turned fifty-five, Tillie promised Lawrence to get back to Carmel and work on the new stories, finishing "*Requa* first," now to be a novella about a "ghostboy," the literally "snotty kid," whose inertia infuriates his Uncle Wes and others. She wrote and rewrote lines to convey Stevie's sense of anomie in the mysterious Requa, but her lines were halting, the story plotless. She proposed a new name for

the enlarged *Tell Me a Riddle*: "*Yonnondio*... 'the word itself a dirge' from
Walt Whitman." Her Christmas holiday in San Francisco stretched into
two months, a "menacing time." The menace included family obligations
and even, she said, a suspected "brain abscess," perhaps an excuse for her
general befuddlement. In March she returned to Carmel and rented a less
grand, more "motelly" place. For Jack's birthday, she made a heart out of a
MacDowell photograph of her wearing a turtleneck jersey with (clearly) no
bra, wistfully looking off camera.[48] She wished, "Happy Birthday/ Happy
Year/Long Life" to "my love/ my lover/ my lovable/ Jack/ in joy that you
got born." He would have been happier to have her with him in St. Francis
Square.

On 4 April, Martin Luther King, Jr., spoke at the Riverside Church in
New York City, joining Civil Rights and antiwar movements' resolution "We
Shall Overcome." As protests over the draft, the Vietnam War, and racial and
sexual discrimination escalated, so did a right-wing backlash in such works
as *Alice in Womanland, or The Feminine Mistake*. "The pill" was blamed
for promiscuity and immorality because, as Tillie noted, birth control had
almost eliminated "that great inhibitor of sexuality, fear of pregnancy."

About when Anne Sexton won the Pulitzer Prize for poetry, Tillie won a
National Endowment for the Arts fellowship of $10,000.[49] On 11–12 May, she
returned to St. Francis Square, where she found Jack so ill that she brought
him down to Carmel. By 22 May, she had returned him to San Francisco and
had "my first free moment in two weeks." She promised to send *Requa* to
Lawrence "within the month," but she told Russell she had worked on new
stories "all simultaneously" and had finished none of them or her "longer
work." She mentioned "torment about my 'facility,'" which explains why she
also wrote to the sometimes suicidal Anne "perhaps we are each other."

As Tillie became more anxious about her broken facilities, she compensated by helping other women writers. She recommended African-American
playwright Alice Childress to the Radcliffe Institute and promoted the
works of Sandy Boucher, Blanche Boyd, and Susan Griffin, among many
others. Her promotions reached an absurd level, however, at Ernest Gaines's
reading of his forthcoming *Bloodline*, when Tillie almost ignored Gaines to
court women writers. A friend suspected her of "acquisitiveness: how many
people can she gather about her at one time; how many people can she
touch & influence simultaneously. Bah."[50] Tillie had begun wearing flowing
long robes, often of Indian patterns and fabrics and taking center stage,
whatever the occasion.

In mid-July, Sam Lerner came to visit. Tillie wrote Gene that Sam had
been "a near corpse" when he arrived, but visiting the Olsens had begun his

"resurrection." Gene had recently traveled to Russia to "fulfill Ida's wishes" and bring back soil that "did not belong to Communists." Moscow relatives, the Dishners, were too frightened of the oppressive Soviet regime to invite Gene to their home, so they met him at the ballet. Through their English-speaking daughter Lisa, they told about the Soviet Union's ugly treatment of Jews. Then Lisa arranged for Gene to address her class, where he incautiously talked about student rebellions in America. Two weeks after he left, Lisa wrote that her father was dead, thanks, Gene feared, to his talk about "free speech in America."[51] Gene's narrative not only established him as Ida's most loyal child but also violated Tillie's sense of the glories of Soviet communism.

In early October, the "Call to Resist Illegitimate Authority" or RESIST placed anti-Vietnam War statements in papers across the country, signed by authors, the clergy, academicians, and medical doctors, including Benjamin Spock. In "Stop the Draft Week," young men turned in or burnt their draft cards. In Washington, D.C., protestors rallied at the Lincoln Memorial and marched across the Potomac to the Pentagon. Their protest began peacefully but unraveled into chaos and confrontation; U.S. marshals arrested nearly seven hundred.[52] A full-time opponent of the war, Dr. Spock spoke as a "baby doctor" who believed, as Tillie did, that a war culture does profound damage to its children.[53] Tillie signed the RESIST document, though she objected to its sexist use of "man" and "brotherhood" to represent the whole human race.

When Tillie turned fifty-six in January 1968, the postman deposited an odd birthday present of about eight hundred remaindered copies of *Tell Me a Riddle* in the stairwell at St. Francis Square.[54] Tillie sent a box to the Radcliff Institute, one hundred copies to Dick Scowcroft, and another hundred or so to the Tovishes, with instructions to "GIVE THEM AWAY," perhaps to a Peace campaign. Nightly news programs listed the Vietnam body count, which totaled about one thousand Americans per month. Students chanted at President Johnson, whenever he left the White House: "Hey, hey, LBJ, how many kids did you kill today?" Churches, synagogues, and universities held peace vigils. In New York, an Auction for Peace solicited work from prominent writers, among them Tillie Olsen. She donated "makings" of "Tell Me a Riddle" with a quotation by Kostelanetz, who now described it as "surely among the great works of American fiction of recent years."

For Tillie, saving her book from the dumpster turned out to be a smart move. Friends gave or loaned copies to people who put the thin book in pockets and purses, read the shorter stories on trains and planes before settling into the title novella. Many passed on the collection but stipulated that it be returned. Thus, the reputation of *Tell Me a Riddle* continued to spread. Its reissue with three new stories promised to be a best-seller.

When Gene Lerner turned fifty-one, in February 1968, he and Tillie exchanged comments on aging. Tillie felt "not *less* capable or eager for life—more." She was however "not really back to work—inflamed with undones—but terribly distractable," though she was now supported by NEA money and had a private study at home. Gene startled her by sending a copy of the photograph of the four oldest Lerner children dressed up for the camera. Tillie wondered when she had "raised reality" by redrawing her eyebrows and hair to cover her ears, perhaps her first self-makeover.

After proposing to Anne Sexton "perhaps we are each other," Tillie sent Sexton an antique Easter card with a poem on sickness and madness in which she asked "All over with me?" and instructed "destroy," which Sexton did not. As if to cover the loss of her ego strength, Tillie became more imperious. Asked to write a blurb for Maxine Kumin's novel *The Passions of Uxport*, she made several unfortunate pronouncements. She accused Kumin of shallow Freudianism and of basing her main characters too clearly on herself and Anne. Tillie thought Kumin insensitive to Anne's suicidal depressions. Her use of an invented word "shallowized" provoked Anne to write Tillie, "Am I shallow? Is my work shallow?" Tillie wondered if she related to writers better through books than in person. Actually, she related to her juniors better than to her peers.[55]

Peace activists celebrated when Lyndon Johnson announced he would not seek reelection. The only true antiwar contender for the presidency was Senator Eugene McCarthy, a long shot. Then Robert F. Kennedy delighted civil rights and peace activists by announcing his decision to run. Delight was followed by horror, however, when Martin Luther King, Jr. was assassinated on 4 April 1968 in Memphis, Tennessee, and Robert Kennedy was assassinated on 5 June in Los Angeles. Grief and fury further catalyzed the antiwar movement; but hundreds of protestors were arrested, and many were jailed, suggesting that change was not "gonna come" after all. Professors Noam Chomsky, Florence Howe, and Paul Lauter wrote about the adverse implications of making criminals out of peace protestors.[56] Tillie supported but did not join the so-called "peaceniks." Though earning a stipend from NEA, she asked Lawrence to support her for three months at $325 a month. Beginning to suspect he was dealing with a con artist, Lawrence said he would send money in return for finished sections of her book.

At all-male, all-white Amherst College, Leo Marx, English Department chairman, realized that his students were ill-prepared to understand the conflicts that provoked protests, riots, and assassinations. The University of Massachusetts in Amherst and the newly founded Hampshire College hired women and African-Americans on their faculty, but Amherst College hired no blacks, only a few Jews, including Marx, and only one part-time woman teacher.[57] Seeing her name, like his, on RESIST petitions, Marx thought Tillie Olsen might shake up Amherst's entrenched conservatism.

That August Chicago police, assisted by the National Guard and the U.S. Army, brutally attacked antiwar demonstrators at the Democratic Convention. When Hubert Humphrey emerged as the nominee, the Right associated him and the Democrats with lawlessness and disorder; much of the Left associated Humphrey with Johnson and the Vietnam War. Republicans and their nominee Richard Nixon seemed above the fray. When a banner proclaimed "Women's Liberation" outside the Miss America pageant in Atlantic City, few noticed, until the media spread the news that women unfurling the banner had also thrown girdles, bras, and false eyelashes into a "freedom trash can."[58]

Tillie won another term at MacDowell and, in late September, flew into Boston for what she called a "botched visit" with an ailing Connie Smith. Then, she wrote Smith: "It will probably be the right year (my books done) (!)." She arrived at MacDowell ahead of her assigned term and so was put in an unplumbed unrenovated studio, where an outdoor privy seat treated with lime produced a violent allergic reaction, after which MacDowell's cook began preparing special meals for her. During her lifetime, Tillie had suffered from pleurisy, pneumonia, flu, diverticulitis, rectal bleeding, kidney or gall bladder trouble, colitis, Artaud's disease, back pain, and now "withdrawal of hormones" (menopause), and perhaps a "brain abscess," though she may have invented that last illness. When young she had learned the usefulness of illness; as she aged she learned the uses of carelessness. When she broke a zipper on a boot, unfitting her for an interview at Amherst, sculptor Deborah de Moulpied, drove her to Keene, New Hampshire, to buy new boots.

Tillie caught a wearying set of buses to Amherst. There, she sat in on classes and pronounced that Amherst faculty members were teaching the wrong books and students were ignorant of lives unlike their own. Her outbursts on such topics convinced Leo Marx that Amherst needed her. Amherst's beauty and generous salaries tempted Tillie. Perhaps she could not teach Karl Marx at Amherst, but she could enlighten students on American inequality. Some members of the English Department opposed hiring someone without a degree and the college president opposed paying a married woman as much as a man with a family. Still, her O. Henry awards, *Harper's* article, and Leo Marx's sponsorship gave her a certain luster.[59] Marx pleased her by sending her back to MacDowell in a chauffeur-driven car.

After the trip, Tillie moved to the cozy two-room Mansfield Studio, which offered an open fireplace, a screened back porch, and plumbing. She called Jack to propose that she spend a year at Amherst alone. In a long "unsatisfactory" conversation, he refused, if they were to remain married. As the leaves fell around her cabin, Tillie read Thoreau's journal to compare his autumn at Walden Pond with hers at MacDowell. Colonists that fall included scholar Peter Viereck, writing a book on Soviet letters, Helen Ansell, a photographer for *Life Magazine,* Cid Ricketts Sumner, a writer of girls' books, and Deborah de Moulpied. Tillie broached a painful subject by mail: "Jack am going to ask: should it be necessary, if can stay through February. Know what a blow that is for you (me too, personally) but no sense unsettling, resettling." She promised to be in San Francisco for the holidays and spend time alone *"with you* 3–4 days of it." After President Johnson pledged that the United States would cease bombing Vietnam, she cast an absentee ballot for Humphrey. She was appalled when Nixon won the presidency.

Jack's routine of night work helped him suppress his "sex hunger for the feel of you."[60] Tillie's coterie of followers kept her from feeling any such hunger. One colonist wrote Hannah about people who "lionized" her. One had gotten "down on one knee in front of Tillie the Queen. It actually happened . . . I was saying to myself, 'That is bullshit, pure and simple.'" Tillie did not tell Jack about playing the queen, but she did tell him guardedly about Deborah de Moulpied coming "at midnight last night to fetch me" for a moonlit drive. With the road iced over, de Moulpied instead bedded down with Tillie, reminding her of lesbian escapades in Omaha forty years before.[61]

Tillie flew home on 19 December but had no time for her promised "3–4 days" alone with Jack. She was back in New York for a 26 December meeting designed to shake up the academic Modern Language Association.[62] The meeting organized a campaign to elect leftist Louis Kampf of MIT as MLA president, instead of the official nominee, and to endorse curriculum reform reflecting diversity, instead of readings in only so-called "dead white males."[63] Tillie confessed to Lawrence: "I won't have Requa to send. I haven't been able to work on it, or on anything. A charred way to end the year."

She was back at MacDowell on New Year's Eve, when other colonists returned merrily and tipsily from a cocktail party in Peterborough.[64] Sitting beside her at dinner, Peter Viereck was "pontificating" about Soviet and American proletarian writers, when he pronounced that he and Tillie Olsen "were the only well-read people there." One colonist ran out; another slapped Viereck and called him a boor. Almost everyone let grievances fly, some over Tillie's magisterial ways. It was not a soothing end for a "charred" 1968.

Tillie began 1969 by writing Jack an endearing letter saying that she hoped the first day of the New Year would be their "last separation." Stomach trouble kept her from eating and writing, but Debbie de Moulpied comforted her with helpful gifts and the staff carried an extra table and a wheeled posture chair to the Mansfield Studio. In a long harried conversation Jack protested that she was not consulting him about Amherst. He wanted to know more about Debbie, whose name appeared in most of Tillie's letters. He was needy and resentful and determined not to be left alone for a whole year.

Kostelanetz's expanded edition of *Great Stories* included ten men and two women, one of whom was Tillie Olsen, a designation earning her further clout for Amherst.[65] She planned to focus her writing course on the "Struggle to Write," but her other course was as daunting to describe as it would be to teach. She considered: "Omissions: myths and realities of human experience" or "Literature of revolution—oppression-poverty." The MacDowell cook checked out a book on gall bladder diets and made special meals for Tillie. She finally sent Leo Marx a course name: "The literature of poverty, oppression, revolution, and human struggle for freedom (or triumph of human spirit)." She suggested offering her writing class twice a week, "the second session to be open as ½ course to those interested in the struggle to write." At the end of January, Tillie slipped on the ice, badly bruising herself. On the *Requa* typescript, she wondered if "I have to fuck up."[66] Perhaps she did.

She rented for the next academic year a big "old fashioned house" two blocks from Amherst's English Department, large enough for herself and Jack and visitors. They would need to feed the cats while the owners were on sabbatical and pay about $220 a month, as opposed to $145 on the St. Francis Square mortgage. She belatedly proposed to Jack that they call each other only on Sundays, at cheaper rates. She suggested that he scrape through, borrowing if necessary, until she could send a check in mid-February for $1500 to 2000.[67] She would tell him about the "colonist I'm most fond of, regard most highly for quality and promise of her work (and feel I can call on in need, she's such a love of a human being) the beautiful Debbie."

Later in February, Jack flew to Boston to visit, and Tillie took the bus down to spend a time of "happiness together." She returned to MacDowell just as Debbie, bringing gifts for Tillie, returned from New York. Having lovers, both Jack and apparently Debbie, being freed from most money troubles, and accepting an academic post, once Robert Frost's, appeared to stimulate Tillie's creativity. She spent a "happy day" walking in the meadows, feeling the "gathering" of her powers.[68] She bragged to Anne Sexton that March 1969 was a time of "writing at the crest time, flood time, into my book," but she did not identify the book. In mid-March, she celebrated Jack's birthday with news that Amherst would pay $14,000 for nine months of teaching, with $1000 extra for relocation expenses. Instructing him on which debts to pay off first, Tillie admitted she "really shorted Julie in not bringing her up to handle money better."[69] At the end of March, at a farewell dinner for Debbie, Tillie drank wine "when I shouldn't have," which upset her digestion. Helen Ansell brought novelist May Sarton to meet Tillie, but Sarton did not offer the adulation that a younger coterie offered Tillie.

When Tillie's sister Lillian called to say that Sam Lerner was in the intensive care unit in the Poughkeepsie hospital with "extremely serious" heart and lung trouble, Tillie booked costly flights into New York City and then Poughkeepsie. Sam's health, her own gall bladder troubles, and Emily Dickinson's poem about a "reportless grave" depressed her. Still assuring Lawrence, "you will have a book to publish," she briefly confronted her "disorganization, litter." Her organizing method was to "just stack, pile stuff up." She remembered her 1961 breakdown: "that anguished January on my back, momentary suicidal thinking: & I cant even die because of the mess everything's in."

Tillie seemed so caring and so vulnerable that Helen Ansell took Debbie's place, knocking "herself out trying to DO things for me."[70] Though she had already signed the contract with Amherst, had arranged to rent the house on Snell Street, and had listed her courses in Amherst's fall bulletin, Tillie told Lawrence on 13 May that she might cancel because "I *must* publish next year." She left MacDowell burdened by commitments and terrified that her inheritance from her mother might include gall bladder cancer. She was home in time to ride with Jack and Kathie up to Reed College for Laurie's graduation. When they returned, Tillie checked into Kaiser Hospital in Oakland on 1 June. She wrote Nolan Miller that she had four to six weeks work left to do on her book which "must be done this summer."

She remained in the hospital a week, relieved that her gall bladder trouble was not cancer.

The Olsens planned to make the arduous trip east and settle into the house on Snell Street in mid-June, but Tillie's operation and subsequent fevers ill-fitted her for either a crosscountry drive or serious writing. She and Jack arranged for someone to feed the cats on Snell Street, borrowed money against her Amherst salary, hired youngsters to drive their car east, and flew to New York, where they spent a few days in Hannah Green's Greenwich Village apartment. Apparently then, Tillie met Florence Howe and her husband Paul Lauter in the lobby of a nearby hotel. Lauter recalled waiting in the hotel lobby until a frazzled, for once rather dowdy woman stood dazed in the doorway. Howe said "that must be she," and the three reformers greeted each other warmly. Tillie opened a big brown envelope and gave them a photocopy of the anonymous *Life in the Iron Mills* from an 1861 *Atlantic Monthly*. She said it was written by Rebecca Harding Davis, of whom neither had heard. That evening, Howe and Lauter disobeyed Tillie's suggestion not to read it at night. Each, as Tillie predicted, cried.[71] Tillie and Jack got to Amherst in time for an old-fashioned Fourth of July fireworks show. She taped writers' pictures in her work room on Snell Street and hung Swan's portrait of Emily Dickinson downstairs. She felt, not a religious but a feminist calling, when Howe and Lauter insisted she write about Rebecca Harding Davis.

When New York's 92nd Street Y offered Tillie one hundred dollars to read in early 1970, it suggested she share the reading with Maxine Kumin to insure a larger audience. Insisting on reading alone, Tillie sent the Y a list of over fifty invitees, including Lawrence, Wasserman, Howe, Frank MacShane of Columbia's writing program, writers Alice Childress, Cynthia Ozick, and Grace Paley, an agent named Elaine Markson, and other influential literary people, including Lola Szladits, curator of the Berg Collection of the New York Public Library, and reviewers Annie Gottlieb and Julian Moynihan. She also listed her Omaha cousin Sam Braude, now a Wall Street broker.

On 7 September Tillie wrote Sam Lawrence that she had been "*six weeks* close" to finishing when she left MacDowell on Ascension Day. She had "lost the summer" thanks to illness, moving, and preparing her class. On 13 September, Jack wrote their daughters that "Mother is still weak but improving markedly each day." Plagued by high cholesterol, he began jogging slowly along Amherst's tree-lined streets where houses stood on "indecently large" lawns. Amherst classes were personalized with usually only fifteen students apiece, but advance publicity and the uniqueness of her topics made students flock to her poverty class, the department's first course to focus on under-represented voices. Her other course was titled "The Struggle to Write: The creative process as revealed in the diaries, workbooks, letters, and lives of writers including Camus, Chekhov, Conrad, Fitzgerald, Gide, Hardy and James." (Here her notion of struggle trumped her feminism.) The term had just begun when Tillie rushed out of class to find a dignified gentleman by the door. He said, "Hello, I'm Nolan Miller." Tillie whooped in delight, hugged him, lunched with him, and said good-bye, forever.

In her assignments, Tillie did include one woman writer, herself. She told students about her hard life, another instance of emphasizing message, not craft. Some were irritated by her obsession with work, but another supposed that boys needed to learn about the lives of working-class women.[72] She carried stacks of quotations on cards and would give them to the students—choosing the phrase that she thought most appropriate for each. She tacked up quotations around her desk. She advised Scott Turow's senior independent study project; and he saw in Tillie a "mythic, maternal sense of humanity." A less enthusiastic student journalist wrote about Tillie's "bureaucratic befuddlement," but he affirmed that her trouble with time was "her only real failure. . . . Class sessions were occasionally more like nightmares, but they were laboratories and, make no mistake, Tillie Olsen was teaching a great amount."[73]

Jack soon secured a job over the hill in Mount Holyoke, printing the *Wall Street Journal*, a job he took, Scott Turow recalled, as "a hoot" for a former Marxist. Though living together, Jack and Tillie conducted much of their lives apart, a habit that baffled Turow who knew Jack independently.[74] Perhaps Jack was bruised by Tillie's many absences. Perhaps he was irritated that Amherst faculty members hardly knew how to talk with a tradesman like him. He certainly resented sexist remarks that he should join the faculty wives' club. Many actual faculty wives were as unhappy to be relegated to tea-serving, white-gloved wifely duties as Jack would have been. They were forming an Amherst Women's Liberation movement, much to Tillie's delight.

Since Tillie had said she was only six weeks away from finishing her book in May 1969, Lawrence assumed she would "beg, borrow and steal" six weeks from Amherst to finish it. Teaching works about the underprivileged, as in *The Souls of Black Folk* and *Life in the Iron Mills*, to privileged young male students, however, kept Tillie from writing all fall. Scouring libraries to uncover information about the free-thinking New England writers who had encouraged Rebecca Harding Davis, Tillie confided in Connie Smith that she was working on, or at least thinking about, a "Rebecca book."

For some time, Anne Sexton had worked on a play titled *Mercy Street*, which began a Broadway run on 3 October. Tillie tried to heal the rift between them with a note to Anne by saying vaguely that she had been "bowled over" by her play. In New York to teach a seminar at Columbia University and earn an extra two hundred dollars, Tillie went by Russell and Volkening offices to ask why she had gotten no income from reprints of her stories. Russell and Wasserman struggled to clarify that earnings were applied against the advances she had already received and spent. Though proud to represent the author of *Tell Me a Riddle*, they were, unlike her acolytes, increasingly irritated with her.

On 10 December, Emily Dickinson's birthdate, Tillie took her writing class to visit the brick, Federal-style Dickinson house, the Homestead. She asked the students to remain in the downstairs parlor, while she went up to Emily's room, for what the students imagined was a séance. She wept to feel herself close to her hero and then to learn that thousands of antiwar demonstrators, singing John Lennon's "Give Peace a Chance," had been tear-gassed in front of the Justice Department. To the right, the antiwar movement meant chaos, subversion, lawlessness, drugs, and bra-burning; to the left, incoming President Nixon heralded fascism.

Tillie and Jack flew home to spend Christmas back on St. Francis Square, where friends and family stopped in everyday until the whole holiday passed "in a haze." Then Tillie flew east alone and gathered her "makings" of *Requa* from the house on Snell Street and on 30 December went by bus to the MacDowell Colony where she planned to bring a "substantial chunk" of *Requa* to closure "by the end of the holidays." From his exasperating "stupor, the lostness, the torpor," Tillie wrote passages showing the thirteen-year-old Stevie at last recognizing that Uncle Wes was "all he has." Then the motherly boardinghouse owner takes the orphan for Decoration Day at ancient cemeteries, including Indian burial grounds. Connecting at last with his past, Stevie "stealthily secretly" begins to reclaim himself. Odd word placing conveys his broken consciousness, as well as Tillie's. She spent New Year's retyping bits, stapling them together, deleting other bits, adding addenda, and struggling to end the first part of *Requa*. Did Tillie's desperate stapling (literally) bits of this story together foretell a loss of her ability to envision a whole? What did she mean when she wrote Smith: "(my books done)(!)"? Certainly, she implied that she had finished her novel. Perhaps instead she meant that she was done attempting to write it and was redirecting her ego strength.

CHAPTER 13

TILLIE APPLESEED

1970–1974

I am close to great yield.
—Tillie Olsen, application to the
Guggenheim Foundation, 29 October 1974

On the calendar, the 1960s were over. In American hearts and minds, though, they seemed endless. Nightly news shows still broadcasted Vietnam body counts. Disaffected citizens still held vigils and teach-ins. President Nixon and Vice President Agnew smeared protesters as effete snobs, pseudo-intellectuals, and cowards. Cities braced for more riots. Tillie stayed at Mac-Dowell until her cobbled together early part of *Requa* could be sent to the *Iowa Review*, which quickly accepted it. By her fifty-eighth birthday, she was back at Amherst, where, as she wrote Miller, "I learn I love teaching—but cant write as I need."

On 9 February 1970, the Olsens took the train into the City. In the apartment of Hannah Green and her husband, Jack Wesley, Tillie changed into a long flowing dress to read from *Tell Me a Riddle* at the Poetry Center of the 92nd Street Y. Hardly dowdy, she swung her shawl about her shoulders and assumed characters' different voices, a performance that made Alice Childress see the stories as "love letters to Walt Whitman's people," women, blacks, and Jews. Listed as a printer, Jack was, as Childress wrote, "so nicely himself," proud to be with Tillie as her husband. Her lengthy guest list and a postreading cocktail party on the Upper West Side secured a large, influential audience.[1]

In March, Tillie traveled to Boston to read about Rebecca Harding Davis in the Widener Library and lunch with Anne Sexton and Maxine Kumin. Tillie meant to reach out to them but instead lectured them on feminist obligations, as she also did at a talk before the Amherst Women's Liberation

Movement.[2] Irritated by her haughty manner as well as her remark that Anne had "shallowized Max's book," Kumin and Sexton walked out on her. Back in Amherst, Tillie sent Anne a 1910 card, bought at Steele's used book store, showing a little girl climbing over a fence, with a little boy holding a ladder.[3] Tillie labeled it now "too late" to cross "over the fence" between herself and Anne.

However much her imperious manner offended some people, seeds sown by Tillie Olsen, Betty Friedan, and others were replenishing the literary landscape. Alice Walker, the daughter of sharecroppers, rediscovered the almost forgotten Harlem Renaissance author Zora Neale Hurston and was teaching the country's first course in black women writers at elite Wellesley College. Robin Morgan's *Sisterhood Is Powerful*, Kate Millett's *Sexual Politics*, Elaine Showalter's *Women's Liberation and Literature*, Mary Ellmann's *Thinking About Women,* and Gloria Steinem's slick magazine *Ms.* all found readers starved for a woman's perspective.[4] Though crusty Diarmuid Russell saw a glut in what he called "women's Lib books," most women, including Florence Howe, saw a drought. One afternoon in March Tillie left her writing class with poet Denise Levertov to meet Howe at the University of Massachusetts Library.[5] Howe hoped to start a commercially viable press for, by, and about women. Tillie agreed to be an adviser, on condition that the press reprint work by lost women writers, beginning with Rebecca Harding Davis's *Life in the Iron Mills.* Howe thought "if that gem had been lost, there must be more," and so agreed.[6]

On 30 April, when Richard Nixon announced that he was sending ground troops into Cambodia, students all over the country went on strike. At Kent State University, the Ohio National Guardsmen, firing on student protestors, killed four; at Mississippi's Jackson State, police, firing on student protestors, killed two. On 3 May, Amherst area students called a strike. By 7 May, Amherst College teach-ins on peace and justice replaced standard classes. Tillie spoke passionately about the horrors of war, repression, injustice, poverty, mass murder, and sexism.[7] At the University of Maryland, Baltimore County, Paul Lauter was fired because, the dean said, they had never had demonstrations until Lauter arrived, forgetting that "Nixon's bombing of Cambodia just might have" provoked the protests.[8] Widespread outrage brought Congress to outlaw troops in Cambodia. Tillie took time from speech-making to take her writing students on 15 May, the eighty-fourth anniversary of Emily Dickinson's death, to visit the Old West Cemetery. Weeping over Dickinson's gravestone's inscription "Called Back," Tillie felt called to her crusading self, now as an orator for peace and for women.

At the close of her appointment at Amherst, Tillie invited the English faculty, at departmental expense, to lunch at a back table in the Faculty Dining Commons. Against the clatter of utensils, the chatter of nearby voices, and Tillie's stammer, the men only gradually realized that she was lecturing on the lack of "political and social range" in their courses. These dedicated teachers were outraged. Professor William H. Pritchard was mystified that she was "a sort of heroine to members of the emerging women's movement," when to the faculty she seemed autocratic and incompetent.[9] Amid a "dementia packing stage," Tillie reflected that she had written no fiction in a year.[10]

She and Jack soon camped near Seneca Falls, New York, site of America's first Women's Rights convention. There in 1848, the Declaration of Sentiments proposing universal suffrage had been passed only after impassioned speeches by Elizabeth Cady Stanton and former slave Frederick Douglass. Stanton's house was marked only by a "rusty 1932" sign, further evidence of society's devaluing women's accomplishments. After their crosscountry trek, the Olsens were glad for family and friends, but Tillie was, as she wrote Gene, "dangerously exhausted" and wanted "to talk to you about Ma." In Jack's absence, his printers' union had lost clout, and he landed on the picket line.[11]

That summer Laurie Olsen studied education in Antioch-Putney graduate school and married on 22 August atop mile-high Putney Mountain. She and the groom wore hand-made wedding clothes, beads, and flower wreaths; the wedding party hauled musical instruments up the mountain, danced, and sang for hours. Except the pastor and his wife, they invited no older people, not even their parents, a testimony to their belief that youth could give peace and love a chance to make a better world.[12]

For a Guggenheim proposal Tillie resurrected her San Francisco novel, supposedly "now near completion" and to be published in 1971, along with "a new 120 page novella, *Requa*." After those books, Tillie proposed to write "about women: Woman."[13] While war resisters practiced what Grace Paley called "combative pacifism," Tillie spoke in safer academic venues, unaware that, on 4 November 1970, the FBI finally closed her case.[14] Florence Howe and others launched the Feminist Press with a reprint series to start with Rebecca Harding Davis's *Life in the Iron Mills*, introduced by Tillie Olsen.

She returned from San Francisco to Boston in late November, disconsolate to find that Connie Smith had just died of cancer. She did not attend the service for Smith, at which Maxine Kumin and Radcliffe President Mary Bunting spoke.[15] At MacDowell, Tillie was thrilled that Hannah Green and Jack Wesley were fellow colonists. She sent Hannah daily notes of love and neediness; for example, "Please if buggy is hale and you can take 20 minutes come and take me for groceries."

Back to San Francisco by Christmas, Tillie enjoyed the usual carol-singing and gift-giving, but she wanted to see no one outside her family. The year 1970 had been a "broken" one. Connie Smith had died. She thought the *Iowa Review* had mangled "Requa." She had not worked on, much less finished, the novella *Requa*. After decades of longing for time to write fiction, she had committed herself instead to write a "Rebecca book," or rather an historical introduction to Davis's novella.

The political and cultural transformations that rattled the country also shook academia and the MLA. Radical MIT professor Louis Kampf became its president, and Florence Howe its second vice president. The organization endorsed, for its late 1971 Chicago meeting, an unprecedented number of sessions on only women writers. Ingrained assumptions about great literature and great authors were under assault. Textbooks featuring only males were suddenly passé. Publishers scrambled to catch up with the revolutionary fervor. Turning fifty-nine, Tillie basked in the light belatedly shed on women's writing. The new feminism did not, however, convince the Guggenheim Foundation to support her "woman book."[16]

For forty years Tillie had identified with Rebecca Harding Davis, author of one classic novella. Now, as she described Davis, she might have been describing herself, except that Davis was a highly prolific writer.[17] Tillie's Rebecca loves husband and children but craves solitude, "longs for a knowing relationship with those outside the bounds of her class," experiences deeply social injustice, suffers under financial and domestic burdens, disdains bourgeois approaches to art, yearns to write, and suffers a breakdown. Tillie poured so much of herself into her introduction that it became longer than Davis's novella.

To oversee its completion, Florence Howe and Paul Lauter visited the Olsens several times that spring. They were surprised that Civil Rights champions like Howe and Lauter knew so little about the labor movement. The women usually formed one pair, the men another; as the couples walked near St. Francis Square in Japan Town or near Fort Point at the base of the Golden Gate Bridge, the Olsens told stories about labor history. Sometimes they drove their guests to an ice cream shop atop a San Francisco hill. When the women went in for cones, labor discussions could turn personal as Jack complained about Tillie's absences and Lauter insisted that her work was essential to the feminist movement. Meanwhile, silly Tillie would ask the shop owner to do something special for a poor old lady like herself who might not live to eat another ice cream cone. Then she and Howe would leave the shop giggling. One of their four cones would be topped with extra ice cream, whipped cream, syrup, and chocolate chips, testimony to Tillie's talent for wheedling special treatment from almost anyone, including Howe and Lauter.[18] They thought her such a treasure Howe gladly edited her idiosyncratic fragments into dramatic sentences. Lauter verified facts and quotations. When Lauter corrected her statement of the Seneca Falls "Declaration of Sentiments" she changed it back. When he proved that his was accurate, she replied, "but mine is better." Here, she lost.[19]

When Martha Foley and David Burnett chose "Requa" for inclusion in the *Best American Short Stories*, Tillie insisted it be reprinted as "Requa I" because it "was *not* a story but the first third of something." She disliked the looks of "Requa I" as much as "Requa."[20] She demanded that both galley and page proofs of the reissued *Tell Me a Riddle* "*must* be sent me for checking." She delayed printing, complained about the delay, and kept revising. (Russell wrote Lawrence "she always has new versions of stories as you know.") She also exasperated her agent and publisher by offering reprint permissions to friends. She gave "I Stand Here Ironing" to Michele Murray for $200, while her agent charged $400, and "Tell Me a Riddle" to Mary Anne Ferguson for an anthology of women writers for much less than Kostelanetz paid. She sent Lawrence such muddled lists for complimentary copies that he hired a man in San Francisco to straighten them out. This agent replied: "Sam, I sent a girl out to Tillie Toiler's chop house and, six hours and four hours typing later . . . the lists are on the way to her and you. I paid the girl. I'll send you a bill, the grief was free."

Since childhood, Tillie had assumed that the chaos she worked in and the grief she gave others were the prerogative of genius. Sam Lerner now regretted spoiling his genius daughter. Jann Lerner Brodinsky and Harry and Clare Lerner visited him often. Jann assumed personal burdens, like telling him of the death of his younger sister Rose. Harry watched his finances and, along with Lillian and Gene, supplemented them. When Gene came from Italy, he took Sam to see Lillian and Joseph Davis; Dr. Davis monitored his health. Tillie had not seen him since 1969 when she impulsively flew to Poughkeepsie. When Sam wrote her that he was "weak and full of pain," resentment of his most favored but least attentive child seeped through his words.[21]

New technologies made the physical task of writing easier for Tillie. She rented IBM Selectric typewriters at home and at MacDowell. Photocopying freed her from endless retypings. At newspapers, though, computers replaced linotype machines, thereby rendering Jack's hard-won skills obsolete. Now he had to learn the "qwerty" keyboard, another humiliating adjustment.[22] Tillie complained that he worked only two days a week and they were too poor to keep oranges in the house. Still, learning that Faber and Faber was going to destroy unsold copies of *Tell Me a Riddle*, Tillie found money to buy them, as she had the old Lippincott copies.[23] With her story collection a failure on both sides of the Atlantic, Tillie again asked the Guggenheim to support a "woman book." She no longer mentioned a novel but said that "*Requa*, a 120 page novella" was coming out in 1972.

Just when money troubles made Tillie feel as shriveled as an unwatered plant, she got a call from Dick Scowcroft, who wondered if she might take on Wallace Stegners's spring writing seminar. Wanting also to teach an original "class on women," she sent him her women's reading list. After considerable politicking with a skeptical English faculty, Scowcroft offered Tillie a Stanford teaching post for 1972 spring quarter.

When a surprise vacancy at MacDowell opened in November 1971, Tillie immediately left California for New Hampshire. Skimming through airport newsstands, she saw in *Cosmopolitan* a story by Edith Konecky, whom she soon met at MacDowell. When Tillie praised her story, Konecky was "flabbergasted" that Tillie Olsen read *Cosmopolitan*.[24] She shared with Konecky her apprehensions (not her history of abortions) when the Supreme Court heard the case of *Roe v. Wade*. Soon Konecky became her devoted acolyte. Tillie's assurance to Jack "love it doesnt stop" was hardly more convincing than hers to Lawrence: "DO not waver, Sam. I will try for a harvest year."

Tillie was one of the featured speakers at an early morning session on women writers on 28 December. Its organizer, Elaine Hedges, was nearly beside herself trying to find Tillie, who showed up very late. She redeemed herself, however, by arguing that the underrepresentation of women had nothing to do with biology but everything to do with denied opportunity. Her admittedly unscientific survey found only "one women writer for every twelve men." Women scholars flocked to Tillie's room and stayed up half the night hearing her talk about lost women writers. Soon her hotel room was cluttered with stacks of writings that female MLA members passed around like contraband. As Hedges later detailed, colleges nationwide now listed seven hundred courses in women's studies. Women's anger had transformed itself into "liberation for the woman writer, critic, and reader as well."[25]

Howe and Lauter were so charmed by Tillie's magnetic personality and impressed by her knowledge of women and labor that they wanted to resurrect her 1930s writings so she called Jack and asked him to search for "The Iron Throat," "The Strike," "Thousand Dollar Vagrant," her unfinished Imperial Valley piece, and "several unpublished stories I'd told Florence Howe about." When she left Chicago, she went back to MacDowell to finish what was now an "Afterword" to *Life in the Iron Mills*.

On 14 January 1972, Tillie's sixtieth birthday, when she went into Colony House for dinner, Tillie found a telegram from Jack: "FOR WHAT ITS WORTH, MY HEAD AND HEART FULL OF YOU TODAY. WANT MORE THAN ANYTHING PRODUCTIVE, HAPPY, CLOSE YEARS TOGETHER IN YOUR SIXTIES." This telegram suggested renewed loving relations with her husband, unless she took to heart his wish not only for productive but "together" years during their sixties.

However much she craved solitude, Tillie interrupted her "Rebecca" with excursions to Steele's book store, New Hampshire cemeteries, and the frozen MacDowell Dam with Hannah Green, Jack Wesley, and Edith Konecky.[26] In San Francisco, Jack began searching through an old trunk of boxes and papers for Tillie's 1930s writings. One night, when she was in the Colony Hall, he called to say he had found, in her words, "not them, but two large envelopes marked '30s, containing all manner of writing, no two pages in order" about a family named Holbrook. After nearly forty years, her lost 1930s novel was found. All she needed to do was to finish it.

At MacDowell, deep snow did not keep the postman from his rounds, so the envelopes Jack had found soon arrived. Tillie hovered in the Mansfield studio rereading her 1930s novel. There were only eight disordered but finished chapters, ending in terrible oppression: at the packing house where 110° heat broils Jim and other workers like the hogs, and in the kitchen, where 107° heat sickens children and Anna, who is canning. Playing with jar lids, however, baby Bess's noises make Mazie, Will, and Anna laugh, momentarily forgetting their misery. Tillie felt "like the archeologist sifting the layers [but] finding only shards." She sent her chapters to Russell, not Lawrence. She was taken aback but pleased to learn that Nixon had opened relations with the People's Republic of China.[27] On 29 February, she finished the afterword to "Rebecca," and, with bright sun promising a spring thaw, she "suddenly broke up. Cried uncontrollably" and "lopped off my hair with rusty kitchen shears," surely a self-defeating gesture.

Invited to the State University of New York at Old Westbury, where Florence Howe now taught, Tillie presented Howe with the "Biographical Interpretation" to *Life in the Iron Mills*. She told a rapt audience about 1840s New England utopian Fruitlands, which she said was all male, except for Mrs. Bronson Alcott and her four "Little Women," including Louisa May. After that amusing, rather inaccurate feminist talk,[28] she flew home, where another Guggenheim rejection awaited her.

Designers at the Feminist Press chose nineteenth-century photographs as possible cover designs for *Life in the Iron Mills*, but none captured the poignancy of Davis's tale of an unschooled miner who creates magnificent sculptures out of korl, left-over mining debris. Marianna Pineda's female figures, however, seemed rather like the "Korl Woman" who crouches "on the ground, her arms flung out in some wild gesture of warning" and of hunger. Pineda offered *Oracle: Portentous* for the cover.[29]

In late March, Tillie at last revealed to Lawrence that she had sent Russell a "partly typed up, partly Xeroxed copy of a 30s mss." She wondered if he might want to publish it. He immediately phoned Russell who told him it was unreadable so Lawrence insisted that Tillie "have it retyped at our expense." Reading a review of the reissued *Tell Me a Riddle*, Tillie was stung by a reference to "writing Tillie Olsen didn't do."[30]

That March, when the Senate ratified the Equal Rights Amendment (ERA), the last barriers to women's rights seemed to be falling. With state legislatures rushing to ratify the Amendment, Stanford women, including nonstudents, rushed to sign up for Tillie's women's literature class, featuring out-of-print or hard-to-find works by Willa Cather, Harriette Arnow, Dorothy Canfield Fisher, Elizabeth Stuart Phelps, Ruth Benedict, and Mary Gray Hughes. Mary Jane Moffat remembered: "the impacted knowledge she wanted to pass on to us brooked no interaction. Her famous stammer and uh-uh-uh kept questions and discussion at bay. Class would start and two hours later clutching her note cards, she would have only covered 1% of the topic of the day and would sigh heavily." When Moffat once asked a formalist question: "how does it stand up as a work of art?" Tillie's anger erupted as it had in the 1930s against "purist" writers like Proust, Jeffers, and Stein. She gave "an hour-long lesson on the misguided nature of my question."[31] In terms of coherence, the class was a disaster; in terms of inspiration, it was a success that brought many students to declare themselves feminists.

Tillie now titled her 1930s novel *Us*, identifying the Holbrook's plight with all humanity's. She followed editorial suggestions Abe Goldfarb had made nearly forty years ago. Though Lawrence had offered to pay for typing, Tillie asked Florence Howe to retype sections of *Us*.[32] With Nixon using words like "Communist menace" to justify an ongoing war, in 1971 former Pentagon official Daniel Ellsberg leaked information to *The New York Times* proving that Nixon had lied to promote the war. He now kept a list of enemies, starting with Ellsberg, and used antifeminist smears about abortion and amnesty against Democrats George McGovern and running mate Sargent Shriver.[33] After a break-in at Democratic National Committee headquarters in the Watergate complex in D.C., Tillie worried that the United States had regressed into a police state.

On 5 August, she got *Us* back from Howe and sent it to Lawrence. He interrupted his holiday to read it and quickly pronounced that *Us* achieved the "quality of Greek Tragedy. I urge you to neglect everything else, *everything*, and complete the final section. It will be a very great honor to publish your book." He insisted, "we are your publishers . . . it would be a mistake to have your work scattered or published piece-meal." Still, Tillie imagined that the Feminist Press could publish the paperback and Lawrence the hardback edition of *Us*, but she finally admitted to Lawrence "there can be no such thing as 'completing the final section.' None exists."

That September Eugene Lerner and Hank Kaufman began rehearsals for a New York production *Berlin to Broadway with Kurt Weill*.[34] Gene's success and her sisters' star-struck visits with him made Tillie long to go abroad, but she had neither passport nor birth certificate so she enlisted her youngest sister to find Omaha records verifying her birth date. Vicki was peeved with the assignment, but on 25 September 1972, she obtained Long Elementary School records saying that Tillie Lerner had been born on 14 January 1912 and entered Long when she was nine. Vicki sent Tillie the information, along with an Affidavit of Birth form for their father to sign.[35]

That fall Tillie made another Guggenheim application. Under the category "compensation," she listed her salaries: $15,000 from Amherst, $200 each for Columbia writing seminars, and $4500 for the Stanford quarter. She did not list any compensation from her Stanford, Ford, Radcliffe, or NEA fellowships. She admitted her proposal was "awkwardly said," as indeed it was, thanks to the scarcity of complete sentences and the presence of phrases like "with partially dones."

From MacDowell, Tillie sent Howe and Lauter her reading list for women's literature classes, which they published in *Women's Studies Newsletter*,[36] the sort of publication ridiculed by mainstream media. TV anchor Harry Reasoner, for example, gave *Ms.* "six months before they run out of things to say."[37] Male professors and reviewers disparaged "lady writers," thought women's fiction was "tainted," and faulted Dickinson for feminine cuteness, but the times were indeed changing at last. Alix Kates Shulman had been a protester at the Miss America contest in 1968; now her *Memoirs of an Ex-Prom Queen*, influenced by Grace Paley and Tillie Olsen, was a best-seller.[38] Meeting Shulman at MacDowell, Tillie took her on as a new protégé.

Washington Post reporters Carl Bernstein and Bob Woodward uncovered the connection between the Watergate break-in and the White House, but on 7 November 1972, 61 percent of voters chose Richard Nixon over George McGovern. Tillie tried to nourish optimism by quoting Walt Whitman's reminder that good is not "quell'd by one failure or two failures or any number of failures."

Throwing new shawls and silk blouses into a suitcase, Tillie left MacDowell in mid-November 1992 for a harrowing two-week lecturing and reading tour, on which she impressed one student reporter mostly by fraught emotions and smooth skin.[39] Between appearances, she stayed in New York with Hannah Green and Jack Wesley, where Laurie joined her. On 19 November, Tillie took Laurie and her hosts, courtesy of Gene, to see *Berlin to Broadway with Kurt Weill* at the Theatre De Lys, where Tillie was literally upstaged. She and Laurie took the train to see Sam Lerner and get him to sign the affidavit Vicki had sent.[40] In Old Westbury, Tillie read chapter four of her 1930s manuscript to a "hushed, raptly attentive, sometimes weeping audience," bringing herself "also near tears." Her theatrical readings seemed apolitical, but they were publicized as part of the protest movement. Despite her diva presentations, Tillie described herself as a "partially destroyed human." Of course, the more she set herself on exhausting lecture circuits and haggled with publishers over reprints and corrections, the less time and energy she had to do the writing she kept promising.[41]

Seymour Lawrence Inc.'s offer to Tillie of $10,000 ended competition between Lawrence and Howe. Tillie promised to finish the book she now called *From the Thirties* for Lawrence by Christmas. But she had no copy of the plan she had sent Donald Klopfer in 1935.[42] She diverted herself from writing by complaining about errors in the new Delta *Tell Me a Riddle*. She told Lawrence that she did not want it or *From the Thirties* ghettoized as working-class or women's literature but sold as "quality literature," a contradiction to her belief that only subject and function, not art, matter.

Even while she claimed not to be a troublemaking, "temperamental egocentric writer," Tillie continued revising her "Rebecca" and then protesting the resulting delays. When *Life in the Iron Mills* finally appeared in December 1972, it created a modest sensation. Here an American classic, reclaimed after 111 years, proved the Feminist Press's contribution to American literature and evidenced Tillie Olsen's authoritative historicism. She was thrilled by Annie Gottlieb's review and a letter from Polly Bunting, Radcliffe's president, relating her recovery of Davis to the Institute's mission.[43] She sent *Life in the Iron Mills*, with her long "Rebecca," special delivery to Jack late in 1972, "the year when it cost you (and me) precious together, holiday days for New York."

Tillie's spirits were buoyed by praise for her historical writing but deflated by phone calls with Jack. He did not want to "interfere with what serenity and single mindedness you need." Nevertheless, he could not "hide my tears and despair." Their calls were such "torture," he proposed it would be better "if we didn't talk at least not now." Like other husbands of prominent women, he was tired of the query "and what do *you* do?" especially when he had no job. His mood improved by lobbying, with others, for a labor studies program at City College of San Francisco. Tillie tried to help, from a distance, by declaring that he knew more about labor than authors of "uncomprehending articles like the blue collar/white collar series" and by getting Florence Howe and Mary Anne Ferguson to suggest that he speak on labor issues at their universities. Jack was most cheered because the printed "Rebecca" should mean Tillie's return.[44]

After nearly thirty years together, Tillie did not want to abandon Jack; after losing her novel for almost forty years, she did not want to abandon it either. She was nearly beside herself, though, trying to finish. She was so depressed another MacDowell regular, *New Yorker* writer Maeve Brennan, wrote her, "When you are so sad that you 'cannot work,' there is always danger that fear will enter and begin withering about." To avoid an invasion of fear, Tillie chose work over love and stayed on at MacDowell.

She was pleased that her search for a birth certificate and hence a passport ended on Christmas day, when Harry Lerner found a Jewish notary willing to go with him to the Workman's Circle home in Media and notarize Sam Lerner's affidavit about Tillie's birth on 14 January 1912. Tillie belatedly announced to Jack that her work would keep her at MacDowell until mid-January. The MacDowell staff heeded her every request for electric blankets, special feasts, bird seed, writing paper, and commemorative stamps. She asked after their families, worried that they worked too hard and risked their health in the sub-zero climate, gave them little curios, and hugged them for their many kindnesses to her.

As 1973 began, the snow became "marble hard," birds froze, and snow-covered branches fell around her cabin. When the temperature rose above zero, Hannah Green and Jack Wesley arrived to celebrate her sixty-first birthday and New Left successes. Florence Howe was now the third woman president of the MLA.[45] The United States ended direct military intervention in Vietnam. In *Roe v. Wade*, the Supreme Court decided that antiabortion laws violated women's rights to privacy. More states affirmed the ERA. Tillie kept delaying her return home, trying to bring order and resolution to the fragments of late chapters that she had written so long ago.[46] Though her creativity seemed as frozen as the landscape, Tillie risked Jack's anger to stay at MacDowell into February.

He responded by asking if she felt any responsibility to their marriage. She wrote and rewrote a letter, acknowledging that she had "forfeited" their home life to her writing. She ended: "Its almost more than I can endure—what its costing me—always in the shadow of the possibility of failure—let alone having to have responsibility for you." He must have noticed that she implied that her costs and fears were worsened by "responsibility" for him. She spent January trying to finish and became almost apoplectic because she could not. Finally, she capitulated to Jack and set off for home in mid-February, after meeting with Sam and Merloyd Lawrence in their Boston office.

Back home on 15 February, Tillie reflected, "I am 61 years, 1 month, 1 day." Her "cocooned sleep at MacDowell" seemed a lost idyll. She chose the title "Yonnondio" for her novel, though she had originally planned to use it for her not-to-be collection of seven stories.[47] She tried to shut herself in her study and pull her novel together. She sent five chapters, "fragments that seemed worth saving" to Lawrence's friend and *Atlantic Monthly* Press editor, William Abrahams. When another feminist instructed her to "stop making idiot comments about female failure," when the Guggenheim rejected her again, when she could not finish *Yonnondio*, she sunk nearly into despair.[48]

Two letters did brighten her outlook. Martha Foley praised her "magnificent" reclamation of Rebecca Harding Davis and sent a glance back to show how far women had come. Just after World War I, Foley had been on a parade route where Woodrow Wilson was to pass and was arrested for "loitering and sauntering," a charge usually for prostitutes; her true offense was a placard reading "Votes for Women." Howard N. Meyer wrote that both he and Tillie had rescued forgotten masterpieces and restored their authors' reputations. He had done so with Thomas Wentworth Higginson, Emily Dickinson's friend and advisor. Feeling his words offered a "hand touch" from Dickinson herself, Tillie startled Meyer with outpourings of gratitude.[49]

Yellowed pages of her novel felt like hand-touches from her own past, from Abe Goldfarb, little Karla, Rae Schochet, Bennett Cerf, Harry Carlisle, Sanora Babb, and fellow jail-bird Jack Olsen. She felt a "grave robber," for resurrecting her characters and also her past. She did not know "what I'm doing. I leave out interpolations, put them back in; fix on one version, go back to another . . . doubt again." She was shuffling old pages, not writing new ones. She was "absolutely at a loss" to add to or to end her novel.

Abrahams, then in California, made editing suggestions. Exasperated that her response was only weeping, he pronounced her "très difficile." Finally, he suggested she give up and publish the novel as it was with an autobiographical afterword.[50] Able to recycle not to reinvent, Tillie excused her inability to invent by circumstances: "1973, in the heaped snow of New England" was not the 1930s or "Faribault, Minnesota, Omaha, Stockton, East Los Angeles, Venice, San Francisco where what you have read was written." Nor was she "that girl who was I, 37–40 years ago." She made these excuses in a brief "Note About This Book" and an afterword beginning "Reader, it was not to have ended here."[51] Her story was indeed such an authentic epic of the 1930s that reenvisioning it in the 1970s was challenging, especially when the idea of salvation through communism was totally discredited and when she felt unprepared for broad research. (She might have consulted Jack, who had founded and now directed a community college labor studies program.[52]) Circling back over the same pages, she feared the "possibility of failure." Although she could not match the tragic beauty of her 1930s writing, she did not want critics to compare her present efforts with her past ones. She dated her explanations February 1973 but sent them off in March, along with the typescript of *Yonnondio* and a note to Lawrence regretting the "wasteful three months since I was in your office."

She and Jack had a bittersweet visit in Los Angeles, staying with his sister Eve Marcus and seeing his brother Max Olsan. Thanks to a postwar investment in containerized shipping, Max had been a millionaire even before selling his vast Anaheim property to Walt Disney, who built Disneyworld there. Then Jack and Tillie escaped to Yosemite, where melting winter snow helped to restore long-ago mountain "honeymoon" memories and rekindle their affections. When they returned, they found the entire country mesmerized by televised congressional investigations of the Watergate break-ins.

Lawrence assured Tillie that *Yonnondio* "is an enduring work of fiction." He did not tell her that the *Atlantic* had rejected an excerpt. By midsummer, Tillie had teaching offers from Louis Kampf at MIT and Mary Anne Ferguson at the University of Massachusetts.[53] Though MIT stood as a bastion of masculine knowledge, junior women faculty had started courses in women's studies and had petitioned the Humanities division to bring Tillie Olsen to campus.[54] Though teaching seemed a "surrender—loss of courage," Tillie accepted and planned a year in Boston, without Jack.

She kept fiddling with the text of *Yonnondio* but complaining, as she had with her "Rebecca," about a "dismaying" delay in its production. The copyeditor said Tillie had "just about rewritten her book in galleys. Practically none of the changes she's making are due to our copyediting." Faber and Faber were waiting to publish *Yonnondio*, but her ongoing revisions meant Delacorte could not deliver it. The entire book needed resetting, at a printer's fee of $800, which Lawrence paid rather than rile Tillie. She seemed willfully ignorant about printing, admitting that she sometimes "reversed" herself about which fragment to include, but insisting that she did not rewrite. Red Tovish later remarked on her "powerful ego" and "jealous guarding of her reputation."[55]

On 11 September, Tillie heard about a military junta's overthrow of socialist Salvador Allende. That night, before reading all of "Tell Me a Riddle," she wept about the tragic coup in Chile, echoing one in Guatemala, and recited Whitman on human liberty. Her novella's references to twentieth-century atrocities produced more tears from author and audience.[56] She repeated this performance two days later at the San Francisco Public Library and then flew to Boston, where she settled into an apartment on Marlborough Street and delivered to Lawrence *Yonnondio*'s new galley proofs, with yet more mark-ups. Alone again, Jack took the dedication of *Yonnondio*, "For Jack," wryly.

Tillie was invited to speak at the dedication of Marianna Pineda's *Aspects of the Oracle III: Portentous*, a gift in memory of Constance E. Smith, which was installed early that fall in Radcliffe Yard. Tillie stayed at the expensive campus Sheraton Hotel and gallantly donated her honorarium of several hundred dollars to a memorial fund.[57] The more she feared that the wellsprings of her creativity had dried up, the more dramatic her performances: "writing is gone, but many come & listen to my talks—at the last one, 'Denied Genius—Blood Kin of Great Writers,' [some] even wept." Such speeches seemed "something in me put to use." She hugged the young women who approached her, urged them to write, and invited them to send their stories to her.[58] Faculty from MIT's Women's Studies program marveled that she was hardy enough to swim in the MIT pool and to walk in snowy Boston. They accepted Tillie's claim she had spent "a lifetime putting her own needs as a person and artist on hold" and rationalized that such sacrifices justified her neediness. Though irritated by her unstructured lectures, they taped them, as a labor of love. From California, Mary Jane Moffat thanked "Tillie Appleseed" for spreading the seeds of women's studies. Moffat affirmed, "Generations will thank you as I do now, far too sparingly." That adoration was replicated among young women who saw prospects opening where only locked gates had been. Tillie's "seeding talks" (one at Michele and Jim Murray's home in Washington, D.C.) germinated in Lee Edwards and Arlyn Diamond's 1973 *American Voices, American Women*, dedicated to Tillie Olsen, and in Michele Murray's *Women in Literature*.[59]

All that fall, Tillie rotated between teaching at MIT, lecturing elsewhere, and hibernating at MacDowell. From there she applied to the Guggenheim, reviving her "book of fiction of novel length," which she said was interrupted when her 1966–1967 NEA "grant period ended." People writing grant applications necessarily make their own best cases. Tillie however came close to deceit. She failed to list grants that funded short periods away from home and did not mention her two-year Ford Foundation grant. In all her Guggenheim applications, she referred to preventive "circumstances" but never explained why supportive circumstances had not enabled her writing. Again and again, she claimed that *Requa* would be in print the year after an application.[60] Perhaps Tillie truly believed that one more grant was the alchemy that would transmute her into a novelist. Certainly, she believed that the state should take care of its artists. Or perhaps, she was wheedling for money to protect her from an unproductive and impoverished old age.

Tillie's October speaking engagements, away from MIT, took her to Nebraska, New Hampshire, and Maryland. At Essex Community College, the audience responded warmly, though they had waited an hour for her to show up. Her afternoon reading at what Tillie called the "all masculine Hopkins air" did not go well, but that night she brought a Towson State audience to tears over "I Stand Here Ironing." (All this happened the day Vice President Agnew resigned, facing charges of graft and tax evasion. Nixon nominated House minority leader Gerald Ford on 12 October.)[61] Back in Boston, Tillie lunched with Adrienne Rich, whom she had asked to recommend her for the Guggenheim.[62] Over Thanksgiving, at MacDowell, Tillie read page proofs for *Yonnondio*, under threat from Lawrence who instructed she "must now call a halt" to revisions. Unaware that Random House had bought this same book almost forty years before, Lawrence assured Tillie: "My commitment to you is for life." To guarantee her reputation with scholars, Tillie sent a *Yonnondio* chapter to Lola Szladits, curator of the Berg Collection of the New York Public Library, and offered her "after makings."

At year's end Tillie went to MacDowell, where Johns Hopkins writing teacher Thelma Nason was working on her "Fictional Autobiography" of Ethel Rosenberg. When Nason took a copy of *Tell Me a Riddle* off Mac-Dowell's library shelf, she found the published book still full of cross-outs and insertions, illustrative of Tillie's inability to let her book go. Her inability to anticipate was comically illustrated one evening when Nason saw her "fly" out of a woman's residence bathroom wrapped only in a Turkish towel.[63] While some found Tillie's screw-ups amusing, others irritating, Florence Howe found everything Tillie did endearing. Howe dedicated her late-December MLA presidential address to Tillie Olsen, "the teacher of us all." With this recognition, courses in Women's Studies proliferating, and her long-lost novel about to appear, Tillie had reason to feel triumphant. Instead, she called 1973 a "bad year."

She stayed on at MacDowell in freezing weather until early January 1974, when she returned to Boston to speak at MIT about the dismal representation of women in science. For such talks, Tillie pulled tiny scraps of paper out of pockets in paisley skirts and spoke associatively way beyond the confines of her scheduled time. Later in January, after she turned sixty-two, Tillie became Distinguished Visiting Professor at the University of Massachusetts, Boston, earning $13,000 for one semester. To celebrate, Mary Anne Ferguson invited her forego her usual rabbitlike food for "steaks and lobster!" which Tillie downed like a trucker.[64]

Almost forty years after Macmillan and Random House had fought over publication rights and two years after Lawrence Inc. and the Feminist Press had sparred over *Yonnondio: From the Thirties*, it appeared in late February 1974. Tillie tried to console Jack with a brief trip home but was back in Boston when news about the granddaughter of her old nemesis, newspaper baron William Randolph Hearst, became a national scandal. Patty Hearst (a.k.a. Tanya), with her supposed kidnappers, demanded from Grandfather Hearst a "ransom" of a multimillion-dollar food program for the poor.

A former Hearst paper now ran Sandy Boucher's article "Tillie Olsen Is a Survivor." To Boucher's surprise, Tillie found this account "nauseating." She was happier when, in the *National Observer*, Michele Murray described *Yonnondio* as a premier American notice "of the existence of the very poor." Tillie was pleased by Annie Gottlieb's saying that in *Yonnondio*, as in Plath's poetry, "motherhood must finally be counted among the circumstances that can simultaneously hinder and nourish genius." Less pleasing was the insinuation that she depicted mostly victims.[65] Most gratifying was Gene Lerner's comment about Ida "so you add to her life and to her eternity."

When Michele Murray died on 14 March at the age of forty, Tillie traveled to Washington, D.C., for a memorial. After close friends and *National Observer* staffers spoke, audience members, including Eugene McCarthy, were invited to speak. Doris Grumbach recalled that Tillie "was given the floor first, and she spoke for more than an hour, on and on, without connections or reasons." Grieving, thirteen-year-old Sarah Murray was irritated by Tillie's posturing, which she later saw as cultivating her role as an iconic woman.[66] Tillie was perhaps compensating for another Guggenheim rejection.

Lola Szladis encouraged that iconic image when she mounted "in what is the 'altar' in the Berg a small exhibition to honor you."[67] After 15 April, well-dressed New Yorkers stared into display cases at Tillie's scribbled attempts to sort chronology, her layout plan for the Holbrooks's house, and pages typed on backs of Public Works Administration papers, with

Tillie's scribbled insertions and those in the unidentified hand of Abe Goldfarb. She lectured and performed at seven colleges that spring, while still teaching at the University of Massachusetts. She tried to "bunch" together people as well as obligations. She scheduled a boat ride around Manhattan with writer friends, dinner with her cousin Sam Braude and his wife Adele, and an overnight stay with Karla's in-laws Harry and Dotty Lutz. About half an hour after the dinner appointment, Tillie called the Braudes saying that she couldn't find where she had parked the Lutzes' car. She made another distressed call and then a third to say that she had found the car and would arrive shortly. "Shortly," Adele Braude recalled, "turned into never." Tillie accepted "all the attention, all the invitations, even if it meant, in the end, not keeping all her commitments." She never contacted the Braudes again.[68]

Tell Me a Riddle, which had failed a decade or so before, now went into its fourth American printing. *Life in the Iron Mills* went into a third printing, *Yonnondio* into a second printing.[69] Saying she abhorred self-promotion, Tillie was an accomplished practitioner. Red Tovish thought her "one of the most self-involved people I know." She somehow managed to seem self-sacrificing, even while she, like Norman Mailer, offered "advertisements" for herself. She distributed favorable reviews to Radcliffe and her siblings. She overcommitted herself to different presses and audiences and agreed to be interviewed by professor Elaine Showalter and *New York Post* writer Jerry Talmer. He reported that her first daughter was the child of "a previous marriage" and that her high school English teacher had been "so outraged by a Tillie Lerner question about Hamlet that she threw a book at the girl and expelled her." Here, Tillie disclosed truths about marrying and getting expelled that she had long hidden. She responded by asking Showalter to destroy her tape.[70]

In a *Washington Post* interview, conducted after the Murray memorial, Tillie added two new fabrications to her persona. She said that because she stuttered, an Omaha "school thought I might be feeble-minded. My foreign-born mother was afraid that they would take me away and institutionalize me. So she kept me at home, and as a result I didn't really start to school and learn to read until I was nine years old. Then I learned almost overnight, I was so overripe. But what this meant was that I kept to the oral tradition much longer." Conveniently omitting her years at Kellom School from age five to age nine, this plot-line embroidered on her transfer to Long Elementary.[71] Tillie's other artifice was more self-serving and more venal: she said she and Jack had "also raised the son of her sister who died of cancer. (The son was killed later in Korea.)"[72] Tillie had actually taken in youngsters like

Leroy King and T. Mike Walker, so why would she invent a dead sister and an adopted, orphaned nephew? Perhaps, she wanted to claim a closer relation to the Lerners. Certainly, she was mesmerized by her power to raise or create new realities. She forgot, however, that Harry and Clare Lerner took the *Post*. After they confronted her, Tillie never told that outrageous story again. Another example of trying to raise her image was making a generous donation to the Connie Smith Memorial Fund in the fall. In late spring, though, Tillie asked the Radcliffe Institute for a $150 refund to help her pay outstanding credit card bills. At the end of her teaching term, after a "woeful—heartbreaking" visit with Sam Lerner, Tillie returned to San Francisco, then retreated to a Mediterranean-style house in Santa Cruz, loaned by leftie friends. It presided over views of both the sun's rising reflection and its setting over the Pacific. In June, she left the gorgeous Santa Cruz house to join Jack in Yosemite. They were relieved that their rebel daughter Kathie, now married to Charles Hoye, seemed settled and domestic after giving birth to a baby, named after her sister Laurie.[73] In San Francisco, despite mysterious pains in her abdomen, Tillie gave a party for women writers, including visiting Alice Walker. During the party, Tillie held forth on the subject of class, insisting that, if "most of the time you have to put your energy toward acquiring bread and rent" you are "working class." Of course, for nearly twenty years, grants, academic posts, and lectureship fees should have freed Tillie from worrying about bread and rent if she had husbanded her money. She seemed "very very old and tired."[74]

After Nixon resigned rather than face impeachment, Tillie was proud that new President Ford was born in Omaha in 1913 but appalled when Ford pardoned Nixon.[75] She could not have invented the conversion of a Hearst heiress to latter-day communism or the resignation of an anti-Communist president. Here reality outstripped imagination and reinforced her decision not to invent an ending for *Yonnondio*. It sold impressively, but Tillie complained that Lawrence had not promoted it. He countered: her ongoing re-writing had caused *Yonnondio*'s delayed release; every book club had turned it down; Delacorte had spent almost one dollar per book on publicity ($5000 for 5400 copies sold); he had urged book store owners to stock *Yonnondio* but "we cannot *force* booksellers to order."

Tillie had surgery for a noncancerous tumor and, on 29 September, asked the Guggenheim Foundation for an extension after "major surgery"; Laurie Olsen testified that her mother was too ill to meet the Guggenheim's 1 October deadline so the Foundation extended its deadline until 1 November. Then Edith Konecky called with the appalling news that on 4 October, Anne Sexton had committed suicide.[76]

By 10 October Tillie was in Santa Cruz. The deaths of Connie Smith and Anne Sexton made it "an infinite presumption to have plans." As ego overcame melancholy, Tillie donned the mantel of survivor, manifested in a long cape she wore to stride along the bluffs to see the Monarch butterflies clustering in eucalyptus trees. After a young graduate student named Candace Falk moved into the renovated window-filled garage behind her, Tillie watched her comings and goings and left notes saying "Learn to say NO." She turned the breakfast nook into a study, putting women writers' pictures around windows overlooking the Pacific. When she invited Falk in, Tillie set a timer to keep them from talking too long. When Falk asked if she could help, Tillie asked her to buy pomegranates. Falk had to ask what they were.

Tillie wrote Marianna Pineda she "almost went under" writing the Guggenheim application, but she finished it on 26 October. She began by proclaiming, "I am close to great yield," and ended so confusedly Guggenheim officials must have wondered if Tillie Olsen really were an accomplished writer.[77] She did come close to explaining her money troubles, though she omitted Jack's undependable income: she had written "on time secured ahead by going into debt and then having to leave writing to work to repay them; or by mortgaging my work to a publisher (a nine year ago $7500 advance is still being repaid through royalties): or by time secured through grants." When she had money, Tillie used it to buy gifts, give cash to others, help educate grandchildren, purchase books and clothes for herself and her family, and to pay for taxis and sometimes first-class plane tickets. She treated advances like income and resented that royalties went to reimburse advances and that interest doubled or tripled unpaid debts.

Tillie was distressed to read that Adrienne Rich in a New York memorial for Anne Sexton proclaimed "we have had enough suicidal women poets." In a *Boston Globe* obituary, Denise Levertov regretted that the suicide linked female creativity with self-destructiveness.[78] Tillie's unfulfilled promises and litanies of excuses underscored the image of self-destructive women artists. As if to compensate, she busied herself recommending dead women writers for the Feminist Press's reprint series and live ones to Radcliffe and other granting agencies. She wrote a seemingly endless stream of letters and cards to friends and strangers, though Alice Walker was unsure how to take the old cards with racist messages that Tillie sent her. Tillie urged women to send her their writing, offered usually wise criticism, and wrote book jacket blurbs for almost anyone who asked. Her generosity disarmed critics and guaranteed a fan club, including a group of what Falk called "Santa Cruz groupies."[79]

All around the country, women met for "consciousness-raising" sessions. Many were distressed that, despite feminism, the media featured few examples of women in positions of authority. Some were mad that successful women writers could be dismissive of others.[80] All were furious that women were paid less than men and struggled harder for promotions. Many were angry to have given up careers for husbands who later left them. Many were mad that their sexual needs were ignored by partners. Many insisted women needed men like fish needed bicycles. Betty Friedan wanted to dissociate feminism from lesbianism, but in Santa Cruz women's sessions, Tillie encouraged inclusiveness. In November, she spoke at a conference on Virginia Woolf at the University of California in Santa Cruz (UCSC). Tillie's amazing memory of Woolf's texts, her understanding of Woolf's politics and philosophies, and her passionate response to Woolf's reading tradition inspired most, though not all, of her academic audience.[81]

Usually more responsive than men to Tillie's talks, women did indeed consider her Tillie Appleseed, spreading seeds that grew a newly confident and self-aware crop of women. A male journalist thought that people "embraced her less as a major force in American literature . . . than as an enricher of spirits."[82] Some seeds, however, fell on fallow ground. Some audiences were irritated by her relying on emotions rather than reason. Some called her an "unstoppable" or "dominant talker" who used her stutter to silence others. Some were angry over an evangelical zeal that kept her from relinquishing platforms. Some considered her litany of complaints about "circumstances" self-pitying excuses. Some thought she used her charisma to cover her inadequacies.

By the end of 1974, a chastened U.S. citizenry seemed to have learned the pitfalls of war-mongering, name-calling, power-abusing, dissent-suppressing, and rights-denying. The Vietnam War was ending and with it 1960s turmoil. The Civil Rights Movement had taught America the evil of racism, and the Equal Rights Amendment promised to end the evil of sexism. With mild-mannered Gerald Ford as president, the country seemed poised for a return to core American values. In her Santa Cruz retreat, with her timer and "just say NO" reminders, Tillie too might be poised for another beginning and her long-delayed great yield. One question was whether the imperious, the irritating, or the inspiring Tillie Olsen would emerge. Another was whether she could or would write again.

CHAPTER 14

QUEEN BEE

1975–1980

A passion and a purpose inform its pages: love for my incomparable medium, literature; hatred for all that, societally rooted, unnecessarily lessens and denies it.

—Tillie Olsen, preface to *Silences*, 1978

As 1975 began, Tillie invited Candace Falk to walk with her. Falk expected to meander along picking up shells or admiring the sunset, but Tillie would don her grand cape and march, undaunted by wind or spray. Trooping toward the Natural Bridges State Beach, Falk once remarked on some tacky little houses they passed. Tillie halted, looked Falk in the eyes, and pronounced that these houses were owned by working-class people without time or money for good taste. She would marvel at the Monarch butterflies, almost covering the park's eucalyptus trees, and then set off again. Because Falk was writing her dissertation on Emma Goldman, Tillie bombarded her with information on communism, labor history, and radical women authors. When they returned, she would dart into the house, leaving Falk feeling she had been sucked up and spit out by a tornado.

Since 1972, when Congress had passed the ERA and the Feminist Press brought out *Life in the Iron Mills* with Tillie's perceptive "Afterword," many books by and about women had been published, and thirty-three states had ratified the ERA. Still, some argued that, thanks to the 1964 Civil Rights Act, the ERA was unnecessary. Others argued that it was dangerous. Phyllis Schlafly gained fame by claiming that the ERA would draft women into battle, force them into men's bathrooms, and rob them of husbands' support. On 16 January, two days after her sixty-third birthday, Tillie gave her talk on "Denied Genius" for the UCSC women's voices group, relating the suppression of nineteenth-century women to the coddling Schlafly

268

claimed modern women needed. Schlafly was, however, taking a toll on even such an ardent feminist as Tillie. She objected to having her work "increasingly ghettoized as Women's Studies, women's stuff only, not literature to be taken seriously." When the Woman Today Book Club chose *Tell Me a Riddle* and *Yonnondio* as selections, ordering one thousand copies of each book, Tillie protested to Lawrence that a woman's book club was "another residue of sexism."

That spring, two awards gave Tillie the support she craved. The American Academy and the National Institute of Arts & Letters recognized her literary achievement with $3000 and the Guggenheim Foundation, despite her confused and late explanation, finally awarded her a fellowship of $12,000.[1] She filled in her Guggenheim budget form as a still needy Tillie: "married, although living apart," with a husband "off social security," and a father "always partially dependent upon my help," the last a definite untruth.[2]

Instead of settling down to write her promised "great yield," Tillie diverted herself writing notes to almost every promising young woman writer, addressed as a "dear true" writer, "bloodkin, heartkin," or "beloved equal younger sister—writer, [of a] beloved future."[3] They were thrilled to receive such tender notes from the iconic Tillie Olsen. Alice Walker even clasped one like a talisman against the notoriously sexist Ishmael Reed. Walker revered Zora Neale Hurston as a lost mother-figure and hoped Tillie could be a living literary mother-figure.[4] Annie Dillard more skeptically supposed that Tillie was "rounding us all up" to secure their loyalty.[5]

Traveling like an itinerant preacher was not only diversion but avoidance. Tillie flew to New York for the American Academy ceremony, and Edith Konecky met her at Kennedy airport, settled her into Hannah Green's apartment, and entertained her with the increasingly wacky Maeve Brennan. Tillie began buzzing in and out of the city for a sojourn at the Yaddo Artists' Colony and various talks and readings.[6] Though Konecky now found Tillie "a bit of a prima donna," she taxied her back and forth to airports.[7] After Tillie read at SUNY Buffalo, the news arrived that the United States was evacuating Saigon. At a reception, Tillie took the floor. Though she credited students and faculty, "You did this," she appropriated the event to herself: "You must not let them take your history from you, the way they did with my generation, the generation of the thirties."[8] She meant the suppression of leftist voices during the McCarthy era, a remark that fit her heightened concern for silenced people. The American Academy held a ceremony on 21 May. Its citation praised her "poetic fiction" that "very nearly constitutes a new form for fiction." Later, Tillie marked up a copy with what even she called "snotty revisings." She crossed out "very nearly"

and wrote "why qualify?" Such revisions were, if not "snotty," arrogant.[9]
She felt her superiority justified her impositions. She wrote Mary Anne
Ferguson, "Dear One: you must not complicate your too-demanded time"
but then suggested "meeting the plane, having dinner, seeing me off on the
bus, even driving me up" to MacDowell. Ferguson met her at Logan Airport
on 20 September, took her to dinner, housed her overnight, drove her to
MacDowell, and loaned her a box packed with electric blanket, linens,
thesaurus, dictionary, and soup pot.

Once settled in, Tillie had the peace, solitude, and now the financial
support she had craved. With Guggenheim money arriving in quarterly
$3000 payments, she could write the novel she had been promising since
1959, or *Requa*, or her woman book. She decided on the latter, as the
simpler, though her copy-outs and notes sometimes seemed "masses of
inchoateness, wellings up, dischargings, addings to the years' now hopeless
disordered accumulations." Facing written gems and detritus, Tillie almost
gave up: "it is fragments, reader—if they live enough in you, you will write
it in your head yourself."[10]

As fall became frigid winter, Tillie began to yearn for the "isolation,
health" back in Santa Cruz. She left MacDowell, depositing a duffel bag
of scarves and warm clothes and Ferguson's box of supplies in Peterborough with Rosellen Brown.[11] She was in San Francisco for holiday parties,
gift-giving, and the yearly MLA meeting, held there in 1975. The MLA
Commission on the Status of Women could celebrate many successes, but
it had not impacted a large session on the "Jewish American Writer." Tillie
was so angry that only male writers were discussed she lowered her reprint
fee to $500 so that "Tell Me a Riddle" could appear in an anthology of
Jewish American Fiction. She insisted to Scott Turow that there was more
Jewishness in *Yonnondio* and one Malamud novel than in all the touted
male "Jewish novelists."[12]

By year's end, Tillie had been recognized by the American Academy,
the Guggenheim, the MLA, Ferguson in her anthology *Images of Women*,
Blanche Gelfant in the *Massachusetts Review,* and Robert Coles in the *New
Republic.* He said: "Everything she has written has become almost immediately a classic. . . . She offers an artist's compassion and forgiveness but
makes plain how fierce the various struggles must continue to be."[13] Despite
all this acclaim, Tillie had written no more fiction. Her woman book defied
organization. Only one more state had ratified the ERA in 1975.

The New Year began poorly, as Tillie turned sixty-four on 14 January
1976. She was in debt to Faber and Faber because English sales for
Yonnondio had not matched advances. With only two Guggenheim
payments left, she asked for an extension, which was against Guggenheim

policy, as its procure explained. She further distracted herself by marking up the Delta *Tell Me a Riddle* for a corrected Laurel paperback. Then, on 18 February, she heard from Harry that Sam Lerner, aged ninety-one, had died at the Workmen's Circle home. Tillie sent her corrected Delta edition to Lawrence, saying "my father died and I am in a mourning time." Gene Lerner was in New York and traveled with Lillian to Bethesda for the funeral. When the rabbi asked the congregation to stand, Gene and Lillian did not, but Jann, Harry, and Vicki did, and Harry recommitted himself in Sam's memory to preserve Yiddish literature. Mary Anne Ferguson recalled that Tillie had "all sorts of guilt feelings" about seeing her father so rarely in the retirement home. Tillie sought to make amends by suggesting that Jann move to Santa Cruz.[14]

When Jann Lerner Brodinsky moved into an efficiency apartment on Cliff Street, Julie and Rob Edwards, Kathie Olsen Hoye, and Tillie welcomed her; her landlord let her borrow an old record player, and Tillie sent her a check, which Jann used for yoga lessons.[15] Harry wrote Tillie he was "really relieved" by "the warm reception you gave her." Jann had never asked for financial help from their father, but she had no job, no permanent home, and only the $1000 Harry advanced her from Sam's estate for moving costs. After funeral and tombstone expenses, Sam's estate left $1417 for each child so Harry proposed that the other siblings waive their shares, which left $6083 for Jann. The siblings agreed, though Tillie asked for $100 for each daughter.

Tillie often blamed presses and anthology editors for "violating" her image.[16] She needed to mold decades of inchoate notes on her reading and speaking into a work of transformative nonfiction, but the messier her organization, the more imperious she became. She sent portions to Delacorte demanding that someone else change every "his" to "her" and check quotations for accuracy and copyright status, even while only she could "make changes in the work."

When Tillie and Alice Walker spoke at a symposium in Portland, Oregon, organizers cut off Tillie's meandering talk so that others could speak. The event went, in Walker's words, "all wrong," but Tillie excused herself by saying she was mourning her father. Walker now found Tillie narcissistic; Tillie thought Walker prideful; their disagreement echoed a quarrel between Elizabeth Cady Stanton and Frederick Douglass. Though the two had worked together for abolition, Stanton patronized the former slave and then resented that black males got the vote before white women, as Tillie patronized Walker and then resented her fame. Tillie had always objected to quarrels among supposed allies: dividing Socialists from Communists, the CIO from the AFL, the ILWU from the Teamsters, and now pro- and antimotherhood and pro- and antilesbian feminists.[17] Yet ignoring Walker's request to endorse her novel *Meridian* divided Tillie from Walker.

Having promised Lawrence to complete the woman book by April 1976, on 1 May, Tillie used a card saying, "I NEED MORE TIME AND I PROB-ABLY ALWAYS WILL" to say "Sorry, dear Sam. But it *will* be worth it." She now agreed with him to title the woman book *Silences*. She invited Bay Area women writers to a party on 25 May for visiting Norwegian scholar Pers Seyerstad. She was mugged by young black women. She excused another delay by describing a Yosemite family holiday as an obligatory "3 week all year planned seemingly unpostponable ungetting-out-of family camping time." When the Olsens left the mountains, they found that the Democratic presidential nominee was Jimmy Carter. Tillie sought out the "curl and indifference of the sea" and moved alone into the Santa Cruz garage apartment formerly occupied by Candace Falk, supported by her last Guggenheim installment.

Disorganized Tillie kept rewriting, reordering, and adding selections, sending different versions to Merloyd Lawrence, nonfiction editor for Seymour Lawrence Inc. Even to Tillie, assembling *Silences* seemed "one fiasco after another." She told the Lawrences she could not even recall what sections she had already sent. Finding the manuscript, as they politely wrote, "difficult to follow," they asked her to prepare, at their cost, "a finished and complete manuscript, clearly typed, without written nota-tions." They begged "please endeavor to make one clean cohesive copy that can be easily understood by a printer." While Tillie drove her publishers nearly mad with her muddled texts and peremptory demands, her loyal coterie thought her beyond criticism. Even when reviewing Adrienne Rich's *Of Woman Born*, Annie Gottlieb put in a plug for Tillie for dignifying the "uniquely female experience as a source of human knowledge."[18] Theatre teacher Bobbi Ausubel staged "I Stand Here Ironing" in New England and wanted to film "Tell Me a Riddle." Mindy Affrime and Rachel Lyon, founding a film company named Godmother Productions, wanted to make "Tell Me a Riddle" their first production.

Tillie had faulted Gerald Ford for pardoning Nixon and was glad that Ford was defeated on 2 November. Like other West Coast lefties, though, she was uneasy that he was defeated by Carter, a Southern Baptist and former Georgia governor. She was worried that no further state had ratified the ERA, and she was distressed by a second request from the Guggen-heim Foundation for a progress report. She wrote that "the term was given over mostly to the work of imaginative fiction, novel length, long in the often-interrupted making. It is nearer to its conclusion as a result of my

Guggenheim year."[19] More honestly, she said: "Because of the urgency of its content, I also worked on the preparation of a book of essays and source material, now in the hands of the publisher (Delacorte)."[20] At year's end, Tillie suffered a concussion. Her daughter Kathie later said she fell on one of her "mighty walks." Tillie wrote friends vaguely that her concussion came from "holiday injuries." Exactly what happened remains a mystery.[21]

The concussion sucked her into what she called the "vortex of the personal," oppressed by knee pain, back pain, confusion, a sense of failure, and paranoia. She attacked Bobbi Ausubel for a "truncated" version of "I Stand Here Ironing." Early in 1977, Lawrence returned *Silences*, begged her yet again to simplify, cut instructions, and send a *"final and complete"* version "ready for standard copyediting." Tillie replied, "You sent it back [at] a wrong time. I could not work on anything." As she turned sixty-five, Tillie feared that she had "lost language." In mid-February, she remailed *Silences* to Lawrence and enlisted Mary Anne Ferguson to proofread it. She recovered enough language to promote herself to Carmen Callil and Lennie Goodings, of the English women's press Virago.[22]

Supposedly finished with *Silences*, Tillie flew into Boston where she met her youngest sister in an airport café. Tillie "got weepy," as Vicki said she always did when talking about their parents, and would not explain a terrible bruise.[23] At Amherst College's week-long colloquium on Family Life in America, Tillie read all of "Tell Me a Riddle" and gave some scheduled but vague "Musings," for which she later apologized to Alice Walker. She read, taught, and lectured in Boston, New York, and Washington, D.C.[24] At George Washington University, she charmed creative writing faculty and students by offering *Forum*, the school's literary magazine, selections from *Silences*.[25] She had earlier offered her *Harper's* and *College English* essays to Alta, the one-named, bisexual founder of Shameless Hussy Press.[26] After Lawrence vehemently protested such violations of her publishing contract with him, Tillie withdrew her essays from Alta, citing her concussion and what she called a "kind of breakdown" as excuses. Following Alta's accusations of "opportunism, stupidity, dishonor, possible senility," Tillie wrote a two-page, single-spaced reply that came off as unresponsive and self-exculpatory. Her ongoing excuses and complaints, often in collect calls to publisher, editors, and agents, exasperated Harriet Wasserman, who decided it was now "impossible for me emotionally to work effectively with you by phone." Tillie quickly fired Wasserman and signed with agent Elaine Markson instead.[27]

Though Tillie described herself as "incapacitated ill most of the time," in late July through mid-August, she joined the family for a camping trip to the Canadian Rockies, telling young writer Marge Piercy it was "my first vacation in 3 years." Rachel Lyon, Mindy Affrime, and Susan O'Connell had raised $50,000 to form Godmother Productions and now courted Tillie with plans to make a major film of her novella. Novelist Joyce Eliason would write the screenplay. Lee Grant, a four-time Academy Award acting nominee and survivor of Hollywood blacklisting, would make her directing debut. Aged Melvyn Douglas, prominent in 1930s leftist movements, would star as David, while the Oscar-winning actress Lila Kedrova would play Eva. Thanks to shared leftist and feminist politics, Tillie gave Godmother permission to make "Tell Me a Riddle" into a movie.

In the fall, the MacDowell Colony assigned Tillie its grandest studio, the Watson, a neoclassic building featuring Doric columns and portico. Another colonist, Elinor Langer, Josephine Herbst's biographer, was delighted to hear Tillie's memories of Herbst from the 1935 Writers' Congress but irritated by Tillie's instructions to emphasize Herbst's communism.[28] Late in October, despite the "$$$$$," as she wrote to Konecky, Tillie flew from the tiny airport in Keene, New Hampshire, into New York. In Greenwich Village, Alix Shulman steered her and Hannah Green to Eighth Street, where a dry cleaner's window was filled with old flat irons, provoking Tillie to hold forth on paintings by Degas and Picasso, both titled *Woman Ironing*, and on toy flat irons readers frequently sent her. On 26 October, she read at Queens College, Flushing, where a young professor named Joe Cuomo had arranged for limousine transportation from Hannah's, a five-hundred-dollar payment, and an interview.[29] Howard Meyer showed up at her reading to report that, as Tillie had instructed him in a "white-hot" letter, he had debunked the giddy portrait of Emily Dickinson in the popular play *The Belle of Amherst*.[30]

The Lerner siblings had circulated a laudatory *New York Times* article about Gene Lerner and Hank Kaufman's plans for a Broadway production based on the life of their friend Josephine Baker, the first African-American movie star. Before Baker died in 1975, Lerner and Kaufman had bought the rights to her story; in 1977, they took an apartment on West Fifty-fifth Street and hired theatre greats to work with them. Though they still needed more than a million dollars, Lerner and Kaufman hoped to open on Broadway on 9 April 1978, the anniversary of Baker's last Paris opening.[31] Flushed with her success at Queens College, Tillie called Gene, and he agreed to make time to see her one midafternoon. She made him wait until 7:30. She greeted him with "I'm sorry." He replied, "as usual— your family is always last." When she came in, he asked, "'Tillie if you had to choose between your writing and Jack, what would you choose?' and without a pause, she said, 'I'd drop him in a minute.' She said it just like that, like a sword in your heart. How could she be so unfeeling?"[32] Whether he recalled the comment accurately, Tillie seemed indeed to have dropped Jack. She had a habit of embracing and then dropping people no longer useful—like Nolan Miller—or no longer needful—like Alice Walker.

Forever grateful to Tillie for inspiring the Feminist Press, Florence Howe gave a party for her, with much laughing, hugging, toasting, and celebrating. If the guests wanted to talk about the Iranian Revolution or crippling inflation, they had little chance. Tillie monopolized conversation with a geyser of talk about history, literature, feminism, and women writers. Shulman now called her a talking *Bartlett's Quotations*. Though she dazzled admirers with her fantastic memory of women's writings, Tillie sometimes fell back on gender stereotypes. She denounced Daughters Press for acting like a "reprehensible male establishment publisher," conveniently forgetting how patient and generous her male publishers were. At Vassar, after reading "Tell Me a Riddle," she spoke of Ida as if she were one of the "peasant women with 'worn bodies' used 'as tools by life'" and "abused by a conventional male society." Recalling the only image that ever moved her deeply, Tillie told a new story, saying that in her dying days, Ida had on Christmas Eve a vision of three wise men who turn out to be women.[33]

Tillie picked up galley proofs of *Silences* at the Delacorte offices before returning to MacDowell and, on 5 November, promised immediately to check them. Instead, she procrastinated until Thanksgiving. She returned the galleys on 2 December, furious over what she called errors and whole "problem pages." Though she had created the very "headaches and penalties" Lawrence had begged her to avoid, Tillie expected him to get corrected galleys and "problem" pages back to her immediately. She wanted the book published in March and "not *only* identified with Women's Studies or the feminist movement" but marketed to a "broad general" audience. She sent a long list of recipients for free copies. Meanwhile, Delacorte editors took *Silences* out of their schedule.

In "almost 1978," Tillie marked up a copy of "Tell Me a Riddle" to indicate what Ausubel should emphasize in staging it, markings which emphasize Eva's hunger for belief. Tillie now elaborated on her remarks at Vassar with a new version of her last visit with Ida, who responds to "a knock at the door":

> Why do you come to me? I am not religious. I am not a believer. And they said O we didn't come to talk with you about that, we wanted to talk with you about books, about ideas . . . Come in, come in then she said, but as they began to talk, she saw that they were not men but women, that they were not dressed in splendid jewel-encrusted, robes, but in the

everyday coarse woven shifts and shawls of the peasant women of her native Russia . . . . They drew closer against the cold, began to sing, and she too began to sing, the clouds of their breaths shining in the air, [they] knelt, the beasts too kneeling, she kneeling.

In 1955, when she last saw her mother, Tillie had neither said nor written anything about Ida having such a vision. Now she said she had seen Ida "but twice in my adult life, separated by the continent, by needs of my own four children, by lack of means." She meant the family's 1954 visit to Washington, D.C., and her 1955 visit alone, omitting times when she dropped off her daughters in Omaha and Ida and Sam's 1947 visit to the Olsens.[34]

Indiana became the thirty-fifth state to ratify the ERA, but equal rights were not established in academia, as Americanist Annette Kolodny found when the University of New Hampshire denied her tenure and promotion. (Always responsive to anti-feminism, Tillie sent Kolodny a generous check to help with legal expenses.) Tillie had always finagled extra time at MacDowell, so she was appalled when the Colony insisted she vacate the Watson Studio by 29 December. She felt "in turmoil in a defenseless time—leaving here, leaving my work; an accumulation of humiliations, mis-timings on Silences." She was so addled that Edith Konecky offered to drive her to Logan airport, but, when Konecky came by, Tillie had not packed. She said she wanted to give Edith one last chance to see the photos and quotations she had taped up. Barely keeping her irritation in check, Konecky threw Tillie's things into bags, boxes, and cases. She broke the speed limit racing to the airport, arriving barely in time for Tillie to get curbside check-in and make her plane.[35] Perhaps Tillie had lost her grip on reality. At any rate, her neediness was useful in extorting favors.

By 6 January 1978 she was at her Santa Cruz retreat, aggravated by an abscessed tooth and a letter from Rachel Klein, lead Delacorte copy-editor, explaining that Silences' publication was delayed thanks to numerous, involved, undecipherable, and extensive author's changes. Klein and her staff were making the changes Tillie requested and also correcting her errors, as when she quoted passages inconsistently; they were left with the time-consuming task of checking each quotation against the original.

Demanding that her book be published immediately was a function of deepening paranoia about money. She lamented to Lawrence: "I am back to the marginality of my pre-M.I.T., pre-Guggenheim earning & saving years. I did not have the rent for this workplace down here this month." Blaming "economic terrors," Tillie could hardly refuse speaking invitations, which came frequently because of pressure to have women on programs.

(Pulitzer Prize–winning author Annie Dillard got more invitations than Tillie but, unlike Tillie, turned them down so she could write.[36]) In a single week Tillie made six impassioned speeches in the East and in the next week several more at the University of "Hawaii!!" (as she marked it on the calendar). She took Jack to Hawaii, but he was not a presence in her letters, an arrangement that sparked rumors of their permanent separation. Tillie called Rachel Klein from Hawaii to insist, in a two-hour collect call, that *Silences* appear in May. Klein countered that an error-ridden book would credit neither of them.

Lawrence wrote that he was doing his "best to preserve 'a national resource,'" but Tillie was preserving neither herself nor her writing. On her 1978 wall calendar, she began scribbling in authors' death ages, circling dates and writers who had died younger than she, now sixty-six.[37] Lawrence admitted to Delacorte editors that he was "having serious problems" with her, but he wanted "to keep Tillie Olsen as an author and to keep her calm. She is in the middle of a long work of fiction which we don't want to lose." He asked them to work overtime to bring out the hardcover *Silences* in June or July 1978. By this time, Lawrence himself had doubts about the "long work of fiction" no one had seen. In late March, Delacorte sent out copies of what Tillie called "still messed up" bound galleys. A review in the May *New Leader* criticized her for showing, not empathy, but "an indiscriminate sympathy for her own gender," for assuming a "messianic" role, and for "crying over her lack of productivity."[38]

Tillie was so scattered Alice Walker heard that she had had a "sort of break-down."[39] Nevertheless, Tillie went back on the speaking circuit. At a Conference on Motherhood in Columbus, Ohio, she argued that, as the "most fleshly sensual perhaps profoundest of experiences," motherhood shapes society. The thirty-plus-page transcript, made from her taped remarks, records her saying "I had a kind of mini-breakdown after the workshop this morning, perhaps occasioned by fatigue." Her internal dam against chaos was weakening, but she blamed the rupture, not on speaking and traveling and stress, but "a lifelong agony . . . my daughterhood and my motherhood," a comment out of sync with her panegyric to mother-hood. Another cause of her mini-breakdown was the appearance of a tall woman with silver glints in her raven-black hair. When she said, "Hi Tillie, I'm Jeanette Gray," they fell into each others arms, weeping. Gone were rivalries over who was the better poet, the better Communist organizer, or the better lover of Eugene Konecky. Calling Tillie the "Shakespeare of short stories," Jeanette soon added pressure on Tillie: "I am sure you have it in you to become the greatest and finest woman author of our times and I am so glad that you are working now."[40]

On 26 June, Sam Lawrence arrived in San Francisco and drove to Santa Cruz to present Tillie with an advance copy of the hardcover *Silences*. The book jacket was bone-colored with "Silences" dramatically calligraphed in a shade of apricot and the words "Tillie Olsen" in black swirling letters, and she was gratified by the book's appearance. The next day, however, she wrote "accident" on her calendar, though not what happened. She occasionally noted "Jack" when he visited or "City" when she went home. Her calendar's fragmented notes suggest she had not yet recovered from her "mini-breakdown."

In July, Tillie led an exhausting daylong meeting with UCSC's Women's Voices group, using her advance copy of *Silences*. With this protective audience, her personal magnetism excused failures in clarity.[41] Also, talk about the ways women's talents are silenced carried special urgency, when some states threatened to retract their ratifications of the ERA. Women petitioned, boycotted, lobbied, and marched on Washington, demanding that Congress extend the deadline, which it did, until 1982.

Reconciling himself to Tillie's absence, Jack and six retired labor activists founded the "Fort Point Gang," which walked once a week to Fort Point near the Golden Gate Bridge. He loved telling stories, talking politics, and reviewing labor history with the gang. He organized and taught in labor education programs at City College. He often drove a pickup truck with a hooded back into the hills to camp with his buddies.

On Lawrence's letter saying that the paperback *Silences* would be out in August 1979, in large black letters Tillie printed the word "Betrayal." As she escalated quarrels, he begged her to "conserve your energy and not dissipate it on messages and phone calls to our publicity people."[42] Replying on a postcard picturing a fire-breathing dragon, she insisted that, if she had "dissipated" her energies, it was her publisher's fault. The evidence tells another story.[43]

The hardcover *Silences* officially appeared on 24 July.[44] It includes her *Harper's* essay and her 1971 MLA talk, as printed in *College English*, her 1972 "Afterword" on Rebecca Harding Davis, long "aftersections" on "Silences" and on the "Writer-Woman," and expansions of nearly fifty years of copy-outs. Tillie admitted that *Silences* is not "orthodox academic scholarship." She said that it was written "with love for my incomparable medium, literature; hatred for all that, societally rooted, unnecessarily lessens and denies it; slows, impairs, silences writers." She dedicated the book: "For our silenced people, century after century their beings consumed in the hard, everyday essential work of maintaining human life. Their art, which still they made—as their other contributions— anonymous; refused respect, recognition; lost."

Tillie was, as Lawrence said, "a good adman. Adwoman. Adperson." She asked Harry Lerner to supply names and addresses of long-lost cousins to be sent publicity. Doing so, he told of a service for "the 24 Yiddish poets and writers that Stalin murdered 26 years ago," a reminder that his politics were not hers. He did not comment on *Silences*; she infuriated her sisters and brothers with her complaints about deprivations and victimhood. Gene reminded her that she had not written fiction after "The Iron Throat" in 1934 by choice.[45]

After shielding her from the condemnatory *New Leader* review, Lawrence was glad to share novelist Margaret Atwood's review. She set a precedent of praising *Silences* for its message about the ways art can be "subverted," while faulting it for its "scrapbook" form, which John Leonard called a "hodge-podge" and Diana Loercher a "pastiche." Joyce Carol Oates faulted Olsen for "numerous inconsistencies and questionable statements offered as facts." She assumed that Olsen's sloppy prose betrayed "an editor's indifference," an infuriating remark to editors who had struggled to correct and clarify Tillie's prose. Joan Peters faulted Tillie for a "standard romantic portrait of the artist as mad recluse." As an argument, Peters declared *Silences* "weak." After Doris Grumbach called *Silences* "useless," Lawrence complained to Katherine Graham, owner of the *Washington Post*, who printed an exchange between Thomazine Shanahan and Grumbach, who said loyalty made Shanahan "overlook the weaknesses, carelessness, and plain failure in both reason and style in *Silences*." Rather than use such remarks as occasion for introspection, Tillie responded with angry letters to Peters, Grumbach, and perhaps Leonard. In response, Grumbach praised Tillie's fiction but faulted *Silences* for including self-described "unwritten speeches" in a "paste and clipping book, put together rather than written."[46]

Despite such criticism, the *New York Times Book Review* named *Silences* an editor's choice. Two book clubs chose Tillie's books for their lists, and Lawrence ordered a third printing of *Silences*. Tillie reacted to her success melodramatically: "for a while at least now, there is enough for rent & food necessities," the sort of remark that provoked both Blanche Boyd and Rosellen Brown to caution her against self-pity.[47] After Tillie wrote NPR's Susan Stamberg praising her interview with Rosellen Brown, Stamberg asked to interview Tillie. She was so obsessed with complaints about "unforgivable" errors in the hardback *Tell Me a Riddle*, she hardly noticed when Jimmy Carter, Israel's Menachem Begin, and Egypt's Anwar Sadat signed the Camp David Peace Accord.[48]

After her concussion, "sort of breakdown," and "minibreakdown," Tillie jotted down names: Hannah Green (who was mysteriously ill), Pablo Neruda (who died at the age of sixty-nine), and Alice Munro (who had

written "Executioners"). Then Tillie wrote the word "Jonestown," where an
entire religious commune died, by mass suicide or murder. The assassinations of Mayor George Moscone and the openly gay city supervisor Harvey
Milk further distressed Tillie.[49] She turned to reflections on death from
Thomas Hardy and others, thinking of making them into an anthology, to
be called a "Death Treasury."[50] In December 1978, reading again at Queens
College, Tillie responded to applause as if she were a soprano called back
for an encore. As "after reading remarks" she read "Dream Vision," a version
(sometimes hyphenated as "Dream-Vision") of "My Mother's Dying
Vision."

When the University of California/Berkeley hired Alice Walker to teach
creative writing and African-American Studies, Tillie found an apartment for Walker in St. Francis Square. Walker hoped that proximity and
mutual admiration would blossom into honest, helpful conversations
about women, race, and writing, but she feared Tillie's mothering might be
smothering. Walker treasured pictures taken by an itinerant photographer
of her parents in the 1930s when they were sharecroppers in Georgia. In one,
Alice's mother, Minnie Lou, wears beads and a straw hat, her Sunday best,
and stands in the middle of a dirt street. Tillie called that picture "beautiful"
but also pronounced "I want" someone to write the "autobiography" of the
Harlem Guild.[51] Her "I want" confirmed Walker's suspicion that Tillie was
trying to "appropriate" black writers, herself included.[52]

From the tape of her recent reading at Queens, Markson had Tillie's
memoir of Ida phoned in to the *New York Times* "Op Ed" page, as a gloss
on the Christmas story, which the *Times* did not print. Markson then began
shopping it around for another buyer.

As 1979 began, Tillie saw clips from Godmother's film *Tell Me a Riddle*.
Eliason had enlarged Jeannie's role to make a more positive and accessible
ending, offending Tillie, who insisted that Rachel Lyon restore the novella's
"international character, the songs they sing, and on the woman part of
Eva's life, the mother part." As she turned sixty-seven, Tillie both requested
a schedule of Godmother's payments to her and attacked it for having "little
understanding" of "the ways in which the content of TMAR can be realized,
transformed" in film. She even hired a lawyer, who told her that she had no
grounds for suing Godmother for departing from her novella.

Tillie gave a party on 18 January 1979 for an apprehensive Alice Walker.
Dressed in a flowing blue robe, Tillie drank little cups of sake and held
court. She was, Moffat remembered, "in fine form." Clinging to one
guest at a time, Tillie recited her accomplishments, giving what Dorothy
Bryant described as "mischievous, double-edged compliments." No

one dared make double-edged compliments about Tillie's nine years without publishing fiction.[53] Lawrence urged "please finish REQUA." She did not reply.

Back in Santa Cruz, Tillie hired an assistant in a "desperate" but "unsuccessful effort to do something about a crushing weight of ever-accumulating, unanswered correspondence." One letter was from English Professor Deborah Rosenfelt, who wanted to publish "Tell Me a Riddle," along with critical essays on it. After her assistant quit, Tillie invited Rosenfelt to help organize files in turn for Tillie's help with the edition.[54]

At Humboldt State University, near Eureka, California, Jayne Anne Phillips, another Lawrence author, invited writers her students were studying to give readings. Tillie was first, to be followed by Rosellen Brown and Annie Dillard.[55] Since Lawrence was in the West, Phillips invited him to hear Tillie. Unexpectedly, he hired a pilot and two-seater plane to fly to northern California, near the setting of *Requa*. In pouring rain, Phillips drove Tillie to the local airport, where they stood under umbrellas on a rain-swept runway listening to the throbbing of an engine circling above purple massed clouds. Soaked and frightened, remembering Amelia Earhart's vanishing into the Pacific, they almost wept when a small break opened and a toylike plane darted through clouds, landed on the shiny tarmac, and taxied up to them. Later at dinner, Sam calmed his nerves with considerable wine, while Tillie, as usual before a performance, ate little or nothing. Then she read "Requa I" on and on, with her publisher sleeping in the front row.

The day after the Humboldt symposium ended, Tillie joined a more theoretical symposium of women academicians at Reed College. When Patricia Meyer Spacks, an authority on eighteenth-century literature, observed that women's memoirs and autobiographies show them using disadvantages and turning passivity into power, Tillie rose to protest, as if she had been attacked personally.[56] She was consoled by Elinor Langer's introduction: Tillie Olsen was "not a woman who lived her life as an artist, but an artist who has lived her life as a woman." Calling Langer's words one of her "proud-joy" testimonies, Tillie instructed Lawrence to "take time to *read it*." Langer, however, soon began to shy away from "a feminist pat on the head" from Tillie Olsen.

Meanwhile, Elaine Markson's efforts on behalf of Tillie's "Dream Vision" took an odd twist. A television show called *Turnabout*, which dealt comically with the paranormal, bought it perhaps for its initial episode about a statue with magical powers, that presumably enables an old dying woman to see three wise men (or women).[57] Harry and Clare Lerner happened to see it, with a credit line to "Tillie Olsen," and Clare fired off what must have been a scathing denunciation and refutation, calling Tillie's vision "a combination of imagination, poetic license & emotion." The old woman was "unidentifiable," her seemingly Christian vision a lie.

Tillie did not know of her sister-in-law's response, for she was lecturing and reading in the east, gathering more disciples. One wrote "whether you are at your most scattered or whether you are entirely present and eloquent" it was "a gift" to hear her. Tillie continued telling women to send her their work, critiquing their stories, recommending them to each other and to grant agencies, and sending notes, calendars, and tiny gifts to them. Her devotees saw her as an ideal but distant godmother. Hannah Green adored her, though her husband was beginning to find Tillie irritating. Though Alix Kates Shulman reviewed *Silences* positively, privately she and Green speculated about Tillie's lack of discipline and productivity. Green fervently believed Tillie was writing; Shulman no longer did.[58]

Lawrence disliked Tillie's self-presentation as a caring mother-figure, when to editors, filmmakers, agents, and publishers she was a dominating harridan, to strangers a queen bee, and to friends a dependent child. She sometimes dined out without money or credit card, making inadequate gestures to repay whoever paid her bill. She forgot the linens, soup pot, blankets, and books she had borrowed from Mary Anne Ferguson four years before, until Rosellen Brown asked, "Who and where is Marian Ferguson, who is supposed to receive your duffel bag of scarves and so on?"

Tillie read and lectured at five or more eastern colleges that spring. Among the piles of letters and papers awaiting her in late March back in Santa Cruz was Clare Lerner's letter denouncing the television version of Ida's last days. In a long reply, Tillie said that she "refused to listen to, see that program, the whole experience [so] nightmarish" that she told only a few family members about it. Though Harry could "feel that nothing mother on TV was 'a stranger,'" Tillie insited that "the dream is true." She even said that she had heard some of it from Clare "though [Ida] had said she dreamed the night before of the *three wise men* dancing, her delight in their dancing and in how beautiful the colors, how they were dressed, and your eerie feeling because it was on Christmas Eve she had dreamt it."

There are several problems with this defense. First, Tillie had not been at Harry and Clare's on Christmas Eve or Christmas but had arrived late on 26 December. Second, Susan Lerner has a distinct memory that when her family celebrated her grandfather's birthday on the first light of Hanukkah in 1955, near Christmas time, her grandmother was barely able to speak, much less to describe an elaborate vision. Third, at that time, and for nearly the next twenty years, Tillie had said nothing about any vision Ida described to her. And fourth, Ida's distrust of Christianity was probably too deeply rooted for even her subconscious to produce a Christian vision. Near the end of her long screed, Tillie replied, "Tell Susan I did not assent to *Turnabout* 'to sell books.'"[59]

When Jack was "discovered ill—at times could not lift a cup to his lips," Tillie left Santa Cruz for San Francisco and subleased an expensive studio on Gough Street, still complaining about being kept from writing. Then an impressive vellum envelope with the embossed logo of the University of Nebraska in Lincoln arrived. It contained the startling announcement that Tillie Olsen would receive an honorary Doctorate of Letters at a ceremony on 12 May. She found that Linda Pratt, an English professor, had nominated her. She sent Harry the news and told him to tell Gene, who then told Harry he had sold the Josephine Baker project. When she donned academic gown and mortar board and was hooded in university colors, Tillie remembered how Woolf, in *Three Guineas*, pokes fun at the "ornate clothes" judges, priests, soldiers, politicians, and academics wear. To Lawrence, she bragged that as a woman she had marched "Not as in *Three Guineas*—at the end—but the beginning of the procession."

Harry had flown in for the occasion, and he, Vicki, and Tillie, with a reporter, returned to the old Omaha neighborhood. The Caldwell Street house had been torn down but other old houses were standing. A blind African-American sitting on her porch swing recognized them by their voices, causing Tillie to reflect that, though the woman's daughter was called "colored," Omaha was not as "ghetto-ized" in the 1920s as it was in the 1970s. She observed that, in the 1920s, people faced "death on the job, death from diphtheria or scarlet fever, accidents all the time" but did not "give in to the fear of them." With Vicki and Harry beside her, she acknowledged, as she usually did not, that she had married at age nineteen. When the Lerner siblings called on the Blumkin sisters and their mother, now one of the country's wealthiest businesswomen, Rose Blumkin insisted that Sam Lerner could have been president of the United States. Posing together for Vicki's camera, Harry and Tillie maintained warmth by not mentioning "Dream Vision."[60]

At the time University of Omaha History Professor Bill Pratt, husband of Linda Pratt, had organized a dramatic exhibit memorializing Omaha's darkest hour, the 1919 lynching of Willie Brown. With narration by local son, Henry Fonda, the exhibit included articles, testimonials, and photos of the courthouse mob and Brown's burned body. Though she was horrified, Bill Pratt recalled Tillie expressed no sign of recognition.[61]

She had promised Lawrence to do nothing but write after her trip to Nebraska; by 2 June Tillie had different plans: "Three more weeks. (Sam I am breaking a promise to you; going to London with Jack for 15 days;

thinking t better to have it over with; punctuating an end.)" By "have it over with" could she have meant ending her marriage with Jack? If not, what? Possibly, she meant settling hassles with Virago, which had rejected *Silences* in 1978 as too long and "a bit scrappy," but now agreed to reissue it, along with *Tell Me a Riddle* and *Yonnondio*. Tillie and Jack spent a day or two in Paris and then flew to England. She imagined seeing innumerable literary sites and did at least visit the Brontë parsonage, Keats's house, the Tate and the National Portrait galleries, and the memorial to Karl Marx in Highgate Cemetery. There she and Jack posed together: he looked weary, Tillie revitalized. On 13 June, Carmen Callil introduced Tillie to an enthusiastic Virago staff and took her to dinner with several British women writers.[62] After her return to Santa Cruz, Tillie created another publishing showdown by sending her three books, each full of inked-in corrections, to Callil, who replied that the changes Tillie requested in *Silences* alone would necessitate "drastic resetting" whose "exorbitant" costs a now unenthusiastic Virago staff refused to undertake.[63]

That summer, Jimmy Carter spoke presciently about the need for Americans to conserve energy and develop alternate energy sources. Some Americans thought the Marlboro Man image under threat by conservation, human rights, and feminism. "Ole boys" complained that women and minorities were hired and promoted over white male counterparts, hardly the experience of Annette Kolodny. College students encountered these issues in political science, women's studies, and now in literature classes. Paul Lauter was editing the two-volume *Heath Anthology of American Literature*, which took space from white male literary lions to include diverse authors, more representative of America. Tillie wrote him, "what a difference this anthology will make."

Tensions between Tillie and Alice Walker had simmered for years but boiled over when Tillie suggested that Walker write on Alice Smedley. Busy finishing *A Zora Neale Hurston Reader* and starting *The Color Purple*, Walker teased, "I'd rather write about you." Tillie responded, "Don't bother to write anything on me, Sweetie." Walker's reply on 18 July 1979 regretted that Tillie had not responded to two requests to write about *Meridian* and thus protect it from antifemale, antiblack reviewers. She accused Tillie of patronizing her as a black writer.[64] Chagrined, Tillie immediately recommended *Meridian* to Virago and asked Bill Pratt for articles about the 1919 lynching.

Laurie's 1970s wedding ceremony dedicated to young love and peace had not insulated her from divorce. She remarried Mike Margolis, a multitalented musician with left political leanings. Laurie passed her thirty-second

birthday in the late stages of pregnancy. Tillie came up from Santa Cruz
for the birth of Jesse Margolis on 26 July 1979. After writing Lawrence
about having "it over with," Tillie did not mention Jack for a time, but
she told Hannah he was "functioning, able to care for himself. But [still]
on dangerous prednisone." She confessed to Hannah that she was "not
writing."

Traveling to Santa Cruz in August, Susan Stamberg was surprised by
"how MODEST [Tillie's] surroundings were for a woman of her age and
literary stature." Her place looked like a graduate student's, except for the
portrait of Dickinson on the wall and valuable books on the shelves. Tillie
was so "wandering and unfocussed," Stamberg stayed for more than two
days, asking and reasking questions in hopes of getting clear answers. They
went out to local spots for meals "on NPR's dime" and Tillie "REALLY
enjoyed her food," as if eating out were a rare treat. Later, Stamberg and an
NPR editor began honing the interviews toward coherence.[65] Tillie reluctantly agreed to a much shortened list of revisions for resetting.

That summer Frank MacShane, a founder of Columbia University's
translation program, was teaching a translation workshop in Rome.
Among his students was Sara Poli, an Italian academic and translator of
technical texts. A Boston friend had given her a copy of *Tell Me a Riddle*,
and MacShane encouraged her to translate it. Meanwhile, Gene Lerner and
Hank Kaufman had sold their villa to help finance the Josephine Baker
movie. Sorting letters and papers, Gene put Ida's few letters and her school
notebook in a drawer.

Tillie deplored colonialist intervention, whether in the Philippines, Cuba,
Guatemala, Chili, or Iran, where the CIA had installed an America-friendly
government so she saw justice when the Iranian Revolution deposed the
Shah of Iran and even when, on 4 November 1979, Iranian revolutionaries
took over the American Embassy and claimed fifty-two hostages. Most
Americans, though, saw the hostage crisis as further proof of an ineffectual,
feminized America. They worried that "ole boys' clubs" were being replaced
by a "helping circle" of women.[66] Many were surprised to hear that, for the
first time, a feature film was written, produced, and directed entirely by
women. Tillie was queen bee when:

Godmother Productions invites you to our
Tell Me A Riddle Celebration
At Oz Atop the Hotel St. Francis
Union Square, San Francisco,
November 17, 1979, 5:30–8 P.M.

At the end of 1979, Tillie sent out a few New Year's cards but apparently no letters.

She wrote that she had been "sometimes functioning, sometimes not—a flu that became a pneumonia," which lingered into February 1980.[67] She began assembling, with Julie's help, a collection of writings on death. On 11 February, she assumed her peremptory persona, writing Lawrence: "About the Death Book. . . . Say yes or no" or she would find another publisher. Nine days later, she sent him the "Death Treasury" proposal.[68] Markson wrote him: "Tillie and her daughter really want to do this although she does say she's working on 'her fiction' (that's a quote Sam)." Having no inkling of Markson's skepticism about her fiction writing, Tillie officially ended her "demeaning" relationship with Harriet Wasserman. She hurled a long list of complaints at Lawrence and an even longer one at the Delacorte staff about royalties. Lawrence explained again that holding royalties on reserve against returns was standard procedure. Her books earned about $7000 for the last half of 1979.

After months of distilling, Susan Stamberg's interview with Tillie Olsen aired on NPR's "All Things Considered" on 3 March.[69] Stamberg assured Tillie that the NPR staff had "felt inspired by your words," but kind words could not save Tillie from a virtual tsunami of depression, illness, fatigue, anger, and fear over money and for her reputation. She besieged the Elaine Markson Agency with complaints that *Yonnondio* was being advertised in Germany to the "female market" rather than to a "class-conscious reader-ship." She forbade filmmaker Midge McKenzie from mentioning "I Stand Here Ironing" in promotions for her film *Ironing*, yet she demanded "50% of all" McKenzie's "net proceeds." She lost her Santa Cruz workplace and needed $15,000 by 18 April to close on a house in Soquel, California. She wanted an advance on the death book, *Requa* or on another "work of fiction," presumably her long-jettisoned novel, a request that infuriated Lawrence, her publisher, not her banker. He now doubted such a novel existed.

On 30 March, the *Washington Post* ran an illustrated article that should have calmed Tillie with its descriptions of her novella as "one of the very best pieces of 20th-century American fiction and also one of the least known. Its author, Tillie Olsen, also fits that description." Lee Grant said the script was so moving that "sometimes I've cried so hard I couldn't say 'Cut!'" She tactfully described Tillie's desire for "more input into the screenplay" as a result of being "crammed, crammed, with much she wants to give, convey, communicate." Proud of the film, she admitted that Tillie Olsen was not "jumping up and down" over it.[70]

Tillie went on another extensive, exhausting lecture tour, thanks again, as she told Edith Konecky, to "economic terrors/necessities." When she read at William James College, a woman said she saw her aura: a "yellow white light around your entire body as you stood there on the stage. (It did not happen until you stood)." The aura also surrounded the copy of *Tell Me a Riddle* "you held in your hand."[71] Tillie was auraless when she complained about a "humiliating" *Los Angeles Times* interview, tried to keep an English scholar from introducing *Silences*, and tried to prevent Lynne Conroy's film based on "I Stand Here Ironing" from being shown, though it had won a red ribbon for adaptation at the American Film Festival.[72]

The arrival of a letter from Sara Poli asking to interview Tillie began a summer buried under an "avalanche" of hopeful plans and disorienting hassles. Lawrence ordered a fourth printing of ten thousand paperbacks of *Silences*, and Tillie made the down payment on a modest two-story house in Soquel with a view of Monterey Bay. She asked Virago to schedule appearances in London, Cambridge, Oxford, and "Leeds or another working class" university,[73] but not to overschedule her for "somehow I am in a 67–68 year old body."

That summer Kathie Olsen conducted oral history interviews with Jack, who talked about labor history, not his marriage. The family moved Tillie's accumulation of books and papers, in boxes and file cabinets, to her new home. Tillie signed change of address notices "Movingly." In her victim persona, she described the move to Hannah Green as "a dreadful mistake."[74]

Even during the move, Tillie kept up a vigilant correspondence about royalties, reprint rights, a trip to England, a possible one to Scandinavia, and Sara Poli's audacity in translating "without realizing permission is necessary." Virago notified Tillie it could not afford to bring her to England so she accepted a post of International Visiting Scholar at Norwegian universities, arranged by Pers Seyerstad. Then, the British Post Office announced that, along with a presentation pack of stamps picturing Emily Brontë, Charlotte Brontë, George Eliot, and Elizabeth Gaskell, it was naming Tillie Olsen as one non-British woman writer continuing their legacy. Tillie took this recognition as "one of my few *true* honors—being linked the century after with these four writers I revere and—[who] in different ways—are, have been, life-giving to me."[75] Post Office publicity prompted Virago now to offer Tillie a one-week publicity tour, to coincide with its September publication of her three books and obligate her for two European tours.[76]

Hassles over the Italian translation continued. Tillie told Poli not to proceed; Lawrence told her to negotiate with Markson; then Markson asked for $2000 because the movie *Tell Me a Riddle* would "increase the commercial value" of her translation.[77] Expecting to earn only $400, at most, Poli begged Gene Lerner to intervene. Tillie threatened to fly to Rome and negotiate with Poli herself. Lawrence felt he was "taking part in a bizarre comic opera," which seemed more surrealistic after he and Markson settled on two contracts: the death book, offering Tillie "$25,000 with $7,500 for reprint permissions and $1,000 for photo permissions," and her novella, offering her $35,000 but only when she completed it.

Tillie's notes from this period are revealing: "Cast a Vote for the Human Race. There is only 1 earth. Creating your future. Let us Preserve it. Teach Peace or We Die. Arms are for hugging. We are the curators of humanity. An animal never accepted environment but changed it." Perhaps for speeches in Scandinavia, these notes suggest her reliance on adlibs, slogans, personal commentary, and ultimately charisma to turn topics into stirring orations.[78] They also suggest why her orations remained unpublished.

In August, Virago Press sent Tillie her busy English schedule. She wrote Sara Poli that she would not go to Rome but could meet her in Paris. Meanwhile, Gene Lerner showed Poli's translation to Italian novelist Alberto Moravia, who found Poli's Italian "elegant." Tillie flew with Jack to London on 15 September and to Paris on 18 September. She failed to meet, as promised, Hannah Green and Jack Wesley. Nor did she call Sara Poli, who got to Paris on 19 or 20 September to find Tillie gone. In tears, Poli called Gene Lerner, who called Tillie in London and "cussed her out for how she treated Sara Poli." He sent a long letter, hand-carried by a friend to London, detailing the ways she had insulted, not just Poli, but him and their family. He reminded her that she alone of the Lerners had not responded when he and Hank Kaufman needed funds for their Josephine Baker project. Furthermore, "it was I who sent you funds in December, 1955, which permitted you to come to Washington to see Mother. If I had not done that, you would have not seen her and there would not have been a TMAR. How much would you estimate my contribution to be worth in dollars and cents?" He had also loaned her $500 in 1959, but she had reneged on promises to repay him. He wanted reconciliation, given the "precious blood we share through the Mother who left me with the special mandate of ambassador to her children." After reading this letter, Tillie relented, at least about Poli, who interviewed her at the Royal National Hotel, on Bedford Way, near the British Library.[79]

In the interviews Virago had arranged, jet-lag made Tillie even more scattered than usual. Reading (or reciting) was easier, so she read the entirety of "Tell Me a Riddle" for about three hours, an event Lennie Goodings and the Virago staff thought a "most astonishing event at a theatre above a pub in Hampstead."[80] Tillie and Jack left London for Moscow on 28 September for their first visit to the USSR, where they got a standard Soviet tour, weighted with propaganda about happy workers. On 1 October, they flew to Stockholm. Tillie's talks at the universities of Trondheim, Bergen, Tromso, and Oslo allowed her little slack time, nor did her own return schedule; she flew to London on 15 October and to San Francisco the next day.[81] She described herself to Hannah Green as "this driven creature," sometimes too weary to smear on face cream. English sales were soon impressive, except for *Silences*. By the end of November, bookstores had returned so many copies that Tillie could buy them for 33¢ each. The Italian soap opera came to its finale when Poli's translation of *Tell Me a Riddle* failed to sell to an Italian readership.

Jimmy Carter had won Tillie's heart with his work for peace and conservation so she was distressed when he lost the 1980 election to Ronald Reagan. The Republican Party removed the ERA from its platform, and Tillie feared an upswing of antifeminism, censorship, red-baiting, and book-banning. She took the murder of former Beatle John Lennon, on 8 December, as an especially bad omen, given that he was killed probably for marrying an outspoken Japanese artist and fellow peace advocate.[82]

Tillie Olsen had become an icon for feminism's best, its inclusiveness and insistence on equal rights for all, regardless of class, color, creed, sex, or sexual orientation. There were, however, cracks in her iconic image, which her devotees refused to see. More objective observers noted her effusive but sometimes short-lived interest in them, her queenly roles and patronizing affect, her controlling talk, her reliance on charm and emotion rather than logic, and her failure to produce what she said she was writing. Tillie's frequent screw-ups invited chauvinist arguments about women's incompetence. Moreover, her complaints about disadvantages, after so many advantageous awards, encouraged a view of women as whiners, wheedlers, and victims. Tillie suspected that some now thought her a detriment to the very feminism she had inspired.

CHAPTER 15

IMAGE CONTROL

1981–1996

*Hoping naturally with my particular brand of egotism that I would be speaking
for many more than myself.*
—Tillie Olsen, University of Nebraska, Lincoln, spring 1982

At the beginning of 1981, images of Tillie Olsen formed an odd palimpsest of
positive and negative impressions. The day after Lee Grant appeared on the
Merv Griffin talk show promoting the movie *Tell Me a Riddle*, a blur of calls
and visits celebrated Tillie's fame and her sixty-ninth birthday. Fame brought
a request from Leonda Finke, who had sculpted busts of Virginia Woolf and
Emily Dickinson, to do Tillie Olsen's portrait. It also brought some local
kids, thinking her rich, to break into the Olsens' San Francisco apartment.
Finding little valuable among a clutter of books, papers, photos, clothes, and
undistinguished furniture, they piled papers on the stove and turned it on.
Smelling smoke, Eno and Edna Herbert, an African-American couple living
below, broke in and extinguished the fire but could not undo the smoke
damage. When Tillie heard, she made a rare call to Jann, who wrote Gene:
"Til phoned me today to tell me she had been in the hospital and that their
apt. in San Francisco had been broken into and set on fire. Her papers were
spared, everything else ruined." Tillie may not have been in the hospital but
illness added to her victimized image. Her papers were spared because she
had them with her in Soquel. Insurance paid for repairs and two months in
the classy Hotel Miyako.

"Felled" by the tally of offenses she had received from Gene Lerner, Tillie
returned $500, insisting that she had gotten only $25,000 from Godmother.
He was grateful for the twenty-two-year-overdue $500 but not for the
patronizing tone in Tillie's offer to "strengthen, sustain" him. She proposed
coming to Rome so he told Jann he would promote "diplomatic relations" if

Tillie would let herself be "just a plain sister, not a legend, a self-promoted deity and downright fraud."

Tillie's double-edged introductions of women writers at her party for Alice Walker had suggested to Dorothy Bryant that a party would be "a good set-up for an old-fashioned murder mystery" about new-fangled feminist infighting. Bay Area women writers attended a party in Berkeley and agreed to be photographed for the cover of her mystery novel. The legendary Tillie was photographed talking, hugging, laughing, singing, and signing autographs. For a *Los Angeles Times* interview, though, Tillie played the victim: "As a writer, her work was limited by class and sex and she lived in a kind of exile, never treated with respect," a complaint that insulted Lawrence and the agencies whose respect had given her the means to write.[1]

Peggy McIntosh had attended the informal seminar Tillie, Hanna Papenek, and Sister William had given at Radcliffe back in 1963. Now a faculty member at Wellesley College, she invited Tillie there for a conference and introduced her saying that "asking Tillie Olsen to speak on a panel is like trying to fit the Pacific Ocean into a teacup," words confirmed as Tillie way overflowed her allotted time limit.[2] When she autographed *Silences*, "To Peggy whom I have learned to love honor but NOT obey (Time)," Tillie established that she consciously refused to obey time limits when talking about the waste of women's talents, but she did not acknowledge that her garrulousness wasted the talents of the other panelists. The next morning she left the secluded Wellesley Club for a walk around the campus lake. When she returned, she found under her door an envelope with a poison pen note inside. McIntosh asked Mary Anne Ferguson to stay with a very shaken Tillie. McIntosh, who adored Tillie, did not see the note, but she assumed some outsider had tracked Tillie down to ask, "You dirty commie, why are you still hanging around?" Mary Anne Ferguson, by this time realistic about Tillie, thought it was from a fellow panelist, saying, "You narcissist, what right do you have to confiscate everybody else's speaking time?" While Tillie thrilled students with her personal response to their work on nineteenth-century women writers, she alienated her fellow adult panelists.[3] After her reading at Columbia, Dick Elman wrote: "You're a great writer, but you're not being great when you read for 2½ hours." That letter ended their friendship.

When Tillie returned to San Francisco, Jack had moved them back to their repaired apartment. Leonda Finke soon arrived, pulling a luggage carrier with a crate full of oil-based clay. As she made a clay "sketch" and took photos on a Saturday, they recited Dickinson's poems and shared nostalgia for 1930s politics, when, as Finke recalled, "everyone with a conscience was a radical." Tillie had failed to say she would not be available on Sunday and had scheduled a shiatsu massage on Monday so Finke had to take photos on Saturday and finish her scuplture back in her Long Island studio.[4]

Thanks to an organized campaign, Mayor Dianne Feinstein designated Sunday, 18 May, "Tillie Olsen Day." Tillie's family sang, someone planted a Chinese Gingko tree in her honor, and Alice Walker told of arguing with Tillie "with nothing held back out of politeness or decorum" until they had learned from each other. Ernest Gaines spoke briefly, saying that "behind this lady here, there's a fella I like very much, Jack Olsen." During the many speeches, Tillie held Jack's hand, and he was often teary-eyed. When the audience rose to applaud, Ann Hershey reported, Tillie sent "the wave of adulation right back, 'well, if you're standing, stand up in recognition of yourself, because of what the people said here about me, that has to do with every one of you.'" Hershey said Tillie's "insistence on the inclusion of everyone is what draws us to her."[5] Five days later, a party for Alice Walker struck a funnier note that Tillie envied: "Your grandmamma survived Taft (!). Your Mama survived Hoover (!@#*&%Z!). You've already survived Nixon and One Hundred and forty days of Reagan. Why? Because *You Can't Keep a Good Woman Down*."

That fall, the assassination of Anwar Sadat, a perverse retaliation for the Camp David Peace Accord, made Tillie feel "battered" by public events. After giving another talk in New York, she retreated to MacDowell for a few weeks, pleased to find *Tell Me a Riddle* playing in Peterborough. She often said that the film was not her "Tell Me a Riddle" but people should see it because it was better than most movies.

Tillie was back in San Francisco when Dorothy Bryant's novel *Killing Wonder*, its cover a collage of Bay Area women writers, was released. Protagonist India Wonder has written one book which "brought her such adulation that she never published anything more." After she dies at her party for women writers, a "Nancy Drew-like protagonist" discovers that almost all "Wonder's 'sisters' had reason to despise her." They suspect that she did not write so she could remain a symbol of the thwarted woman artist. The *Nation* made the connection explicit: *Killing Wonder* is about "the mysterious death of a feminist novelist from California whose initials are T. O." It was "irresistible fun" to read as a *roman à clef*.[6] Clearly, Bryant shared little of McIntosh's or Ann Hershey's adulation and much of the realism of Mary Anne Ferguson and the irritation of Dick Elman and Gene Lerner.

As Tillie entered her seventies, the break between adulation and scorn intensified. At a Virginia Woolf Centennial Conference, Joanne Trautman said "no one alive knows or understands Virginia Woolf and her work better than Tillie Olsen." Woolf scholars might well have felt insulted, but seventy-year-old Tillie almost required such hyperbolic praise. At a conference on "The Feminist Aesthetic," she justified her narcissism as "'My Female Aesthetic,' hoping naturally with my particular brand of egotism that I would be speaking for many more than myself." According to the transcript, she said she had "disorganized my talk."[7] She was not at her best talking about aesthetics, especially after a wearying string of other appearances. Why she put herself through these paces is a riddle with at least three answers: a mission to convince women of their talents and the justness of their cause; a compulsion to earn money; and, like India Wonder, an excuse for not writing. She applied for a fellowship from the National Endowment for the Humanities, to write, not fiction, but nonfiction. Privately, briefly introspective, she admitted "years of deferring" and even "megalomania." Though she acknowledged "what might have been & never will be now," she was still promising to finish *Requa* by summer's end. The more terrified she was that she would "like most of my class and sex fall into oblivion and failure," the more protective she was of her reputation.[8]

On 16 March 1982, when Helen Caldicott spoke at Grace Cathedral in San Francisco on the "Medical Consequences of Nuclear War," Alice Walker and Tillie Olsen were on the podium. In one paragraph, Walker introduced Tillie by speaking of her respect for all "human beings whether she is like them or not." Rather than introduce Caldicott similarly, Tillie began: "On that August morning, 37 ½ years ago" and told of reading about the atomic devastation that had convinced her to act and write "on the side of life, and to keep life on earth." She continued speaking from notes and reading from "I Stand Here Ironing." She had yet to mention Caldicott, when officials silenced her. On Tillie Olsen Day, Alice Walker had praised her tolerance and Ann Hershey had praised her inclusiveness, but on this day Tillie wanted only to praise herself.[9]

She left Soquel on occasional Thursdays that summer to join the Fort Point Gang, including former *People's World* editor Al Richmond, as they walked to touch the fence at Fort Point, singing an old labor song "Hold the fort, for we are coming." On Laguna Street, Tillie eyed the Chinese Consulate. Even as a teenager, Tillie had empathized with the Chinese against Japanese imperialism. She had read Pearl Buck, Grace Boynton, and everything she could find by Ding Ling, an aristocratic Chinese writer, who had read Marx and Lenin in solitary confinement. Released in 1975,

Ding Ling was "rehabilitated" by the Communist regime to be "accepted into the ranks of ordinary people."[10] If she joined a group of American women writers traveling to China, Tillie would benefit from Richard Nixon, after all.

When the extended deadline for ERA passage expired without its ratification, Tillie felt even more intensely a "tremendous pressure of words."[11] Though she feared "turning into India Wonder," she spoke on Ding Ling in Brooklyn and gave talks on women in Amherst and Boston. When a film adaption of "I Stand Here Ironing" was shown at an event honoring Tillie, she sat on the front row between Arlyn Diamond and Annette Kolodny. When the film's voice-over recited the story's opening words, Kolodny's eyes filled with tears, while Tillie began muttering. As tears ran down Kolodny's cheeks, Tillie grumbled that this woman could not afford a lace tablecloth. When the film showed Emily clowning like Charlie Chaplin, Tillie groaned that Emily would not borrow from Chaplin. While Kolodny wept, Tillie fumed. The audience gave a standing ovation, but Tillie sat, angry that her story had been appropriated.[12]

When she returned home, Tillie found an impressive letter, dated 14 October 1982, from the United States-China Peoples Friendship Association inviting prominent women writers to China in summer 1983; each needed to pay her own expenses of about $3,000. Then Tillie got another impressive letter inviting her to speak at an Italian convention on women and culture. When she discovered, though, that the Italians would not pay her, she wrote Sara Poli: "they took me away from my writing, the lectures I could have given, the money I could have made." Here Tillie equated writing, which the Italians did not take from her, with earning money, which they did.[13] She was literally invested in public readings and speeches which provided her a guaranteed fee and a mostly adoring audience. Tillie told Lawrence that, "carrying out the Reagan policy" the Social Security Administration had declared that "as *Silences* was published after my 65th birthday, royalties should have been declared." Clearly, she, not Reagan, caused her tax problems by not declaring income from *Silences* on her tax returns.

Just after Tillie turned seventy-one early in 1983, she heard from William Bennett, then chairman of the National Endowment for the Humanities, that she had won an NEH fellowship to publish a collection of speeches called "Harvestings." Tillie hoped "not to go under again," an apparent reference to a breakdown.[14] She fretted so much about China that Edith Konecky offered to loan her the money. Speaking in San Antonio and at a "Tillie Olsen Week and Symposium," in Iowa and Illinois, Tillie must have earned enough for the China trip, but she asked Konecky for a loan of $1000 and joined the writers' delegation, which left the West in early June to be greeted in the East by the head of the Chinese Writers' Association. When he called them "pigeons of peace," the Americans stifled giggles. But when a Chinese actress sang "My Old Kentucky Home" and "Ole Black Joe" in honor of the Americans, they had to stifle groans. Alice Walker and Paule Marshall explained that such songs romanticized slavery and hence were inappropriate; the Chinese reacted as if the actress had lost face. Tillie worsened cultural divides by telling about being mugged in San Francisco by black women.

For more than two weeks, the group traveled from province to province, joining Chinese women for panel discussions of women and writing. The Chinese women told of rising early to care for houses, husbands, and children, of being sent to work in gulags, and of having husbands' and colleagues' heads chopped off during the Cultural Revolution. Ding Ling's husband had been executed, but she and the other women somehow had found the energy to survive and to write, though many humbly said "we do not know why we could not follow the dead." In city after city, Tillie trotted out her personal protocol of complaints about lacking the circumstances to write because she had a husband, a job, and four daughters. Her self-absorption was as unresponsive to others as her sponging up time. She talked so long about Paule Marshall's immigrant childhood, as daughter of West Indian parents, that Marshall had no time to tell her own story.

In Beijing, the China Writers' Foundation held a ceremony for the Americans, who were on stage sitting on stiff chairs, upholstered in wine-colored velvet, topped by protective antimacassars, listening to the ancient Madame Huang describe the Long March in Chinese. After an hour, while the Americans were politely applauding, Tillie rose from her chair, knelt before the old woman, and kissed her tiny feet. Madame Huang seemed at a loss, until she deduced that kneeling was an American custom and also knelt before Tillie. Again, fellow Americans stifled giggles.

Nellie Wong, who roomed with Tillie, reported that she sobbed in bed at night. When they visited Agnes Smedley's grave, she wept publicly. Tears usually created sympathy and concern, but not with fellow writers. Before the trip ended, fatigue, cultural clashes, and Tillie's histrionics had created what Lisa Alther described as "junior-high-like" bickering over who was sitting by whom and whether Tillie always got the window seat. For all her talk of inclusiveness, Tillie had aggravated the bickering through cultural insensitivity, long-windedness, and sentimentality. After Tillie appropriated Marshall's personal narrative, Alice Walker stopped speaking to her.[15]

When Julie wrote a memoir about the birth of her daughter, Tillie gave up the idea of a "Death Treasury" and began collecting writings about motherhood.[16] Florence Howe agreed to publish her collection to be called *Mother to Daughter, Daughter to Mother*.[17] Tillie did not tell Lawrence or NEH that she was assembling it, rather than her death treasury or her "Harvestings" collection. She did write snatches of prose meditations, called "bluies" because they expressed "the blues" on blue paper that Mary Anne Ferguson supplied from Boston. She also added descriptions to her "*Requa* notebook."

Elinor Langer's biography of Josephine Herbst delighted Tillie until she read that Katherine Anne Porter had informed on Herbst.[18] Though Langer had solid evidence, Tillie accused her of siding with the FBI. She pronounced "Katherine Anne Porter did not turn in Josephine Herbst." She needed to have both writers sanctified, regardless of truth, as she needed to paint the mural of her life, sanctified and sealed from an intrusive biographer.

When she woke at four in the morning on 1 August, with terrible pain on her side, Tillie feared she was dying. Sleepless, she made journal entries, wondering if she had cancer or a brain hemorrhage. She puzzled over confusing financial advice that predicted losing money whatever she did with it. She decided "this house—insanity" and soon passed it on to Julie and Rob Edwards. She vowed to "leave them the feeling of my tenderness," a phrase conjuring up the impression, not the reality, of tenderness. She sent Edith Konecky a check for $100. "In what may be insanity" she planned another tour.[19]

Tillie proclaimed that the year 1984 would be a "crucial year" and "all will be tested." She moved "back to my beloved city, home" but left for Iowa to give another lecture, to be taped and published as "The Word Made Flesh." After the American-Soviet Friendship Society invited her on a cultural exchange, she flew with Jack to Yalta and thence to Moscow. She returned such an adamant defender of the Soviet Union that Grace Paley avoided the topic when she talked to Tillie on the phone.[20]

For a *Publishers' Weekly* interview, anticipating the 1984 *Mother to Daughter* collection, Tillie painted herself as an early mother with a first baby born "out of wedlock." Just half an hour into the interview, Tillie broke down, sobbing "we're all dying off, and no one has told our stories." Tears were handy substitutes for answers. The reporter confronted her with both adoring and scornful judgments: "Tillie Olsen's name is revered by some women, excoriated by others." Her critics wanted her to quit making excuses and just "*do the work.*"[21] Tillie countered that her understanding of women's lives "simply has not been articulated in our time," except by herself.

In October, Tillie applied for a Bunting Fellowship, the new name for Radcliffe Fellowships, founded in 1961 by Mary Ingraham Bunting. Her project summary included: "1) Completion of a work of fiction long in process. 2) Continued sporadic work on a memoir-of-sorts. . . . 3) Completion of a collection of essays based on some unwritten talks given over the last decade and spoken from preserved notes."[22] Her impressive list of major talks was, however, "unwritten." In December, Tillie turned in her NEH report, saying evasively that her "imaginative fiction" had been "immeasurably illumined" by her year of support. She was "more committed than ever to the subject, the significance, the beauty, the importance of my *Harvesting.*" Here vagueness about her fiction and braggadocio about her nonfiction hid her failure to keep her promise to NEH. After a year of funding, she could not blame "circumstances" for preventing writing, but she refused to blame herself.

Mother to Daughter included "Dream Vision," and Tillie sent a copy to Gene early in 1985, saying "I mourn that life has estranged us." Reading the "Vision," he concluded, as he wrote Lillian, that "Til is going Catholic on us." He thought that the "particular Christlike mysticism" she attributed to Ida was a stand-in for Marxist idealism. Tillie had created "an alternate reality" about their mother, who "no longer is our Mother but the Mother Til has formed, in private fantasy."

Having lost a fortune on the unproduced Josephine Baker project, Gene wrote Tillie that he and his new partner Augusto Rosati wished to buy an apartment in Rome for which he needed help on the down payment. This time, Tillie responded generously with a $1000 check, which was also a down payment on a better relationship with Gene, whom she and Jack were to visit. They stopped briefly in Greece and then arrived in Rome on 7 June. She had much to prove to Gene, as he to her. Both dressed their parts: Gene "in my aquamarine silk shirt & white trousers," and Tillie in a long, flowing green dress. She carried her "green-eyed, graceful head" and her age "extremely well. . . . She wore huge dark glasses that suited her mystique—and she has it. Jack also looked well, tho heavy." At his apartment, Gene irritated Tillie by talking of Lillian's kindness, her "amazing tourist capacity," and her knowledge of art and architecture. Even worse was his account of his 1967 Soviet tour. Unlike Tillie, he had visited Kiev, "beloved to Mother." Unlike Tillie, he found their cousins in Moscow. Unlike Tillie, he had taken vials of earth from Ida's Maryland grave to Minsk and dug up soil there to scatter on their parents' Bethesda graves. Tillie preferred to talk about their "Jewish heritage, that need to change the world and eradicate those breeding grounds for hatreds and ignorances."[23]

Tillie was taken aback to see on Gene's desk a framed picture of Karla, Ida, and Gene, taken in 1936, just before Ida had insisted that he return Karla to her mother. Seeing Tillie's interest, he said, as he reported to Lillian, "if you as much as touch that photo, you're going to find yourself with two bloody arms and no hands." He invited Sara Poli, now reconciled with Tillie, for lunch with actress Lila Kedrova, whom he jokingly called "our mother," offending Tillie. When she complained about Godmother Productions, he said she needed a good agent: "By the way, didn't you have a brother who was one of the best in the world?" Jack wisely observed, "we always have a private self that we never reveal to others." Though "affable," he seemed worn out. Gene caught a taxi and put them on a train to Florence that afternoon.[24] Long-term wounds had been cauterized, barely.

Tillie returned to California in time to join a writers' protest against the University of California, Berkeley, for investing in South Africa and hence supporting apartheid.[25] She won a Bunting for 1985–1986, a $15,250 stipend provided by a private fund for retired academic women, though she was hardly the former teacher that fund was meant to serve. She would live at 83 Brattle Street, where she need not be, as officials wrote, "distracted." She flew to Boston alone early in September, taking cardboard cartons of photos, letters of praise, tiny irons, and other keepsakes. She left this paraphernalia in the Brattle Street apartment for weeks while she stayed at MacDowell, returning to Cambridge in mid-October. Among the Brattle Street residents was Yvonne Noble, whose story illustrated English academic sexism and snobbery.[26]

Tillie was still battling the IRS. She wrote Lawrence that the Internal Revenue Service and the Social Security Administration were taking more than $5000 from Social Security payments to cover back taxes. She praised his companion Joan Williams for her book *Country Woman*.[27] As requested, he wrote a California judge, who dismissed Tillie's case and sided with the IRS. Attempting to avoid taxes, failing to understand why Social Security extracted them from her checks, and blaming the Reagan administration show Tillie as disconnected from legal realities, as she was from publishing and speaking constraints.

On New Year's Day 1986, Tillie was alone in her Brattle Street apartment, suffering from back pain that could only be eased by lying flat with her feet up on a table. Physical pain provoked metaphysical reflections in her private journal:

spilt milk the voices of Karla and Jack my still littered desk so begins my
74th year kissing the face of my mother, smiling in her yard, the print dress,
its bright colors, her flowers in the border behind the next year she was
dead I know nothing of my birth if it was hard or easy or where it was

Momma I know I gave you pleasure those baby years, before Harry,
before you were too overworked to ever sit you gave me life and listening
love the listening only those baby years when I laid my head on your breast
the war years when I stopped overnight in Omaha and we slept together

I have not done well with my life, momma some things I am proud of
some things were of use but I have not harvested dear one I have never
written that gone life the dead my living dead to write them

the call of R. [Russia?] another year the unknown wanting bells at
midnight as new years, bubbles, a horn then singing to be out in the night
to be able to walk without my back hurting without back spasm abide
with me

do you remember of course I do the vow? The aspiration? The
litany?[28]

Gene's tribute to Ida on 29 January 1986, the thirtieth anniversary of her
death, only aggravated Tillie's sense that she had failed Ida.

At Radcliffe, the several faces of Tillie Olsen appeared on different days.
The unconventional Tillie came to a select formal dinner at Harvard's
Adams House in jogging clothes. The confrontational Tillie scolded another
Radcliffe fellow, a theologian writing on Jewish women's history, for not
covering secular Jewish figures, like Bund leaders and labor organizers. The
generous Tillie would not accept an invitation to be the keynote speaker for
Women's History Month until Yvonne Noble was also invited.[29]

Tillie left Cambridge at the end of March to be Hill Visiting Professor at
the University of Minnesota. Mary Anne Ferguson remembered that Tillie
left "under very hectic conditions, getting books and possessions ready to
ship." In the East, Ferguson was her chief organizer and package-mailer. In
the West, Jack was. Sometimes, though, Tillie provided the wrong address,
and her things went missing. Then she would weep over the notes, pictures,
irons, and keepsakes she would never see again.

In Minneapolis, Tillie might have recalled her tender times with Abe
and baby Karla in 1932–1933, but she was busy gathering notes for formal
lectures with catchy titles like "Oral/Aural in Literature and in Our Time"
and "Sex and Death in the Nineteenth Century." As always, she impressed
audiences with her vast knowledge and her passionate response to literature and the human condition, which seemed in peril after the Chernobyl

nuclear disaster, on 26 March 1986. The inspirational Tillie returned to Radcliffe to give her Bunting Seminar at April's end to an overflow crowd that mostly forgave her disorganization. Her comments on motherhood brought the *Boston Globe* to interview her for a Mother's Day article. Scholarly Tillie said Mother's Day was the idea of Julia Ward Howe, first president of the New England Woman Suffrage Association. Incendiary Tillie insisted that a once-a-year respect for mothers was "unforgivable," "hypocritical," a "travesty," and "almost obscene."

She was back in Minneapolis to read "Tell Me a Riddle," at a benefit for the feminist Foot of the Mountain Theater, to observe on 15 May the centennial of Dickinson's death, and to speak at the Jewish Community Center. There she tried simultaneously to honor her Jewish inheritance, her secularism, her atheism, her latent Christianity, and her commitment to social justice. On 13 June, the *American Jewish World* printed a letter headed "Olsen not appreciated in talk at JCC" because she was confusedly and "publically sorting out the threads of a past in which she, as a Jew, was tangled in knots."

After more honors and talks, Tillie felt like a marathon runner whose legs were getting wobbly. Worse, she feared that her mind too was wobbling. That summer and fall, she lived in San Francisco with Jack but continued traveling to give lectures and readings on a frenzied schedule hardly good for body or mind.[30] Death was a constant presence. Meanwhile, the Stanford Libraries hired a new curator of British and American literature named Bill McPheron. Working with John L'Heureux, head of creative writing, he contacted former Stanford creative writing students about an exhibit to be called "First Drafts, Last Drafts." He asked them, including Tillie, for an original note on the writing program and a manuscript sample written at Stanford.[31]

The Olsen family gathered in the St. Francis Square apartment on 14 January 1987 to present a "Tillie Olsen Birthday Book" of tributes to her generous, meaningful life.[32] When she heard that Stanford English Professor Diane Middlebrook was writing Anne Sexton's biography, Tillie feared a less generous image of her would emerge. She sought, unsuccessfully, to keep Middlebrook and others from reading her letters to Sexton, at the University of Texas, Austin. She agreed to an interview with Middlebrook but insisted on approving what Middlebrook wrote. Before the interview, was half over, Tillie was in tears, not over Sexton's suicide, but over, Middlebrook thought, "finding herself unable to control" her image. After hours of trying to get precise answers, she was "tremendously frustrated by Tillie's decision to rewrite the past." Before she left, Middlebrook too cried, "furious for letting myself be set up like this by agreeing to let her see the manuscript."

Canadian writer Adele Wiseman, who headed an artists' program at the Banff Conference Centre in the Canadian Rockies, was one of Tillie's devotees. Though Tillie described her project only as "writing," Wiseman saw that she was given a three-month stay, beginning 1 September, in a studio with windows overlooking wooded "magnificence." When writer-in-residence, Betty Jane Wylie asked her to autograph her well-marked up *Silences*, Tillie wrote detailed, time-consuming responses to Wylie's remarks. She told Wylie she was writing a novel.[33] For a Colony newsletter, Tillie donned her working-class persona to praise the "cooks, the cleaners, the house-keepers. I lived most of my life working on everyday jobs, like waiting on tables." She affirmed: humankind has "transcended slavery, feudalism and the caste system. No totalitarian government has remained forever."[34] She was at Banff when Al Richmond died on 6 November 1987. Jack kept obituaries, showing that Richmond had died as fierce a stickler for clear English as he had been in 1938, when he apparently fired Tillie over her contradictory statements about working mothers. Richmond had been not quite seventy-four. Almost seventy-six, Tillie considered her mortality and worried about posterity's judgment.

Working on what he called the "difficult and convoluted task" of getting Tillie to finish the note about her Stanford years, McPheron gave her a deadline. Middlebrook sent Tillie her chapter titled "1963: Tillie Olsen and Anne Sexton at the Radcliffe Institute." Tillie's reactions reveal a desperate attempt at image control. For example, Sexton did, as her letters prove, push "for Olsen's appointment to the Radcliffe Institute," but Tillie insisted that Middlebrook delete any reference to Sexton's special pleading for her.[35] Tillie repeatedly attacked quotations Middlebrook had taken from the actual tape recording: "My language? no"; "never did I say this"; "out of context"; "quote me exactly"; and "never would I over-simplify." Where Middlebrook described Sexton's copying quotations from "bundles of loose pages [Tillie had] collected over the years, all shapes and sizes," Tillie added that Sexton also copied "so many of my own" original thoughts, later expressed in *Silences*. She insisted: "No No No not just this I was source, teacher." Middlebrook observed "the "psychodynamics of her narcissism" took over whenever Tillie encountered a version of her persona she wanted to suppress.[36]

Early in December, Clark University invited May Sarton, Gwendolyn Brooks, and Tillie Olsen to its campus, after students had read their work. The Associated Press called their discussion on motherhood and writing a "spirited fight" among septuagenarians.[37] Afterward, Sarton called Tillie "an impossible woman who always talks too much in a pious inflated way that makes me crawl." A jealous Sarton later asked Hanna Papenek what made Tillie Olsen "so important to you feminists?"[38] In the first full length book on her, Elaine Orr offered an answer: "only Olsen seems to be exploring as her primary interest the implications for culture and for being human of women's traditional caretaking roles." Orr wrote of the "spirit and faith" that Olsen expressed, most explicitly, in "Dream Vision."[39] When she was asked to contribute to a book honoring Wallace Stegner, Tillie told John L'Heureux she would send him that "Vision."

Despite McPheron's deadline for the "Drafts" exhibit, Tillie went to New York City in early 1988 for the Y's "Selected Shorts" program. She had been asked to choose stories for actress Linda Lavin to read. Tillie chose ones by Mansfield, Cather, and Mary Jane Moffat, who felt "in lofty company. It was typical of Tillie's generosity to choose an unknown, little-published, late-starter to introduce to that sophisticated audience."

With Joan Williams, Sam Lawrence had moved to Oxford, Mississippi, where he was negotiating with the university to purchase his books, art, and correspondence with authors, including Katherine Anne Porter, Kurt Vonnegut, Jayne Anne Phillips, Susan Minot, Tim O'Brien, Mississippian Barry Hannah, and Tillie Olsen. He begged her, "Please finish REQUA. Please. On bended knee." At Stanford, L'Heureux was mired in "endless phone calls to Tillie," made worse by an answering machine that left no time to leave a message. She showed what L'Heureux called, "a writer's customary paranoia carried to an extreme." She continued dithering with McPheron over the "First Drafts" exhibit. Procrastination for Tillie meant avoidance, but why she avoided finishing *Requa* and made such persnickety demands on others is a mystery only partly explained as writer's paranoia. She admitted to Mary Gray Hughes, "this is a hard time and I am not weathering it well—let alone transcending." She was distressed by the successful appeal to racism in George Herbert Walker Bush's defeat of Michael Dukakis in the 1988 presidential race. Reading Virginia Woolf's late letters about the blitz of London did not help weather her own time, but her main worry was protecting her image from those who excoriated it.

The Modern Language Association met in New Orleans at year's end with a program vastly expanded since the 1960s when relatively few male scholars made presentations before huge audiences. Now scholars representing different specialties and politics spoke at a plethora of sessions. That year in a session devoted to "*Silences*: Ten Years Later," panelists celebrated the salubrious influences of her book on lives and careers, on the ways literature was taught, and on the life of the country. No one mentioned its disorganization, awkward prose, or occasional problems in logic. It would be heresy to criticize either *Silences* or Tillie Olsen. Both the book and the woman were revered symbols of feminist survival.

L'Heureux's *The Uncommon Touch: Fiction and Poetry from the Stanford Writing Workshop* prints Tillie's scarcely comprehensible note about the roots of "Dream Vision" in a year of "resurrection" at Stanford, when Ida died; then "through thirty-three years [the memory?] has fed, feeds, comprehension, caring, expression; come tangible, present, in all I have published since—and my as yet unpublished, unharvested."[40] The volume was presented to Stegner at a huge banquet. Tillie was not there.

On 26 February 1989 Jack Olsen died at age seventy-seven of heart failure. At the funeral, Georgie Kaye threw a wreath in the Bay and sang "Take me over the sea where Franco can't get to me." Laurie's husband Mike Margolis said he learned to be a father from Jack. Before he sailed his best hat into the grave with the coffin, Karla's husband Arthur Lutz said he learned to be a husband from Jack. Amid much singing, Tillie stood alone to sing: "I could search the world over and never find a sweet man like him." Soon after, she arranged to read the whole of "Tell Me a Riddle" at San Francisco State University. She copied a Käthe Kollwitz naked, sagging self-portrait onto blue cards and printed on them "How I am now." She invited recipients to hear "my personal/public liturgy for Jack—Al, too, and I want some friends I love to be there." Of course, the wrenching story of Eva's journey toward death was based on Ida's, not Jack's, death, and Tillie's reading was about her, not Jack. She may have been too absorbed to respond to news that Vicki's daughter Sandy had died.

With the catalog for the "Drafts" exhibit about to go to press, Tillie finally wrote her piece on Stanford and relinquished a few pages of "Requa I," but she was too paranoid to trust them to the Post Office and insisted that McPheron meet her in the Palo Alto bus station to receive them in person. Then she flew to Bethesda, for once attending a Lerner family affair, the wedding of Harry and Clare's son Howard Lerner and Elizabeth Goll on 9 April 1989 at the Lerners' home. All the siblings attended, and all, excepting Harry, stayed in a nearby hotel. According to Gene, the wedding was "most original and simple," a Jewish wedding with international overtones, a testimony he attributed to Ida's ongoing influence. Afterward, Gene proposed that he and his sisters take the rare opportunity to talk together. Because Jann was the eldest, they met in her room; they had barely settled on chairs and bed and voiced a few pleasantries about how well they looked, when Tillie began to speak. According to Gene, she went "on and on and on and on about the death of Jack and all the people who came, that none of us had ever heard about or cared about." With Tillie acting as if she were on stage, he broke in to say, "Well, Tillie, you know that Vicki had a tragedy just a month ago?" When the siblings rose to leave, he walked Tillie to her door, and she said "maybe I talked too much." Gene replied, "You know you are a star and we know you're a star, but we matter too." She slapped him, said "you can't talk to me like that," and slammed the door in his face.[41]

Several weeks later, when she spoke at a writers' forum at the Denver Public Library, Tillie strolled into Denver Books, a family-owned used and rare book store near the university. The wife asked, "may I help you?" The haughty Tillie replied, "don't you have any of my books?" The woman retorted, "How do I know? Who are you? What is your book?" Tillie gave her name but left in a huff. Then the husband, according to his wife not given to chauvinist opinions, made one: Tillie Olsen "must not have a husband because no man could live with her."[42] Star-power had again interfered with civility.

While Tillie was in the East, McPheron's "First Drafts, Last Drafts" opened in the grand Green Library gallery. Attending the exhibit after she returned, Tillie thought seriously about selling her papers to Stanford, but she balked at the idea that strangers could read them. McPheron refused to sequester papers, but he assured Tillie that Stanford would pay generously.

Tillie gladly talked with Constance Coiner, a UCLA graduate student writing a dissertation on Meridel Le Sueur and Tillie Olsen, in the context of history, feminism, Marxism, the Old Left, and Paul Lauter's Olsen-inspired attention to labor history. Tillie said that the Communist Party was ahead of the times in granting women's rights. To Coiner, she insisted that women must "agitate, educate, organize."[43]

Though she had recently slammed a door in his face, Tillie began writing Gene conciliatory letters, saying that she wanted to see Ida's night school book when she got to Rome that fall. Her efforts reminded Gene, he wrote Vicki, of the "undeclared race your elder sisters and brothers entered" as they had walked to Central High, along different routes, always conscious of who arrived first at school." Now, even as Jann's eightieth birthday approached, he felt "we continue that race in life, a relay of years." For him, the relay meant making 12 October "Tillie Day." Augusto stayed up late cooking. Gene got up early to prepare for Tillie and for Anna Magnani the next day. He met Tillie at the Nationale Airport and brought her to the new apartment for lunch. Examining his collections of autographed movie star and family photographs, including one of Lillian, Tillie remarked, "she's the real beauty of the family." She still wanted a copy of the photo of Gene and Karla with Ida, and she insisted that Gene retrieve Ida's night school book. Augusto had prepared an excellent lunch, Gene recorded, of "cold pasta, cold onion omelet, salad, macedonia de fruitta. T ate with relish. Talk *in the main* of racism & the Jews, Israel." He got her on a train by midafternoon.[44]

In Sardinia, at an Italian–North American Studies Association Conference, Tillie settled into her hotel, a former castle with watch towers from which she could see Africa. Conference topics included Italian/American anarchists, Italian/American movie stars, and *Yonnondio*. Later Tillie returned to Rome with Sara Poli. The death of a young black man, beaten to death for trying to organize African immigrants, galvanized Italians against racism. Tillie and Poli joined marchers, carrying placards of Martin Luther King, Jr., and Frederick Douglass, making Tillie proud of Italy and of her country too. She was pleased to have made peace with Gene at last and exultant that she had managed to sneak away a page from Ida's notebook, which became one sacred object that she never lost.[45]

Then she traveled to Florence where conference organizer Liana Borghi offered her a spare bedroom. On the flight home, the pilot announced that the San Andreas fault under northern California had shifted, creating a massive earthquake. He made an emergency landing in Las Vegas, where Tillie spent panicked hours waiting in pay phone lines. Finally, she reached Kathie. Though plates and cups, lamps and television sets, had jumped off shelves and tables, the Bay Bridge had partially collapsed, and the World Series had stopped in the third inning, Kathie assured her that the Olsens were safe.[46]

Leveraging her star-power with Middlebrook, L'Heureux, McPheron, her siblings, Denver book sellers, and others cost Tillie some of her aura. L'Heureux thought that she deprived herself of friendly support and of time for writing by interminable wrangling. He posed the same riddle May Sarton had: Why was Tillie Olsen so important to feminists and others? The other side of this riddle was: Why was Tillie Olsen so selfish with some people and so generous with others, like Noble, Moffat, Wylie, and Coiner? Other riddles were: how genuine were her frequent tears? How vulnerable physically and mentally was she in her late seventies? And especially why did she not write?

Back in 1977, Tillie had quoted some of Thomas Hardy's "Human Shows," and she and Grace Paley had debated what each would most mourn at death. In 1986, Tillie had reflected on "the dead my living dead" and recalled her vows to her mother. At the end of 1989, she sent Mary Gray Hughes the Hardy quotations and copied passages from Ecclesiastes. As 1989 ended, she had Jack's death to mourn, unfinished "harvestings" to regret, physical vulnerabilities to fret over, and mental slippage to fear.

In the early 1990s, family, friends, and beneficiaries worked to bring long-deserved, though posthumous, recognition to Jack with a Jack Olsen Scholarship in Labor Studies.[47] The tributes to him made Tillie even more determined that working-class struggles figure in the heroic mural of her life, as they had in 1930s WPA murals celebrating the honest work of farmers and factory workers. In an interview with Linda Pratt, Tillie's humble vignette told about her family living in poverty in South Omaha and her father working in nearby packing plants.[48] To Abby Werlock, she added a good mother vignette saying "only once did she send Karla to relatives."[49] Then she presented a grandiose self when Gene Lerner, in the United States for checkups and visits to his siblings, came to San Francisco. Tillie donned a long print dress with pockets stuffed full of dollar bills. As they walked to a Japanese restaurant, she dispensed money to homeless people, who would say "bless you." Tillie replied, "Don't bless me; curse the system."

Suffering from heart trouble and diabetes, Sam Lawrence began to fear that he would die without publishing *Requa*. He offered Camille Hykes, his chief editor, an expense-paid week in San Francisco under assignment to get Tillie to give up her fiction. Tillie enjoyed picking up Hykes at the Hotel Miyako and driving her up and down the San Francisco hills at breakneck speed, which terrified Hykes. One day they sat on the floor in Tillie's apartment, with pages strewn around them, and Tillie held a manuscript of parts of *Requa* in her hand and read to Hykes, who found the prose beautiful. Tillie amused her by telling about a visit with Lawrence when her stutter set off his until neither could produce sounds other than "ah, ah, ah" and "uh, uh, uh." She said the manuscript of *Requa* was too poorly typed to be taken to him and that she could not afford to hire a typist. Hykes offered to type it herself, but Tillie refused. Then Lawrence offered to hire a California typist or to pay for Tillie to go away where she could concentrate and finish. Again, she refused. Instead, she promised to type up *Requa* and mail it in a month. She never did.[50]

Tillie tentatively agreed to let Peter Howard, owner of Serendipity, a Berkeley rare book store, appraise her collection for Stanford. She was used to people marveling at her books, which extended from 1901 and 1902 *Comrades*, through American literary classics, to Virginia Woolf's works, to piles of current books, but Howard alarmed her by recording each book in a bulky portable computer. He horrified her by burrowing into file cabinets and box after box of disordered papers. She tried to intervene, but the gruff Serendipity owner ordered her out. For days, it seemed, he desecrated her sacred spaces, while Tillie could only wring her hands.

When Peter Howard submitted his appraisal, Tillie was livid. She took his evaluation of $27,500 as a personal insult and told McPheron that she would not sell for twice that much. She was appalled that Howard listed early diaries and "letters to Jevons." Intent on keeping the image of herself as an abandoned single mother in the mosaic of her life, she told McPheron that Abe Jevons Goldfarb was Karla's father but only a brief "drifter" in her life and irrelevant to her work. Stanford would buy everything, or nothing. While she was dithering over selling her papers and thus exposing herself or not selling and thus losing the money, Tillie got a request from Paul Mandelbaum to submit something for a collection of famous writers' juvenile efforts. Tillie sent him her high school "Fuzzy" story and the poem "At Fourteen Years," which Howard had just unearthed.

Tillie found a new artist retreat in Hedgebrook, an island colony for women writers, where she went in August 1991.[51] There, while some colonists gossiped that she only pretended to write, a new protégé, young Hawaiian Kiana Davenport, defended her. Tillie was honored in Omaha that fall.[52] At the Jewish Community Center, she read aloud the purloined page of Ida's letter beginning "Dear Teacher: I am glad to study with ardor." Tillie enhanced her picture of Ida as an uneducated peasant by asking, "Where did she pick up that word?" After her talk, a gray-haired woman stood and said, "I'm Ruthie." Tillie rushed off the stage to meet her former neighbor (now Ruth Stein Fox), which began a tear-fest among older residents.[53]

Back at MacDowell, Tillie acquired yet another protégé in Joyce Winslow, who wept to meet "the best short story writer of our time." Tillie responded in kind, saying that Winslow's "Born Again" was "the best short story I've read in ten years."[54] Winslow toasted her: "it is rare that one's hero is as marvelous in person as in print."

When Tillie turned eighty Laurie sent her a long birthday letter celebrating her adored "Mama who cares so passionately and deeply about the world and its people, and is so determined that we all need to and can turn around the forces of corruption and greed." Laurie said she would be privileged to "care for you." In February 1992, doctors concluded that Harry Lerner had a brain tumor and could not live, so Lillian gave a dinner party for him, surrounded by family and friends, but Tillie did not attend. Nor did she attend his funeral in April.[55] In May, she went to New York City to examine her papers in the Berg Collection and stick post-it notes on them. She made imperious but not always accurate notes like "TLO—5/12/92—This is *all* 2 and 3." She wanted copies of everything, including the "Fuzzy" story, now titled "Not You I Weep For" for Mandelbaum's *First Words*. Editing her story, Mandelbaum asked if it were "an abortion Fuzzy hints at?" She replied truthfully, "you are right—an abortion."

Tillie's scattered manner, factual manipulations, evasions, and excuses exasperated people seeking information. Now she blamed her lack of clarity on her brother's death.[56] When a graduate student named Anthony Dawahare interviewed her, Tillie rocked back and forth, sobbing. Her anguished talk about human inhumanity was incomprehensible.[57] Though relieved when Bill Clinton and Al Gore defeated George H. W. Bush and Dan Quayle, Tillie had become too obsessed with her papers and her legacy to follow national politics very carefully. McPheron negotiated with Stanford officials to consider Howard's appraisal as only a base for a much more substantial purchase price.[58] Finally, Tillie signed a contract selling all her pre-1985 papers to Stanford. After she delivered those papers, Stanford committed itself to purchasing all her post-1985 papers. Tillie began going through them, adding notes on post-its that were sometimes clarifying, often obfuscating. She inked over names and hid the letters to Jevons. She congratulated herself on her youthful writing: "how sometimes observant, true, deep and yes witty, yes precociously I was writing then." She was reshaping her past by "constituting my working-class experiencing," when she was "in grade school Kellom Long." She used Bill Pratt's research to incorporate the 1919 lynching of Willie Brown into her life picture: "for years I thought it was some kind of recurring nightmare—a black man's burning body . . . my face against my father's waist not to see." She fabricated an ego-supporting tale about helping "care for and support her five siblings." Sorting and censoring, she wondered "how many years by now out of disorder?"[59]

While Tillie was reconstituting autobiographical recollections, she got a call from *Newsweek* editor Jonathan Alter, who was celebrating the magazine's sixtieth anniversary with six short essays, each covering a decade and written by a major American author. He offered Tillie Olsen an assignment to treat the 1930s in about two thousand words. Tillie was thrilled to have a new chance to put her imprimatur on the 1930s. Recalling FDR's voice, she insisted "we could not see his face" yet he was "that personal." Then she sidetracked to reflect: "There are few pages I have written since to equal Anna and Mazie under the catalpa tree that spring morning. . . . Yes I came to love them more and more as I created them, and I myself," a disguised admission of self-invention. She made a poignant note about "the strange difficult way I write now," an admission that she could not gather words. That page ends with a non-word: "typyply" or "tyfyply," apparently an attempt to spell "typify." Despite all she had to say, broken mental synapses now made writing a complete sentence laborious.

Because she submitted nothing, Alter began calling. Her answering machine cut off after thirty seconds, so he dialed again and again to leave bits of frustrated queries. Finally, Tillie replied, almost incoherently: "With all the other personal pages I set aside or excised from there are pages & pages on my times 'in the can' (30s expression)," where she had "languished 5 (6?) weeks—no money for bail." She recalled campaigning "in classic if filmed documentary weather. A near blizzard gloveless, wet feet, a stupid YCL leaflet (not all of it) about how getting 3.2% beer was not going to end the depression." She remembered the bonus marchers, heroes, and then bums. She told him to read *Yonnondio* as if it would substitute for her inability to tell more about the 1930s.[60] Alter was alarmed.

As oblivious to word limits in writing as to time limits in speaking, in mid-December, Tillie sent Alter a mishmash of personal experience and history; he asked her to focus on the decade itself. Her new draft was better, but his deadline was at hand. Unsure why the author of the great *Tell Me a Riddle* produced so few coherent sentences, he praised her splendid images and phrases but wanted revisions, thereby making Tillie threaten to withdraw. She seemed such a "control freak," he asked screenwriter Billy Wilder to "pinch hit." Instead, Alter himself attacked with his red pencil. He deleted pages of undistinguished prose, lifted important phrases, inserted needed verbs, and strung jewels of poignant adjectives from different drafts together. Feeling like a miner hacking sparkling diamonds from dull rock, he congratulated himself: "Wow, I helped Tillie Olsen write a few good sentences." He probably wrote the last powerful one himself: "It was a time of human flowering, when the country was transformed by the hopes, dreams, actions of numerous, nameless human beings, hungry for more than food."[61]

When Seymour Lawrence died on 4 January 1994, at the age of sixty-seven, Tillie was too excited to notice. When she saw the finely honed essay Alter had mined from her jumbled prose, Tillie forgot her threat to withdraw. The 3 January 1994 *Newsweek* printed "The '30s: A Vision of Fear and Hope" by Tillie Olsen. This two-page, 2,500-word essay begins with memories of Depression misery. In FDR's first hundred days, his achievement was "to redefine what being American meant," while Eleanor Roosevelt's was to dedicate her widowhood to "the 1948 Universal Declaration of Human Rights." Alter included a side-bar as payback to Billy Wilder, with his photo and a remark about 1930s movies designed to "get people out of the doldrums." Though she complained that the article was "not what I intended," Tillie sent multiple copies to friends and family. In turn, Gene wrote that Rome's head rabbi respected "Tell Me a Riddle" as among the "outstanding literary words of the diaspora." Tillie was giddy: "Did it really happen? Is it so? I hug myself—the Chief Rabbi of Rome—not only has read my work—said that?" His words confirmed that an atheist belief in the human race could "equal Judaism—Religion. I feel vindication for ma and Daddy . . . their 'Yiddishkeit.'"

More than thirty years had passed since *Tell Me a Riddle* was published, more than twenty-five since Lawrence had resurrected it, and more than twenty since "Requa I" appeared, gaps Tillie did not want explored; thus she was "adamant about" trusting only some people with her reputation.[62] She had trusted Linda Pratt with an interview but now complained to Gene that Pratt's essay about their Omaha Jewish background was "narrow" and did not cover "the qualities of my work."

Having explained that Stanford would pay nothing for her papers until it received them, Bill McPheron begged her to pack up boxes. When she said she had, say, fifteen boxes ready for Stanford, McPheron would drive to San Francisco to pick them up. As often as not, however, as she began showing him the contents of each box, she removed notebooks and files, so that when he finally left, he had perhaps only ten of the original fifteen boxes. Still, in July 1994, he managed to extract the first of the Tillie Olsen Papers for cataloging at Stanford. While Tillie put on a show of a clever mind and retentive memory at another celebration in Omaha in September, her daughters worried about her. A former carriage house behind Laurie's and Mike shingled Berkeley home might be redone as a "mother-in-law" apartment, if she would move.

In early 1995, Tillie used her first Stanford money to begin renovating the carriage house's upstairs, designating the barnlike space below as repository for her many file cabinets. Julie's daughter Rebekah, a Berkeley graduate student, settled in for the time being. By this time, library shelves held more books about Tillie Olsen than by her.[63] Still feeling pressure to finish *Requa*, though Lawrence was dead, Tillie read a version at San Jose State University in 1995.[64] For the rest of that year, she fiddled with *Requa*, packed and unpacked her boxes, and contemplated moving.

Linda Pratt had cited Gene (then Morris) Lerner's August 1934 letters about the "Iron Throat" and Tillie's arrest. Omaha historian Oliver Pollak sent Pratt copies of those 1934 letters, and Tillie wrote to praise Gene's prescience.[65] He said he was glad to have her scribble, "even if undated, unsigned, coherently incoherent and unstreamed by consciousness. It is evident that you are under severe pressures." She did not appreciate such analysis but sent him, as requested, Pratt's article with her retorts scribbled in. Irritated, he replied:

Dear, dear, *dear* (the last in the trio underlined with a touch of exasperation) Til, is it not, was it not possible for you to have arranged for me to
have a copy of the Pratt as actually, finally printed??????? I mean, well,
understandable your 'compulsive, impulsive talk-back' ... interrupting
the thread of thought and shredding context? (Interesting. I made a typo,
first writing "threat" of thought.) I mean, well can't your fame and prestige
be transferred into a request to somebody to please send your illiterate
brother Gene a final copy as actually printed??????

Over the years, Hannah Green had survived several bouts with cancer,
but now tumors reappeared in her lungs. When Tillie heard the news, she
called Hannah and Jack Wesley, Edith Konecky, Alix Kates Shulman, and
others to weep. As Hannah needed more and more help, Shulman and
friends helped Wesley administer the appropriate but heart-wrenching
care. When Tillie arrived in May 1996, Shulman was so busy dealing with
Hannah's day-by-day decline that she found Tillie's tears irritatingly
useless.

Tillie traveled on from New York for engagements that culminated in
D.C. with recording at the Library of Congress. She spent a night with Clare
Lerner, having a grand time trying, as she wrote Gene, "to up each other
with acerb" (acerbic remarks). In the morning, she packed to move to a
hotel and found Clare on a porch transferring plants from pot to pot. When
Tillie kissed her sister-in-law good-bye, "knocking over the sprinkling can
full of water, deluging all her soil under the table," Clare screamed, "Get the
hell out of here before I kill you." Later Clare, elegantly dressed in navy and
white, came to hear Tillie reading. Clare confided, "you know I'm rather
glad I didn't kill you." Narrating this tale to Gene, Tillie congratulated
herself on reading for three days at the "sacred" library, making five hours
of recordings, with "each day's reading better."

Now fiction editor of *Modern Maturity*, the magazine of the American
Association of Retired People, located in D.C., Joyce Winslow asked her
hero for a story. Before Tillie was to read at the Library of Congress, she
contacted, not only Clare Lerner but Winslow, Eileen McClay, Vicki's son
Cory Richards, and perhaps others. McClay brought two of her poems to
Union Station, the only spot and time Tillie had available. Weeping over
the poems, she made McClay feel that she alone, out of all Tillie's acquaintances, mattered. When Cory Richards took Tillie to dinner, she charmed
waiters and staff people by asking if their feet hurt, if they were properly
paid and protected, and if they had children. She carried such a special aura
that Cory forgave her for dropping into and then completely out of his life.

She swept people up in her wake and then forgot them, just as she extended generous invitations, only to be unavailable to execute them.[66]

During Tillie's last day reading at the Library, she and Winslow went to an outdoor café, where their sandwich plates came decorated with fat summer strawberries. A homeless man paused on the sidewalk, staring at the strawberries until Tillie invited him to join them. Winslow, who was paying for the expensive lunch, found the man "smelly and a little nuts and I didn't want to sit next to him at lunch. Tillie shushed me, 'He's hungry,' she said." Winslow was pleased that the man took Tillie's half-sandwich and her strawberry and did not sit down, but then Tillie was hungry, so Winslow had to buy her a large dessert and coffee. On the next day, Tillie was interviewed at the AARP radio station. She did not eat breakfast "so I won't burp on the radio." Winslow took her, courtesy of AARP, to a posh Washington restaurant for an inside lunch where Tillie sent her cheesy pasta and her vegetable vinaigrette salad back for redoing twice until the chef's third effort met her demands. When she could not finish her rich pasta, she asked for it to be boxed. That evening she called Winslow to report that she had food poisoning and needed a ride to the emergency room, where she stayed overnight to be rehydrated. Not wanting to throw away expensive food, Tillie had carried her box of cheesy pasta all afternoon in the June heat and then eaten the spoiled pasta in her hotel room. Still, she blamed the restaurant for poisoning her. She had agreed to be interviewed as a favor to Winslow and was offended that the station did not air the session. (Actually, the AARP radio editor could not edit out her stutters and uh-uh-uhs.) She told Winslow that she could not send a story to *Modern Maturity* because she was working on a novella that could not excerpted. She had been magnanimous to her nephew, solicitous to the staff at one restaurant, thoughtful toward the homeless man, autocratic to the chef at another restaurant, accusatory of everyone but herself, and needy and dishonest with her protégé. Still, Winslow felt "privileged to know her. She picks my spirits up whenever I talk with her."[67]

Rosenfelt's edition of "Tell Me a Riddle" included seven essays on the novella, among them the third version of Pratt's essay. Tillie sent the volume to Gene, this time only scribbling a few retorts on it. Although Tillie condemned Pratt for not praising her enough and not making the Lerners underprivileged enough, Gene was impressed with Pratt's insight. He responded to Tillie's description of her interaction with Clare: "at least in my experience, [you] aren't one to make fun of yourself, and your doing so in this case came to me as a delicious surprise. Remember, once upon a time, you wrote with laughter in your pen? A pity that it no longer seems to be instrument of your talents."

Tillie found it harder and harder to laugh. Constance Coiner's dissertation on Olsen and Le Sueur was now a book, but Coiner and her daughter Ana were on Trans World Airlines flight 800 when it crashed, killing all passengers. Mary Anne Ferguson survived cancer surgery in August. In October, Hannah Green died of lung cancer. In November, Marianna Pineda died of pancreatic cancer.[68]

With so many friends dying or in peril, Tillie felt more intensely the "pressure of words." After an ever-extended Omaha presentation, Oliver Pollak offered double-edged comments: "Ms. Olsen spent an hour on the soap box extolling the virtue of the International Declaration of Human Rights. Then she read from *Yonnondio*, castigating dehumanizing technology and brutality in factories, mines, and the South Omaha stockyards."[69] These were of course crucial issues for humanity, but Pollak had heard them before.

When Tillie returned to Radcliff for the thirty-fifth anniversary of the Bunting Institute, she and Hanna Papenek were irritated to hear gifted women spouting clichés about "role models." Tillie rose to scold "you people don't understand lack of opportunity." Despite all her writing and speaking, despite the courses she had taught on the literature of women and the underprivileged, despite courses on social responsibility taught by Robert Coles and others, these privileged women at her beloved Radcliffe felt little empathy with the less advantaged. Nor did they know much about Tillie Olsen. Eighteen years after *Silences*, she had assembled (with Julie's help) readings for *Mother to Daughter* and had written briefly for "First Drafts" and fragmentedly for *Newsweek*. Otherwise she had given mostly "unwritten" talks. At almost eighty-five, Tillie could hardly bear to consider that her creativity was splintering into bits and her reputation sinking into oblivion.

CHAPTER 16

ENTER BIOGRAPHER

1997–2007

What a sleuth you are!!!!!!!!!!!!!!!!
—Tillie Olsen to Panthea Reid, 15 March 1999

When I finished writing *Art and Affection: A Life of Virginia Woolf,* it occurred to me that a biography of a living author would be fun to write. When I happened on Tillie Olsen's name and address in the roster of the Virginia Woolf Society, it seemed serendipity. I knew nothing about her except that she was the author of "I Stand Here Ironing," which I had taught decades before, and "Tell Me a Riddle," which I was then teaching. She was a great writer, shared my appreciation of Woolf, had led a long, no doubt fascinating life, and was a good woman, adored by many. She had published little but was said to be working on a masterpiece.

I dashed off a letter telling her about my students' enthusiastic response to "Tell Me a Riddle." In February 1996, I received a note written in a very tiny hand. With a magnifying glass, I deciphered Tillie's thanks for describing my students' reactions. I was thrilled by her closing "Yrs. For Art & Affection, Tillie Olsen." Three months later, she signed herself "Affectionately—Tillie." I was ecstatic—if this great writer felt "affection" for me, she should be pleased to have me write her life. I carefully penned a letter saying that I wanted to be her biographer.

I received no more "affectionately" signed notes. After a year's silence, I contacted Laurie Olsen, who became an intermediary for increasingly warm conversations between Tillie and me. When I proposed traveling to California to see if we liked each other, Tillie replied, "Oh, I like you already, but that doesn't mean I want you to write about my life." We agreed that I should visit on a fall teaching break, before Halloween 1997. I sent her five pages of questions about her memories and opinions. Living with my maternal grandmother had prepared me, I expected, for dealing with old women. Reading the snippets about her life in print had prepared me, I thought, for Tillie Olsen. I was wrong on both counts.

On 27 October 1997, Tillie Olsen arrived an hour late at the motel she had recommended in San Francisco's Japan Town, wearing tennis shoes and a jogging outfit. She was shocked to find me in a basement room by the kitchen. Though I had not complained, she used her clout to get me moved into an upper room with a view. As we walked through San Francisco's Filmore District, we were greeted by shopkeepers, waitresses, and grocery men. Tillie kissed many of them on each check. ("I kiss like an Italian," she told me.) Along the way to her place, she tried, unsuccessfully, to get a special rate for me at the grand Hotel Miyako, though she had already improved my quarters at the Miyako Motel.

Inside the Laguna Street entrance to her building, Tillie bounded up the steps to her third floor apartment two at a time, lamenting that she could no longer take them three at a time. After admiring her view of the Square's courtyard and the miniature irons on her coffee table, I took my tape recorder, legal pad, and pages of questions from my briefcase. When I read a question aloud, Tillie popped up to search shelves to pull out books with scraps of paper marking their pages, telling me that hers had been called the "most read books" someone (I could not catch his name) had ever seen. She talked at such a fast pace, punctuated by stuttering pauses while she sought the right word, that I was often unsure what she was saying, especially when the combination of speeding and stopping made it impossible to interrupt her. She told about picketing to keep books in the San Francisco Public Library, which brought up her walking with husband Jack Olsen in the 1943 "march inland" when, she said, daughter Kathie was conceived. Clearly, Tillie Olsen's life story fit no stereotypes; nor would my biography.[1]

Tillie kissed pictures of her "most belovedest" departed, including ones of Harry Lerner, Hannah Green, and Marianna Pineda. Her talk ranged from San Francisco neighborhoods, to the Spanish Civil War, to the first Russian Revolution, to her parents' refusal to marry, to Karl Marx on religion, to Yiddishkeit values, and then to a 1919 lynching in Omaha, Nebraska. Her long story elaborated on ousted politicians, who bribed a mob with liquor, and the *Omaha Bee*, which printed inflammatory journalism. She said her father went out to investigate the troubles. Though only seven then, Tillie told me that she had "insisted on going with him. And it was several blocks away and . . . there were all men, there were no women there; this man wanted his kid to get through all these other bodies [of men] who were out to cut off ears and other things and he gave him a knife and he wanted him to go up and this kid did not want to and his father began to beat him up. And I remember the smell." That narrative of racist brutality brought us both near tears. She said she "used to think this was a nightmare" until 1979, when historian Bill Pratt had shown her an exhibit on Omaha's darkest day. Later, he sent her articles that, she said, proved she had been a witness.

Our conversation (or rather her monologue) ran all afternoon. In the evening, we walked through the Square's courtyard, past children of mixed heritages playing on slides and swings. Tillie introduced me to an African-American woman with tennis balls on her walker's front feet and complained, as we walked on, about some residents putting up guard rails. Inside a Japanese restaurant, the song "I believe in yester year" played endlessly, while ceiling fans kept wind chimes tinkling. Telling about her father's threatened exile to Siberia, she sang "Cling, clang, Cling, Clang. Chains Dragging," a dissonant refrain against the wind climes cheerful tinkle. She spoke of her mother's openness about sex and said her "baby" brother was gay and president of the Anna Magnani Society in Rome.[2]

At eighty-five, she seemed undaunted. At fifty-seven, I was exhausted, as I trudged back to the motel. In my new room, I listened to tapes of our conversations. Between Tillie's speeded-up phrasing, her stammer, and her rushing over unknown names, not to mention the wind chimes and the unrelenting "yester year" song in the restaurant, I realized that making sense of Tillie Olsen's voice might be more of a struggle than reading her minuscule handwriting.[3]

I carried my tape recorder to her apartment late the next morning, giving up on my list of questions. When I mentioned the impact of her 1963 "Silences" talk at Radcliffe and her 1971 talk at MLA, Tillie modestly said: "It was just the right time. I put together what people knew but had not put together." Agreeing that the times had been ripe for a feminist resurgence, I said it took her to awaken women. Then Tillie said, "You know I'm a Marxist, honey. It was context." She did not, however, like the context in which two women scholars wrote about her: Linda Pratt had ignored the profundity of her stories; Jane Marcus had dared to write about her stutter.[4] Such complaints were at odds with her initially modest self-effacing self-presentation.

Walking, we met a fierce wind racing down Geary as we plodded up the street. "They call this pneumonia gulch," Tillie informed me. "Don't you need a coat?" Her hair was so short and frizzled that the wind hardly disturbed it, while mine was blown either into my eyes or behind my ears.

I told her my sweater was warm, which it was in Louisiana, but it did not protect me from the San Francisco wind. She steered me up Ellis Street toward St. Mary's Cathedral. At the steps before its massive doors, Tillie began climbing in an odd zig-zag pattern—moving up at a diagonal, across and down at another diagonal—showing off her "squirrel-in-the-cage routine" and her spry, healthy body.

At the top of the steps, we marveled at the view of the bay. I was shivering so we ducked inside. I was awed by the building's modernist simplicity, but Tillie preferred the cluttered look of a small side chapel filled with Mexican folk art. We sat in silent contemplation, and I wondered if she were praying, like the mother in the closing lines of "I Stand Here Ironing." As if she knew my thoughts, Tillie whispered that she found solace in St. Mary's Cathedral's peace work but could not imagine a religion in which one goes to a service, confesses, is cleansed, and is free to sin again. Without transition, she said she regretted only one abortion because maybe "we could have made him happy, or been happy with him too."

Back at her apartment, I kept on my sweater. We lunched on apples and a cheese torte I had brought. She discussed Jack's enlisting in World War II, a fire in their apartment, and her work on the staffs of *Peoples' World* and the *Labor Herald*. When she and Jack had visited the Soviet Union, she said they found food cheap and "everything for children was free, wonderful illustrated books, the circus. If Madeleine Albright knew the Universal Declaration of Human Rights she would not be so down on China."[5] She gave me ten copies of that Declaration. She praised the Chinese for educating all their children and the Cubans for having "the world's best health care."

That afternoon, between singing Satchmo snatches like "Fooderacky Sacky . . . I want some seafood, Mammy,"[6] Tillie talked about the Cold War, the FBI infiltration of the Communist Party, and Kathie's yelling "Garbage, Mom" when the FBI came to call. Here Tillie said, "I did regret giving up Jack's warm Army overcoat." When I queried the connection to the FBI, she shrugged. She gave me a copy of the unfinished talk she had given at Grace Cathedral and spoke of her post-atom-bomb decision to write "utterances on the side of life." She scheduled a shiatsu massage the next morning so we did not meet again before I flew back to Baton Rouge, miserable with the coughs and chills that by Halloween became walking pneumonia. Clearly, Tillie Olsen was scattered and hard to follow, but she had participated in or witnessed the great events of the twentieth century and had written powerful, beautiful fiction. Writing her life would be both a challenge and an honor.

In early 1998, when Tillie celebrated her eighty-sixth birthday, I read a review that presented her in a rather different light. In a novel, an old writer "compares his own small output with that of Tillie Olsen, who makes him seem 'prolific' by comparison, but who . . . shrewdly turned her life-long writing block into a badge of feminist honor."[7] I hoped that Tillie had not seen the review, a distinct likelihood, given the stacks of unread newspapers all over her apartment. That review raised the puzzle of why this great writer had written so little.

Still, Tillie complained about being "INUNDATED" by honors and obligations. On 1 March, Cabrillo College Women's Studies Program held "A Tribute to Tillie Olsen" and the mayor of Santa Cruz proclaimed "Tillie Olsen Day." Over the phone, Tillie read me her daughter Julie's tribute: "my parents held out the continual message of justice, and they lived their lives in an ongoing effort to bring about social change," providing "the one safe haven in the world of work." Clearly, Tillie liked to complain but loved to be honored. She seemed, however, rather gruff when I said I was going to read papers in the Anne Sexton and Knopf collections at the University of Texas at Austin.

From its first appearance in 1995, I subscribed to *DoubleTake*, a magazine co-edited by Robert Coles and Alex Harris and dedicated "to the written word and the visual image, to renderings of the world as it is and as it might be." I wrote the editors to ask if *DoubleTake* might be interested in an article on Tillie Olsen and was thrilled by an immediate, positive response. (I later learned that Coles had commissioned Rosellen Brown to write about Tillie, but Brown had given up after a day's attempts to break her out of a cycle of canned answers.).

By this time, Tillie and I were on teasingly good terms. On my way to California that spring to explore the Tillie Olsen Papers at Stanford, I asked if I could do anything for her. She suggested I hold a parasol over the right side of her face after minor surgery. I joked, "I thought you lacked vanity." She said vanity about her looks was acceptable because she had "a lot to be humble and crestfallen about. All I have to do is just walk into my room." Her chore of sorting papers to send to Stanford paled, I thought, before my task of reading them.

By 6 April 1998, I had checked into a small bed-and-breakfast hotel in Palo Alto. The next morning, I stood on the street corner until the Marguarite, a free shuttle bus, picked me up and dropped me on Stanford's campus. With advice from the driver and students, I walked among handsome Italian Renaissance buildings until I found the Green Library, where Special Collections had pulled from the stacks boxes 15 through 19, dealing mostly with Tillie's early life. I was taken aback. These are huge boxes filled with papers and notebooks of all sizes and many degrees of legibility.[8] On a quick glance through box 17 I found some early diaries written in a large and clear script, making me wonder when and why Tillie had shrunk her handwriting. I was mystified by 1930s letters addressed to "Mrs. Goldfarb," but I began reading methodically through the diaries. In the evenings, though rather agog over young Tillie's zany cleverness and morose self-pity, back in my B&B, I began working on my article for *DoubleTake*. I started with Tillie's horror at seeing, when she was seven, a black man's burned and mutilated body dragged into her mixed-race neighborhood as warning, she said, to "uppity" blacks.

By the weekend, I was rather proud of the twelve pages I had written and took Caltrain into San Francisco to show them to Tillie. I imagined she would make a few suggestions, but she spent the afternoon going over every comma, semicolon, and phrase. She objected to my tone, crossed through anything that seemed even slightly critical, including my reference to her limited output, and cut out my entire treatment of the 1919 lynching. I acquiesced, not wanting to offend the woman whose biography I was now committed to writing. Still, it seemed odd, after she had described at length the grisly aftermath of the lynching, that she did not want me to publish it, so I contacted Bill Pratt. He remarked that the lynching occurred after midnight at the courthouse, a long way from Tillie's home. He thought it unlikely that her father would have taken her, as Tillie told friends, "to see the dragging of the body."[9] He agreed to send me the articles he had sent Tillie.

Back at Stanford, plowing through the early papers, I found innumerable passages Tillie had inked out, apparently to keep words and sentences hidden from her biographer. Still, occasional references to an Abe, Jevons, and AJG had escaped her efforts at censorship.[10] Gradually I realized that these names belonged to one man: Abraham Jevons Goldfarb and that Tillie had been "Mrs. Goldfarb." When I next visited her, I asked about him. Startled, she fired back: "Where did you hear that name?" When I said "from your old letters and diaries," she seemed crestfallen, perhaps angry. It dawned on me that her life story was a huge maze, and I had no annotator to lead me through it, as I had had when writing Virginia Woolf's life.

Before my husband John Fischer came to visit me midway during that research trip, Tillie asked him to bring something to introduce himself. He brought Jonathan Swift's "On Poetry: A Rapsody," whose attack on monarchies had been censored in Swift's lifetime. As John read aloud lines accusing kings of being the lowest of beasts, Tillie roared with laughter.[11]

We stayed up late talking about Swift's seditious writings in eighteenth-century Ireland. John and I left after midnight. As we walked along Laguna Street, something caught our eyes, and we looked up to find charming Tillie blowing bubbles to us out of her bedroom window.

After John went back to Baton Rouge I spent another couple of weeks at Stanford. Though distressed to find that Tillie had hidden much of her life story, I warmed to the challenge of uncovering facts. I shivered, however, to discover that, though I searched box after box of papers, including ones labeled "unidentified fragments," "potential story," and "miscellaneous writings," and looked through boxes of "makings" of her published writings, I found no evidence of the masterpiece that she was said to be writing. Her mysterious publication record and her long, cluttered life seemed like a brier patch. Writing her life might be less honor than entrapment. I thought of laying low or giving up. Instead, I applied for an NEH fellowship to write the biography and also edit a selected edition of her letters. I began to sense that my life story might forever be entangled with hers.

I contacted the journalism teacher at Omaha's Central High School, who gave several senior journalism students extra credit for finding Tillie's "Squeaks" column in ancient copies of the school *Register*. When I next visited Tillie, she asked if I had heard about the time she "almost became a corpse." Of course, I wanted to hear. She said that the organizer of an Italian conference had offered her a room in her Florence apartment. Tillie had climbed four flights of stairs, struggled to open the heavy door, and had fallen inside. Only when the door slammed did she realize that she had left her purse outside and locked herself in. She had no phone, no bathroom, nothing to eat or drink except cheese and a water bottle in her pockets. Needing to pee, she used a cup. Using her suitcase to reach the window, she dumped out her urine, called "help," and wrote notes to throw out the window. She tried to rattle the ancient door, but no one came, so she prepared to die a slow death by starvation, without even an English book to read. Finally, a woman called at the door. Tillie rushed over and called back. Then she heard a key in the lock. When the door opened, Tillie fell into the arms of a woman who spoke no English. Tillie's story was so dramatic and funny—she was so lovable—that I was very grateful she had not become a corpse. I spent my last night in California in her back bedroom in a narrow bed squeezed between file cabinets, which she opened to show me drawings of Karla as a sexy young woman. After Tillie said good-night, rather than engage myself in a moral debate about whether to search the cabinets for clues, I fell asleep.

Before she went on a speaking jaunt—receiving her ninth honorary degree (this one from Amherst College)—I tried to get her blessing. In July 1998, she wrote a letter saying that Panthea Reid was "engaged in writing a biography on my life and work" and "would appreciate an interview, or correspondence with you, to share memories and letters, etc."

The Stanford collection had only a few letters from Tillie, mostly ones her family returned to her or drafts of more formal epistles. On 10 September 1998, Curator Bill McPheron and I cosigned a letter asking Tillie's friends to donate to Stanford letters that they had received from her. Soon a half-century of correspondence began appearing in my LSU and Stanford's Special Collections mailboxes. Old friends, including Sister William and Dick Scowcroft, contacted Tillie for the first time in decades. Barbara Swan sent me a copy of her lithograph of Tillie. On 21 September, Gene Lerner wrote from Rome on impressive stationery from the Anna Magnani Society. He asked to see my Woolf biography and hoped "you can achieve a bio of Til which is dimensioned as well as definitive." Reading my book, he focused on Woolf's struggle writing her Fry biography. He asked me, "does not the subject who still lives make the task more difficult, confusing the role of arbiter?" I had hardly considered myself an arbiter, but when I read the articles Bill Pratt sent I became one. Recognizing that the stories Tillie had told tracked these articles, I suspected that twenty years of brooding over the lynching had transformed information into memory, hence perhaps her deletion from my *DoubleTake* article.[12]

Laurie Olsen and Mike Margolis had begun working on Sunday afternoons to move Tillie to her new place behind their Berkeley house. Working with her, though, soon became working against her: As they packed boxes for Stanford, she would pull out old books and papers and reread and describe them. When she left for a triumphal visit to Omaha, appearing at Creighton and Omaha universities, they tackled her apartment alone. They packed up her keepsakes, including Barbara Swan's portrait of Emily Dickinson, and furniture that would fit in a one-bedroom apartment. After *Omaha World-Herald* proclaimed that "A legend walked the streets of Omaha one recent Wednesday," the legend returned to California, where Laurie and Mike settled her into the apartment, which she called her "tree house," in their back garden, where roses, camellias, and jasmine flourish. They made regular trips across the bay to pack more book boxes, which McPheron trucked to Stanford, while they hauled the last file cabinets for storage beneath Tillie's apartment.

My work got a tremendous boost when I heard from William Ferris, chairman of NEH, that I had won a Fellowship for University Teachers for

1999–2000. With LSU's assistance, by summer 1999, I would be freed of teaching duties to work full-time on editing Tillie's letters and writing her biography. All biographies begin with some coverage of heritage, but Tillie had only three or so stories about her parents' early lives, few names, and no dates so I called the Anna Magnani Society and hoped to find Gene Lerner. A voice answered, "Chaio, hello, this is Gene Lerner." As we talked, he asked if our conversation was confidential. I said it was because I had promised Tillie not to publish the biography while she was alive. He said that he, his other sisters, and brother Harry, before his death, vehemently objected to the picture of their childhood that Tillie had displayed for public consumption. Among her falsehoods were that their father was born in Odessa, had lived in South Omaha, and had worked in mines and packing houses. He asked if Tillie had ever mentioned Abe Goldfarb, the Sappho Club, or her expulsion from Central High. He thought she was "haunted by the past yet unable to embrace it" or to distinguish between "reality and fiction." He suggested I listen to everyone, balance different opinions, and check records. I agreed, as those are the obligations of any biographer. He soon sent me the letter he had written to Jann five years before, announcing that Tillie "cannot be our historian nor inscribe the 'family bible' in her images and her mirrors." Clearly, he expected me to become the historian who would right wrongs that Tillie had done, a rather bigger assignment than the one for which I had bargained. Still, uncovering facts is the biographer's obligation so my courage held.

On 21 February 1999, Tillie called Gene to say, "I'm not calling because of your birthday, but because Clare died." Gene called Howard and Liz Lerner to express grief over the "terrible news," but Liz asked, "what news?" Howard assured his uncle that he would call himself, as he did when Clare did die on 17 March 1999 at the age of eighty-five.[13] Why would Tillie invent her sister-in-law's death before it happened? Gene thought it continued her lifelong tendency to sacrifice truth for drama.

My connections with Mississippi authors took an odd turn when I drove there to work on Tillie Olsen, who had never been to Mississippi.[14] In the Williams Library at the University of Mississippi, across from the William Faulkner Room, the Seymour Lawrence Room contains a treasure trove of letters, to and from Tillie, dated and filed by year from 1965, when she had first signed with Lawrence. I ordered copies of every page, naively thinking that missing facts were mostly found. Gene Lerner had volunteered to research genealogy.[15] While he would cover early history, the Seymour Lawrence files, along with letters arriving in my mailbox almost daily, should cover late history.

Along with letters from Tillie, people began sending memories and comments, which were oddly split between positive raves and negative dismissals. Some people wrote me about Tillie's "radiant sincerity," "tremendous generosity," and her "aura." They thought of her as a legend, a treasure who deserved every woman's adulation. But some wondered why she spoke about her wonderful family mostly as a burden. Many complained that she kept her audiences captive, saying little but repeating it endlessly. Others said she had made a career out of not-writing, had done less with more grants than any other living writer, and used tales of deprivation to extort privileges. How she could be both genuine altruist and self-promoting pretender mystified me. Though she tried to hide information from me, she generously revised our contract for an edition of letters in my favor. She ended a note with a mixture of, I think, resentment and admiration: "What a sleuth you are!!!!!!!!!!!!!!"

Tillie was fond of saying "Visualization creates reality." By the end of the twentieth century, she seems to have thought that if she could keep her early diaries invisible to me, the events they detailed would lose reality. Clearly, she and I were locked in a hide-and-seek game. One of my seeking ventures uncovered the organizer of the 1989 Italian-American conference, Liana Borghi. When I wrote her about Tillie's story of almost becoming a corpse, she was "vastly amused." She said that the ancient door of her Florentine apartment was stiff and hard to open, but Tillie's account of being locked in was a complete fiction.[16] When Tillie could invent such an elaborate, funny story, I wondered why she did not invent new fiction.

In November 1999, the *Progressive* published an interview that began by noting a "self-effacing" Tillie Olsen, who told about sitting "on Eugene V. Debs's lap and given him red roses" and extolled Debs's reminder to telling his listeners that they were not heads or brains but "hands," cowhands or farmhands, to the rich. Repeating the lynching story to good purpose, she said that she used the word "racist, but never 'race': "Race is not a fact. There is only one race: human. Skin color is less than 2 percent of the DNA."[17]

On New Year's 2000, Tillie called Gene Lerner to say, lightheartedly, "I suppose Panthea Reid has been after you." She told him I had "bribed" Central High Students to copy her old "Squeaks" column.[18] Meanwhile, one of Tillie's friends asked about my relationship with her because "all her friends feel very protective of her," which meant, I feared, protecting Tillie's self-image, regardless of facts. Because biography shapes the paraphernalia of a life into a coherent and even plotted narrative, it is like fiction, though based entirely on evidence. The need to "invent the truth," or, in Annie Dillard's words, to "fashion a text," was made more difficult, I was discovering, by a subject who had already invented or fashioned much of her life story.[19]

That January, Gene Lerner came to the United States to see Lillian Lerner Davis in Horsehead, New York, Jann Lerner Brodinsky near Seattle (where they celebrated her ninetieth and his eighty-third birthdays), Tillie Lerner Olsen in Berkeley, Howard and Liz Lerner in Bethesda, and Vicki Lerner Bergman and Hank Kaufman near Miami. He recorded their recollections. In Berkeley, Tillie booked him into a B&B near Laurie and Mike's house and astonished him by paying his hotel bill. For nearly five days, he could not manage "concentrated conversation, what with the telephone calls and constant interruptions and her from time-to-time lame efforts to make order out of her horde of papers," but Gene nonetheless had a "meaningful and warm" reunion with Karla.

His last night in Berkeley was a "truly festive" exhibition of the family community that Tillie and Jack had fostered. Hosting four generations for dinner, Laurie and Mike played "violin and guitar, with shifts from time to time to other instruments. All of us were singing. The songs were mixed: Yiddish, Spirituals, Gershwin's 'Summertime.'" Gene recorded the high-point of the evening when he and little Annie "concocted an improvised ballet. Annie, Til's great-granddaughter, Karla's grand-daughter, Erica's daughter, is studying ballet. I studied modern ballet for nearly three years. And there we were, this five-year-old and this eighty-three-year-young, going at it, with twirls and arabesques as Mike and Laurie accompanied us. It was just great. And everyone was delighted, no one more so than Annie. And me." Gene and Tillie laughed as if there had never been a breach, and Ann Hershey photographed them in a dramatic kiss. They had at last achieved harmony, before he declined into obscurity and she rose into further celebrity. Ann Hershey had begun filming a *Tillie Olsen Story*. That April, Tillie won a Lannan Fellowship to write her memoirs. Mary Anne Ferguson handled recommendations to procure the hand-some award.[20]

Leon Edel, biographer of Henry James, called a biographer a Sherlock Holmes of the library.[21] My detective work took me into scores of libraries, kept me for days and days turning microfilm reels of ancient newspapers, necessitated innumerable calls and letters, sent me to a long list of archives, and also required odd research trips. On 29 May 2000, I flew into Omaha, where the public schools' office pulled records from 1917 into the 1930s from Kellom, Long, and Central High schools. These records prove that Tillie's story of about being kept out of school because she was thought retarded was utterly false. Among other matters, they also establish that she had dropped out of high school in both her junior and senior years.[22]

My most curious research trip was out on the Nebraska plains, where I happened to spot the Saunders County museum, whose curator showed me early twentieth-century land plats and census records. After he called the school board in the tiny town of Wahoo, I drove there and found the office and an almost forsaken outbuilding behind it in which I uncovered the 1916 list of pupils at school #38 in Saunders County that included "Fannie Lehrner." I did not see the farm where the Lerners had share-cropped because the flat land was crossed by indistinguishable, unmarked roads running at right angles to each other and the day was so cloudy I could hardly tell west from east. Finally a slight glow in the west helped me turn east toward better marked roads leading me back to Omaha. On the next day, I interviewed several oldsters who had known Tillie as a girl. I astonished Tillie with my discoveries and the people from her past I had "resurrected." Like Gene, she now called me "detective." Less flatteringly, she said, "You ought to work for the FBI."

When I told her that I would accompany John Fischer to Germany, for the Fourth Münster Symposium on Jonathan Swift, she said, "Oh, you must go to Rome and meet my baby brother." Having already planned to inter-view him, I agreed. After the symposium we set off for Rome. One of Gene Lerner's former employees, now manager at the Hotel Nazionale, made reservations for us at discounted rates; this made me wonder if the rivalry between Tillie and Gene included finagling special hotel rates for friends. Gene preferred to meet me "in a corner of the bar/lounge which was the seat of my 80th birthday celebration" at the Nazionale. He spent three mornings talking to me with verve and wit, hardly taking a break. Noisy tourists arriving from the Piazza Montecitorio, near the Italian parliament, assumed that the handsome gray-haired man in crisp white pants with the impassioned voice was a celebrity conducting an interview for the tabloid press. When John and I visited Gene and Augusto at their apartment on Via Vetulonia, we admired huge photos of movie stars and Augusto's abstract paintings that nearly covered the walls.[23]

Back from Europe just long enough to recoup some energy, I flew into Oakland on 14 July 2000 and checked into the pleasant B&B hotel in Berkeley where Gene had stayed. Tillie had had a spinal block a few days before and was supposed to stay in bed, but she had awakened at three in the morning and had scrubbed her sink, kitchen, and bathroom floor before getting back to bed and trying to read. When I came over, she was still in bed, hunting under the covers for Philip Roth's *I Married a Communist* and wondering how he got so much insider information. Wearing a fleece vest and apron over a granny gown, she showed me around her new quarters, which had a living room and bedroom on either end and kitchen and bath between. On her bulletin board were post cards of W.E.B. Du Bois and one of Abraham and Tad Lincoln, obituaries of old friends, and many photos, including one of a horse named "Tillie" at Flyaway Farms, New York.

She saved me a large hotel bill by offering me the key to an absent friend's nearby apartment. About noon the next day I told her I had a confession. She asked if I wanted to go into a closet nearby. I said no, that she (as priest) should be hidden in the closet. Then I "confessed" that I was to see Alice Walker at two in the afternoon so we had better have lunch. We walked to her favorite restaurant with Tillie stopping along the way to rub her aching back against street signs, in what she called her "doggie routine." At lunch, she talked on and on, apparently forgetting my "confession." By the time we walked back to Tillie's place and I settled her in, I had to call and tell Alice Walker that I would be late. After narrating various stories about Tillie's befriending her and then colonizing her and others, Alice Walker ended graciously by saying that Tillie "has a good heart." Walker warned, "What a job you've got to do." I agreed. When we parted, she said, "It's going to be rich." I hoped so.[24]

When I got back, Tillie was curious. Looking east, she kept saying "where Alice Walker lives." She asked if Walker displayed photos of her parents as sharecroppers and she wanted to know what we had talked about. Apropos of nothing, Tillie proclaimed that she had been asked to make a speech at Grace Cathedral. Then she began a monologue about the trip to China, both outbursts clearly intended to counter whatever Alice Walker had told me.

While Tillie rested, I settled at a small desk in her living room and began trying to organize a huge cardboard box labeled "Jack." I found wonderful war letters mixed up with old bills, credit card receipts, and union business records. I separated out the letters and sorted them into decades which I put in large labeled envelopes. Tillie fretted that her letters to Jack were hasty and ordinary because everybody wrote to servicemen. She said that she had a wartime job, with a staff and responsibility for the servicemen's center and canteen, and had driven all about northern California; thus, she had no time to write literary letters. She laughed that her real claim to fame was being a three-time answer in the *New York Times* crossword puzzle.

Because I was driving to Stanford early the next morning, I wanted to take Tillie, Laurie, Mike, and their younger son Josh, to an early dinner by the bay. As the afternoon wore on and Tillie remained in her granny gown and vest, I kept asking how long it would take her to get ready. Finally, she said it would only take her ten minutes because she didn't wear makeup. While I sorted more letters, she disappeared and returned in a handsome black velvet pants suit, with a blue silk scarf, earrings, black dancing slippers, black socks with little flowers on them, and perfume. Only later did she recall that she had not had a bath since having the spinal block. Her outfit and perfume nicely covered any failure of hygiene but could not disguise evidence that, at eighty-eight, though still hearty and witty, she was slipping.

I drove down to Stanford the next day and returned after the Green Library closed. At Tillie's that evening, I found my envelopes of Jack's letters emptied out and everything scattered into a virtual rat's nest on her sofa. I needed to make copies to take home, but, without acknowledging that I had only days, not months, in California, she wanted me merely to take notes about the letters. I met Julie Olsen Edwards for the first time the next morning. Scrambling eggs, she disclosed that Tillie was terrified about money and afraid to pay someone to clean or do secretarial work so the family had hired a devoted graduate student named Michelle Matz for a combination of paper-sorting and overseeing. Julie gave her mother a bath, washed her hair, and settled her back in bed because she felt dizzy from heart palpitations. Julie told me that Tillie psyched herself up to dazzle friends and doctors—making people protest that she could not be eighty-eight—but such performances left both friends and physicians ill-prepared to assess her actual troubles. When I found a lunch-box poem about the ill-fated egg-salad sandwich she had intended to make for Jack,[25] the indefatigable Tillie rose from bed to read it aloud with such verve we were all convulsed in laughter. Julie and Laurie said that I could copy letters from their father and grandfather so Tillie agreed; I rushed to a photocopy shop before she changed her mind.

I stayed in Palo Alto for several more days searching the Tillie Olsen Papers. I took notes on everything and ordered photocopies of important papers to study at home. I still found no evidence of a near-finished *Requa* and only snatches of the unfinished novel. I returned to Berkeley on the weekend when Rebekah Edwards joined Tillie and me for lunch. Her great-uncle Gene had sent her the family tree that I had diagrammed from his discoveries. When I said that relatives in Moscow had told Gene that Ida's father had been called "Rabbi," Tillie seemed flummoxed. When I told them about Mendel Lerner running a small school, as well as a mill and tavern, she was upset. When Rebekah said she had never heard of Abe Goldfarb before, Tillie changed the subject to writer Paul Auster, who, she said, had been better paid for his archive than she for hers, although she was a "much more important writer." Later, Bill McPheron remarked that, if Tillie had sent on her papers when she signed the contract, instead of haggling and prevaricating, she could have banked Stanford's large payment and received income, even as her capital from Stanford increased in value. After ten days of yo-yoing, to use her phrase, between Berkeley and Palo Alto, I returned to Baton Rouge, daunted. Tillie had always been an unreliable narrator of her own life, thus the errors in published critical accounts were not the critics' fault, except in that they took her word. Her determination to protect her image, along with her failing memory, now made her an even more untrustworthy narrator. Still, she was losing her ability to hide her past, while I was honing my ability to discover it.

Gene Lerner put me in touch with Lillian Lerner Davis, who drew the layout of the Caldwell Street house and its neighborhood. I sent Gene one of Rae Schochet's blasts at Tillie and Abe over their neglect of Karla. He recalled that "their behavior made our Mother Ida weep, other times angered her, as it infuriated me and others in the family." Gene had spent more than a year consulting with family, gathering and organizing old letters and records, cataloging Lerner papers, and writing a narrative about the Lerner clan and its ancestry. After Peter Howard gave a modest estimate of their value, Stanford purchased his "Lerner Family Papers." Bill McPheron wrote Gene: "How beautifully structured and finely written is your account of the Lerner family!" (He would never have similarly complimented Tillie for her supposedly explanatory post-it notes and indeed her "makings" and "blueies," which are neither structured nor finely written.[26])

Ann Hershey and Julie accompanied Tillie to the East, where Ann filmed Tillie and Julie singing together in a New York taxi and in Boston visiting her old friend Red Tovish. Tillie complained, "I have this woman attached to me with a camera, like an umbilical cord," but she loved being a film star, just as she loved my *DoubleTake* article. I was proud of it, too, except that Tillie's deletions turned my article from biography to hagiography.

When John Fischer chaired LSU's English department, we started a town-gown support group called "Readers and Writers," which, with the College of Arts and Sciences, in early 2001 invited Tillie and Ann Hershey to Baton Rouge. Laurie Olsen was scheduled to be in Lafayette, Louisiana, for a conference on bilingual education so we timed Tillie's visit to coincide with hers. At the airport, we were unnerved to see Tillie emerging from the plane's corridor leaning on Ann on one side and a cane on the other. Because they stayed with us, John and I saw that Tillie ate breakfast, went to bed early, had a not-too-tiring tour of Acadiana, with time to rest before our Saturday party. Needing no cane, she amazed guests with her beauty, wit, and vitality. On Sunday, 4 February 2001, we took Tillie and Ann (now "Annie" to us) to a Cajun restaurant in an old country store. When I recommended the oyster and artichoke soup, Tillie said that, after being pregnant in Stockton where she had little to eat but artichokes, she would never eat another.[27] When she wondered why there were no blacks in the restaurant, except presumably in the kitchen, I volunteered, lamely, that Oprah had recently visited and that Ernest Gaines was a known patron. John, more usefully, pointed out that most local blacks were in church.

Laurie Olsen arrived by late afternoon to hear her mother reading "I Stand Here Ironing." After the last line ("she is more than this dress on the ironing board, helpless before the iron"), a tearful audience could hardly stop cheering, until I took over to suggest that they speak with Tillie in the lobby where she could sit and sign books. As hundreds lined up to get her autograph, Tillie told Malcolm Richardson, then chair of the department, "You owe it to your readers—your readers complete your writing." When one of my older students told her that she too had been a single mother, Tillie rose to hug her, both of them in tears. As people waited for her blessing and her signature, Annie Hershey kept filming. Later I found that Tillie had signed many books in unusually large letters, "Visibility Creates Reality." I wondered if Annie and I too had been "colonized" by Tillie Olsen. Annie was making her public persona more visible. I would illumine the real Tillie beneath the facade, if I could find her.

While Tillie was still signing books, John and I went home to set the table and warm up the pot of soup I had made in advance. Our California guests returned just before ten in the evening, and we made sure Tillie ate something and then got to bed. The next day, she spoke at a luncheon session with women's studies students, at which she ate nothing. She promised to read papers and stories from these enthusiastic young women, though Annie and I knew she would not. When the campus paper reported that Tillie Olsen "had to work to support her family during the Great Depression instead of attending high school," I wondered if the student reporter had misunderstood or if Tillie had really made that claim.

Tillie and I did not talk about the 2000 election, which Al Gore won, barely, in the popular vote but the Supreme Court gave to George W. Bush to avoid a Florida recount. Just after inauguration day, I happened to call a long-time lefty named Marvin Gettleman. He was just back from D.C. where he had held up signs saying "Hail to the Thief." I suspect Tillie wanted to be there, too.

Her terrific performance in Baton Rouge emboldened her to accept other invitations. At the end of March, she was keynote speaker at a South Carolina conference on Charlotte Perkins Gilman. She read a pastiche of prose from Gilman and herself. She no doubt had failed to eat and, with no one watching over her, probably to sleep. Before she got to the end of "I Stand Here Ironing," under bright spot lights, she collapsed on the stage. Later, when I talked to her on the phone, she was mightily impressed with the drama of being whisked to a hospital with sirens screeching. On 5 April, she was honored in San Francisco.[28] Then, on 23 April, with Annie Hershey, she flew to the Midwest to read at Grinnell College and receive a plaque at Central High's centennial. She fainted at Grinnell and was sent to the hospital. Her readings were cancelled, but students came to the hospital to read to her from her works. In Omaha, Annie drove Tillie to the home of Oliver and Karen Pollak, where she collapsed again, and was sent by ambulance to another hospital. Under oxygen, she returned to the Pollaks, where she received guests from her bed. Apparently near death, Tillie recited phrases she would have included in the "Death Treasury." Back in her Berkeley apartment, when Annie scolded her for not wearing her doctor-ordered support hose, a spunky, very much alive Tillie said, "Remember, I refused to wear a girdle."

I feared that I would never finish Tillie's life while teaching, grading papers, reading dissertations, and serving on committees at LSU. Reluctantly, John finally agreed to make a drastic move, and we retired from active duty in May 2001. Several farewell speeches made it sound as if my main accomplishment in twenty-five years at LSU was bringing Tillie Olsen to campus. Our move to Princeton, New Jersey, was a long and complicated process, but by late summer we had our house and his Swift and my Olsen files in order. I started contacting people again, provoking a call from Tillie in a pique after a protective friend read her the questions I dared ask.

That fall, having heart palpitations, Tillie feared being left alone so family and friends took turns being with her. Michelle Matz told me that, when Tillie was obstreperous, she would threaten to "tell Panthea on you." Tillie began talking of anointing a family member to write her life story, a sad attempt, I thought, to checkmate me. Belatedly, it dawned on me that Tillie had never signed a statement specifically allowing me to put her unpublished materials into print. However much I had honed my investigative skills, if I could not publish my findings, she would win our hide-and-seek game. I quickly wrote up a permission statement for Tillie to sign. To my horror, she refused. I had spent years tracking down the facts of her life and had resigned my job for, it now seemed, nothing. Annie feared that Tillie would die before she could finish her film; I, however, feared that she would live on and on, preventing publication of my biography.

Tillie had seemed oblivious to the 9/11 destruction of the World Trade Towers and the backlash to it until she told a pharmacologist wearing a head scarf, "You must be having a very hard time right now." As they embraced, the compassionate, still crusading Tillie said, "We're all sisters trying to take care of our children." The Muslim woman said, "You're the first person to treat me well since 9/11."[29]

Despite her collapses in South Carolina, Iowa, and Nebraska, and her heart palpitations, in 2002, Tillie revved herself up for more grand appearances. When she received a plaque in Los Angeles at the Western Workers Labor Heritage, the entire audience rose to sing "Happy Birthday, Dear Tillie," for her ninetieth birthday. On another trip to Los Angeles, Tillie seemed as proud of being picked up at the airport by her brother-in-law Max in his Rolls Royce as of receiving the Kirsch Award from the *Los Angeles Times*. Then she flew to San Antonio to give another moving performance of "I Stand Here Ironing." Afterward, she kissed a local reporter on the mouth, giving her "almost a religious experience. I felt kissed by a saint."[30] Following Dylan Thomas, Tillie told herself: "Do not go gentle into that good night." I think she imagined dying on stage, under the spotlight. Certainly, she gave herself opportunities to do so.

When John and I drove to western New York State, Lillian Lerner Davis confirmed stories about Tillie's early scandalous misbehavior. While I felt buffeted one way by her testimony, a letter from Mary Anne Ferguson buffeted me the other way. She and others were "worried about your vision of Tillie. She has defects but in my opinion her good qualities far outweigh any eccentricities and difficulties." I reevaluated: did I resemble Janet Malcolm's picture of the biographer as professional burglar "breaking into a house, rifling through certain drawers that he has good reason to think contain the jewelry and money, and triumphantly bearing his loot away."[31]I honestly think I am not such a biographer. For one thing, there was no "loot," figurative or literal, in trying to unravel the riddles of Tillie Olsen's fame and failings, grandeur and pettiness. Fearing I had wasted years, money, and job, all for naught, I asked Annie Hershey to try again to get Tillie to grant me permission to quote from her unpublished papers. Annie gave her the letter, but it soon disappeared inside a haystack of papers. By this time, I felt biased toward the generous Tillie, but biased against the controlling Tillie. With help from the Authors' Guild and my son Reid Broughton, an attorney, I wrote a new permission letter

At the end of August, Tillie was suffering from stomach pains, leg pains and dizziness, but she avoided another hospital stay, and I traveled to California in September 2002, yo-yoing again between Stanford and Berkeley,

where I stayed with Laurie and Mike. Whenever I questioned Tillie, she kept
to her familiar stories, evading actual details, while I struggled to probe
beneath canned answers. We were locked in an ever fiercer battle between
hiding and finding. Tillie seemed to be winning.

One day, Annie drove with me to Stanford to film some of the Tillie
Olsen Papers. She particularly wanted to see the early 1930s scrapbooks
Tillie had made out of Omaha and San Francisco phone books, but they
turned out visually as confusing as her handwriting. On the way back,
Annie confided that Tillie told people she was writing two hours every
morning but was doing no such thing. She was, I observed, trying to keep
the tapestry of her life intact, regardless of reality. One evening Annie
and Carol Osmer-Newhouse invited Tillie and me to dinner. Driving up
to El Sobrante, Tillie seemed like my grandmother, reading signs aloud
and telling me "left" when Annie's directions said "right." I talked about
the trove of letters from Rae Schochet that I'd gone through at Stanford;
I did not remind Tillie that she said she had given them to Karla. I said
that her undated early diaries were a puzzle, but a universal calendar
could identify, say, "Friday, the 15th" by month and year, so I now could
date entries and piece her early life into chronological order. Suddenly the
befuddled old woman reading road signs became the perceptive genius
realizing the implications of my ordering system. She responded, "I wish
I hadn't left all those diaries to Stanford." Since she had, though, she
accepted that she might lose the hide-and-seek game. On 14 September
2002, I showed her my revised letter that thanked her for making her
unpublished materials available to scholars and asked her permission
to "quote from original documents and cite information that you have
provided." Exclaiming, "What a nice letter," she signed with a flourish,
though she did add a comma, as Sara Vore Taylor had taught her nearly
seventy-five years before, between "September" and "2002."

Riddles posed by the life of Tillie Lerner Olsen center on her productivity, her self-invention, and the disparity between the admirable and the
unadmirable Tillie. Early diaries, poems, satires, and letters leave no doubt
about the literary brilliance and easy productivity of Tillie Lerner. Early star
power, however, I realized, had encouraged overconfidence and excused
a lack of discipline. Then the Communist Party spoiled her as much as
her parents had. Party members disregarded bourgeois values and encouraged her to conceptualize through ideology. When she began her 1930s
novel, she created clearly realized members of the Holbrook family, but
the further disasters she had planned before communism and the salvation
she intended after it were abstract, as indicated by the difference between,

in Bennett Cerf's words, the "glowing and alive" chapters she wrote mostly in 1932–1933 and the tedious list of catastophes (Appendix C) she sent to Donald Klopfer in 1935. In the 1950s, weaned from communism, Tillie produced the great stories in *Tell Me a Riddle*, all based on actual people, mostly her family, and on actual events, not ideology.

The grants she began winning in the 1950s, along with the advances she received from Malcolm Cowley and then Sam Lawrence, however, spoiled her. Once again a residue of party ideology was the culprit. Rather as Tillie Lerner had expected Bennett Cerf, in Ella Winter's word, to "keep" her, Tillie Olsen believed that, after the insults and deprivations she suffered during the Depression and the McCarthy years, she was entitled to be kept by foundations and artists' colonies.

Tillie often spoke of being a partially destroyed human being, blaming years of doing others' typing for her painstaking writing method. She spent years reworking sentences in "Tell Me a Riddle" and produced a brilliantly distilled masterpiece. She never, however, managed such specificity, distillation, and wholeness again, except when heavily edited. Though grants gave her years to write, she was an easily distracted procrastinator. Squabbling over what she had already written kept her from writing new works. Laudable activities like researching history, rereading favorite books, and writing blurbs for friends also kept her from writing. Her exhausting lecture tours were a means of avoiding writing. Following what she once privately acknowledged as megalomania, Tillie reinvented herself as a *grande dame*, celebrated for performing her famous stories, rather than writing new ones.

On several occasions Tillie spoke of having a "breakdown" or a "mini-breakdown," and perhaps she did have one in 1961. Over the years, the liberties she took with language developed into a disregard for clarity, as well as legibility. Bits of the novel she had promised the Ford Foundation, the Radcliffe Institute, NEA, and the Guggenheim suggest a fragmented mind-set, as do the unfinished "Requa I" and *Yonnondio*, the scrapbook-like *Silences*, and the unpublished papers at Stanford (see note 26). The pieces she sent to Jonathan Alter at *Newsweek* offer evidence that Tillie had lost her ability to synthesize. Such a loss would be natural in an old woman, especially one doomed to develop Alzheimer's, but I think this loss began as early as her fifties. And it terrified her. In a very few diary entries and letters, she expressed the gnawing fear that she had lost the ability to write, even while she publicly claimed to be almost finished writing a novella, a novel, and a collection of her talks. She occasionally spoke of writing her autobiography, clearly in hopes of preserving her preferred self-image without acknowledging how much of her life story she had exaggerated or fabricated. The Lannan Fellowship to write her memoirs was the last in a long list of grants she won with promises she did not keep.

Since the mid-1930s, Tillie feared that, if she did not write, no one else would speak for lost, forgotten people. Telling their stories seemed her moral obligation, her way of honoring her mother and expressing her own conviction that the proletariat, when not thwarted, can make profound contributions to civilization. Fearlessly speaking up for women and minorities, she finally saw herself as more a catalytic speaker than a writer. Possibly her inspiring presence did mean more than her unwritten novel would have. Certainly, her resurrection of nearly forgotten women writers was an invaluable contribution to human history. But I wondered how she got away with winning so many awards and advances on what one of my correspondents calls the "greatest book never told." The principal riddle growing out of my discoveries about the life of Tillie Olsen is how she managed to hide the terrible secret that she could no longer write.

My emphasis on twentieth-century American history answers, at least in part, that question. Tillie Olsen was the hero twentieth-century American culture needed: a writer capable of producing powerful, moving prose that exposed women's actual lives, outlining the effects of sexism on women's minds and bodies, ensuring that motherhood is not understood as a subject for once-a-year cards and flowers but a determinate of everyone's life, pointing out how sexist power structures were, and still are, in American society.[32]

Furthermore, we needed a feminist hero who had been oppressed by a male exploitative society and was rescued by herself with the help of other women. We believed that women would make love not war, that women would be kinder, gentler leaders of corporations, universities, and countries. Such beliefs further spoiled Tillie. When I have suggested to those who see her as savior that she was inclined to falsify, these devotées seem not to care about her fabrications, though they would like to silence me. Their reaction suggests that perhaps Tillie's casual attitude toward facts anticipated a late twentieth-century and early twenty-first century disdain for what George W. Bush reputedly called "truthiness."

Maybe, if Tillie Olsen had not been so lionized, if she had had to be accountable to foundations, publishers, and audiences, she might have gotten her life and mind in order and written the long-promised great novel and some promised new stories. Or, if fiction-writing was simply beyond her power, she should have stopped promising publishers and foundations an illusory output. With an editor, she might have gathered her most insightful speeches into the "Harvestings" volume. Or maybe she could have enjoyed her old age without putting herself on one treadmill after another.

As she turned ninety-two in 2004, Tillie's decline accelerated. She could not remember dates, could not answer her message machine, and panicked because she could not remember her next invented lecture date. She continued to claim that she was writing every day. As her short-term memory failed, her long-term inventiveness thrived. She fooled family and caretakers with stories about nonexistent visitors and newly scheduled appearances. Family and friends rallied around her. Laurie and Mike did the cooking, shopping, laundry, and pill-monitoring, while Karla, Julie, Kathie, grandchildren, and friends spelled them. Annie came over in the mornings to make breakfast and was sometimes there to tuck Tillie in at night. The strain was physically and emotionally wearing on everyone, though moments when Tillie read the funnies aloud, told silly jokes, and hugged visitors and caretakers helped to compensate. The family sent papers from the downstairs files to Stanford, which then made its final payment.

Tillie fretted about her lost children and also her lost parents. She took a postcard with a picture of a tree in a storm, wrote a note, and asked Laurie to mail it for her. It read:

Dearest Mom and Dad:
I am in jail here. No, no charges against me that I know. I don't know how I got here. Please get me a good lawyer. This is a nightmare.
                              Love Always, Tillie Lerner Olsen.

P. S. my new book is just out. I wish you could see it. Am not sure your address now, or if you have moved or not. I don't know where you are. I feel like this tree blowing in the wild wild winds. Stay well dear ones. Write when you can. Try to find me if you can.

That sad note was the last that Tillie Lerner Olsen, as she so clearly signed herself, wrote. She was soon diagnosed with mid-stage Alzheimer's. A letter, signed by Scott Turow, Grace Paley, and Florence Howe, asked friends in "the spirit of the rent parties she and Jack gave during the 1930s and again in the 1950s," for contributions to help Tillie, now a "comrade in need." Contributions, the Stanford money, and Tillie's social security and royalties, along with heroic efforts from her family and friends, kept her at home as long as possible.

Meanwhile, Lillian Lerner Davis fell, cracking her hip, and died on 12 March in the Finger Lakes region of New York. On 31 May, Jann Lerner Brodinsky died, from Alzheimer's. And on 20 July, Gene Lerner also died of Alzheimer's. In November, Tillie's family moved her into a residential Alzheimer's facility in Oakland. Karla Lutz visited her mother every day and supervised her care with vigilance and compassion. Friends and other family members visited regularly so Tillie was rarely alone. She seemed at peace.

Once, Annie Hershey walked out of the elevator there and heard Tillie's voice singing to herself, hearty and content, from one of her labor song books. She did not seem to notice other residents mumbling mindlessly. She seemed to have disappeared inside herself. Once when Julie was with her, however, an aide was giving a resident a hard time and, out of her own fog, Tillie emerged to say to the other woman, "Remember you are a human being."

I visited Tillie in the Lakeview Home in summer 2006. On my first visit, I came with Annie Hershey, and Tillie seemed to know neither of us. A week later Julie picked me up in front of the San Francisco Public Library to drive to Oakland. Julie went over old scrapbooks and photographs with Tillie, trying to keep family names and faces alive in her memory. When Julie left, Tillie and I shuffled out into the residents' garden. She brought along a well-worn copy of Emily Dickinson's poetry and read aloud in a still strong voice. Unless I turned the page for her, however, she would read to its bottom and then begin reading from the top of the same page. She had no idea who I was but seemed comfortable enough. When I asked her if she would like me to read to her, she nodded, so I took the book and found "The Snake," which seems a "whip-lash/ Unbraiding in the sun" and causes "a tighter breathing,/ And zero at the bone." Dramatizing my reading for Tillie's benefit, I found her looking up at me with a glimmer of recognition. But when Julie and I took her to dinner in a place by the bay where she could watch the boats and the gulls, she seemed to have faded inside herself again. As I kissed her good-bye, I told her again that I loved her.

Tillie died early on New Year's Day 2007, with her family around her, singing the old songs she loved. Laurie thought she saw a tear trickle down her mother's cheek before she slipped away.

EPILOGUE

On 17 February 2007, at the First Congregational Church of Oakland, family and friends held a memorial service called a "Celebration of the Life of Tillie Olsen." Mike Margolis called the community together by blowing on a conch shell; Karla Lutz and Tillie's caregivers danced and sang an Amharic welcome chant in honor of Tillie. Annie Hershey showed clips from her retitled film *Tillie Olsen: A Heart in Motion.* Julie, Kathie, and Laurie gave moving tributes to their mother. Ronnie Gilbert, a member of the Weavers, sang "Bread & Roses," Melanie de More sang "Lift Every Voice and Sing," grandson Jesse Olsen Margolis played his "Song for Tillie." Other friends and close family members celebrated her life and work. The community sang together. During this beautiful tribute, hundreds of people wept. Certainly I did.

On 11 September, the Feminist Press held another memorial, this one in New York City. Laurie and Karla came east for the occasion. Laurie delighted the audience with the talk she had given in Oakland. Bad weather had prevented Florence Howe from making the Oakland celebration so she presented her remarks in New York. Women writers, including Marilyn French, Edith Konecky, and Jane Lazarre, spoke of Tillie's influence through her fiction and friendship.

At the MLA meeting in Chicago at the end of December, two sessions were devoted to Tillie Olsen. One offered an advance viewing of Ann Hershey's film, which shows mostly the adored and adorable Tillie. The other was to be an assessment of Tillie's life and work. At that session, I argued that we honor Tillie's legacy by understanding facts rather than perpetuating falsities. I began by listing erroneous but accepted tales about her life: that the Lerners lived in south Omaha where her father worked in the meat-packing houses, that she was kept out of school until age nine because she was thought retarded, that she dropped out of high school to support her family. I had intended to offer instances from her entire life, but before I could proceed further, I was told that my time was up.

Because other speakers had taken much more time, cutting me off seemed an attempt to censor me by those who want to canonize Tillie.

However heartfelt were my tears at the Oakland celebration, I have never adored Tillie. I wept then for an ideal evoked by powerful words and music. I suppose I also wept realizing that my discoveries about this larger-than-life woman would diminish her idealized public image. I feared too that my discoveries might tarnish the progressive causes in which I also believe. My biographer's obligation, however, is to try to tell the truth as artfully as possible and not to let love hamper honesty.

I think that true love accepts the complete person, but adoration does not. My more than ten years working on this book have been filled with exasperation and excitement, fury and fascination, tedium and love, but not adoration. Early in *Two Lives*, Janet Malcolm makes a case for Gertrude Stein as the writer "whose work most cries out for the assistance of biography in its interpretation." Because the public images of Tillie Olsen are such products of her times, I believe that her life cries out even more for this objective biography, with its mixed verdict on Tillie Lerner Olsen and with, I hope, most riddles solved.

I expected writing this biography would be fun. Alice Walker said it would be rich. My forays into history as far back as czarist Russia and as far east as mainland China, into times poignantly mixed with pain and hope, have been deeply enriching for me. I hope my readers will find this book enriching for them as well.

BIBLIOGRAPHY OF PRIMARY WORKS BY TILLIE LERNER OLSEN

(excluding most reprints)

[* indicates works I have discovered and added to Olsen's bibliography.]

[** indicates minor works not usually included in Olsen's bibliography.]

Tillie Lerner. "At Fourteen Years" and "Not You I Weep For" [1926–1929]. In *First Words: Earliest Writing from Favorite Contemporary Authors*, edited by Paul Mandelbaum. Chapel Hill: Algonquin Books, 1993.

———. "I Want You Women Up North to Know." *The Partisan* (March 1934). Reprint, *Feminist Studies* (Fall 1981); *Writing Red: An Anthology of American Women Writers, 1930–40*. New York: The Feminist Press, 1987.

———. "There is a Lesson." *The Daily Worker* (5 March 1934). Reprint, *The Partisan* (April 1934).

———. "The Iron Throat." *The Partisan Review* 2 (April/May 1934).

———. "Thousand-Dollar Vagrant." *The New Republic* (29 August 1934).

———. "The Strike." *The Partisan Review* (September/October, 1934). Reprint [with small changes], *The Young Worker* (25 September and 9 October 1934).

———.* "The Yes Men of the Sacramento Court: Fake Witnesses Stutter Their Parts Despite Many Careful Rehearsals." *The Western Worker: Western Organ of the Communist Party U. S. A.* (22 November 1934).

———.* "Why They're Trying Don." *Young Worker* (18 December 1934).

———.* Review of *Call It Sleep*, by Henry Roth. *Pacific Weekly* (18 November 1935).

———.* "Burlesque With Dignity—The Secret of Gilbert and Sullivan." *Daily People's World* (1 January 1938).

———.* "'Suspect' Lets Down San Francisco Audience." *Daily People's World* (3 February 1938).

———.* "Lowdown on 'Women.'" *Daily People's World* (11 February 1938).

———.* "Franklin, Champion of Freedom." *Daily People's World* (17 February 1938).

———.* "Simplicity of Portrayal of Workers Makes 'The Wave' a Great Picture." *Daily People's World* (25 February 1938).

————.* "Noted Publisher Here: To Visit Tom Mooney." *Daily People's World* (26 February 1938).

————.* "'Golden Boy' Most Thrilling and Important Play of Year, But Odets Pulled Punches." *Daily People's World* (16 April 1938).

Tillie Olsen. * "Price Gouge Rackets Raise Price, Lower Quality—Watch Close." *Labor Herald* (5 February 1943).

————.* "TILLIE OLSEN SAYS: No Time for 'Household Hints.'" *Daily People's World* (18 April 1946).

————.* "The Struggle to Maintain Women's Wartime Gains." *Daily People's World* (2 May 1946).

————.* "Wartime Gains of Women in Industry." *Daily People's World* (9 May 1946).

————.* "There's a New Job for Jobless Women." *Daily People's World* (16 May 1946).

————.* "WHAT DO YOU THINK? 'Politically Active' Mothers—One View." *Daily People's World* (23 May 1946).

————.* "TILLIE OLSEN SAYS: Back to the Slave Shops?" *Daily People's World* (6 June 1946).

————.** "On the Writing of a Story." In *Stanford Short Stories, 1956*, edited by Wallace Stegner and Richard Scowcroft. Stanford: Stanford University Press, 1956.

————. "Help Her to Believe." In *Stanford Short Stories, 1956*, edited by Stegner and Scowcroft. Reprint, *Pacific Spectator* (Winter 1956). Reprint, as "I Stand Here Ironing," in *Best American Short Stories, 1957*, edited by Martha Foley and David Burnette. Boston: Houghton Mifflin, 1957.

————. "Hey Sailor, What Ship?" In *New Campus Writing, No. 2*, edited by Nolan Miller, assisted by Judson Jerome. New York: G. P. Putnam's Sons and Bantam Books, 1957.

————. "Baptism." *Prairie Schooner* 31 (1957). Revised as "O Yes," in *Tell Me a Riddle*.

————. "Tell Me a Riddle." In *New World Writing No. 16* (1960). Reprinted in *Best American Short Stories, 1961*, edited by Martha Foley and David Burnett. Boston: Houghton Mifflin, 1961.

————. *Tell Me a Riddle: A Collection*. Reprints of "I Stand Here Ironing," "Hey Sailor, What Ship," "O Yes," and "Tell Me a Riddle." Philadelphia and New York: J. B. Lippincott, 1961.

————. "Silences: When Writers Don't Write." *Harper's Magazine* (October 1965).

————. "Requa." *Iowa Review* (Summer 1970). Reprint, "Requa I," in *Best American Short Stories, 1971*. Boston: Houghton Mifflin, 1971.

————.** "Momma's Revolt." [Transcribed by Katha Amatnick (Sarachild) from remarks made at Old Westbury College, March 1972], *Woman's World* (July-September 1972).

————. "Women Who Are Writers in Our Century: One Out of Twelve." *College English* (October 1972).

————.** "Tillie Olsen's Reading Lists." *Spectrum: Women's Studies Newsletters* (1972–1973).

————. "A Biographical Interpretation." Afterword to Rebecca Harding Davis, *Life in the Iron Mills*. New York: Feminist Press, 1972.

————. *Yonnondio: From the Thirties*. New York: Delacorte Press/Seymour Lawrence, 1974.

————.** "Excerpts from a talk by Tillie Olsen." *Trellis* [University of Southern California at Santa Cruz] (Summer 1978), 35–42.

————. *Silences*. New York: Delacorte Press/ Seymour Lawrence, 1978.

————.*An unidentified episode, apparently using "Dream-Vision," on "Turnabout" television series, early 1979.

————.** "Foreword" to *Black Women Writers at Work*, edited by Claudia Tate. New York: Continuum, 1983.

————. "Dream-Vision." In *Mother to Daughter: Daughter to Mother: Mothers on Mothering; A Daybook and Reader Selected and Shaped by Tillie Olsen*. Old West-bury, N.Y.: Feminist Press, 1984.

————.** "The Word Made Flesh." 12th Annual Reninger Lecture, in *Critical Thinking/ Critical Writing*. Cedar Falls, Iowa: Educational Service Publication, 1984.

————. "Mothers & Daughters." With Julie Olsen Edwards, in *Mothers and Daughters: That Special Quality: An Exploration in Photographs*, edited by Tillie Olsen, Julie Olsen Edwards, and Estelle Jussim. New York: Aperture, 1987.

————.** [On a Year of "Writing Resurrection"]. In *First Drafts, Last Drafts: Forty Years of the Creative Writing Program at Stanford*, edited by William McPheron. Stanford: Stanford University Libraries, 1989.

————.** "Introduction." To *Allegra Maud Goldman*, by Edith Konecky. New York: Feminist Press, 1990.

————.* "A Homage to Agostino Rosati." [Translated as "Omaggio ad Agostino Rosati"] *Rosati Exhibit Catalogue*. Il Quadrato di Idea, Via Panisperna 261, Rome, 1992.

————.** ["To Sam."] *Seymour Lawrence Publisher: An Independent Imprint Dedicated to Excellence*. Boston: Houghton Mifflin and Seymour Lawrence, Inc., 1990.

————. "The '30s: A Vision of Fear and Hope." *Newsweek* (3 January 1994).

————.** "Foreword" and "Afterword." To *Bright Web in the Darkness*, by Alexander Saxton. Berkeley: University of California Press, 1997.

————.** "Response." *Frontiers: A Journal of Women Studies* (November 1997).

FAMILY TREE

OLSEN, LERNER, GOLDBERG, AND GOLDFARB FAMILIES

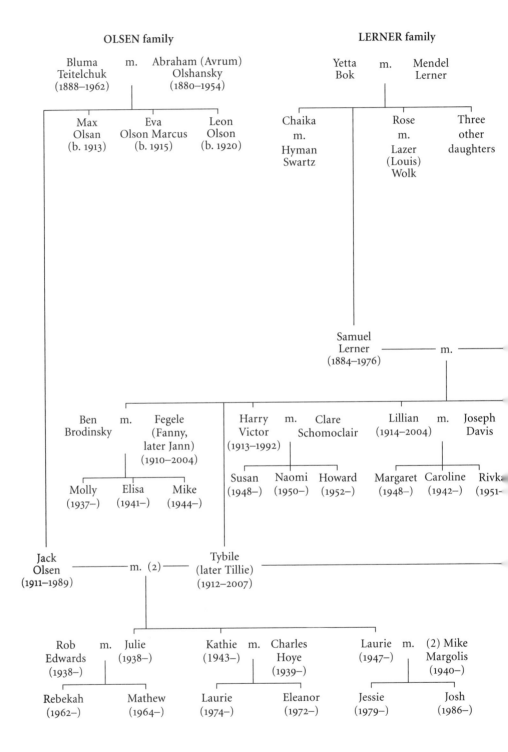

OLSEN family

Bluma Teitelchuk (1888–1962) m. Abraham (Avrum) Olshansky (1880–1954)

Max Olsan (b. 1913)

Eva Olson Marcus (b. 1915)

Leon Olson (b. 1920)

LERNER family

Yetta Bok m. Mendel Lerner

Chaika m. Hyman Swartz

Rose m. Lazer (Louis) Wolk

Three other daughters

Samuel Lerner (1884–1976) ——— m. ———

Ben Brodinsky m. Fegele (Fanny, later Jann) (1910–2004)

Molly (1937–) Elisa (1941–) Mike (1944–)

Harry Victor (1913–1992) m. Clare Schomoclair

Susan (1948–) Naomi (1950–) Howard (1952–)

Lillian (1914–2004) m. Joseph Davis

Margaret (1948–) Caroline (1942–) Rivka (1951–

Jack Olsen (1911–1989) ——— m. (2) ——— Tybile (later Tillie) (1912–2007)

Rob Edwards (1938–) m. Julie (1938–)

Rebekah (1962–) Mathew (1964–)

Kathie (1943–) m. Charles Hoye (1939–)

Laurie (1974–) Eleanor (1972–)

Laurie (1947–) m. (2) Mike Margolis (1940–)

Jessie (1979–) Josh (1986–)

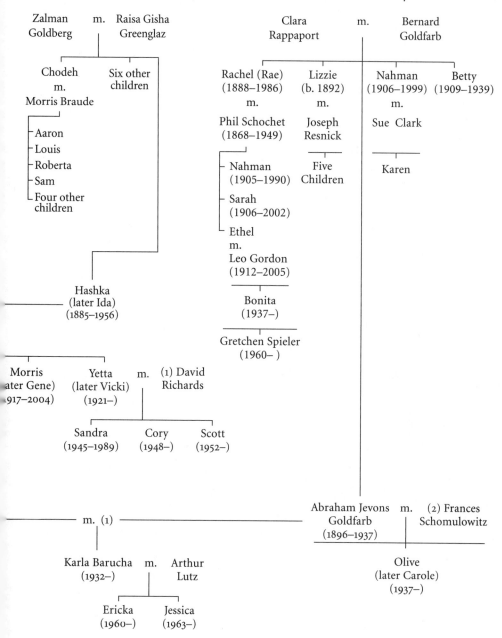

GOLDBERG–GREENGLAZ family

Zalman Goldberg   m.   Raisa Gisha Greenglaz

Chodeh m. Morris Braude   Six other children

- Aaron
- Louis
- Roberta
- Sam
- Four other children

Hashka (later Ida) (1885–1956)

Morris (later Gene) (1917–2004)   Yetta (later Vicki) (1921–)   m.   (1) David Richards

Sandra (1945–1989)   Cory (1948–)   Scott (1952–)

m. (1)

Karla Barucha (1932–)   m.   Arthur Lutz

Ericka (1960–)   Jessica (1963–)

GOLDFARB family

Clara Rappaport   m.   Bernard Goldfarb

Rachel (Rae) (1888–1986) m. Phil Schochet (1868–1949)   Lizzie (b. 1892) m. Joseph Resnick   Nahman (1906–1999) m. Sue Clark   Betty (1909–1939)

- Nahman (1905–1990)
- Sarah (1906–2002)
- Ethel m. Leo Gordon (1912–2005)

Five Children

Karen

Bonita (1937–)

Gretchen Spieler (1960–)

Abraham Jevons Goldfarb (1896–1937)   m.   (2) Frances Schomulowitz

Olive (later Carole) (1937–)

1935 PLAN FOR THE
1930s PROLETARIAN NOVEL

Tillie Lerner sent this plan for completing (or almost completing) her 1930s novel to Donald Klopfer in 1935. I reprint it as written, without corrections. It remained in the Random House files and is now at Columbia University; thus, it was unavailable to Tillie Olsen in 1973 when she was trying to revise her 1930s novel as *Yonnondio*. This list of disasters would have been of little help anyway because she named but did not develop new characters, imagined endless disasters, and subsumed plot to ideology.

The Strike: The battlecamp of the children, how the women marched, and the slow defeat, the slow betrayal. Kryczi and Jim and Kelly. The race hatred, Jeff kicked and kicked by Jim in a temper while Ben and Jimmie cry and do not understand; the final defeat, the sellout, and Jim blacklisted; his hatred.

After Strike—I. The search for work, the slow disintegration and bitterness. Will selling papers. Anna when she has to stop the insurance payments on the kids. They hunt for dandelion greens in Summer. Anna at the grocer's begging for credit, and thrown out, and Ben watching, how it breaks his heart, and Will trying to kill the man. The slow laceration. And in Fall, the fear, at school, the hunger scene and Smoky expelled. Dog meat. Down on the railroad tracks hunting for coal, the r.r. bull, beating up the kids. Jim drunk, the fight, and afraid, he hops a freight.

After Strike—II. The cold—they sleep all in one bed for warmth and go down to the station and pretend to be waiting for a train, and huddle in the department store. The baby found buried on the dump by the kids. The eviction. The attempt at charity, and Anna, "you're what they call edjicccated?" The one room near the skid row they get for taking care of the rooming house. The long year of horror, the things seen, and Annas disintegration.

Ben dies—ptomaine poisoning. Wills nose broken by the drunk. Mazie working that summer at the peanut factory—her fright at the Italian. Jimmie and the whores. And Annas state. Mazie and the roomer—the money she gets and she and Will go to a movie, and that night Baby Bess playing with the gas jets, laughing and laughing and Anna what are you laughing for, and smelling the gas, the idea comes, and while Will and Mazie roar at the Charlie Chaplin, the suicide, and they come home—

That Winter and Early Spring. Will at the orphanage—the wolf—the having to eat his vomit. Mazie in the small town with Annas cousin, Edith, unwanted, except by Edith. Edith. The kids, so alien, the school torment, the sickness, and getting well again, somehow so bruised, this brother of Ediths, Arthur there following Edith around the house, reading to her, and the strange scene of love with Mazie. All this very short, kaleidoscopic.

The Beetfields. With the Evans, her uncle Jerry, educate them what for? let them learn how to fill their bellies, his bitterness, but a broken man, a windbag, and Aunt Margaret, a deathly sick woman. All the kids, wild and rebellious. The thinning in the fields, then the summer heat, the mexican family, the dead baby, and Jerrys talk with the Mexican, the songs in the night, in the late fall, the topping, Mazies hands cracked from the frost the scene with the mountain ranges tumbled. And Will, run away, comes there, but no words between him and Mazie, what could he say of? And then the horrors he thinks in his mind.

The City. With Will in the reformatory for running away. School and how alien it and the kids are. Mazie friendship for Ellen her cousin and their dreams together. The neighborhood, the poverty, the sense of being a burden and Jerry bitter tongue, the men around. The work for room and board, and falling asleep in school over her lessons, the shame. Adolescence, all that smolders. Margaret makes her come back to live with them. Ellen goes her way, and now narrowly Mazie escapes. Working in the cafeteria at school, the shame and her friend Kay, their talks. And then, 15, after the happenings and the flunking, she quits school, and remembering Anna and what she had said for Education—and what Anna did not know of it.

The Work. Lard pail at the packinghouse, and casings, and then the tie factory, the weariness. The day she comes home and the shrunken stranger there—her father this man? it cannot be, and the silence between them, and how it hurts her, the whole coming back, the seeing him. His going away, The five oclock hysteria at the factory. Walking home, the sound from the dance halls. The ride Mazie takes with Ed's friend, Alan, in the hearse with the corpse in the back.

The hole-up. Will there, and the ride in the locked cooler car, for the three days and nights from Seattle to Chicago (to teach them kid 'boes a lesson). Then talk then. Pauline and Ethel.

The scene between Ed and Jerry at Eds not having a job yet. (I left all that out the two chapters above, not meaning too about Ed and Ellen). The barbecue and the talk among all the youngsters. Alan and Mazie, and Ed lams out, not bearing being a leech, and takes to the road. And the year at the ice cream factory—everywhere horror—Margaret and Jerry and Ellen, hearing her story, and Alan disappears (I cant give you any resume of this part because its mostly psychological) the walk and all the things that happened. And Will, trying to get into a flophouse that below zero night, so feverish, the delirium, with the white snow piling up and the smell of bread, and an old bum, (it might be Jim even) gathering him up and staggering around with him trying to get him in somewhere, and finally, Will freezes there stiff—

It sounds like tripe said like that. You cant have any idea what its like. It seems as if everything is left out. Its not even a skeleton, the dev't of the people, all the atmosphere, the real feeling and purpose of the book isn't there—

And as you see, the revolutionary part which was in the novel as I wrote it in Faribault isn't in. It cant be—there's too much in this, and I cant have a 800 or more page tome. There doesnt seem anything outside of chapter 5 and 6 (before and [after] the strike) I can cut down, and theres still the last chapter in here I'm not certain what it'll be. And the revolutionary part demands a whole book by itself. (And theres only two characters in this book that continue on, Mazie and Arthur, and then not as main characters.)

NOTES

CHAPTER 1 — 1880S–1916

1. Ida's notebook is now in the Lerner Papers.

2. Later, Harry Lerner and his family celebrated Sam Lerner's birthday on the first licht (light) of Hanukkah, the 25th of Kislev on the Jewish calendar. Because most records were lost and memories often suppressed, I made here a construct from family recollections and history. I have relied particularly on the research of Eugene (formerly Morris) Lerner and the cooperation with him of sisters Jann (formerly Fannie) Lerner Brodinsky, Lillian Lerner Davis, and Vicki (formerly Yetta) Lerner Richards Bergman. (I have used their original names when those names applied and the new names after the three siblings changed their names.) Prime historical sources, listed in the bibliography, are works by: Baron, Gassenschmidt, Gitelman, Glenn, Hyman, Löwe, and Weinberg. Also, the website www.jewishgen.org has provided particular information about these families, their locations, and their means of earning a living.

3. These were former Lithuanian territories, within the Bobruisk District of the Minsk Province, near the bank of the Svishlock River. Taking the 1881 assassination of Czar Alexander II as an excuse to crack down on progressives and Jews, Alexander III tightened regulations and condoned pogroms against already-oppressed Jews.

4. Gene Lerner, conducting an extensive genealogical search, gleaned information from relatives still in Russia.

5. One of her grandsons, Samuel Braude, supplied Gene Lerner with her photograph (illustration 1).

6. For gender roles in Russia, see Magnus.

7. Glenn, 10. Quoted from *Jewish Grandmothers*, 125.

8. See Mendelsohn, 11–14, for information about working conditions in the Jewish Pale.

9. Such home schools varied in quality because they lacked supervision (see Bergelson, 15). According to Jewish law (*halakha*) women were exempt from the study of the Torah, an exemption that would adversely affect the transmission of Jewish traditions in an increasingly mobile world. See Hyman, chapter 2.

10. When she told me this story, Tillie mentioned Peretz's story "Buntcheh the Silent" (see Peretz, 59). Possibly other details in her account were borrowed from her reading.

11. Tillie's siblings said that their father swam perfectly naturally, though Tillie's youngest daughter did think she remembered Sam's brief dog paddling. Interviews with TO, 27 October 1997; with Gene Lerner, 1 July 2000; with Laurie Olsen, 15 September 2002.

12. Tillie Olsen maintained that Jews "really believed that God had this huge golden

cup and in it he collected human tears, and when all the tears would [overflow] the Messiah would come." Interview, 27 October 1997.

13. See Gendler, 75–82.

14. Jann Lerner wrote a useful narrative she called "How Dad Escaped from Russia." Her narrative and research are now in the Lerner Papers. Written records, produced in consultation with an informant, are more reliable than stories produced later. See also Levin, 261-63.

15. Nearly a third of Bund members were young, unmarried women, eager for enlightenment and change. See Hyman, 78–79, and Davis-Kram, 27–41.

16. Interview with TO, 27 October 1997. Richmond, 7, 8. Interview with Gene Lerner, 3 July 2000.

17. One revolutionary paper was *The Minsk Laborer;* another was "Der Veker" [The Alarm]. See Gitelman and Hertz for details of Bund activities. Sam, Ida, and Genya are not among the young people listed by Hertz in *Generations of Bundists.*

18. Tillie remembered nothing about Olga, while her siblings remembered the story their mother told about Olga. They had never heard of Genya.

19. Tillie said that Samuel later recognized that his father simply wanted him "under God's protection going across the ocean" and was sorry for his angry departure. Interview, 27 October 1997. Gene Lerner also heard "that Samuel refused to kiss the mezuzah and was beaten by Mendel" (to PR, 30 January 2003). The obituary for Sam Lerner followed this story, with amusing confusion: "He escaped from prison with the aid of his sister Ida, who smuggled him out under her skirts" (*The Jewish Week,* 4–10 March 1976).

20. No one now knows whether the three sisters who stayed behind were on better terms with their father or whether they simply lacked an opportunity to escape.

21. Both Sam, as recorded by Jann, and Rose Lerner Wolk, as remembered by Gene, said that their mother died of epilepsy after Sam's departure. Further, "there is absolutely no evidence in the Lerner family of any such thing as a picture of her which he wrapped in black" (Gene Lerner to PR, 30 January 2003).

22. The Lerner children never knew that two of their aunts and their mother were all officially "Ida"; they called the aunts by their Yiddish first names or their married surnames. For them (as henceforth in this biography) their mother was the only Ida.

23. See Larsen and Cottrell who use "Gate City" in their title.

24. The two separate Omahas are divided by Dodge Street, which runs due west from the Missouri River dividing the city in half. North of Dodge, early in the century, the immigrant neighborhood was largely eastern European, especially German, Russian, and Lithuanian. Packing houses, in South Omaha, chiefly employed Italian and Irish immigrants, later Polish and Czech, and finally African-American workers. As Omaha spread west from the river toward the suburbs, street numbers climbed over thirty, and distinctions between North and South evaporated.

25. In 1905, Omaha had a far larger population of Jews than did Des Moines, Sioux City, or Lincoln. By 1912, Jewish populations numbered: Lincoln, 1,200; Sioux City, 1,400; Des Moines, 5,500; Kansas City, 8,000; and Omaha, 12,000 (Pollak, 1999).

26. The Bebers were in Canada around 1904 and in Omaha by 1910. While Ida's mother Raisa Gisha Shapiro married Zalman Goldberg, Ida's aunt married Abraham Greenglaz. A Greenglaz daughter named Rachel, first cousin of Ida, married Israel Beber, also of Minsk, born in 1871. On 10 January 1912, he filed a Declaration of Intention with the

District Court in Douglas County, Nebraska. The Bebers, including Samuel (later a judge), had five children born before arriving in Omaha. Rachel and Israel Beber were especially fond of cousin Ida Goldberg.

27. Omaha had built the school where the first territorial capital building had stood. An 1870 photograph shows a crowd of gentlemen in topcoats and ladies with parasols admiring the new Omaha High School, with its towers, gables, four-storied chimneys, and fancy roofs. Omaha Historical Collection.

28. See Weiner, 8–13.

29. The pawnbroker was Max Lerner, but he does not seem to have been kin to Sam.

30. Conversation with TO, 11 June 2000. A letter from Jann to Gene Lerner, dated 5 October 1997, and his transcription of a conversation with her in February 2000, are in the Lerner Papers.

31. Gendler, 135.

32. The Burmeister's land stretched through sections nineteen, twenty, and twenty-one of Marble precinct, eight miles southeast of Mead and seven miles north of the smaller hamlet of Memphis.

33. Three years later Fannie enrolled in school #38 in Marble precinct; school records state that she had to walk a half a mile on an open road to get to that school. Mr. Burmeister's farm, across the road from school #38, was the only farm in the area with two houses on it, the smaller one being about half a mile away from the school. Land ownership records are on file at the Saunders County Museum in Wahoo. When Charles Burmeister died on 11 September 1941, the *Wahoo Wasp* noted that he had "farmed on a large scale"; such a scale would have required a tenant farmer.

34. During World War II, this area became a U.S. Military Reservation. It now contains the University of Nebraska's Field Laboratory or agricultural station and the Nebraska National Guard training post.

35. *Saunders County Nebraska: History.*

36. One such paper was the *New Era* in Wahoo, Nebraska. See Paul Olson.

37. Conversations with Raymond Screws, curator of the Saunders County Museum, on 1 June 2000 and Tillie Olsen on 11 June 2000. Information supplied by Gladys Cajka of the Saunders County Genealogical Seekers, 10 October 2001.

38. Conversation with TO, 11 June 2000.

39. Harry's middle name was a tribute to Eugene Victor Debs whose fourth bid for president of the United States had garnered 6 percent of the vote in 1912; Debs was the most successful Socialist Party nominee ever.

40. Harry's birth certificate lists the birthplace as Marble precinct in Saunders County and the physician as a Dr. Thomas from Memphis, who gave Memphis as the Lerners' residence.

41. Again, Dr. Thomas presided at the birth, this time registering the residence as Mead. This uncertainty about naming their residence suggests, not that they moved about, but just how isolated and difficult it was to locate the farm.

42. Perky, 250. Fussell is my source for World War I information.

43. Conversation with TO, 11 June 2000.

44. I examined these records at school board offices in Wahoo, Saunders County, Nebraska.

45. There were eight Gehrmanns, seven Wagners, five each of Ohms and Karloffs, three each of Polzins, Leinemanns, and Youngs, two each of Wittes and Deans. Families

with only one child in school #38 were Klotz, Wilgus, Kennec, Burmeister (age nine), and "Lehrner."

46. Interview of 7 December 1999. Liberty Bonds did not go on sale until the United States entered the war in April 1917, by which time the Lerners had left the farm.

47. Interview with TO, 27 October 1997.

CHAPTER 2 — 1917–1924

1. TOP, box 17.

2. Tillie's birth date was correctly registered as 1912, but her name was recorded as "Ida Tillie Lerner." Tillie's kindergarten class of thirty had only seven children whose parents were native born—and only three of them were from Nebraska. Sixteen children were of Russian parentage. (Omaha supported the education and acculturation of diverse children with two teachers in most elementary classes.) Both Fannie and Tillie loved Kellom School. Interview with Lillian Lerner Davis, 24 January 2002.

3. Family lore had both Ida's and Tillie's birthday as 14 January, but Ida's death certificate lists her birth as 24 January 1885.

4. Interview with TO, 11 June 2000.

5. Lillian Lerner Davis to PR, December 2000. Interview with Gene Lerner, 3 July 2000.

6. She had learned to obtain pessaries or diaphragms, although they were illegal Interviews with TO, 27 October 1997 and 2 July 2000. See Chesler, for information about the underground market in birth control devices and the story of Margaret Sanger's campaign for reproductive rights.

7. Sam Braude to PR, 7 September 2001. Aaron Braude to PR, 11 March 1999. Aaron Braude, "As Time Goes By" [unpublished private autobiography].

8. Tillie also said she had a very good friend Jo Eva Crawford, a name that does not appear in Tillie's early diaries.

9. Interview with Eugene Lerner, 3 July 2000.

10. Aaron Braude to PR, 11 March 1999.

11. She assumed it recognized women's equality, not realizing that the Nineteenth Amendment was payback for women's war efforts.

12. Omaha's black population doubled between 1910 and 1920. While the *Bee* printed such irresponsibly slanted coverage, the *Omaha World-Herald* won a Pulitzer Prize for its editorial "Law and the Jungle" about these horrible events.

13. About one hundred federal troops arrived after the burning, too late to save the victim or indeed the courthouse; they did disperse the crowd before the violence further escalated and spread beyond the city center. Laurie, 137.

14. Shapiro, 75. See Pollak, 1999, 129.

15. The deed is only in Sam's name perhaps because the Married Women's Act was not passed by Congress until 1922 or perhaps because Ida was not legally Sam's wife. Record No. 444 records the purchase on 6 January 1920, for a deed dated late in 1919.

16. Interview with Lillian Lerner Davis, 24 January 2002.

17. See Kugler, 40. Though vehemently anti-Zionist, the Circles fostered a general sense of Jewish identity or "Yiddishkeit," a word Tillie Olsen said "distinguished a secular from a Judaic Jew. . . . It refers to having a real social conscience—which presumably Jews are born with." Interview with TO, 27 October 1997.

18. Over the years, Omaha's one Jewish printer kept a running tab for Sam Lerner's

printing orders, which indicate that the Workmen's Circle raised money to benefit its people, keep Yiddish alive (though records were kept in English), and support the Socialist Party. A letterhead on bond paper reads: "Nebraska State Committee Socialist party, S. Lerner, Financial Secretary, 2512 Caldwell Street, Omaha, Nebr."

19. Gene Lerner, "Lil: A Memoir for her Eightieth Birthday," 14 December 1994, Lerner Papers, and to PR, 2 February 2002. Lillian's quietness and lack of energy were later found to be the results of low blood pressure. Interview with Lillian Lerner Davis, 24 January 2002.

20. Record No. 634. My thanks to Oliver Pollak for sending me copies of Sam's printing charges and the Lerner property deeds.

21. Lerner, "From Czarist Russia," 4; Lerner Papers.

22. Conversation with TO, 14 September 2002.

23. With immigration slowing in the 1920s and membership declining, Workmen's Circles began a national campaign to enlist children in permanent membership. The Circles offered Socialist Sunday Schools and sponsored the Young People's Socialist League. The refrain of the Workmen's Circle Hymn or (Arbeter Ring Himne) reiterates "Stand all for one and one for all. The working class ideal." Another version of the hymn ends with "Socialism triumphing and liberty." Another song asked, after all their hard work, "what my people, do you earn?" The Lerner children all sang such songs, read socialist articles, poems, and delighted in socialist cartoons. Interviews with TO, 11 April 1998 and 27 October 1997.

24. A number of black men who survived the riot appealed nationally to such groups as the National Urban League and the National Association for the Advancement of Colored People. The American Red Cross pitched in, as did some white churches, and at least one courageous woman journalist. My thanks to Eddie Faye Gates for information. Structures in the decimated Greenwood area were not rebuilt; it became the site of the Oklahoma State University-Tulsa campus.

25. The North Omaha Workmen's Circle branches donated $49.10 toward supporting strikers at the meat-packing companies. Pollak, 1995.

26. Jann Lerner Brodinsky to Gene Lerner, February 2000. Interview with Lillian Lerner Davis, 24 January 2002. Interview with TO, 29 October 1997.

27. Interview with Gene Lerner, 3 July 2000. Gene Lerner to PR, 11 February 2002.

28. Bill Pratt to PR, 20 May 2000.

29. Also the much larger Brandeis theater downtown began in 1919 to stage Yiddish plays. Sometime in the early 1920s, Sam's brother-in-law Louis Wolk performed there in a play staged by a traveling troop of Yiddish players. Pollak, 1999, 129, 159.

30. Articles on the book's acceptance appeared in "Bark," a newsletter of the Woodmen of the World, and in the Central High newspaper, which quoted a few mild lines from "Infidelity": "Have you watched how the sun/ Through the winging hours/ Enfolds the tremulous/ Amorous flowers?" I can find no record of Dorrance's publication of Konecky's *Trail 'O Spring* in 1923. Eugene and Eva Konecky had a second son, born in 1925, but Gene was less and less a presence in his sons' lives. Documents from and interview with Pollak, 25 April 2002.

31. Lillian Lerner Davis to PR, December 2001. Interview with Lillian Lerner Davis, 24 January 2002.

32. Jann Lerner Brodinsky to Gene Lerner, 1999.

33. There were lessons on "Articulation" (or pronunciation), spelling, and handwriting,

the latter called "Lend a Hand (Script)." Typical titles were "Courage and Cowardice," "Beware of the First Drink," "Don't Kill the Birds," and "Which Loved Best?" *McGuffey's Third Eclectic Reader*.

34. Here and below, my source is Gene Lerner, 1, 2, and 3 July 2000.

35. *Omaha Evening World Herald* (10 and 11 October 1923) and *Omaha Bee News* (12 October 1923).

36. She refers to Tennyson's "The May Queen" and the line "For I'm to be Queen of the May, mother. I'm to be Queen of the May."

37. In 1978 Leonard Nathan remembered that, when his mother was president of the Council of Jewish Women, she taught Ida, who "made a very deep impression" because of her "strong convictions and her intellect." Tillie later maintained that her mother learned more English on jobs than in night school (interview with TO, 27 October 1997). Ida, however, did not take jobs outside the home, except briefly in perhaps 1934 when she left Sam and took a job in the school cafeteria, much to her younger son's embarrassment. See Lerner Papers and TOP, box 19.

38. Tillie Olsen's transcription of the passage quoted here in chapter 1 ends "feverish hungry eyes." Gene Lerner's transcription, labeled "Ida Lerner: From a Page Missing from Her Notebook," does not include the word "hungry." Lerner Papers.

39. In his 1986 memoir, Gene Lerner quoted these as "*Her words* of more than sixty years ago." Lerner Papers.

40. Lillian Lerner Davis to PR, December 2000. Lillian did not think the candy business failed. She thought it was so successful Sam talked of incorporating. Interview with Lillian Lerner Davis, 24 January 2002.

41. Interviews, 27 October 1997 and 11 April 1998.

42. Interview, 4 April 1998. Gene Lerner said Chodeh Braude's attendance would have offended Ida. When I asked Aaron Braude if he had heard anything about his mother attending Tillie's graduation, he replied, "I don't recall my mother ever discussing Tillie" (to PR, 5 July 1999). More specifically, he said, "I doubt that my mother attended Tillie's graduation" (to PR, 17 November 2001).

43. She recalled finding it in the *McGuffey Readers*; they include various "supposed speeches," but apparently not this particular one. The Lerners owned a number of leftist anthologies, among them *The Ancient Lowly: A History of the Ancient Working People from the Earliest Times to the Adoption of Christianity by Constantine*, which could have included a simulation of a Spartacus speech entreating Roman slaves to rebel against their serfdom. TOP, box 18.

44. Because Morris was photographed with a neighborhood child, the photographer was likely offering a special on pictures of children from the predominantly Jewish neighborhood. None of the family could recall why baby sister Yetta was not in either picture.

45. Lerner Papers.

CHAPTER 3 — 1925–1929

1. My thanks to Gary Thompson, principal of Central High School, who in 2001 and 2002 provided me with information on Central High, its teachers, and Tillie Lerner's permanent record.

2. Gene Lerner to Oliver Pollak, 13 April 1997. Jann Lerner Brodinsky to Gene Lerner, 5 October 1997.

3. Thus, when Tillie later spoke of "crossing the tracks" to Central she was not being literally accurate.

4. The journals and diaries Tillie kept over the next years offer an unusually frank glimpse into the formation of her character and career, even as they convey the self-absorption, moodiness, and, often, silliness of a very young woman. Along with other documents, they have enabled me to detail a period most biographers can only guess about. Tillie kept extensive records from her high school years into her early twenties. Though never in an easy-to-decipher, dated format, they contain enough clues to date by a universal calendar. These diary entries are scattered among clippings, poems, letters, and miscellaneous notes in several boxes, especially boxes 15 and 16. TOP, box 17, holds most of them, including the 1930 notebook, which offers consecutive entries.

5. Pollak, 1995, 162.

6. Milton Konecky to PR, 25 October 1995. Gene Konecky, 1918 diary. The *Bulletin* was so radical that, years later, the Jewish Community Center's library refused a gift of its complete run from 1916 to 1921. Interview with Minette Louis Katz, 18 August 2001. Tillie told a story of Chodeh's putting a son who tried to run away in chains, interview, 4 April 1998. Aaron Braude and Roberta Braude Diamond conceded that their mother was capable of such extreme abuse; to PR, 17 November 2001 and 23 February 2002.

7. Interview with Frances Blumkin Batt and Cynthia Blumkin Schneider, 2 June 2000. In 1978, writer Leonard Nathan wrote Tillie recalling her being "at camp on our farm." Though she elsewhere mentioned her camp name, Tillie noted on this letter, "I think he has me mixed up with someone else," some affluent camper. TOP, box 26.

8. Interview with Gene Lerner, 3 July 2000.

9. Tillie described the cartoon as showing "the dual Carnegie." "But look at how grateful so many of us are." Interview, 27 October 1997. See Pollak, 2005, xi.

10. Interviews with TO, 27 October 1997 and 21 March 2002. Tillie said that Ida was contrasting the "gossip and hypocritical high morality" of the Omaha Jewish women with Anna Karenina's great passion.

11. Most of Tillie's early poems are in TOP, box 15.

12. Interview with Ruth Stein Fox, 3 June 2000. Gene Lerner's transcription of conversations with Vicki Lerner Richards Bergman and Lillian Lerner Davis, February 2000, are in the Lerner Papers.

13. Interview with Ruth Stein Fox, 3 June 2000.

14. Hurwitz, 57–58. Neither Ida nor Sam read the Communist Yiddish paper called the *Freiheit*. Interview with TO, 27 October 1997.

15. Words for the first song included "Tack Hammer, Tack Hammer, Strike." The peddler's song ran: "See my bag is filled to overflowing with gold brocades and velvets rare. How it strains 'gainst my aching shoulders, how my back my burdens bare." Gene Lerner with Lillian Lerner Davis, February 2000.

16. The "Tillie the Toiler" comic strip, by Russ Westover, featured a fashionably dressed career woman and her male chauvinist colleagues, a strip Tillie called "under the table pornography." Interview with TO, 27 October 1997. A side panel in the comic strip pictured Tillie Jones in her underwear with a dress beside her. Readers could cut out Tillie and dress or undress her like a paper doll.

17. Interview with TO, 27 October 1997.

18. Interview with TO, 14 September 2002.

19. Interview with TO, 11 April 1998.

20. TOP, box 15.

21. Tillie later said that her "Squeaks" column won a national "Quill and Scroll" award. It certainly deserved to win, but perhaps her teachers were too offended with Tillie to nominate her. She is not listed in the *Best Creative Work in American High Schools* between 1927 and 1930.

22. Interview with Gene Lerner, 3 July 2000. He was reading to me from his unpublished autobiography.

23. Lillian Lerner Davis to PR, December 2000. Seventy-odd years later, contemporaries from the old neighborhood, who described Tillie's "hell-cat" behavior, asked to be anonymous. They still seemed mystified that in high school Tillie had non-Jewish, wealthy friends, whose names they did not recognize.

24. His cousin George Creel was a prominent journalist and friend of the muckraker Lincoln Steffens, whose *The Shame of Cities* the Lerners owned.

25. Interview with TO, 27 October 1927. Tillie's recollections of being on the lake with Agnes were meant to prove that she was not marginalized; see Linda Pratt, "The Circumstances of Silence," in Nelson and Huse. Tillie wrote her reflections on these poems when she reread them before depositing them at Stanford. TOP, box 15.

26. Interview with Gene Lerner, 2 July 2000.

27. Conversation with TO, 21 September 1999.

28. Albert Einstein (1879–1955) won the Nobel Prize in 1921 for the theory of relativity. Hermann Keyserling (1880–1946) founded the School of Wisdom in 1920.

29. Ida's attitude further alienated her from Sam's family, for his cousin Hannah LaBook Sogolow's husband Morris Sogolow was athletic director at the Center.

30. Gene Lerner to PR, 7 December 1999. Interview with Gene Lerner, 2 July 2000.

31. German philosophers Arthur Schopenhauer (1888–1860) and Friedrich Nietzsche (1844–1900) appealed to Tillie's nascent sense of personal power, though Schopenhauer recommended frustrating that power. Tillie may not have understood Nietzsche's irony but appreciated his aphoristic pronouncements like the death of God, the overman, the will to power, and the usefulness of sickness.

32. Conversation with Gene Lerner, 10 January 2000.

33. Yetta, renamed Vicki, mentioned this flirting in a February 2000 interview with her brother Gene. Neither she nor her siblings thought Sam responded to other women's advances.

34. Ida's cousin Rachel married a Beber and lived in Omaha. Sam Lerner's older sister Chaika married Hyman Swartz. They first settled in Omaha, then moved to Des Moines, where the Lerner children sometimes visited them.

35. Chodeh's sons Hyman (Herman), Harry, Louis, and Aaron all ran away from home. Aaron Braude to PR, 31 March 1999 and 5 July 1999. Adele, who married Sam Braude, explained that the "Braude kids survived and achieved and were self-motivated, intellectually curious, compassionate . . . with a strong sense of humor through it all." To PR, 22 February 2002. Roberta Braude Diamond said that her mother was "inflamed with ideas & took out her frustration on her kids. " She was never "complacent or even smug—she was always too aggravated or angry!" Roberta Braude Diamond to PR, 23 February 2002.

36. Tillie told me that the pilot was the older brother of one of her friends. Of the few pilots registered to fly in Omaha in the late 1920s, only E. D. Fox had a sister who knew Tillie. My thanks for Les Valentine of the University of Nebraska, Omaha, for uncovering these records.

37. Conversations with TO, 7 February and 20 March 2002.

38. Interviews with Ruth Stein Fox, 3 June 2000, and Lillian Lerner Davis, 24 January 2002.

39. According to the *World-Herald*, Jeanette's aristocratic Russian family, with literary and religious connections, had encouraged her to write from the age of five.

40. Interview with Frances Blumkin Batt and Cynthia Blumkin Schneider, 2 June 2000. In 1996, the Riviera was renovated as the Rose Blumkin Performing Arts Center.

41. Her physics class was incomplete, but for the spring term of 1928 she received all As in English history, Expression, Glee Club, and English. Tillie did not acknowledge this withdrawal. I discovered it in the "Annual Registers of the Board of Education," Omaha, Nebraska.

42. TOP, box 19.

43. None of Tillie's papers mention a man named Thomas. Eugene Konecky's tutelage in poetry and "free love" and her passionate adoration of him, along with the absence of any other man in her life at that time, all suggest that he was the father of her child.

44. Newspaper mentions of these transgressions have not surfaced. Gene Lerner's interview with Jann Lerner Brodinsky, February 2000.

45. Interview with Gene Lerner, 2 July 2000.

46. Someone took a photograph of Tillie holding a large battered doll. Tillie labeled it "Myself at 14 (?)." TOP, 1998–242. Perhaps this posed picture was, like her poem, "The Mother Who Died too," a way of objectifying her loss.

47. Aaron Braude to PR, 31 March 1999 and 26 April 2002.

48. "The People's Business of Nebraska: Devoted to the Principals [sic] of the Socialist Party," Omaha (October 1928). TOP, box 18.

49. A diary entry refers to an actual girl called "Fuzz": "Fuzz came—talked about ourselves. Thoroughly disgusted Fuzz—partly myself & Jeanette." Later Tillie could not recall who the actual "Fuzz" was. TOP, box 17.

50. Her American history notebooks list some ninety items she studied, including John Marshall, Monroe Doctrine, Harrison, Land Law of 1829, Panic of 1837, spoils system, gerrymander, potato famine, City of Monuments, Queen City of the West, Jay's Treaty, and Vanderbilt. TOP, box 16.

51. Her "Squeaks" attack was titled: "Ode to Mrs. Jensen's VII hour chorus class"; Irene H. Jensen was one of the four members of CHS's music faculty. Many students kept Taylor's style book and "Practice Sheets in Sentence Structure and Punctuation" all their lives. Gene Lerner to PR, 1 March 2000; interview, 1 July 2000.

52. Editing these "First Words," more than seventy years later, Mandelbaum asked if the operation were an abortion. Tillie replied, "you are right—an abortion." TOP, box 15.

53. The original of this untitled story is in the Berg Collection. In 1991, Tillie Olsen added a note wondering "how old was I? 17? 18?—perhaps even 19." "The original of this, typed on butcher paper, (and my favorite version) is also at the Berg." TOP, box 15. Because the Berg copy is crude and written on normal paper, my guess is that she romanticized her memories of the "original" story.

54. Gene later recalled a "brawny wise guy I didn't know sauntered up" and asked if he were the brother of Tillie Lerner, who was "really hot stuff." Morris tried to defend his sister's honor, but his chivalry brought him only bruises. Interview with Gene Lerner, 2 July 2000.

55. Interview with Ruth Stein Fox, June 2000.

56. "Any Man" and anticulture poems, "At the Teachers' Convention" and "Culture," are in TOP, box 15.

57. Interview with TO, 21 March 2002. Anel Creel heard the account of the teachers'"roasting" Tillie from a teacher she called only "Mary." TOP, box 19.

58. Tillie later said she forgave Sara Vore Taylor because she had been under great pressure because "she had a mother dying and she lived with her." Interview, 27 October 1997. This example of creative recollection is contradicted by the 1932 City Directory, which lists Miss Taylor's mother as still alive.

59. Gene Lerner's interview with TO, 1 March 2000.

60. Interview with TO, 27 October 1997.

61. Gene Lerner to PR, 8 December 1999. The reprimand can be found in the Berg Collection, NYPL, with a copy in TOP, box 20. In her junior year, Tillie was absent eleven times before withdrawing. In her senior year, she was absent seventeen times before withdrawing. Her permanent record does not use the word "expelled."

62. Gene Lerner to PR, 7 and 3 December 1999. Gene said that teachers at Central confirmed to him that Tillie had been expelled. In 1974, Tillie's interview with Jerry Tallmer confirms the expulsion story.

63. TOP, boxes 19 and 17.

64. Gene Lerner's notes from his conversation with TO, 1 March 2000, also include his statement that he could not get her to explain what Konecky and Jeanette had to do with the *Hamlet* story.

65. My thanks to Stacy Carlson for her diligent searching of Omaha City directories and newspapers for pertinent information.

66. Interview with TO, 22 July 2000.

67. Conversation with TO, 25 May 2000.

68. The unmarried Szold first appears in the Omaha City Directory in 1929 with a job teaching at the Studio of Expression and Dramatic Art.

69. The two pages discussed above can be found only at Stanford. In that collection, they appear as an introduction to the eight original pages, which are in both the Berg and Stanford collections.

70. This version was published in 1993 in Mandelbaum's *First Words*.

71. Tillie only kept a fragment of this letter. Apparently, she recopied and mailed it to Marian whose letter seems to have been a response. TOP, boxes 19 and 24.

72. TOP, 1998, box 24.

73. TOP, box 16.

74. She recorded these reflections on 14 October on the back of homework, meticulously identified: "Harry Lerner, October 8, 1929, fourth hour, section II." TOP, boxes 15 and 16.

75. The plight of women mill workers, for example, inspired at least six novels. See McElvaine, 46–50, 65–66, and Cook, 36–37.

76. She left this note (torn out of a book from apparently 1929) within pages of a diary where a few brief entries can be dated from April and May 1930. TOP, box 17.

77. A detail she reused in her Fuzzy story.

78. TOP, box 17.

79. From a clipping of 3 October 1931, Douglas County Historical Society.

80. In a typical pattern, the father Bernard emigrated first (in 1902); his wife Clara followed in 1903 with the three eldest children: Rachel (15), Lizzie (11), and Abe (6). Thanks to Gretchen Spieler, Rachel's great-granddaughter, for this and other family information.

81. Among his papers is a 1929 letter from another editor of the *Modern Quarterly* who refers to Abe's paper or journal. I have yet to find a publication edited by Goldfarb.

82. Anel Creel's cousin George Creel had worked for President Wilson on a peace treaty with Mexico during the postwar period, which Abe apparently spent in Mexico. See Steffens, *Letters*, 557–58.

CHAPTER 4 — 1930–1933

1. Interview with TO, 27 October 1997.

2. Morris Lerner remembered the table cloth, the candles, and his father's reaction to Jeanette Gray. The visiting cousin called "Dee" could have been David Beber, younger brother of Sam Beber. Rose and Louis Wolk, who were leaving Omaha for Washington, D.C., had a daughter named Tillie, who might have been called "Dee" to avoid confusion. Interview with Gene Lerner, 2 July 2000.

3. TOP, box 17. This little book interrupts the sequence of her diary written in an "Our Leader" composition book and shows a rather open handwriting. Tillie wrote the name Gitlow, who had run with William Z. Foster as Communist candidate for vice president in 1924. Later the party split between the Communist Party (Foster) and the Communist Labor Party (Gitlow).

4. Records list his occupation before enlisting as a "Clerk-Stenographer" in Minneapolis. The Army placed him in a motor training division. He spent time in a detention brigade in Florida. Then Abe served in a motor transport repair unit in El Paso. He was honorably discharged there in April 1919 and returned to civilian life, as his military record states, "to finish school." He worked as a stenographer for businessmen traveling on fast trains. His niece Ethel thought he joined the Mexican rebels.

5. She returned to the "Our Leader" diary, on a "Sunday" (26 January 1930), mentioning her Buddha again. Two versions of these passages can be found in TOP, boxes 15 and 17.

6. This January 1930 registration subtracted a whole year from her age, a fiction she clung to for much of her life. She described Sam's profession as "interior decorator," inflating his occupation here while later deflating it. Douglas County, Nebraska, Board of Education Registers.

7. Tillie described Meryl as "opposed to us, seductions, etc." TOP, box 15.

8. TOP, box 17. Edited by V. F. Calverton and S. D. Schmalhausen, the *Modern Quarterly* printed serious discussions of art and society in Volume Five. Calverton wrote, "Revolt and Reaction in Contemporary European Literature"; "Whither Art?"; "The Revolution-in-the-Wordists"; and "Art in the Ancient World."

9. TOP, box 17.

10. *Omaha Bee News*, 19 March 1930. Gene Lerner to PR, 26 July 2002.

11. Tillie threatened to stop this diary if her writing did not improve. There were only seven Lerners because Jann had left home. TOP, box 17.

12. On 10 April, Anel wrote that she had sold a poem, though the magazine folded before printing it. Anel had lived in Omaha, New York, Illinois, and Missouri and was now moving to California. TOP, box 15.

13. TOP, box 17.

14. Interview, 15 July 2002. Freda spelled inventively to amuse Tillie: she was "Freeda," the cities were "Soo City" and "Des Monies." Tillie may have worked in Iowa at the Ottumwa Railway & Light Company. She used its stationery for years. She kept the pamphlet, which may have been privately printed.

15. Tillie bragged so much to Freda about men that Freda instructed her to stop writing about "*boys boys* of Omaha." One of the "boys" Freda mentioned was named Abe, and Freda asked Tillie, on 13 May 1930, to send her "Abe Frais '*Address.*'" (She underlined the word five times and put it in quotation marks.) Probably this was another Abe.

16. Abe gave this pamphlet to Rae. In May 1930 Rae told Abe that she was copying out Konecky's *Secrets* for a man friend. She hoped Abe would remain in school that summer.

17. In a letter to an unidentified "Darling," Tillie gave the address as #1811, 40 East Oak, Chicago. She knew nothing about Greenwich Village and thought Chicago was the center of the artistic and literary world. Conversation with TO, 15 June 1998.

18. This Ben was a known entity because when Freda wrote to ask Tillie "How is Chi?" she also wrote, "did you ask Ben about *me* going to school?" Ben might have been a Ben "Belitt" or "Bulitt," a name in Tillie's diaries. Tillie later tore pages out of this book. TOP, box 19. Later she remarked that Meryl offered Tillie to these men to keep from sleeping with them herself. Conversation, 15 September 2002.

19. Gene Lerner's record of his conversation with Jann Lerner Brodinsky, February 2000. Jann's notes on "Personal" family history (written probably in the 1960s) include "1930 = I in Minneapolis. . . . T in Chicago [when I stopped there] on [my] way to D. C." Lerner Papers. Given Jann's animosity, this recollection might be suspect, except that Tillie recalled Meryl's offering her to men and she had Fuzzy pose in the nude.

20. Interview with Ruth Stein Fox, 3 June 2000.

21. Now at Stanford, this Omaha phone book, for winter 1931–1932, must have been fresh off the press in August 1930. This and a scrap book, made from a San Francisco phone book, are both in TOP, box 1998–242.

22. A letter about Communist youth saving a Mexican family, mailed to the "Voice of Youth, 37 Grove Street," San Francisco, in August 1930, offered the sort of testimony Tillie collected, though that letter probably came into her possession after 1934.

23. Freda Rosmovsky hoped Tillie would catch a ride from Des Moines to Sioux City. TOP, box 19.

24. His new address was 1517 S. 33rd Street, a large enough street number to be beyond the slums of South Omaha. School records list Jeanette's birthday as 3 January 1915.

25. By "we," she probably meant the CP, for she seems not to have been in Omaha. Armour had packing houses in several midwestern cities, including Kansas City.

26. Historian Fred Whitehead describes Kansas City as a "grand scene" for radicalism.

Tillie was walking over the Inter-City Viaduct that connects the two Kansas Cities. Whitehead to PR, 22 April 2003.

27. TOP, box 19. Phil Sharpe, whose address was 3833 W. 14th St., Chicago, was probably the Chicago artist for whom Tillie posed in the nude. It is unusual for her to have kept such a damning letter.

28. She was in the Oak Grove Cemetery in Kansas City, where an Amelia Parker is buried. That cemetery looks over the "bottoms," Fred Whitehead tells me, "just as Tillie Olsen described it." TOP, box 17.

29. The old Union Pacific/Missouri Pacific bridge stretched over the Kansas River, and the Missouri Pacific Rail Road went from Kansas City, KS, to Leavenworth, KS.

30. When she placed these diaries at Stanford, Tillie bitterly noted Konecky "harmed me so." TOP, box 15.

31. This was at a shop Tillie called "Allison's," but no shop was registered under that name either in Omaha or Kansas City. Fred Whitehead tells me that small, personally owned shops were not always registered.

32. TOP, box 15.

33. This typescript is in the Berg Collection of the New York Public Library. The penciled-in additions are not in Tillie's hand but match samples of Abe's handwriting.

34. When she reread this poem before boxing it for Stanford in the 1990s, Tillie wrote a comment: "What was this 18–19 yr. Old—as I read her now—striving to articulate—I want to write about this—understand it—her—who did not understand herself—what was happening? Revulsion at surrender to an act, a situation, a relationship dragging (not the right word) me away from—pinning me down—away from—'running with crying heart.'" TOP, box 15. The gist of those comments is that Tillie, in her eighties, wondered why the nineteen-year-old Tillie had been concerned about a love relationship that, for a while, gave her ease and might have kept her from "running with crying heart." That reflection, of course, begs the question of why the eighty-year-old Tillie tried to erase all evidence of Goldfarb from her papers.

35. One copy of "The Realist" was headed "T Lerner/ R.F.D.#4, Box 74-d/ Stockton, Calif." Later, Tillie noted that it was written in "the same desperate Stockton time . . . that I typed up one of the 'Fuzzy' story versions to send out, hopefully for money." Tillie tore the Stockton back address off another version of "The Realist," trying to hide evidence of her early marriage from her biographer. TOP, boxes 19 and 15.

36. One man arrested for selling the *Daily Worker* died working on a rock pile. Another wrote in the *Daily Worker* (4 July 1931) of being "stripped to the waist, chained, and beaten across the bare back with a rubber hose" by the superintendent of prisoners. With such outrages gaining publicity, Paul Cline told the *Star* that the Communist Party worked only for "the welfare of all."

37. My thanks to Fred Whitehead for Kansas City information, including the *Star* article. Cline, 3–4.

38. Sam wrote almost all the family letters because Ida never learned written English proficiently.

39. Tillie destroyed, tore off, or inked out so much information in diaries from this period that the summer of 1931 is a near blank. The possibility that she had a child is explored here, in chapter 6, note 12, and chapter 7, note 12.

40. Because Ethel blamed the young women for the house's artistic slovenliness and

since Tillie was clearly in Kansas in September, summer 1931 seems the correct time for Ethel's unmailed letter.

41. Anel Creel wrote on 19 November 1931; by that time Tillie was definitely in Kansas City. TOP, box 19.

42. TOP, box 19.

43. Tillie's notes criticize the central Communist bureau for "choking membership by giving decisions as orders" for the Hunger March; clearly, though, the complicated agenda for the march necessitated such "orders."

44. Discovered riding the rails in a boxcar with the nine young black men, the white girls were, apparently, talked into accusing the blacks of rape. The trial substituted racial hysteria for evidence. Tillie followed the appeals, which continued for years. The *Daily Worker* (12 February 1932).

45. During a 1916 "preparedness" parade in San Francisco, a bomb exploded, killing nine or ten people. Local radical Tom Mooney was arrested and jailed. His incarceration on flimsy evidence was a rallying call for two decades. No published version of Tillie's account survives. TOP, box 4.

46. "The Kansas City Labor History Tour," printed in October 1992, based on Archives of the International Ladies Garment Workers Union, Cornell University. Courtesy of Fred Whitehead.

47. Probably, she was jailed near the end of the school term at the close of 1931. Already weakened, she became seriously ill in jail. Though Tillie invented and exaggerated many events in her life, early references to "Argentine" and the "horror" establish that she did not invent this jail term, though she exaggerated its length.

48. Fred Whitehead, interview with Clara Cline Lutz, 11 November 1980. Winston, 17.

49. TOP, boxes 16 and 19. These are labeled "Silone."

50. TOP, boxes 17 and 15.

51. See Shutt.

52. Whitehead's unpublished 1980 interview with Clara Cline Lutz.

53. TOP, box 15.

54. TOP, box 15. The cigarlike pods of catalpa trees remain attached in winter. When she deposited her materials at Stanford, Tillie wrote a note attached to this poem wondering whether it was written in "Omaha or Faribault." She knew it was written when she was "back with J[evons]." She reflected: "How many years until winter again—1962—[in Massachusetts] . . . the 1st snow—Jeanette—Gene—J[Jevons]—Paul."

55. Gene Lerner talked about "casting" because he had partnered with Hank Kaufman to form the Lerner-Kaufman Film agency. Interviews with Gene Lerner, 1 and 2 July 2000 and 1 February 2002.

56. The fliers in her scrapbook were ones she handprinted herself; conversation with TO, 15 September 2002.

57. See Coiner for a copy of this picture.

58. Conversation with Roberta Braude Diamond, 9 November 1999. She had never before mentioned this incident with Jevons.

59. *Daily Worker*, 16 February and 10 March 1932. Tillie later identified Henry Winston as "Head of the party School for YCL'ers then . . . A great human being . . . (black). Became Nat'l leader CP. Smith Act prisoner. Blind." Historian and collector Laird Wilcox

tells me that Henry's brother Sylvester Winston was a police officer in Kansas City, MO (to PR, 30 August 2002). Tillie also said that Bud Reynolds was head of the party school in Kansas City. Nancy Schimmel, daughter of Bud and Malvina Reynolds, does not remember her father "saying anything about Kansas City or heading a Communist Party School there or anywhere" (to PR, 25 April 2002).

60. Tillie later explicated these abbreviations: "Cain—Gene's pseudonym—" and "Storms, YCL name for J" (here Jeanette). TOP, box 19. An envelope postmarked 8 December 1931, kept with her novel-in-progress, is from "Kane, 3343 Manderson St., Omaha Neb" to "Miss Catherine Storms, c/o Marie Kvaternik, National Café and Hotel, 402 n. 5th Street, Kansas City, Kansas." Berg Collection. Tillie used the name Marie Kvaternick in her novel. Fern Pierce sounds older than sixteen, as Tillie described her in October.

61. TOP, box 1. Elsewhere (TOP, box 15), Tillie referred to Kansas City as a "place of horrors." Tillie was thinking of both Omaha and Faribault as a retreat from the horror of Kansas City.

62. Tillie used the backs of stationery from the company for her own letters, diaries, and bits of fiction.

63. Unfortunately, these letters have not thus far surfaced.

64. His absence meant that he and Tillie exchanged letters; she kept hers, inking out his name on some and tearing it and expressions of affection off others. Her mutilated letters to Abe are in TOP, boxes 17 and 19.

65. She named the family Holbrook after a fellow revolutionary who apparently died in Kansas City. TOP, box 1998–192.2.

66. Her diary also mentions a "yen" for a man named Matt and for another named Puninski. TOP, box 19.

67. TOP, box 15.

68. Lizzie's and Joe Resnick's first child was born in the year of their marriage, 1910. Little Bernard, born in 1931, was a very late child.

69. TOP, box 17.

70. Her notes on "Neighbor Rosicky" are in TOP, box 17 Tillie labeled them "Mpls—1932."

71. Possibly, instead, Monroe responded critically and Tillie destroyed the letter. TOP, box 19.

72. Cowley, 26.

73. Among them were Sherwood Anderson, Erskine Caldwell, Malcolm Cowley, John Dos Passos, Theodore Dreiser, Granville Hicks, Langston Hughes, Edmund Wilson, and Lincoln Steffens. McElvaine, 205, 123–134, 204.

74. Tillie clipped a headline from the *Minneapolis Tribune*, on 8 July 1934, "Jobless March on City Hall." Whether Abe's failed speech was there or elsewhere is unclear.

75. Olsen private papers. Tillie did not know that Abe had made a pass at Roberta Braude. The City Directory listed them as: "Goldfarb A Jevons bkpr Tailors Service Co. r 625 S 9th and Goldfarb Abe (Tillie) tailor h623 [or 625] S 9th Apt 3. This area held numerous, reasonably priced apartment buildings close to downtown.

76. Interview with Ruth Stein Fox, 3 June 2000.

77. Vicki Lerner Bergman's recorded conversation with Gene Lerner, February 2000. She said her disease was "Dermatitis Venanata Thrombophlebitis of the left leg."

78. The song was by Jay Gorney and Edgar Y. Harburg. See Gorney, 14.

79. A September *New Masses* feature, "How I Came to Communism," was signed by prominent writers, many of whom were now supporting Roosevelt.

80. "Stalin in the American Commission."

81. TOP, box 19. The new Kansas District Organizer was Katherine Erlich. Fern Pierce seems to have referred to a published letter by Abe Goldfarb when she said—"I guess the YCL letter fits the League there [in Minneapolis] like a glove."

82. TOP, box 19.

83. Tillie wrote different versions of this letter. The draft for Jeanette is in TOP, box 15; the finished letter to Ethel is in TOP, box 1998–242.

84. The expectant couple had moved to an apartment near Goldfarb cousins named Kassler. Clara Rappaport Goldfarb, Abe's and Rae's mother, had a sister Sarah Rappaport who married a Kassler. Rae hoped Tillie would accept help from these cousins.

85. Perhaps he also told Tillie that he was only twenty-seven. Karla's birth certificate lists the Goldfarbs' address as 529 S. 9th Street. The City Directory placed them earlier at 623 and 625 S. 9th Street.

86. Ethel later argued that Tillie had wanted disciples; Ethel wrote that she and Jeanette had been "two preliminaries, two husks for [Tillie] to practice on, to warm up on." She supposed Yetta would be next.

87. Olsen private papers. She kept no letter thanking her for money or a birth announcement; perhaps she failed to send them.

88. Abe's youngest sister Betty, born in 1909, reported that Calverton, editor of the *Modern Quarterly,* was "flattered" to be compared to Abe. References to Abe's writing suggest that he was a modestly prominent leftist intellectual, using a pseudonym.

89. The day before Roosevelt's inauguration, more than five thousand banks closed. See Alter for coverage of the "defining moment" when people put money back in the banking system.

90. TOP, box 19.

91. When Gretchen Spieler asked Ethel, her grandmother, about Abe's writing, Ethel no longer remembered.

92. Interview with Lillian Lerner Davis, 24 January 2002.

93. Interview with Gene Lerner, 1 July 2000. Five years before, Abe had written this sort of advice, in an affectedly clever style, to his younger brother Nahman. Perhaps he rationalized kissing or making a pass at Roberta Braude in 1932 and then Yetta Lerner in 1934 as similarly useful initiations.

CHAPTER 5 — 1934

1. See McElvaine, 154. Mervin Le Roy's 1933 *Gold Diggers* was an allegory showing a Broadway production called "We're in the Money" closed down and replaced by a new production in which Joan Blondell sings "Remember My Forgotten Man" because otherwise "you're forgetting me." Behind her, "forgotten men" dance in a rousing routine, which saves the production and, implicitly, the country.

2. TOP, box 18, includes the book jacket from Emma F. Langdon's *The Cripple Creek Strike: History of Industrial Wars in Colorado, 1903–4–5.* Tillie was using this book about mining conditions and protests as a resource for her novel. Felipe Ibarro, "Where the Sun Spends the Winter," *New Masses* (9 January 1934).

3. Named for the radical journalist John Reed (1887–1920), the first of these clubs was founded in New York about 1930 to support radical writers and their work. By 1934, there were around twenty such clubs across the country, several of them publishing their own journals: *Leftward* (Boston), *Left Review* (Philadelphia), *Left Front* (Chicago), *Partisan* (San Francisco, Carmel, and Hollywood), and *Partisan Review* (New York City).

4. See McElvaine, 153–54.

5. McWilliams, 84, writes of Bridges's "shrewd practical approach to trade-union problems." McElvaine is my principal source for Depression history; Quin for details of the San Francisco strike; McElvaine, Gurko, and Denning for the cultural history of the period. Tillie's bitter diatribe against the CWA and Roosevelt is in TOP, box 16. Party letters to Jack Olsen are in TOP, box 1998–242. Archie Brown, who would be the Communist candidate for state treasurer, wrote Olsen on 14 February about holding meetings in the east Bay, specifically in Berkeley and Stockton. A letter to Jack Olsen, dated 18 June, says that Brown, jailed in Los Angeles, had been put in "the black hole"; mail to him should be stopped. TOP, box 19.

6. *San Francisco Chronicle* (15 February 1934). TOP, box 16, includes an even more didactic poem, "Our Miracle" that celebrates rebels, whatever their fate, against fascism. Communists had broken up a Socialist protest against Dollfuss in Madison Square Garden, further deepening divisions between leftists.

7. Phelps, 49.

8. TOP, box 19.

9. Ida's maiden name is often incorrectly given as Beber. See Appendix B.

10. See McElvaine, chapter 9. Tillie's unfinished "Imperial Valley" piece is in TOP, boxes 4 and 16. She kept a letter from Ramona, the only female YCL worker in Calexico, in the Imperial Valley, to Caroline Decker in jail, TOP, box 19, and one from Dorothy Ray, later Healey, to Jack Olsen from "Il Prisoners des Valle Imperial." TOP, box 1998–24.

11. See Quin, 31. Bruce Nelson says "the Embarcadero was known as the 'slave market,'" 106. Nelson interviewed Jack Olsen in 1981, note 5, 295.

12. TOP, box 16. Depositing her papers at Stanford, Tillie wrote on this note: "1933–4 (?) Consciousness [of] Nazi's Death Camps." Her point was that the CP knew of Nazi atrocities before the Allies discovered them.

13. By, respectively, Jay Gorney and Jimmy Durante.

14. Later Tillie gave 71 Diamond Street as an address because it was "a nonexistent number," but for several months she did receive mail at 73 Diamond Street. In the 1934 San Francisco City Directory, Nahman Goldfarb appears as a salesman living with Sue Goldfarb at 4595 18th Street.

15. The full title was: *Western Worker: Western Organ of the Communist Party U.S.A.* See Quin, 39.

16. TOP, box 15, includes this unpublished version of "The Strike."

17. TOP, box 33.

18. TOP, box 16. This fragment is undated, but references to the searchlights and the bay seem to place it in San Francisco during the strike of 1934.

19. Conversation with Vicki Lerner Richards Bergman, 9 November 1999, and her further recollections from February 2000, which were recorded by her brother Gene Lerner.

20. The *Western Worker* (11 June 1934).

21. Olsen declared his candidacy on 13 June 1934. My thanks to Genevieve Troka, of the California State Archives, who uncovered election materials for me. The CP's note is in TOP, box 19.

22. In her 1994 *Newsweek* article Tillie said there were 100,000 mourners.

23. Ella Winter's article is in TOP, box 18.

24. See Winter and Kaplan. Kaplan's title for his seventeenth chapter is "Guru of the Left."

25. See McElvaine and Quin for further details.

26. Denning reproduces one of her photographs: "San Francisco Waterfront Strike, 1934" from the San Francisco Museum of Modern Art.

27. TOP, box 16. In another version, Tillie added lines beginning: "If I go round and round,/ then they'll go round and round/ wooooooo ooo/ my stooges here,/ Ive got them so well wound/ Whatever I expound/ wooooooooo/ thats what they'll sound. . . .'"

28. Perhaps she meant Tom Courtney who gave Abe and Tillie $50. Yetta mentioned Tom in January 1934. "Is Jevons home? Are you well yet? Have you seen or heard from Agnes? If so, how is she? Tom?" TOP, box 19.

29. TOP, box 18. *Western Worker* (16 April 1934).

30. Hearst papers were the *Examiner* and the *Call-Bulletin*. The *Chronicle* proclaimed itself "The City's Only Home-Owned Newspaper," but it was said to be controlled by shipping interests. The Scripps-Howard *San Francisco News* was more objective.

31. Seeley, 310. See Nasaw, 492, for details of how Hearst coordinated newspaper coverage to make readers fear armed insurrection in San Francisco. Typically biased reporting was the *Chronicle*'s 19 July headline: "Bridges Admits Failure of Plot to Starve City Into Defeat."

32. A reporter for the *Examiner* named Tillie as Jack's manager. California State Archives do not list managers. Louise Todd worked to get several Communist candidates on the ballot in 1934 and became Olsen's manager.

33. See Tillie Olsen, "The '30s." Actually, Marian Chandler was arrested too but from 2270 Geary Street.

34. Many of the clippings quoted here were saved (but not identified) by Tillie Olsen and are in TOP, box 18. Thanks to Bill Lynch who identified them and other sources to help complete the story of Tillie's arrest.

35. The paper also named William Newman and Sam Prinze. Going over these materials fifty years later, Tillie Olsen wrote on this clipping: "Did I say I'd been at U.C.? None of us knew Dave was heir to Phillip Morris fortune." In "The '30s" she wrote that Dave was a "Reynolds tobacco heir." His photo is in TOP, box 18.

36. Tillie sometimes talked of being beaten herself—while trying to help another prisoner. Later, she dropped that part of her story.

37. There are several versions of this song, dating from the early twentieth century and the Wobbly or Industrial Workers of the World movement. A version by Faith Petric continues: "If you marched or agitated/ Then you're bound to hear it said./ So you might as well ignore it/ Or love the word instead./ Cuz ya ain't been doing nothing/ If ya ain't been called a Red." Coiner, 241, gives later dates.

38. Winter and Shapiro, 260. An example of such fear-mongering was Elizabeth Dilling's *The Red Network*, which accused everybody from Eleanor Roosevelt to Mahatma Gandhi of being a Communist menace.

39. The first headline is from the *Examiner*. TOP, box 4 includes a typed copy of an editorial, originally printed in the *Pacific Rural Press*, 4 August, reprinted in the *Carmel Pine Cone* on 10 August, attacking the Steffens, who called the latter paper the *Swine Cone*, TOP, box 19.

40. Bill Lynch found this photograph.

41. See Atkinson for evidence of just how political and relevant Faulkner's 1930s fiction actually was.

42. TOP, box 33. Friede's firm was Covici and Friede. Mangione was an editor at Robert M. McBride Publishers.

43. One of the prisoners, a union organizer named Caroline Decker, wrote a piece for the *New Masses* (28 August 1934) titled "California's Terror Continues."

44. On 17 August 1934, the *New Republic* wrote Tillie Lerner on Dolores Street accepting her essay on the strike. Tillie tried to ink out her address. TOP, box 33.

45. All letters to and from Bennett Cerf and Donald Klopfer, including those from William Saroyan, Sanora Babb, and Ralph Reynolds, are in the Random House Collection at Columbia University.

46. Anderson forwarded such letters to Tillie; many are now in TOP, box 19.

47. This column, which Tillie pasted in her scrap book, by Sender Garlin, was from the *Daily Worker* (11 August 1934). See chapter 2 for Tillie's meeting, when she was almost twelve years old, with Eugene Debs.

48. He sent a similar telegram of support to Anderson. TOP, box 33.

49. TOP, box 33. Tillie did not preserve a story about tie-factory girls; perhaps she intended to but did not write it. Nineteen years later, Cowley wrote Tillie that Cantwell had gotten "spooked" in the San Francisco inquisition. He did not recall that Tillie and Cantwell had met, but Saroyan's letter establishes that they had.

50. Vicki brought her autograph book for these famous people, including Saroyan and Hughes, to sign.

51. Arthur Caylor, "The Whirligig," *San Francisco News* (14 August 1934). In addition to the publishers mentioned here, TOP, box 33, includes 1934 letters to Tillie from many other publishers.

52. TOP, box 19. See Kaplan, 318–19, for more on the harassment of Steffens and his family.

53. These rules would be published in the introduction to his forthcoming *The Daring Young Man on the Flying Trapeze and Other Stories*. See Leggett, 29.

54. Enamored of a would-be novelist named Leo Gordon, Ethel was taking classes, keeping books at the New York Workers School, and trading on her relationship with the famous Tillie Lerner.

55. Conversation with TO, 19 July 2003. See Quin, 189–90.

56. TOP, 1998-24.

57. TOP, boxes 16 and 17.

58. *Chronicle* reports on the jailed Reds, on 11 and 14 August, do not mention Jack Olsen or Tillie Lerner. On 14 August, Louise Todd was released from jail. Jack Olsen definitely was free on 5 September when he signed the "Candidate's Affidavit of Receipts and Expenditures for Primary Election."

59. "Former Omahan Headed For Bright Career as Authoress," *Weekly Omaha Jewish Press* (24 August 1934), from the archives of the Jewish Community Center, Omaha,

TOP, box 18. In December 1934, Tillie wrote Cerf that Morris had publicized "my arrest and shame."

60. See Rideout for discussion of such shop-worn formulas in radical American novels.

61. She was in the hospital until about 25 September. The Knopf editor marked a letter to her "Sept. 25. This was returned from St. Luke's. I'm sending it c/o Gen. Delivery." TOP, box 1998–24.

62. The *Partisan Review*'s note on Tillie Lerner said she had been arrested but was "recently released on bail, and is now completing a novel, part of which appeared in the April-May issue of *Partisan Review.*"

63. Apparently, Tillie was fabricating on 10 September when she wrote Cerf. She had been out of jail a month but said "they waited till now to get him." The *Whirligig* article had identified her without mentioning the name "Goldfarb." An unidentified "JM" wrote Abe in September that Nahman Goldfarb could not get a job with SERA while his brother worked for the agency, thus suggesting that Abe had not been fired after all. This "JM" told Abe that Jack Olsen sent "greetings to T and hopes for her rapid recovery." According to the *Western Worker* (20 September 1934), "SERA Workers in San Francisco" were demanding "$10 Weekly."

64. Tillie did not mention Karla. Coiner blames a masculine press for disinterest in the "mother-content" of Tillie's writings, but Tillie's private letters also omit Karla.

65. The *Young Worker*, published in New York by the Young Communist League of the USA, reprinted "The Strike" in two parts: 25 September and 9 October 1934. The *Young Worker*'s version of "The Strike" breaks up the article into shorter paragraphs (one of which it prints twice) and cuts some of the treatment of "OUR BROTHERS," Tillie's tribute to the two strikers shot by policemen.

66. Saroyan had been in court when Lyon, called "Red" in the trial with Tillie, defended himself.

67. While potential publishers had had trouble finding her, Tillie belatedly kept Random House informed of her frequent relocations that fall: from Broderick Street in San Francisco, to Spruce Street in Berkeley, to the RFD post office box in Stockton, to General Delivery in Sacramento, and then in December 1934, to Rhode Island Street in San Francisco. Macmillan addressed a last letter to "Mrs. Tillie Goldfarb" on Rhode Island Street.

68. When a mutual friend asked "when does T. expect her baby?" Sue Goldfarb replied that Tillie had had a miscarriage; then she wrote Tillie to say that a "miscarriage" was her explanation. Letters from Sue and Nahman Goldfarb follow the loss of their baby. Sue's reference to Saroyan's radio talk dates this letter after 14 October 1934 so Tillie's interrupted pregnancy was definitely in fall 1934. TOP, box 1998–24.

69. Sue Goldfarb thought Saroyan's "Aspirin Is a Member of the NRA," in the *American Mercury*, "nonsense." She termed Abe's response to the story "rib cracking" but did not indicate whether his response was private or published. Ethel Schochet began, as she wrote Tillie, "collecting statements of Saroyan for your amusement." TOP, box 1998–24. *Stand Up and Cheer*, featured Shirley Temple, "Aunt Jemima," and "Stepin Fetchit."

70. Tillie kept a booklet on "The Pacific Coast Maritime Strike," TOP, box 18. See Kirchwey for an account of California's Criminal Syndicalism law, enacted as a "concrete expression of war psychology" during the U.S. participation in WWI. The 18 November

1935 issue of *Pacific Weekly* describes Michael Quin as "the author of a decently published pamphlet, *The Criminal Syndicalism Case Against Labor,* the assignment first offered to Tillie Lerner. By May 1935, Grace Lumpkin was writing for the *Labor Defender.*

71. *Western Worker* (22 October 1934).

72. Sinclair had won the nomination over George Creel (cousin of Tillie's Omaha friend Anel Creel). Olsen's article appeared in the *Young Worker* (23 October and 4 November 1934).

73. An article titled "Sacramento" from Tillie's scrapbook (TOP, 1998–242) carries no byline. It came from the *Western Worker* (22 October 1934), before Tillie got her assignment. This article and a later one by Dave Lyon end with pleas to write protests, a liberal notion of working within the system. The *Labor Defender's* purpose was to "provoke indignation in fellow Communists and win support from liberals with a heart" (Fried, 22).

74. After the *Anvil* and the *Partisan Review* merged, "Skeleton Children" was not printed until it appeared as an early section of *Yonnondio* (1974).

75. Ella Winter signed her letters by Steffens's pet name for her "Peter." They are in TOP, box 33. Abe wrote Sue that Tillie had finished the "Imperial Valley" piece. TOP, box 16, includes some twenty-five pages of this article, in various stages of incompletion and revision.

76. Tillie's intercession with Granville Hicks on Saroyan's behalf bore fruit: in the *New Masses* (23 October 1934), Hicks printed a Saroyan story and letter saying that he was not a member of any party, though the CP was the "most valid and decent" he knew; Hicks's editorial commentary advised Saroyan to read Marx.

77. After the Modern Library had reissued *Three Lives* in 1933, Gertrude Stein signed with Random House.

78. TOP, box 19.

79. At the end of 1934, the editors of *Controversy* split. Steffens, Winter, and W. K. Bassett started a new journal called *Pacific Weekly: A Western Journal of Fact and Opinion.*

80. See Buhle and Wagner, 62, and McElvaine, 228–37. McElvaine points out that these "dirty tricks" were only surpassed in the presidential election of 1972.

81. Among other scapegoating tactics, Coughlin tried to blame FDR and the Jews for the Great Depression. The issue of the *Young Worker* that printed "Why They're Trying Don," included an article on Coughlin written by Al Richmond, who would play a part in Tillie's life. TOP, box 18, includes "Truth about Father Coughlin," several *Maritime Strike News Bulletins*, from San Pedro in December 1936, and a clipping on Cartagena Spain.

82. Perhaps Jack Olsen was also at the trials, for Winter wondered if "the CS kids got over the bone Jack made?"

83. Tillie sent this letter to Cerf during the week of 19 November. In her 7 November letter to Klopfer she had mentioned "the day I went into Frisco to meet Doletsky," so perhaps she met him twice.

84. After having his gift of *Three Lives* returned from the Berkeley address, Cerf remailed it to Stockton, and hedged his bets by sending a letter to Tillie at General Delivery in Sacramento.

85. TOP, box 17.

86. TOP, box 15, and TOP, box 1998–242. This article appeared in the *Young Worker*

(18 December 1934). Though Tillie misspelled Bigham's name as "Bingham" and made a few mistranscriptions, most of her changes are decidedly literary.

87. Ida's letters are in TOP, box 19, and in Lerner Papers. She probably wrote this letter in 1934, after Tillie had Philip Rahv send the *Partisan Review* to Sam Lerner. Tillie's twenty-one-page draft version of Anna's thoughts is in the Berg Collection of the NYPL.

88. TOP, box 16.

89. The passage survives in the first part of *Yonnondio*. The manuscript with the instructions to delete the passage is in the Berg Collection, NYPL.

90. Christmas was on a Tuesday so she was speaking of Friday or Saturday, 21 or 22 December 1934.

CHAPTER 6 — 1935–1936

1. See Denning, 4 and *passim*, for a discussion of the socialist-leaning groups that together formed a "Popular Front" and changed American values.

2. A telegram from Macmillan, dated 12 January 1935, is addressed to "Mrs. Tillie Goldfarb" at the Rhode Island Street address. TOP, box 33.

3. Harry (Mink) Johnson was known as a great storyteller; Peter Quince wrote for the Federal Writers' Project, the *Anvil*, and the *Young Worker*.

4. Faulkner was in his early thirties when he perfected a similar technique in the Benjy section of *The Sound and the Fury*. Faulkner paraphrased words he had given the beleaguered Dilsey, who remarks, near the end of *The Sound and the Fury*, "I does the bes I kin."

5. Courtesy of "The Family Songbook" collected by Laurie Olsen.

6. That January, the *Young Worker* memorialized "Red Rosa" Luxemburg, who had been arrested in the uprisings of 1905 and escaped. Later she helped transform the "Spartakus League" into the German Communist Party and was "lynched by a Fascist crowd of officers." In February 1935, the *Young Worker* also eulogized Joe York, the YCL leader Tillie had tried to write about three years before, who had been "Murdered by Ford's thugs, at Dearborn."

7. See TOP, box 33, and *New Masses* (29 January 1935).

8. On her desperate telegram, the Random House accountant penciled in "Sent $100 Jan."

9. He sent her basic instructions on how wide to make her margins, where to place her name, and how to achieve legibility by writing only on one side of a page. TOP, box 33.

10. Karla now wore a truss over her stomach hernia.

11. TOP, box 16. This long letter narrated both her departure and her return in a jumbled order. Both the salutation and the signature are torn off, but evidence, especially Rae's comments, indicates that Tillie wrote it to Abe and that the date is late January 1935.

12. This "Tom" might be the Tom Courtney who gave Abe $50. Perhaps by "have him," she meant have his support. If this Tom were a child Tillie had, Rae might have meant having a way to be in touch with him. TOP, box 16, holds Tillie's reference to a "love story of long ago; he at the school for the feeble minded." During the 1950s, under the name Emily Hulot Olsen, she wrote a story and poem about having a retarded child

and keeping him. TOP, box 15. If Tillie and Abe had a son, perhaps named Tom, a birth date of 1931 seems likely; being adopted or put in an institution would perhaps explain the absence of birth records.

13. TOP, box 19. Ella Winter's invitation was written on 18 December 1934. In her letter of 22 February 1935, she asked, "How are Karla and J [Jevons]?" assuming that Karla and Abe were with Tillie.

14. The *Western Worker* reported on Strachey's San Francisco talk on 25 February 1935. He debated anti-Soviet thinkers in cities across the country; Cerf attended a New York debate on 24 March.

15. Strachey narrated these events in letters to Tillie, none of which mention her daughter. TOP, box 19.

16. According to the *New Masses* (26 March 1935), the Hearst papers were calling for Strachey's deportation because his public appearances were persuasive. Though being investigated for "peddling Marxism," Strachey thought his troubles would seem "tame stuff" to the supposedly intrepid Tillie.

17. Stewart had written *Going Hollywood* (1933) and *The Barretts of Wimpole Street* (1934). He would write the Academy Award-winning script for *Philadelphia Story* (1940). He was a committed member of the Hollywood Anti-Nazi League.

18. These claims, on a draft of this letter, are mixed in with scenes from her book. Berg Collection, New York Public Library.

19. See Gurko, 66–70, for the "flood of novels" about similar disasters.

20. Berg Collection, NYPL.

21. See Appendix C for the planned disasters she sent Donald Klopfer. Tillie wrote on the backs of sheets of paper from the Common Brick Manufacturers Association of Northern California, the Civil Works Administration letters sent to "AJG," a Farmer Labor Party, a Federal Study of Local School Units, and a savings and loan receipt form. Berg Collection, NYPL.

22. Sometimes Karla's "tummy" referred to her stomach hernia, sometimes her appendix.

23. For the *Western Worker*, Carlisle wrote "Calif. C.S. Trial Goes to Jury: Victims of Terror Raids Face Possible Prison Terms" (1 April 1935). Without bylines, the *Western Worker* printed "Steffens Fights War on his 69th Birthday" (8 April 1935) and "45 Facing Gallup Murder Frame-Up" (22 April 1935).

24. Tillie sent a copy of the *Brothers Karamazov* to the Tehachapi Women's Prison, where Nora Conklin and Louise Todd were imprisoned, with a letter about this talk on Ukraine. See the *New Masses* (12 March 1935) for a letter from Donald Bigham and Martin Wilson.

25. The Holbrook passages about unemployment were definitely written in spring 1935 when she was in Venice.

26. McElvaine lists sixty to seventy-five million movie tickets a week, with 60 percent of the population seeing movies, 208. John R. Chaplin uses similar numbers for yearly sales. He defines the Hollywood mentality, as "empty laughter lulling the masses to sleep, cutting them off from thought, from culture, from enlightenment." *International Literature* (December 1934) ran a series on "The Myth and Reality of Hollywood."

27. Wixson, 395. Tillie remembered Carlisle telling her about meeting a woman wearing a violet-colored hat and veil, a matching violet suit with a short skirt and shiny

silk stockings. After marrying the woman, he became appalled by her indifference to the working classes. Conversation with TO, 22 July 2000.

28. Wixson, 395.

29. The *New Masses*, on 14 and 21 May 1935, covered the kidnapping and "frameup" in Gallup.

30. Years later, Tillie said that she had taken Karla with her and dropped her off in Omaha on the way east, but this letter and Babb's recollections establish that Karla was not with Tillie. TOP, box 16.

31. Interview with Lillian Lerner Davis, January 2002.

32. Wixson, 395, 559. Wixson to PR, 24 October 2000.

33. When they set off, neither Babb nor Carlisle knew that Tillie was married. See Wixson, 395, 388.

34. To Tillie, Bein regretted the "de-balled" writers' congress, perhaps referring to tiresome debates about bourgeois and proletarian writing, TOP, box 19. Dealing with attempts to unionize mill workers, *Let Freedom Ring* opened at the Broadhurst Theater on 6 November 1935 and ran for 108 performances.

35. Chairman Waldo Frank made this plea, but he was a token, non-CP leader, while other members of the executive committee were CP members or "fellow travelers." See Aaron, *Writers*, 284.

36. One speaker argued that the American writer should "stir the worker himself to create art." Malcolm Cowley argued that the middle class and the proletariat could profit from each other. See the *New Masses* (2 and 23 April, and 7 May 1935) and Aaron, *Writers*, 286. In the 14 May *New Masses*, Granville Hicks criticized Faulkner's *Pylon* not for its actual artistic failures but because Faulkner was too much of a capitalist.

37. The Twenty-first Amendment, repealing the Eighteenth, officially passed on 5 December 1933, ending Prohibition. A play about coal miners called *The Black Pit* opened at Theatre Union in 1933.

38. Unaware that the *Partisan Review* was planning to take over the *Anvil*, Tillie dutifully took notes about making the *Anvil* "a Party magazine," TOP, 1998–242. She was an unwitting accessory to an anti-Conroy coup, staged by eastern, more intellectual, non-working-class Communists.

39. Interview with TO, 4 April 1998. See Cerf, 105, for a slightly different account of the evening. Sylvia Sidney was two years older than Tillie and also born of immigrant parents.

40. Wixson to PR, 28 November 2000. Among the marchers were fiction writers Josephine Herbst, Meridel Le Sueur, Nelson Algren, and Richard Wright; poet Langston Hughes; playwright Albert Bein; Earl Browder, president of the CP-USA; and editors Malcolm Cowley (of the *New Republic*), Granville Hicks, Isidor Schneider, and Mike Gold (of the *New Masses*), Philip Rahv and James Farrell (of the *Partisan Review*), and Jack Conroy, fiction writer and editor (of the *Anvil*). See Aaron, *Writers*.

41. Herbst appears only as a profiled head with a large hat; cartoons of the men end at the chin or shoulders; two men are shown with an outline of their backs.

42. Wixson, 395.

43. An advertisement ran in the *New Masses* (7 May 1935).

44. When Vicki needed to submit original poems in Sara Vore Taylor's English class, Tillie told her to submit her own juvenile poems as hers; if queried, Vicki should re-

member that "silent, mysterious, hokum goes over big." Vicki Lerner Richards Bergman, with enclosures, to PR, 29 December 2001.

45. Actually, Cerf had visited the USSR with some admiration but much disgust over self-inflicted suffering and assumed martyrdom. See Foley and Gurko for analyses of the proletarian social novel in the 1930s.

46. Tillie said she had given her word that she would write her novel to Earl Browder and "Trachty," Alexander Trachtenberg, cultural head of the CP-USA. Clearly, the party was as eager for Tillie to finish her novel as was Cerf. See Aaron, *Writers*, 281–84.

47. Olsen organized the first Youth Congress in Southern California in February 1935.

48. TOP, box 17. This penciled entry was partly crossed through .

49. When she began her film about Tillie Olsen, Ann Hershey did not know that Tillie had had a husband before Jack. After I told her otherwise, Hershey made inquiries and was told that Abe had walked out on Tillie, leaving a note saying that he would no longer endure her treatment of him.

50. Internal references to the "San Francisco General Strike Diary," *International Literature* 2 (February 1935), 43–51, establish that the letter-writer was Peter Quince. See TOP, box 33. Wixson, 395.

51. *Time* (January 1935). The *Western Worker* (10 January 1935). Future President John F. Kennedy was one of Joseph Kennedy's sons.

52. Fragments in the Berg Collection from the first seven or so chapters, include several self-directed notes about her "lousy" writing. One page is labeled "CHAPTER TWELVE" and numbered 319, but there are no intermediary chapters.

53. Winter was generous with her own and Steffens's money and may have received money from the USSR for political leaflets and party organizing. See Billingsley, 29–30.

54. Interview with Schulberg, 22 July 2000.

55. Billingsley, 56.

56. In *Footlight Parade*, for example, James Cagney plays a Broadway producer saved by New Deal lyrics. Billingsley plays up, while Buhle and Wagner play down, Communist attempts to use Hollywood.

57. Interview with TO, 22 July 2000.

58. The narrator in Budd Schulberg's *What Makes Sammy Run* earns $350 a week. In the early 1940s, Faulkner earned a humiliating $300 a week, while "top" writers might earn $2,500. See Blotner, 1121.

59. Her principal characters are young New York intellectuals trying to start a leftist magazine. The Hunger March and the campaign to free the "Scottsboro Boys" form part of the background. The future editor concludes "Down with revolutions, resolutions, magazines. . . . We believe in nothing but aspirin and sex," *The Unpossessed*, 326. The Communist Party thought the book "unsound" for giving comfort to capitalists.

60. At novelist Samuel Ornitz's Los Angeles home, Lawson had met Ainslee, who helped him learn film technique, Buhle and Wagoner, 35.

61. The note to Tillie is from Louise Maxson, TOP, box 19. Ashe wrote for the *Western Worker* and organized a party cell in Hollywood. See Billingsley, 52 and 228–29.

62. The *New Masses* (23 April 1935) ran an ad about the American Writers' Congress.

63. From the USSR, Ainslee sent Tillie "greetings to Matt and Louise and Jerry and

Sylvia." Matt Pelman and Louise Maxson were CP colleagues of Jack Olsen. (Louise Todd was in prison.) Jerry and Sylvia were Goldfarb friends or family. These greetings establish that Ainslee knew Tillie's activist comrades and Goldfarb connections. TOP, box 19.

64. Before Social Security most of the elderly were destitute. See McElvaine, chapters 11 and 12.

65. Eleanor Roosevelt brought Sidney Kingsley's *Dead End* to Washington for the first-ever White House command performance in December 1935.

66. Berg Collection. The benefit concert was on 27 October 1935. Cerf mentioned, in a January 1936 letter, going with Sylvia and Tillie to a cocktail party in Los Angeles near the end of October 1935.

67. Tillie had disappeared from the roster of *Pacific Weekly* (the journal replacing *Controversy*), but on 12 August she was again listed among its contributors, though it had yet to print anything by her. Perhaps she helped secure its interview with Harry Bridges in that issue.

68. *Pacific Weekly* (18 November 1935). This review, reprinted here for the first time, partly echoes the *New Masses* (12 February 1935): "it is a pity that so many young writers drawn from the proletariat can make no better use of their working class experience than as material for introspective and febrile novels."

69. Billingsley, 56–57. His source is Schwarts, *Hollywood Writers' Wars*, 92.

70. Billingsley, 65; Navasky, 244.

71. TOP, box 19. See Healey and Isserman, 61–64, for more about working for the YCL in San Pedro and for quotations from Jack Olsen. In southern California's YCL, proletarian workers dubbed middle-class volunteers "artists or petty bourgeoisie youth that are bored with the present system." Olsen was mostly opposed to expelling the volunteers. The Southern California Regional American Youth Congress, in February 1935, was meant to settle these differences. TOP, box 1998–242, holds many letters on this topic.

72. TOP, box 17. Tillie's adolescent poems and diary entries often anticipate death, as in a poem about snow covering the earth that "will also be my shroud" (TOP, box 16). This 1935 experience was "first" probably because it seemed genuine. A letter from Marian Ainslee, written then, is in TOP, 1998–242.

73. The *Labor Defender* (July 1935) says CS prisoners Caroline Decker, organizer for the Cannery and Agricultural Workers Industrial Union, and Nora Conklin, organizer of the Unemployment Council, had been "carried to Tehachapi to begin their sentences of one to fourteen years each." Tillie collected letters to and from these prisoners and lacerated herself for not being among them. TOP, box 19.

74. TOP, box 17. Many pages are torn out of this tiny book. In the 1930s, train steward-esses could be hired to care for children traveling alone.

75. Reel 297 of the CP-USA at the Library of Congress includes District 13 (California) records. Minutes for 5 November 1935 include instructions: "T. to go to Sacramento." A month later JG [perhaps Jevons Goldfarb] should "be given one-month leave of absence" and "T. to be sent out by TU Dept. from time to time for trade union work in sections." Whether "T." is Tillie Lerner, though, cannot be known.

76. Established early in Roosevelt's presidency, the CCC gave young unmarried men

jobs conserving the nation's natural resources. To restore the Roman Empire, Mussolini's troops invaded Ethiopia in 1935.

77. TOP, boxes 16, 17, and 1998–242.

78. Dated 30 December 1935, this issue of *Pacific Weekly* actually appeared in 1936.

79. Though she was almost twenty-four that New Year's, Jack thought she was twenty-two.

80. TOP, box 16.

81. In the 1934 City Directory Harry and Celia Dinkin were listed at an address on McAllister Street; he was a clerk, perhaps on the docks. They are not listed in the 1936 directory, apparently because they had moved to Fell Street and did not have a telephone.

82. Interview with Gene Lerner, 3 July 2000.

83. At the time, medical schools in the East had quotas limiting the number of Jews admitted.

84. My thanks to Ruth Stein Fox for giving me a photo of Vicki in the Lerners' living room. Interview with Lillian Lerner Davis, 24 January 2002.

85. The list included Josephine Herbst, Jack Conroy, Erskine Caldwell, John Dos Passos, and André Gide. Tillie told Cerf to write her in care of an Alice Owens at General Delivery in San Francisco; when he did this, however, his letters were returned.

86. Erik Matilla to PR, 7 November 2000. The "Woman Question" was a pamphlet by Clara Zetkin, a colleague of Rosa Luxemburg. The relationship of women's issues to Marxist issues was much debated in the 1930s. Olive Schreiner's *Woman and Labour* (1911), a favorite of Tillie's, was widely circulated. Mary Inman was studying Lenin and Zetkin, in preparation for her *In Woman's Defense* (1940). A *New Masses* (19 February 1935) featured an article on "Women and Communism." Grace Hutchins published *Women Who Work* in 1934.

87. On her note, Tillie also wrote "1935–36 Matt?" TOP, box 17.

88. Those words are from a handsome sailor named Gehn, who after a drunken brawl in which someone was killed, "took the rap" and was sent to Alcatraz. Interview with TO, 22 July 2000. TOP, box 19.

89. Tillie took notes, imitating these sailors' stories. TOP, box 16.

90. Saunders wrote Tillie he told Hawaiian sailors "that they ought to knock off singing long enough to chase Dole and the other sugar barons to hell out—then they could really sing—they think it is a swell idea." TOP, box 24. He also advised sailors to "go to Soviet Russia" for safety. Tillie often typed up Saunders's columns to deliver to Mike Quin at the *Western Worker*. TOP, boxes 18 and 19.

91. The dialogue seems partly authentic, mostly drunken. TOP, box 1998–242.

92. The FBI said that Tillie and Jack married in 1936 and that a Rev. Floyd Seaman—possibly a joke about a seamen or semen—married them.

93. On 28 February 1959 Jack sent Tillie a telegram: "REMEMBERING A VALENTINES DAY 23 YEARS AGO THAT STARTED THE FINEST THING IN MY LIFE." In 1945, when Tillie was at a California Labor Conference in the mountains, near Fresno, she wrote Jack about being there earlier on "(our honeymoon) trip." Olsen private papers.

94. TOP, box 19.

95. The photograph is dated 22 April 1936. Courtesy of the San Francisco History Center, San Francisco Public Library.

96. TOP, box 18 contains many instances, including a printing receipt dated 5 March 1936 for Tillie Lerner of the "Youth Press Committee" for 500 stickers and 500 dance tickets and a YCL bulletin on the framing of Tom Mooney with the call to "Be LOYAL, not to the bosses, but to yourself—to your class" and to join the YCL, written in the name of Jack Olsen, YCL State Secretary, at the 37 Grove Street address.

97. *Western Worker*, 11, 14, and 21 May, and 4 June, 1936. Ella Winter and Lincoln Steffens had withdrawn from the editorship of *Pacific Weekly*. Winter began writing for the *Western Worker*, and Steffens reviewed Hicks's biography of John Reed there on 11 May 1936. Steffens died in August. Tillie does not seem to have noted the loss of her early sponsor.

98. One photograph, courtesy of the Jewish Community Center, Omaha, Nebraska, shows "Morrie Lerner, Lil Lerner, Karla Goldfarb, Ruthie Fox, Yetta Lerner (Vicki), and Phil Shoolein." Another shows Ida, Karla, and Morris (Gene). The quotation from Ida is in Gene Lerner's memoir. Lerner Papers.

99. Jack, Tillie, and Karla lived at 1250 Montgomery Street, San Francisco, TOP, box 19.

100. Sanora Babb saw them together and remembered: "after she brought Karla to SF Tillie turned her care over mainly to Jack Olsen." Doug Wixson to PR, 24 October 2000.

101. The chapter headings were: I-Idyll; II-The Mine; III-The Farm; IV-The City; V-Some Laughter & a Portent of Weeping; VI-The Strike; VII-The Man Without a Country; VIII-The Street; IX-And Night Descended—Anna's; X-The Poem. Berg Collection.

102. Presumably, she meant Japanese advances into China. Berg Collection. TOP, 1998–242.

103. Tillie kept the first issue (dated 1 October 1936) of the *Maritime Mirror: "Reflecting the Opinions of the Rank and File,"* written "For Union Labor. BY Union Labor," probably by Tillie herself.

104. Assigning comrades to posts, regardless of their personal lives remained a common practice in the CP. Tillie Lerner's voter registration in Los Angeles was dated 23 September 1936. For the 1935 Los Angeles City Directory she listed herself oddly at 2612 ½ W. Pico as "Tillie Olsen." She recommended to students: Jack London's "South of the Slot," Bellamy's *Looking Backward*, Shaw's *Major Barbara*, Dickens's *Bleak House* and *David Copperfield*, and Scott's *Heart of Midlothian*. TOP, box 1998–242. The party reprimand is in TOP, box 16.

105. See McElvaine, 280–81.

106. McWilliams wrote *Factories in the Field*. Steinbeck's articles, in preparation for *Grapes of Wrath*, were appearing in various magazines and papers.

107. Mike Quin wrote Tillie about transportation to the conference. TOP, box 19. She took Karla and left her with Nahman (who now worked for SERA) and Sue Goldfarb. See Rae Schochet's letter to Abe, TOP, box 1998–353. The *Western Worker* (16 November 1936) included details about the Congress.

108. Schulberg to PR, December 2001. He said Tillie was expected to be "even better than Clara Weatherwax," the author of *Marching! Marching!* (1935), which was awarded the *New Masses*'s "best novel" award, though James T. Farrell quipped that it should have been titled "Stumbling! Stumbling."

CHAPTER 7 — 1937–1939

1. The address she used in early 1937 was 3745 Whiteside Avenue. Tilda Olsen appears in the 1937 Los Angeles City Directory living at 645 E. Washington Blvd.

2. FDR set up a commission on slums, which resulted in government funding for safe, low-income housing.

3. Within the next two and a half years, Court retirements enabled Roosevelt to appoint liberal justices: Hugo Black, Stanley Reed, William O. Douglas, Frank Murphy, and Felix Frankfurter.

4. One 1937 letter was addressed to him at CP headquarters in Los Angeles. TOP, box 19. An undated reference to Jack Olsen in a little notebook shows him looking for a nursery for Karla, TOP, box 17.

5. A letter from "AF of L—Sam" was sent on 30 April 1937 to Tillie at the Whiteside address. A 1937 envelope to Tillie Lerner from *International Literature* in Moscow was sent to the Whiteside address but forwarded to the Winter Street address. (Tillie kept these envelopes, not, apparently, the letters.) Marian Ainslee telegraphed Tillie at the Winter Street address. TOP, box 19.

6. A letter to Tillie, with its signature torn off, dated 3 March 1937 says that the Los Angeles YCL is "going to town, with four new branches, recruiting etc. Our work both in the East-bay and San Francisco is not making as rapid progress as we should. Dorothy Rae [Healey] is working at the present time and cannot devote as much time as County Organizer as she should. Of course, the best branch in the city is the 'waterfront,' they recruited 70 during the strike!" TOP, box 19.

7. TOP, boxes 19, 17, and 16.

8. The *Western Worker* maintained that "Trozkyites Work With Fascists for War, Against Labor." It urged liberals to disregard "principles of civil liberties" and stop defending Trotsky. Mike Gold called Trotsky "the most horrible Judas in all history." Ella Winter compared him to John Wilkes Booth, failing to note that Lincoln was no dictator, while Stalin was, or that Booth was an assassin, while Trotsky was not; *Western Worker* (18 and 22 February and 8 March 1937). See Mangione on the debilitating effects of Marxist ideology in the WPA Writers Project, 136–37.

9. Abe maintained to Rae that "even" Malcolm Cowley and Edmund Wilson of the *New Republic* had seen the wisdom of Marx and Lenin, though Wilson had regressed into a Trotskyite. Abe recommended Steffens's autobiography. Gretchen Spieler's private collection. Rae wears overalls, perhaps for work, in one photo. TOP, box 48.

10. TOP, box 16.

11. This accounting dates from March 1937.

12. Tillie dated this note, Sunday, 28 February [1937]. A notebook she dated 1937 includes stories about Spain and one (she later explained on an attached post-it) is about "A pregnancy (I had an abortion) A new story—setting Spain." TOP, boxes 17 and 16. The miscarriage or abortion Sue Goldfarb wrote about can be dated 1934. Thus Tillie had had abortions in 1928, 1934, and now 1937. Also perhaps she had placed a 1931 child "Tom" with a couple for adoption. The "dead rich" baby quotation is in TOP, 1998–353.1.

13. She was referencing Cab Calloway: "Folks, here's a story about Minnie the Moocher./ She was a red hot hoochie-koocher."

14. Born on 15 April 1937, Olive later changed her name to "Carole."

15. Lillian and Joseph had secretly married in Atlantic, Iowa, in September 1936. By the time Rae brought Karla to Omaha, their marriage was no longer a secret.

16. The *Western Worker* (21 June 1937).

17. TOP, box 17.

18. Mike Gold's "Tribute to the *Western Worker*" was printed in New York in the *Daily Worker* and reprinted in the *Western Worker* (29 July 1937).

19. She wrote this to Jerre Mangione; records of her FWP work have not surfaced.

20. The *Mariner* is in TOP, 1998-242.

21. TOP, boxes 19 and 18.

22. In 1934–1935, Tillie had written only two of her promised articles on the Criminal Syndicalism trials. When the accused "syndicalists" finally were set free, the *Western Worker* (4 October 1937) turned to Paul Cline, not Tillie Lerner, for some perspective on this "signal victory."

23. In a letter to Amy, dated 13 October 1937, apparently Tillie asked "how your chest is, your general health, how your book goes." An envelope to Tillie in the hospital from Louise Maxson in San Pedro is dated 20 October 1937. A letter from Jean [Wertheimer] to "Kiddo" says Maxson told her "you were in the hospital." TOP, box 19. Who cared for Karla while Tillie was hospitalized is not clear.

24. TOP, box 19.

25. See the *Western Worker* (14 October 1937) and Billingsley and Buhle and Wagner for more on union rivalries. The letter to Tillie from "AF of L—Sam" (see note 5) might relate Tillie to these rivalries.

26. Tillie said she tried not to cause Abe pain but later tried to cross out that statement. Her tiny handwriting attributes the story to an unidentified writer with a name like "Komroff."

27. She also wrote: "I had to get flu to round out things—and granulation in my incision so the darn thing drains all the time . . . now all I do is cough just a little bit, and after the eighty-ninth probing, digging, cauterizing it looks like the zipper will heal up."

28. The *Western Worker* ran the photograph on Thanksgiving, 25 November 1937, courtesy of the Resettlement Administration. The official title of Lange's photograph is "Migrant Mother, Nipomo California, 1936." See Denning, figure 7, and 137–38.

29. *Western Worker* (18 and 22 November 1937). Walker Evans authored the "racketeering" article, saying that Capone promised big business, before being sent to Alcatraz, to "save the country from Communism."

30. The Social Security Administration records that Abe Goldfarb, also listed as "A. J." or "Albert" Goldfarb, was working for the Edison Brothers Stores earlier in 1937, when he resisted getting a Social Security card. He had acquired one by the time of his death.

31. Both the *Van Nuys News* (18 November 1937) and the *San Fernando Sun* (19 November 1937) carried error-filled accounts, the former calling him "Filbert" and the latter "Albert." The Van Nuys paper also said that he had been using an alias, Al Alton, a name not listed in a Los Angeles city directory. The death certificate gives his correct name but lists his age as thirty-seven, when it should have been forty-one. The FBI and the LA police had infiltrated the CP by this time, perhaps on the trail of AFL-CIO rivalries. Billingsley, 64.

32. An envelope in TOP, box 19, was from "Mr. Tillie Lerner, 1250 Montgomery St., San Francisco" to "Mrs. Jack Olsen, 3018 Winter Street, Los Angeles." The postmark is 4 December 1937.

33. TOP, box 17. A companion reference to Spain dates these entries from this period.

34. TOP, box 16. In the 1990s, Tillie dated this page "1936" without explanation. It seems more likely to date from 1935 when she fled Hollywood or from 1937 when she castigated herself for falsity.

35. The family only heard from Tillie about once a year so possibly Tillie simply forgot she had not already told them that Abe was dead. Conversation with Vicki Lerner Richards Bergman, 9 November 1999.

36. TOP, box 17. This is the same memo book in which she mentioned "my pregnancy," late February 1937.

37. See Appendix A for the previously unlisted contributions of Tillie Lerner to the *Daily People's World*, also known as *Peoples' World*.

38. *DPW*'s weekly magazine soon printed Martin Wilson's "Songs of San Quentin" after he was released from jail. The *DPW* magazine in this period published fiction by Jack Conroy, Meridel LeSeuer, Upton Sinclair, Genevieve Taggard, John Steinbeck, and Sanora Babb, but none by Tillie Lerner.

39. There is no correspondence with either Mooney or Bridges in the Random House files at Columbia. After Steinbeck's *Grapes of Wrath* was published in 1939, Random House rejected Sanora Babb's novel about migrant workers, probably since Cerf saw no market for a second book on the topic. See Wixson, 396.

40. Perhaps embarrassed by her article "Noted Publisher Here," Tillie did not send it to Cerf. He found out about it when Marian Spitzer, a short story writer, sent him a copy.

41. Al Richmond explained this argument to the San Francisco YCL, probably at Tillie's invitation.

42. Billingsley, 71-73.

43. TOP, box 18.

44. *Daily People's World* (26 March and 15 April 1938). TOP, boxes 17 and 16.

45. *Daily People's World*, "The Stars Aid Spain" (26 March 1938). Representing the League of American Writers, Franklin Folsom accompanied Ella Winter when she brought the writers' protest to the editors of the *Times*. See Folsom for details.

46. Tillie added the comment about working for Western on a Post-it note in the 1990s. She often told about working at the Palace Hotel and, as a maid, being prevented from hearing an address by Pearl Buck, but no contemporary references seem to have survived. They lived on Wallace Street, Divisadero Street, and Roosevelt Way. TOP, boxes 15 and 16.

47. In September 2002, Tillie could or would not explain why she had been so unsuccessful in following the lessons in birth control that Ida had imparted to her, her sisters, and their friends.

48. A letter to "Mrs. Olsen" at 2008 O'Farrell Street instructs her to report to the chest clinic on 31 May 1938. TOP, box 19.

49. *People's World* (7 June 1938). When Sanora Babb visited the Olsens, she concluded

that Jack had assumed primary responsibilty for Karla's care. Doug Wixson to PR, 24 October 2000.

50. Chamberlain explained ceding much of Czechoslovakia to Hitler as buying "peace in our time," alluding to the English hymn "God the Omnipotent!," written by Henry F. Chorley and John Ellerton, asking God for "peace in our time, we pray."

51. Gurko sees this event as harbinger of the country's "girding itself for war." See Gurko, 222–26.

52. Two comrades running for office did not dare attack FDR or Democrats. They were Nora Conklin, former CS prisoner, and Dave Saunders, writer and sailor. TOP, box 1998-242.

53. TOP, box 19. Mussolini was then preparing to invade tiny Albania.

54. TOP, box 19.

55. Eleanor Roosevelt spoke to the Freshman Club on 12 January 1938. In his letter thanking her, Gene called her the "personification of democracy." All references to Gene Lerner's correspondence with Eleanor Roosevelt are courtesy of the Franklin D. Roosevelt Library. An Omaha newspaper article, perhaps by Gene, includes a photograph of "Eugene Morris Lerner" and emphasizes the brilliance of all six Lerner children "noted for jumping grades in school, earning A grades and things like that. They are all products of Central High school, with Yetta the only one still a student there, collecting A grades."

56. TOP, box 16.

57. TOP, box 19.

58. TOP, box 15.

59. Hundreds of microfilm reels of CP-USA minutes and instructions now at the Library of Congress show the CP bogged down in minutiae and in-fighting.

60. The Hitler/Dies article, by Donald Odgen Stewart, is from *DPW* (21 January 1939).

61. *DPW* (21 Feb and 1 Mar 1939).

62. TOP, box 19, also contains a letter from a former San Francisco comrade who had moved to Herrin, Illinois, where "75% of the people live on WPA or relief. WPA pays $44 a month." This letter from "Evelyn" is a well-written, detailed reminder that the Depression continued and all classes suffered.

63. Interview, 27 October 1997. Tillie sometimes confused Eggan, who died in 1938, with Kaye, who stayed with Tillie and Jack in 1939 when Julie was a baby.

64. TOP, box 17.

65. Jack's younger brother Leon wrote on 8 May 1939 to congratulate Jack on "landing a job with the snap of a finger." Olsen private papers.

66. From Tillie's letter to Rae Schochet. Abraham Olshansky, born 25 October 1880, and Bluma Testelchuk Olshansky, born 25 December 1888, both in Russia, lived at 25 Dudley Avenue in Venice. Jack's brother Max Anglicized the name as "Olsan," his brother Leon as "Olson."

67. See Navasky, 239–42. Communist Party-U.S.A. records at the Library of Congress show a totalitarian and inefficient bureaucracy log-jammed by expulsions for "conduct unbecoming" a party member (which usually meant criticizing or disobeying leadership) and for being a "counter-revolutionary Trotskyite." Records also include manifestos, directives, copies of long, redundant speeches (all said to be greeted by

"loud applause"), acceptances or denials of applications to leave the United States, instructions for agit-prop departments, arrangements for publishing pamphlets at 10¢ apiece, with an irregular system of discounts, assignments to "smash up" rival meetings, and lengthy letters censuring members, answering complaints, and granting or denying permission to leave districts. Reports from all twenty-eight districts were due every Saturday at the central office. Holding the tedious post of "section functionary" was considered an honor.

68. Tillie told Rae she was in Venice three weeks, but her letters to Jack suggest a much longer stay. Possibly she spent two visits there. If so, they were both in summer 1939, judging from details about Julie.

69. Jack's brother Leon's 1939 letter establishes that in 1939 Jack was acting state secretary of the YCL, TOP, box 1998–242. Though it is convenient to assume that Tillie resigned from the party over its insensitivity to women's issues, two loyal Communists said she did not. Robert Treuhaft, Jessica Mitford's widower, remembered that he and Jessica ("Decca") took Tillie, not Jack, to CP meetings in the 1940s. His law partner, Doris Walker remembered that Tillie "certainly acted like a member" in the 1940s until the mid-1950s when "people began leaving in droves." She said that some California Communists did receive benefits from Moscow but assumed that Tillie Olsen did not. Interviews, 2 April 2000.

70. The library card was issued to Matilda Lerner, 3019 Winter Street, Los Angeles. She checked out nineteen books in October and twenty-one in November. She last used the card on 29 November 1939, when she checked out two books. TOP, box 18. Perhaps Jack's parents took care of Julie while Tillie worked for the CP.

71. Jann Lerner Brodinsky translated it from the Yiddish. She did not share it with Tillie. The poem reads:

> It's not white and not black
> In the depths of my heart
> Also not red and not yellow.
> It is never light, never white.
> I ache with my sorrow.
> To what purpose this burden?
> What will be tomorrow?
> Day in and day out
> It tortures my soul
> Drawing this very life away,
> In my loneliness, cold I become,
> Instead of living, dead I become.
> And strong I feel my pain.
> To what my life?
> I know I stand on the cross road
> Where it leads to a dark road,
> I look around me in anguish,
> I cry, "Come, Help Me,"
> But no reply to my cry.
> I become frozen
> Like a stone.

72. Sam inked out this old address and added the new one on this letter. Tillie later maintained that her parents had moved "during the war." She often said "my dad sold the house without asking" her mother, but the Caldwell Street deed had been in Ida's name for nearly twenty years.

73. Sam told her to send flowers in the names of the Workmen's Circle, Branch 173, and the Ladies Auxiliary of Branch 258. On the day he wrote, Tillie was checking out books as Matilda Lerner in Los Angeles. Disparate dated records have enabled me to piece together these events; still the word "apparently" is necessary.

74. The recipes she copied out seem, however, unused. TOP, box 17.

CHAPTER 8 — 1940–1945

1. The famous industrialist and aviator were members of the American First Committee to avoid war.

2. TOP, box 15. Steve Nelson, 260.

3. TOP, box 15, includes scattered "makings" of an undeveloped work called "Lost Women."

4. Olsen private papers, returned to her by Ethel Schochet.

5. Apparently, Rae assumed that, after May 1937 when she cursed Abe for neglecting Karla, he did not want to see her, and she did not know how to find Frances. Because Tillie was in Los Angeles when two papers ran reports of his death and because many people knew he was her husband, it is odd that Tillie said she had not heard. Marian Ainslee telegrammed Tillie five days after his death asking her to call "IMMEDIATELY."

6. The *New York Times* named *The Great Dictator* as one of the ten best films of 1940.

7. Under Chamberlain, Britain had made insufficient war preparations. Churchill became British prime minister and minister of defense on 13 May 1940, when he gave this speech.

8. About this time, Ida's former English teacher saw Ida walking along Farnam Street in downtown Omaha convulsed in tears because Harry had drawn such a low draft number. Leonard Nathan to Tillie Olsen (Lerner Papers). On 29 October 1940, the secretary of war, blindfolded, drew the first draft numbers for the first U.S. peacetime conscription.

9. In Gene Lerner's "Story of the Lerner Family," he tells of getting Eleanor Roosevelt to address the Student Forum, of which he was president. On 10 June 1940, as class president, he delivered the graduation address and Senator John Thomas (R., Idaho) inserted it into the *Congressional Record* of 15 June 1940. Thomas then offered Gene the post of legislative secretary. Lerner papers.

10. TOP, box 17.

11. Whether Rae denounced her in stronger words than she had used before or whether they simply drifted apart is unclear—unless more letters turn up.

12. Tillie had been thrilled to see Hemingway support Republican Spain. She was less thrilled with his 1938 play *The Fifth Column*, which blames the Communists for betraying the cause.

13. TOP, box 17.

14. See Navasky, 244.

15. See Schulberg, 68, 303, and 72.

16. TOP, box 17.

17. See Folsom, chapter 17. Split between pacifist and prowar factions, the League of American Writers soon dissolved.

18. Zinn's sixteenth chapter, 407–442, is titled "A People's War?" See Gilbert, 198–211; he does not mention an expected Chinese protection of Russia from Japan. The "Louise" was either Louise Maxon or Louise Todd.

19. A picture of Tillie, Jack, and three-year-old Julie seems to date from just before Tillie caught a train for this convention, not, as Julie later thought, from a trip to New York City. See Zandy, 338, for the photo of an unhappy Julie, an apparently resigned Jack, and a glamorous Tillie wearing a fantastic hat.

20. Tillie apparently neither wrote Jack then, nor did he keep her letters. Being "oh so lonesome for you," he wrote her several letters.

21. Hearing that they named Julie for Jack Eggan, a communist, Harry, as an adamant socialist, had sent Tillie a disapproving letter after Julie's birth.

22. An attorney for Pacific Gas and Electric Company wrote Jack, at 50 Divisadero Street on 6 July 1940, hoping to settle their unpaid bill of $24.03 in "an amicable manner." TOP, box 19.

23. Against Japanese advances into Burma, Allied forces had withdrawn to India. See Gilbert, 316, 321, 336–37. Harry managed to find and save Indian and Chinese Jews. Despite the objections of Senator Thomas, Senator Robert Taft, and Vice President Harry Truman, as a conscientious objector, Gene withdrew from politics lest his pacifism reflect adversely on Senator Thomas. Interview, 2 July 2000.

24. She is sometimes credited with establishing San Francisco's first public child-care center. Newspaper accounts, however, establish that there were several such centers emerging in this period.

25. Ida and Sam sent a postcard to Karla from New York City in February 1942, which dates this incident. Interview with Gene Lerner, 2 July 2000. Tillie did not know the story about Ida's "wedding" ring.

26. A typescript of the broadcast is in TOP, box 18.

27. The Emergency Milk Committee Conference was held on 17 June 1942 in Oakland. TOP, box 19.

28. They did not know that Warren appeased his xenophobic supporters by seeing to the removal of Japanese-Americans to internment camps.

29. Wallace gave the speech on 8 May 1942 to the Free World Association in New York City.

30. The *Dispatcher: Official Newspaper of the International Longshoremen's and Warehousemen's Union, CIO* was published at 150 Golden Gate Avenue, with Harry Bridges as president. There was a separate edition for Local 6, which had 15,000 warehouse members.

31. Interview with Gene Lerner, 1 July 2000.

32. She sent the girls to Omaha while she and Jack "honeymooned" in December and then joined the March Inland in January before the girls returned home. Sam's clearly dated letters are from late January and February, after the girls had returned to California. Tillie told the story about the baby's conception and later described Kathie as a "ten-month" baby. Conversation with TO, 19 July 2000.

33. In, respectively, *Arise My Love* (1940), *His Girl Friday* (1940), and *Woman of the Year* (1942).

34. See Appendix A, Bibliography of Primary Works for first-listings of previously unknown writings by Tillie Olsen. Many articles mentioned here and below had no byline but were probably also hers. Meat quota articles appeared on 19 February 1943 in both the *Herald* and the *Dispatcher*. A picture from the *San Francisco Examiner* (17 February 1943) shows her as the only woman on the "emergency meat committee." After her KYA broadcast, the *Dispatcher* printed "How to Look For and Fight Black Market" (26 March 1943). The "McKinley Newsletter," June 1943, featured an article about a summer child-care center for working mothers, who were to "Phone Mrs. Olsen." On 16 July, the *Herald* wrote about her work to establish "10 Child Care Centers." By August, Tillie was one of the vice presidents on the National Congress of Women's Auxiliaries of the CIO. She endorsed Cleta O'Connor Yates, the only woman running for supervisor in San Francisco, whom the FBI called "a well-known Communist." The USO (United Service Organizations) was formed, at FDR's request, to improve the morale of American troops. The "ILWU Auxiliary Bulletin" mentions Tillie's work on 1943 consumer issues. TOP, boxes 17 and 18.

35. See Gilbert, chapter 32.

36. TOP, boxes 15 and 17.

37. No records of her participation survive. See TOP, box 19 for the Office of War Information's letter.

38. Tillie remained in the hospital with her baby for about a week. Later she said she wanted to write about "Empey & Chris and that wartime maternity ward," but these names do not appear from that time.

39. Interview, 4 April 1998.

40. Lillian Lerner Davis lived in the Bronx with her two daughters and worked as a clerk stenographer in the Selective Service. Jann lived in Washington, D.C. Gene was writing plays while working for peace in New York City.

41. Tillie Olsen's personal files, undated.

42. The *Labor Herald* pictured Tillie, as "State Auxiliary Pres" and one of two women in a group of ten, discussing rationing problems. TOP, box 18.

43. The announcement was in the 11 February 1944 *Labor Herald*. There would be twenty-four weekly classes. Only male teachers were listed.

44. Among them was the WWI film *Sergeant York* (1941). WWII films included *Wake Island* (1942), *Casablanca* (1943), and *Watch on the Rhine* (1943). James Cagney won the Oscar for best actor in the patriotic musical *Yankee Doodle Dandy* (1943). The 1943 film of Hemingway's *For Whom the Bell Tolls* served to translate antifascism from the Spanish Civil War to WWII. Other rousing war films were *Commandos Strike at Down*, *So Proudly We Hail*, *Action in the North Atlantic*, and *Guadalcanal Diary*.

45. Canon John P. Craine officiated. Believing that Tillie and Jack had married in February 1936, in her "Statement for Daddy's Memorial Program" Kathie Olsen identified 17 February 1989 as "just two days before [Jack and Tillie's] 53rd wedding anniversary."

46. Probably near Mt. Hamilton and the Henry W. Coe State Park.

47. She took over the duties of Claudia Williams who become director of the CIO's political action machinery. Steve Murdock, who had been state CIO legislative director, was leaving for the army. The FBI put this photo of Tillie on file.

48. Durante, jazz musician and entertainer, joked about appropriating from George Gershwin's *Rhapsody in Blue* to write a symphony but writing "Inka Dinka Do" instead.

49. In pages torn from spiral notebooks, Tillie calculated her debts haphazardly and argued for "public ownership of utilities." TOP, box 17.

50. The *ILWU Dispatcher* was also published from this address, though it was a national paper.

51. On 25 August 1941, British and Soviet ambassadors in Teheran had forced the Shah of Iran to resign in favor of his son. In 1942, the United States sent aid to the USSR through Iran's capital Teheran. Iran declared war on Germany. On 29 November 1943, in Teheran, Churchill, Roosevelt, and Stalin made postwar plans. Gilbert, 226, 367, 478, 517.

52. TOP, box 17.

53. She explained how the CIO had countered its historical problems by "breaking out of the isolation of wages-hours-conditions into the broadest community mobilization for victory, for post-war planning, and the common good." The report exceeds two thousand words. Olsen private papers.

54. TOP, box 19.

55. Tillie planned to take Julie and leave her in Washington, D.C., with Jann, but Sam wrote Tillie that Jann's health was too poor to care for another child. Someone, perhaps Karla, typed a note to Jack that Julie dictated: "KARLA AND ME ARE VERY HAPPY THAT YOU ARE COMING TO SEE US SO IS THE WHOLE FAMILY I AM TOO SAD THAT I CANT GO WITH MOTHER TO WASHINGTON." From the train, however, Tillie wrote Jack: "Your daughters [Julie's] ear is being puffed to bursting by our fellow passengers—they solemnly keep telling her she's smart and so brilliant—and who is she to contradict these authoritative grownups, damn them all." The letter remained in a purse-size spiral tablet. Whether she copied and mailed it is unknown. Julie is absent from other accounts of this journey. TOP, box 19.

56. Smedley's only novel was *Daughter of Earth* (1929). She lived in China from 1928 to 1941. Tillie was instrumental in helping the Feminist Press reestablish her reputation. TOP, box 16.

57. She kept paper and envelopes from every hotel she stayed in, including the Wellington and Allerton House in New York and the Sherman in Chicago, where she seems to have stayed on 4 June.

58. Ida apparently said: "Zie vel nib gehn tzu a chazena abi zie vel zeen die Kala, und zie vel net gehm zu a livia abi qie vet zien die Kerper." To Tillie's question about originality, she probably said "oisgetrocht-shmorsgetracht, Alt hat been gesagt. Epes vegen viefiel torsente yohrem menshen haben sochen gezugt." My thanks to Faye Bradus for the Yiddish translation.

59. All that spring, the *Labor Herald* devoted pages to voter registration drives. On 31 March, it ran a special supplement headed "Support the President."

60. This surprise "weekend" together began on 11 June.

61. The convention lasted from 31 August to 3 September. One speaker was Senator Claude Pepper. *Labor Herald* (18 August and 8 September 1944).

62. *Labor Herald* (8 September 1944) also tells of Jack's Alabama assignment.

63. Six or seven years later, Tillie would tell Julie a story that implied that Jack had

not been able to spend time with her before leaving for nearly two months in further training near Dothan, Alabama.

64. Part of a letter headed "Appeal of Tillie Olsen" tells something of her activities: "Although the appellant is not compensated directly by the Red Cross, she receives Red Cross funds as part of her salary and for the use of her car for the performance of Red Cross activities. . . . She should therefore be allowed sufficient preferred mileage to perform those Red Cross activities." Olsen private papers.

65. The phrase is DeBattista's.

66. The minutes of a meeting of the Servicemen's and Veterans' Committee tells of the debate between "Brother Bridges" and "Sister Olsen." TOP, box 18. The second quotation is from a "Hot Cargo" column.

67. Reeva Olson started a seaman's canteen and was then working at AYD (American Youth for Democracy) with younger merchant seamen at 937 Haight.

68. In early 1962, Tillie wrote Anne Sexton that in the late autumn of, probably, 1944, she had gone to Boston for four days. Her contemporary records, however, do not mention Boston.

69. Actually, in 1944 she was already thirty-two.

70. A page remained in a small ring-binder notebook. TOP, box 19. Letters to soldiers had to be sent to a New York post office address, from which they were forwarded to the troops, wherever they were stationed. Tillie wrote Jack that "letters reaching the east Fri, Sat & Sun (the 13th, 14th, 15th)" of October should be sent in care of Lil Davis.

71. Tillie's letter to Jack does not mention her parents, who must have already left for Omaha.

72. Miller's American Band of the Expeditionary Forces had been stationed in London after the Normandy invasion. Flying to France to arrange a Christmas concert, Miller's plane went down on 15 December 1945.

73. TOP, box 19.

74. Pauline's baby Jan Rosenthal was not with them. After Sam Rosenthal died, his parents raised Jan to keep her from Pauline's "Commie family" connections. Julie Olsen Edwards to PR, 28 May 2005.

75. In addition to violating Tillie's rights to privacy and free speech, the FBI report is remarkable for its carelessness. One page reports that the Omaha field office can find no record of her birth in 1930.

76. His cryptic letters suggest that he was part of the Allied operation in the Ardennes, in which 14,000 Allied soldiers died.

77. For General Dwight D. (Ike) Eisenhower, General Douglas MacArthur, and Joseph Stalin.

78. The man's name was Harry Bottcher. Jack wrote about him in early March 1944.

79. Fifty-six years later, Tillie Olsen told students at Louisiana State University about Robeson's marvelous serenade. One student thought Tillie had said that she and Robeson worked together.

80. The 23 March 1945 *Dispatcher* printed the news of his medal and promotion but gave no details because Tillie knew no more than bare facts.

81. NBC radio played the *Adagio* across the country all day long. This elegy was also played after the assassination of John F. Kennedy and after the terrorist attacks of 11 September 2001.

82. A list of powerful and famous women: Eleanor Roosevelt, first lady; the Duchess of Windsor, formerly Wallace Simpson, for whom Edward VIII had abdicated the throne of England in 1936; Ingrid Bergman, beautiful, passionate actress and film star; and Virginia Gildersleeve, dean of Barnard College, and the only woman other than Eleanor Roosevelt in the U.S. delegation to the UN founding.

83. Among the articles on these horrors were ones in the *Dispatcher* 4 and 8 May 1945 and the *San Francisco Chronicle* on 6 May 1945. See also Gilbert 663–64.

84. Julie Olsen Edwards to PR, 28 May 2005.

85. See Gilbert, chapter 47.

86. She was counting from Hitler's invasion of Poland, 1 September 1939.

87. Tillie saw that the story about Jack's letter was printed, *Labor Herald* (11 May 1945). See TOP, 1998–242, box 1, for clippings that she kept.

88. There was a 29 February in 1936 as well as in 1944. In her entry, Tillie misdated her birth as 1913 but did give the correct place—"Omaha, Nebr."

89. Sandra Joy Richards was born on 25 April 1945.

90. TOP, box 18.

91. Interview, 28 October 1997. See Gilbert, 701, for more on the UN.

92. According to the FBI's report. TOP, box 18.

93. The death toll in Hiroshima soon reached 92,233. Forty years later it was tallied as 138,890. Thirty years after the bombing of Nagasaki the death toll there was calculated at 48,857. For the rest of the century, people continued dying from the effects of atomic radiation. Gilbert, 712–19.

94. That was as specific a description of the killing fields as Jack ever wrote. Interview, 28 October 1997.

95. These words are excerpted from the transcript of an impromptu talk Tillie gave in 1982 when she was to introduce antinuclear activist Helen Caldicott.

96. Interview with TO, 28 October 1997.

97. Back in March, the *Dispatcher* had reported that Jack's brother Leon should be rotated home in September. Such rotations were based upon the number of days in combat. After Labor Day, Leon spent about two months at Camp Beale.

98. The letter from Ruth Sutherland or "Rootie Thoity" ends: "im with ya to the finish see say Hello to karlawhiteyjacktilliejuliepaulinemarycharliejanlouisereevale- onavrumblumkeevabobbiesimmiemaxjudydorothy and familywhaddyasay." Separating the names, we find it mentions Judy, daughter of Max and Dorothy Olsan, born in 1941; it does not mention baby boomers Ken Marcus, son of Eva Olsan and Simson Marcus, or Margie Olson, daughter of Leon and Reeva Olson, both born in 1946. So it must date from the 1945 Labor Day Parade, the first one since fall 1941. TOP, box 19.

99. The "displaced persons" program was founded as the United Nations Relief and Rehabilitation Administration.

100. On 18 September 1945, the Lerners sold their house at 3419 Lafayette for $6350. Their new house, at 3504 Lafayette Avenue, was not so charming but was large enough for Sam to make a separate apartment upstairs for the Richards to rent for $45 a month.

101. *Labor Herald* (21 September 1945). Notes for more speeches on labor issues are in TOP, box 17.

102. An accomplished publicist, Tillie placed Jack's argument about demobilized

veterans in the *Labor Herald* (21 September 1945). See TOP, box 17, for her notes for her own speeches on labor topics.

103. Julie Olsen Edwards to PR, 28 May 2005.

104. Jack was a member of the Black Panther Division of the 66th Battalion of the United States Infantry.

105. The *Dispatcher* (30 November 1945) featured an editorial insisting that the troops should be returned and showed a cartoon of an "OVERSEAS VETERAN" tied down by cobwebs.

106. *All Quiet on the Western Front* was filmed in 1930. The 1945 film *G.I. Joe* was about war correspondent Ernie Pyle.

CHAPTER 9 — 1946–1950

1. Julie Olsen Edwards to PR, 28 May 2005.

2. Later Tillie wrote on the first letter "Lindsay's notes when she turned over her apt. to us for our 'after the war honeymoon.'" Olsen private papers. Tillie later said Mary Lindsay committed suicide.

3. Marvin Gettleman on CP labor schools, to PR, 23 January 2001. *Daily People's World* (14 and 19 January 1946).

4. See Gilbert, 728–29.

5. Records at the Holocaust Museum in Washington, D.C., indicate that, on 29 March 1946, Jewish Displaced Persons in Stuttgart, Germany, staged a riot. Harry took their side and confronted authorities over mistreatment. Gene Lerner saw Harry's courage as another instance of Ida's legacy. Interview, 2 July 2000.

6. See Black, 151. "The World Through Hollywood's Eyes—truth or falsehood?" by Alvah Bessie, *Daily People's World* (15 February 1946); "'We are with you' . . . in [the] fight on native Fascists" by Dalton Trumbo, *Daily People's World* (5 April 1946). "STOP the UN-AMERICAN COMMITTEE," *Daily People's World* (19 February 1946). Though leftist, many screenwriters avoided controversy. Slessinger and Davis, for example, wrote the screenplay of *A Tree Grows in Brooklyn*; Albert Maltz wrote *Pride of the Marines*.

7. *Daily People's World* (16 March 1946).

8. This announcement mentions her three children, her recent accomplishments in the CIO, and Jack's position in the ILWU; it does not mention any writing by "Tillie Lerner," not even her earlier *People's World* writings.

9. Tillie had argued in the second column, on 2 May, that such discrimination had been eliminated. Notes for these articles are in TOP, box 16.

10. In 1969, Richmond complained about leftist writers who were so "preoccupied" with theories that they neglected "what *did* happen." See the *San Francisco Sunday Examiner & Chronicle* (13 December 1987).

11. In March 1945, the month before his death, FDR had appointed Wallace secretary of commerce.

12. Tillie later said that after his experience "shepherding" German POWs, Jack was convinced that the United States was giving ex-Nazis "privileged access" to immigration. Interview, 27 October 1997.

13. He defeated three-term Congresswoman Helen Gahagan, wife of liberal actor and activist Melvyn Douglas. Because she opposed the fascistic methods of HUAC, Nixon branded her a Communist.

14. TOP, box 17. Her late 1945 letters to Jack had mentioned Christmas, but this seems to have been the first time the Olsens observed Christmas. However domestic were the gifts to the younger daughters, both in number and cost, they suggest favoritism for Julie and Kathie over Karla, at least on this list.

15. Congress was unmoved when a "FLOOD OF PROTESTS SWAMPS SENATE AT ZERO HOUR" to stop passage of Taft-Hartley. *Daily People's World* (23 June 1947).

16. *Daily People's World* (3 June 1947). The Guthrie's first son was Arlo. *Dispatcher* (27 June 1947).

17. Budd Schulberg and Samuel Ornitz wrote the script for *Little Orphan Annie.* John Ford directed the film *Grapes of Wrath.* Trumbo's novel *Johnny Got His Gun* was not adapted for film until 1971.

18. Tillie proposed names "Anita Jean," after Anita Katherine Whitney and Jean Wertheimer, women who defied elitist backgrounds to join the CP. Interview, 4 April 1998. The baby's full name was Anita Laurie Olsen.

19. Julie Olsen Edwards to PR, 28 May 2005.

20. Rob Treuhaft remembered that Jack held a prominent place in the union, did good work helping integrate the union, and made a good salary. Interview, 22 March 2000.

21. TOP, box 17. Later Tillie said GI's sweethearts were publicly urged to write lovingly.

22. He later became a regional director of the ILWU, a Civil Rights leader in San Francisco, and a founder of St. Francis Square, a cooperative housing development for low- and middle-income people.

23. TOP, box 16. Oleta Yates ran a door-to-door campaign "particularly in working-class neighborhoods," according to *Daily People's World* (19 September 1947). She won only 13 percent of the vote.

24. Interview with TO, 28 October 1997. "Backstage at UN meeting," *Daily People's World* (25 September 1947).

25. Tillie's old mentor and lover Eugene Konecky wrote "Monopoly Steals FM," exposing networks colluding with the FCC to sabotage independent FM stations. *Daily People's World* (22 October 1947).

26. Paulette Goddard, heroine in *The Great Dictator*, complained about the removal of a sympathetic black character from the film *Hazard, Daily People's World* (23 October 1947). "Most censored Films of 1947," *Daily People's World* (5 January 1948).

27. "Call to defend Howard Fast," *Daily People's World* (17 September 1947). Hollywood figures who condemned HUAC hearings included Ava Gardner, Paulette Goddard, John Huston, Danny Kaye, Burt Lancaster, Lucille Ball, Edward G. Robinson, Audie Murphy (most decorated war hero), William Wyler, and Melvyn Douglas. Bertolt Brecht decamped to Germany, Donald Ogden Stewart to England. The remaining eight of the "Hollywood Ten" were Samuel Ornitz, Lester Cole, John Howard Lawson, Herbert Biberman, Albert Maltz, Alvah Bessie, Adrian Scott, Edward Dmytryk, Ring Lardner, Jr., and Dalton Trumbo. *Daily People's World* (22, 23, and 28 October, 25 November 1947). Tillie knew Stewart, Lawson, and, possibly, Lardner and others of the "ten."

28. TOP, boxes 18 and 16. *Dispatcher* (12 December 1947)

29. Julie Olsen Edwards to PR, 7 December 2007. Julie says new dresses were a rarity. Perhaps the green jumpers were a gift from Ida and Sam.

30. DiBattista, 329–30.

31. Luckily, their family doctor, Asher Gordon was so dedicated to the lefties and the Olsens that he came to the house and sat by her bed with Tillie when Kathie had an attack. Domestic details here are from an interview with Kathie Olsen Hoye, 8 April 2006.

32. She later said that she recognized one of these women as a jail-bird, arrested for prostitution back in Kansas City, now living a respectable life. Interview with TO, 28 October 1997.

33. The November 1948 conference was to have been headed by women and about "Women as Heads of Families," but a man, Dr. Lester W. Sontag, was a major speaker. TOP, boxes 17 and 18.

34. Nancy Scott, on Al Richmond, *San Francisco Examiner & Chronicle* (13 December 1987). Tillie's old friend from Kansas City days, Henry Winston, was arrested. *Daily People's World* (3 December 1948).

35. *Daily People's World* (6 December 1948).

36. TOP, box 16.

37. TOP, box 15. Mary E. Wilkins Freeman's "Revolt of Mother" (1891) could be considered an exception.

38. Given Sam's verbal skills, this accusation seems plausible, but Jann's story of Sam's escape from Russia says nothing about a "secret radical press."

39. Tillie said that she left the Party that year over its sexism, as when it censored her for bringing baby Laurie and her ironing to meetings. FBI informants considered her still an active member.

40. TOP, box 16. At least she does not seem to have kept rejection letters.

41. Conversation with TO, 15 July 2000.

42. Five years before, Sam had told Tillie he could not help her financially because he had invested in this farm; perhaps he had contributed to the Davis's down payment before Joseph Davis's medical practice was established. A farmer managed the tree nursery for the family. The cottage consisted of two large rooms (an eat-in kitchen and a living-bed room with bath) over a garage.

43. They moved to Washington, D.C., in fall 1949.

44. Interview with TO, 28 October 1997. Her photographs from the period show both women and men of different races and ethnic groups at union meetings.

45. Quotations from Jack Olsen here and in the next chapter are from Kathie Olsen's oral history project, interviews with her father conducted in spring 1980. Permission granted by Kathie Olsen Hoye.

46. *San Francisco Downtown Shopping News*, 2 February 1950. Tillie kept the article without the citation; my thanks to Bill Lynch for the detective work that uncovered it.

47. See Stone, 374–93.

48. Tillie quoted Paul Chown, an ILWU official with Jack who became a professor at the University of California: the "purpose of anti-communism was to kill the left and kill democracy too. The right wing on the one hand and the Teamsters on the other ruined most unions." Interview with TO, 27 October 1997.

49. Interview with TO, 28 October 1997.

50. *National Guardian* (19 April 1950). TOP, 1998–242, box 1.

51. Interview with Gene Lerner, 3 July 2000; "Lil: A Memoir for her Eightieth Birthday," Lerner Papers.

52. In July 1950, Sam inquired if Karla was "progressing in her cloueing [clowning]"?

53. The Army did withdraw MacArthur's accusation. In 1935, Tillie had been expected to review Smedley's *Daughter of Earth* for the *New Masses*. Smedley's article on Chinese wood-engraving appeared in *DPW* (11 February 1949). Smedley's obituary from the *New York Times* is in TOP, box 18. A page of Tillie's notes on her is in TOP, box 16.

54. TOP, box 16. This draft letter ends with mostly illegible handwritten notes; perhaps she retyped and mailed it. Constant Coiner's version was that Tarantino accused Tillie of being an "agent of Moscow" trying "to take over the San Francisco Public School System by tunneling into the PTA," 150. Tillie later recalled that many people stood by her, including the school principal. Interview with TO, 28 October 1997.

55. The workshop was taught by Margaret Heaton. Julie Olsen Edwards later said that Heaton's emphasis on children's rights and the importance of a child's emotional well-being affected Julie's career decision to teach early childhood education. To PR, 2 August 2005.

56. Interview with TO, 28 October 1997.

57. McCarthy was then chair of a Permanent Investigations Sub-Committee of the Senate Committee on Government Operations. Margaret Heaton signed the loyalty oath, but other California teachers refused, citing the freedoms guaranteed in the Constitution of the United States. They were not reinstated. Tillie kept the "Composite Statement of Public School non-signers, San Francisco, Nov. 8, 1950." TOP, box 18.

58. California Senator Sheridan Downey had resigned.

59. Union contracts allowed the employer to lay off new workers in the first ninety days without cause.

60. TOP, box 18.

61. TOP, box 16.

62. Calling herself a "traitor," Tillie acknowledged "writing of you yes" and crossed out a man's name, possibly Cline's. She also wrote: "need: only my own subjects / horror over my papers, my litter, my undones thinking of Lawrence [?] Powell [?] sitting in that tower room." TOP, box 16. No Powell living then in San Francisco lived where a house with a tower would be. Paul Cline and Helen and Virginia Oprian did live in such a place. Conversation with Virginia Oprian Cannon, 22 February 2006.

63. See Boyer's last chapters.

64. TOP, box 16. She labeled these reflections: "1950 at work."

65. Interview with TO, 28 October 1997.

CHAPTER 10 — 1951–1955

1. Information about Paul Cline, Helen Oprian, and her daughter from conversations with Virginia Oprian Cannon and her son Carl Cannon, 22 and 23 February and 11 March 2006.

2. She invited a ninety-one-year-old former pupil of Kennedy's, whose chief school-time fear was getting ink stains on her pinafore. Her remarks reminded Tillie that genteel nineteenth-century cultural prescriptions belittled children, especially girls. The old woman sent a thank-you note to Tillie and the PTA, written so perfectly it looked like calligraphy. TOP, box 19. Interview with TO, 28 October 1997.

3. TOP, box 16.

4. *San Francisco Sunday Examiner & Chronicle* (13 December 1987).

5. Navasky, 245, 239, 281–83.

6. She later attended Bard College on a dance scholarship.

7. TOP, boxes 16 and 17.

8. Jack had "nurtured" Al Addy for union leadership and as a photographer. Julie remembers "it was a painful betrayal for my Dad who was very fond of Al and had invested a lot of himself in the young man." Julie Olsen Edwards to PR, 7 December 2007. Interview with TO, 28 October 1997.

9. See Coiner, 253–54, for the text of Jack's speech before the California HUAC in 1952. Jack B. Tenney, who had tried to outlaw the CP from elections, headed HUAC committee hearings in California. See Burke, 156–57.

10. Kathie Olsen to PR, 12 August 2005.

11. Interview with TO, 27 October 1997.

12. Chaplin sailed in September 1952. Historian Henry Steele Commager, sociologist C. Wright Mills, theologians Reinhold Niebuhr and Paul Tillich, and Dean Virginia Gildersleeve of Barnard College were among the signers of a public warning against Eisenhower sent to the *New York Times*. See Carter, 25.

13. From a letter to Jack when he was away in 1953 or 1954.

14. Exactly what else she did or did not say was inked out when the report was supplied to Tillie Olsen much later under the Freedom of Information Act. TOP, box 18. Interview with TO, 28 October 1997.

15. The desegregation case was first argued in December 1952. Tillie recalled: "Once I haunted the Salvation Army and Goodwill for long underwear, warm sweaters, and coats we could afford and packed them for the cold in Tule, the concentration camp, for we might be placed there." Olsen private papers.

16. That was their 1980 title. The book was translated as *Hollywood Sul Tevere* (Milano: Sperling & Kupfer, 1982.) Its subtitle lists Anna Magnani, Ava Gardner, Anita Ekberg, Simone Signoret, Rossano Brazzi, Margaret Truman, and Robert B. Aldrich. The further list of famous names with whom they worked includes Josephine Baker, Ingrid Bergman, Richard Burton, Maria Callas, Charles Chaplin, Bette Davis, Dino De Laurentis, Federico Fellini, Mel Ferrer, Audrey Hepburn, Sophia Loren, Else Martinelli, Irene Papas, Burt Reynolds, Roberto Rossellini, Frank Sinatra, Susan Strasberg, Elizabeth Taylor, Shelly Winters, and Franco Zeffirelli.

17. From Gene Lerner's memoir for Ida. Lerner Papers.

18. Lerner Papers.

19. TOP, box 17. Sometimes she made fun of her difficulty finishing: "stories are due stories are due/ the birds sing all the day/ stories are due stories are due/ but mine aint on the way." TOP, box 16.

20. Though Tillie later labeled these notes "Excerpts from my notebooks, June 1963," the notes include the reference to 1953–1954 and thus date from then. Tillie later used these notes for a speech given, apparently, in the 1980s. I have slightly reordered the notes for clarity and emphasis. TOP, box 12. In another notebook, she wrote "TIME IT FESTERED AND CONGESTED . . . writing in my sleep." TOP, box 16.

21. Kazan had planned an exposé of dockworkers as Communists, which Arthur Miller refused to write for him. Schulberg had no qualms about replacing Miller.

22. Conversation with Kathie Olsen, 9 July 2005.

23. According to the FBI, she was unemployed then, but she may have held temporary jobs that they did not track down. Another unfinished story is in TOP, box 15.

24. Though Emily is a schoolgirl with midterms and a school counselor, Tillie left her age as nineteen, Karla's age when Tillie began writing. Pearlman and Werlock assume she wrote accurately: "Olsen's feelings of anguish and longing when leaving Karla with relatives is surely significant in her depiction of the ironing mother who, like Olsen, lacked the means to encourage and enhance the talent of her eldest daughter," 30.

25. An undated letter from Lillian to Tillie reads, in its entirety: "I'm mad. You might have answered my letters—especially since I asked you to do so as soon as possible. Lil." Olsen private papers.

26. Sam described the house just after their move in a February 1954 letter to Tillie.

27. Harry and Clare's three children were present. Whether Jann and her children, who were about to move from D.C. to New Jersey, were there is unclear.

28. TOP, box 17.

29. Conversation with Kathie Olsen, 9 July 2005.

30. Tillie told Joanne Frye about "Margaret Heaton's attending with Olsen the black church. . . ." Tillie also told Frye that "it was Margaret who fainted," Frye, 64, 65. Kathie Olsen said that she and her mother were the only white people in the African-American church and that she herself almost fainted. She also said that Tillie did not sing in a Gospel choir, as Frye implies, 61. Conversation with Kathie Olsen, 7 July 2005.

31. Ida wrote Gene "in her own handwriting" about this time, and he wrote back hoping to hear more about the Olsens' visit. Lerner Papers.

32. TOP, box 17. This box also includes several undeveloped story ideas. This is the version Tillie told me (28 October 1997). In a 1990 interview, she told Abby Werlock that "so great was his respect for her talent that he later told her not to come to class, for he felt he had nothing more to teach her." Pearlman and Werlock, 28. Conversation with Kathie Olsen, 9 July 2005.

33. TOP, box 16. Olsen private papers.

34. At least no reference to any response from Tillie survives.

35. This outstanding program, then chaired by Wallace Stegner, had among its fellows Robert Stone, Larry McMurtry, Ernest Gaines, and Wendell Berry. See Stegner and Etulain. They mention Tillie but misspell her name as "Olson," 14–15.

36. TOP, box 16. In the December 1954 vote the Senate censured him for conduct "unbecoming a Member of the United States Senate," not for his anti-Communist rampage.

37. Like one of his characters in *The Crucible*, Miller refused to name names. In 1955 he was convicted for contempt of Congress, a conviction reversed by 1957.

38. See Halberstam, chapters 34 and 35.

39. Tillie received $2,000 for the academic year 1955–1956 as a nonmatriculating student. She needed to pay $65 a quarter in fees. The young faculty member was Richard Kraus. The other Jones Fellows were Bill Wiegand and Denise James. After Stegner's retirement, these fellowships were renamed for him.

40. Lerner Papers.

41. Gleason's sister wrote Tillie regretting that he drank so much around the children. TOP, box 1995-130. Julie remembered that her parents would tell Whitey not to come back unless he was sober, but they would relent because he had been such a good friend.

To PR, 2 August 2005. Having lost his restaurant, Walker's father had insisted that Mike drop out of school and move with the family. He refused and was left behind.

42. Julie Olsen Edwards has said this was "the *least* fictional of all Mom's stories." To PR, 28 May 2005.

43. Rossano Brazzi (1916–1987) was the popular Italian hero in *The Barefoot Contessa* (1954) and *Summertime* (1955).

44. Adele Braude to PR, 7 September 2001.

45. Filling out a form in 1958, Tillie wrote that "the class in advanced fiction was attended two afternoons a week; all other time was devoted to writing." Sometimes she said she went to class only once a week.

46. Casa Marinero is inside Rizal Park in Manila, Philippines. Recollections here are those of Bill Wiegand, interview, 30 April 2000.

47. She quoted Ralph Abernathy saying: "they cannot speak for themselves so I must speak for them." She also recorded: "Walk together children, don't you get weary, for there's a great camp meeting in the promised land." And she noted "why don't you hep you own brother, you so highamighty." There is also a curious reference to Philip Wylie's accusations against "momism," the supposedly bogus authority of matriarchs, in his *Generation of Vipers*, which went into its twentieth printing in 1955. TOP, box 16.

48. Gene Lerner translated some of Ida's words from the Yiddish and included them in his memoir for Ida's grandchildren on 29 January 1989, the thirtieth anniversary of her death. Lerner Papers.

49. Harry wrote Gene, on 2 October 1955, that Ida had only six months to live. See also "Lil: A Memoir for her Eightieth Birthday, December 14, 1994." Lerner Papers.

50. Lawrence Ferlinghetti's San Francisco City Lights Bookstore published "Howl" and more Beat writings.

51. Gene deposited his copy of her transcription in the Lerner Papers at Stanford. What happened to the copy that Lillian sent Tillie is unknown. Almost fifty years later, Lillian wrote, "I regret I did not keep a copy—perhaps Tillie still has my letter. I do not recall it exactly . . . Tillie should find the letter with my translation." Lillian Lerner Davis to PR, 25 January 2002.

52. Ida said "seetert" or "tzitert." Lillian translated that word as "hung" or "shivered" in the air. My thanks to Yiddish expert Bob Eisenberg who suggests: "for music I would translate it as 'vibrated in the air' or even better 'pulsated in the air' or best 'electrified the air.'" To PR, 15 July 2005.

53. Lerner Papers. *Glory Brigade* was a 1953 Korean War film starring Victor Mature, with Lee Marvin in a minor part. The film shows how rivalry between Greeks and other ethnic groups must be set aside for the greater good of defeating communism. Clearly Ida was touched by the Greek music and dance. Lillian's shorthand was "hard to decipher" so she was unsure whether Ida had said "cultural" or "spiritual." Bob Eisenberg thinks "spiritual" is correct.

54. Lillian Davis to Gene Lerner, 2 November 1955, and to PR, 25 January 2002

55. Conversations with Richard Scowcroft, 6 January, 25 February, and 5 November 2000; with Bill Wiegand on 30 April 2000.

56. Gene telegraphed Tillie from the Hotel Weylin on 10 December 1955 asking her to support Ida's going immediately to Omaha. Soon, he realized that he should take her to Harry and Clare's instead. Gene Lerner to PR, 29 January 2001.

57. Conversation with Gene Lerner, 30 January 1999. Lerner Papers.

58. Tillie wrote that she had spent Christmas morning at home in San Francisco before beginning her flight to Washington, D.C. She wrote home about staying in a luxury hotel and flying first class into D.C. She mentioned Julie's application to Mills College, as she did in 1956. Olsen private papers.

59. Clare and Harry Lerner recognized Sam's birthday as "on the first licht (light) of Hanukkah, the 25th or 26th of Kislev on the Jewish calendar." They celebrated it around 25 December on the Gregorian calendar. Susan Lerner to PR, 2 July 2008.

60. From an introduction to *The Sound and the Fury* written in 1933 for a limited edition that Bennett Cerf hoped to print. Faulkner called the image of Caddy climbing the pear tree to look in on her grandmother's funeral while the other children look up at the "muddy seat of her drawers" "the only thing in literature that will ever move me very much." Philip Cohen and Doreen Fowler explain the composition of various versions of this introduction in *American Literature* (June 1990).

61. TOP, box 17.

CHAPTER 11 — 1956–1961

1. In "On the Writing of a Story," Tillie writes coherent, logical, long sentences, unlike the barely coherent notes on similar topics she wrote for McPheron and L'Heureux in the 1980s.

2. Her death certificate names death from: "Cancer of gall bladder w metastasis to liver."

3. Her daughters, except Laurie, were old enough to wear, not play with earrings. Tillie addressed this undated letter to Jann in a discussion of family business, with copies to the other siblings. Lerner Papers.

4. Halberstam devotes chapter 31 to the importance of Elvis.

5. TOP, box 17.

6. Elman, 29, 31.

7. Conversation with Julie Olsen Edwards, 2 August 2005.

8. He thought her first scene was too long, Whitey's relationship to the family unclear, and her lack of quotation marks puzzling. Conversation with Nolan Miller, April 1999.

9. Later, as a policeman in the San Francisco Police Department, he followed advice from Tillie and Jack to observe carefully, advice he put to use in his novel: *Voices from the Bottom of the World: A Policeman's Journal* (Grove Press, 1970).

10. TOP, box 17.

11. TOP, box 19.

12. Stanford, box 25.

13. Helen D. Kline gave the eulogy a year after Ida's death. Lerner Papers.

14. TOP, box 19.

15. "San Francisco Type Club Newsletter" (17 February 1957). TOP, box 18. This experience influenced his dedication to the union's Political Action Committee. He helped develop the Martin Luther King Apprenticeship Training Program to increase minority membership in the trade.

16. Cowley wrote Tillie that Millgate was "an English Fulbright Fellow with a wide knowledge of American literature and American labor problems." Later Millgate blamed

himself for being "unable to take advantage of" Tillie's conversation. Millgate to PR, 15 October 1999.

17. After accidentally breaking an egg, for example, Tillie wrote a rollicking poem to accompany Jack's reduced lunch, which she called "Melancholy apology poem written in the midst of egg wreckage & fish stink at 7 this morning."

18. Wallace Stegner, Malcolm Cowley, and Karl Shapiro were among the team of writer-teachers who selected the winning entries from different college writing programs.

19. He wrote: "Mrs. Olsen's only previous publication was a story in *Pacific Spectator,* Winter, 1956, but she has recently had a story accepted by Karl Shapiro for the *Schooner.*" *New Campus Writing: No. 2,* 275.

20. To fight back, she collected evidence showing that the Society of Internal Medicine tried to blackball leftist doctors in spring 1956. Though she inflated her image for Miller, saying that the Society had bought an $800 IBM Selectric typewriter to bribe her into staying, the Society assured the FBI that it was firing her. TOP, boxes 17, 18, and 19.

21. She made this melodramatic conclusion after finding Thomas Hardy's *Jude the Obscure* and Olive Schreiner's *Story of an African Farm* in a book trough for 5¢ apiece.

22. Conversation with Kathie Olsen Hoye, 9 July 2005. TOP, box 16.

23. The eulogy was by Ricky Johnson, whose parents were Tillie's old friends Lillian Dinkin and Harold (Mink) Johnson. TOP, box 19.

24. Sputnik was in orbit only about three months, but it seemed, in Halberstam's words, a "technological Pearl Harbor," 623. It also spurred another anti-Red backlash.

25. Her reading notes include quotations from Marcel Proust, Walt Whitman, Lord Byron, F. Scott Fitzgerald, Paul Valery, Honoré Balzac, Herman Melville, Edgar Allen Poe, Nathaniel Hawthorne, Henry James, Somerset Maughan, Rainer Maria Rilke, and four women: George Sand, Willa Cather, Rebecca Harding Davis, and Emily Dickinson. TOP, box 17.

26. Among them were Scribner's and Simon and Schuster and *Discovery* and *Atlantic Monthly* magazines.

27. TOP, box 33.

28. Julie Olsen Edwards to PR, 18 May 2006.

29. Tillie revised the poorly typed copy after it was rejected.

30. She may have recopied this letter to Scowcroft but kept a draft. TOP, box 16.

31. She applied to write a story collection and lost because the fellowship sponsored a novel.

32. Others authors, including Sherwood Anderson, Ernest Hemingway, and William Faulkner, had also published collections of interrelated stories as novels.

33. Back in 1934, Macmillan had assumed she had agreed to an option contract; Random House, without imposing such an option, had nonetheless lost the money it advanced her.

34. This syndrome results from excess pressure in the inner ear and creates fluctuating hearing loss, vertigo, ringing in the ears, and a feeling of enormous pressure that seems to threaten the inside of the head.

35. Her recommenders were Malcolm Cowley, Blanche W. Knopf, Nolan Miller, Richard Scowcroft, Wallace Stegner, and William Maxwell of *The New Yorker,* whom Stegner hoped would take Olsen under his wing.

36. This incomplete draft letter is emended by hand, often illegibly. Presumably she polished the letter before sending it to the Ford Foundation. TOP, box 16.

37. This time extended from Karla's third birthday at the end of 1935 until June 1936, when Ida asked Gene to return her to Tillie.

38. The cancelled check to Tillie Olsen is in the Lerner Papers.

39. Huntington Hartford was heir to the A & P grocery chain fortune. He devoted a great deal of money to the arts, publishing, and show business.

40. Possibly an allusion to David Reisman's *The Lonely Crowd*.

41. See Reid, "From Osipovichi to Omaha."

42. Pearlman and Werlock confuse the Stanford and Ford awards, 29. Tillie listed the Ford Foundation Creative Writing grant, 1959–1961, as an award of $4000 a year.

43. Tillie gave no details but said that her absence was "hard on Jack" and their phone bill. Interview, 28 October 1997.

44. Frye, 177.

45. Tillie sent a story to Hannah Green saying it was a "not ready story. Started at Stanford, then put aside (couldn't continue because of the coincidence of my mother). . . . Tell me what you think, specific." Hannah had already responded to "Tell Me a Riddle," so this seems to have been another story, now lost.

46. This note is dated 1959. TOP, box 16.

47. Agee and Evans had been on assignment for *Fortune Magazine* in 1936 to report on sharecropping in Alabama, but publisher Henry Luce had rejected their efforts. Houghton Mifflin published *Let Us Now Praise Famous Men* in 1941. Largely unnoticed then, in 1960, five years after Agee's death, it spoke to a renewed awareness of human dignity and economic injustice.

48. William Piehl sent me, among other correspondence, Tillie's invitation to her open house.

49. One was John Gilgun, who applied for a Saxton after their conversation. A year later he won a Saxton and wrote to thank Tillie: "I owe it to you!" TOP, box 21.

50. Sexton, 103. Miller had published Sexton earlier in the *Antioch Review*. She had attended a writing workshop at Antioch in summer 1957. The originals of her letters are in TOP, box 27. Carbon copies of many of them are at Texas, along with Tillie's letters to Sexton.

51. A bank loan to Jack and Tillie Olsen, dated 10 August 1960, is for $160. They agreed to repay it in five installments. Tillie wrote Cowley in October 1960 that she was having "six tooth yankings, a bridge, etc."

52. Karla had married Arthur Lutz a year earlier. They met at Bard College. Then he entered graduate school at the University of Wisconsin. Ericka Lutz was born on 7 October 1960.

53. *New York Times* (20 November 1960). In fall 1961, *Time* featured President Bunting on its cover and *Newsweek* ran an article on her.

54. Sexton, 117, 127–28.

55. Tillie said Kathie picketed "what was then the Outer Row, to get them to integrate pupils." Interview, 28 October 1997.

56. Sexton first wrote Tillie on 5 April 1960; Tillie replied in November with her "dear related to me" note. Anne's letter saying that Tillie's letters look as if they were written by a fairy is dated "November noon." Though the editors add "[1961]" the correct date is

November 1960. Tillie's long letter trying to dispel any "fairy" image dates from January 1961, when she had a new grandchild and before she was hospitalized.

57. Jack was fifty on 16 March 1961. See the *New Republic* (17 February 1941) for Westcott's article. Elman's letter is in TOP, box 21; he apparently did not keep her note. A letter addressed to Tillie at Kaiser Hospital was forwarded to the Swiss Avenue address on 30 March 1961, TOP, box 25.

58. TOP, box 17. In the 1990s, Tillie labeled this notebook "1960 with my now small shattered brain." Letters from Cowley and Elman establish that the correct date was 1961.

59. Electroconvulsive therapy (ECT) breaks the repetitive patterns symptomatic of depression. Other important writers given shock therapy in this period include William Faulkner (1952), Sylvia Plath (1953), and Ernst Hemingway (1961). ECT's usefulness has since been questioned because it sometimes causes permanent memory loss. (See Andre.) Tillie read an article, "Is Affection Good for the Heart?" which assured her that the "power of affection can overcome the physical impact of electric shock," reading which establishes her interest in shock treatment; TOP, box 16. Kathie Olsen calls my suggestion that her mother might have had shock therapy "almost blasphemous." She says that Tillie used the word mad "to describe her deepest feelings—she was 'driven mad' with despair at so much that was terrible in this world, or she was 'mad with worry' about things (money, health of her family, war)," to PR, 11 May 2008. Julie Olsen Edwards checked with Tillie's physician who replied that Tillie had never mentioned any treatment for depression; psychiatric records, however, are closed. He also thought that it would be irresponsible for me to argue that Tillie stopped publishing because of shock therapy; Julie Edwards to PR, 1 June 2008. I am not making that argument, but I am noting that Tillie's own words suggest depression and shock therapy.

60. Among them were Erich Maria Remarque, Glenway Westcott, Elizabeth Madox Robert, Katherine Mansfield, Olive Schreiner, Franz Kafka, Charles Dickens, Anton Chekhov, and Joseph Conrad.

61. Interview, 28 October 1997. The actual title to the collection for which Woolf wrote a preface was *Life as We Have Known It.*

62. Rechecking this letter in the Berg reveals that Tillie wrote this improbable assortment of words and letters. What "k. woman" means eludes me, unless it is the "korl woman," from *Life in the Iron Mills.*

63. TOP, box 17.

64. TOP, box 13, does include a long "unidentified story" that Tillie could have intended to turn into a novel. Some characters, Jeannie, Carol, and Len, are carryovers from the stories in *Tell Me a Riddle.* Others are new, as is a grandfather's death. Tillie borrowed names from Arne Matilla's Finnish family and the story of an amputated leg from Jack's sister. These more than forty pages offer fragments of conversations and snatches of direct addresses, but in no way do they approximate even an unconventional novel.

65. TOP, box 16.

66. Hannah Green was working as a research assistant for Matthew Josephson, author of *The Robber Barons*, a 1934 Marxist analysis of industrialization. While she worked on her own fiction, Hannah was helping Josephson with his memoirs.

67. Conversation with Julie Olsen Edwards, August 2005.

68. Including Anne Sexton, Malcolm Cowley, Nolan Miller, and Blanche Knopf, who

dropped out of the competition to publish Tillie's novel. An advertisement in *College English* read: "Mrs. Olsen, honored as one of the important talents in America today has collected all her fiction in this first book." It was priced at paper, $1.65; cloth, $3.50.

69. *San Francisco Chronicle* (9 September 1961). TOP, box 1998–242.

70. She gave 1913 as her birth date and listed Scowcroft as her only recommender.

71. She had been involved in discussions with her siblings in 1957 about whether or not he should go to this home. He moved in October 1961. See Lerner Papers.

72. Jann did write a birthday card saying: "I enjoyed your tribute to Mom in your book." Olsen private papers. Rivka Davis remembered that her mother "expressed considerable anger at the way Ida and Sam were depicted in 'Tell Me a Riddle.' She thought that the account falsified both the facts of her parents' lives and her mother's death, and the nature of their characters." Gene's defense of the book as fiction did not impress Lillian, who said "people took it as accurate." To PR, 4 September 2005.

73. Robert R. Kirsch, "Books," *Los Angeles Times* (31 December 1961).

74. *San Francisco Examiner* (17 December 1961). The "literary breadline" phrase was an accurate quotation, which Tillie also used it in her Guggenheim application. Her beleaguered-housewife persona depended on denying ever having household help.

CHAPTER 12 — 1962–1969

1. For her biography of Sexton, Diane Middlebrook gave Tillie a draft of the chapter about Radcliffe. When she read that Sexton had pressed for her appointment, as she indeed had, Tillie insisted "not accurate."

2. From John Leonard's introduction to the Dell Edition of *Tell Me a Riddle*. On 6 August 1962, Leonard sent Elman the tape of Tillie reading "O Yes," which Elman asked to rebroadcast. TOP, box 21.

3. Dick Elman sent the recording to Malcolm Cowley, then president of the National Institute of Arts and Letters, who engineered the award for her. Tillie's last day working at the hospital was 18 January 1962.

4. Rebekah Edwards, daughter of Julie and Rob Edwards, was born on 3 April 1962.

5. Divorced in 1959, Jann Lerner Brodinsky moved alone to Boston. Gene was sending Jann funds to help her fulfill her dream of going to college. Lerner Papers.

6. Once when Gene admired Jann's "enviable posture, rapid graceful walk," she replied that Ida's ambitions for her children might have been wrong: "we all should've been dancers, athletes or physical education instructors." See Gene Lerner's "From Czarist Russia" in the Lerner Papers.

7. TOP, 1998–353, includes her clippings on James Meredith, integration, and race.

8. The Mississippi legislature passed a bill aimed specifically at keeping Meredith out of "Ole Miss."

9. For accounts of Tillie at Radcliffe, I tried to contact all alumnae and interviewed (by phone or mail) Mildred Goldberger, Sister William (Helen Kelley), Maxine Kumin, Eileen Morley, Hanna Papanak, and Barbara Swan. Harold Tovish was exceedingly helpful.

10. Ursula Niebuhr's husband was famous theologian Reinhold Niebuhr; Mildred Goldberger's husband was Marvin Goldberger, winner of the Heineman Prize for mathematical physics; Maria Teresa Moevs's husband was Robert Moevs, composer, Rome Prize winner, and a current Guggenheim Fellow; Barbara Swan's husband Alan

Fink was a director of the Boris Mirski Gallery in Boston; Maxine Kumin's husband Victor Kumin, a chemical engineer, was a manager at the Kendall Company in Boston; Anne Sexton's husband Alfred (known as Kayo) was a salesman. Only Tillie and Anne Sexton seem to have been married to nonprofessional men.

11. Middlebrook, 195. The unpublished letter from Sexton is in TOP, box 27.

12. After the botched U.S. invasion of Cuba, known as the "Bay of Pigs," Castro had implored Premier Nikita Khrushchev for protection; he responded with a missile installation in Cuba. After Kennedy quarantined Cuba, Khrushchev ordered missile-carrying Soviet ships to reverse course and Cuban missile installations to be dismantled. In turn, America promised not to invade Cuba and to dismantle U.S. missiles near the Soviet border in Turkey.

13. The notebook is in TOP, box 17. Boxes 16 and 1998–242 also hold jottings on Jeannie. In her list of late-starting writers, Tillie listed Joseph Conrad, Angus Wilson, Sherwood Anderson, and Elizabeth Madox Roberts.

14. Conversation with Harold Tovish, 20 June 1998. His article "Sculpture: The Sober Art" in the *Atlantic Monthly* (September 1961) shows him a sensitive artistic critic.

15. Interview with Hanna Papanek, 15 January 1999. Tillie might have been trying to counter the effect of Aleksandr Solzhenitsyn's *One Day in the Life of Ivan Denisovich*, his autobiographical novel about life in a 1950s Soviet labor camp, available in English in 1963.

16. From Laurie Olsen's talk at the Memorial for Tillie Olsen, 17 February 2007. Hope Davis, one of the mothers, wrote Tillie that her husband, Robert Gorham Davis recalled Tillie Lerner from his political days. He later gave a favorable review to Tillie's "Hey Sailor." TOP, box 21.

17. From Olsen's mark-up of Diane Middlebrook's chapter 10. The Radcliffe College press release of 4 February 1962 said that a "social psychologist, Mrs. Benjamin W. White, of Lexington, Mass.," was appointed to conduct a study of Radcliffe fellows.

18. In her "Biographical Interpretation" to *Life in the Iron Mills*, Tillie said she uncovered the author's identity in 1958. She learned more about Davis only after arriving at Radcliffe.

19. Charlotte Perkins Gilman, Genevieve Taggard, Mary Austin, and Olive Schreiner had one child each. (Schreiner's died quickly). Dorothy Canfield Fisher had two children. Sarah Orne Jewett, Mary E. Wilkins Freeman, Alice Dunbar-Nelson, Agnes Smedley, and other women writers she read about were childless.

20. On 22 January 1963, Cowley explained: "We wanted the first book to be bigger & have a wider sale." Lippincott's story series "lost too much money for them & had to be abandoned."

21. Texan Ted Daffan wrote "Born to Lose" in 1949. Ray Charles made it a hit in 1962. Tillie cited Albert Camus as background for Jeannie's and Lennie's reflections. A crematory foretold "the fate of humanity." TOP, boxes 17 and 16.

22. Higginson (1823–1911) was an abolitionist, minister, teacher, and soldier who lead a Civil War regiment of former slaves. He was a literary advisor to Emily Dickinson. TOP, box 16, includes a note on "the Emilys [*sic*] and their fathers."

23. From a transcription, purchased by Anne Sexton, now at Texas. Tillie's notes for this talk in TOP, box 16, mention her "hungry snatched reading—interred in the 31 cartons"; speaking "in voices not my own," and fearing "I am being destroyed."

24. Middlebrook, 198. Sexton's transcriptions occupy nearly seventy single-spaced pages. The value she placed on them expressed "her feeling of being undereducated." Diane Middlebrook to PR, 23 March 2006.

25. See *Marianna Pineda*. In 1970, the Institute received the gift of Pineda's *Aspects of the Oracle III: Portentous*. This six-feet-high sculpture sits beside the Institute library on a natural rock garden pedestal.

26. Sister William (Helen Kelley) became president of Immaculate Heart College in Los Angeles within months of leaving the Radcliffe Institute.

27. She recommended Hannah Green to her agent and publisher, Dick Elman for a Ford grant, and T. Mike Walker for a Stanford writing fellowship. TOP, boxes 18 and 27.

28. Tillie jotted down ideas for an "embryo story" about mother/daughter rivalry, based on Kathie's resentment." TOP, box 16.

29. Middlebrook, 213.

30. TOP, box 16. Grolier's billed the Institute for her books at a 10-percent discount.

31. Theodora Ward was the editorial associate for volumes of Dickinson's poems and letters. She authored several articles on Dickinson. Her grandparents had been friends of the Dickinson family.

32. Radcliffe College Archives holds an untranscribed tape recording.

33. Radcliffe fellows who were critical of Tillie Olsen asked to remain anonymous, but Middlebrook confirmed that she heard similar stories. Diane Middlebrook to PR, 23 March 2006.

34. She overlooked her residency at Huntington Hartford and the previous summer alone in Arlington.

35. Olsen private papers.

36. TOP, box 33.

37. Julie and Rob Edwards's second child Matthew was born on 4 November 1964. TOP, box 28.

38. TOP, box 16. Tillie did take time to read and critique a novel about China by an elderly colonist named Grace Boynton, whose parents had been missionaries. Tillie's good deed interfered with her own work.

39. Wilder and Sexton were traveling together that May. Afterward, in San Francisco, Tillie almost drove Wilder "batty" by teasing her about her lesbian affair. Diane Middlebrook to PR, 23 March 2006.

40. The contract's terms were, after Russell's fee: $5370 on signing; $840 on 3 January 1966; and $1290 on delivery, plus a 10-percent royalty on the first five million hardback copies and a 6-percent royalty on paperbacks.

41. Diarmuid Russell secured the release.

42. See TOP, box 28.

43. The writers named on the cover were Norman Podhoretz, Gore Vidal, Isaac Bashevis Singer, Louis Simpson, and David Dempsey; the "and others" were Robert Kotlowitz, Alan Levy, and Tillie Olsen. Demsey wrote the article on the Foundations.

44. Olsen private papers.

45. Lyon was not, as Tillie liked to say, an heir to a tobacco fortune. He was born in Montreal and became a senior vice president of Cecil & Presbrey in charge of the Philip Morris account. Michael Lyon to PR, 30 December 2006.

46. Her undergraduate thesis at Goddard College—"What Kind of World?"—focused on the need for empathy and understanding. Her graduate thesis at Goddard was titled "Creative Dramatics: For a Human Relations Centered Curriculum."

47. Caroline Eckhardt, Rivka Davis, and Cory Richards to PR, June 2008.

48. Tillie said that bra-less-ness was "in the spirit" of the writers' colony in the 1960s. Interview, 15 July 2000.

49. In a 1970 Guggenheim application, Tillie said that NEA "had requested the application."

50. The author asked not to be identified.

51. Interview with Gene Lerner, 2 July 2000. Gene told amusing tales about actor John Gielgud's butler driving him in a red Mustang convertible, which the KGB lectured to him about keeping clean. When Gene told the KGB that James Baldwin had been scheduled to join them, they thought he meant James Bond.

52. See Norman Mailer's *The Armies of the Night* for a dramatic account of the "March on the Pentagon."

53. She made notes in this period about "teaching our youth" not to be "pawns, followers" and "future killers" but to be "believers in democracy." Olsen private papers.

54. The collection only sold 809 copies in the United Kingdom. Colin Penman, Faber and Faber archivist, to PR, 11 May 2000.

55. See Middlebrook, 301. Diane Middlebrook to PR, 23 March 2006.

56. "Reflections on a Political Trial," *New York Review of Books* (22 August 1968). Howe and Lauter taught in Mississippi Freedom Schools in 1964 and 1965. Lauter to PR, 28 August 2007.

57. Marx authored an important study of American literature called *The Machine in the Garden.* Information about Amherst is from a 1998 seminar paper by Leslie Cole Manace, available from the Amherst College Library.

58. Organizer Robin Morgan described the pageant as "a perfect combination of American values—racism, materialism, capitalism—all packaged in one 'ideal' symbol, a woman." See Isserman and Kazin, 235–36.

59. Interview with TO, 18 July 2000.

60. Olsen private papers.

61. Deborah de Moulpied chose not to discuss her relationship with Tillie Olsen; letter to PR, 16 June 2007.

62. See "Reforming the MLA," *The New York Review of Books* (19 December 1968). Signers were Noam Chomsky, Frederick Crews, Florence Howe, Richard Ohmann, Paul Lauter, and Louis Kampf.

63. The reading list from Tillie's course on the literature of poverty would be published in radical newsletters associated with the New University Conference and the Students for a Democratic Society.

64. The party was given by George Kendall, general director of the Colony from 1952 to 1971, and his wife.

65. The title was *12 from the Sixties: Selected and Introduced by Richard Kostelanetz.* Tillie had appeared uninvited at Kostelanetz's first poetry reading in sculptor Red Groom's loft. Kostelanetz to PR, 20 December 1998.

66. TOP, box 13.

67. She apparently was expecting this large revenue from the Kostelanetz story collection.

68. TOP, box 16.

69. See Julie Olsen Edwards, in Zandy, for her attitude toward money.

70. A woman named Sally Johnson also asked if Tillie would "honor" her with her laundry. A man named Norman addressed Tillie as "my beloved guru." TOP, boxes 24 and 25.

71. Florence Howe to PR, 8 July 2007. Conversation with Paul Lauter, August 2007. In her "Biographical Interpretation," Tillie said, "I never envisioned writing of [Davis] until Florence Howe and Paul Lauter, to whom I had introduced *Life in the Iron Mills*, suggested that The Feminist Press issue it and that I write the foreword." In fall 1969 she mentioned a "Rebecca book"; thus, Lauter's recollection of meeting Tillie in New York in 1969 seems accurate, though Howe dates it in the spring of 1970.

72. Conversation with Robert DeMaria, 6 December 2001.

73. Lee Richards, "Tillie Olsen at Amherst," *The Amherst Student* (4 June 1970).

74. Scott Turow to PR, 5 September 2001.

CHAPTER 13 — 1970–1974

1. My thanks to Steven W. Siegel, literary director and archivist, the Y Library, for these records.

2. Lorna M. Peterson to PR, 14 November 2001. TOP, box 16. Interview with TO, 18 July 2000. Tillie sent a copy of her reading list to Radcliffe.

3. Tillie valued old cards because they showed a longing for self-expression in people who could write little.

4. In 1984 *Women's Studies Quarterly* published a chronology of milestones in the women's movement; it listed many books by and about women published in trade presses in the 1970s.

5. TOP, box 24. Levertov lived in Somerville, Massachusetts, and taught occasionally in nearby institutions. Tillie invited her to the class and then left it in her hands.

6. Florence Howe to PR, 8 July 2007.

7. Tillie's undated test was a list of quotations to identify from Bronowski, Blake, Goya, Whitman, Hardy, Agee, Du Bois, and other men.

8. Paul Lauter to PR, 28 August 2007.

9. William Pritchard to PR, 22 September 2001 and 8 June 2007. Professor Howell Chickering was away but later talked to students who said they "benefited more" from Tillie's "personality than from her instructional skills." To PR, 26 September 2001.

10. She did not count "Requa" as writing apparently because she assembled it from already written bits.

11. A note from Sandy Boucher, dated 9 July 1970, mentions Jack's picketing in San Rafael. TOP, box 20.

12. The *Brattleboro Reformer* covered the wedding. Tillie sent the illustrated clipping, with handwritten annotations, to the Radcliffe Institute.

13. Among other women, she would write about Alice, Dorothy, and Sophia, lesser known sisters of Henry James, William Wordsworth, and Henry David Thoreau, and about Mary Moody Emerson, aunt of Ralph Waldo Emerson.

14. In 1963, J. Edgar Hoover had called pro-integration, antiracist protests Commie-inspired and had ordered files on old Commies reopened. The Boston FBI did not pursue her, but her file was not closed until 1970.

15. Held in Harvard's Memorial Church, the remarks of four speakers were published by Radcliffe in a pamphlet.

16. In this proposal, she did not address Merloyd Lawrence's criticism: "we are surrounded by Women's Lib ideas: what we need is someone to make shape out of them."

17. On 24 February 1971, Tillie wrote to Jerre Mangione at the University of Pennsylvania asking him to check out and mail to her Helen Woodward Schaeffer's "Rebecca Harding Davis: Pioneer Realist," an unpublished 1947 University of Pennsylvania dissertation. She promised to return it "immediately after reading." In a letter of almost two years later, she again asked him to check out the dissertation for her.

18. At the Feminist Press's memorial for Tillie Olsen on 11 September 2007, Howe told this story as a single event to illustrate Tillie's dynamic personality. Lauter confirmed that Tillie "would wheedle a little extra" and more than once "did her 'little old lady' routine." To PR, 3 October 2007.

19. Lauter to PR, August 2007.

20. When I met Tillie Olsen in October 1997, I carried a photocopy of "Requa I" with me. She made corrections on sixteen of its twenty-six pages.

21. The Lerner siblings felt similar resentment. On 9 January 1973, Jann wrote Gene that many of Sam's fellow residents asked if she were the famous daughter. She assumed that they had hardly seen Tillie Olsen. Letters about finances are also in the Lerner Papers.

22. The standard "qwerty" keyboard refers to the top left letters on a standard typewriter's keyboard.

23. Tillie also told Nolan Miller she had to take a job, a development she does not mention elsewhere. She bought the remaining copies for £6.40 apiece.

24. Konecky was Edith Konecky's married name. Through her, I found Eugene Konecky's son Milton and his recollections of his father, Tillie Lerner, and Jeanette Gray in the late 1920s and early 1930s. Edith Konecky to PR, 11 April 2000. Her "Love and Friendship" appeared in the September 1971 issue of *Cosmopolitan*.

25. In the pamphlet *Elaine Hedges: A Tribute*, Emily Toth describes how dealing with Tillie had brought Hedges near a nervous breakdown.

26. Konecky was at MacDowell as an artist. She stayed on in the Annex (now the Heyward studio) from August 1972 until April 1974 in exchange for winterizing and upgrading that lodging. In the summer months, she formally applied and was accepted as a MacDowellite. To PR, 11 April 2000.

27. Since 1934, when General Chiang Kai-shek had forced Chinese Communists on the "Long March," Tillie had denounced him. Since 1949, when he retreated to Formosa (now Taiwan) and Mao Tse-Tung established the People's Republic of China on the mainland, Tillie had railed against the isolation of Communist China.

28. Kathie Amatniek [Sarachild] wrote up Tillie's presentation as "Momma's Revolt and Other Remarks," a title borrowed from Mary E. Wilkins Freeman's "The Revolt of Mother." Tillie's notes are in TOP, box 15.

29. Harold Tovish spoke of Pineda's great generosity as a near fault.

30. *The Nation* (10 April 1972). Reviewer Elizabeth Fisher edited the new feminist literary magazine *Aphra*. Tillie offered to read Fisher's novel-in-progress and let her

reprint "The Iron Throat" from the *Partisan Review* (Spring 1934) in *Aphra* (Summer 1972).

31. Moffat to PR, 21 January 1999.

32. She told Lawrence that "Florence has had them [the manuscript pages], and FP wants to publish it all." After starting competition between Lawrence and Howe, she now hoped it could be "worked out happily."

33. Near the end of 1971, Ellsberg was indicted for espionage and conspiracy. Thanks to government misconduct, the charges against him were dismissed in 1973.

34. Apparently, the Lerners (except Jann and Vicki) chipped in to help with production costs. Whether Tillie did is unclear.

35. Tillie had first written the State of Nebraska; it instructed her to get a delayed birth registration using such evidence as school records and a parent's affidavit. TOP, box 48.

36. See Robin Dizard in Hedges and Fishkin for discussion of the enormous impact of those reading lists.

37. *Woman's World* was a noncommercial publication of "Redstockings" a founding women's liberation group from the 1960s. Kathie Amatniek [Sarachild] was a contributor. *Ms.*, edited by Gloria Steinem, published articles not only on women's issues but also, at its inauguration, printed an interview with Daniel Ellsberg.

38. Shulman was an organizer of the Women's Liberation Movement.

39. Mara Kelly said Olsen's "mouth is sad and mobile, her skin smooth and young, although she is in her late 50s. Her voice is punctuated by sighs. She seems ready to weep." *The Mass Media* (6 March 1972).

40. Gene Lerner wrote: "Jann, Lil and Vicki all agree that any theory about T's being retarded because of the stutter should be thrown into the ash can and that her stutter was in no way a worry for our parents, and I join them in that point of view"; to PR, 27 May 2000.

41. Tillie Olsen's readings and talks were advertised on mailing lists to progressive groups, making her appearances virtual rallies for peace and justice. Paul Lauter to PR, 28 August 2007. She wrote about being "partially destroyed" on 21 November 1972. TOP, box 24.

42. The chapter outline is in the Berg. The letter to Klopfer is printed here as Appendix C.

43. Gottlieb, *The New York Times Book Review* (31 March 1973). TOP, box 20.

44. Perhaps Tillie referred to an article in *Time Magazine* called "The Blue Collar Blues" (24 July 1972).

45. Previous women presidents of MLA were Louise Pound in 1955 and Marjorie Hope Nicolson in 1963.

46. See Coiner, chapter 6; she says authorial insertions ask "who will speak for the oppressed workers," 190.

47. The allusion is to Walt Whitman's poem on aborigines, people "utterly lost" from history: "unlimned they disappear," as poor people of the 1930s also disappeared.

48. The writer was Ellen Moers. TOP, box 26.

49. Foley's letter is in the Lawrence Collection. Meyer's *The Amendment that Refused to Die* was nominated for a Pulitzer Prize in 1973. He wrote the introduction to Higginson's *Army Life in a Black Regiment.* Conversation with Meyer, 21 January 2000.

50. Abrahams to PR, 19 May 1998, through assistant Philippe Tapon.

51. TOP, box 4, includes attempts to finish *Yonnondio*. She sent broken notes on it to Hannah Green but was able to write only fragments.

52. The full title was the San Francisco Community College District Labor Studies Program.

53. Ferguson had earned a Ph.D. in Anglo-Saxon studies but had not been hired to teach Old English. Her collection *Images of Women*, her work on the MLA Commission on the Status of Women, and the advent of Women's Studies resulted in a tenured professorship and then an administrative position as chair of the English department.

54. This group of "young Turk" faculty women included Ruth Perry, Barbara Sirota, Patricia Cummings, and Janet Horwitz. Ruth Perry to PR, 10 December 2004; Barbara Sirota to PR, 26 March 2008.

55. Conversation with Harold Tovish, 20 June 1998.

56. Sandy Boucher described Tillie's response to the events in Chili. See note 65.

57. Tillie thought she spoke poorly, but Susan Lyman, acting dean of the Radcliffe Institute, thanked her for her "beautifully chosen words, expressed with such generous sincerity." Erika Duncan thanked Tillie for "photos of the beautiful ceremony for Connie," meaning this dedication. TOP, 1998–353.1, box 10.

58. One who wept was Mary Fran Breathitt, a young manic-depressive writer, who said she could only communicate with Tillie Olsen. TOP, box 20.

59. Ruth Perry and Barbara Sirota to PR, 28 and 31 March 2008. Arlyn Diamond was the daughter of Tillie's first cousin, Roberta Braude Diamond. Hardly an anthology of women's writing appeared during this period without thanks to Tillie Olsen.

60. In previous applications, she listed the Ford money inconsistently as $7000, $8000, and $9000. In 1973, she mentioned the Ford award in her text but not in her itemized list of grants and fellowships. There she listed her Amherst position at $14,000, her 1966 NEA Fellowship at $10,000, her spring 1972 quarter at Stanford at $4,500, and her fall semester at MIT at $10,000. (She earned $13,000 for the spring term at the University of Massachusetts/Boston.) Tillie earned $300, plus expenses, for each appearance; TOP, box 24. In 1974, according to the 1984 *Women's Studies Quarterly*, women academicians averaged $10,357 a year, compared to men's $17,188.

61. The phrase "masculine Hopkins air" comes from Tillie Olsen's letter to Thelma (Tema) Nason. Hedges's letter about these events mentions no problems at Johns Hopkins. TOP, box, 24.

62. Because Tillie asked Rich to recommend her only once and because their friendship ended, perhaps Rich faulted Tillie for the tone of self-pity and defeatism in her work.

63. Conversation with Nason, fall 2001.

64. Sirota to PR, 26 March 2008; conversation with Ferguson, 9 October 1999.

65. Boucher's article appeared on 10 February in the conjoined *San Francisco Examiner & Chronicle* and in *Ms.* in September. Gottlieb, *New York Times Book Review* (31 March 1974). Catharine Stimpson said Olsen rendered the "consciousness of victims"; *The Nation* (30 November 1974).

66. See TOP, box 26. Sarah Murray thought that Tillie's "aphoristic poetic" expressions, like her impossible handwriting, conveyed unresponsiveness. Conversations with Sarah and Jim Murray in March 2000. Grumbach to PR, 27 January 1999.

67. The *Bulletin of the New York Public Library* said that Tillie Olsen "has honored our Berg Collection with the gift of a portion of the very early manuscripts of her novel *Yonnondio: From the Thirties.*"

68. Conversation with Shulman, 29 September 1999. Adele Braude to PR, 7 September 2001.

69. Lawrence wrote her on 13 April that *Yonnondio* had sold out in San Francisco. In 1974 Faber's *Tell Me a Riddle* sold only 809 copies. Its edition of *Yonnondio* sold only 631 copies in 1974, but it sold more than 1000 copies in each of the next nine years, rising to 1281 in 1983. Colin Penman to PR, 11 May 2000.

70. TOP, box 16.

71. In the interview with Elaine Showalter, Tillie gave a slightly different version of this tale: "they thought I was feeble-minded . . . the truant officer found me reading *David Copperfield* and thought I was lying when I said I wasn't going to school." She also fabricated living "first in the slaughterhouse section of Omaha."

72. Ellen Ficklen Mitchell, "San Francisco's Tillie Olsen," *Washington Post* (2 June 1974).

73. Laurie Hoye was born on 8 August 1974.

74. Among other partygoers on 19 July 1974 were Jessica Mitford, Susie Griffin, Mary Jane Moffat, Charlotte Painter, J. J. Wilson, and Alta, of the Shameless Hussey Press. Laurie Olsen, who was editing *Nonsexist Curricular Materials for Elementary Schools* (1974) for the Feminist Press attended with a staff member from the Feminist Press. Sandy Boucher to PR, April 2000.

75. The Supreme Court had ruled unanimously that Nixon could not hide his involvement in the raid on the Democratic National Headquarters.

76. Anne Sexton put on her mother's fur coat, poured herself a big glass of vodka, shut the garage door, and turned on the ignition, filling the garage and car with carbon dioxide. See Middlebrook, 397.

77. She wrote this explanation: "to hopelessly hope my application arrives deadline day. It was to have been taken care of here, where I've come for swifter recovery: solitude, the sea, and not to be trapped in our third [floor] walkup S. F. shelf [?] apartment with stair climbing forbidden for six weeks. But my help never showed, nor do bookstores have *Yonnondio* here or Rebecca, so I sent the makings to my occasionally angelic daughter in S. F. to xerox, assemble, get book copies, mail. The makings went special (a mistake?) but a phone call just now tells me they're still not there. Nor can she register all for the p. o. will be closed this [Saturday] afternoon and Monday . . . a federal holiday. Just explanatory."

78. Middlebrook, 397. Rich seems to have similarly objected to Tillie's pose of victimhood. (See note 62). Rich has not answered my queries so I am speculating here.

79. Thanks especially to Tillie, the Feminist Press reprint series, after Davis, resurrected the work of Alice Smedley, Charlotte Perkins Gilman, Kate Chopin, and Zora Neal Hurston, and many other women authors. Conversation with Candace Falk, 29 March 1999.

80. Both Martha Foley and Ellen Moers in letters to Tillie made this complaint. TOP, boxes 21 and 26.

81. Conversation with Candace Falk, 3 February 1999. Woolf scholars Madeleine Moore and J. J. Wilson, along with the UCSC English faculty invited Tillie. Wilson

found Olsen's talk on Woolf a "breath of fresh air." Wilson to PR, 4 November 2007. William Abrahams and Peter Stansky, Stanford professor of British history, however, found Tillie's talk tiresome. Interview with Stansky, April 1998. On 10 January 1975, Tillie wrote Lawrence that she was surprised to hear that "Billy and Peter were at the Woolf symposium when I spoke. I did not see them." They had left long before she finished.

82. Colman McCarthy, in the *Washington Post* (1 December 1976). He had attended the private reading at the Murrays' home in 1972.

CHAPTER 14 — 1975–1980

1. Since 1958, when she first applied to write what she then called "a long gestated novel of San Francisco," Tillie had made nine Guggenheim applications, but she withdrew one.

2. Gene Lerner periodically sent Jann checks from which she parceled out $60 a month to Sam. There is no record of financial aid from Tillie. See Lerner Papers.

3. Among recipients were Annie Dillard, Jane Lazarre, Cynthia Ozick, Alice Walker, Rosellen Brown, Norma Rosen, Jane Cooper, Alix Kates Shulman, Maxine Hong Kingston, Blanche Boyd, Marge Piercy, Mary Gray Hughes, and Mitsuye Yamada. TOP, box, 34, holds requests for Tillie's endorsement.

4. After Alice Walker had found Hurston's unmarked 1960 grave in 1973, her "In Search of Zora Neale Hurston" appeared in *Ms.* March, 1975. Walker credited her story "Everyday Use" to the influence of Tillie Olsen and Ernest Gaines.

5. Annie Dillard to PR, 11 April 2008.

6. When Jack Wesley won a Guggenheim, he and Hannah Green began spending every summer in France until 1995. Conversation with Wesley, 5 April 2000. In her 1989 *A Place at the Table*, Edith Konecky fictionalizes a brilliant writer's decline into a "bag lady," based on Mauve Brennan.

7. Poets and Writers, which began in 1970, helped colleges invite writers to campus by subventing costs. Thanks to its help, Tillie earned $600 from C. W. Post and $500 from Sarah Lawrence during this period. When Tillie received an invitation from one place, she sought others in the same regions, like Buffalo this time; thus she "bunched" speaking engagements, much as she did people.

8. Lillian Robinson witnessed this event; see *The Nation* (20 January 1992). Coiner recounts it, 3.

9. She left the corrected citation for Hannah Green and Jack Wesley.

10. TOP, boxes 16 and 4.

11. TOP, box 20.

12. Tillie perhaps had in mind Philip Roth's *My Life as a Man*.

13. Tillie was, however, not famous enough to prevent Gelfant from misspelling her name as "Olson" in the *Massachusetts Review* (Winter 1975). Coles's review of the Delta paperback of *Tell Me a Riddle*, first appeared in the *New Republic* (6 December 1975).

14. Mary Anne Ferguson to PR, 9 October 1999. Jann had lived in an apartment Lillian and Joseph Davis rented for her, near their winter home in Florida.

15. See Jann Lerner Brodinsky's letter to Tillie and Jack Olsen, 16 May 1976. Lerner Papers. Despite her lauded master's thesis in education, Jann was thought too old to find a permanent job as an educator.

16. She kept rewriting her life for different editions of *Working Papers*, edited by Sara Ruddick and Pamela Daniels, and *Images of Women*, edited by Mary Anne Ferguson.

17. Joanne Russ wrote Tillie that feminists with children should not expect those without to "share your trap." She also said that Alta bullied others in "lesbian space." TOP, box 27. Olsen files at Radcliffe include many discussions of motherhood versus careers.

18. In the November 1976 *Mother Jones*, Gottlieb cited Alta's *Momma: a start on all the untold stories* and Lazarre's *The Mother Knot* as examples of Tillie's influence.

19. Twenty years later, Tillie placed the "makings" of this novel at Stanford, which cataloged them as "Unidentified manuscripts." See TOP, box 13.

20. Paul Lauter thinks that, by this time, Tillie saw herself "as a political figure as much as a writer." Lauter to PR, 28 August 2007.

21. Kathie Olsen to PR, June 2008. Tillie mentioned the concussion in several January letters.

22. Callil said that playwright Arnold Wesker had suggested Tillie Olsen's work to Virago. Wesker's east European Jewish background and leftist politics were compatible with hers. TOP, box 33.

23. Conversation with Vicki Lerner Richards Bergman, spring 1999.

24. After the week at Amherst, she spoke at the Caravan Theatre about *Tell Me a Riddle* and Connie Smith's legacy, read "Tell Me a Riddle" at the University of Massachusetts, Boston, and taught a class at Columbia University, before reading and lecturing at George Washington University.

25. Faculty members she charmed included A. E. Claeyssens and Eileen McClay. An adoring women's studies and writing student was Thomazine Shanahan. There is no evidence she called her brother Harry Lerner while in D.C.

26. Feminist publishers chose such names as *Ms.*, *Aphra*, *Sinister Wisdom*, *Up From Under*, *Spare Rib*, *Viva*, *Persephone*, and *Mother Lode* for magazines and Daughters, Virago, and Shameless Hussey for presses.

27. Markson had been on Tillie's guest list in 1970 for her first reading at the Y's Poetry Center.

28. Conversation with Langer, 8 March 2000. Tillie told Langer that both she and Herbst spoke at the 1935 conference.

29. Cuomo edited *A Shout in the Street: a journal of literary and visual art*. When he asked Tillie for permission to publish his conversation with her, she refused.

30. Meyer presented a "Second Look at 'The 'Belle'" at Hofstra University in 1980. In the published version, in *Nineteenth-Century Women Writers of the English-Speaking World*, he mentions the "instigation" of Tillie Olsen. Conversation with Meyer, 21 January 2000.

31. John Corry, "Broadway," *New York Times* (1 April 1977). Despite lavish plans, the Baker project did not make it to the stage; Lerner-Kaufman lost their investment.

32. Interview with Gene Lerner, 2 July 2000.

33. Carol Verderese, "Tillie Olsen: A Women of Sensitive Insight and Emotional Depth," in Vassar's *Miscellany News*, 4 November 1977. Two of Tillie's former Amherst students, Robert DeMaria and Frank Bergon, were on Vassar's faculty and researched this article for me. Conversations, May and June, 2008.

34. There are at least thirty-six pages of jottings toward "Dream Vision." Most are

a mix of typed and inked additions, without a clear copy. I have quoted from one of the more legible versions. Inconsistencies include whether the vision occurred on Christmas Eve (in some versions) or Christmas Day (in others). TOP, box 13.

35. Konecky told this story at the memorial for Tillie Olsen, sponsored by the Feminist Press in New York City on 11 September 2007. Her appointment book dates the event as 30 December 1977. She had visited Tillie at the Watson Studio on several occasional that December and so had already seen Tillie's photos.

36. To PR, 11 April 2008. Dillard also pointed out that "if it weren't so hard for women to be taken seriously, there would be a lot more famous women from whom to draw."

37. Tillie allowed me to copy this 1978 calendar, perhaps the only preserved one.

38. Isa Kapp, *The New Leader* (22 May 1978), 5–6.

39. TOP, box 28.

40. Jeannette Gray Nagel then lived in Cleveland. She wrote Tillie several times during the next three years. She did not mention hearing from Tillie. TOP, 1995-135.1, box 1.

41. Among her devotees there were Maggie Anderson and Marcy Alancraig. Anderson printed her edited transcription of Tillie's talk in *Trellis*. Marcy Alancraig blamed "any problems with your talk on the length of time and tiredness." She tactfully wondered if next time "we should plan a shorter talk?" TOP, box 20.

42. For example, Rachel Klein tallied up $29 in phone calls to and from Tillie. She worked on the jacket copy of a new Dell reprint of *Tell Me a Riddle*, which Tillie approved on the phone but then completely rewrote. Lawrence noted that such reversals were "all part & parcel of publishing Tillie."

43. Beside the dragon, the card said, "Don't be afraid to hurt my feelings; All you risk is my unbounded rage." Delacorte/Lawrence and Olsen/Lawrence correspondence make it clear that Tillie created the problems she blamed on her publisher.

44. The Lawrences wrote her that a first printing was of 7500 copies at $10.95 apiece.

45. Interview, 2 July 2000. In her acknowledgments for *Silences*, Tillie contradicted her fabrication about not going to school until she was nine by mentioning being "a child at Kellom and Long Schools. . . ."

46. Margaret Atwood, *New York Times Book Review* (30 July 1978). John Leonard, *New York Times* (31 July 1978). Diana Loercher, *Christian Science Monitor* (18 September 1978). Joyce Carol Oates, *The New Republic* (29 July 1978). Doris Grumbach, *Washington Post Book World* (6 August 1978). Joan Peters, *The Nation* (23 September 1978). Shanahan and Grumbach, *Book World* (10 September 1978). Grumbach to PR, 27 January 1999. The exchanges in the *Post* brought a letter from Clare Lerner to Tillie; she thought "your admirers (in the 'Letters to the Editor' section). . . . shrill and unbalanced—by the time I finished reading them I found myself wondering how I should approach you the next time we meet. Should I enter bowing low and exit backwards as before royalty—or what? Let me tell you its quite uncomfortable to have a guru as a sister-in-law!" Lerner papers.

47. See TOP, box 20. Having written a blurb for Blanche Boyd's *Mourning the Death of Magic* (1977), Tillie felt Boyd's advice a violation of a code of loyalty.

48. She discovered that changes she had insisted on in the Laurel edition were not in the hardback *Tell Me a Riddle*. The three heads of state signed the Accord on 17 September 1978, establishing the Israel-Egypt Peace Treaty of 1979.

49. "Executioners" was in Munro's 1974 collection *Something I've Been Meaning to Tell You*. Jim Jones had founded the "Peoples' Temple" at Jonestown in the mid-1970s

in North West Guyana. Rumors of cultism and abuse had brought an investigation, headed by Congressman Leo Ryan. As Ryan and his colleagues were about return to the United States, they were gunned down on 18 November 1978; then more than four hundred people, the entire population of Jonestown, died too. The assassinations, in San Francisco's city hall, occurred on 27 November 1978.

50. She sent Elaine Markson a proposal for this collection dated 1979. To Sam Lawrence, though, in early 1980, Tillie said she had "sent it originally on July 20, 1978."

51. A community of writers of African descent founded in Harlem in 1950. Tillie referred to Rosa Guy, the one woman among its four founders. By 1983, Guild members had produced some four hundred books.

52. Framed photographs of her mother, Minnie Tallulah [or Lou] Grant Walker and her father, Willie Lee Walker hang on Alice Walker's walls. Comments about her relationship with Tillie are from her speech on "Tillie Olsen Day" (TOP, box 28) and from my interview with Walker, Berkeley, California, 15 July 2000.

53. Moffat to PR, 21 January 1999. Bryant had not met Tillie until she was invited to this party. Bryant had observed the infighting and posturing at a feminist conference and was thinking of writing a novel on the subject. Bryant to PR, 20 December 2007.

54. Tillie signed a contract allowing Deborah Rosenfelt to edit a critical edition of "Tell Me a Riddle" and obligating her in June and July 1979 to organize Tillie's files and correspondence. Rosenfelt agreed to submit her work to Tillie and not to use of any of Olsen's materials without written permission.

55. In January she gave the commencement address at Pitzer College, in Claremont, earning a sizable honorarium. Then Humboldt paid Tillie $600 plus expenses.

56. Spacks was speaking from her 1975 *The Female Imagination*. My thanks to Jane Kyle and Elinor Langer for details.

57. Evidence about the show is mostly lost, but Tillie's response to Clare's letter (see below) leaves no doubt that the writers for *Turnabout* made some use of her "Dream-Vision."

58. Conversation with Jack Wesley, 5 April 200. Alix Kates Shulman, "Overcoming Silences: Teaching Writing for Woman," *Harvard Educational Review* (November 1979). Conversation with Shulman, 29 September 1999.

59. TOP, box 13. Conversations with Susan Lerner, 2 July 2008 and 14 April 2009.

60. Tim Norris, *Omaha World-Herald* (May 1979), quoted Tillie rather inconsistently as saying: "People back then would call Jo Eva [Crawford] 'colored,' but we didn't have that kind of barrier then."

61. Conversation with Bill Pratt, 15 April 1998.

62. Among them were A. S. Byatt and Cora Kaplan.

63. See TOP, box 33. Despite agreeing to curtail her demands, Tillie asked Virago to make "endless corrections," which were "quite grueling." Lennie Goodings to PR, 8 February 2008.

64. On 26 October 1979, Tillie sent Walker a $10 check, which Walker returned uncashed. See TOP, box 28.

65. Wendy Blair was the editor who worked on the tapes. Stamberg to PR, 28 April 2000.

66. Valerie Trueblood, *American Poetry Review* (May/June 1979), talks of Tillie Olsen's "helping circle."

67. Tillie's illnesses might have resulted from exhausting schedules or been what we now call "chronic fatigue immune deficiency syndrome."

68. This proposal does not include selections but rather a list of authors whose work would be included. Tillie said it would "have to be adequately budgeted for secretarial help and necessary permissions fees. It will have 'terrible beauty' and be a much used, much loved book."

69. On 9 July 1980, a sixty-minute version of Stamberg's interview played on NPR's "Options." Copies are no longer available.

70. Kenneth Turan, "Million-Dollar Miracle: How Three Untried Producers Are Bringing a Fiction Masterpiece to the Screen," *Washington Post* (30 March 1980). The article featured information about Godmother and photos of Lee Grant with Lila Kedrova, the Godmother filmmakers/producers, and a scene with Lila Kedrova and Melvyn Douglas.

71. See TOP, box 25, for this letter from Judith Minty.

72. Tillie's paranoia about finances prevented her from being generous to Conroy, who had taken on considerable debt to film "I Stand Here Ironing." Tillie made both Conroy and McKenzie change the titles of their films to dissociate them from her fiction. TOP, boxes 21 and 25, contain correspondence with Conroy and McKenzie.

73. "Requa I" was reprinted in a 1979 issue of English journal *Granta*. Tillie complained about the printing, getting American editor Bill Buford to apologize. TOP, box 33.

74. She wrote to Wasserman and Lawrence: "The Delacorte royalty statement for the period ending December 31 1979 was incomplete. . . . . there is no listing of hardcover sales of *Silences* in this period; only a debiting for returns amounting to $1,557.86."

75. To Elaine Showalter, 1 February 1981. Tillie did not mention Jane Austen, whose sense of manners and class Tillie found bourgeois.

76. The Unitarian Women's Federation awarded her its annual "Ministry to Women" award, and Tillie went to a convention in Omaha on 20–24 July to accept a joint award from the Federation of Business and Professional Women's Clubs and the British Post Office. Julie Zelenka, in "Old Neighborhood Stays With Her," *Omaha World-Herald* (1 August 1980), quoted Tillie's saying that she did not like to be "separated from other women" by titles like "Mrs. or Miss."

77. Elaine Markson negotiated for about $1837 for a French translation of *Tell Me a Riddle*. She sent the *Washington Post* article to Poli.

78. She scribbled these notes on an article by Sara Ruddick in *Feminist Studies 6* (Summer 1980).

79. Interview with Gene Lerner, 2 July 2000. He called his letter to Tillie of 25 September 1980 "a very tough and perhaps brutal letter" about her treatment of Sara Poli. See Lerner Papers. Sara Poli incorporated her London interview with Tillie into her introduction to *fammi un indovinello* (Savelli Editori), the Italian edition of *Tell Me a Riddle*. Conversation with Sara Poli, 30 August 1999.

80. Goodings to PR, 8 February 2008.

81. The Norwegian universities paid for her flight (business class), gave her $75 a day, and a substantial honorarium. They kept her busy for nearly two weeks.

82. Tillie kept a note from a young man saying that the death of Lennon was more important to his generation "than the assassination of John Kennedy was to your generation." TOP, box 24.

CHAPTER 15 — 1981–1996

1. Kay Mills's interview appeared in the *Los Angeles Times* on 26 April and was afterward syndicated with different titles emphasizing either victimhood or survival.

2. Titled "Breaking the Sequence: Women, Literature, and the Future," the conference took place 30 April–2 May, 1981.

3. Conversations with McIntosh, 22 August 1999, and Ferguson, 13 March 2008.

4. Interview, 19 April 2008.

5. Ann Hershey, "In Honor of An Uncommon Common Writer," *San Francisco Sunday Examiner & Chronicle* (5 July 1981).

6. Leah Garchik, "Who is India Wonder?" (*Review*, 15 November 1981). E. P., the *Nation* (27 February 1982).

7. Tillie made no effort to revise the transcription; it remained among her papers. TOP, 1998, box 192.1.

8. TOP, box 16, and TOP, 1998–353.1, box 10.

9. Among Caldicott's books was her 1978 *Nuclear Madness: What You Can Do*. She left her medical career in 1980 to found Woman's Action for Nuclear Disarmament. See Walker's letters to Tillie in TOP, box 28.

10. Tillie owned copies of many writings by and about Ding Ling. The article quoted here is titled "Veteran Writer Ding Ling."

11. On 14 July 1982 the ERA was reintroduced, as it has been in every session of Congress.

12. Diamond, the daughter of Roberta Braude Diamond, was an assistant professor at the University of Massachusetts, Amherst. Kolodny was an assistant professor at the University of New Hampshire. Neither recalls which film adaptation was shown then.

13. By this time, her minimum fee was $1500 a lecture.

14. TOP, box 14.

15. My thanks to Alice Walker, Blanche Boyd, Valerie Miner, Nellie Wong, and Lisa Alther, who shared with me memories of the trip to China. Paule Marshall did not answer my queries.

16. Mary Jane Moffat had superseded Tillie's "Death Treasury" idea with the 1982 collection, *In the Midst of Winter: Selections from the Literature of Mourning*.

17. Tillie continued to inspire new volumes from the Feminist Press, including *Writing Red: An Anthology of American Women Writers, 1930–1940* (1987), with an introduction by Toni Morrison.

18. Elinor Langer, *Josephine Herbst* (Boston: Little Brown, 1983).

19. TOP, box 16. TOP, 1995–135.1, box 5.

20. Conversation with Paley, 8 March 2000.

21. Lisa See, "Tillie Olsen," *Publishers' Weekly* (23 November 1984).

22. She listed her keynote address at the Woolf conference; her MIT and UCSC lectures on women and literature; talks on Motherhood, Ahistoricality, Literature and Film; The Writer and Social Responsibility; the Thirties; the Fifties; international women's literature; 1982 and 1984 commencement addresses; an "afterpiece" to *Silences*; and her talk on Constance Smith from the dedication of Pineda's *Oracle*.

23. These topics were on her mind after her interview with Naomi Rubin, "A Riddle of History for the Future," *Sojourner: the New England Women's Journal of News, Opinions, and the Arts* (July 1983).

24. See Lerner Papers for Gene's diary. Lillian Lerner Davis traveled more after her husband died on 1 February 1983.

25. Tillie tallied this as her third arrest (after 1931 in Kansas City and 1934 in San Francisco). She said the group, which included Maya Angelou, Lawrence Ferlinghetti, and Alice Walker, was too famous for jail.

26. Though she held a Yale Ph.D. and had been tenured at the University of Illinois, Noble had not found a position in England after she left the United States to marry an Englishman.

27. Merloyd and Sam Lawrence, who had been living apart for some years, divorced in 1985. Williams had been William Faulkner's protégé and sometime mistress. In the 1950s, Faulkner's agent placed a story of hers and then two of Faulkner's short essays with Lawrence at the *Atlantic Monthly*.

28. I have preserved here Tillie's habit of using little punctuation or capitalization and substituting spaces for periods or commas. Olsen private papers.

29. Judith Plaskow was the theologian.

30. In October, she was in New York City for a benefit reading for the Feminist Press; in November she was in Cambridge, Massachusetts, giving a benefit reading for *Sojourner*; in December she spoke at Brandeis University and Cambridge City Hall.

31. McPheron holds both a Ph.D. and an M.L.S. After this exhibit, he began expanding Stanford's collection to include Stanford graduates and Charles Olson and Allen Ginsberg, among others.

32. Julie and her sisters gathered and assembled this collection of letters from admirers.

33. Conversation with Betty Jane Wylie, November 1999.

34. Ena Spalding, "Leighton Artist Colony Newsletter" (May-November, 1987).

35. Here she was the opposite of Gertrude Stein, who, Janet Malcolm observes, offered a magical picture of good things just happening for her (*Two Lives*, 13-14).

36. Diane Middlebrook to PR, over several years, most particularly on 23 March 2006.

37. *Omaha World Herald* (11 December 1987).

38. *Selected Letters of May Sarton: 1955–1995*, 331. Conversation with Hanna Papanek, 15 January 1999.

39. *Tillie Olsen and a Feminist Spiritual Vision*, x, xi.

40. John L'Heureux found Tillie Olsen "terrifically self-important"; to PR, 13 March 2008. *The Uncommon Touch*, was dedicated to Wallace Stegner on his eightieth birthday, 18 February 1989.

41. Interview with Gene Lerner, 3 July 2000.

42. Conversation with Hanna Margan, October 2003. Louise Witonsky put me in touch with Margan.

43. Coiner's principal source for Tillie's life is Deborah Rosenfelt's 1981 interview.

44. Kaufman and Lerner's *Hollywood sul Tevere* is filled with photographs of stars.

45. Tillie's theft of this page is confirmed by the fact that it was in the papers she deposited at Stanford. When Gene Lerner deposited the Lerner Papers at Stanford, Ida's notebook was among them, but missing the one page in the Tillie Olsen Papers.

46. Roughly seven points in magnitude on the Richter scale, the earthquake occurred on 17 October 1989, the largest quake in the Bay Area since the earthquake of 1906.

47. At a memorial, the Board of Supervisors of the City and County of San Francisco presented a posthumous Certificate of Honor to Jack Olsen.

48. She told Elaine Orr that Sam was blacklisted at the plants after the workers' strike failed; Orr, 23.

49. Pearlman and Werlock, 19. It is impossible to know how much time Karla spent with Sue Goldfarb, but Karla was definitely away from her mother 8 June to 10 August 1934; a week or two in February 1935; from early April to late May 1935; from 21 November 1935 to June 1936; for a few days in November 1936; from late May until 13 or 14 October 1937; at the end of 1938; in October and November 1939; and, along with Julie, from December 1942 until January 1943. For Werlock, Tillie also made Sam Lerner sound illiterate, 9.

50. Conversations with Camille Hykes, September 2000 and July 2008.

51. Inspired by *Silences*, Nancy Nordhoff used her trust fund to found Cottages at Hedgebook, built by local artists on Whidby Island near Seattle, as a sanctuary for women writers.

52. She won the Mari Sandoz award, named for a Nebraska writer (1896–1966). The Nebraska Library Association gives this award sporadically.

53. Omaha's Jewish Community Center holds many Lerner/Olsen clippings, including articles by Oliver Pollak; Pratt's article, first published in *Memories of the Jewish Midwest*; a copy of the *Nebraska Jewish Historical Society's Newsletter*, with a photo of Tillie; several photos of Ida and Sam Lerner, some among Workmen's Circle officials; and an article from the *Omaha World-Herald* (4 November 1991).

54. Winslow's "Born Again" won the 1993 Raymond Carver Short Story Contest. Its heading includes the words "written at The MacDowell Colony with the encouragement of Tillie Olsen."

55. The *Washington Jewish Week* (23 April 1992) describes Harry as "founder and past president of Yiddish of Greater Washington, a retired Bethesda lawyer and Air Force Reserve lieutenant colonel."

56. Aruna Sitesh to PR, 10 October 2000.

57. Conversation with Anthony Dawahare, 2 April 2000. He abandoned his hope of printing the interview in the *Critical Response to Tillie Olsen*.

58. Stanford does not disclose what it pays for special collections.

59. TOP, box 17.

60. TOP, 1998–242.1 contains some thirty pages of these notes.

61. Conversation with Jonathan Alter, 4 April 2008. He cited the second paragraph with its catalogue of evocative phrases as an example of such editing. Tillie's notes do not suggest the poignant final image of America's hunger. Rereading it fourteen years later, Alter found it so familiar he thinks it was his. He had read "Tell Me a Riddle" in Robert Coles's Harvard seminar on social and moral responsibility. Alter credits Tillie with partly inspiring his *The Defining Moment: FDR's Hundred Days and the Triumph of Hope*.

62. Arlyn Osborne at UCSC to PR, 5 April 1999.

63. See the Bibliography for books by Martin, Orr, Pearlman and Welock, Faulkner, Hedges and Fishkin, Nelson and Huse, Coiner, Frye, and Rosenfelt.

64. Apparently it was not a complete *Requa*.

65. Gene had apparently made a carbon copy of his letter and later shared it with Pollak, who copied it to share with Linda Pratt and then Tillie. See Lerner Papers.

66. Once Betty Jane Wylie made a special trip to see Tillie in San Francisco, only to find Tillie on her way out of town and unable to see her. Conversation, November 1999. Jessica Mitford and Bob Treuhaft tired of Tillie's vague invitations, saying "we must get together" since she would back out when they proposed a date. Conversation with Treuhaft, 2 April 2000.

67. Conversation with Cory Richards, 28 June 2008. Joyce Winslow to PR, 27 February 2001.

68. Tillie sent Red Tovish $100 for a commemorative fund. He sculpted *In Memoriam*, now in the National Gallery of American Art. Tillie seems not to have commented on the reelection of President Clinton.

69. *Jewish Press* (25 October 1996).

CHAPTER 16 — 1997–2007

1. See Wagner-Martin for analysis of ways in which women's biographies have been distorted to fit stereotypical expectations.

2. She did not mention her brother's book or the many American-Italian films he shepherded into production. I later learned that Anna Magnani and Anita Ekberg had feted Gene Lerner with a grand birthday party at the Hotel Nazionale on 20 February 1997. News photos of the event show Ava Gardner, Margaret Truman, Elsa Martinelli, and Hank Kaufman, among other celebrities, toasting Gene.

3. My transcription of her virtual monologue on 27 October 1997 ran to fifteen single-spaced pages. She gave no dates and spelled no names so I wrote down, for example, "Sugula," "Broomklin," and "Brodie," which I later learned were Sologow, Blumkin, and Braude.

4. "Working Lips, Breaking Hearts: Class Acts in American Feminism," *Signs: Journal of Women in Culture and Society* (Spring 1997). Not having read the laudatory article, Tillie thought Marcus had exposed a private foible.

5. Sworn in early in 1997, Madeleine Albright was President Clinton's second secretary of state, the first woman to hold that position.

6. That's a least what she seemed to be singing. Laurie Olsen agrees.

7. The reviewer was William Pritchard, who had known Tillie when she taught at Amherst in 1969–1970. He was reviewing Brian Mortons's *Starting out in the Evening*, *New York Times Book Review* (18 January 1998).

8. Some hold ½ linear feet of papers, some hold 1 & ½ linear feet, and box 17 holds thirty volumes of journals and diaries. There were then forty-nine boxes. Because so much material remains unprocessed, even the librarians cannot give an accurate count of the volume of the Tillie Olsen Papers. Leon Edel said such archives made him groan; Pachter, 24.

9. Conversation with Bill Pratt, 15 April 1998. When I told Gene Lerner that Tillie said she observed these horrors, his reaction was: "Forget it! Logic's logic. Dad certainly would not have taken her into such a situation—it wasn't some lovely parade." Interview, 2 July 2000. Lillian Davis agreed that Sam "wasn't one go leave the family and go traipsing about" amid such danger. Interview with Lillian Lerner Davis, 24 January 2002.

10. For example, in a letter to Goldfarb she inked out the name after the "Dear" but later in the letter addressed "O Jevons."

11. A. C. Elias, Jr., John Irwin Fischer, James Woolley, "The Full Text of Swift's 'On Poetry: A Rapsody' (1733)," *Swift Studies* (1994).

12. When Elaine Orr interviewed her in 1986, Tillie said that Sam Lerner organized union members to go to Tulsa and help the black people rebuild after the 1921 disaster, probably another instance of transforming information into memory." See chapter 2, note 24, and Orr, 25.

13. Howard Lerner confirmed this story to PR, 28 April 2008.

14. First, I spoke in Jackson at a symposium honoring Ellen Douglas, whose most recent novel was *Truth: Four Stories I Am Finally Old Enough To Tell.* I was editing a collection of "Conversations" with Douglas for the University Press of Mississippi. I then drove to Oxford and, at the University of Mississippi, checked into the same place I had stayed when I spoke at several Faulkner and Yoknapatawpha conferences.

15. On 2 December 1999, he wrote: "I have been in touch with relatives in ten states of the USA, Canada, Israel and England, and have been in contact with or done research on family branches including the Lerners, Bebers, Braudes, Sogolows, Swartzes, Wolks, Alloys, Gils, Books (LaBooks), Goldbergs, Shapiros, and Greenglasses and sought the help of the Nebraska State Historical Society, etc." Thanks to his contacts, reinforced by my access to Jewishgen.org and Jewishgateways.org, I drew family trees and wrote Tillie "I found your grandfather—Zalman Goldberg! . . . in the district of Bobruish, in Minsk." I also found a Brandeis graduate student in Women's History in Czarist Russia whom I hired to search records from the 1880s in Bobruisk to uncover more history of the Lerners and the Goldbergs. I reimbursed Gene Lerner for his research expenses.

16. Tillie had so elaborated this story that Americans often greeted Borghi by saying "you must be the one who incarcerated Tillie Olsen." Liana Borghi to PR, 24 September 1999.

17. Anne-Marie Cusac, *The Progressive Interview: Tillie Olsen* (November 1999).

18. The "bribe" was extra credit from their journalism teacher and thanks from me in my *DoubleTake* article.

19. See Zinsser, passim., especially Dillard's "To Fashion a Text."

20. Julie Olsen Edwards thought the award was for $25,000. Ferguson thought it gave her twice that. The Lannan Foundation does not disclose the amount of its awards. Hershey's *Never Give Up—Imogen Cunningham, 1883-1976* had won a Blue Ribbon at the American Film Fesitval.

21. See Pachter, 25.

22. I visited Oliver Pollak and Linda Pratt. I checked out the Western Heritage Museum, the Douglas County Historical Society, the Omaha Public Library, and the Jewish Community Center, where Mary Fellman and Dottie Rosenblum put me in touch with Ruth Stein Fox, Frances Blumkin Batt, Cynthia Blumkin Schneider, and other old-timers.

23. We bought a 3' x 3' Rosati painting, which sits over my study table as I write.

24. Interview with Alice Walker, 15 June 2000.

25. See chapter 11, note 17.

26. A large densely packed box among the late arrivals at Stanford, for example, includes packets and bundles of "quotations from other writers; responses to other

writers; critiques of other writers and modes of thought; word lists that suggest a searching for associations and synonyms; fragmented ideas and phrases; longer sentences and prose fragments." Annette Keogh to PR, 2 July 2008.

27. Like a poem and a story (in TOP, boxes 15 and 16) about having a retarded child, like Rae Schochet's saying "and then you had Tom," like Tillie's regret, voiced to me in St. Mary's Cathedral, about a son whom "we" could have kept and made happy, the specificity of this remark buttressed my speculation about a son born to Tillie and Abe Goldfarb in 1931 and perhaps adopted or institutionalized.

28. She received the Fred Cody Lifetime Achievement Award for her contributions to creative writing and to the city of San Francisco's New Main Library from the Bay Area Book Reviewers Association (BABRA). Jonah Raskin's account appeared in the *San Francisco Chronicle* (1 April 2001).

29. I thank Ann Hershey for the on-going account of Tillie's health after autumn 2001.

30. Jan Jarboe Russell's tribute appeared in the *San Antonio Express-News* (14 July 2002). Privately, she said that Tillie had kissed her and told her to write fiction because her view of life "was needed." To PR, 18 July 2002. Stories and poems, which Tillie invited women to send her, piled up, unread, in her apartment, but she continued making such invitations and endorsements.

31. Janet Malcolm, *The Silent Woman*, 110.

32. Working Women for Change, for example, protests that women currently enjoy less union representation, less advancement, fewer benefits, and lower wages than men. Minorities suffer the same disadvantages more acutely.

BIBLIOGRAPHY

Aaron, Daniel. "The Thirties—Now and Then." *American Scholar* 35 (Summer 1966): 490–516.

———. *Writers on the Left: Episodes in American Literary Communism.* New York: Harcourt, Brace & World, Inc., 1961.

"Agitprop Activity: Raising the Political Level of Comrades." *The Party Organizer* 4, no. 1 (February 1931): 24.

Ain, Abraham. "Swislocz: Portrait of a Jewish Community in Eastern Europe," *YIVO Annual of Jewish Social Science* 4 (1949): 86–114.

Alperin, Robert Jay. "Organization in the Communist Party, U.S.A., 1931–1938." Ph.D. diss., Northwestern University, 1960.

Alter, Jonathan. *The Defining Moment: FDR's Hundred Days and the Triumph of Hope.* New York: Simon & Schuster, 2006.

Andre, Linda. *Doctors of Deception: What They Don't Want You to Know about Shock Treatment.* New Brunswick, N.J.: Rutgers University Press, 2009.

Andrist, Ralph K. *American Heritage History of the 20's and 30's.* New York: American Heritage Publishing, 1970.

Antin, Mary. *The Promised Land.* Boston: Houghton Mifflin, 1912.

Armitage, Susan, ed. "Responses To and By Tillie Olsen." *Frontiers: A Journal of Women Studies* 18 (1997): 130–60.

Atkinson, Ted. *Faulkner and the Great Depression: Aesthetics, Ideology, and Cultural Politics.* Athens: University of Georgia Press, 2006.

Baron, Salo W. *The Russian Jew Under Tsars and Soviets.* 2nd ed. New York: Macmillan, 1976.

Bergelson, Dovid. *Descent.* Edited and translated by Joseph Sherman. New York: MLA, 1999.

Billingsley, Kenneth Lloyd. *Hollywood Party: How Communism Seduced the American Film Industry in the 1930s and 1940s.* Rocklin, Calif.: Prima Publishing, 1998.

Black, Allida M. *Casting Her Own Shadow: Eleanor Roosevelt and the Shaping of Postwar Liberalism.* New York: Columbia University Press, 1996.

Blotner, Joseph. *Faulkner: A Biography.* 2 vols. New York: Random House, 1974.

Boyer, Paul. *By the Bomb's Early Light: American Thought and Culture at the Dawn of the Atomic Age.* New York: Pantheon, 1985.

Browder, Earl. *What is Communism.* New York: Vanguard Press, 1936.

Brown, Frank. "From a Report to the Agitprop Dept. C. C." *Daily Worker* (15 January 1932), 4.

Brown, Michael E., Randy Martin, Frank Rosengarten, and George Snedeker. *New Studies in the Politics and Culture of U.S. Communism.* New York: Monthly Review Press, 1993.

————. "Echoes of a Crime." *New Republic* 84 (28 August 1932), 9.

————. *Think Back on Us: A Contemporary Chronicle of the 1930's.* Edited by Henry Dan Piper. Carbondale: Southern Illinois University Press, 1967.

Brune, Adrian. "Tulsa's Shame: Race Riot Victims Still Wait for Promised Reparations." *The Nation* (18 March 2002), 11–14.

Buhle, Paul, and David Wagner. *Radical Hollywood.* New York: The New Press, 2002.

Burke, Robert E. *Olson's New Deal for California.* Berkeley: University of California Press, 1959.

Carter, Paul A. *Another Part of the Fifties.* New York: Columbia University Press, 1983.

Cerf, Bennett. *At Random: The Reminiscences of Bennett Cerf.* New York: Random House, 1977.

Chaplin, John R. "The Myth and Reality of Hollywood." *International Literature* 6 (December 1934): 131–35.

Chesler, Ellen. *Woman of Valor: Margaret Sanger and the Birth Control Movement in America.* New York: Simon & Schuster, 1992.

Cline, Paul. "Problems of Organization: New Forces Can be Developed." *The Party Organizer* 4, no. 3 (April 1931): 3–4.

Coiner, Constance. *Better Red: The Writing and Resistance of Tillie Olsen and Meridel Le Sueur.* New York: Oxford University Press, 1995.

Cook, Sylvia Jenkins. *From Tobacco Road to Route 66: The Southern Poor White in Fiction.* Chapel Hill: University of North Carolina Press, 1976.

Cowley, Malcolm. *Exile's Return: A Literary Odyssey of the 1920s.* New York: Viking Press, 1951.

Davis-Kram, Harriet. "The Story of the Sisters of the Bund." *Contemporary Jewry* 5, no.2 (1980): 27–43.

Dawahare, Anthony. "'That Joyous Certainty': History and Utopia in Tillie Olsen's Depression-Era Literature." *Twentieth Century Literature* 44 (Fall 1998): 261–75.

Denning, Michael. *The Cultural Front: The Laboring of American Culture in the Twentieth Century.* New York, Verso, 1996.

DiBattista, Maria. *Fast-Talking Dames.* New Haven: Yale University Press, 2001.

Dick, Bernard F. *Radical Innocence: A Critical Study of the Hollywood Ten.* Lexington: University Press of Kentucky, 1989.

Dunaway, David Kind. *How Can I Keep From Singing: Pete Seeger.* Rpt. Cambridge, Mass.: Da Capo Press, 1990.

Duncan, Erika. "Coming of Age in the Thirties: A Portrait of Tillie Olsen." *Book Forum* 6 (1982): 207–22.

DuPlessis, Rachel Blau. *Writing Beyond the Ending.* Bloomington: Indiana University Press, 1985.

Durant, Will, and Ariel Durant. *A Dual Autobiography.* New York: Simon & Schuster, 1977.

Elman, Richard. *Namedropping: Mostly Literary Memoirs.* Albany: State University of New York Press, 1999.

Faulkner, Mara. *Protest and Possibility in the Writing of Tillie Olsen.* Charlottesville: University of Virginia Press, 1993.

Foley, Barbara. *Radical Representations: Politics and Form in U.S. Proletarian Fiction, 1929–1941.* Durham: Duke University Press, 1993.

Folsom, Franklin. *Days of Anger, Days of Hope: A Memoir of the League of American Writers, 1937–42.* Niwot, Colo.: University of Colorado Press, 1994.

Freeze, ChaeRan Y. "The Litigious *Gerusha:* Jewish Women and Divorce in Imperial Russia." *Nationalities Papers* 25, no.1 (1997): 89–101.

Fried, Albert. *Communism in America: A History in Documents.* New York: Columbia University Press, 1997.

Frye, Joanna S. *Tillie Olsen: A Study of the Short Fiction.* New York: Twayne Publishers, 1995.

Fussell, Paul. *The Great War and Modern Memory.* New York: Oxford University Press, 1975.

Gallup, George Horace, ed. *Best Creative Work in American High Schools.* Cedar Rapids, Iowa: National Honor Society for High School Journalists, 1928, 1929, 1930.

Gassenschmidt, Christoph. *Jewish Liberal Politics in Tsarist Russia, 1900–1904.* New York: New York University Press, 1995.

Gendler, Carol. "The Jews of Omaha: The First Sixty Years." M.A. thesis, Department of History, University of Omaha, 1968.

Gilbert, Martin. *The Second World War: A Complete History.* Rev. ed. New York: Henry Holt and Company, 1991.

Gitelman, Zvi. *A Century of Ambivalence: the Jews of Russia and the Soviet Union, 1991 to the Present.* New York: YIVO Institute for Jewish Research, 1988.

———. *Jewish Nationalilty and Soviet Politics.* Princeton, N.J.: Princeton University Press, 1971.

Glenn, Susan A. *Daughters of the Shtetl: Life and Labor in the Immigrant Generation.* Ithaca: Cornell University Press, 1990.

Goodwin, Doris Kearns. *No Ordinary Time: Franklin and Eleanor Roosevelt: The Home Front in World War II.* New York: Simon & Schuster, 1994.

Gorney, Sondra K. *Brother, Can You Spare a Dime? The Life of Composer Jay Gorney.* Lanham, Md.: The Scarecrow Press, 2005.

Gurko, Leo. *The Angry Decade: American Literature and Thought from 1929 to Pearl Harbor.* Rpt. New York: Harper & Row, 1968.

Halberstam, David. *The Fifties.* New York: Villard Books, 1993.

Healey, Dorothy Ray, and Maurice Isserman. *Dorothy Healey Remembers: A Life in the American Communist Party.* New York: Oxford University Press, 1990. Rpt: *California Red: A Life in the American Communist Party.* Champaign: University of Illinois Press, 1993.

Hedges, Elaine, and Shelley Fisher Fishkin, eds. *Listening to 'Silences': New Essays in Feminist Criticism.* New York: Oxford University Press, 1994.

Hellman, Lillian. *Scoundrel Time.* Boston: Little Brown, 1976.

Hertz, J. S., ed. *Doires Bundistn* [Generations of Bundists]. New York: Farlag Unser Tsait, 1956.

Hobsbawm, Eric. *The Age of Extremes: A History of the World, 1914–1991.* New York: Vintage Books, 1994.

"How We Organized a Neighborhood Mass Meeting." *The Party Organizer* 5, no. 2 (February 1932): 21–22.

Howe, Florence, ed. *The Politics of Women's Studies: Testimony from Thirty Founding Mothers.* New York: The Feminist Press, 2000.

Hurwitz, Maximilian. *The Workmen's Circle: Its History, Ideals, Organization and Institutions*. New York: The Workmen's Circle, 1936.

Hyman, Paula E. *Gender and Assimilation in Modern Jewish History: The Roles and Representation of Women*. Seattle: University of Washington Press, 1995.

Isserman, Maurice. *Which Side Were You On? The American Communist Party during the Second World War*. 1982; rpt. Urbana: University of Illinois Press, 1993.

Isserman, Maurice, and Michael Kazin. *America Divided: The Civil War of the 1960s*. New York: Oxford University Press, 2000.

Johanningsmeier, Edward P. *Forging American Communism: The Life of William Z. Foster*. Princeton, N.J.: Princeton University Press, 1994.

Johnpoll, Bernard K. *A Documentary History of the Communist Party of the United States: Toil and Trouble, 1928–1933*, Vol. 2. Westport, Conn.: Greenwood Press, 1994.

Kaplan, Justin. *Lincoln Steffens: A Biography*. New York: Simon & Schuster, 1974.

Kazan, Alfred. *On Native Grounds: An Interpretation of Modern American Prose Literature*. New York: Harcourt, Brace, 1942; rpt. Garden City, N.Y.: Doubleday Anchor, 1956.

Kirchwey, George W. *A Survey of the Workings of the Criminal Syndicalism Law of California*. Los Angeles: California Committee, American Civil Liberties Union, 1926.

Klehr, Harvey. *Communist Cadre: The Social Background of the American Communist Party Elite*. Stanford: Hoover Institution Press, 1978.

Klehr, Harvey, David Earl Haynes, and Kyrill M. Anderson. *The Soviet World of American Communism*. New Haven: Yale University Press, 1998.

Kramer, Sydelle, and Jenny Masur, eds. *Jewish Grandmothers*. Boston: Beacon Press, 1976.

Kugler, Israel. "Life in the Workmen's Circle: Reminiscence and Reflection," *Labor's Heritage* 3 (October 1991): 36–49.

Larsen, Lawrence H., and Barbara J. Cottrell. *The Gate City: A History of Omaha*. Enl. ed. Lincoln: University of Nebraska Press, 1997.

Laurie, Clayton D. "The U.S. Army and the Omaha Race Riot of 1919." *Nebraska History* (Fall 1991): 135–43.

Leggett, John. *A Daring Young Man: A Biography of William Saroyan*. New York: Alfred A. Knopf, 2002.

Lerner, Eugene. "From Czarist Russia to Omaha, Nebraska, and Beyond: The story of the Lerner Family Over More than One Hundred Years." Unpublished family history, Lerner Papers, Stanford University.

Levin, Nora. *While Messiah Tarried: Jewish Socialist Movements, 1871–1917*. New York: Schocken Books, 1977.

Los Angeles: A Guide to the City and its Environs. Compiled by Workers of the Writers' Program of the Work Projects Administration in Southern California. New York: Hastings House, 1972.

Löwe, Heinz-Dietrich. *The Tsars and the Jews: Reform, Reaction and Anti-Semitism in Imperial Russia, 1772–1917*. Switzerland: Harwood Academic Publishers, 1993.

McElvaine, Robert S. *The Great Depression: America: 1929–1941*. 1984; rpt. New York: Times Books, 1993.

McGilligan, Pat, ed. *Backstory: Interviews with Screenwriters of Hollywood's Golden Age*. Berkeley: University of California Press, 1986.

McGuffey's Third Eclectic Reader. Rev. ed. Van Nostrand and Reinhold. © 1907 and 1920 by H. H. Vail.

McPheron, William, ed. *First Drafts, Last Drafts: Forty Years of the Creative Writing Program at Stanford*. Stanford: Stanford University Libraries, 1989.

McWilliams, Carey. *The Education of Carey McWilliams*. New York: Simon & Schuster, 1979.

Madden, David, ed. *Proletarian Writers of the Thirties*. Carbondale: Southern Illinois University Press, 1968.

Magnus, Shulamit S. "Pauline Wengeroff and the Voice of Jewish Modernity." In *Gender and Judaism: The Transformation of Tradition*, edited by T. M. Rudavsky. New York: New York University Press, 1995. 181–90.

Malcolm, Janet. *The Silent Woman: Sylvia Plath and Ted Hughes*. New York: Alfred P. Knopf, 1994.

———. *Two Lives: Gertrude and Alice*. New Haven, Conn.: Yale University Press, 2007.

Mangione, Jerre. *The Dream and the Deal: The Federal Writers' Project, 1935–1943*. Boston: Little, Brown and Company, 1972.

Martin, Abigail. *Tillie Olsen*. Boise, Idaho: Boise State University Press, 1984.

Menard, Orville D. "Tom Dennison, the *Omaha Bee*, and the 1919 Omaha Race Riot." *Nebraska History* 68 (Winter 1987): 152–65.

Mendelsohn, Ezra. *Class Struggle in the Pale: The Formative Years of the Jewish Workers' Movement in Tsarist Russia*. Cambridge: Cambridge University Press, 1970.

Middlebrook, Diane Wood. *Anne Sexton: A Biography*. Boston: Houghton, Mifflin, 1991.

Nadel, Ira Bruce. *Biography: Fiction, Fact, and Form*. New York: St. Martin's Press, 1984.

Nasaw, David. *Chief: The Life of William Randolph Hearst*. Boston: Houghton Mifflin, 2000.

Navasky, Victor S. *Naming Names*. New York: Viking Press, 1980.

Nekola, Charlotte, and Paula Rabinowitz, eds. *Writing Red: An Anthology of American Women Writers, 1930–1940*. New York: The Feminist Press, 1987.

Nelson, Bruce. *Workers on the Waterfront: Seamen, Longshoremen, and Unionism in the 1930s*. Urbana: University of Illinois Press, 1988.

Nelson, Kay Hoyle, and Nancy Huse. *The Critical Response to Tillie Olsen*. Westport, Conn.: Greenwood Press, 1994.

Nelson, Steve. *Steve Nelson: American Radical*. Pittsburgh: University of Pittsburgh Press, 1981.

"New Cadres in Our Party." *The Party Organizer* 3, no. 2 (March 1930): 4–7.

Nisbet, J. F. *The Insanity of Genius, and the General Inequality of Human Faculty Physiologically Considered*. New York: Charles Scribner's, 1912.

Old Favorites from the McGuffey Readers, 1836–1936. New York: American Book Company, 1936.

Olson, James C. *History of Nebraska*. Lincoln: University of Nebraska Press, 1955.

Olson, Paul A. "Scandinavian Chapter." In *Broken Hoops and Plains People: A Catalogue of Ethnic Resources in the Humanities: Nebraska and Surrounding Areas*. Lincoln: Nebraska Curriculum Development Center, 1976.

Orr, Elaine Neil. *Tillie Olsen and a Feminist Spiritual Vision*. Jackson: University Press of Mississippi, 1987.

Pachter, Marc. *Telling Lives: The Biographer's Art*. Washington, D.C.: New Republic/Smithsonian, 1979.

Pearlman, Mickey, and Abby H. P. Werlock. *Tillie Olsen*. Boston: Twayne Publishers, 1991.

Peretz, I. L. *In This World and the Next*. Translated by Moche Spiegel. New York: Thomas Yoseloff, 1958.

Perky, Charles, ed. *Past and Present of Saunders County: A Record of Settlement, Organization, Progress, and Achievement*. Chicago: S. J. Clarke, 1915.

Phillips, Cabell. *The 1940s: Decade of Triumph and Trouble*. New York: Macmillan Publishing, 1975.

Pineda, Marianne. *Marianne Pineda: Sculpture—1949–1996*. Boston: The Alabaster Press, 1996.

"The Political Development of the New Member." *The Party Organizer* 4, no. 2 (March 1931).

Pollak, Oliver B. *A State of Readers: Nebraska's Carnegie Libraries*. Omaha, Neb.: Lee Booksellers, 2005.

———. "The Workmen's Circle and Labor Lyceum in Omaha, 1907–1977." *Nebraska History* 76 (Spring 1995): 30–42.

———. "The Workmen's Circle in the Midwest." Unpublished paper, 21 December 1999.

Pratt, Linda Ray. "Tillie Olsen's Omaha Heritage: A History Becomes Literature." In *Memories of the Jewish Midwest: Journal of the Nebraska Jewish Historical Society* (Fall 1989), 1–16. [Revised as "The Circumstances of Silence: Literary Representation and Tillie Olsen's Omaha Past," in Rosenfelt, 113–31].

Quin, Mike. *The Big Strike*. 1949; rpt. New York: International Publishers, 1991.

Raskin, Jonah. Interview with Tillie Olsen, April 2000; unpublished notes, courtesy of Raskin.

Reid, Panthea. "From Osipovichi to Omaha: Sources behind Tillie Lerner Olsen's 'Tell Me a Riddle.'" In *Studies in Jewish Civilization 18: Love—Ideal and Real—in the Jewish Tradition*, edited by Leonard J. Greenspoon, Ronald A Simkins, and Jean Cahan. Omaha: Creighton University Press, 2008.

———. "Tillie Olsen: Utterances on the Side of Life." *DoubleTake Magazine*, Spring 2000.

Richmond, Al. *A Long View from the Left: Memoirs of an American Revolutionary*. New York: Dell/Delta, 1972.

Rideout, Walter B. *The Radical Novel in the United States, 1900–1954*. Cambridge: Harvard University Press, 1956.

Riesman, David, in collaboration with Reuel Denney and Nathan Glazer. *The Lonely Crowd: A Study of the Changing American Character*. New Haven: Yale University Press, 1950.

Rosenfelt, Deborah Silverton, ed. *"Tell Me a Riddle" by Tillie Olsen* (Women Writers, Texts and Contexts Series). New Brunswick, N.J.: Rutgers University Press, 1995.

Sarton, May. *The Selected Letters of May Sarton, 1955–1995*. New York: W. W. Norton, 2002.

Saunders County, Nebraska: History. Wahoo, Neb.: Saunders County Historical Society, 1983.

Schulberg, Budd. *What Makes Sammy Run?* New York: Random House, 1941.

Schwarts, Nancy Lynn. *The Hollywood Writers' Wars*. New York: Knopf, 1982.

Seeley, Evelyn. "War on the West Coast II: Journalistic Strikebreakers." *The New Republic* (1 August 1934), 310–12.

Sexton, Linda Gray, and Lois Ames, ed. *Anne Sexton: A Self-Portrait in Letters*. Boston: Houghton Mifflin Co., 1977.

Shapiro, Judah J. *The Friendly Society: A History of the Workmen's Circle*. New York: Media Judaica, 1970.

Sharistanian, Janet. "Afterword" to Tess Slesinger, *The Unpossessed: A Novel of the Thirties*. 1934; rpt. Old Westbury, N.Y.: The Feminist Press, 1984.

Shepherd, Naomi. *A Price Below Rubies: Jewish Women as Rebels and Radicals*. Cambridge, Mass.: Harvard University Press, 1993.

Showalter, Elaine. *A Literature of Their Own: British Women Novelists from Brontë to Lessing*. Princeton, N.J.: Princeton University Press, 1977.

Singer, Peter. *A Darwinian Left: Politics, Evolution and Cooperation*. New Haven, Conn.: Yale University Press, 1999.

Slesinger, Tess. *The Unpossessed*. 1934; rpt. Old Westbury, N.Y.: The Feminist Press, 1984.

"Stalin in the American Commission." *Party Organizer* 5 (November-December 1932): 32.

Steffens, Lincoln. *The Letters of Lincoln Steffens*. 2 vols. Edited with introduction by Ella Winter and Granville Hicks, with a memorandum by Carl Sandburg. New York: Harcourt Brace & Company, 1938.

Stegner, Wallace, and Richard W. Etulain, *Conversations with Wallace Stegner on Western History and Literature*. Rev. ed. Salt Lake City: University of Utah Press, 1990.

Stone, Geoffrey R. *Perilous Times: Free Speech in Wartime, From the Sedition Act of 1798 to the War on Terrorism*. New York: W. W. Norton, 2004.

Tobias, Henry J. *The Jewish Bund in Russia: From its Origins to 1905*. Stanford: Stanford University Press, 1972.

"Two Lessons from the San Francisco General Strike." *The Party Organizer* 7, no. 8 (August 1934): 1–3.

Wagner-Martin, Linda. *Telling Women's Lives: The New Biography*. New Brunswick, N.J.: Rutgers University Press, 1994.

Weber, Myles. *Consuming Silences: How We Read Authors Who Don't Publish*. Athens: University of Georgia Press, 2005.

Weinberg, Sydney Stahl. *The World of Our Mothers: The Lives of Jewish Immigrant Women*. Chapel Hill: University of North Carolina Press, 1988.

Weiner, Miriam. *Jewish Roots in Ukraine and Moldova: Pages from the Past and Archival Inventories*. New York: YIVO Institute for Jewish Research, 1999.

Weizmann, Chaim. *Trial and Error: The Autobiography of Chaim Weizmann*. Selected and arranged by B. Horovitz. Great Britain: Harper and Brothers, 1949.

Wengeroff, Pauline. "Memoirs of a Grandmother." In *The Golden Tradition: Jewish Life and Thought in Eastern Europe*, edited by Lucy S. Dawidowicz. Syracuse: Syracuse University Press, 1996.

Who's Who in Labor. New York: Dryden Press, 1946.

Wilson, Edmund. *To the Finland Station: A Study in the Writing and Acting of History*. Garden City, N.Y.: Doubleday, 1935.

Winston, Harry. "An Understanding of the Y. C. L. Convention." *The Party Organizer* 10 (June 1937): 17–20.

Winter, Ella. *And Not to Yield: An Autobiography*. New York: Harcourt, Brace & World, 1963.

Winter, Ella, and Herbert Shapiro, eds. *The World of Lincoln Steffens*. New York: Hill and Wang, 1962.

Wixson, Douglas. *Worker-Writer in America: Jack Conroy and the Tradition of Midwestern Literary Radicalism, 1898–1990*. Urbana: University of Illinois Press, 1994.

Zandy, Janet, ed. *Liberating Memory: Our Work and Our Working-Class Consciousness*. New Brunswick, N.J.: Rutgers University Press, 1994.

Zinn, Howard. *A People's History of the United States, 1492-Present*. New York: Perennial Classics, 2001.

Zunser, Miriam Shomer. *Yesterday*. New York: Stackpole Sons, 1939.

INDEX

429

ABOUT THE AUTHOR

Panthea Reid is the author of *William Faulkner: The Abstract and the Actual* and *Art and Affection: A Life of Virginia Woolf.* She has edited books on Walker Percy and Ellen Douglas. She attended Randolph-Macon Woman's College and the University of Alabama and holds a Ph.D. from the University of North Carolina. She taught at Virginia Tech and, for twenty-five years, at Louisiana State University. *Newsweek* online carries her "How I (Almost) Lost My Mind," which bears some relation to writing this biography. A native of Kentucky and Alabama, she now lives with her husband, John Irwin Fischer, in Princeton, New Jersey.